THE LORD

THE
LORD

BY ROMANO GUARDINI

With a New Introduction by
JOSEPH CARDINAL RATZINGER

Gateway Editions
REGNERY PUBLISHING, INC.
WASHINGTON, D.C.

Copyright © 1954 by Regnery Publishing, Inc.
Copyright © renewed 1982 by Elinor C. Briefs

Translated from the German by Elinor Castendyk Briefs

Library of Congress Cataloging-in-Publication Data
Guardini, Romano, 1885–1968.
    [Herr, English]
    The Lord / by Romano Guardini : with an introduction by Joseph
Ratzinger ; [translated from the German by Elinor Castendyk Briefs].
        p.   cm.
    Previously published: c1954.
    "A Gateway edition."
    ISBN 0-89526-714-4 (alk. paper)
    1. Jesus Christ—Biography.   I. Title.
BT301.2.G8413   1996
232.9'01
[B]—DC20   96-22678
                                                            CIP

Published in the United States by
Gateway Editions
A Division of Regnery Publishing, Inc.
One Massachusetts Avenue, NW
Washington, DC 20001

Visit us at www.regnery.com

Distributed to the trade by
National Book Network
4720-A Boston Way
Lanham, MD 20706

Printed on acid-free paper
Manufactured in the United States of America
2002 Printing

Books are available in quantity for promotional or premium use.
Write to Director of Special Sales, Regnery Publishing, Inc.,
One Massachusetts Avenue, NW, Washington, DC 20001, for information
on discounts and terms or call (202) 216-0600.

Nihil obstat
Rt. Rev. Msgr. J. G. Kealy
Censor
26 August 1954

Imprimatur
✠ Samuel Cardinal Stritch
Archbishop of Chicago
26 August 1954

CONTENTS

PART THREE • *The Decision*

PART FOUR • *On the Road to Jerusalem*

PART FIVE • *The Last Days*

PART SIX • *Resurrection and Transfiguration*

INTRODUCTION

by Joseph Cardinal Ratzinger
Prefect of the Congregation for the Doctrine of the Faith

Romano Guardini's book *The Lord* has helped more than one generation of Christians enter into a deeper relationship with Jesus Christ. When the book first appeared, it offered a new approach to the spiritual interpretation of Scripture for which young people in particular longed; a longing, I might add, which is being felt again in our own day.

The First World War was everywhere experienced as the collapse of the liberal dream of ever-advancing progress engendered by reason alone. This crisis of liberalism had great consequences for the Church and theology. Every "rational Christianity" which the liberal theologians had managed to develop was affected by it. Liberal Biblical interpretation, or exegesis, had actually prepared the ground for this crisis by its attempt to discover behind the "veneer of dogma" the true "historical" Jesus. Naturally, by the liberal's way of thinking, the historical Jesus could be only a mere man. The liberals thought that everything supernatural, everything pertaining to the mystery of God that surrounded Jesus, was merely the embellishments and exaggerations of believers. Only with everything supernatural removed could the true figure of Jesus finally come to view! Already by the turn of the century, however, Albert Schweitzer had established that such an attempt would result only in contradictions: such a "sanitized" Jesus would not be an actual person, but the product of a historian.

As a student Romano Guardini had himself experienced the drama of liberalism and its collapse, and with a few friends he set out to find a new path for theology. What came to impress him in the course of this search was the experience of the liturgy as the place of encounter with Jesus. It is above all in the liturgy that Jesus is among us, here it is that He speaks to us, here He lives.

Guardini recognized that the liturgy is the true, *living* environment for the Bible and that the Bible can be properly understood only in this living context within which it first emerged. The texts of the Bible, this great Book of Christ, are not to be seen as the literary products of some scribes at their desks but rather as the words of Christ Himself delivered in the celebration of holy Mass. The scriptural texts are thoroughly imbued with the awe of divine worship resulting from the believer's interior attentiveness to the living voice of the present Lord. In the preface to his book, Guardini himself tells us of the way in which these texts have arisen: "We can only reverently pause before this or that word or act, ready to learn, adore, obey."

Clearly Guardini did not view his book as theology in the strict sense of the word, but more as a kind of proclamation or preaching. Nonetheless, he certainly did not fail to take into account the theological significance of what he had to say. Throughout *The Lord* Guardini struggled to come to the correct understanding of Jesus: All attempts to "cleanse" the figure of Jesus of the supernatural result in contradictions and meaningless constructions. One simply cannot strip "the Wholly Other," the mysterious, the divine, from this Individual. Without this element, the very person of Jesus Himself dissolves. There simply is no psychological portrait of Jesus which can render His different features comprehensible solely from a human perspective. Repeatedly the attempted analysis of this Man takes us into that realm which is incomprehensible, into "an incomprehensibility, however, full of measureless promise." The figure and mission of Jesus are "forever beyond the reach of history's most powerful ray," because "their ultimate explanations are to be found only in that impenetrable territory which He calls 'my Father's will.' "

Guardini spoke in a similar way in 1936 in a small but invaluable book entitled *The Picture of Jesus the Christ in the New Testament*, the result of his characteristically methodical reflections:

> Perhaps we will not even succeed in arriving at the portrait of a 'person,' but rather only at a series of sketches which stretch beyond our range of vision. Perhaps we will experience that the Ascension was not simply a unique occurrence in the life of Jesus, but rather above all, the manner in which He is given to us: as one vanishing into heaven, into the Unconditional which is God. However, if that is the case, then these bare sketches are most precious: They are signposts pointing us to the 'stepping beyond' of faith; and insofar as they go beyond our vision, in fact, precisely because they go beyond our vision, they teach us to worship.

It is from such a way of thinking that the meditations arose which together make up this book. For Guardini the first step is always attentive listening to the message of the scriptural text. In this way the real contribution of exegesis to an understanding of Jesus is fully acknowledged. But in this attentiveness to the text, the listener, according to Guardini's understanding, does not make himself to be master of the Word. Rather, the listener makes himself the believing disciple who allows himself to be led and enlightened by the Word. It is precisely by repudiating a closed, merely human logic that the greatness and uniqueness of this Person becomes apparent to us. It is precisely in this way that the prison of our prejudices is broken open; it is in this way that our eyes are slowly opened, and that we come to recognize what is truly human, since we have been touched by the very humanity of God Himself.

One of Guardini's favorite expressions was, "that which is truly real will arise from the rich, varied expansiveness of our existence, of our being fully Christian, and will lead us to the One who is truly real." As we are taught by Guardini, the essence of Christianity is not an idea, not a system of thought, not a plan of action. The essence of Christianity is a Person: Jesus Christ Himself. That which is essential is the One who is essential ["*Das Wesentliche ist der Wesentliche*"]. To become truly real means to come to know Jesus Christ and to learn from Him what it means to be human.

Our time is in many respects far different from that in which Romano Guardini lived and worked. But it is as true now as in his day that the peril of the Church, indeed of humanity, consists in bleaching out the image of Jesus Christ in an attempt to shape a Jesus according to our own standards, so that we do not follow Him in obedient discipleship but rather recreate Him in our own image! Yet still in our own day salvation consists only in our becoming "truly real." And we can do that only when we discover anew the true reality of Jesus Christ and through Him discover the way of an upright and just life. Guardini's book *The Lord* has not grown old, precisely because it still leads us to that which is essential, to that which is truly real, Jesus Christ Himself. That is why today this book still has a great mission.

(TRANSLATED FROM THE GERMAN
BY JOHN M. HAAS, S.T.L., PH.D.)

AUTHOR'S PREFACE

Anyone who undertakes the task of writing about the life and person of Jesus Christ must know from the start what he means to do and recognize clearly the limitations which the subject necessarily imposes. One might comply with the present tendency and attempt a psychology of Jesus; the trouble is that a psychology of Jesus is an impossibility. A psychology of St. Francis, yes—at least to the point where something beyond mere human nature stirs: that superhuman reality through which true humanity in God's sense is established. St. Paul touches on the elusiveness of the spiritual man when he writes that he can judge everything, "and he himself is judged by no man" (I Cor. 2:15).

It would be possible, and most inspiring, to trace the roots of St. Francis' marvelous personality; to inquire into what conditioned this or that trait, or permitted, often in spite of highly conflicting elements of the man's nature, the essential oneness of the Franciscan spirit.

But no such study of Jesus Christ, save the most limited, is feasible. Anyone who attempts to overstep the obvious limitations only loses sight of the authentic figure, core of which is the *mysterium Dei,* canceler of all psychology. Here lies the secret of grace: participation in the divine mystery; hence the impossibility of "analyzing" any true Christian. All one can do is demonstrate from ever new points of departure how all attributes, all characteristics of Christ terminate in the incomprehensible, an incomprehensibility, however, of measureless promise.

Or one might attempt to add still another biography of Christ to the already lengthy list. But strictly speaking, a biography of Christ is another contradiction in terms. A biography of St. Francis, yes— possible at least to the point just mentioned, beyond which the mystery of rebirth and guidance by grace contradicts all why's and wherefore's. Still, one could try to see the man as he stood in his age; to show how he was sustained by the century he formed; how all its forces converged in him, its purest expression, while he remained himself, Francis. It would be possible to trace his spiritual pilgrimage to the One in whom all fulfillment lies, to note its detours, the confusions of the road, the milestones reached and passed, the breaches made in the journey by grace. But though Christ also lived in a specific historical milieu, and though knowledge of the forces at work in it does further an understanding of him, a biography of Christ is practicable only within the narrowest confines. Neither his personality nor his works are immediately traceable to the conditions of the times, for he came to us out of the fullness of time contained in the mystery of God, and it was to this mystery that he returned after he had "moved among us" (Acts 1:22). We can point to certain decisive events in his life, can recognize specific directions in it and watch their sense evince and fulfill itself; but we shall never be able to ascertain a genuine evolution of character in the life of Jesus. It is equally impossible to motivate the unwinding of his destiny or the manner in which he accomplished his designated mission, for their ultimate explanations are to be found only in that impenetrable territory which he calls "my Father's will"—territory forever beyond the reach of history's most powerful ray. All we can do is to ponder such words as: "And Jesus advanced in wisdom and age and grace before God and men" (Luke 2:52), or the passage in the Epistle to the Galatians which describes him as one "in the fullness of time," ripening to maturity deeply conscious of the history about him. We shall make no attempt to loosen the close bonds which did exist between him and his time, as certain modern historians have attempted to do. We can only reverently pause before this or that word or act, ready to learn, adore, obey.

The meditations that follow make no claim to completeness. They do not attempt to recount Jesus' life in any chronological order or logical sequence; rather they select from it this or that teaching, event, trait, miracle for thought, as it happens to warm to life. This book is no scientific documentation of history or theology. Its chapters are the spiritual commentaries of some four years of Sunday services undertaken with the sole purpose of obeying as well as possible the Lord's command to proclaim him, his message and works.

The author wishes to point out that he offers nothing "new": neither a new understanding of Christ nor a better Christological theory. Religion is not a question of new things, but rather of things eternal. If, however, current history were to succeed in re-establishing contact with eternal history, then something new indeed, uncontaminated and free from the dust of usage would appear.

Occasionally, the reader may encounter unaccustomed ideas, turns of thought meant only to stimulate reflection on the mystery of God "which has been hidden for ages and generations, but now is clearly shown to his saints. . . ." (Col. 1:26–27).

In the face of this mystery, human conceptions weigh little. They may be used or discarded. What counts is the realization that Christ forces upon us when he himself "interprets Scripture" and our hearts start "burning within us" (Luke 24:27 and 32).

ROMANO GUARDINI

PART ONE

The Beginnings

I

ORIGIN AND ANCESTRY

If someone in Capharnaum or Jerusalem at the time had asked the Lord: Who are you? Who are your parents? To what house do you belong?—he might have answered in the words of St. John's gospel: "Amen, amen, I say to you, before Abraham came to be, I am" (8:58). Or he might have pointed out that he was "of the house and family of David" (Luke 2:4). How do the Evangelists begin their records of the life of Jesus of Nazareth who is Christ, the Anointed One?

John probes the mystery of God's existence for Jesus' origin. His gospel opens:

> In the beginning was the Word,
>   and the Word was with God;
>   and the Word was God.
>   He was in the beginning with God.
> All things were made through him,
>   and without him was made
>   nothing that has been made. . . .
> He was in the world,
>   and the world was made through him,
>   and the world knew him not. . . .
> And the Word was made flesh,
>   and dwelt among us.

And we saw his glory —
  glory as of the only-begotten of the Father —
  full of grace and truth. . . .

                                    (JOHN 1: 1–14).

Revelation shows that the merely unitarian God found in post-Christian Judaism, in Islam, and throughout the modern consciousness does not exist. At the heart of that mystery which the Church expresses in her teaching of the trinity of persons in the unity of life stands the God of Revelation. Here John seeks the root of Christ's existence: in the second of the Most Holy Persons; the Word (*Logos*), in whom God the Speaker, reveals the fullness of his being. Speaker and Spoken, however, incline towards each other and are one in the love of the Holy Spirit. The Second 'Countenance' of God, here called Word, is also named Son, since he who speaks the Word is known as Father. In the Lord's farewell address, the Holy Spirit is given the promising names of Consoler, Sustainer, for he will see to it that the brothers and sisters in Christ are not left orphans by his death. Through the Holy Spirit the Redeemer came to us, straight from the heart of the Heavenly Father.

Son of God become man—not only descended to inhabit a human frame, but 'become' man—literally; and in order that no possible doubt arise, (that, for example, it might never be asserted that Christ, despising the lowliness of the body, had united himself only with the essence of a holy soul or with an exalted spirit,) John specifies sharply: Christ "was made flesh."

Only in the flesh, not in the bare spirit, can destiny and history come into being; this is a fact to which we shall often return. God descended to us in the person of the Savior, Redeemer, in order to have a destiny, to become history. Through the Incarnation, the founder of the new history stepped into our midst. With his coming, all that had been before fell into its historical place "before the birth of Our Lord Jesus Christ," anticipating or preparing for that hour; all that was to be, faced the fundamental choice between acceptance and rejection of the Incarnation. He "dwelt among us," "pitched his tent among us," as one translation words it. "Tent" of the *Logos*—what is this but Christ's body: God's holy pavilion among men, the original tabernacle of the Lord in our Midst, the "temple" Jesus meant when he said to the Pharisees: "Destroy this temple, and in three days I will raise it up" (John 2:19). Somewhere between that eternal beginning and the temporal life in the flesh lies the mystery of the Incarnation. St. John presents it austerely, swinging its full metaphysical weight. Nothing here of the wealth of lovely characterization and intimate detail that makes St. Luke's account bloom so richly. Everything is concentrated on the ultimate, all-powerful essentials: Logos, flesh, step into the world; the eternal origin, the tangible earthly reality, the mystery of unity.

Quite different the treatment of Christ's origin in the Gospels of Matthew, Mark, and Luke. St. Mark does not mention the Incarnation. His first eight verses are concerned with the Forerunner; then immediately: "And it came to pass in those days, that Jesus came from Nazareth in Galilee and was baptized by John in the Jordan" (Mark 1:9). Matthew and Luke, on the other hand, painstakingly trace Jesus' genealogy, the course taken by his blood through history.

In Matthew this line of descent opens the gospel. It begins with Abraham and leads via David and the succession of the Judean kings through Joseph "the husband of Mary" (Matt. 1:16). In Luke the genealogy is to be found in the third chapter after the account of Jesus' baptism: "And Jesus himself, being—as was supposed—the son of Joseph," whose line reaches back through Heli, Mathat, Levi through names about which we know nothing but their sound; back to David; then through his forbears to Juda, Jacob, Isaac and Abraham, who in turn are linked with the spiritual giants of prehistoric ages—Noah, Lamech, Henoch, and finally through Adam, to God (Luke 3:23–38).

It is often asked how two such different genealogies came to be recorded. Some scholars consider the first the lineage of the law, that is of Joseph, who counted legally as Jesus' father. The other genealogy, then, would be that of the blood, of Mary. Since according to

Old Testament law, no line could continue through a woman, Joseph's line was substituted. A third theory is that of the levirate marriage required of an unmarried man to his brother's widow if that brother died childless. The first issue of such a union belonged to the line of the deceased, while subsequent children continued the genealogy of the natural father. Because of these different approaches to the question, Jesus' ancestry was recorded variously.

It is very possible that this last explanation is the correct one, especially since it is Mary's line that is recorded by St. Luke, the Evangelist who brings the Mother of the Lord particularly close to us.

Study of the genealogies makes one thoughtful. Aside from the dignity lent them by the word of God, they possess *per se* a high degree of probability, for the ancient races had a very true memory. Moreover, the recorded lineage of the nobility was preserved in the temple archives. We know, for example, that Herod, the nameless upstart, had such records destroyed because he wished to curtail the pride of the old families by depriving them of the possibility of comparing their background with his.

How their names sing! From them, during long dark centuries, emerge the great figures of the morning of time: Adam, word still heavy with nostalgia for a lost paradise; Seth, born to him after Cain's murder of Abel; Henoch, who walked with God and was said to have been spirited away by him. Then comes Methusalah, old as the mountains; and Noah, encompassed by the terrible roaring of the flood. One after another they appear, milestones on the road through the millenia leading from Paradise to him whom God called from his home and people to enter into his covenant: Abraham, who "believed" and was a "friend of God"; Isaac, the son given him by a miracle and returned to him at the altar; Jacob, the grandchild who wrestled with the angel of the Lord. These powerful figures personify the strongest element of the Old Testament: that wonderful ability to stand firmly implanted in earthly existence, yet to wander under the eyes of God. They are solidly realistic, these men, bound to all the things of earth; yet God is so close to them, his stamp so indelible on all they are and say, on their good deeds and bad, that their histories are genuine revelations.

Jacob's son Juda continues the line through Phares and Aram to King David. With David begins the nation's proudest era—interminable wars at first, then long years of glorious peace under Solomon. But already towards the end of Solomon's life the royal house turns faithless. Then down plunges its course, deeper and deeper into the dark. Occasionally it reascends briefly, then it continues downhill through war and famine, crime and atrocity, to the destruction of the empire and the transfer to Babylon. There the radiance of the house is utterly extinguished. From now on, the strain barely manages to survive, its descendants muddling through darkness and need. Joseph, Mary's husband, is an artisan and so poor that for the traditional presentation offering of a lamb, he can afford only two young pigeons, the poor man's substitute (Luke 2:24).

The history of God's people emanates from these names, not only from those listed, but also from those conspicuously absent: Achab and his two followers, struck from the files, we are told, because of the curse that the prophet put upon them. Some names leave us strangely pensive. They are names of women, mentioned only in brief asides and included, so some commentators explain, to stop the mouths of those Jews whose attacks were directed against the Mother of God; they should reflect on the dishonor of their royal house, rather than attempt to discredit Mary's honor.

David's grandmother, Ruth, does not belong in this company. To the juridically minded Jews, she as a Moabite was a blemish on the royal escutcheon; hadn't David's veins received from her the taint of foreign (forbidden) blood? Yet to those of us who know her through the little book that bears her name, she seems very near. On the other hand, it is recorded that Juda, Jacob's eldest son, begot Phares and Zara with Thamar, his own daughter-in-law. Originally the wife of his eldest son, who died early, she was then, in accordance with the law, wedded to Onan, brother of the deceased, against his will. Onan angered God by withholding Thamar's mari-

tal rights, and therefore had to die. Juda refused the woman his third
son, fearing to lose him too. So one day when Juda set out for the
sheep-sheering, Thamar donned the raiment of a harlot and waylaid
her father-in-law at the lonely crossroads. Twins, Phares and Zara,
were their offspring; Phares continued the line (Gen. 38).

As for Solomon, it is recorded that he begot Booz with Rahab, the
"mistress of an inn" or "harlot" (in the Old Testament the terms are
interchangeable) who received Joshua's spies in Jericho (Joshua 2).
King David begot Solomon with "the wife of Urias." David was a
kingly man. The shimmer of his high calling had lain upon him from
earliest childhood; poet and prophet, he was filled with the spirit of
God. In long wars he had established the foundations of Israel's empire. His were the virtues and passions of the warrior: he was magnanimous, but he could also be adamant; even merciless when he
thought it necessary. The name of Bethsabee recalls a very black spot
on David's honor. She was the wife of Urias the Hethite, one of
David's officers and a loyal and valiant man. While Urias was away at
war, David dishonored this marriage. Urias returned home to report
on the battle raging about the city of Rabba; the king, suddenly
afraid, attempted to conceal his deed by far from kingly subterfuges.
When these failed, he sent Urias back to the war with a letter: "Set
ye Urias in the front of the battle, where the fight is strongest: and
leave ye him, that he may be wounded and die" (2 Kings 11:15). So
it occurred, and David took "the wife of Urias" for his own. When
Nathan the prophet revealed God's wrath to him, David was stricken
and repented with prayer and fasting. Nevertheless, he had to watch
the child of his sin die. Then David arose, dined and went in to
Bethsabee. Solomon was their son (II Kings 11 and 12).

St. Paul says of the Lord: "For we have not a high priest who cannot have compassion on our infirmities, but one tried as we are in
all things except sin" (Hebr. 4:15). He entered fully into everything
that humanity stands for—and the names in the ancient genealogies
suggest what it means to enter into human history with its burden
of fate and sin. Jesus of Nazareth spared himself nothing.

In the long quiet years in Nazareth, he may well have pondered these names. Deeply he must have felt what history is, the greatness of it, the power, confusion, wretchedness, darkness, and evil underlying even his own existence and pressing him from all sides to receive it into his heart that he might answer for it at the feet of God.

II

THE MOTHER

Anyone who would understand the nature of a tree, should examine the earth that encloses its roots, the soil from which its sap climbs into branch, blossom, and fruit. Similarly to understand the person of Jesus Christ, one would do well to look to the soil that brought him forth: Mary, his mother.

We are told that she was of royal descent. Every individual is, in himself, unique. His inherited or environmental traits are relevant only up to a certain point; they do not reach into the essence of his being, where he stands stripped and alone before himself and God. Here Why and Wherefore cease to exist: neither "Jew nor Greek," "slave nor freeman" (Gal. 3:27–28). Nevertheless, the ultimate greatness of every man, woman, and child, even the simplest, depends on the nobility of his nature, and this is due largely to his descent.

Mary's response to the message of the angel was queenly. In that moment she was confronted with something of unprecedented magnitude, something that exacted a trust in God reaching into a darkness far beyond human comprehension. And she gave her answer simply, utterly unconscious of the greatness of her act. A large measure of that greatness was certainly the heritage of her blood.

From that instant until her death, Mary's destiny was shaped by that of her child. This is soon evident in the grief that steps between herself and her betrothed; in the journey to Bethlehem; the birth in danger and poverty; the sudden break from the protection of her home and the flight to a strange country with all the rigors of exile—until at last she is permitted to return to Nazareth.

It is not until much later—when her twelve-year-old son remains behind in the temple, to be found after an agony of seeking—that the divine 'otherness' of that which stands at the center of her existence is revealed (Luke 2:41–50). To the certainly understandable reproach: "Son, why hast thou done so to us? Behold, in sorrow thy father and I have been seeking thee," the boy replies, "How is it that you sought me? Did you not know that I must be about my Father's business?" In that hour Mary must have begun to comprehend Simeon's prophecy: "And thy own soul a sword shall pierce" (Luke 2:35). For what but the sword of God can it mean when a child in such a moment answers his disturbed mother with an amazed: "How is it that you sought me?" We are not surprised to read further down the page: "And they did not understand the word that he spoke to them." Then directly: "And his mother kept all these things carefully in her heart." Not understanding, she buries the words like precious seed within her. The incident is typical: the mother's vision is unequal to that of her son, but her heart, like chosen ground, is deep enough to sustain the highest tree.

Eighteen years of silence follow. Not a word in the sacred records, save that the boy "went down with them" and "advanced" in wisdom, years and grace "before God and men." Eighteen years of silence passing through this heart—yet to the attentive ear, the silence of the gospels speaks powerfully. Deep, still eventfulness enveloped in the silent love of this holiest of mothers.

Then Jesus leaves his home to shoulder his mission. Still Mary is near him; at the wedding feast at Cana, for instance, with its last gesture of maternal direction and care (John 2:1–11). Later, disturbed by wild rumors circulating in Nazareth, she leaves everything and goes to him, stands fearfully outside the door (Mark 3:21, and 31–35). And at the last she is with him, under the cross to the end (John 19:25).

From the first hour to the last, Jesus' life is enfolded in the nearness of his mother. The strongest part of their relationship is her silence. Nevertheless, if we accept the words Jesus speaks to her simply as they arise from each situation, it seems almost invariably as if a cleft gaped between him and her. Take the incident in the temple of Jerusalem. He was, after all, only a child when he stayed behind without a word, at a time when the city was overflowing with pilgrims of all nationalities, and when not only accidents but every kind of violence was to be expected. Surely they had a right to ask why he had acted as he did. Yet his reply expresses only amazement. No wonder they failed to understand!

It is the same with the wedding feast at Cana in Galilee. He is seated at table with the wedding party, apparently poor people, who haven't much to offer. They run out of wine, and everyone feels the growing embarrassment. Pleadingly, Mary turns to her son: "They have no wine."

But he replies only: "What wouldst thou have me do, woman? My hour has not yet come." In other words, I must wait for my hour; from minute to minute I must obey the voice of my Father—no other. Directly he does save the situation, but only because suddenly (the unexpected, often instantaneous manner in which God's commands are made known to the prophets may help us to grasp what happens here) his hour *has* come (John 2:1–11). Another time, Mary comes down from Galilee to see him: "Behold, thy mother and thy brethren are outside, seeking thee." He answered, "Who are my mother and my brethren? Whoever does the will of God, he is my brother and sister and mother" (Mark 3:32–35). And though certainly he went out to her and received her with love, the words remain, and we feel the shock of his reply and sense something of the unspeakable remoteness in which he lived.

Even his reply to the words, "Blessed is the womb that bore thee," sometimes interpreted as an expression of nearness could also mean distance: "Rather, blessed are they who hear the word of God and keep it."

Finally on Calvary, his mother under the cross, thirsting for a word, her heart crucified with him, he says with a glance at John:

"Woman, behold, thy son." And to John: "Behold, thy mother" (John 19:26–27). Expression, certainly, of a dying son's solicitude for his mother's future, yet her heart must have twinged. Once again she is directed away from him. Christ must face the fullness of his ultimate hour, huge, terrible, all-demanding, alone; must fulfill it from the reaches of extreme isolation, utterly alone with the load of sin that he has shouldered, before the justice of God.

Everything that affected Jesus affected his mother, yet no intimate understanding existed between them. His life was hers, yet constantly escaped her. Scripture puts it clearly: he is "the Holy One" promised by the angel, a title full of the mystery and remoteness of God. Mary gave that holy burden everything: heart, honor, flesh and blood, all the wonderful strength of her love. In the beginning she had contained it, but soon it outgrew her, mounting steadily higher and higher to the world of the divine beyond her reach.

Here he had lived, far removed from her. Certainly, Mary did not comprehend the ultimate. How could she, a mortal, fathom the mystery of the living God! But she was capable of something which on earth is more than understanding, something possible only through that same divine power which, when the hour has come, grants understanding: faith. She believed, and at a time when in the fullest sense of the word probably no one believed. "And blessed is she who has believed. . . ." If anything voices Mary's greatness, it is this cry of her cousin Elizabeth.

Mary believed blindly. Again and again she had to confirm that belief, and each time with more difficulty. Her faith was greater, more heroic than that of any other human being. Involuntarily we call to mind Abraham and the sudden, terrible sublimity of his faith; but more was demanded of Mary than Abraham. For years she had to combat an only too natural confusion. Who was this "Holy One" whom she, a mere girl, had borne? This "great" one she had suckled and known in all his helplessness? Later she had to struggle against the pain of seeing him steadily outgrow her love, even purposely flee it to that realm of ineffable remoteness which she could not enter. Not only did she have to accept this, but to rejoice in it as in the fulfillment of God's will. Not understanding, never was she to lose heart, never to fall behind. Inwardly she accompanied the incomprehensible figure of her son every step of his journey, however dark. Perseverance in faith even on Calvary—this was Mary's inimitable greatness.

And literally, every step the Lord took towards fulfillment of his godly destiny Mary followed—in bare faith. Comprehension came only with Pentecost. Then she understood all that she had so long reverently stored in her heart. It is this heroic faith which places her irrevocably at Christ's side in the work of redemption, not the miracles of Marianic legend. Legend may delight us with deep and gracious images, but we cannot build our lives on imagery, least of all when the very foundations of our belief begin to totter. What is demanded of us, as of her, is a constant wrestling *in fide* with the mystery of God and with the evil resistance of the world. Our obligation is not delightful poetry but granite faith—more than ever in this age of absolutes in which the mitigating spell is falling from all things and naked opposites clash everywhere. The purer we see and understand the figure of the Mother of God as she is recorded in the New Testament, the greater the gain for our Christian lives.

Mary's vital depths supported the Lord throughout his life and death. Again and again he left her behind to feel the blade of the "sword"—but each time, in a surge of faith, she caught up with him and enfolded him anew, until at last he severed the very bond of son-ship, appointing another, the man beside her under the cross, to take his place! On the highest, thinnest pinnacle of creation Jesus stood alone, face to face with the justice of God. From the depths of her co-agony on Golgotha, Mary, with a final bound of faith, accepted this double separation—and once again stood beside him! Indeed, "Blessed is she who has believed!"

III

THE INCARNATION

The Christmas liturgy includes these beautiful verses from the eighteenth chapter of the Book of Wisdom: "For while all things were in quiet silence and the night was in the midst of her course, thy almighty word leapt down from heaven from thy royal throne. . . ." The passage, brimming with the mystery of the Incarnation, is wonderfully expressive of the infinite stillness that hovered over Christ's birth. For the greatest things are accomplished in silence—not in the clamor and display of superficial eventfulness, but in the deep clarity of inner vision; in the almost imperceptible start of decision, in quiet overcoming and hidden sacrifice. Spiritual conception happens when the heart is quickened by love, and the free will stirs to action. The silent forces are the strong forces. Let us turn now to the stillest event of all, stillest because it came from the remoteness beyond the noise of any possible intrusion—from God. Luke reports:

"Now in the sixth month the angel Gabriel was sent from God to a town of Galilee called Nazareth, to a virgin betrothed to a man named Joseph, . . . and when the angel had come to her, he said, 'Hail, full of grace, the Lord is with thee. Blessed art thou among women.' When she had heard him she was troubled at his word, and kept pondering what manner of greeting this might be.

"And the angel said to her, 'Do not be afraid, Mary, for thou hast found grace with God. Behold, thou shalt conceive in thy womb and shalt bring forth a son; and thou shalt call his name Jesus. He shall be great, and shall be called the Son of the Most High; and the Lord God will give him the throne of David his father, and he shall be king over the house of Jacob forever; and of his kingdom there shall be no end.'

"But Mary said to the angel, 'How shall this happen, since I do not know man?'

"And the angel answered and said to her, 'The Holy Spirit shall come upon thee and the power of the Most High shall overshadow thee; and therefore the Holy One to be born shall be called the Son of God.' . . .

"But Mary said, 'Behold the handmaid of the Lord; be it done to me according to thy word.' And the angel departed from her."

How quietly everything occurred is clear from the following: as it became evident that Mary was expectant, Joseph, to whom she was promised, wanted to nullify the betrothal, for he thought she had been unfaithful to him; he is praised for planning "to put her away privately" so as not to expose her to scandal, for she was certainly very dear to him (Matt. 1:19). What has happened is so impenetrably deep that Mary cannot speak of it even to her future husband, and God himself must inform him.

Underlying depths that with sufficient reverence we can at least begin to fathom, the unfathomable depths of God, for it is to him that the opening verses of this chapter refer:

> In the beginning was the Word,
> and the Word was with God;

God is being described. With him is someone else, someone called "the Word"; he is the expression of the meaning and fullness of God, the First Person, Speaker of the Word. This Second Person is also God, "was God," yet there is only *one* God. Further, the Second Person "came" into his own: into the world which he had created. Let us consider carefully what this means: the everlasting, infinite Creator not only reigns over or in the world but, at a specific "moment," crossed an unimaginable borderline and personally entered into history—he, the inaccessibly remote one!

How can we best picture God's relation to the world? By imagining him as one who, having created the world, lived somewhere 'up there,' endlessly remote and blissfully sufficient unto himself, content to allow creation to roll automatically along its once established course? Or is he to be considered as something *in* the world, the world's own original cause and *Urgrund,* a creative Power permeating all things, which are but the material expression of his essence? The first conception isolates him in celestial unapproachability. The second would make him the essence of all that is. And the Incarnation? Was there once a man so completely in the extraordinary clutch of the divine idea, so inflamed by divine love, that it could be said of him: God Himself speaks in him? Or perhaps: God is expressed in all things, in all people, but in one particular person that expression was so powerful and clear that it may be said: in him God appeared bodily on earth. It is immediately evident that neither interpretation is founded in Holy Scripture.

Revelation's account of the Incarnation and the relation of God to the world is something fundamentally different. According to the Bible, God entered into time in a specific manner, acting on an autocratic decision made in complete freedom. The free, eternal God has no destiny which is a matter for mortals living in history. What is meant is that God entered into history, thus taking destiny upon himself.

However, this journey of God from the everlasting into the transitory, this stride across the border into history, is something no human intellect can altogether grasp. The mind might even oppose the apparently fortuitous, human aspect of this interpretation with its own 'purer' idea of godliness; yet precisely here lies hidden the kernel of Christianity. Before such an unheard of thought the intellect bogs down. Once at this point a friend gave me a clue that helped my understanding more than any measure of bare reason. He said: "But love does such things!" Again and again these words have come to the rescue when the mind has stopped short at some intellectual impasse. Not that they explain anything to the intelligence;

they arouse the heart, enabling it to feel its way into the secrecy of God. The mystery is not understood, but it does move nearer, and the danger of "scandal" disappears.

None of the great things in human life springs from the intellect; every one of them issues from the heart and its love. If even human love has its own reasoning, comprehensible only to the heart that is open to it, how much truer must this be of God's love! When it is the depth and power of God that stirs, is there anything of which love is incapable? The glory of it is so overwhelming that to all who do not accept love as an absolute point of departure, its manifestations must seem the most senseless folly.

Time unrolls further. Joseph, instructed by God, takes his promised bride to him. How deep that instruction must have gone to decide this sober man! How must he have felt before he realized that God had laid hand on his future wife, and that the life she had conceived was of the Holy Spirit! In that realization awoke the great and blissful mystery of Christian chastity (Mark 1:19–5). Luke continues: "And Joseph also went from Galilee out of the town of Nazareth into Judea to the town of David, which is called Bethlehem—because he was of the house and family of David—to register, together with Mary his espoused wife, who was with child. And it came to pass while they were there, that the days for her to be delivered were fulfilled. And she brought forth her firstborn son, and wrapped him in swaddling clothes, and laid him in a manger, because there was no room for them in the inn."

What we have just attempted to grasp in the obscurity of divine action now presents itself to us in visible form. At first a child like any other, it cries, is hungry, sleeps, and yet is "the Word . . . become flesh." It cannot be said that God "inhabits" this infant, however gloriously; or that heaven has set its seal upon him, so that he must pursue it, suffer for it in a manner sublimely excelling all other contacts between God and man; this child *is* God in essence and in being.

If an inner protest should arise here, give it room. It is not good to suppress anything; if we try to, it only goes underground, becomes toxic, and reappears later in far more obnoxious form. Does anyone object to the whole idea of God-become-man? Is he willing to accept the Incarnation only as a profound and beautiful allegory, never as literal truth? If doubt can establish a foothold anywhere in our faith, it is here. Then we must be patient and reverent, approaching this central mystery of Christianity with calm, expectant, prayerful attention; one day its sense will be revealed to us. In the meantime, let us remember the directive "But love does such things!" The tenor of the infant's destiny is now fixed. What one is by birth determines the general theme of the life to follow; everything else is necessarily supplementary. Incident and environment are certainly influential—they sustain and burden, promote and destroy, effect and form. Nevertheless, it is the first step into existence with its heritage of blood and spirit that is decisive. Christian thinkers have spent much time and thought probing Jesus' inner life, now from the psychological, now from the theological side, in an effort to discover what must have taken place there. But all psychology of Jesus shatters on the rock of what, essentially, he is. An analysis of Christ might be valid for the periphery or outmost surface of his being, but any significance or image it manages to construct is almost immediately consumed by the power of the center. As for theological analysis, however true in itself and fundamentally important to Christian thought, it is necessarily abstract. Hence, in order to advance at all in our faith, we are bound to call some concrete train of thought to our assistance. Let us try this one:

The young creature in the stall of Bethlehem was a human being with human brain and limbs and heart and soul. And it was God. Its life was to manifest the will of the Father: to proclaim the sacred tidings, to stir mankind with the power of God, to establish the Covenant, and shoulder the sin of the world, expiating it with love and leading mankind through the destruction of sacrifice and the victory of the Resurrection into the new existence of grace. In this accomplishment alone lay Jesus' self-perfection: fulfillment of mission and personal fulfillment were one. The Resurrected himself points this out: "Did not the Christ have to suffer these things before entering into his glory?" (Luke 24:26). It was as if Jesus' self-realization meant that his human being "took possession" of the divine being he had always intrinsically been. Jesus did not "experience" God; he was God. He never at any given moment "became" God; he was God from the start. His life was only the process by which this innate divinity came into its own. His task was to place divine reality and power squarely in the realm of his human consciousness and will; to reflect holy purity in his relation to all things, and to contain infinite love and divinity's boundless plenitude in his heart of flesh and blood. The Lord's life might also be called a continuous penetration, infiltration of self, a hoisting of his being to ever higher levels of self-containment. For him self-conquest is seizure of his own superabundance. All external speech, struggle, action is simultaneously an unbroken advance of the man Jesus Christ into his own divinity. The thought is certainly inadequate. It does not pretend to be perfect theological argument but only a stimulus when we reflect on the frail child in the crib and on all that stirs behind its small forehead.

The public life of the Lord lasted at the utmost a brief three years; some say scarcely two. But precisely for this reason how significant the preceding thirty years in which he did not teach, did not struggle, did not work miracles. There is almost nothing in Jesus' life which attracts the reverent imagination more than the prodigious silence of these thirty years. Once something of the enormity behind it breaks through: the incident in the temple when the twelve-year-old is for the first time allowed to accompany Mary and Joseph on the annual pilgrimage to Jerusalem which custom demanded. His parents start for home believing the child to be with the group of relatives also making the pilgrimage, but the boy has stayed behind. At last he is definitely missed, and three days of anguished searching follow, first among the relatives, then in Jerusalem. When the boy is finally found in the temple, he answers astonishment with astonishment: "How is it that you sought me? Did you not know that I must be about my Father's business?" (Luke 2:41–49). Jesus enters the temple, and something in him seems to rise and grip him. His mother, Joseph, his traveling companions are utterly forgotten! His reply to Mary's shaken questioning best reveals how remote from theirs is the world in which he stands even then.

Nevertheless, he obediently returns to Nazareth with his parents to grow with the years in wisdom and grace before God and men.

IV

THE FORERUNNER

Befor the Lord—pale by comparison with him, yet powerful—stands the great figure of John the Precursor. Luke suggests the mystery woven about the birth of this child of aged
parents given them by God with the promise: "For he shall be great
before the Lord; . . . and shall be filled with the Holy Spirit even
from his mother's womb. And he shall bring back to the Lord their
God many of the children of Israel, and he shall himself go before
him in the spirit and power of Elias, . . . to prepare for the Lord a
perfect people."

All who hear of it are deeply stirred and wonder: "What then will
this child be?" Then comes the further statement: "And the child
grew and became strong in spirit; and was in the deserts until the day
of his manifestation to Israel" (Luke 1:15–17, 66, 80).

John has been called to a great and difficult destiny. The hand of
the Lord has placed him in the midst of solitude, far removed from
all that ordinarily comprises human life. There, set apart, he lives in
strictest abstinence, his spirit growing in strength and his entire
being concentrated on the sacred will bent upon him. For any true
insight into this life we must open the books of Samuel and Kings
and read the earlier prophets: Samuel and Elias and Eliseus, who
lived, all of them, such supernatural lives in the grip of the Holy
Spirit. Now they are elevated to the summits of power and illumination, now flung back into impotency and darkness, according to
the Spirit's will. One moment they are filled with superhuman
greatness; the next humbled below the measure of common respect.

Nothing in themselves, they are mere instruments of the force that rules them, parts in the mystery of that active divine guidance operating within the nation. John is one of these, the last of the line, but so close to the stupendous event the others have indicated that he actually brushes it. For that which the Evangelists call "the fullness of time" now approaches. The womb of the present swells; the hour is ripe (Gal. 4:4). John's whole life is a growing toward this fulfillment; this is the hour to which he points. Of all the prophets to proclaim the Messiah, he is the one privileged to say: "Behold, the lamb of God," see, over there—that is he!

One day the sacred calling reaches John. The exact time is recorded in the opening of St. Luke's third chapter with the formal precision usual in the prophetic books when describing manifestations of God's word. Then comes his message, with

> *The voice of one crying in the desert,*
>   *"Make ready the way of the Lord,*
>   *make straight his paths.*
> *Every valley shall be filled,*
>   *and every mountain and hill shall be brought low,*
> *And the crooked shall be made straight,*
>   *and the rough ways smooth;*
>   *and all mankind shall see the salvation of God."*

All Judea hears the powerful voice. In reply to its summons, the people of Jerusalem flock to the Jordan to confess their sins and be baptized (Mark 1:5). It is a baptism of preparation, "with water," anticipating the baptism to come, "with the Holy Spirit and with fire" (Luke 3:16).

When the rumor begins to circulate among the people that John himself is the Messiah, the Jews in Jerusalem send priests and Levites to him to inquire: "Who art thou?" He tells them plainly: Not the Messiah.

"What then? Art thou Elias? . . ."

"I am not."

"Art thou the Prophet? . . ."

"No. . . ."

"Who art thou? that we may give an answer to those who sent us. What hast thou to say of thyself?" And John tells them he is the voice of one crying in the wilderness, foretold by Isaias. To their question why he baptizes if he is not the Christ, he replies: "I baptize with water; but in the midst of you there has stood one whom you do not know. He it is who is to come after me, the strap of whose sandal I am not worthy to loose."

Among the many who come to the Jordan to be baptized by John is Jesus. Startled, John tries to refuse: "It is I who ought to be baptized by thee, and dost thou come to me?" But Jesus insists on placing himself completely within human law: "Let it be so now, for so it becomes us to fulfill all justice." So John receives him in baptism, and as Jesus steps from the water, the mystery of the Spirit is revealed above him: heaven opens—the barrier between Creator and created has fallen—and the Spirit of God descends in the shape of a dove to hover over Jesus. Now John *knows* (Matt. 3:13–17).

Driven into the desert by the Spirit, Jesus fasts, returns, collects his disciples, and begins to teach. He goes the way indicated by the Father's will; John goes his. But the two roads often touch; back and forth between them run hidden paths of sharpened attention, suspicion, and jealousy.

One day John's disciples complain: "Rabbi, he who was with thee beyond the Jordan, to whom thou hast borne witness, behold he baptizes and all are coming to him."

John answers with the profound word of renunciation: "He who has the bride is the bridegroom; but the friend of the bridegroom, who stands and hears him, rejoices exceedingly at the voice of the bridegroom. This my joy, therefore, is made full. He must increase, but I must decrease" (John 3:22–30).

Another time John's disciples cross-question Jesus: "Why do we and the Pharisees often fast, whereas thy disciples do not fast?"

(Matt. 9:14–15) and the Lord replies that now, in this one brief period of festivity in which the Bridegroom is with them, there can be no fasting—there will be ample time for that later. Once it is Jesus' disciples who beg him to teach them to pray, "even as John also taught his disciples" (Luke 11:1). And he teaches them the Lord's Prayer.

Then comes the moment when the fate of the prophet John is sealed. To be a prophet means to speak the word of God, whether timely or untimely. John therefore addresses Herod, one of the tetrarchs of the country. He is a dissolute, violent man corrupted by outer power and inner weakness. He has helped himself to his brother's wife, Herodias, and is living with her. John confronts him:

Not even you may do such things!

The crime of daring to criticize a prince, and the still greater crime of opposing the passions of a woman like Herodias must be expiated. John is thrown into prison. Herod is strangely affected by the mystery behind this man and often sends for the prisoner to discuss his affairs with him and ask his advice. But he is unable to find the strength to pull himself out of the mire (Mark 6:17–21). So John, the mighty prophet, spends his days in a dungeon. Finally he sends a messenger to Jesus with the question: "Art thou he who is to come, or shall we look for another?" (Matt. 11:3).

It has been claimed that John did this for the sake of his disciples, that they might hear the confirmation from Jesus' own lips. Possibly this is true; but it is also possible that John sent to Jesus for his own sake. If he did, it would by no means conflict with his calling. Often, naively, we imagine the illumination of a prophet as a fixed thing, as though he had only to behold, once, in order to know without wavering forever after; as though once gripped by the Spirit, he stood fast for all time. In reality even a prophet's life is shaken by all storms and saddled with all weaknesses. At times the Spirit hoists him far above the heights of human accomplishment or being; then he beholds, drawing from his vision the power to unhinge history. At other times, the Spirit drops him, and back he plunges headlong into darkness and impotency, like Elias in the desert when he flung himself down beneath a bush and begged for death. (No more moving and powerful picture of the essence and destiny of the prophetic life exists than that found in the seventeenth to nineteenth chapters of the first Book of Kings.) Perhaps John did ask for his own sake; if this is true, what agonizing hours must have shaped that message to Jesus! The Lord replies:

"Go and report to John what you have heard and seen: the blind see, the lame walk, the lepers are cleansed, the deaf hear, the dead rise, the poor have the gospel preached to them." Then come the curious words: "And blessed is he who is not scandalized in me" (Matt. 11:4–6 and Is. 61:1–4). Reading them, one stops short. What does it mean, this gentle warning? Certainly, it is spoken generally; confidence is essential to Christianity. But it is spoken specifically too, to John. What is its meaning for him? But let us leave the passage for a moment.

"Then, as they went away, Jesus began to say to the crowds concerning John, 'What did you go out to the desert to see? A reed shaken by the wind? But what did you go out to see? A man clothed in soft garments? Behold, those who wear soft garments are in the houses of kings. But what did you go out to see? A prophet? Yes, I tell you, and more than a prophet. This is he of whom it is written, *Behold, I send my messenger before thy face, who shall make ready thy way before thee.*

" 'Amen I say to you, among those born of women there has not risen a greater than John the Baptist; yet the least in the kingdom of heaven is greater than he' " (Matt. 11:7–11).

Never was human being given such a testimonial. The Lord calls him the greatest of those born of woman, and his judgment holds. What dark, mysterious grandeur rises here! Would you but "receive it," continues the Lord, John is the promised Elias. He is the crier in the desert, he whose entire life was a constant: Not I—he!

The time comes for the Baptist's destiny to be fulfilled. Herodias wants him out of the way. When her daughter Salome delights a company of birthday guests with her dancing, and the king recklessly promises to grant her any wish she may have, her mother instructs her to demand the head of John "right away . . . on a dish." Herod shudders with horror, but weakling, he yields (Mark 6:21–29).

Now John is dead. He was allowed little more than thirty years of life. We are likely to forget this. The greatest of all prophets, the greatest of all mankind, destroyed by the hatred of a sinful woman and the weakness of a degenerate little tyrant!

In the Gospel of St. John there are several passages that shed light on the soul of this man.

One day Jesus goes to the Jordan alone—and how strangely stirring it is, this solitary approach: not a word of proclamation, not yet a single disciple with him. Everything is still open, but over him hovers the unspeakable. John sees him from afar and calls: "Behold, the lamb of God, who takes away the sin of the world! This is he of whom I said, 'After me there comes one who has been set above me, because he was before me.' " Then follows the formal testimony: "I beheld the Spirit descending as a dove from heaven, and it abode upon him. And I did not know him. But he who sent me to baptize with water said to me, 'He upon whom thou wilt see the Spirit descending, and abiding upon him, he it is who baptizes with the Holy Spirit.' And I have seen and have borne witness that this is the Son of God" (John 1:29–34).

At this point let us inquire into the heart of the prophet. At first he does not know who the Messiah is; he knows only that he is there somewhere among the living: ". . . but in the midst of you there has stood one whom you do not know. He it is who is to come after me, who has been set above me, the strap of whose sandal I am not worthy to loose." Then the baptism is performed, the heavens open, the Spirit descends, and at last he can say: "And I have seen and borne witness that this is the Son of God" (John 1:34).

The next day John was again standing with two of his disciples when he caught sight of Jesus approaching: " 'Behold the lamb of God!' . . . And the two disciples heard him speak, and they followed Jesus.

"But Jesus turned round, and seeing them following him, said to them, 'What is it you seek?' They said to him, 'Rabbi (which interpreted means Master), where dwellest thou?' He said to them, 'Come and see.' They came and saw where he was staying; and they stayed with him that day. It was about the tenth hour" (John 1:37–39). Andrew and John the Evangelist have left their master and gone to the One "who was with thee beyond the Jordan." Jesus' "increase" and the Baptist's "decrease" have begun.

The greatness of the Precursor lies in his eye for the fullness of time; in his selfless: Not I—he! But then, what do the words about not being "scandalized in me" signify?

It has been contended that John hoped for the re-establishment of an earthly Messianic glory, and that in these words of Jesus lay a rebuff. I believe they go deeper. The Lord called John the greatest of those born of woman; therefore he was the greatest. Moreover, he could not possibly have remained unconscious of his greatness: of the immeasurable power and weight of his existence.

It was John's mission—and greatness—to proclaim the advent of the kingdom. Nor was he in any way unworthy to do so, he who "even from his mother's womb" was filled with the Holy Spirit (Luke 1:15). It could only mean that his particular vocation was to lead the way to the promised realm, to direct others to it, but in some special sense to remain without. One is reminded of Moses close to death, standing on Mount Nebo and looking down on the Promised Land. He is not allowed to enter. Not until he has passed through death does he come into the true land of promise (Deut. 34:1–6). For Moses this was punishment; he had failed in an hour of trial. For John it was not punishment but vocation. Everything in him cried out to be with Christ, in that kingdom of God about to dawn in Messianic abundance, ushering in the new creation. For us its bliss is unimaginable, but for the prophet, who had felt it deeply, it was the object of his most powerful longing. Yet he was not allowed to enter. No psychology, indeed no one who has not personally penetrated deep into the mystery of the divine will, can explain this. This side of death, John was to remain Precursor: herald of the kingdom.

Let us concentrate for a moment on his fate. He lies in prison, a powerless victim of wretched paltriness and fully aware of the death threatening him from Herodias' hatred. Must not the knowledge of his own greatness have revolted against the apparent senselessness of it all? Surely his darkest hours came then, and with them danger of rebellion and doubt: Can he who allows such things to happen to his servants really be the Messiah?

If it was thus, the heart must overflow at the mystery of love demanding the utmost, yet so gently; so all-knowing in spite of the distance between them, so calmly trusting. Into the depths of John's lowest hour then would Jesus' word have been spoken: "*Blessed* is he who is not scandalized in me." The Lord knows his herald; knows his need. The message sent by the mouth of his uncomprehending disciples into the darkness of the dungeon is a divine message. John understood.

V

BAPTISM AND TEMPTATION

Just how the period of retirement in the life of the Lord came to an end is not recorded. The Evangelists write only that one day, as John stands preaching and baptizing on the Jordan, Jesus suddenly appears and demands baptism. Startled, John replies: "It is I who ought to be baptized by thee, and dost thou come to me?" but Jesus only answers: "Let it be so now, for so it becomes us to fulfill all justice." And John acquiesces.

The heavens open, the dove descends, and the voice is heard: "This is my beloved Son, in whom I am well pleased" (Matt. 3:13–17).

Jesus arrives at the Jordan, the profound experience of childhood and the long process of maturity behind him. He is fully aware of the stupendousness of the task before him and of the powers that rise to meet it from the depths of his being. Yet his first gesture, first words are an expression of deep humility. No claims to special privileges; no: that may be the law for others, but not for me! He goes up to John and asks to be baptized. To demand baptism implies readiness to accept the word of the baptizer, to admit oneself a sinner, to do penance, and to accept willingly all that God sends, however difficult. No wonder John is startled and tries to dissuade him! But Jesus quietly takes his place in line. He refuses to be an exception; voluntarily, he places himself within the law that is valid for all.

This humble descent to the human level was immediately answered by an outpouring from above. Since the fall of man (and the resultant corruption of nature—Rom. 8:20–22) a barrier had separated us from the beatific presence of the omnipresent God in his heaven. For a moment this barrier was removed. While Jesus stood there praying, writes Luke, stressing that it was a spiritual event, an infinite encounter took place: the illimitable abundance of the divine Father streamed into the Son's human heart. Event "in the spirit" obviously; yet also an act as real, or more real, than any tangible reality.

The Holy Spirit lifts man beyond himself in order that he may experience God the Holy One and his love. We have already spoken of the mystery of Jesus' existence: he is the actual Son of God, bearer of the living Godhead which streams through him, illuminating every cell of his being; yet he is also true man, like us in all things, sin excepted. In other words, he grows, increases with the years in wisdom and grace, and not only in the eyes of the world, but also in the eyes of God. . . . At this point the mystery deepens: Jesus is the Son of the Father. At all times "I am in the Father and the Father in me" (John 14:11–12). Yet it is also said that he "comes" from the Father and will return to the Father, and what is still more baffling, upon the cross he cries out in an agony of forsakenness (Matt. 27:46).

Jesus' every act is governed by the Father; hence the Spirit (through which the Lord was conceived and made man) is always with him, for it is the bond of love uniting Father and Son. Yet we read that the Holy Spirit "comes" over Jesus, just as one day, sent forth from the Father, it will come over all whom Jesus calls his own. The intellect cannot cope with such paradoxes, though it somehow senses the reality beyond all reality, the truth beyond all truth. Precisely here lies the danger. The mind must never allow itself to be misled into seeming 'comprehension,' into facile sensations or phrases with nothing solid behind them. The whole problem *is* a mystery, the sacred mystery of the relationship of the triune God to his incarnate Son. We can never penetrate it, and knowledge of this incapacity must dominate our every thought and statement concerning Jesus' life.

The power of the Spirit descends upon Jesus. Into the rapture of this encounter, into the divine superabundance of the moment, stream the words of paternal love which Luke records in the form of direct address: "Thou are my beloved Son, in thee I am well pleased." "Now Jesus, full of the Holy Spirit, returned from the Jordan, and was led by the Spirit about the desert for forty days, being tempted the while by the devil" (Luke 3:22 and 4:1–2). Jesus is driven by the force of the *pneuma*. Mark uses a stronger verb direct from the realm of prophetic experience: the Spirit "drove" Jesus out into the wilderness and solitude far removed from those he knew and loved, but also from the crowds along the Jordan. Here there is no one but the Father and himself. Mark also stresses the wildness of that solitude, "with the wild beasts" forty days and forty nights (1:12–13). Forty days is the Biblical idiom used to express a long period of time. It is borrowed from one of the elementary rhythms of life.

Jesus' body fasts while his soul stands before God. How can what happens here be expressed? Once on the Mount of Olives we were permitted to hear his prayer: complete surrender of his personal will to the will of the Father. Perhaps this praying in the wilderness was much the same, save that it rose from the joyous eagerness of the beginning. Then follows the story of the temptation. Please read the account in Matthew 4, verses 2–11.

Filled with the Spirit, Jesus goes into the wilderness, swept along by an immeasurable consciousness of mission and of strength. He fasts. What real fasting means—not the going without food imposed by necessity, but spontaneous self-denial—we may learn from the great masters of the spiritual life. Today doctors and educators again know a little more about it. At first only the lack of nourishment is felt; then, according to the strength and purity of the individual nature, the desire for food vanishes, not to return for several days. When the body receives no nourishment from without, it lives on its own substance; however, as soon as this self-calorification begins to attack the vital organs, a wild, elementary hunger is aroused, and life itself is threatened. Such was the hunger of Jesus in the wilderness.

Simultaneously, another, a psychic process takes place: the body becomes more supple, the spirit freer. Everything seems to grow lighter, detached. The burden of gravity itself grows less perceptible. The limits of reality begin to withdraw; the field of the possible to widen as the spirit takes things in hand. The enlightened conscience registers with greater sensitivity and power, and the will becomes increasingly decisive. The protective mechanisms of human nature which shield man from the hidden, threatening realms of existence beneath, above, and beyond him begin to fall away. The soul stands stripped, open to all forces. Consciousness of spiritual power increases, and the danger of overstepping the set limits of human existence, of confusing its dignity and its possibilities, grows acute: danger of presumption and magic, general vertigo of the spirit. When a deeply religious person undergoes these processes his soul can become involved in crises of extreme gravity and danger.

In just such a moment came the temptation by him who recognized in Jesus his greatest enemy.

How that temptation is expressed—oh, the dubiety, the provocativeness of the very first words! "If thou art the Son of God," we are reminded of the temptation that so successfully confused humanity's original progenitors: "Why hath God commanded you, that you should not eat of every tree of paradise?" (Gen. 3:1). "Of every tree"—hellish obscurity poisoning the simplicity of obedience and trust, twilight that fakes everything, worse than the definite lie. Here it is essentially the same thing, only much more dangerous for the soul at the apex of human spirituality.

"If thou are the Son of God, command that these stones become loaves of bread." Hunger is aroused; the sensation of miraculous power and the consciousness of divine sonship are questioned and accordingly enlivened. Greed is tempted to break its bonds and abuse the miraculous powers meant only for the needs of the divine mission. Everything is lured away from the pure service of the paternal will into the wilderness of confusion. But what happens? Greed is not aroused—not even its opposite, violent suppression of greed. With the complete composure of one entirely free, Jesus answers: "It is written, 'Not by bread alone does man live. . . .' " Man does live by bread, and it is good that he does, but not only by earthly bread. Even more vital is the bread "that comes forth from the mouth of God." For this bread above all should he hunger. Confronted by such freedom, the blow can only glance off powerless.

Next Satan leads Jesus into the holy city. Suddenly he finds himself looking down from the pinnacle of the temple upon a swarm of people far below.

Again the voice: "If thou art the Son of God, throw thyself down"; mortal and immortal danger veiled in the pious words: "for it is written, 'He will give his angels charge concerning thee; and upon their hands they shall bear thee up, lest thou dash thy foot against a stone.' " The thrust is a sure one, touching the very spot that must prove fatal for anyone made uncertain by sin. That soaring spirit which long fasting seems to have made independent of gravity, that blurring of the borders between the possible and the impossible, fantastic desire for the extraordinary, and most powerful of all, the terrible lure of the abyss—who has not felt something of this when he stood on a great natural height or at the top of a high building? Shall I try it? The atmosphere *might* bear me! Or even the fatal attraction of the fall itself, cloaked in the reference to the charge given the angels! Delusion enough for anyone not sharply on his guard. But Jesus is—and more. Again the temptation glances off: "It is written further, 'Thou shalt not tempt the Lord thy God.' " Likewise no mere parrying blow, but an answer straight from the core of the test.

Once more forces collect for the assault—the mountain-peak view of the vast glory of the world, offering itself to him who is truly competent to rule! How the sensation of spiritual strength must swell the breast at Satan's words! The will to power increased with the sense of exalted dignity and importance! Never was the costliness of earth more deeply felt than by Jesus' greatest and most sensitive of hearts; sweet and potent, it must have hummed in his blood, calling up all his powers of creativeness and ownership. The greatness you feel in you, mighty one that you are, what are you going to do with it? Squander it on the paltriness of the poor or the stuffiness of the pious? On the mission of a wandering preacher? You were born to rule; the power and responsibility of a true sovereign await you! Tremendous temptation! The price, of course, is the falling away from God: "All these things will I give thee, if thou wilt fall down and worship me." It is the showdown. Now comes the answer that puts an end to the combat: "Begone, Satan! for it is written, 'The Lord thy God shalt thou worship and him only shalt thou serve.' " At that the devil left him, Luke adds, "for a while" (4:13).

Jesus returns to the world, and quiet days follow, peaceful days spanned by a wonderful awareness of coming greatness. Soon, one after another, his disciples gather about him.

How forcefully Jesus' life unfolds in these events—in the quiet as well as in the tempestuous. From the plentitude and power of year-long silence they stir, one by one: the humility of the baptism answered by heaven; voice of the Father himself expressing eternal satisfaction; the wilderness and temptations less overcome than dissipated in the face of divine freedom; then the return to the prescribed circle of the mission and the calm waiting for the hour of beginning.

VI

INTERIM

After Jesus' return from the solitude of the desert and before his first public proclamation, between past and future, stands a moment big with the unclouded purity of the present. The protective aegis of childhood and youth is gone; work and struggle in the field of historical reality have not yet begun. For a brief span it is as though Jesus were completely free. Once he begins to teach, every word will bring a response, every action a reaction; effect will be met by counter-effect, and gradually that fateful clinging tissue of historical fact will be woven that is to become his winding-sheet. But for the moment the Lord walks untrammeled.

Since the baptism, the abundance of the Spirit has streamed into him. Spirit is creative; it must find an outlet in word and act. It is eager to measure its strength. Now, in this interim, its direction yet undetermined, it simply streams, self-sufficient and brimming with endless possibility.

Let us pause for a moment and try to realize something we too often forget. Intellectual habit has made the fact that Jesus lived to be little over thirty almost self-understood. Automatically we think of him as one crucified after a short period of public activity. Actually, the prematureness of that death was not nearly as self-understood as we may suppose. True, he did say: "Did not the Christ have to suffer these things before entering into his glory?" (Luke 24:26). But this was a 'must' of love—God's love. From the human point of view, Golgotha was anything but 'necessary.' It was a monstrosity terrible beyond conception that this vessel overflowing with divine potentialities should have been broken so soon!

Had the words, "and Jesus advanced in wisdom and age and grace with God and men" (Luke 2:52), suddenly ceased to be valid? Unthinkable! Let us not be overbold, either, about formulating so-called necessities. Who dares to state that man is so antagonistic to things divine that any encounter between him and the incarnate God *must bring God death?* What if the masses had accepted him, if he had been allowed to continue to grow in wisdom and favor, through his fortieth, sixtieth, eightieth year—to ripest age—what mortal and immortal glory would have been the result! Think, Jesus at the age of an Abraham, a Moses! Certainly, the mystery of divine providence necessarily reins the Christian imagination. It is not allowed to go too far. But surely it should go far enough to realize something of the unfathomable depths of the love which embraced such renunciation!

It is John, "the metaphysician" and disciple "whom Jesus loved" (John 13, 23), who gives us an inkling of that suspended moment's plenitude.

We recall the incident on the Jordan. Jesus walks by, and the Baptist points him out as the lamb of God and relates how the heavens opened at his baptism. John's two disciples are silent. One feels their gaze full of reverence on the fading figure of the Lord, but neither moves. The next day the same scene. Again John calls out, "Behold the lamb of God!" This time the disciples follow him.

Thus it is the world that takes the first step: two of the Baptist's followers withdraw from their master and accompany Jesus home, to remain with him from the tenth hour on—from four o'clock to sundown.

What words must have passed back and forth through the late afternoon between these enthusiastic votaries of John and Jesus, through whom the endless fullness and promise of time so richly streamed! What purity of thought they must have had, purity of a fountain just breaking from the earth. As yet nothing has been soiled

by the world: not one word has been misunderstood, not one rejection has fallen, or suspicion or accusation. Everything still shimmers
in the unspeakable clarity of beginning.

The two are Andrew and John the Evangelist, the writer. The
Bible says little about Andrew. Legend has it that he ardently adored
the cross of Christ, and that in Achaja he went to a death closely re-
sembling that of his Master. John writes of him: "Now Andrew, the
brother of Simon Peter, was one of the two who had heard John and
had followed him. He found first his brother Simon and said to him,
'We have found the Messias [which interpreted is Christ].' And he
led him to Jesus. But Jesus, looking upon him, said, 'Thou art
Simon, the son of John; thou shalt be called Cephas [which interpreted is Peter]' " (1:40–42). A new contact. Like lightning from
Jesus' eye and will, flashes the thought:

You shall be called the Rock! That is vision—insight that sees and
determines what is to come. And it is command. Vision and command that take their place in history, history-making as long as history will be made.

John continues: "The next day he was about to leave for Galilee,
and he found Philip. And Jesus said to him, 'Follow me.' " Philip
understands and goes with him.

Then: "Philip found Nathanael, and said to him, 'We have
found him of whom Moses in the Law and the Prophets wrote,
Jesus the son of Joseph of Nazareth.' And Nathanael said to him,
'Can anything good come out of Nazareth?' Philip said to him,
'Come and see.'

"Jesus saw Nathanael coming to him, and said of him, 'Behold a
true Israelite in whom there is no guile!' Nathanael said to him,
'Whence knowest thou me?' Jesus answered and said to him, 'Before Philip called thee, when thou wast under the fig tree, I saw
thee.' Nathanael answered him and said, 'Rabbi, thou art the Son of
God, thou art King of Israel.'

"Answering, Jesus said to him, 'Because I said to thee that I saw
thee under the fig tree, thou dost believe. Greater things than these

shalt thou see.' And he said to him, 'Amen, amen, I say to you, you shall see heaven opened, and the angels of God ascending and descending upon the Son of Man' " (John 1:45–51).

Infinite, eternal vision of the prophet and more than a prophet beginning to reveal itself! Nathanael feels himself 'seen' in the powerful sense of the Old Testament, the seeing of God that revolutionizes men's lives (Gen. 22:14).

Jesus is still free. He walks in the streaming abundance of the Spirit, but the world which he is about to enter already moves toward him. Its feelers reach out to explore him. He accepts their advances, and the brief hour draws to a close.

Those who come to Jesus (already attracted more than they know), these men whose faces the Master scans and accepts, are marked once and for all time. The lightning that has struck deep into their souls will never burn out. Their missions and their fates are sealed. At first they return to their old occupations; this has been only a preliminary contact. Not until later will they leave everything to follow in the literal sense of the word. Henceforth Jesus too is somehow bound. His hour of perfect freedom is over.

Now let us glance briefly at that other event which falls into this early period: the wedding-feast in Cana. It helps us to see how in Jesus the fullness of the Spirit is poured to fill the need of the moment (John 2:1–11).

That this incident still belongs to the earliest period of his public activities, 'hovering' between family and public life, is evident from the opening lines: "And on the third day a marriage took place at Cana of Galilee, and the mother of Jesus was there. Now Jesus too was invited to the marriage, and also his disciples." Then we read of the embarrassment about the failing wine-supply and of Mary's whisper to her Son.

But he only answers: "What wouldst thou have me do, woman? My hour has not yet come." In other words, your request, based on a momentary need, can have no authority for me. Only the bidding of my Father in the given hour governs my actions—no other.

Again and again Jesus speaks of his Father's will. This paternal will is not to be understood as a fixed, preconceived program including everything that will ever occur in the course of time. Rather, it lives, takes shape in Jesus, directing him during the progress of events according to the need of the hour. The Father and his will are with him always, upholding, surrounding, fulfilling and urging him constantly on. Jesus, who stands alone in the world, is at home in this will; so much so that its fulfillment is "food" to him (John 4:34). From time to time this volition 'condenses' to a specific demand or decree. For every situation in which Jesus finds himself, the paternal will issues its precise instructions. It is to these that Jesus is referring when he speaks of his "hour." This direct and intimate bond between Father and Son is wonderful, but it is heavy too, and often inflicts severe pain. We are reminded of the conflict that is the prophet's constant lot. He stands squarely in the turmoil of a daily life moved by necessity, pleasure and earthly values. Men desire to eat and drink; to live and possess; to work, create, reap honor and power. In a world of such desires, comprehensible to all, the prophet is necessarily a foreign body. He obeys a different logic, the logic of God: "For as the heavens are exalted above the earth, so are my ways exalted above your ways, and my thoughts above your thoughts" (Is. 55:9). Thus the prophet's acts must seem folly, if not a source of actual danger to those about him (Jeremias). He reacts to a different stimulus, that of the Spirit, wind that "blows where it will" (John 3:8). The sudden, inexplicable words and actions that it inspires must often seem arbitrary and senseless to those 'outside' that will.

If this is already so true of the prophets, how entirely true must it be of Jesus! John's gospel is filled with references to the impression Jesus makes on the practical Pharisees and Sadducees. They are uneasy, shocked, indignant. They feel their order shaken and the safety of their people dangerously undermined. This alone explains that otherwise blasphemous passage: "Are we not right in saying that thou are a Samaritan, and hast a devil?" (John 8:48—In other words, half pagan and at the mercy of demonic forces.) A ray of light falls from here upon that strange verse in Mark's account (3:20–21): "And they came to the house, and again a crowd gathered so that they could not so much as take their food. But when his own people had heard of it, they went out to lay hold of him, for they said, 'He has gone mad.' And the Scribes who had come down from Jerusalem said, 'He has Beelzebub,' and, 'By the prince of devils he casts out devils.' " Then follow the lines telling how his mother and brothers, alarmed, appear outside and call him.

From incidents such as these we sense something of that holy, awful law under which Jesus stands; the deep, intimate, inexorable power that guides him, slashing like a sword into his daily life and into that of his loved ones, causing infinite pain to all. We feel the terrible loneliness about him and realize what it must have cost to believe in him and to follow him to the end.

And yet, the Father's will is the Father's love. Through his complete acceptance of it, Jesus enters into the intimacy of God, where all things are luminous with his tenderness and power. This will is constantly forming directives for all needs as they present themselves.

Thus also here at the wedding-feast Jesus' "hour" is to come. Mary is little daunted by her Son's rebuke. She feels the approaching moment of decision and instructs the servants: "Do whatever he tells you." Then it happens: water is transformed into choicest wine—symbol of the divine abundance which streams from above, waiting to find its way into human hearts.

VII

BEGINNINGS

J esus' term of untrammeled freedom in the plenitude of the
Spirit is soon over. We have seen how people crowd into his life,
how soon its strands are gathered together and the weaving of
his fate is begun.

It is difficult to order the events of this life; some of them we shall
never be able to place exactly. But the main events stand fast, and
about each twines a wealth of further happenings, deeds, speeches—
usually grouped by the Evangelists according to similarity, that the
memory may retain them more easily. What may seem trivial from
the historical standpoint, may be particularly profound from the spiritual, for there is no such thing as a 'history' of the Son of God in the
human sense of the word. Through birth he became part of human
history; living in it, working and suffering; on the cross he fulfilled his
human destiny, and in the Resurrection he crossed the border between time and eternity. Granted, within these prescribed events he
was completely historical, yet always he remained God. Everything
he did was done from the eternal; everything he experienced was
caught up into the eternal. Living in time "under guardians and
stewards" (Gal. 4:2), by his act of complete surrender and obedience
he remained Lord of time, Creator of the new creation. Though we
cannot separate Jesus from the historical situation of his age, uncertainty of date in his life suggests more than a mere lack; it emphasizes
here in time the ever active presence of eternity.

Following the Evangelist John, we find Jesus at the Easter festival
in Jerusalem immediately after his first contact with his future disci-

ples. Here a preliminary 'offensive' in the fullness of the Spirit takes place: the radical cleansing of the temple. We feel the coolness of the official world toward this outburst of divine passion; sense the impotency of the spiritual act before the smiling unbelief of the world's mighty and wellborn. This is the first revelation of that mysterious "dispossession" that St. Paul mentions in the second Epistle to the Philippians.

Then, apparently by way of Samaria, Jesus returns to Galilee. In Sichar he encounters the Samaritan woman at Jacob's well, and a despised, half-breed adventuress is the first to recognize the Messiah. He also visits Capharnaum and decides to make it the center of his activities.

One of the Synoptics concludes the account of the journey: "And after John had been delivered up, Jesus came into Galilee, preaching the gospel of the kingdom of God, and saying, 'The time is fulfilled, and the kingdom of God is at hand. Repent and believe in the gospel' " (Mark 1:14–15).

Thus Jesus begins his public life with the proclamation of the glad tidings: "The kingdom of God is at hand."

The Gospels are filled with the Lord's teachings of the kingdom. It was the theme and content of his mission, the distaff around which his fate was spun. It is impossible to state briefly what the words mean. We must read the Gospels, the Acts, the Epistles; must broaden our appreciation of what actually became a radiant, soaring possibility only to fade and disappear. We must familiarize ourselves with the specific spoken words, yet also sense the unspoken thought that runs through them and through the figures they evoke. Then, intuitively, we may gain some comprehension of all that the kingdom of God stands for. Before then, it would be senseless to try to explain. We shall speak of the kingdom often in the course of our meditations, and ultimately it will take shape before us—not in so many words, but envisioned and experienced none the less. For the moment, let us simply examine Jesus' testimony . . . by accepting literally what the witness states. Jesus says: "The time is fulfilled, and the kingdom of God is at hand." God's kingdom therefore is no fixed, existing order, but a living, nearing thing. Long remote, it now advances, little by little, and has come so close as to demand acceptance. Kingdom of God means a state in which God is king and consequently rules. What does this mean?

Let us put it this way: what is it that actually has power over us? What rules me? People, mainly. Those who speak to me, whose words I read; those with whom I associate or would like to associate; the people who give or withhold, who help or hinder me; people I love or influence or to whom I am bound by duty—these rule in me. God counts only when people permit him to, when they and their demands leave me time for him. God rules only in spite of people; when under their influence I am not too strongly tempted to feel that he does not exist at all. He reigns only inasmuch as consciousness of his presence is able to force itself upon me, to coexist with the people in my life. . . . Things also rule in me: things I desire, by the power of that desire; things that bother me, by their bothersomeness; things I encounter wherever I go, by the attraction they have for me or by the attention which they demand. Things in general, by their very existence, fill the spiritual 'space' both within and around me, not God. God is present in me only when the crowding, all-absorbing things of my world leave room for him— either in or through them, or somewhere on the periphery of their existence. No, God certainly does not dominate my life. Any tree in my path seems to have more power than he, if only because it forces me to walk around it! What would life be like if God did rule in me?

Then I would know—not by strenuous, conscious effort, but spontaneously, from the vitality of constant encounter: *He is!* His would be the one name, the one reality before all others. I would know him as I know the beauty and freshness of a meadow in full bloom, and I would be able to speak of him, as I speak of its richness, deeply conscious of what I meant. His essence would be as real and clear to me as that of a person I knew intimately and understood—to my good or harm: someone with a certain face, a familiar gait, whose mind and spiritual powers responded in a specific manner to my own.

Then God would stand with all the power of his being in my soul, as the point of departure, the sense and goal of everything. My heart and will would experience him as the Holy Being who appraises every value, the Sense behind all senses; as the One who rewards not only ultimately, but who alone, here and now, lends the most insignificant earthly act its intrinsic justification and meaning. Then his summons would really reach me, and shaken and blissful, I should know that my human personality consisted of nothing but the manner in which he calls me and the response I make to that call. . . . From that moment on my conscience would clearly recognize its duties, and overstepping mere conscience, the ultimate in human experience would stride into my life: love fulfilling its holy destiny between God and me alone.

Where this is so, there is the kingdom of God. But with us it is the kingdom of people, kingdom of things, kingdom of earthly powers and events and arrangements and interests. They stifle God, crowd him out of our lives. Only in the pauses of our existence, or on its fringes, do they allow him to come into his own. Who can understand how God can be what he is, how everything that is has its being through him alone (so much so, that were he to withdraw his hand, it would dissolve like a shadow in the sun), yet that I, who am nothing in myself, who exist only as he made me, a symbol or image of my Maker, can be so ignorant of him? How is this possible that the tree in the road is more real to me than he? That God remains but a word to me? That he does not stream overpoweringly into my heart and consciousness?

Thus one might suggest what the kingdom of God must be. . . . And now Jesus proclaims that the time for it has come. After the kingdoms of people and things, yes, and in one terrible sense, of Satan, now God's kingdom is to be established. That for which the prophets have waited so long is actually on its way at last—to the chosen people and to all people. The power of God forces itself into the world ready to take over: to forgive, enlighten, lead, sanctify, to transform all things to the new existence of grace.

Not by physical violence was this to come about, but by faith, by the voluntary surrender of the individual. Hence the admonition: "Repent and believe" (Mark 1:14–15). People were to trust Jesus' promise and to make a complete right-about-face from things to God—then his kingdom would be there.

What would have happened if the masses had responded to this message? To have an idea, we must ask the prophets. Something new, almost incomprehensible to us today would have taken place. Isaias speaks of it, telling of the stock of Jesse yet to burgeon and bring forth a scion, one whom the spirit of the Lord will rule in justice, who will help the helpless to their right and trample injustice. Then follow the beautiful words of the mystery of divine love among men:

> The wolf shall dwell with the lamb:
>> and the leopard shall lie down with the kid.
> The calf and the lion and the sheep shall abide together:
>> and a little child shall lead them.
> The calf and the bear shall feed,
>> their young ones shall rest, together:
>> and the lion shall eat straw like the ox.
> And the sucking child shall play on the hole of the asp;
>> and the weaned child shall thrust his hand
>> into the den of the basilisk.
> They shall not hurt,
>> nor shall they kill in all my holy mountain:
>> for the earth is filled with the knowledge of the Lord,
>> as the covering waters of the sea.
>
> (Is. 11:6–9)

What do the words mean? (This is no fairy-tale, no attempt to construct an utopia.) Inspired poetry, they suggest the prophet's vision of things to come. They sing of peace, abundance, truth and purity pulsing through all creation; of that holy state of being beyond the reach of direct words. Supreme impossibility only images of the impossible can imply.

It was decisive for the future that the tidings of the kingdom were first announced to the chosen people, the people of the covenant that Abraham had sealed on Mount Sinai. Had this people believed and the kingdom of God been accepted and allowed to unfold, who knows what might not have been achieved? A new state of being would have been launched, a new creation, new history. The promise of Alpha and Omega, "Behold, I make all things new!" would have been fulfilled literally (Apoc. 21:5). High tide of the world—unending transformation in the storm of Pentecostal love!

But the Jewish people did not believe. They did not change their hearts, so the kingdom did not come as it was to have come. To this day it remains pending, straining toward us in a continual Advent. Sometimes it reaches out and touches individuals or small groups; sometimes, briefly, even a whole community; then it recoils again.

What a privilege it must have been to see the Lord in that early period of abundance when he carried holiness into the crowds. How straightly he spoke to the souls of men! Pressed forward by the *élan* of the Spirit, he reached out to people with both hands. The rush of the Holy Spirit swept the kingdom of God forward, and the human spirit, shaken by the force that demands entry, felt it beat against the door. The accounts of these first events are vibrant with spiritual power. Thus from Mark: "And they were astonished at his teaching; for he was teaching them as one having authority, and not as the Scribes" (1:21–22). They were "astonished," literally shaken out of themselves. Such was the divine power that poured from his words. Jesus' sentences were not merely correct and pointed as were those of the Scribes, they were the words of one "having authority." His speech stirred; it tore the spirit from its security, the heart from its rest; it commanded and created. It was impossible to hear and ignore.

The account continues: "Now in their synagogue there was a man with an unclean spirit, and he cried out, saying, 'What have we to do with thee, Jesus of Nazareth? Hast thou come to destroy us? I know who thou art, the Holy One of God.' And Jesus rebuked him, saying, 'Hold thy peace, and go out of the man.' And the unclean spirit, convulsing him and crying out with a loud voice, went out of him" (Mark 1:23–26). Obviously a case of "possession." Science insists that the New Testament's "possessed" were simply insane; the age did not recognize their symptoms and therefore held demons responsible for them. In this respect it concludes, Jesus was a man of his time. True, the external manifestations then were probably very similar to the symptoms recorded by specialists in our clinics today; but what is *behind* those symptoms no psychiatrist can tell. When the Lord commanded an evil spirit in one who was mentally ill, he worked from an approach that no modern doctor can share. Evil does not function so that one can say this or that is unnatural, therefore demonic. Neither the supernatural nor the unnatural in Christian life makes its appearance by stepping into some gap in the natural order. Everything is also 'natural'; the chain of natural events never breaks. Everything is the result of something else—but it is precisely here, in natural cause and effect that Satan works as well as God. Therefore, when Jesus addressed the demon in a sick man, he did so because he knew that 'something else' lay at the bottom of the psychosis.

This then the answer of the fiend to the tidings of the kingdom—certainly not the response of an equal! (Facile linking of the words God and devil can only be a result of thoughtlessness or of disbelief.) Satan is and remains creature, created thing that in its revolt from God retains a certain power and superiority over purely worldly forces.

The listeners receive these words of the fiend as answer and confirmation. "And they were all amazed, so that they inquired among themselves, saying, 'What is this? What new doctrine is this? For with authority he commands even the unclean spirits, and they obey him.' "

Then, also buoyed by the stream of the Spirit, come the first heal-ings: "Now Simon's mother-in-law was keeping her bed sick with a fever, and they immediately told him about her. And drawing near, he took her by the hand and raised her up; and the fever left her at once, and she began to wait on them" (Mark 1:29–31). First the sin-gle old woman in her house, then the many; stirring accounts of in-numerable sick being carried through the cool of evening to the Master's door. In the loving, healing strength of the Spirit, Jesus looms like a rescuing cliff above the tides of human suffering.

After this great outpouring, the opposite: quiet withdrawal, col-lecting of forces: "And rising up long before daybreak, he went out and departed into a desert place, and there he prayed" (Mark 2:35).

It is that solitude again with its stillness and overflow of spirit in which he once spent forty days.

VIII

Scandal in Nazareth

What was the response to the tidings of God's kingdom proclaimed in the superabundance of the Holy Spirit? How did people receive the revelation of that mystery so difficult to convey to the intellect yet so close to the heart? In Luke's account of the beginnings of Jesus' public life we find an incident that answers the question darkly enough.

"And Jesus returned in the power of the Spirit into Galilee; and the fame of him went out through the whole country. And he taught in their synagogues, and was honored by all.

"And he came to Nazareth, where he had been brought up; and according to his custom, he entered the synagogue on the Sabbath and stood up to read."

The synagogue was not the temple, but the meeting-house of the faithful. Here they gathered to pray and to listen to the sacred teachings. In the synagogue, interpretation of the word was not a formal duty of the priests; any adult member of the congregation who desired to explain the doctrine was free to do so. Thus Jesus was able to preach in the synagogues without difficulty whenever he saw fit, and he often did, both in his native city and in the surrounding country.

According to custom, the servant of the synagogue brought him a scroll, and Jesus rose to read.

"And the volume of Isaias the prophet was handed to him. And after he opened the volume, he found the place where it was written, *The Spirit of the Lord is upon me because he has anointed me; to bring good news to the poor he has sent me, to proclaim to the captives release, and sight to the blind; to set at liberty the oppressed, to proclaim the acceptable year of the Lord, and the day of recompense"* (Luke 4:17–19 and Is. 61:1–2).

We have the scene before us vividly enough. Jesus opens the book handed him, and his eye falls on the great prophecy at the beginning of chapter sixty-one. The passage is allotted him in the highest sense of the word, and the hour is ripe for him to speak openly. He reads, hands the book back to the attendant, seats himself, and begins: "Today this Scripture has been fulfilled in your hearing."

The words just read concern the Messiah, on whom the Spirit of the Lord has fallen, God's *"anointed."* Anointment means the permeating of the whole being with the sanctifying power of the Spirit; it is that seizure, setting apart, and "sealing" of a person by which the Lord makes him his servant and delegate: his prophet, priest or king. However, the full power of consecration rests upon him whose very essence is that of *"the anointed One"*: the Messiah, Christ. It is his mission to proclaim to the poor that the kingdom is at hand. ('Poor,' first of all, are the needy and despised of the world; but also those, however rich and honored, who recognize themselves as participants in the universal poverty of fallen creation.) He is to bring prisoners liberty—and again, all mankind is 'prisoner,' fettered by sin, if only it would admit it. He will open the eyes of the blind to heavenly light, make men aware of God's proximity, restore the broken-hearted, bringing them the breadth and abundance of holy freedom. For all he proclaims the year of acceptance by the Lord, year of the great pardon, and his message of the coming kingdom stirs mind and heart.

"And all bore him witness, and marvelled at the words of grace that came from his mouth. And they said, 'Is not this Joseph's son?' . . . 'Amen I say to you, no prophet is acceptable in his own country. In truth I say to you, there were many widows in Israel in the days of Elias, when heaven was shut up for three years and six months, and a great famine came over all the land; and to none of them was Elias sent, but rather to a widowed woman in Sarepta of Sidon. And there were many lepers in Israel in the time of Eliseus the prophet; and not one of them was cleansed, but only Naaman the Syrian' " (Luke 4:22–27).

Mark notes that Jesus teaches as one "having authority not like the Scribes," and Luke points out that all "marvelled at the words of grace that came from his mouth." Here "grace" must be understood in its full Greek sense: simultaneously pure heavenly gift that can be neither demanded nor forced, and loveliness, delicate, mobile beauty. The words amaze and delight his hearers with their power and charm. Yet, swift as an adder, the objection strikes: "Is not this Joseph's son?" Into the moment, luminous with the beauty and holiness of Jesus' message, darts something malignant. It comes from the blackest, basest dregs of human nature. The Lord recognizes it at once: the enemy. Deftly he forces him out into the harsh light: "but only Naaman the Syrian."

"And all in the synagogue, as they heard these things, were filled with wrath. And they rose up and put him forth out of the town, and led him to the brow of the hill, on which their town was built, that they might throw him down headlong" (Luke 4:28–30).

Here counter-revelation—revelation of scandal and hate. Outburst of man's irritation against God and the essence of God: holiness. Scandal is revolt against the living God. At the bottom of the human heart, side by side with longing for the eternal source and fulfillment of all things, lurks resistance to that source: elementary sin in its lair. Seldom does it confront holiness openly; almost always it strikes at the bearer of holiness: at the prophet, the apostle, the saint, the confirmed believer. Such people do irritate. Something in us finds the very presence of one dedicated to God unbearable. We revolt against him, 'justifying' our distaste with his shortcomings (naturally, there are always shortcomings) or with his sins. How could such a person be a bearer of sanctity! Or perhaps it is only his weaknesses (which from our dour viewpoint of rejection immediately swell perniciously), or his eccentricities that are so maddening—nothing is more trying than the eccentricities of a saint! In short, the fact that he is a human, finite being is too much to bear.

And the sharpest criticism, the most impatient rejection of holiness is always to be found in the prophet's own home. How can we admit someone whose parents we know, who is 'exactly like anybody else' to be allied with holiness? What, So-and-so, whom we've known all our lives, a chosen one! This is scandal, Jesus' most powerful adversary. It closes peoples' ears and hearts to his message, however joyful; arms men against the kingdom for which he stands. Danger of such scandal was closely allied to the person of Jesus. When John the Baptist sent his disciple to him from the dungeon to inquire whether he was the Messiah, the Lord answered with the same words he had used in Nazareth to identify himself and to proclaim the nearness of the kingdom: ". . . the blind see, the lame walk, the lepers are cleansed, the deaf hear, the dead rise, the poor have the gospel preached to them. And blessed is he who is not scandalized in me" (Matt. 11:4–6 and Is. 61:1–4).

Tidings of God's kingdom, confirmed by the Holy Spirit, proclaimed by human lips? There lies the root of the offense. That is what irritates to the point of murderous violence. Blessed is he who does not succumb to this unholy irritation.

In Nazareth, scandal, flickering since Jesus' very first words, now flares up. Then it glimmers hidden under the ash. At the end, its roaring conflagration closes over Christ's head: eternal revolt of the human heart against the bearer of its own salvation.

Scandal—source of the power that Jesus' enemies organize against him. They use any 'reasons' for their hatred that they can find: that he heals on the Sabbath; that he dines with people of ill repute; that he does not live as an ascetic, and so on. The real reason is never given; invariably it is this mysterious, inexplicable impulse of the fallen human heart revolting against the holiness that is God.

Thus into the hour glowing with the fullness of holy beauty and truth slash the words: "Is not this Joseph's son?" and Matthew adds: "Is not his mother called Mary, and his brethren James and Joseph and Simon and Jude? And his sisters, are they not all with us? Then where did he get all this?" (Matt. 13:55–56).

Jesus forces the enemy to step from his ambush: You doubt me? You whisper: Why doesn't he work the miracles he has worked elsewhere here in his own city? Let me tell you! There I could work, because there they believed in me; but you do not believe. And why not? Because I am one of you! Beware, what happened to those nearest Elias and Eliseus will happen to you: their own people refused to believe and fell from grace, and the holiness which they denied was given to strangers!

But the hour is Satan's. From those who had just witnessed, amazed and moved, the grace and beauty of Jesus' words, a paroxysm of rage breaks lose. They thrust him out of the synagogue and through the streets of the city to the precipice of the hill on which it lies, to hurl him from it. Rejection of the kingdom's eternal, inexpressible abundance has become a living possibility. Already the cross stands waiting.

However, the hour in which "the power of darkness" has its will entirely has not yet come (Luke 22:53); the incident is turned into a demonstration of spiritual power. The strongest things are the stillest. The scene in the temple before Easter, when Jesus singlehanded overthrows the tables of the money-lenders and drives the crowds of bartering pilgrims from his Father's house is striking enough (John 2:14–17). But what occurs here in Nazareth is an even greater proof of spiritual force. The excited mob, infuriated by neighborly hate and general demonic hysteria, surrounds Jesus, drives him up the hill to the brink of the precipice and tries to force him over it to his death. Suddenly, in the thick of the clamor and chaos, the quiet words: "But he, passing through their midst, went his way." No return of violence for violence. Soundlessly, effortlessly, divine freedom walks right through the seething mob, its irresistible force bound by nothing on earth but its own "hour."

IX

THE SICK

"Now when it was evening, and the sun had set, they brought to him all who were ill and who were possessed. And the whole town had gathered together at the door. And he cured many who were afflicted with various diseases, and cast out many devils; and he did not permit them to speak, because they knew him" (Mark 1:32–34).

The picture is a moving one. The heat of the day is over, and from the mountains comes a breath of coolness. It is as though the world around Jesus were opening its heart. From all sides human suffering streams to him; on foot, on the shoulders of the sturdy, on stretchers. And Jesus walks through the flood of pain, and the power of God flows from him in a wave of healing, and the words of the prophet are fulfilled: "Surely he hath borne our infirmities and carried our sorrows" (Is. 53:4). The Spirit within him has the power to heal—to heal from the root of the evil. He recreates original life new and unspoiled. Jesus' salutary powers are inexhaustible—more than adequate for all the misery. He does not recoil before the wounds, the distorted limbs and faces that gather at his door. He holds his stand. He does not select, does not choose this malady as particularly urgent, that sufferer's faith as particularly promising; he receives them all, simply, accepting each burden as it comes. His "Come to me, all you who labor and are burdened" is practiced before it is preached (Matt. 11:28).

Suffering is a shoreless ocean that surged in on Jesus, tide upon tide. Has anyone seriously determined to help set out and not been so overwhelmed by what he found, that he counted himself fortunate if he managed to keep afloat? Jesus felt it all and was rocked by pity. He opened the dykes and let in the terrible flood, but he mastered it always.

We know of no word from him that reveals him as an utopian. He never even suggests that pain will be banished from the world. Still less does he exalt himself above it in transports of pity or enthusiasm. With customary realism he looks it straight in the eye; he never loses courage, never grows tired or disappointed. The sympathetic, all-comprehending heart of Jesus Christ is stronger than pain.

Sometimes, roughly sketched in the Gospels, we find the figures of individuals picked from the crowds of the healed. Peter's mother-in-law is among the first.

Another time Jesus is walking along the road accompanied by a large crowd. A blind man in the street hears the clamor of excited voices, inquires, and calls out: " 'Jesus, Son of David, have mercy on me!' And many angrily tried to silence him. But he cried out all the louder, 'Son of David, have mercy on me!' Then Jesus stopped and commanded that he should be called. And they called the blind man and said to him, 'Take courage. Get up, he is calling thee.' And throwing off his cloak, he sprang to his feet and came to him. And Jesus addressed him, saying 'What wouldst thou have me do for thee?' And the blind man said to him, 'Rabboni, that I may see.' And Jesus said to him, 'Go thy way, thy faith has saved thee.' And at once he received his sight, and followed him along the road" (Mark 10:46–52).

Or again, Jesus sits teaching in a typical single-roomed Galileean cottage crowded to the walls with eager listeners. A paralytic is brought to the door, and because the stretcher-bearers are unable to reach Jesus through the packed room, they climb up on the flat roof, remove part of it, and lower the sick man on his bed into the Master's presence. The crowd grumbles, but Jesus, touched by the simple faith behind this operation, says to the frightened patient: "Son, thy sins are forgiven thee."

The murmuring increases: Blasphemy! Who can forgive sins but God? Jesus seals his words with the divine deed: "I say to thee, arise, take up thy pallet, and go to thy house" (Mark 2:1–12).

One day while Jesus is standing in the midst of a distrustful, hostile crowd that watches his every move, a man with a "withered hand" is brought to him. It is the Sabbath, and everyone waits to see what he will do. Jesus orders the sick man into the middle of the room so that all may see his misery. "Is it lawful on the Sabbath to do good, or to do evil? to save a life, or to destroy it?"

Sensing the sullen stubbornness of the hearts around him, Jesus glances about threateningly, as if to force the truth upon them. Then he commands the invalid: "Stretch forth thy hand." And the hand is healed (Mark 3:1–6). One after another they appear: the lame, the halt, the blind—living witnesses of the healing power that radiates from the Son of God.

Sometimes it is as though we were allowed a glimpse behind the scene. A blind man again. Jesus lays his hands on the man's eyes for an instant, then takes them away: Dost thou see anything? Excitedly the man replies: "I see men as though they were trees, but walking about." The healing craft has seized the extinguished nerves; they are animated but do not yet function properly. The figures beheld are still disproportionate, blurred and strange. Again Jesus places his hands for a moment on the man's eyes, now he sees clearly. It is almost like watching the miracle unfold from within (Mark 8:22–26).

Once Jesus is making his way through a huge milling crowd. A woman who has suffered for years from a hemorrhage that no medicament, no doctor has been able to alleviate, sees him. "If I touch but his cloak, I shall be saved." She goes up to him from behind, touches his garment and notices at once on her body that she is well. But Jesus, aware of the power that has flowed from him turns around: "Who touched me?"

Amazed, his disciples answer: "Thou seest the crowd pressing upon thee, and dost thou say, 'Who touched me?'" But the Lord knows what he is saying. He has felt "that power has gone forth from him" and he scans the crowd. Frightened, the woman throws herself at his feet and tells him what has happened; Jesus dismisses her tenderly. It is as though he were so charged with healing power, that he must not even consciously will a cure. One has but to come to him in faith to receive of his strength and health (Mark 5:27–34).

What are these healings to Christ? Modernity, with its vital social and caritative sense, has tried to define the Lord as the great philanthropist, the friend of mankind who saw and helped its sufferings wherever possible. But modernity is over-simplifying. Love, yes; and deepest sympathy—his heart overflows with them. Even the Gospels, usually so reticent about feeling, frequently refer to these: "And when he landed, Jesus saw a large crowd, and had compassion on them, because they were like sheep without a shepherd. And he began to teach them many things" (Mark 6:34). Yet Jesus is not merely a great figure of charity with a boundless heart and tremendous capacity for service. He makes no attempt to track human suffering to the root in order to eradicate it. He is no social reformer fighting for a more just distribution of material wealth. The social reformer aims at lessening suffering; if possible at removing it. He tries to meet human needs in a practical manner: to prevent misfortune, to readjust conditions in order that happy, physically and spiritually healthy people inhabit the earth. Once we see this clearly, we realize that for Jesus the problem is quite a different one. He sees the mystery of suffering much more profoundly—deep at the root-tip of human existence, and inseparable from sin and estrangement from God. He knows it to be the door in the soul that leads to God, or that at least can lead to him; result of sin but also means of purification and return. This is obviously what is meant by his words about taking up the cross and following him (Matt. 16:24). Perhaps we come nearer the truth when we say: Christ did not avoid pain, as we try to. He did not ignore it. He did not insulate himself from it. He received it into his heart. Sufferer himself and realist, he took people as he found them, with all their shortcomings. Voluntarily he shared their afflictions, their blame, their need. Herein lies the immeasurable depth and breadth of Christ's love. Its power is the triumphant power of truth in a love which seizes reality and lifts it out of itself. Jesus' healing is divine healing; it reveals the Universal Healer and directs towards him. It is inseparable from faith. In Nazareth he is unable to work miracles because the people there do not believe. To force the supernatural upon them would be to destroy its intrinsic sense: the faith from which it springs. The disciples are unable to cure the sick boy because they are faint-hearted, and the strength which should operate from the Holy Spirit is thus fettered (Matt. 17:14–21). When the paralytic is first brought to Jesus his physical disorder is apparently ignored. Before all else Jesus sees the sufferer's faith. Responding to this faith, the Lord forgives his sins; then, almost as a finishing touch, he cures him. To the father of the sick boy who begs Jesus: "But if thou canst do anything, have compassion on us and help us," Jesus replies: "If thou canst believe, all things are possible to him who believes," and the miracle is performed (Mark 9:23–25).

Then we have the captain who confronts Jesus with military simplicity: "Now when he had entered Capharnaum, there came to him a centurion who entreated him, saying, 'Lord, my servant is lying sick in the house, paralyzed, and is grievously afflicted.' Jesus said to him, 'I will come and cure him.' But in answer the centurion said, 'Lord, I am not worthy that thou shouldst come under my roof; but only say the word, and my servant will be healed. For I too am a man subject to authority, and have soldiers subject to me; and I say to one, "Go," and he goes; and to another, "Come," and he comes; and to my servant, "Do this," and he does it.'

"And when Jesus heard this, he marvelled, and said to those who were following him, 'Amen I say to you, I have not found such great faith in Israel. . . . Go thy way; as thou hast believed, so be it done to thee.' And the servant was healed in that hour."

In the ears of the blind man echo the wonderful words: "Go thy way, thy faith has saved thee" (Mark 10:46–52).

X

"WHAT WAS LOST"

Around the image of Jesus we often find other images more or less familiar, and it is important to understand his relation to them. We have just mentioned his approach to the mentally and physically ill, so fundamentally different from that of the average social worker or reformer. Next to the sick and the "possessed" stand the "publicans and sinners." Jesus does not avoid them. Indeed, he is seen so often in their company, that his enemies accuse him of being the "friend of publicans and sinners" (Matt. 11:19). The accusation is a sharp one, spoken as darkly as its accompanying epithets of glutton and winebibber. Association with these outcasts was more than questionable, and to this day when we carefully examine the attitudes—whether positive or negative—reserved toward Jesus' choice of companions, we almost invariably find at least an echo of the same questioning surprise. We should know, therefore, what the terms actually stand for.

In the ninth chapter of the first Gospel the following passage may be found: "Now as Jesus passed on from there, he saw a man named Matthew sitting in the tax-collector's place, and said to him, 'Follow me.' And he arose and followed him. And it came to pass as he was at table in the house, that, behold, many publicans and sinners came to the table with Jesus and his disciples" (Matt. 9:9–10). The Evangelist is describing himself—it is the story of his own bitter and blissful experience.

The publican or tax-collector of the Roman Empire was a black figure indeed. A central tax system did not exist. Instead, a private collector answerable for a certain sum was appointed to each province. How this sum was to be obtained was not specified. This was left to the ingenuity (and conscience, where existing) of the individual publican, who was given free rein and full powers of execution. Often enough, he demanded several times the imposed amount. The urban collectors usually sold their rights to bleed the rural areas to country friends or relatives, who in turn lined their pockets. Consequently the people's money was ruthlessly extorted, and the whole system was little better than well organized and legally supported robbery. Palestine was no exception. Here too the publican was the chief oppressor of the people. In addition, as an ally of the Romans he was considered a traitor and enemy and was accordingly ostracized.

Such a man Jesus commands to leave the customs-house and follow him. He is invited to join the circle of the Lord's most intimate disciples. Not only does Jesus speak with him openly—scandal enough—he accepts his hospitality! The man's friends also gather: more "publicans and sinners," a despised company, and Jesus sits at table in their midst. Terrible offense, for community of table was a symbol of brotherly union and had a definitely ceremonial, if not ritualistic, character. To dine with the 'untouchables' was to manifest an inner bond with them and to become, oneself, impure. Thus the Pharisees' shocked question is understandable: "Why does your master eat with publicans and sinners?"

Why does Jesus do this? One might suspect a certain romantic 'anti-bourgeois' tendency that led him to despise the assured, orderly lives of the protected strata of society and to acknowledge only the outcasts and underdogs as full-fledged human beings. However, any such conception is entirely modern and was undreamed of in Jesus' day. Romantic idealization of the downtrodden (fallacy of super-civilized and degenerate ages) was as unknown to the first century as it was foreign to Jesus' character. His words and deeds are rooted elsewhere. He would be the last to consider social ostracism *per se* something desirable, or any established order of property as necessarily detrimental. Every known human condition can lead either to God or away from him. Jesus' point of approach is entirely simple: the sick, not the well, need the doctor. Then follow words of grave irony: "I have come to call sinners, not the just." In other words, consider carefully before you decide to count yourselves among the virtuous. It is not to them that I have come. If you wish me, admit yourselves to be sinners, and then—where is the difference between you and these?

The scene is repeated in much the same form, only magnified and with greater vividness in Luke's account of the chief publican, Zacchaeus, for the incident was too typical of conditions in any Roman province to remain isolated.

"And behold there was a man named Zacchaeus; and he was a leading publican, and he was rich. And he was trying to see Jesus, . . . but could not, on account of the crowd, because he was small of stature. So he ran on ahead and climbed up into a sycamore tree . . . And when Jesus came to the place, he looked up and saw him, and said to him, 'Zacchaeus, make haste and come down; for I must stay in thy house today.' And he made haste and came down, and welcomed him joyfully" (Luke 19:2–6).

How vivid the picture of this little man strangely caught up in the excitement that ripples through the city. Suddenly he must see for himself the Master whose name is on every tongue. Too short to peer over the heads of the crowd, he flings dignity to the wind and climbs a sycamore tree. Jesus sees him and instantly recognizes the deep readiness that has placed him there. Calling Zacchaeus down from his perch, he demands his hospitality. At once the indignant: "He has gone to be the guest of a man who is a sinner." Zacchaeus senses the danger that threatens the incredible honor, and he stands his ground upright. Deftly he throws all possible weight on his side of the balance: "Behold, Lord, I give one-half of my possessions to the poor, and if I have defrauded anyone of anything" (probably he was not much different from the others in this respect) "I restore it fourfold."

We must repeat: Jesus is not influenced by any resentment against the mighty. He has been accused of it. It has been claimed that he lacked the natural, healthy impulse to rule in good conscience which every real man knows; that he was too weak or too degenerate to take his place among the great. Instead, succumbing to a strange split in his personality, he took up the banner of the poor against those to whom he really belonged. Such arguments are also artifices of our day—false from a purely historical point of view and falser still from that of all Jesus was and desired. No secret envy, no impotent rage, no mistrust of earthly greatness here. The Lord knew none of these offspring of fear because he was free—completely and innately free. He championed the despised and abandoned because nobody else lifted a finger for them. He does not say that they are more deserving; he insists only that they too receive their rights. Likewise, he does not oppose the powerful and recognized because greatness and power in themselves are evil; this is true only in so far as they divert their representatives from God. Jesus sweeps all worldly differences aside and addresses himself to the essential human being in rich and poor alike: "he, too, is a son of Abraham." Here again the Lord is guided only by his Father: "For the Son of Man came to seek and to save what was lost" (Luke 19:10).

The eighth chapter of John's Gospel recounts the story of the adulterous woman: "Now the Scribes and Pharisees brought a woman caught in adultery, . . . 'Master, this woman has just now been caught in adultery. And in the Law Moses commanded us to stone such persons. What, therefore, dost thou say?' Now they were saying this to test him, in order that they might be able to accuse him. But Jesus, stooping down, began to write with his finger on the ground.

"But then they continued asking him, he raised himself and said to them, 'Let him who is without sin among you be the first to cast a stone at her.' And again stooping down, he began to write on the ground. But hearing this, they went away, one by one, beginning

with the eldest. And Jesus remained alone, with the woman standing in the midst.

"And Jesus, raising himself, said to her, 'Woman, where are they?
Has no one condemned thee?' She said, 'No one, Lord.' Then Jesus
said, 'Neither will I condemn thee. Go thy way, and from now on
sin no more' " (John 8:3–11).

Again we must take care not to be misled. A superficial reader
might interpret Jesus' act as a defense of sin against virtue, defense of
the individual who has broken the law at the risk of life as against that
law. Here too such an interpretation would be far from the truth.
Jesus is no romantic revolutionary. He does not stand for the rights of
passion as against the hypocritical severity of a moral code that is
brittle with dust and age. If we look closely, we see that the core of
the incident is the same bitter core we have found before in other encounters. The Pharisees have not come for the sake of justice, but in
order to set Jesus a trap. Their own virtue is simulated, for they themselves by no means practice what they demand of others, or when
they do, then in a spirit of such harsh self-righteousness that they are
deaf and blind to the essence of Christ's message. Jesus therefore remains silent, and his silence is the voice of truth. He does not question the justice of the law, but slowly the indicters understand why
they are making the charges they make, realize what they themselves
are. Ashamed, they file out "one by one, beginning with the eldest."

The woman's acts are by no means accepted. She has sinned, and
in addressing her, Jesus does not mitigate the verb. He defends her,
not in the eyes of God, but from her earthly accusers and from the
narrow spirit behind their law. Thus a higher, heavenly justice
widens the heart and reveals "the grace of God our Savior" to all,
and another "lost" one is summoned home by the simultaneously
just and merciful Father (Tit. 2:12).

Then, the divinely beautiful account of the sinner in St. Luke
(7:36–50):

"Now one of the Pharisees asked him to dine with him; so he
went into the house of the Pharisee, and reclined at table. And be-

hold, a woman in the town who was a sinner, upon learning that he was at table in the Pharisee's house, brought an alabaster jar of ointment; and standing behind him at his feet, she began to bathe his feet with her tears, and wiped them with the hair of her head, and kissed his feet, and anointed them with ointment.

"Now when the Pharisee, who had invited him, saw it, he said to himself, 'This man, were he a prophet, would surely know who and what manner of woman this is who is touching him, for she is a sinner.'

"And Jesus answered and said to him, 'Simon, I have something to say to thee.' And he said, 'Master, speak.' 'A certain moneylender had two debtors; the one owed five hundred denarii, the other fifty. As they had no means of paying, he forgave them both. Which of them, therefore, will love him more?' Simon answered and said, 'He, I suppose, to whom he forgave more.' And he said to him, 'Thou hast judged rightly.' And turning to the woman, he said to Simon, 'Dost thou see this woman? I came into thy house; thou gavest me no water for my feet; but she has bathed my feet with tears, and has wiped them with her hair. Thou gavest me no kiss; but she, from the moment she entered, has not ceased to kiss my feet. Thou didst not anoint my head with oil; but she has anointed my feet with ointment. Wherefore I say to thee, her sins, many as they are, shall be forgiven her, because she has loved much. But he to whom little is forgiven, loves little.' And he said to her, 'Thy sins are forgiven.' And they who were at table with him began to say within themselves, 'Who is this man, who even forgives sins?' But he said to the woman, 'Thy faith has saved thee; go in peace.' "

Let us not spoil the sacred beauty of the passage with analysis. For anyone who reads it carefully, no explanation is necessary. We must guard against one thing only: sentimentality.

The woman enters a room full of cold-hearted, disdainful guests. From all sides glances, gestures indicate only too clearly that she be asked to leave at once. When Jesus accepts her ministering, the Pharisee thinks he has trapped him: if he is a prophet he must know that she is a harlot and send her away. Apparently, though, he is ignorant of the fact—consequently, no prophet. If he does know what she is and still suffers her, then he is as wicked as she!

Is Jesus siding with the harlot against the Pharisees?—with the life of dishonor against lives of decency and order? Certainly not. But he is exposing the self-satisfied accuser in all his worldliness as one who is cold, hard, blind, and deeply enmeshed in the prejudices of his class. Simultaneously, he reveals the true position of the woman they so crudely judge: the depths of her contrition, the heights of her love place her, the redeemed one, on the plane of her Redeemer, far above anyone present. The woman whom you call sinner, Jesus seems to say, ceased to be a sinner before she entered this room; for no one can love as she loves who has not already been forgiven for sins that were great indeed.

Here is no romanticizing of sin, no siding with passion against law and order. The Savior demonstrates sharply that for him one thing only is important: the human being, whether its name is Mary Magdalen or Simon the Pharisee. Both are addressed here, not as they measure up to worldly standards, but as they measure before God. This sinner was one of the very few who really believed. Was there any other besides the Lord's own Mother, Mary of Bethany and John?

Jesus does not champion the cause of the free individual against society. He does not stand for the heart as against the law. He does not side with the outcast against the prudent and the respected. He does not consider the sinner as such more valuable than the virtuous. Jesus is far from both romanticism and class-consciousness. He is interested only in the individual soul whom he places before God. He possesses the godly power that springs from divine freedom, power to stir all manner of men: the poor and lost simply by accepting them as human beings and bringing them the tidings of God's mercy; the great and admired by making them realize that they dangerously overrate themselves and risk losing their salvation.

Jesus came—he and no other—to bring about the "Great Revaluation" through God's message to the world. The New Testament does say that the poor, despised, the sinful are more open to the tidings of the coming kingdom than are the prosperous and the powerful whose one interest is to preserve the status quo. Naturally, the wealthy have little desire for a revaluation. The others are readier because they are freer. And though it must never be forgotten that poverty can also lead to separation from God, revolt against God, it is an accepted fact that the poor and the disinherited experience more deeply the illusoriness of earthly existence. The world itself sees to it that they realize where they stand. Need can make one apathetic or desperate; still there remains a deep bond between the sinners, the "little ones," and the divine Herald of God's kingdom, himself poor and homeless.

Once the danger of distorting Jesus' portrait has been removed, let us remember the mystery of poverty, of rejection and "folly for God's sake" that is relevant indeed to Christ: the mystery and folly of the cross.

XI

DISCIPLES AND APOSTLES

After Jesus' death, the question of the traitor's successor is put to the apostles; Peter says: "*And, His ministry let another take.* 'Therefore, of these men who have been in our company all the time that the Lord Jesus moved among us, from John's baptism until the day that he was taken up from us, of these one must become a witness with us of his resurrection' " (Acts 1:20–22). It is as though the chief apostle were taking stock of the period just ended, as though he sensed the imponderable weight and responsibility of their years in Jesus' presence.

As soon as Jesus begins his preaching and healing, crowds eager for health and salvation cluster about him; but individuals come to him too, men desiring to associate their lives exclusively with his. And Jesus does not address himself to the crowd only; he binds those who seek him out firmly to him. Thus a community of disciples closely attached to the Master and to his destiny springs up around him.

After John and Andrew, the Baptist's disciples, come to Jesus, Andrew takes his brother Simon to the Lord, who promptly names him Cephas, the man of rock. Later they announce their discovery to Nathanael. At first condescending, skeptical, soon he too believes (John 1:37, 42, 49).

After the preliminary contact, these men apparently returned to their old occupations: "And passing along by the sea of Galilee, he saw Simon and his brother Andrew, casting their nets into the sea (for they were fishermen). And Jesus said to them, 'Come, follow me, and I will make you fishers of men.' And at once they left the nets, and followed him. And going on a little farther, he saw James the son of Zebedee, and his brother John; they also were in their boat mending the nets. Immediately he called them. And they left their father Zebedee in the boat with the hired men, and followed him" (Mark 1:16–20).

The "man named Matthew sitting in the tax-collector's place" describes his own summons: " 'Follow me.' And he arose and followed him" (Matt. 9:9).

And there are others—among them the Scribe who comes to him: "Master, I will follow thee wherever thou goest." Jesus warns him: Be careful! "The foxes have dens, and the birds of the air have nests; but the Son of Man has nowhere to lay his head" (Matt. 8:10–20). Do you really want to go with such a one?

Another expresses the desire to follow him—later: " 'Lord, let me first go and bury my father.' But Jesus said to him, 'Follow me, and leave the dead to bury their own dead' " (Matt. 19:22).

Among Jesus' followers were also women: Mary Magdalen, Mary of Bethany, and her sister Martha. The sisters were not among those who literally followed Christ from place to place; they remained in their own house, but were among his most intimate friends. There are others of whom we know nothing save that: ". . . he was journeying through towns and villages, preaching and proclaiming the good news of the kingdom of God. And with him were the Twelve, and certain women who had been cured of evil spirits and infirmities: Mary, who is called the Magdalene, from whom seven devils had gone out, and Joanna, the wife of Chuza, Herod's steward, and Susanna, and many others, who used to provide for them out of their means" (Luke 8:1–3).

These are women Jesus has helped in their bitter need, who now in their turn lovingly tend him and his disciples. On Calvary they prove more courageous than the men. "And many women were there, looking on from a distance, who had followed Jesus from

Galilee, ministering to him. Among them were Mary Magdalene, and Mary the mother of James and Joseph, and the mother of the sons of Zebedee" (Matt. 27:55–56; see also John 19:25).

We meet them again at the tomb where they go to tend the body and are told by the angel, before all others, that the Lord is risen. Salome is also named as one of them (Mark 16:1). Finally, we read of them in the upstairs room in Jerusalem where, after Christ's ascension, they gather with the disciples to wait and pray for the descent of the Spirit (Acts 1:14).

Thus the circle of those who desire to be nearer the Master grows. This does not mean that certain people felt a spiritual "kinship" with him and therefore sought his company. Neither does it mean that he selected "personalities," an elite who understood him better than the others, to share in his work. To the end of his life Jesus was intrinsically alone. No one was every really close to him—close enough to understand his thoughts or to help him essentially with his task. He summoned certain people and kept them with him; these he trained, filling them with his will and his truth for one purpose only: that later he might send them forth as his witnesses and messengers.

From this crowd of disciples he did choose a small number to be his special messengers, his "apostles."

"And going up a mountain, he called to him men of his own choosing, and they came to him. And he appointed twelve that they might be with him and that he might send them forth to preach. To them he gave power to cure sicknesses and to cast out devils. There were Simon, to whom he gave the name Peter; and James the son of Zebedee, and John the brother of James (these he surnamed Boanerges, that, Sons of Thunder); and Andrew, and Philip, and Bartholomew, and Matthew, and Thomas, and James the son of Alpheus, and Thaddeus, and Simon the Cananean, and Judas Iscariot, he who betrayed him" (Mark 3:13–19).

What the Evangelists have recorded are only brief fragments of those years big with the bounty of the Lord's coming and going among them. They watched his life unfold from day to day, heard his words, shared his experiences from the beginning of his public appearance to his ascension. The record is fragmentary indeed, but there is enough to give us insight into his method of training those who are to carry on when he is gone.

His disciples are with him always. At the beginning of the Sermon on the Mount we have the words: "And seeing the crowds, he went up the mountain. And when he was seated, his disciples came to him. And opening his mouth he taught them. . . ." (Matt. 5:1–3). After he had spoken his disciples began to ask what the parable meant. "He said to them, 'To you it is given to know the mystery of the kingdom of God, but to the rest in parables . . ." (Luke 8:9–10).

And again: ". . . privately he explained all things to his disciples" (Mark 4:34).

They also come to him with questions, Peter's for example: "Lord, how often shall my brother sin against me, and I forgive him? Up to seven times?" And Jesus: "I do not say to thee seven times, but seventy times seven" (Matt. 18:21–22).

The message of the kingdom is prodigious, its demands heavy indeed. The disciples are often stricken: "Who then can be saved?" Jesus, seeing how bewildered and helpless they are, how utterly incapable of fulfilling God's demands alone and unaided, looks at them compassionately: "With men this is impossible, but with God all things are possible" (Matt. 19:25–26).

On one occasion, startled, they realize how rashly, how completely they have delivered themselves up to him, and Peter asks: " 'Behold, we have left all and followed thee; what then shall we have?' And Jesus said to them, 'Amen I say to you that you who have followed me, in the regeneration when the Son of Man shall sit on the throne of his glory, shall also sit on twelve thrones, judging the twelve tribes of Israel. And everyone who has left house, or brothers, or sisters, or father, or mother, or wife, or children, or lands, for my name's sake, shall receive a hundredfold, and shall possess life everlasting. But many who are first now will be last, and many who are last now will be first' " (Matt. 19:27–30).

He teaches them how to appear before God in prayer—the form, the frame of mind and soul that are most acceptable. He shows them what is essential in his Father's eyes. Then, one day at their request, he teaches them the Our Father.

When they are troubled because those who for them still represent authority—the Scribes, the rabbis, the mighty—are against Jesus, he calms their fears, renews their courage, and binds them the more closely to him: "Do not be afraid, little flock, for it has pleased your Father to give you the kingdom" (Luke 12:32). Gently he prepares them for the coming persecution: "No disciple is above his teacher, nor is the servant above his master. It is enough for the disciple to be like his teacher, and for the servant to be like his master" (Matt. 10:24–25). And remember: "Are not two sparrows sold for a farthing? And yet not one of them will fall to the ground without your Father's leave. But as for you, the very hairs of your head are all numbered. Therefore do not be afraid; you are of more value than many sparrows" (Matt. 10:29–31). Whatever happens will serve God's holy purpose.

Jesus leaves them no illusion about their own strength and faith. When they vainly try to heal the crazed, suicidal boy and finally have to go to him for help, he rebukes them: "O unbelieving and perverse generation, how long shall I be with you? How long shall I put up with you? Bring him here to me," and he heals the youth with a word.

Afterwards, when they are alone, the disciples ask why they failed, and Jesus replies: because you had no proper faith. They had tried to effect a cure by an effort of the will, possibly bordering on magic. He teaches them that the healing of God's disciples is healing in confidence of mission and in faith—pure faith utterly submissive to the will of God (Matt. 17:14–21).

Another time the disciples are on the lake when a storm comes up. Jesus walks over the waves to meet them, and they are terrified. But he reassures them, and Peter calls: "Lord, if it is thou, bid me come to thee over the water." Jesus does so, and Peter steps confidently over the side of the boat and starts walking toward him. But suddenly he becomes conscious of the danger; fear fills his heart and weights him down. He starts to sink and cries out in terror. Jesus: "O thou of little faith, why didst thou doubt?" (Matt. 14:22–31).

One day the mother of James and John, the Zebedee brothers, comes to Jesus with a special request: will he not promise her sons seats of honor in heaven—one on his right hand, the other on his left? (We see here how closely the hopes and ambitions of the little community are linked to the sacred tidings.) Christ questions them: "Can you drink of the cup of which I am about to drink?" And they, little dreaming what they say: "We can." But Jesus only replies: "Of my cup you shall indeed drink"; (though you have no idea what you are saying) "but as for sitting at my right hand and at my left, that is not mine to give you, but it belongs to those for whom it has been prepared by my Father" (Matt. 20:20–28).

Again he reprimands them when they try to restrain the children who have come to see him. "Let the little children be, and do not hinder them from coming to me, for of such is the kingdom of heaven" (Matt. 19:13–15). And when Peter, after his inspired recognition of the Christ at Caesari Philippi relapses into worldliness and tries to prevent the Lord from returning to Jerusalem where the passion awaits him, he must hear the words: "Get behind me, satan, thou art a scandal to me; for thou dost not mind the things of God, but those of men" (Matt. 16:20–23).

Once Jesus sends the Apostles out to test the powers entrusted to them and to observe the people's reactions: "And he summoned the Twelve and began to send them forth two by two; and he gave them power over the unclean spirits. And he instructed them to take nothing for their journey, but a staff only—no wallet, no bread, no money in their girdle; but to wear sandals, and not to put on two tunics. And he said to them, 'Wherever you enter into a house, stay there until you leave the place. And whoever does not receive you, or listen to you—go forth from there, and shake off the dust from your feet for a witness against them.' And going forth, they preached that men should repent, and they cast out many devils, and anointed with oil many sick people, and healed them" (Mark 6:7–13).

They return and report joyfully all they have done, and the Lord receives each one and sees to it that he has rest and refreshment: " 'Come apart into a desert place and rest awhile.' For there were many coming and going, and they had no leisure even to eat" (Mark 6:30–32). Thus he schools them.

Before sending them abroad the first time he tells them exactly what they are to do and gives them the rules by which they must live. (Please consult Matthew 10 and Mark 6.) The whole sense of Christian teaching is based on Christ's living command as it is contained in Scripture. It is from there that we must take our departure, and there that we must constantly return.

Jesus gives his parting disciples instructions valid for all time. Everything depends upon the authority behind them: "He who receives you, receives me; and he who receives me, receives him who sent me" (Matt. 10:40). As for the strength and wisdom that he lends them: "For it is not you who are speaking, but the Spirit of your Father who speaks through you" (Matt. 10:20). The Apostles receive powers to heal the sick, cleanse the lepers, cure the possessed and raise the dead—in short, miraculous powers. Miracles are not an end in themselves, but are to be used, as Jesus himself says later, because those who do not yet believe have need of a sign. Once he chides his opponents: "If I do not perform the works of my Father, do not believe me. But if I do perform them, and if you are not willing to believe me, believe the works" (John 10:38). Moreover, it is given the Apostles to bring peace with them, "their" peace, which is his. The household whose door they enter is faced with the momentous decision of acceptance or rejection. If it rejects the Apostle, his proffered peace returns to him. Such peace is not to be had for the mere asking. It is the carefully tended fruit of heroic detachment and self-denial:

"Do not think that I have come to send peace upon the earth; I have come to bring a sword, not peace" (Matt. 10:34). Christ's message challenges men to free themselves from earth's natural bonds. The one is ready to do so, the other is not; thus we understand the words about his coming: ". . . to set a man at variance with his father, and a daughter with her mother, and a daughter-in-law with her mother-in-law; and a man's enemies will be those of his own household. He who loves father or mother more than me is not worthy of me; and he who loves son or daughter more than me is not worthy of me" (Matt. 10:35–37). However, he who accepts this sword, receives with it holy peace.

It is clear that the bringers of such tidings travel a dangerous road: "Behold, I am sending you forth like sheep in the midst of wolves. Be therefore wise as serpents, and guileless as doves" if you would survive. The disciples can expect no better treatment than that accorded their Master. If people called him "Beelzebub, how much more those of his household!" They will be dragged "before governors and kings" on Jesus' account and hated for his name's sake. But they are not to fear, for they are in good hands; ". . . what you are to speak will be given you in that hour . . . it is not you who are speaking, but the Spirit of your Father who speaks in you." And even if they should kill the body, the soul that has given itself to Christ is invulnerable. "He who finds his life will lose it, and he who loses his life for my sake, will find it" (Matt. 10:16–39).

Reading the Gospel, we do not gain the impression that during Jesus' lifetime the disciples really grasped his meaning. The Lord was not privileged to live among them as among people who understood him, who saw who he was and the goal before him. Again and again situations arise which show how utterly alone he remained in their midst. Is there a single hour in which his words, pure and undistorted, are really comprehended, really received by heart and mind? I doubt it. How often we are struck by the smallness, the narrowness, the paltriness of the disciples' reactions; how often the heavenly message is degraded to an earthly one! Involuntarily we wonder what might have happened had great and daring men walked with him—all the way. But then we halt; had he not come to bring that which is great by other than worldly standards of great-ness, by that greatness to which the "little ones" are called? . . . If only these at least had opened their hearts to him! Instead, we see how stubbornly they cling to the Messiah-conceptions of the day—till the very moment of the Ascension (from that same Mount of Olives where Christ's agony began) when they ask: "Lord, wilt thou at this time restore the kingdom to Israel?" (Acts 1:6).

Once, just after the miracle of the loaves and fishes, they put out to sea together. Still in the grip of the wonderful hour behind them, Jesus speaks as though from a deep reverie: "Take heed; beware of the leaven of the Pharisees, and of the leaven of Herod!" But the disciples only "began to argue among themselves, saying, 'We have no bread.' " Jesus noticed this and upbraided them: "Why do you argue that you have no bread? Do you not perceive, nor understand? Is your heart still blinded? Though you have eyes do you not see, and though you have ears do you not hear? And do you not re-member? When I broke the five loaves among five thousand, how many baskets full of fragments did you take up?" (Mark 8:15–19).

Again, on the way to Jerusalem he tries to prepare them for the coming passion: "But they did not understand . . . and they were afraid to ask him about this saying" (Luke 9:45). Consequently, when the terrible events of Good Friday run contrary to their ex-pectations, the ground beneath their feet begins to rock. Though Golgotha, the world's response to the sacred message, best proves that it is a heavenly message and must first revolutionize earthly standards, the disciples are utterly confounded. They desert the cross and flee—all but the one of whom it is written that the Lord "loved" him (John 19:26).

First, Pentecost must come. The Holy Spirit must open their eyes and unseal their hearts before the truth is really theirs. It is as if everything Jesus had said and done, as if the tremendousness of his personality and destiny have sunk into their consciousness only as seed sinks into dumb and passive earth. The disciples seem to have seen and heard only physically, registering the impressions and storing them away in their minds. Until now they have been untouched by act and word. But when the Spirit descends, the dormant seed suddenly swells and unfolds, and at last the men who were to be his faithful witnesses spring up, who in turn spread the seed of the Master's sacred word abroad.

What is an apostle really? Frankly, the impression we get from the New Testament hardly permits us to claim that these men were great or ingenious in the worldly sense. It is difficult even to count them 'great religious personalities,' if by this we mean bearers of inherent spiritual talents. John and Paul were probably exceptions, but we only risk misunderstanding them both by overstating this. On the whole, we do the apostle no service by considering him a great religious personality. This attitude is usually the beginning of unbelief. Personal importance, spiritual creativeness, dynamic faith are not decisive in his life. What counts is that Jesus Christ has called him, pressed his seal upon him, and sent him forth.

"You have not chosen me, but I have chosen you, and have appointed you that you should go and bear fruit . . ." (John 15:16). An apostle then is one who is sent. It is not he who speaks, but Christ in him. In his first Corinthian epistle Paul distinguishes nicely between the instructions of "the Lord" and what he, Paul, has to say. The Lord's words are commands; his own, suggestions (7:12). The apostle is filled with Christ, saturated with thought of Christ; the Lord, whom he represents, is the substance of his life. What he teaches is not what he has learned from personal 'experience' or 'revelation,' it is God's word, uttered upon God's command: "Go, therefore, and make disciples of all nations . . . teaching them to observe all that I have commanded you" (Matt. 28:19). To this end alone has the apostle been called, and his very limitations seem an added protection to the truth he bears. When Jesus says: "I praise thee, Father, Lord of heaven and earth, that thou didst hide these things from the wise and prudent, and didst reveal them to little ones," it is an outburst of jubilation over the unutterable mystery of God's love and creative glory (Matt. 11:25). Spiritually, the apostle is seldom more than a "little one"; precisely this guarantees the purity of his role of messenger.

To be nothing in oneself, everything in Christ; to be obliged to contain such tremendous contents in so small a vessel; to be a constant herald with no life of one's own; to forego once and forever the happy unity of blood and heart and spirit in all one does and is— something of the trials of such an existence dawns on us when we read the first letter of St. Paul to the Corinthians, of that Paul who experienced so deeply the simultaneous greatness and questionableness of apostledom: "For I think God has set forth us the apostles last of all, as men doomed to death, seeing that we have been made a spectacle to the world, and to angels, and to men. We are fools for Christ, but you are wise in Christ! We are weak, but you are strong! You are honored, but we are without honor! To this very hour we hunger and thirst, and we are naked and buffeted, and have no fixed abode. And we toil, working with our own hands. We are reviled and we bless, we are persecuted and we bear it, we are maligned and we entreat, we have become as the refuse of this world, of the off-scouring of all, even until now!" (I Cor. 4:8–13).

XII

THE BEATITUDES

And seeing the crowds, he went up the mountain. And opening his mouth he taught them, saying, . . ." What follows is known as the Sermon on the Mount. It is reported by two Evangelists: by Luke in the sixth, by Matthew in the fifth, sixth, and seventh chapters of his Gospel. The pith of the message, which made a profound impression upon all who heard it, is the same in both. In Luke, clearly sketched, it stands alone, that remarkable annunciation on the mountainside that begins with the Beatitudes and ends with the comparison of the two men, one of whom builds his house on solid rock, the other on rubble. Matthew uses the Sermon to introduce a long row of Jesus' teachings imparted on different occasions, though probably from the same period of his life, since the same joyful plenitude underlies both.

Both accounts of the Beatitudes proper begin with the word "Blessed." In Luke there are four Beatitudes: "Blessed are you poor, for yours is the kingdom of God. Blessed are you who hunger now, for you shall be satisfied. Blessed are you who weep now, for you shall laugh. Blessed shall you be when men hate you, and when they shut you out, and reproach you, and reject your name as evil, because of the Son of Man."

But after the words: "Rejoice on that day and exult, for behold your reward is great in heaven. For in the selfsame manner their fathers used to treat the prophets," come the four adverse prophecies: "But woe to you rich! for you are now having your comfort. Woe to you who are filled! for you shall hunger. Woe to you who laugh now! for you shall mourn and weep. Woe to you when all men speak well of you! In the selfsame manner their fathers used to treat the prophets."

We have cause to stop and ask what the four warnings mean. Here something unfamiliar, revolutionary, lifts its head—what is it?

Matthew also records these four Beatitudes, but he colors them differently, spiritualizes them and includes four more:

"Blessed are the poor in spirit, for theirs is the kingdom of heaven.

"Blessed are the meek, for they shall possess the earth.

"Blessed are they who mourn, for they shall be comforted.

"Blessed are they who hunger and thirst for justice, for they shall be satisfied.

"Blessed are the merciful, for they shall obtain mercy.

"Blessed are the clean of heart, for they shall see God.

"Blessed are the peacemakers, for they shall be called children of God.

"Blessed are they who suffer persecution for justice' sake, for theirs is the kingdom of heaven.

"Blessed are you when men reproach you, and persecute you, and, speaking falsely, say all manner of evil against you, for my sake.

"Rejoice and exult, because your reward is great in heaven; for so did they persecute the prophets who were before you" (Matt. 5:3–12).

Praise for the meek, those who have become quiet within, humble and kind. Theirs an attitude of genuine selflessness, of clarity and quiet before God. Such as these will inherit the earth. In the *ordo* of things to come they will be masters, ruling not with weakness, but with that strength become mild which is capable of ruling straight from the center of truth. The merciful are praised because they will find mercy with God. Love of neighbor and love of God belong together: "Thou shalt love the Lord thy God with thy whole heart . . ." and "thy neighbor as thyself." By that same token: "And forgive us our debts, as we also forgive our debtors" (Matt. 22:37–39; 6:12). The love Christ means is a live current that comes from God, is transmitted from person to person, and returns to God. It runs a sacred cycle reaching from God to an individual, from the individual to his neighbor, and back through faith to God. He who breaks the circuit at any point breaks the flow of love. He who transmits purely, however small a part of that love, helps establish the circuit for the whole.

Blessed are the clean of heart, for they will see God. Purity of heart means not only freedom from confusion through the senses, but a general inner clarity and sincerity of intent before God. Those who possess it see God, for he is recognized not by the bare intellect, but by the inner vision. The eye is clear when the heart is clear, for the roots of the eye are in the heart. To perceive God then, we must purify the heart; it helps little to tax the intellect.

Finally, blessed are the peacemakers, for they shall be recognized as sons of God. God is God of peace because He is a God of strength and goodness. It is as difficult to establish genuine peace as it is easy to inflame conflict. Conflict brings with it all the narrowness, contrariness of earthly existence; in order to establish peace, intrinsic peace, one must have deep, all-resolving all-overcoming strength. Those who can build such peace are truly "of God."

We have already discussed the claim that Jesus sided with the weak; hence he himself was fundamentally weak. The theory goes on to explain that the ancient vigor of his blood (which once filled the veins of a David, a Solomon, and still flowed in the later mutinous kings), had spent itself, and consequently Jesus was highstrung, delicate and good, but sadly decadent. Thus it was natural for him to take his stand with the underlings: the poor, the hunted, the oppressed, the suffering and resigned. The best reply to such assumptions is the question: Is a man's strength to be measured solely by his insistence on getting his own way, if not by his brains, by his fists? Obviously there is a higher kind of strength; one, however, which renders all others questionable.

The above interpretation of Jesus' character is the product of very definite prejudices of a none too superior nature. Much nearer the truth would be another, one at least indicative of a certain warmth of heart: namely, that here we are dealing with an overflowing of pure divine love, which by its very purity, is directed especially toward those who need it most: the poor, the sorrowful, and the persecuted. But not even this interpretation quite strikes home. We can arrive at the truth only from the inside, from the heart of the Christian tidings. In the eleventh chapter of his Gospel Matthew writes: "At that time Jesus spoke and said, 'I praise thee, Father, Lord of heaven and earth, that thou didst hide these things from the wise and prudent, and didst reveal them to little ones. Yes, Father, for such was thy good pleasure.' "

Here something so glorious, so powerful seems to fill Jesus' heart that it overflows with gratitude and praise. Isn't this part of the same mystery as that of the Beatitudes? That consciousness of razing all that the world calls great in order to erect authentic greatness?

Jesus did not come to add a new link to mankind's already existing chain of cognition; he did not come to scale new peaks of existence higher than any previously glimpsed; nor did he come to establish a new ideal, a transvaluation for which the time was at last ripe. It is the other way around. From the abundance otherwise reserved for heaven, Jesus brings divine reality to earth. He is the stream of living water from the eternal source of the Father's love to the thirsting world. From 'above' he establishes the new existence it was impossible to establish solely from below, existence which, seen only from the natural level, must seem subvertive and incoherent.

To participate in this new order, man must open his heart. He must free himself from the clutches of natural existence and advance to meet the things to come. He must eradicate the old, deeply rooted claim that this world is sufficient unto itself, the essential and only reality; he must admit that earthly existence even at its best is stained and discredited in the eyes of God. Naturally such self-emancipation is particularly difficult for those for whom the world holds the most delights—for the powerful and creative, for all who have a large share in earth's greatness and beauty. These are the rich, the sated, the laughing, the praised and honored ones—hence, the woe that threatens them. On the other hand, blessings on the poor, the mournful, the hungry and persecuted, not because their condition in itself is blessed, but because it helps them to realize that more than just this world exists. Need teaches them only too well how inadequate existence is, and once taught, they turn more easily from earth to heaven for something better.

Of course the reaction is not guaranteed. Nothing on earth ever, of itself, guarantees heaven. Poverty can make men greedier than wealth. Among families long accustomed to property one often finds great detachment. This freedom from things is of course earthly freedom, product of a high degree of culture and likewise no guarantor of grace; it can immediately shrink from any contact from above. Hunger can harden; pain can drive to despair; contempt can inwardly destroy. Then they too are woes. But on the whole, Jesus' "Blessed are you" is correct. He spoke from experience: it was the poor, the suffering, the despised publicans, sinners and harlots who at least attempted to believe. The powerful, the learned, the wealthy, the secure were provoked by his message, or laughed at him, or hated him, whom they considered a danger to the political existence of the nation: "But one of them, Caiphas, being high priest that year, said to them, 'You know nothing at all; nor do you reflect that it is expedient for us that one man die for the people, instead of the whole nation perishing.' " And they acted accordingly.

In all Jesus says and does stalks a disturbing, antagonizing demand for a general revaluation. Healthy common sense says that wealth is blessing; blessing, the fullness of possessions; blessing, happiness and pleasure and fame. Our natural reaction to the Sermon on the Mount is one of distaste, and it is much better to face that distaste openly and try to overcome it, than to unthinkingly accept Jesus' words as pious platitudes. That is the last thing they are. They come from heaven, but they shake, palpably, the foundations of earth.

The Sermon on the Mount is abused not only by those who resent all questioning of earth's supremacy, or by those who accept the words heedlessly, without making the slightest effort to realize in their own lives the thought behind them. All the mediocre men and women who attempt to justify their weakness to the strong demands of the world with the Beatitudes distort them shamefully, as do those wretched representatives of false piety who attempt to degrade the beauty and costliness of earth from 'the Christian' viewpoint.

Only he does not betray Christ's wonderful words from the mountainside, who keeps his eye clear for the great and beautiful things of life, yet at the same time understands that even the best earth has to offer is paltry and stained and lost by comparison with that which comes from heaven.

In the Beatitudes something of celestial grandeur breaks through. They are no mere formulas of superior ethics, but tidings of sacred and supreme reality's entry into the world. They are the fanfare to that which St. Paul refers in the eighth chapter of his Roman epistle when he speaks of the growing glory of the children of God, and what the last chapters of the Apocalypse suggest in their reference to the new heaven and the new earth.

Here is something new, cosmic, incomparable to anything that has ever been. Jesus can express it only by turning all comprehensible values inside out. When a human being in the grip of divine power attempts to convey something of God's holy 'otherness' he tries one earthly simile after another. In the end he discards them all as inadequate and says apparently wild and senseless things meant to startle the heart into feeling what lies beyond the reaches of the brain. Something of the kind takes place here: "Eye has not seen nor ear heard, nor has it entered into the heart of man, what things God has prepared for those who love him" (I Cor. 2:9). They can be brought closer only by the overthrow of everything naturally comprehensible. Flung into a world of new logic, we are forced to make a genuine effort to understand.

After the Beatitudes, which dart like great jets of flame from the heat and power of the love that awaits us, there follows a row of instruction as to how, now that we have heard, we are to conduct our lives: "But I say to you who are listening: Love your enemies, do good to those who hate you. Bless those who curse you, pray for those who calumniate you."

Do we read correctly? It is enmity Jesus is discussing. What that is only he who has had a real enemy knows, he whose heart has burned with insult; who has never been able to recover from the loss of all an enemy has destroyed. And now, that enemy is not only to be forgiven, but loved! No misunderstanding is possible: "And if you love those who love you, what merit have you? For even sinners love those who love them. And if you do good to those who do good to you, what merit have you? For even sinners do that. And if you lend to those from whom you hope to receive in return, what merit have you? For even sinners lend to sinners that they may get back as much in return. But love your enemies, and do good, and lend, not hoping for any return, and your reward shall be great, and you shall be children of the Most High, for he is kind towards the ungrateful and evil. Be merciful, therefore, even as your Father is merciful."

This is no longer mere justice or even goodness. It is no longer the voice of earthly reason that speaks. Something entirely different is demanded—the positive, heroic act of a bounty that can be acquired only from above, a divine generosity that is its own measure. And again: "And to him who strikes thee on the one cheek, offer the other also; and from him who takes away thy cloak, do not withhold thy tunic either. Give to everyone who asks of thee, and from him who takes away thy goods, ask no return. And even as you wish men to do to you, so also do you to them."

This most certainly does not mean that one must behave like a weakling or surrender oneself to force. Rather, that man should extricate himself from the whole earthly business of defense and aggression, of blow and counterblow, of right and usurpation. He should emerge from the hue-and-cry of terrestrial forces and affiliations to share in the freedom that God alone has to give. The gist of the message lies in the words: ". . . and you shall be children of the Most High, for he is kind towards the ungrateful and evil."

Now we begin to see what Jesus is driving at: a bearing in our relationship to others that is no less than divinely free—not what law and order demand, but what true liberty gives. The measure of that liberty is love, the love of God.

Something of the superabundance of the mood is poured into the words: "Be merciful, therefore, even as your Father is merciful . . . give, and it shall be given to you; good measure, pressed down, shaken together, running over, shall they pour into your lap. For with what measure you measure, it shall be measured to you" (Luke 6:38).

To this we can only reply: But how can we possibly behave like God? And the question, which is really an observation, is sound. Alone we certainly cannot. But Christ does not stand by, a noble taskmaster, urging us to climb by ourselves heights far beyond our strength. What he desires for us is the supernatural life of the children of God. As long as we think from the worldly standpoint, this is of course out of our reach. But Christ says: "With men this is impossible, but with God all things are possible" (Matt. 19:26). He shows us that God not only demands this of us, but that he gives us his own understanding, his own strength, thus enabling us to accomplish his demands. We must accept this on faith. When the mind cries: But that is impossible! faith replies: It *is* possible! Our faith is "the victory that overcomes the world" (I John 5:4).

Every day will close with the realization that we have failed. And still we dare not ignore the command. Ruefully we must place our failure at the feet of our Maker and begin again in the indomitable faith that we will succeed, because God himself gives us both the necessary will and the appointed way (Phil. 2:13).

PART TWO

Message and Promise

I

THE FULLNESS OF JUSTICE

The meditations in Part One dealt with the origin of the Lord and that season of his life which is often referred to as the spring of his public activity. It was then that the power of his personality and the vital truth of his gospel gripped all who saw him. Everywhere hearts unfolded; miracle flowered on miracle, and it seemed as though now surely the approaching kingdom of God must appear in all its unconcealed abundance.

The records of this period are climaxed by the Sermon on the Mount. At the end of Part One we treated the first half of the Sermon, beginning with the powerful and disquieting Beatitudes. It has been claimed that the Sermon on the Mount promulgated Jesus' ethics, in which he clearly revealed the new relationship of man to himself, to others, to the world, and to God: in short, Christian ethics as differentiated from those of the Old Testament and from all other existent ethical codes. But this interpretation is not exact. Once we restrict the word ethics to its modern, specific sense of moral principles it no longer adequately covers the Sermon on the Mount. What Jesus revealed there on the mountainside was no mere ethical code, but a whole new existence—admittedly, one in which an *ethos* is also immediately evident.

Consciousness of this new existence breaks through forcefully in the Beatitudes. Startling words define as "blessed" those whom we naturally consider far from blessed, whereas those we naturally count blessed, the Beatitudes insist are threatened with woe! (Luke 6:24–26). We have tried to interpret this as a transvaluation from 'above' so great and revolutionary that it can be expressed only by the complete reversal of our natural sense of values. How does the resultant new life with all it includes compare with the traditional norms of the Old Testament?

Jesus himself gives the answer: "Do not think that I have come to destroy the Law or the Prophets. I have come not to destroy, but to fulfill" (Matt. 5:17). His message is new, but it does not destroy what was; it challenges it to develop its highest potentialities.

Now follows a row of sketches in which these potentialities are illuminated: Matthew 5:21–30; 33–42; 45–48; and Luke 6:34–35. They all have the same pattern. First: "You have heard that it was said to the ancients . . ." then: "But I say to you . . ." followed by the clarification of the seeming contradiction. Four of these precepts are concerned with man's attitude to his neighbor, three treat the relationship of justice and love, the fourth the relationship to the opposite sex. In between come instructions on man's attitude to God: "Again, you have heard that it was said to the ancients, 'Thou shalt not swear falsely, but fulfill thy oaths to the Lord.' But I say to you not to swear at all: neither by heaven, for it is the throne of God; nor by the earth, for it is his footstool; nor by Jerusalem, for it is the city of the great King. Neither do thou swear by thy head, for thou canst not make one hair white or black. But let your speech be, 'Yes, yes'; 'No, no'; and whatever is beyond these comes from the evil one" (Matt. 5:33–37).

The old Law demanded that when you said something under oath, it be absolutely true; that when you made a vow to God, you keep it. The Lord says: You should not swear at all. Why not? Because everything you could possibly swear by belongs to God, the Majesty above all things, unapproachable, untouchable, holy.

What does the act of swearing under oath actually mean? That what I say is true, so true that I make God my witness. It is as true as God's existence, as his truth. He who swears thus brings God into his statement. He couples his truth with that of God and demands that God vouch for it. Jesus says: How dare you? All the majesty of the Hebraic conception of God (which to avoid all danger of personification forbade even the creation of his likeness) revolts here. Jesus goes straight to the heart of the problem; he no longer draws the line between right and wrong, true oath and false, but much sooner: between divine truth and human truth. How can man, who is full of untruth, place himself with his testimony beside God, the Holy One? He should not swear at all; divine majesty should loom so huge in his heart that his simplest 'yes' or 'no' is as reliable as an oath. Thus the commandment forbidding perjury is supplanted by a far profounder general love of truth, which does not swear at all because it knows and loves God's holiness too well to associate it with any personal testimony. An added dimension of truth permeates and guarantees everything that is said with an entirely new conscientiousness. Then come the words: "You have heard that it was said, 'An eye for an eye,' and 'A tooth for a tooth.' But I say to you not to resist the evildoer; on the contrary, if someone strike thee on the right cheek, turn to him the other also; and if anyone would go to law with thee and take thy tunic, let him take thy cloak as well; and whoever forces thee to go for one mile, go with him two. To him who asks of thee, give; and from him who would borrow of thee, do not turn away" (Matt. 5:21–24).

The old commandment, fifth of the Ten from Sinai, runs: Thou shalt not kill. Jesus seizes upon the wickedness that is expressed by murder and traces it back to its origin in the murderer's heart. What breaks out in violence is already present in the evil word or intent, or rather, everything that follows is the result of that intent. The intent then, not the deed that expresses it, is decisive. Notice that Jesus does not even mention downright hatred; a brother's irritation or having "anything against thee" is enough to sow the dragon-seed of evil. From irritation grows anger; from anger the word; from the word the deed.

"You have heard that it was said to the ancients, 'Thou shalt not kill'; and that whoever shall kill shall be liable to judgment. But I say to you that everyone who is angry with his brother shall be liable to judgment; and whoever says to his brother, 'Raca,' shall be liable to the Sanhedrin; and whoever says, 'Thou fool!', shall be liable to the fire of Gehenna. Therefore, if thou art offering thy gift at the altar, leave thy gift before the altar and go first to be reconciled to thy brother, and then come and offer thy gift" (Matt. 5:21–24).

The Old Law used justice as its norm of human behavior. As others treat you, so shall you treat them. Violence may be returned for violence, evil for evil. The justice of the day consisted in not returning more evil than the amount received, and naturally one was allowed to protect oneself from anything that seemed threatening. Christ says: That is not enough. As long as you cling to "justice" you will never be guiltless of injustice. As long as you are entangled in wrong and revenge, blow and counterblow, aggression and defense, you will be constantly drawn into fresh wrong. Passion, by its very definition, surpasses measure—quite aside from the fact that the claim to vengeance in itself is wrong because it lies outside our given rôle of creature. He who takes it upon himself to avenge trampled justice never restores justice. The moment discussion of wrong begins, wrong stirs in one's own heart, and the result is new injustice.

If you really want to get anywhere, you must extricate yourself from the whole embroilment and seek a position far removed from all pro's and con's. You must introduce a new force, not that of self-assertion, but of selflessness; not so-called justice, but creative freedom. Man is really just only when he seeks more than mere justice. More not merely quantitatively, but qualitatively. He must find a power capable of breaking the ban of injustice, something strong enough and big enough to intercept aggression and disarm it: love.

"You have heard that it was said, 'Thou shalt love thy neighbor, and shalt hate thy enemy.' But I say to you, love your enemies, do good to those who hate you, and pray for those who persecute and calumniate you, so that you may be children of your Father in heaven, who makes his sun to rise on the good and the evil, and sends rain on the just and the unjust. For if you love those that love you, what reward shall you have? Do not even the publicans do that? And if you salute your brethren only, what are you doing more than others? Do not even the Gentiles do that? You therefore are to be perfect, even as your heavenly Father is perfect."

The thought is underlined again, deepened in the words: "And if you lend to those from whom you hope to receive in return, what merit have you? For even sinners lend to sinners that they may get back as much in return" (Luke 6:34). The Old Law had taught man to render love for love, hate for hate. It was a question of feeling, a so-called justice of the heart. Precisely for this reason its "love" was unfree. It was a partial reaction, counterpart to equally legitimate hate. Such love lived from the love it received. It was still a piece of immediate human existence, mixture of attraction and repulsion. And now the Lord says:

Your "justice of the heart" is, in itself, an impossibility. 'Justifiable' hatred will always be greater than the hatred to which it responds; it will only create fresh injustice and with it the 'justification' for fresh hatred. As for love that is dependent on the love of another, it will always be trammelled, unsure of itself and uncreative. It is not yet genuine love, for that is so all-inclusive, that there is no room for any other sentiment beside it.

True justice then is possible only when exalted by a bearing justified not by the emotions, but by the free creative power of the heart. There lies the starting-point of all true love. Independent of the attitude of the other, it is free to fulfill its intrinsic possibilities. It stands much higher than justice. It is capable of loving also when it apparently has all grounds for hate. Thus it gains the power to unseat that hate and to overcome it. By this process true justice of the heart is established, that justice which enables a man to look into the heart of his adversary. There he perhaps learns that the 'wrong' inflicted was not really a wrong at all, but the result of inheritance, destiny, necessity; now, as a brother in their joint human guilt, he can concede even his natural enemy his rights before God.

"You have heard that it was said to the ancients, 'Thou shalt not commit adultery.' But I say to you that anyone who so much as looks with lust at a woman has already committed adultery with her in his heart.

"So if thy right eye is an occasion of sin to thee, pluck it out and cast it from thee; for it is better for thee that one of thy members should perish than that thy whole body should be thrown into hell" (Matt. 5:27–30).

The sixth is the commandment that protects the honor and order of family life. But Jesus teaches that its meaning goes much deeper. It demands not only respect for those of the opposite sex, who are also children of the same Heavenly Father, but also respect for one's own purity, which is not private property, but part of the mystery of love between the redeemed individual and his God.

From the disposition comes the deed; thus a glance, an unspoken thought can profane a marriage. As long as you judge behavior solely by the presence or absence of the actual evil deed, you will be unable to avoid that deed. You cannot cope successfully with the evil act until you tackle it as the root of all action: the attitude of the heart as expressed in glance and word. What is really demanded is not superficial order, but intrinsic purity and respect. These in their turn require spiritual self-control and careful guarding of the natural reactions.

A little reflection on Jesus' interpretation of the Commandments will make us realize what he wants for us: the awakening of the whole human being as God meant him to be. In other words, through the Commandments given Moses, God's holy will reveals itself. It must be obeyed; by obeying, man best attains his own perfection. Unfortunately, appalled by the greatness of the demands, he 'protects' himself from them by limiting their sense. This he does primarily by artificially distinguishing between interior and exterior conduct, judging only the visible, tangible misdeed as really evil. What does not come to the surface is not very important.

But the Lord says: Man is an entity in which there are no compartments. His every act has its degrees of being, first of which is inevitably the attitude of the heart as reflected in word, gesture, bearing. If you draw the line only at the actual deed, you are bound to overstep it. If you tolerate the evil word, the subsequent deed is already half accomplished. If you establish evil in your thoughts, you have sown the seed for the subsequent act. The man, not only his hand, must be good inside and outside. Indeed, essentially the heart is more important than the hand, though the hand is apparently responsible for the greater effects. Once a thought has become deed, it is already a piece of world continuity and no longer contains itself. When yet dependent on the liberating act for expression, its intrinsic virtue or malice is more apparent. It is the first yes or no to passion that decides. Thus Jesus elevates the current conception of mere physical prohibition to a positive command, and substitutes for the mere omission of sin, active virtue.

The other protective covering that man has constructed between himself and God is rationality. It says: Certainly man should be good, but everything within reason. He should be philanthropic—with moderation. He should consider the welfare of others—but of course with an eye to their deservingness and strictly within the boundaries of his own interests. The Lord replies:

You won't get far with that! Man is incapable of justice as long as he aims solely at justice. True justice can be obtained only from above, from a vantage point higher than itself. Man invariably metes out injustice when he tries to distribute a certain measured amount of justice. Justice is only for those who act in the strength of love, which does not measure but gives and creates. You will not even be capable of rendering good for good before you gain a higher level of being than that of mere goodness: that of love. Not until your goodness is protected by love, will it be pure.

To desire no more than justice, "Do not even the Gentiles do that?" That is ethics. You, though, have been summoned by the living God. With ethics alone you will neither satisfy God nor fulfill your intrinsic possibilities. God is the Holy One. Goodness is one of the names of him whose essence is inexpressible. And he desires not only obedience to the commands of an "abstract good," but also your personal affection. More, he wants you to risk *love* and the new existence which springs from it. Only in love is genuine fulfillment of the ethical possible. Love is the New Testament!

Admittedly, this is beyond human power. To purify the heart so completely that from the very start respect for the dignity of the other controls the natural passions; to disarm hatred, surrounding it and overcoming its would-be violence in the perfect freedom of love; to return good for evil, benefit for enmity, all this surpasses human strength, and one should not treat such demands lightly. It is better to struggle against them, or to remain in fear and hope on the threshold of grace than to speak of them glibly as principles of that higher code of ethics generally accepted since Jesus Christ. Actually, they are no less than a vocation to a new life.

We are invited to participate in the sanctity of him whose omnipotence and holiness are contained in the pure freedom of love; hence, of one who stands above good and evil, just and unjust. Truly, this is no longer a question of mere ethics—ethics which made such demands would be immoral—but of faith, of self-surrender to a command that is simultaneously a promise, promise of grace, without which all hope of fulfillment would be futile.

In the measure that man attains that which is higher than ethics, does he awaken the new *ethos* in which the Old Testament is simultaneously fulfilled and transcended.

II

SINCERITY IN VIRTUE

The Sermon on the Mount then demands that the Christian regulate his conduct not according to "justice," but according to *Caritas,* for only through love is true justice (and goodness) possible. But how can we be sure that our love is sincere? Human nature is all too prone to self-deception.

Jesus says: "Be merciful, therefore, even as your Father is merciful. Do not judge, and you shall not be judged; do not condemn, and you shall not be condemned. Forgive, and you shall be forgiven. . . ." And again: "For if you forgive men their offences, your heavenly Father will also forgive you your offences" (Luke 6:36–37; Matt. 6:14–15). "For with what measure you measure, it shall be measured to you" (Luke 6:38).

Pity is a troublesome sensation; it saddles one with a sense of obligation. Man's egoism is therefore eager to protect him from it by isolating him from his neighbor: He is he, not I. He is there, not here. I recognize, honor and regret his need; however, it is not really my concern. . . . As long as we think thus, our so-called justice cannot possibly be taken seriously, and our "love" is illusory. To this attitude Jesus says: Your love will become genuine only when you lower the barrier between yourself and the other, when you put yourself in his place with the question, If I were he, what would I wish in the way of help? The measure of your response to that wish, is the measure of your love. (See Matt. 7:12.)

The thought is clear enough; but what demands it makes! If we go into them deeply enough we begin to feel the fundamental safety of our personal existence dangerously questioned. How can anyone meet such requirement? How can I, when others do not? Naturally, if everyone acted accordingly, if human life were so ordered—but Jesus mentions no such if's and and's! He simply commands us to follow his instructions. Only from the depths of a great faith is it possible to obey. One must be utterly convinced that such obedience evokes a divine reaction in our relationship to God, that when we act according to his will we participate in divine creation, in the forming of a new world, for it is creative conduct that is demanded here.

When man so acts, he not only becomes good in himself and before God, but the divine goodness dormant in him becomes active power. This is what the Lord means when he speaks of "salt" that has not lost its flavor, "light" which lights the whole house.

"You are the light of the world. A city set on a mountain cannot be hidden. Neither do men light a lamp and put it under the measure, but upon the lamp-stand, so as to give light to all in the house. Even so let your light shine before men, in order that they may see your good works and give glory to your Father in heaven" (Matt. 5:14–16).

Divine goodness is incarnated in the person who opens his heart to it; it radiates from him. The will that advances in virtue, the soul that progresses in sanctity is a dynamic force that stirs also the recipient of good, disarms and encourages him. Through the God-reflecting act of a fellow creature, God and his holy will become apparent, and the receiver of good in his turn recalls his own potentialities for good, feels himself summoned by God. But isn't it dangerous to execute God's will with the desire to resemble "the salt of the earth," the "city set on a mountain," "the light of the world"? Precisely; hence the warning: "Do not give to dogs what is holy, neither throw your pearls before swine, or they will trample them under their feet and turn and rend you" (Matt. 7:6). "What is holy" is the flesh from the sacrificial altar. When the sacred rites are over, beware of flinging the remains to dogs! Neither should he who has "pearls" cast them before swine, those half wild herds like the ones we encounter in the incident at Gerasa, who (enraged to discover that they are not edible) only trample upon them and furiously turn on him who has flung them.

These parables clearly warn against indiscriminately presenting the mystery of divine life to the crowd. One must never allow it to be profaned, must avoid goading the general sense of earthliness until it becomes a hungry, disappointed beast that turns upon one in fury. A warning to be prudent, for men are as they are; the Lord is no idealist. But the admonition goes deeper. This more perfect justice must, above all, be selfless. The Lord warns us also to guard against ourselves, against the deeply rooted human traits of vanity, complacency and egoism.

"Therefore when thou givest alms, do not sound a trumpet before thee, as the hypocrites do . . . that they may be honored by men. Amen I say to you, they have received their reward. But when thou givest alms, do not let thy left hand know what thy right hand is doing, so that thy alms may be given in secret . . ." (Matt. 6:2–4).

Give unperceived. He who gives in order to be seen and praised already has his reward. Then his works are not displayed that people might praise God as revealed in him, but that they praise his own personal excellence. Indeed, it is not enough that no third person witness one's generosity, the giver's own right hand should not see what the left does! Not even before oneself should an act of charity be paraded or revelled in. Send that inner, applauding spectator away, and let the act, observed only by God, stand on its own. It is a question here of virtue's intrinsic modesty, of that delicacy essential to the purity from which alone God can radiate.

We have it again in the words: "And when you fast, do not look gloomy like the hypocrites, who disfigure their faces in order to appear to men as fasting. Amen I say to you, they have received their reward. But thou, when thou dost fast, anoint thy head and wash thy face, so that thou mayest not be seen fasting by men, but by thy

Father, who is in secret; and thy Father, who sees in secret, will reward thee" (Matt. 6:16–18).

Here is a suggestion superior to any commandment, though
mentioned in none; one that gives all we do its ultimate value: when
you fast—in other words, when you inflict heavy penance on yourself for your sins—perfume your head and wash your face bright.
Let all you do seem effortless, self-understood. More: disguise it
under an air of festiveness from others and from yourself to protect
it from the least cloud of self-approbation or ambiguity. Then the
purity of the act will truly radiate God. Christ stresses this doing of
good before God alone a second and a third time:

"Again, when you pray, you shall not be like the hypocrites, who
love to pray standing in the synagogues and at the street corners . . . go into thy room, and closing thy door, pray to thy Father
in secret; and thy Father, who sees in secret, will reward thee" (Matt.
6:5–6).

Again the warning. Naturally "thy room" does not mean domestic privacy in preference to temple or church, but underlines the
private, rather than public spirit of the act, for it is possible to be private in church, and 'behind closed doors' on the market-place.
When you pray, do not be wordy. Do not suppose for one moment
that God can be influenced by the number or choice of your words.
Remember, you are conversing with him who knows everything.
Actually, your words are superfluous, yet he does want them. They
too should be modest. When you pray remind yourself that he sees
better than you what you need, though he wants you to ask for it.
When you speak to God, he 'hears' you before the words are uttered, for everything in you stands open before him—even your innermost thoughts. When you really know this, not only with the
brain but with the heart, your praying will be as Jesus wants it.

In these teachings of Christ one often repeated word gives us
pause: reward. Contemporary ethics have declared: The motive of
recompense belongs to a lower moral plane than that to which we
have progressed. The superior modern has no use for it.

Obviously, the claim is not void of truth. If I perform an act in order to reach some particular goal, I am necessarily somehow bound to the connecting link between its means and its end. If though, I do it simply because it is right, I am not even conscious of means or end, but only of its ethical sense, the fulfillment of duty. In the first instance I am bound by practical necessity; in the second I am also bound, but differently, in conscience, freedom. I can attain the end without freedom, but the sense never. There is something rich, magnanimous, kingly in freedom of this kind which considers itself degraded by the mere thought of 'payment.' The purely moral value has majesty. When I do something good, that good bears its own sense within it; it needs no further justification. Indeed, any additional motive would only lessen its intrinsic worth. The purity of the act is threatened by thought of "reward." I do not *want* to do a thing for reward; I prefer to do it for its own sake, which for me is sufficient. We cannot but agree. Yet Jesus speaks of reward—repeatedly and at decisive moments.

At this point we realize how much depends upon our own personal acceptance of Holy Scripture as the word of God. If I see in the Bible only a profound religious text, I most likely resort to my own discernment and interpret it myself. In so doing I am almost bound to conclude that the idea of virtue for the sake of reward is a remnant of the old, still unpurified morality, and that on this point Jesus' ethics have since been surpassed.

If, however, I accept *a priori* every word of the New Testament as the word of God, then, seeing how much emphasis Jesus places on reward, particularly here where he is proclaiming the very essence of Christian behavior, I conclude that the idea of reward must be profounder than most moderns suspect, and that underlying these teachings' ethical intent there must be a subtler motivation that completely escapes the attention. And there is. As we understand it, what the New Testament says is this: At the root of your "pure ethics" lurks the possibility of a monstrous pride that is particularly difficult to unmask. To desire good for its own intrinsic dignity, and

so purely that the pleasure of goodness is the sole and entirely satisfying motive behind our virtue—this is something of which God
alone is capable. Only God can perform good in the pure freedom
of self-expression; only he finds fulfillment rather than self-denial in
majestic magnanimity. Yet modern man has assumed this prerogative
for himself. He places the moral attitude and the divine attitude on
a par. He has so determined the moral attitude that the ego behind
it can only be God, tacitly taking it for granted that human ego, indeed all ego, actually is God. Here lies the moral pride of the age, at
once as terrible as it is tenacious.

Jesus' idea of reward is a warning-call to humility. He says: You
man—with all your possibilities of perceiving and desiring good—
you are nevertheless creature! With all your possibilities of free choice,
you remain creature! Anselm of Canterbury wrote of this moral danger. The almost illimitable possibilities of free choice tempt man to
omnipotence without God, to feel himself God's equal. It can be
overcome by reminding ourselves that even in the practice of virtue
we are subject to God's judgment. The fruit of the good deed (of the
moral decision and the effort spent on performing it) does not follow
autonomously, but is God-given as "reward."

But we must go still deeper.

The idea of reward can be undignified, but only when coupled
with a false conception of God. The God of whom Jesus speaks is
he who urges me to love him by enabling me to love with his divine
power. It is from him that I receive both the love necessary for my
act and its "reward": his esteem, itself love. As genuine love grows it
begins to say: I love God because he is God. I love him because he
is worthy to be who he is. I wish my act to affirm him to whom the
multitudes of the angels cry: "Worthy is the Lamb who was slain to
receive power and divinity and wisdom and strength and honor and
glory and blessing" (Apoc. 5:12).

And suddenly all thought of reward has vanished. No, it is still
present in the humility of the beginning, but vanished as a direct
motive, and that to which autonomous virtue aspired but could not

attain unaided is accomplished: pure good for its own holy sake. Never has purity of intent been more exalted than in the bearing of the saints, who completely overlooked themselves in their burning desire to be possessed by God for God's sake. Only by not aspiring to that purity which is his alone, were they able to avoid running amuck in delusion and pride.

III

POSSIBILITY AND IMPOSSIBILITY

We have just made an attempt to understand something of the uniqueness of the Sermon on the Mount: its revolutionary tidings; the energy with which it insists upon progression from the outer, specific act of virtue to the inner, all-permeating state of virtue; its demand that the degree of identification-of-self-with-neighbor be the sole measure for purity of intent, and consequently, its definition of love as the essence of man's new disposition.

Such demands necessarily raise the already mentioned question: is man capable of satisfying them? Can he be so minded, can he so act? To arrest and overcome violence in goodness; to respond to hate not with hateful deed nor even thought, but with love; to honor those of the opposite sex from the very core of one's being; to be so completely renewed by the divine tidings as to actually consider earthly sorrowing blissful and earthly rejoicing suspicious and dangerous—is this humanly possible?

The moment we accept the words of the Sermon not only emotionally or rhetorically but literally, the question becomes inevitable, especially when we read towards the end: "Enter by the narrow gate. For wide is the gate and broad is the way that leads to destruction, and many there are who enter that way. How narrow the gate and close the way that leads to life! And few there are who find it" (Matt. 7:13–14). Once we accept the question as justifiable, we find it cropping up again and again (see Matt. 13; 20:16, and 11:15), and we must face it. Is it possible to fulfill the demands of the Sermon on the Mount? Are the Christian tidings addressed to all or only to a few chosen ones? Of course, divine choice is made irrespective of the individual's natural traits, (ignoring the world's opinion that only he can perform great deeds who was born with a fearless heart and powerful will; that only he can produce masterpieces who bears within him the plumbless mystery of creative genius). Jesus did not come to bring his message to the particularly gifted, but to "seek and to save what was lost" (Luke 19:10). The "chosen" referred to here can only mean those upon whom God's grace is outpoured, enfranchising the human heart from the bonds of self, instructing it to differentiate between false and true reality, and fortifying it so that it may become capable of performing genuine deeds of faith.

What follows would depend on the nature of the individual. In one who is markedly talented, as was St. Francis, the outcome of grace would be a Christian greatness that is simultaneously worldly greatness. Grace, however, can also work in a person of the most ordinary make-up. Such an individual would live as inconspicuously as those about him, yet his heart would be in God. Whatever its "raw material," grace and its road are open only to those summoned by the autonomous decree of divine Providence. The idea that few are chosen is hard to accept and profoundly discouraging—more discouraging than the apparently harsher supposition that, strictly speaking, no one is capable of fulfilling the Christian demands.

For also this thought seems at times near—as in the conversation with the rich young man. By the end of the dialogue it is obvious that the would-be follower is loathe to sacrifice his belongings, and Christ seizes the occasion to demonstrate the "woe" that threatens the man of property. Logically enough the disciples conclude: If this is so, who can be saved? Christ looks at them and says: "With men this is impossible, but with God all things are possible" (Matt. 19:26). Here it is apparently question of the very essence of Christian existence, and the individual is shaken to hear that no one is exempt from the general impossibility of its realization. Then, one of the great mass of humanity, he calls upon God's mercy, knowing that after all, there must be good reason for Christ's coming: our salvation. In the Sermon on the Mount God demands fulfillment of his laws. We feel that he has the right to demand this; we concede that his demands are just—only to hear that what is expected of all can be fulfilled only by a very few: by those to whom fulfillment is given. This is indeed difficult to accept.

It is essential to remember that the truths of Holy Scripture should never be isolated. Always they must be fitted into the whole, where further truths develop or limit their sense, or balance them with some important counter-truth. For example, the message of the angels on Christ's birth night is one of peace to all who are of good will (Luke 2:14), and Jesus himself says he has come "to seek and to save what was lost." Again and again he pities the many who wander restlessly about "like sheep without a shepherd" (Matt. 9:36). This sounds quite different from the word about the few who are chosen. Yet it too must be included. Both are true. Intellectually we cannot unravel the contradiction; we must try to accept it as it stands, each as best he can before God. If we understand correctly, what Scripture asks is this: How do you know that you are *not* among the chosen? The choice is God's secret; no one knows whether or not he is included, but everyone has the right, no, duty to hold himself open to the possibility. Listen to the Word; weigh the full earnestness of a calling—then see if you dare to say you have not been chosen!

Perhaps you reply: How shall I know? I feel nothing! What is it like to be called? . . . To this Holy Scripture answers: You must not put the question that way. Your task is to accept the commandments of the Lord and to act accordingly. A vocation is no label marked "chosen" which can be fixed to a human existence once and forever. It is a living intention of God, efficacy of his love in the chosen one. Only through the action taken by that person can it become reality. . . . But surely one who is called must behave in a certain recognizable manner? In a certain manner—which? Where is the absolute norm that officially expresses the attitude of the Sermon on the

Mount? Jesus once spoke of turning the other cheek when struck, yet when he was brought before the high priest and one of the officers struck him on the cheek he defended himself: "If I have spoken ill, bear witness to the evil; but if well, why dost thou strike me?" (John 18:23). He called upon the order of the court. This shows how little we can bind ourselves to any one point. No one has the right to judge whether or not another lives according to the spirit of the Sermon on the Mount. There is no specific outward behavior that expresses it. Indeed, not even the chosen one himself can be certain how things stand with him. St. Paul says it explicitly: God alone is judge. Dare then to hope that you are chosen! The chance is taken in faith, and neither from the world's point of view, nor from that of inner or outer experience, can there be any possible objection. But I cannot love my enemy! You can bring yourself to the point of no longer hating him. That is already the beginning of love. . . . I can't even do that! . . . Then try at least to keep your dislike out of your speech. That would be a step in the direction of love. . . .

But surely that would be watering the wine? Isn't it a question of everything or nothing? To be quite frank, the Either-Or people seldom appear to practice their own severity. Their uncompromising attitude often looks suspiciously like rhetoric. No, what the Sermon on the Mount demands is not everything or nothing, but a beginning and a continuing, a rising again and plodding on after every fall.

What then is the main thing? That we accept the Sermon on the Mount not as a fixed, inflexible decree to be carried out to the letter, but as a living challenge and activating force. It aims at establishing a contact between the believer and his God that is gradually to become effective; at instigating action geared to continual progress. But we still have no answer to our question. So far all that has been said is that we are concerned not with a program but with vital action, and that we should begin at once. Is there no cue that might help us at least intellectually to see what we're about? I believe there is, and I should like to explain how I have tried to clarify things for myself; it may be of help to others.

When Jesus preached his Sermon on the Mount—and not only that one sermon, but also others in the same powerful but simple vein—a tremendous possibility stood behind his words. Everything was keyed to the one great hope: "the kingdom of heaven is at hand" (Matt. 3:2). He said specifically that it was near; "at hand" cannot be solely an enthusiastic phrase or rhetorical warning—Jesus always means what he says, and if he says something is "at hand," it is. As far as God was concerned, Isaias' prophecy of the new existence stood ready to become reality. It is idle to try to imagine what that kingdom would have been like. The prophet suggests it in visionary words when he writes in his eleventh book of the calf that shall graze with the lion, of the lamb playing peacefully with the wolf. Then no hurt shall be done, no life taken, and knowledge of the Lord shall lie deep as ocean waters over the face of earth. From the all-renewing power of the Spirit a holy existence was to dawn. Everything was to be different. It is primarily in view of this great possibility that the commands of the Sermon on the Mount were given. The people to whom they are addressed are those who were to participate in this great renewal, and in the new existence these instructions were to be the generally obeyed commands of a God lovingly accepted by all. Such then, the kingdom that would have come if Christ's message had found belief—belief not only of a few individuals, but of the nation that had bound itself to God in the covenant of Sinai. Those in authority: the high priests and the Sanhedrin, the scribes and doctors of the faith should have accepted this belief; when they failed to do so, it was up to the people to thrust them aside and proclaim their faith for themselves. Instead, Christ was rejected by his entire race; so he turned elsewhere—to death. Not in a burst of faith and love and all-renewing spirit did salvation take place, but through Jesus' destruction. Thus he became the sacrifice of expiation. . . . Those addressed by him after this momentous refusal are no longer the same people to whom Jesus first spoke. Now they had become those responsible for Christ's death, the second fall—men from whom the kingdom had recoiled. The harshness of history remains unmitigated.

And still Christ upholds his demands. But now he balances them with something else—his Church, which stands in the closest possible relation to him. She is the continuation of the Reincarnation in history. She is, as St. Paul teaches, the eternal consummation of Jesus' saving and renewing vitality in time. Simultaneously she seems to stand in yet another relationship to him. The Church was founded on the Lord's final journey to Jerusalem, after the decision that he was to die had fallen. (Immediately afterwards he speaks of the violence awaiting him at the hands of the leaders of the people: Matt. 16:13–23.) The Church was established after the Son's return to his Father, upon the descent of the Holy Spirit of Pentecost, Spirit that continually forms Christian history. Christ seems to have made her our weakness' defendant, counter-poise of himself and his demands. She is the advocate of the possible, true mother; reminder, in view of God's tremendous requirements, that after all we are only human.

I am not referring to the limitations of the Church: to her indolence, intolerance, tyranny, narrowness, or to any other form of evil that might be present in her. All these are simply improper, and we shall have to answer for them before God. No. Here I wish to point out the specific task that the Church has been given to fulfill: to reconcile Christ's demands (which seem to exceed human strength), with man's present possibilities; to create a pass, a bridge between them; to come to our aid. Her role can of course become hazardous. It can endanger the purity of divine command; can allow the human element to take the upper hand. Precisely this qualifying element, the wish to mediate, seems to cloud the genuine spirit of the divine tidings. Nevertheless, Christ demands precisely this service of the Church, and it must be rendered in loyalty and humility. So much seems to depend on its proper interpretation and performance! There is a Christianity which stresses the harshness of Christ's demands. It says: everything or nothing and brands the slightest consideration of human weakness as apostasy. The result is that it is forced to conclude either that only very few indeed are capable of following Christ's trail (to the eternal damnation of all others), or it declares that man can do nothing at all by himself and therefore the only course open to him is to accept the consequences and fling himself upon the mercy of God. In both cases the Church must appear a human institution—worse, apostate.

All this sounds extremely Christian; however, on closer examination, we begin to suspect that we are dealing with a grave case of sur-exaltation—excess of so-called strength behind which weakness lies concealed—combined with an unconditional attitude founded on ignorance of human nature. Or worse: possibly it is an unconscious strategy of human nature which attempts to place Christianity in the absolute in order to distance it from the world, that the world be freer for worldliness. On the other hand, behind the Church's attitude, lies a profound sense of realism, a will to Christianize that begins with the possible in order to end on the peaks of sanctity. It is no accident that the 'absolutist Christianity' just mentioned implicitly denies the whole conception of sanctity as 'unchristian.'

Whatever the immediate questions that arise from all this: question of the enormity of the demands as opposed to the weakness of men; of the all or the few or none can live up to them; of absolutism or adaptation to human possibilities; of divine severity or divine tolerance—we must concentrate on the ultimate. Every one of these questions must be considered with a single end in view: God. It is to him that the Sermon on the Mount refers, to God the Father. Jesus focuses the attention on him, precisely here in connection with these difficult demands. Here he does not say as usual, "your Father" in the general plural sense of the adjective, but *thy* Father, thou specifically summoned one! Here God is no exalted and distant lawgiver heaping mankind with ponderous burdens in order to judge and condemn later; he commands in love and helps us to obey. He himself brings his laws to men, lives among them, with them, and is personally concerned with the problem of their acceptance. Here is the all-seeing Father who knows every need before it is expressed because his providential eye is constantly upon us. This the God we must keep in mind when we weigh these questions. Only then will they come into their own deepest sense, and the promise receive its answer: love.

IV

SEED AND EARTH

W hen we study the Sermon on the Mount—that purest expression of Christ's message preached at a time when
there was yet no public opposition to him—we unconsciously ask ourselves: to whom essentially was it addressed, and what
were its chances, from an earthly point of view, of being understood.

We moderns are inclined to answer: Jesus spoke first of all to the
individual, then to mankind in general. Both answers are correct,
for only since Jesus Christ does it exist, this double calling of the individual and of all men irrespective of race. Nevertheless, the reply
is a little too modern to be wholly true; its simultaneously individualistic and international conception must be readjusted and purified. Jesus himself thinks more historically. Primarily concerned
with divine history, he never forgets that he was sent first of all "to
the lost sheep of the house of Israel" (Matt. 15:24). His tidings especially concern those bound by the Covenant of Sinai, race whom
the prophets have taught to expect the coming of the Messiah to the
chosen people under the domination of regent and official. This
then the nation Christ "officially" (the word used here in its fullest
sense: as a charge and mission) calls upon to believe. Its Yes would
have brought about the fulfillment of the jesajanic prophecy, the all-
transforming dawn of the kingdom. When, instead, the people refused Christ, the repercussions were felt far beyond the limits of
personal salvation, also beyond the historical confines of the Jewish
nation. As the response of the people duty-bound to God, it was the
response of the whole human race. What followed meant not only

that the tidings were passed on to others, but that now the whole problem of salvation itself was profoundly altered. The failure of the Jewish people to accept Christ was the second Fall, the import of which can be fully grasped only in connection with the first.

Those who heard Christ during his life heard his voice across one and a half thousand years of history, a circumstance which simultaneously helped and hindered. Israel's history had been shaped by its faith in God. Through this faith the little nation had been able to assert itself against the surrounding empires of the Assyrians, Babylonians, Egyptians and Greeks. Secure in its monotheistic belief, it had been able to overcome the spiritual and religious forces around it. However, in this belief in the one-and-only God, it had also begun to grow harsh and rigid. Consequently, when Jesus' divine message was proclaimed, revealing a God so intrinsically different from the God they had conceived, the Jews were angered. With super-human courage and tenacity they had fought for the Sabbath, for the temple and its rites; but in the process, Sabbath, temple and ritual had become idols.

Such then the background of the people Jesus was addressing.

How did the leaders of the people respond to these tidings? Negatively, from first to last. From the start we see the watching, suspicious faces of "the Scribes and Pharisees." The grounds for criticism are usually ritualistic: that Jesus heals on the Sabbath; that his disciples pluck handfuls of grain on this day; that they do not wash before eating and so on. The real reason, however, lies deeper. Jesus' opponents feel that here is a will foreign to their own. What they desire is the perpetuance of the old covenant. God's dominion is to be established in the world, to be established by his chosen race. Granted, some pneumatological event will bring it about, but so as to eternalize the victory of the old covenant in the world. When they notice that the new Rabbi mentions neither the temple nor the Kingdom of Israel; that he questions the world and the value of earthly existence, proclaiming the divine government of perfect freedom, they feel that he is an alien spirit, and cannot rest until they have him safely under ground. So much for the Pharisees, the strictly orthodox, nationalistic 'conservatives.' Their hated rival group, the Sadducees—liberal, progressive, and influenced by Greek culture—at first pay no attention whatsoever to the 'dreamer.' However, once the movement becomes suspiciously powerful, they join forces with their despised opponents long enough to put an end to the dangerous one.

And the masses? When those in authority failed, it was up to them to obey the impulse of Palm Sunday, and fired by the spirit that the prophet Joel calls Messianic, to recognize the Messiah and proclaim their allegiance to him. But this does not happen. The people do have a certain instinct for Jesus. They come to him for help in their need: they listen to his words, are shaken by his miracles. At times they sense the Messianic mystery that enfolds him and they try to make him king. But their conduct is confused. At the very beginning, in Nazareth, a wave of such jealousy sweeps them that they attempt to take his life (Luke 4:16–30). Later, in Gerasa when he heals the possessed boy, and the herd of swine plunges into the sea, they conclude that he must be dangerous and urge him to go elsewhere (Luke 8:22–37). When he passes through Samaria on his way to Galilee they receive him amicably (John 4:1–42); however, when he returns from the opposite direction on his way to hated Jerusalem, they do not allow him to enter the city. (See Luke 9:51–55.) The masses sense his power and significance, but indeterminately. What is felt is not coordinated into responsible action. For this a guiding hand is needed, and it is not there. How fittingly one of Jesus' friends or disciples might have bridged the gulf between him and the masses, might have gathered the hearts of the crowd and led them to decision! But Jesus' followers are afraid and remain in the background. Thus the people are delivered over to the Pharisees, who make easy game of them, deftly leading them from the enthusiasm of Palm Sunday to the apostasy of Good Friday.

The political forces of the day should also be mentioned; they remain neutral. The actual power was in the hands of the Romans. Pilate only learned of Jesus' existence through his denunciation and at first took the prisoner for one of the many hotheads of the times. He soon realized, however, that he was dealing with someone extraordinary—belief that higher beings or sons of God appeared on earth was not uncommon to the age, and he grew uneasy and tried to free him. But in the end he too conceded to the pressure of the accusers.

Then there are the local princes, among them Herod, tetrarch of Galilee and Jesus' immediate sovereign. His portrait is sketched clearly enough in the Gospels. He is one of the many small oriental despots who are simultaneously vassals of the Roman Empire. Weak and spoiled, he is apparently not shallow, for he loves to talk with his prisoner, John the Baptist, whom he takes seriously. But his depth is without character, for on the strength of a lightly given 'word of honor,' he orders the holy man's execution. When news of Jesus' miracles reaches him, he is seized by a superstitious fear that John has reappeared (Luke 9:7–9). Jesus mentions him once: when the Pharisees tell him he should leave the country, for Herod wishes to kill him: "Go and say to that fox, 'Behold, I cast out devils and perform cures today and tomorrow, and the third day I am to end my course' " (Luke 13:32). During the trial Pilate sends the prisoner to his sovereign. It is a gesture of courtesy by which Pilate hopes to rid himself of the disquieting affair. When Jesus remains mute before Herod, he ridicules him and sends him back in the trappings of a royal fool. The two authorities, formerly enemies, now become friends (Luke 23:12).

And what of the intimates of the Lord? Mary was linked closely with him. We have already spoken of their relationship; there is not much more to be said. With Jesus' next of kin, his "brothers," it is a different story. In chapter seven St. John describes a typical incident. The Pasch is approaching, and they are planning the customary annual pilgrimage to Jerusalem. Jesus' relatives try to persuade him to go with them: anyone who can do what he can should not remain in the provinces; he should go there where all really impor-

tant events take place and make a name for himself! Jesus replies: My
time has not yet come. Your time, it is true, is always there.

We feel the distance between them, even a hint of disdain. Finally, St. Mark reports how once, while Jesus was teaching, and the
crowds streamed to him from all sides, his family try to restrain him:
"But when his own people had heard of it, they went out to lay
hold of him, for they said, 'He has gone mad' " (Mark 3:20–21).
Pique, incomprehension, closed hearts and violence all the way
along the line.

And the disciples? It must be admitted that during Jesus' lifetime
not one of them suggests a great personality. Before Pentecost they
are still all too human. It is depressing to see Jesus among them. Uncomprehending they degrade everything, are jealous of each other,
take advantage of their position, and when the test comes, fail. Already in Capharnaum when Jesus introduces the Holy Eucharist, his
followers begin to murmur among themselves. Many of his disciples
declare: How can one listen to such things? And they turn away
from him. At this the Lord asks the Twelve if they too want to go;
the answer hardly rings with vital conviction. Shaken, bewildered,
they rescue themselves in blind faith: "Lord, to whom shall we go?
Thou hast words of everlasting life." (See John 6:60–69.)

Among these Twelve is Judas who has already lined his pockets
from the common purse (John 12:6). And when it comes to the
seizure, they all flee, and Peter denies his Master (John 18:15–27).

Who then was really open to Jesus' message? First of all, quiet individuals, people inclined by nature perhaps to enthusiasm or aloof-
ness. They distanced themselves from the constant influx of political
events in Jerusalem, from the differences of the Pharisees and Sadducees. They lived completely in the tradition of the prophets, quietly waiting for the fulfillment of God's promise. To these belonged
Zachary the priest, Elizabeth, Mary's cousin, Simeon the prophet,
Anne, the ancient seer, Lazarus with his two sisters, and a good many
others. They came closest to understanding the Lord. But perhaps
also not rightly—possibly for that they were too individualistic.

Then there were the social outcasts, the "publicans and sinners": the ones hated as the enemies of the people because they sided with the Romans for economic considerations, the others despised as dishonorable. What was otherwise their misfortune was perhaps here their salvation. Having no social position to lose, they were more open, readier for the out-of-the-ordinary. They considered Jesus an overthrower of worldly opinion, and they flocked to him; was he not accused of being a "friend of publicans and sinners"? But, of course, when it came to the ultimate decision, such people had no influence whatsoever.

And finally there is a third group: the heathen. Jesus' manner of speaking of them is notable. His words seem to take on a special warmth, almost longing. When the captain tells him it is unnecessary for him to come personally to his sick servant, he has but to command the illness to leave and it will obey, Jesus is both delighted and saddened. "Amen I say to you, not even in Israel have I found so great a faith" (Luke 7:9). Something similar occurs in the incident of the Chanaanite woman. Her faith is great enough and humble enough to allow her to understand that Jesus has been sent first of all to the children of the house of David: to the chosen people, and that she herself is like one of those little dogs that hope for the crumbs "that fall from their masters' tables" (Matt. 15:27). But her faith in divine abundance for all is unshakable. The general impression of the heathen that the Lord must have had is evident in the words with which he threatens the cities of Israel at the time of the Galilean crisis: "Woe to thee, Corozain! woe to thee, Bethsaida! For if in Tyre and Sidon had been worked the miracles that have been worked in you, they would have repented long ago in sackcloth and ashes" (Matt. 11:21).

It was among the heathen that Jesus found open souls and fresh, ready hearts. Only too often, ancient religious tradition, long training, and hard and fast usage stamp the ground hard. The spirit no longer takes any imprint; the heart remains cool or undecided, and rarely does feeling become that passion which demands absolute earnestness. So it must have been then with the Jews. The heathen, on the other hand, were rich virgin soil, frontier country of endless possibilities. But they too had little effect on the imminent decision, for it was not to them that Jesus had been sent. The ground on which Jesus' words fell was hard ground indeed.

We are accustomed to accepting the course of the Lord's life on earth as predetermined. Because it was as it was, we conclude that it was meant to be so. We judge everything by its outcome and forget how monstrous—in the eyes of both God and man—the means by which it was accomplished. We have entirely lost the middle ages' reaction of horror at thought of God's murder. We must strip ourselves of our customary callousness and realize how frightful the whole procedure was, how hardened men's hearts, how paltry Jesus' reception!

Not until we have felt our way back to this attitude will we understand Christ's word: "but this is your hour, and the power of darkness" (Luke 22:53). He knew that in the last analysis, mankind's unique, limitless possibility was not frustrated by human will alone. For this, humans, in spite of all their presumption and violence, are much too insignificant.

It is incomprehensible that things could go as they did when, after all, he was who he was! *Why* was none of those in power receptive and courageous? Why was no one there to lead the people to Christ? Why were his disciples, humanly speaking, so inadequate?

Who is this God who seems to lack the power to bring about his Son's due reception? What a strangely disturbing impression of weakness he makes! And what wicked, dogged power is this thing called "world" that is capable of hardening itself against God's summons and cold-bloodedly making an end of his envoy? What kind of God must this be to remain silent before such things!

We live so thoughtlessly that we no longer feel the impact of such unheard of conduct. How do men imagine the advent of divinity on earth? The myths suggest outpourings of dynamic radiance. Buddha is an ascetic, but he thrones in more than royal esteem. The sage Lao-tse is venerated as a god. Mohammed gallops across the world at the head of victorious armies. Here though, God himself becomes man. He has a divinely grave 'interest' in Jesus' human existence; his own honor is at stake, his omnipotence—and what happens! The long history of the Old Testament has been painstakingly directed towards the coming of the Messiah, yet when he does come, this mysterious hardening of people's hearts, this inexplicable fate! What God is this that such things could happen to his Son?

Surely we begin to feel the otherness of Christianity. Those other 'divinities' were earthly powers, and earth recognizes and loves what is hers. When something truly from elsewhere comes, how different the response! Gradually we sense what it must be to be a Christian: to be allegiance-bound to such a God in a world that is as it is. No wonder it means estrangement. And doesn't "world" in reality, mean ourselves—not only that which is about us? That in us which is close to the divine is somehow alien to us, and we have good grounds for the Christian fear that what happened once might be repeated in us: the second fall, the closing of our own hearts to God!

V

THE "KINDNESS OF GOD"

St. Luke's eighth chapter tells how Jesus once shipped across the lake, and immediately upon landing was surrounded by a large crowd. A ruler of the synagogue, Jairus by name, pushes his way through the crowd to Jesus and desperately begs him to rescue his dying child, a little girl of twelve. Moved, Jesus accompanies the man to his home. On the way they are stopped by the density of the crowd, and the woman with the issue of blood touches Jesus' garment and is healed. Soon after, a messenger arrives and announces to the father: "Thy daughter is dead; do not trouble him." The parents had placed everything on this one last hope, and now it too is gone. But Jesus turns to the man: "Do not be afraid; only have faith and she shall be saved." They arrive at the house, where they are met by the uproar which is the typical Oriental accompaniment of death. Jesus speaks the mysterious word: "Do not weep; she is asleep, not dead." Understandably, the crowds laugh. Jesus sends them away, and taking only the father and mother and his three most trusted disciples with him (those who are to witness his Transfiguration and to remain with him on the Mount of Olives) he goes up to the bed of the child. Taking its hands in his own he says: "Girl, arise!" and she opens her eyes, rises, and evinces such vitality that the Lord, very likely with a smile, instructs the parents to give her something to eat, as she is doubtless hungry (Luke 8:40–56).

The scene suggests another already reported by St. Luke. Once in his wanderings, Jesus neared the city of Naim. Just as he was about to enter its gates, the body of a young man, the only son of a widow, was carried through them. The woman's grief touched the Lord and he said: "Do not weep" and he laid his hand on the stretcher. The bearers stood still, and Jesus commanded the dead one: " 'Young man, I say to thee, arise.' And he who was dead, sat up, and began to speak. And he gave him to his mother" (Luke 7:11–17).

A similar event is described in the eleventh chapter of St. John. After Jesus' meeting with Zacheus, he left Jericho and headed for Jerusalem. On the way he said to his disciples: "Lazarus, our friend, sleeps. But I go that I may wake him from sleep." The disciples, knowing that Lazarus was ill, answered: If he is asleep he will be restored. Then Jesus spoke plainly: "Lazarus is dead; and I rejoice on your account that I was not there, that you may believe." So they continued up the road to Judaea (where Jesus had recently been threatened with stoning) with the sensation of walking toward something stupendous, possibly death, for Thomas said to the others: "Let us also go, that we may die with him."

When they arrived in Bethany, they found the dead man already in his tomb. The house was loud with the coming and going of mourners, visitors and the curious. When each of the sisters greeted the friend and Master, it was with the same words: "Lord, if thou hadst been here my brother would not have died."

A shudder passes through Jesus (literally, he looked fierce and was deeply stirred). "Where have you laid him?" he asks, walks up to the tomb, shudders violently again, and weeps. Then he commands that the stone be rolled away, and imploring his heavenly Father to hear his prayer, calls in a powerful voice: "Lazarus, come forth!" Hands and feet still bound with linen strips, his face veiled, the dead man obeys. Jesus gives the order to free him.

The events are varied. Once the father of the girl comes and fetches Christ. Next, the Lord meets the funeral procession in the street. Finally, with Lazarus, he seems to see in spirit everything that happens. At the lakeshore it is a child that has died; in Naim a youth; in Bethany Lazarus, the grown man. It is as though with each instance death were experienced more and more strongly, by increas-

ingly riper and more conscious life. And each time mortal fulfillment seems more complete: the child has just died; the youth is already being carried to the grave; for days Lazarus has lain in the
tomb. The child's parents have scarcely realized that it is all over.
The mother of the youth knows only too well and is desperate with
grief. For days the cold and emptiness of death have settled in
Lazarus' house. In all the essential fact remains the same: Christ calls
the departed spirit back to earthly existence. The broken thread is
caught up again and further spun. Each time something stupendous
occurs: the rudely severed existence begins anew.

In Naim Jesus' act had the character of an effortless service of love
rendered almost *en passant;* in the house of Jairus it was as though
the Lord were stepping into the quiet inner chamber of intrinsic
trust; but in Bethany he walked out of Lazarus' house to the publicly
exposed grave to bring about there, before the eyes of all and with
tremendous pathos, the resurrection. In the presence of his friend's
death, Jesus "groaned in spirit and was troubled" (John 11:33). The
words are repeated, expressly. In Lazarus' death Christ foresaw his
own. He flung himself upon death to wrest from it the life of his
friend. The cry that woke the dead in the tomb of Bethany reminds
one of that other mighty cry from the cross: "But Jesus again cried
out with a loud voice . . ." (Matt. 27:46–51). In the struggle for his
friend's life, Christ himself wrestled with death, and his victory anticipated the triumph of his own resurrection.

What does this all mean? First, probably the greatest demand that
can be made upon our faith. Nowhere is such overcoming of "the
world" demanded as here, save perhaps in the account of the Incarnation or of the feeding of the thousands and the quieting of the
storm. We feel the objection swelling within us: Can such things be?
And if so, to what end?

Of the two questions, the first is less important. If we believe that
Christ is the Son of God, the answer is self evident; it is convincing
to the exact degree that our faith is sincere. And our faith is sincere,

or rather firmly grounded, only when we properly understand the relationship of the self-revealing God to the world. For us, heirs of a scientific age which is expected to deny the possibility of miracles, the conception of natural law is an added hindrance. However, when we look closely, we soon discover that this conception really means something entirely different. For when a miracle takes place, natural law is not 'interrupted,' but rather, at a given moment forced to obey a higher law, a law that is absolutely realistic and significant. All matter is subordinated to life, producing forms which from the standpoint of mere inanimate matter appear "miraculous." In much the same way, the reactions of a spiritual person, as opposed to those of the merely biological one, also present something inexplicably new. Venturing one step farther, we begin to realize what must be possible when the full power of God breaks into human spirituality.

And we see that the objection raised was really concerned with something quite different: not so much with the question of natural law as with the orderliness of natural conduct. This remains untouched. Logic and natural science rest on the assumption that the world comprises an entity, complete in itself, in which other than natural factors have no place. To this faith replies:

The world lies in God's hand. He *is* Power, Creator in the pure and infinite sense of the word, and when he commands, the ordered world obediently and constructively submits to his will. He is "the Lord." His relation to the world is not naturalistic but absolutely personal; indeed, the world itself is not encysted in the natural, but directed toward the personal, because it was created by the free act of love of a living God. Thus history is allowed to unfold: not only human history, but also divine history, the sacred history of salvation. When God summons nature to participate in sacred history, he 'acts,' and the world 'obeys.' What then occurs is a miracle in which natural law is not suspended but fulfilled on a higher level.

With this the first question is resolved, making way for a profounder one: What is the sense behind such happenings? Not whether they happen, but why they happen is the problem that really concerns us. The mind capable of grasping this taps something very deep. Suddenly it beholds the world from an entirely unaccustomed angle, from that of the heart. Jesus is touched by some human fate. A human sorrow presents itself to him: sorrow of a mother, a father, bereaved sisters, confronting him with the image of an existence uprooted and flung into the inexplicableness of death. It is expressly stated how profoundly shaken Jesus is by these encounters. At such times he seems to step into the fate of the individual, ordering the events of the world from the inside. For one instant created by the Savior's love, a human heart forms the decisive center of world reality.

And otherwise? How does the world appear the rest of the time? One philosopher has given us a thought-provoking answer to the question of how human existence 'really' appears: Somewhere in infinite space a tiny speck may be seen whirling about: earth. On its surface appears a thin coating of mould otherwise called landscape, life, civilization, habitat of barely visible motes known as people. The whole thing lasts only a moment, then it is over. Schopenhauer is right. Seen from the cosmic point of view, we actually appear so, and it is often difficult to rid ourselves of the feeling that any other conception is illusory. But in events like those just described, the perspective shifts. It becomes evident that for God those mites on the grain of sand lost in immeasurable space are more important than the Milky Way or the whole universe; that the short span of time in which life endures on earth is more important than all the light years of astronomy. The few years of human existence, the ten years of solitude that a widow perhaps has before her, weigh more in God's eyes than all the aeons that solar systems require to evolve and decline. God would never sacrifice a single human heart for the preservation of Sirius or the Andromadae, yet when his holy omniscience confronts human suffering incapable of recognizing its hidden significance any other way, he commands natural law to a higher service than that to which it would be capable alone. And it is well that this is so, and significant—also from the standpoint of natural law, provided that it is grasped realistically and not made a fetish.

The miracle reveals the world as it appears to God: the world viewed from within, from the perspective of the human heart and human fate. It also teaches us who God is: him to whom man's fate means so much. He is no mere astronomical God of systems (that God too, certainly, but the cosmos is only the throne of his glory). He is also no mere God of history, Shaper of human fates to patterns of divine profundity, though he is also that. He is the God of hearts.

In all truth one may claim: Tell me what moves you, and I will tell you who you are. God is moved by the suffering human heart; the pain of it clouds his face, and we understand who he is and what St. Paul means when he speaks of the "goodness and kindness of God" (Tit. 3:4). It is inadequate to speak of him as philosophy speaks—as the Absolute, the eternally Immutable. He is the Living One, the Close One, the One forever drawing near in holy freedom. He is the Lover who not only operates, but specifically acts in love. God is he who responds to a cry for help by re-commanding natural law.

But why? Why, when after all, the world continues as before? Everywhere children die, mothers weep and fathers tremble, sisters are left alone. Everywhere human life is torn off unfulfilled. What is the good of these glimpses of divine reality?

They are given us to strengthen our faith, to suggest to us how things really stand with the world, only that we have not the eyes to see and must take Christ at his word. God looks upon every one of us as he looked upon the widow behind the bier. Every one of us should know that God holds his particular existence far more important than Sirius or the Milky Way. For him the heart and fate of each of us is the center of the world, but the visible unrolling of the cosmos conceals this from us. To mere intellect, the course of history seems really little more than microscopical stirring in the mould and my life only an instant in eternity. Therefore, I must believe, silencing by faith the overwhelming protest against divine reality in all I see. That is "the victory that overcomes the world" (John 5:4). With these few miracles Christ pulls the curtain aside, allowing us a glimpse of things as they really are—here too only in faith, but faith walks more easily here than in the traffic of the world.

VI

THE WILL OF THE FATHER

When the twelve-year-old Jesus, after his first pilgrimage to Jerusalem, remained behind in the temple and Mary, after a long search chided him, he quietly counter-questioned: "How is it that you sought me? Did you not know that I must be about my Father's business?" (Luke 2:49–50).

Years later, his youth gone, his public career ended, and all things achieved according to the will of the Father, he meets with the two disciples on the way to Emmaus. It is Easter Monday. Mournful and hopeless, they are discussing the terrible destruction of the past days.

Jesus interrupts: "O foolish ones and slow of heart to believe in all that the prophets have spoken! Did not the Christ have to suffer these things before entering into his glory?" (Luke 24:25–26). Both words issue from the same depths. Through both rings the same astonishment at finding uncomprehended by others what for him is self-understood. Both voice a necessity that is not compulsion, but the intrinsic necessity of a justice as sacred as it is eternal. What is demanded of Jesus' filial heart is precisely what it freely desires from the roots of its being: that wherein its own purest fulfillment lies. Will and necessity have become one.

The first step from youth to maturity leads Jesus to the Jordan, where John administers the baptism of penance, since Jesus too wishes to "fulfill all justice." As he climbs out of the water, the heavens open, and over him stream the words: "This is my beloved Son, in whom I am well pleased" (Matt. 3:15–17).

The Father's joy over the pure hearer, doer who throws his whole soul into the accomplishment of his commands; the boundless jubilation of divine will, seeing its fulfillment at hand, flows down upon Jesus. So powerful is the flood that, as Mark says in one translation, it "flings" Jesus out into the solitude of the desert. Filled with the power of the Spirit, he hastens to be alone. There in the deep silence of the wilderness, in prayer and fasting, the storm within him swings itself still; and when temptation comes, it is not repulsed by struggle, but seems rather to ricochet effortlessly against the invulnerability of freedom sprung from divine necessity. Then Jesus begins his task. He goes to Jerusalem and from there via Samaria back to Galilee. In Samaria at Jacob's well he meets the Samaritan woman. Deeply shaken, she summons her people. In the meantime Jesus' travelling companions, who had left him to buy food, return and urge him: Master, eat! Thoughtfully he replies: "My food is to do the will of him who sent me" (John 4:6–7; 31–34). In the Sermon on the Mount Jesus calls those blessed who "hunger and thirst for justice," and he knows from experience what he is saying: accomplishment of the Father's will alone is fulfillment and reality. It replenishes him, making him forgetful of earthly food and drink.

One day Jesus is seated in a house in Capharnaum, surrounded by listeners, so many that even the doorway is blocked. Someone announces his family: "Behold, thy mother and thy brethren are outside, seeking thee." But he replies: ". . . whoever does the will of God, he is my brother and sister and mother" (Mark 3:35).

Whenever Jesus meets someone in whom the will of God is alive, a warm breath seems to envelop him. Spiritually the paternal will is to him what blood is to natural life. He feels himself more closely 'related' to one whom divine will animates, than to any mere blood relation.

For him whom the Father had sent, this driving will was food, companionship, work and struggle, joy and pain, the content of his existence. All thought and effort was concentrated on the one desire: that his brothers recognize and accomplish this sacred will from which everything depends, sharing in the holy concern for its realization. When the disciples asked him to teach them to pray, he gave them the Our Father, core of which is undoubtedly ". . . thy will be done, on earth, as it is in heaven."

About this will must hover an unspeakable, overwhelming mystery. For when the disciples whom Jesus has sent into the world return and report what they have done, overpowering joy breaks from him: "In that very hour he rejoiced in the Holy Spirit and said, 'I praise thee, Father, Lord of heaven and earth, that thou didst hide these things from the wise and prudent, and didst reveal them to little ones. Yes, Father, for such was thy good pleasure' " (Luke 10:21).

Such will is truth—inevitable, constant; it is divine necessity exalted far above all human conceptions of necessity, yet free gift that stirs to blissful wonderment at the miracle of its own existence.

In his farewell words, Jesus' reference to his Father's will touches the ultimate: "As the Father has loved me, I also have loved you. Abide in my love. If you keep my commandments you will abide in my love, as I also have kept my Father's commandments, and abide in his love." Here we see what fundamentally that will is: love.

Love flowing from the Father to Christ; from Christ to his disciples; from the disciples to all who hear God's word. Not sensation or emotion, but "truth and deed" as John is to call it, fulfillment of God's command to justice and holiness. He who obeys "abides" in Christ's love, as Christ abides in the love of the Father whose commands he obeys. To such souls Christ reveals himself—himself and the Father and all truth. For divine recognition comes not through intellectual comprehension, but essentially through the living act, creator of the new becoming and the new being: "If anyone desires to do his will, he will know of the teaching whether it is from God, or whether I speak on my own authority" (John 7:17). The mystery of God's will is the mystery of his truth.

"A new commandment I give you, . . . that as I have loved you, you also love one another. By this will all men know that you are my disciples" (John 13:34–35). The chain of love is to reach still further:

from one believer to another. Each is to be to the other as Christ is to him who does his Father's will. This will is to create spiritual consanguinity: all are to be brothers and sisters in faith, that Jesus may be "the firstborn among many brethren" (Rom. 8:29). In sacerdotal prayer Jesus reveals the mystery of the divine will: "I have glorified thee on earth; I have accomplished the work that thou hast given me to do. . . . I have manifested thy name to the men whom thou hast given me out of the world. . . . Thy word is truth. Even as thou hast sent me into the world, so I also have sent them into the world. And for them I sanctify myself, that they also may be sanctified in truth.

"Yet not for these only do I pray, but for those also who through their word are to believe in me, that all may be one, even as thou, Father, in me and I in thee; that they also may be one in us . . ." (John 17:4–21). God's will then is the unity of life—that life whose content is truth (the word preserved) and justice (the command obeyed), not in the coldness of will and personal ability, but in the love of God, in which we accomplish what we never could alone; in the unity that makes Father and Son one, and one with them all mankind.

This is the power that sustained Jesus, the plentitude that nourished him, the "bond of blood" between him and all who believed. For this he worked, struggled, suffered. It was to this gift, simultaneously the most powerful and the most vulnerable, that he opened people's hearts, exulting when he felt its power surge within him. This the will that guided his action, not as a fixed program, complete to the last detail, but as a living impetus, constantly renewing itself, enfolding him from instance to instance in each new situation. This he means when he calls the will of the Father his "hour"; hour that has not yet come, he says when the situation is still open, and the paternal will has not yet pronounced its Now! We recall the wedding-feast at Cana, when his mother asks him a favor which he must refuse as premature until, a moment later, his "hour" is there, and he is able to comply with it. (See John 2:1–8.) Or we remember the conversation with his relatives when they cynically suggest his going to

Jerusalem to show what he can do, and Jesus replies: "My time has not yet come, but your time is always at hand" (John 7:6). In other words, they have no appointed hour because they live in the coldness of will and personal ability, not in the love of God, in which we accomplish what we never could alone; in that unity which makes Father and Son one, and one with them all mankind. Passages such as that on the marriage at Cana, in which Jesus speaks of his "hour," are further references to the divine will. (See John 7:3–9.)

The Father's will indicates the hour for all things: it guides Jesus to the Jordan; into the desert and back among people; to Jerusalem and back to Galilee, where he finds his disciples; to his public mission among the crowds and back to the individual; from publican and sinner to scribe and Pharisee; from the educated to the ignorant—teaching, helping, healing; fighting for the acceptance of God's Kingdom in faith and obedience among the people of his covenant. And when that faith and obedience are denied, the will of God guides his Son down the dark passages of the Passion. Unhesitatingly, he accepts this too and sets his face toward Jerusalem, knowing what is ahead: "But I have a baptism to be baptized with; and how distressed I am until it is accomplished!" (Luke 12:50).

To what extent the Father's will is personal command, demand made from countenance to countenance, how far removed Christ's obedience is from mere fatalistic surrender, transport, or coercion, is best revealed in the hour of Gethsemane: "And going forward a little, he fell on his face, and prayed, saying, 'Father, if it is possible, let this cup pass away from me; yet not as I will, but as thou willst.'" "As thou willst" not "as I will"—so sharply are the two wills differentiated, that for a moment it seems as if the divine unity were about to split. Then in perfect freedom follows the decision, the beginning of that supreme proof of love foreshadowed in Christ's farewell words, and with it the new union, deeper than ever before (Matt. 26:36–46). With the acceptance of its dark command begins the accomplishment of the agony from which sprang our salvation and Jesus' glory.

VII

THE ENEMY

Then there was brought to him a possessed man who was blind and dumb; and he cured him so that he spoke and saw. And all the crowds were amazed, and they said, 'Can this be the Son of David?' But the Pharisees, hearing this, said 'This man does not cast out devils except by Beelzebub, the prince of devils.'

"And knowing their thoughts Jesus said to them, 'Every kingdom divided against itself is brought to desolation, and every city or house divided against itself will not stand. And if Satan casts out Satan, he is divided against himself; how then shall his kingdom stand? . . . But if I cast out devils by the Spirit of God, then the kingdom of God has come upon you' " (Matt. 22–28).

Frankly, the whole incident strikes us as strange. Not that we consciously reject it; our resistance is unconscious, rising from habits of thought and emotion that are centuries old. Nevertheless what is reported here is essential to any genuine understanding of the New Testament. Therefore, we must brush aside the instinctive opposition and allow the word of God to guide not only our understanding, but also our sentiments.

The account suggests similar cases of possession that Jesus has cured. Not as a doctor cures; not even as Jesus himself has usually cured, by simply applying his miraculous powers of healing to the ravaged body. Here, behind the torment of body and soul, the Lord recognizes an evil power: the Demon, Satan. It is he who has made the invalid his abode; the physical pain involved is a result of his terrible habitation. It is he whom Jesus attacks, dislodging him by sheer spiritual force, and with him the accompanying ailment.

Reading this, our first reaction is an intellectual objection. Isn't this simply the interpretation of inadequate medical knowledge? Hasn't primitive medicine always looked for evil powers behind the malady—surely something similar occurs here? Wouldn't the Jesus of a scientifically advanced age have seen things quite differently? Yet modern research, which is beginning to free itself from the chains of rationalism, admits that earlier ages were more sensitive than our own; that they employed faculties later stifled by intellectual development. Thus we begin again to suspect the religious qualifications of health and sickness.

Next comes a moral objection. It protests against the existence of intangible powers. Willingly enough it recognizes natural reality on the one hand, spiritual norms on the other: given conditions of being and of intention. But then it balks, afraid of fantastic folly. Somehow, all reference to the demonic smacks of the unclean, of things belonging to a lower level of religion that must be overcome. The conscience is perfectly right to protest against the ambiguousness and murk that are the counterparts of demonic leanings. Nevertheless, here lies the crux of our attitude toward Jesus: do we accept him, once and for all, as our ultimate authority in everything, or do we rely solely on our own judgment? Judgment likely to lead us to consider Jesus as belonging in this respect to a level of consciousness since outgrown, as a victim of the inadequate medical knowledge of his age, and so on? If we think as Christians, we accept him as starting point and norm of all truth, and we listen to everything he says with open minds, eager to learn, particularly when we are dealing, not with chance remarks of Jesus, but with a fundamental attitude that asserts itself again and again.

The Lord's acceptance of the inevitable struggle with satanic powers belongs to the kernel of his Messianic consciousness. He knows that he has been sent not only to bear witness to the truth, to indicate a way, to animate a vital religious attitude, to establish contact between God and man; but also to break the power of those forces which oppose the divine will.

For Jesus there is more than the mere possibility of evil as the price of human freedom; more than the inclination to evil, fruit of individual or collective (inherited) sin. Jesus recognizes a personal power that fundamentally wills evil: evil *per se*. It is not satisfied by the achievement of positive values through wicked means; does not simply accept the evil along with the good. Here is something or someone who positively defies divinity and attempts to tear the world from God's hands—even to dethrone God. God being who he is, this is possible only by leading the world into apostasy and self-destruction.

This is what Holy Scripture means when it says that Satan creates that darkness which refuses the light that comes from God and is the seducer of mankind; that "He was a murderer from the beginning" for "by the envy of the devil, death came into the world" (John 8:44; Wisdom 2:24). The Bible often speaks of him as lord of a "kingdom," founder of a perverted order in which the hearts and minds of men—their creations, their deeds, their relations to things and to each other—seem sensible and coherent, but actually are senseless and incoherent. Long passages in John's gospel describe Satan's attempts to establish a kingdom of evil in opposition to God's holy kingdom, antiworld to the new divine creation unfolding. These verses have nothing in common with that romanticist conception which tries to make Satan God's antipode, and which speaks of darkness and evil as necessary to light and good, indeed to the whole economy of existence sustained by the opposition of these two fundamental powers. Such ideologies are unchristian and cannot be taken seriously. God has no antipode. He exists in pure freedom and holiness in himself, sufficient unto himself. All true being is contained in him, and there is nothing that exists 'beside' or 'opposite' him. Satan is no principle, no elementary power, but a rebellious, fallen creature who frantically attempts to set up a kingdom of appearances and disorder. He has power, but only because man has sinned. He is powerless against the heart that lives in humility and truth. His dominion reaches as far as man's sinfulness, and will collapse on the Day of Judgment—a term long in itself, for every moment of evil is dreadfully long for those who stand in danger of Satan—but only a moment as compared with eternity. "Soon," as the Apocalypse reveals, it will be over (3:11; 22:7).

Jesus knows that he has been sent forth against Satan. He is to penetrate Satan's artificial darkness with the ray of God's truth; to dispel the cramp of egoism and the brittleness of hate with God's love; to conquer evil's destructiveness with God's constructive strength. The murkiness and confusion which Satan creates in men's groping hearts are to be clarified by the holy purity of the Most High. Thus Jesus stands squarely against the powers of darkness; he strives to enter into the ensnared souls of men—to bring light to their consciences, quicken their hearts and liberate their powers for good.

But Satan resists. He even takes the offensive. The temptation in the desert is one such attack: attempt to force upon Jesus a lower conception of his mission, to lure his will to save into channels of egotism (Matt. 4:1–11). It is Satan who leads people to be irritated by truth and to harden their hearts to its sacred tidings. He creates the great self-deception by which—ostensibly to protect the honor and glory of God—men turn against his Son. It is his triumph when in the hour of infinite possibility the incomprehensible happens: the earthly partner of the covenant refuses faith, yes, turns upon God's Envoy and grinds him under heel.

But Jesus stands unshaken. He upholds salvation in all its clarity. Not by a syllable does he alter his message. Nor is he swept by hate into revenge, by force into the brutality of force, by trickery into unrighteous cunning. Undaunted, he advances the divine tidings of sacred reality to the end. Satan is powerless against Jesus' spirit, so he attempts to annihilate his person. But the death on the cross which shatters the tremendous Messianic possibility, establishes salvation. Jesus sees that his immediate strength will not succeed in breaking through the world's spiritual crust. Love and grace, life "that was the light of men" are 'weak,' unable alone to dispel the dark. So the Savior's spirit rises to the incomprehensible greatness of self-sacrifice: Jesus accepts defeat and death and *uses* them as propitiation! What was to have destroyed, ushers in world-salvation (John 1:4).

The following is a direct reference to this invisible conflict: "When the strong man, fully armed, guards his courtyard, his property is undisturbed. But if a stronger than he attacks and overcomes him, he will take away all his weapons that he relied upon, and will divide his spoils" (Luke 11:21–22).

John refers to the same thought at the end of chapter sixteen, where Christ says to his disciples: "I have overcome the world" (John 16:33). And again, "Now is the judgment of the world; now will the prince of the world be cast out" (John 12:31).

The two statements are reinforced by Luke's description of the return of the disciples whom Jesus has sent into the world. Triumphantly they report that the evil spirits have obeyed them in the name of Christ. Jesus replies: "I was watching Satan fall as lightning from heaven" (10:18). This word comes from the same depths as the thought which closes the eighth chapter of St. John: "Amen, amen, I say to you, before Abraham came to be, I am."

Behind the speeches, healings, teachings visible to everyone, dark terrible battle against the invisible foe is being waged. With all the readiness and power of heart and spirit, Jesus stands in its midst; utterly alone he faces the enemy in ultimate, inexorable war.

We suppose that it should have been easy for him to conquer. Surely the power of the Spirit in him is not only stronger than the spirit of deceit and impurity, but is the essence of absolute strength. Yet apparently (and here we glimpse something of all that Incarnation and salvation mean) the God-given mission was to be accomplished not by a simple outburst of divine omnipotence, but so that the incarnate God, with only a mysteriously limited amount of power at his disposal, was to 'stand his man' on the battlefield of the world. Apparently *kenosis,* the self-"emptying," as Paul describes the Incarnation (Phil. 2:7) meant that the Father ordered his Son to contend in weakness and vulnerability, that in all fairness victory might be attained by either one—"victory" in the original sense, which was to pull down the walls of darkness and allow truth to stream into the spirit, love into the hearts of enslaved humanity. This battle lost, the other victory, victory through defeat, was to be won: surrender transformed into triumphant sacrifice.

Into this terrific tension, on which the powers of utmost vigilance and supreme spiritual energy are concentrated, into the amazed questioning of the multitude, "Can this be the Son of David?" falls the word of the enemy: "This man does not cast out devils except by Beelzebub, the prince of devils" (Matt. 12:23–24).

Jesus replies: Don't you see how I war against Satan? Don't you recognize the uncompromising, eternal enmity? How can you say that he works through me, which is the same as saying that we join forces to found one kingdom!

There are moments when even God's enemies are speechless; when even the angels must deride and laughter peal through heaven at the stupidity into which the mighty, the cultivated, the intelligentsia falls when it becomes godless.

A terrible earnestness settles on the room, earnestness of that battlefront on which Jesus stands face to face with his ancient enemy. From depths far beyond his hearers' comprehension, the Lord flings his challenge: "He who is not with me is against me, and he who does not gather with me scatters.

"Therefore I say to you, that every kind of sin and blasphemy shall be forgiven men; but the blasphemy against the Spirit will not be forgiven . . . either in this world or in the world to come" (Matt. 12:30–32).

What has happened? These men have blasphemed against the Holy Ghost. Not only have they turned against God and his dominion; not only against the person, word and deed of Christ, but against the very heart of God. They have falsified his relationship to himself and to mankind, degraded his sacred intentions. Let us think for a moment in earthly terms. A man hurts his friend: he has been inconsiderate, or has misjudged him, or walked roughshod over some sensitive spot, or whatever the trouble may be. Any one of these things can upset a friendship, the extent of the damage depending on the degree of the carelessness or the importance of the dispute. However, something totally different would occur should the man attack not only the work, the words, the conduct of his friend, but his very character. If he were to say: Your motives are impure; you are entirely false and wicked! Such an accusation would necessarily shatter the friendship. Something similar happens here. Jesus is saturated with the essence of God. To accuse him of working through the power of Satan, is to touch the absolute in ill will. Only the man whose spirit has consented to darkness can speak thus. Here forgiveness is impossible because a state has been reached which lies outside the domain of man's earthly experience: that of ultimate petrifaction in evil.

Modern man has done away with Satan and his realm. The process has been a strange one. Banishment to the world of the ridiculous is one of the earliest means employed. Gradually the demon was allowed to become a comic figure. Something of this attitude is in our blood; it is almost impossible to present the devil in any form that does not slide off into comedy. As a matter of fact, this humorous conception has Christian roots; originally it was the banter of the emancipated at the expense of the former master. But from ridicule in faith has grown the empty laughter of faithlessness, which once again serves Satan's purpose. Nowhere does he rule more firmly than where people poke fun at him. Next, the demon was made a tragic hero garbed in the majesty of Evil, the exaltation of Despair. Men tried to promote him to a dark Power, 'necessary' for the fruitfulness of existence. ". . . Part of that power which wills evil and yet produces good" (Goethe: Faust, Studierzimmer). Thus he appears worthy of a strange veneration. Now modern psychology has 'proved' that Christian knowledge of Satan was the same as that demonism which crops up on certain religious levels the world over and which has only gradually been overcome. It is supposedly the product of certain psychological tensions which vanish as soon as man becomes healthier and freer, and so on and so forth.

Consciously or unconsciously (then all the more ardently) modern man imposes his spiritual will upon the cosmos. According to that will, existence is to be natural, an interweaving of natural powers and substances. At the same time, it must be ideal, an interweaving of laws, values, norms. Never is it to be personal. Only impersonal (abstract) reality, impersonal norms are granted existence. The idea of a personal power behind nature is all very well in poetry; however, as soon as it becomes serious prose, it is branded mythology and superstition. Christianity contradicts: Ultimately all being must be personally determined. That is what it is waiting for. But someone else is also waiting—waiting to determine it personally for evil. He does not declare himself, but hides behind logic and objectivity, in the ambush of so-called disenchantment. He throws sand in the eyes of science that prides itself on its "pure rationality," blinding it to the obvious. He makes much research a never ending contradiction in which the first claim is constantly made void by the second, spiritual unity is destroyed, and the specialist forced to rescue himself again and again in the routine of his windowless department. In place of technical but humanly directed rationality, he has constructed the enslaving mechanical order of current industrial life. Man has duped himself by his very cleverness; mistaking means for ends, he has degenerated from a master of the machine to a slave-mechanic. Such deterioration is an expression of the demonic, as is much else. Naturally, it is not easy to see clearly, to differentiate with nicety when our own eyes are blinded. Blurred vision, confused action, coldness of heart and falsely directed will—all are part of the same labyrinth. He who is caught in it sees only objects, facts, consequences, logic. He does not see the enemy.

Jesus brought Satan to a standstill. He alone was able to stare him down. To the extent that we succeed in looking with Christ's eyes, we too shall see him; to the extent that Christ's heart and spirit become alive in us, we shall dominate him. The clever will of course smile at this.

VIII

THE MISSION

We have already mentioned the apostle: who he is, what he is, and the consequences of that being. Nevertheless, let us return to him once more, this time in relation to Jesus' own mission. We saw that the Lord spoke not only to the masses, but also to the small circle of disciples, the twelve apostles, who swiftly gathered about him, men whom he trained to spread his message.

The dispatching of the Twelve is described by Mark in the sixth, by Matthew in the tenth, and by Luke in the ninth chapter. Jesus sends them out two by two with the tidings that the kingdom of God is at hand. He gives them powers of physical and spiritual healing, and warns them against the use of earthly aids, such as money or influence. They are to stop and teach where they are invited to do so, to depart when they are rejected.

These instructions are given relatively early in Jesus' public life. Shortly afterwards he dispatches "seventy-two others," disciples in the broader sense of the word. They likewise are to go in pairs, peaceably; for the time being, to the cities and boroughs of Judea. (Not yet to the heathen nor to the Samaritans, but only to the Jewish people.) They are warned what to expect: they may be welcomed and are then to give the peace of God; they may also be rejected; then they are to leave at once, and their peace will go with them.

And again just before the Ascension: "All power in heaven and on earth has been given to me. Go, therefore, and make disciples of all nations, baptizing them in the name of the Father, and of the Son, and of the Holy Spirit, teaching them to observe all that I have commanded you; and behold, I am with you all days, even unto the consummation of the world" (Matt. 28:18–20). Now the mission is to spread to the ends of the earth.

Another appointment to a mission is the dramatic seizure of Saul, the persecutor of Christians, whom the Lord transforms to Paul the Apostle, the "chosen vessel," who is to carry his name before "nations and kings" (Acts 9:15).

Here, deeply buried, runs a connecting link already hinted at in the words spoken to the departing seventy-two: "He who receives you, receives me; and he who receives me, receives him who sent me" (Matt. 10:40). Again after the Resurrection: "As the Father has sent me, I also send you" (John 20:21). And the sacred chain of vocations becomes apparent. Jesus knows himself sent by the Father, who "dwells in light inaccessible" (I Tim. 6:16). No one has ever seen him, "except him who is from God" (John 6:46). The Father is utterly remote; concealed to all but himself. His revelation is his Son, the living Word. "He who sees me sees also the Father" (John 14:9).

Every attempt to reach the Father directly ends in a generalized divinity. It is impossible to arrive at the ultimate mystery, the true Father, save through the Son, who does not speak for himself, but for his Father. Similarly, the apostles are not to speak for themselves, but for Jesus—and to the end of time. This means that they will always be there, perpetually renewed in the apostolic succession.

"He who receives you, receives me . . ." (Matt. 10:40). He who listens attentively to the apostle, entering with him into the spirit of the tidings, is reached by Christ. ". . . And he who receives me, receives him who sent me." Jesus can neither be proven by concepts, nor 'recognized' by airy experiences. What he is can be conveyed only by his message, for he is not an idea, but history. Likewise the Father cannot be facilely labled the essence or foundation of all things, for he is hidden, to be revealed only through Christ.

Once again a dispatchment is reported—during the forty days after Christ's Resurrection. In one of the modern encounters typical of this period, Jesus appoints the apostles his witnesses: " 'As the Father has sent me, I also send you.' When he had said this, he breathed upon them, and said to them, 'Receive the Holy Spirit; whose sins you shall forgive, they are forgiven them; and whose sins you shall retain, they are retained' " (John 20:21–23). Christ the Intermediary is a sacred living artery through which divine purity and forgiveness flow; through the establishment of the Eucharist he becomes a permanent artery, supplying all generations with the superabundance of divine life. "Amen, amen, I say to you, unless you eat the flesh of the Son of Man, and drink his blood, you shall not have life in you. He who eats my flesh and drinks my blood has life everlasting and I will raise him up on the last day. For my flesh is food indeed, and my blood is drink indeed. He who eats my flesh, and drinks my blood, abides in me and I in him. As the living Father has sent me, and as I live because of the Father, so he who eats me, he also shall live because of me" (John 6:54–57).

As further reference to the continuity of love: "As the Father has loved me, I also have loved you. Abide in my love. If you keep my commandments you will abide in my love, as I also have kept my Father's commandments, and abide in his love" (John 15:9–10). "And the word that you have heard is not mine, but the Father's who sent me" (John 14:24).

All giving and receiving of love takes place "in the Holy Spirit." In his farewell speeches, Jesus explains more fully: "I will ask the Father and he will give you another Advocate to dwell with you forever, the Spirit of truth whom the world cannot receive, . . . he will bear witness concerning me. And you also bear witness, because from the beginning you are with me" (John 14:16–17; 15:26–27).

The Holy Spirit "will teach you all truth," for he too will speak not of himself, but will take from Christ's wealth and give it to the faithful, just as Christ has taken all that he has and is from the Father.

From Father to Son, from Son to the Holy Spirit, from the Holy Spirit to the apostles and thence to all nations—this is the course taken by divine love. Christ's parting words, spoken the moment before his Ascension refer to this: ". . . when the Holy Spirit comes upon you, and you shall be witnesses for me in Jerusalem and in all Judea and Samaria and even to the very ends of the earth" (Acts 1:8).

The apostle is God's emissary in the Holy Spirit. Not until Pentecost is he 'full-fledged.' The Holy Spirit is the living interiority of God. "For the Spirit searches all things, even the deep things of God" (I Cor. 2:10). He effects God's loving self-measurement, self-possession. Inhabiting the Holy Spirit is the Father's eternal Word, the Logos, Son he sent into the world, and it was by the Holy Spirit that Mary conceived (Matt. 1:18). Through him the Son steps into human history, history's true substance. In the Holy Spirit of Pentecost the apostles at last realize who Christ is, at last comprehend, and in the Spirit they proclaim his word to those who (again in the Spirit) hear him (Acts 2:1–41). For outside the Spirit it is heard only by the ear and the mind, not by the sacred, inmost depths of man's being, as it should be, since it is from the sacred, inmost depths of God that it comes. The Holy Spirit alone establishes this intimate contact.

The mass-dispatchment of the apostles suggests a great urgency, knowledge that the time has come: ". . . lift up your eyes and behold that the fields are already white for the harvest" (John 4:35). Time is ready and waiting for the apostles to bring the Christ. It is the fulfillment of time so eagerly anticipated in St. Mark's opening Gospel, the coming of God's Son. St. Paul refers to it in his Roman epistle (Chap. 8) when he speaks of creation lying in birthpains and longing for the expected arrival of the glorious children of God.

Hence one would expect the divine teachings to sweep through the country on a wave of enthusiasm. Yet even before Jesus sends out the Twelve the first time, he prepares them for the possibility of rejection; and when he dispatches the seventy-two he speaks still more earnestly. They must know that they are being sent "like sheep in the midst of wolves. . . . Yes, the hour is coming for everyone who kills you to think that he is offering worship to God" (Matt. 10:16; John 16:2). What the prologue of John's Gospel says of Christ is valid also for his emissaries: that he who is sent will come into the world, but the world will not receive him; he is the light, but the darkness will not suffer it to penetrate. We find it again in Matthew: "No disciple is above his teacher, nor is the servant above his master. It is enough for the disciple to be like his teacher, and for the servant to be like his master" (Matt. 10:24–25).

These instructions to the departing apostles suggest an extreme vulnerability. Something infinitely precious, on which man's salvation depends, is being launched into a hostile world. In all probability it is bound for catastrophe, yet everything depends on the acceptance and spreading of its message. Here lies a profound mystery, we must try to understand. God is the Omnipotent One. In him will and power are inseparable. As for truth, he *is* Truth. When infinite divine truth speaks, we suppose that by its sheer irresistible power it must make itself heard. Surely, the strength of that truth called "light" must radiate in the human soul like sun over dark land! Then how was it possible that such a mission could meet with such a fate?

It seems that upon entering the world, God renounced his omnipotence; he, Truth, left his mantle of irresistibility outside the gates of earth, in order to enter in a form that would permit people to close their hearts to him if they so desired. Purposely God limited his illimitable radiance, wrapping himself in a darkness which enabled men to withstand and even to reject his rays. Perhaps in imposing these limitations on himself, God was conforming to the weakness of the creatures to whom he descended. (An intended weakness, obviously, by the very definition of the word "creature.") For isn't power essential to the awareness of approaching power? Doesn't the impact of a personality or an event vary in degree according to the power of the personality touched by it? The weakness of the recipient weakens the donor; it constrains him. What jubilation therefore when one strong soul meets another! Perhaps it is man's weakness which renders God 'weak.' And not only man's natural limitations, but his sin, his incoherence, his balking contrariness. Self-revealing truth needs the will to truth on the part of the listener in order to penetrate. Sanctity demands readiness for sanctity on the part of the one called. Where this is lacking, truth is bound, light obscured, and the embers are smothered.

Thus, in spite of all its unnaturalness, the necessity for the possibility of rejection. Faith then requires not only the simple will to God's truth, but also a certain responsiveness to precisely this 'weakness' of God. It must possess that holy chivalry of the heart which flies to the defense of defenseless truth; that watchfulness of spirit which recognizes truth even in the dark; the sharp ear of love, and the intuitive strength of sacred desire. In truth's very defenselessness must lie an unspeakable mystery of love. By that act of self-renunciation, known as the Incarnation, God's Son shed his glory to enter the world "in the nature of a slave" (Phil. 2:7).

Aren't the instructions which the Twelve receive before departing on their missions (to take nothing for the voyage, neither breadbag nor money nor begging-sack; no second coat, no second pair of sandals; to teach without reward and to heal without pay) given to preserve that divine helplessness? Isn't this the real reason why money and power endanger the divine tidings, which remain so much stronger in weakness? (I Cor. 1:25). The word made known by force does not bring Christ. Influence based on money and power does not bring God, for such means make void the means by which God himself entered the world. Here we glimpse a new facet in the life of the apostle. He must accept and constantly renew within himself this basic secret of his mission: the vulnerable Christ he bears within him in his sacred word is only endangered when power, property or strategy of any sort contribute to the reception of his tidings.

IX

FORGIVENESS OF SINS

And they came, bringing to him a paralytic, carried by four. And since they could not bring him to Jesus because of the crowd, they stripped off the roof where he was, and, having made an opening, they let down the pallet on which the paralytic was lying. And Jesus, seeing their faith, said to the paralytic, 'Son, thy sins are forgiven thee' " (Mark 2:3–5).

A thought-provoking account. What must have taken place within the man who was healed? He had suffered from paralysis—severely and for a long time; when he was brought to Jesus he could no longer walk. His disease was painful and apparently allowed no hope of improvement. So there he had lain. Perhaps he had done some thinking. (Illness can be thought-provoking if the invalid does not succumb to the torpor or self-indulgence of the sick-bed, but proceeds into the sphere of quiet beyond suffering.) Reviewing his life as he lay there, had he realized that much of it was disordered: here a neglected duty, there an injustice, and only too often surrender to passion? Had he begun to understand what it is that lies at the root of wrong-doing: not only offense against a law or a person, but against something eternal that is no mere moral code, something immeasurably great and precious? Perhaps he recognized this as sin, and saw whom it was directed against: holy God. Terrible sin, that touches the ultimate Majesty.

Possibly he had continued to think: of the injustice perpetrated around him by his relatives, friends, fellow citizens, countrymen.

He began to see how one injustice leads to another, how impossible it is to isolate the single wrong. He saw how one huge network of injustice is woven, so intricate that with all due recognition of individual responsibility, it is impossible to speak exclusively of the sin of the one, which only contributes its particular features to the face of collective wrong. Perhaps he began to consider also his malady in a new light. He realized how often need and suffering result from sin; how evil ushers them in or accentuates them, or at least enables them to do their worst. And perhaps one day it dawned on him that fundamentally sin and pain and death fuse to form a dark wedge. The name of its edge is sin; of its bulk pain, and its blunt end is death. Then someone told him about the Master who had brought men such powerful succor. Now friends have carried him to Christ, and he lies before him and hears the words: Man, thy sins are forgiven thee. And he knows now with certainty: Yes, that is the main thing, forgiveness! He is filled with a quiet clarity; at last everything is in order. Then he is also cured and understands how it all hangs together: One thing leads to another—good as well as evil—but through this Stranger everything is made new. And when the biting skepticism of the Pharisees darts into the crowd: "Who can forgive sins, but God only?" Jesus' reply does not stand alone; the invalid too knows the answer: Here *is* God!

It all might well have happened this way, but equally well quite differently. Perhaps the man had lost himself in his illness: in pain and the alleviation of pain, in the privations and small pleasures of infirmity. Perhaps he had entered no inner sphere, but had slid from one externality to another, living exactly as all superficial people do, only in a sickbed. If conscious of sin at all he had said: It might have been worse; I've neither stolen nor murdered. Besides, the others are just as bad—it is human nature. For the most part, however, he had kept all thought of sin far from him.

He never admitted that illness, pain and death have any connection with sin (naturally, each was a thing in itself) or that, for example, dishonesty or unscrupulousness could ever have anything to do with the spreading of contagion. All in all, he was not prone to speculation on the collective responsibility of mankind.

Borne before the Master, he finds it strange, indiscreet of him to mention sin. After all, he has come to be cured—what is the man driving at! And when, finally, he is healed, he secretly concludes that the whole scene has been a bit on the dramatic side. This man has failed to comprehend what sin is. He has neither penetrated its depths nor allowed its significance to rise to the surface of his consciousness; thus he also fails to experience what forgiveness is.

Or has the paralytic pleaded personally guilty and accepted his illness as a just punishment? The idea that everyone is involved in sin would never have occurred to him. No, every man stands on his own responsibility, his own free will. He would have had equally little patience with the thought of the oneness of wrong and suffering, sin and death. The conscience and its responsibility lie here, the corporal-spiritual processes of sickness and need there. Hearing Jesus' words of forgiveness, he does not understand. Wrong is wrong and must remain wrong. This is essential to man's dignity. Though one must try to improve, full responsibility for the past remains. Who dares to lighten the load? Possibly he even feels hidden strength in his sin and stubbornly shuts himself up with it (the obstinacy would likely remain even if he began to suspect hidden weakness there instead). He wants help—not forgiveness!

Forgiveness of sins. The words stand there so guilelessly in the gospels! How readily we reach for facile comparisons between the forgiveness of God and that of an earthly father or friend, convinced that we have solved the whole problem! In reality, it is packed with questions. Yet it is one of the main points of the good tidings, for Jesus said: "I have not come to call 'the just,' but sinners" (Mark 2:17). Naturally, this does not mean that he excludes the just, but that there is no such thing. People who do not regard themselves as sinners are non-existent for salvation; or rather, for them salvation consists first of all, of admitting their sinfulness.

What does it mean to be a sinner? To sin not only against a certain person or thing, but to fail sacred truth and justice? To stand in opposition not only to the eternal moral code, but also to the living and holy God, imitating Satan's age-old attack, the creature's senseless but profoundly exciting attempt to dethrone, degrade and destroy his Creator. Earthly sin is likewise directed against the sacred, god-drawn life in man, and works itself out in the degradation and destruction of natural life. Sin does not remain in the solitary cell of the individual conscience, but swiftly spreads to become a community of error and fate. Stronger or weaker, overt or clandestine, conscious or unconscious, hesitant or determined, its ultimate sense is destruction. What then must take place if forgiveness is to be experienced?

Man must admit the general profundity of sin, must overcome his attitude of superficiality and cowardice, and earnestly attempt to face sin in whatever form he may encounter it. He must not make it a mere matter of judgment or of will, but must feel, and deeply, for its core. He must not stubbornly insist upon the justice of a mere judge, but must consent and accept—*with* all his moral dignity, his freedom and responsibility—a Father's love. (And how many refuse precisely this!) He must discard defiance and that fatalistic pride which insists on doing everything alone and living one's own life in spite of everything, God included, if not first of all. Instead he must learn the humility that seeks grace. This is the summons in Jesus' first words: "The time is fulfilled, and the kingdom of God is at hand. Repent and believe in the gospel" (Mark 1:14–15). Before all else, men must learn that they are sinners; they must take stock of what they have become through sin, and *de profundis* call to God that they may be forgiven.

Forgiveness does not mean that God says to me: Your evil deed shall be undone. It was done and remains done. Nor does it mean that he says: It was not so bad. It was bad—I know it and God knows it. And again it does not mean that God is willing to cover up my sin or to look the other way. What help would that be? I want to be

rid of my transgression, really rid of it. Again, were one to say: Forgiveness means that I remain a sinner, but that God in his magnanimity attributes me with sanctity, thus giving me a share of his own
unimaginable divine grace, the thought would be so complicated
and so full of reservations that it would be untenable with the meaning of Scriptures. Forgiveness also does not mean that God gives me
the strength never to repeat my sin. Even if this were so, my old sin
would still be there; forgiveness could never spirit it away. That
would be deceitful and impure. How could God's immaculateness
ever reconcile itself to such a thought?

What possibility then does exist? Only one: that which the simplest interpretation of the gospel suggests and which the believing
heart must feel. Through God's forgiveness, in the eyes of his sacred
truth I am no longer a sinner; in the profoundest depths of my conscience I am no longer guilty. That is what I wanted—only that! If
such complete eradication of my sin cannot be, then it should stand.
But it can be; that is the sense of Christ's message.

Whether or not such forgiveness is possible cannot be determined by you or me according to any ethical or religious principles.
The question can be answered by revelation only, which clearly reveals who God is. He is the God of Justice, who not only rejects sin,
but absolutely condemns it; the Holy One who hates sin with divine
hatred; the True One who neither veils nor covers, but penetrates to
root and essence. And now, Christian revelation continues, in a
mysterious and supremely holy sense infinitely far from mitigating
the majesty of virtue, God lives beyond the reaches of good, and
therefore of evil. He himself *is* the good—but in inconceivable freedom; freedom from all ties, even from ties as ultimate as the conception of good. Such freedom renders him more powerful than sin.
It is the freedom of love. Love is not only kinder, more alive than
mere justice, it is more than justice—higher, mightier, in sense and
essence. Such then the love that enables God to rise and, without in
the least impairing truth and justice, to proclaim: Thy sin no longer
exists!

"Enables God"—what non-sense have we here? Yet precisely this is the decisive point. Here lies the enormity of it all: without diminishing the majesty of goodness, without bringing the reality of my sinful deed into phantastic abeyance, God in all holiness and truth is able not only to declare, but actually to make me free of guilt. This is the climax of the story as told by St. Mark. When the Pharisees object, Christ replies: "Why are you arguing these things in your hearts? Which is easier, to say to the paralytic, 'Thy sins are forgiven thee,' or to say, 'Arise, and take up thy pallet, and walk'?"

Yes, which is easier? To make a sick man well or to unburden a sinner of his sins? We are used to the reply that they are equally difficult, for only he can forgive (recreate) who can create. But the answer is not correct. Forgiveness, truly efficacious forgiveness is possible only for him who is 'above' God. The idea is of course preposterous, but in its very absurdity lies a grain of truth. Christ has really come to proclaim the "God above God"! No "supreme Being," but the Father concealed in unapproachable light, him of whom we knew literally nothing before the Son revealed him. We must take revelation seriously. Men actually did not know that God must be as he is in order to be able to forgive, for what they formerly meant by forgiveness was no true forgiveness, but a covering up, a looking away, a gracious ignoring, cessation of anger and punishment. Genuine forgiveness is as far superior to creation, as love is to justice, and if the mystery of creation out of nothing is already impenetrable, all human concepts are completely lost when faced with the mystery of God's power to render a sinner sinless. Such creative power emanates from the pure liberty of love. Between the states of sinfulness and sinlessness lies a death, a destruction in which the sinner is submerged, in order to be lifted from it into a new existence.

And into a new justice—naturally, as the Gospels clearly state it—a justice that is not of man. The justice he now possesses comes from God. It is the gift of love, grace-given share in God's justice. How it is possible that God's justice becomes my own (is not merely cast over me, or reflected by me, or attributed to me, but is genuinely mine) that is the impenetrable secret of the new existence.

The tidings of this transformation, of the new justice, of the God capable of such things are Christ's themes. That these things might be, he lived, taught, and died. The letters of the apostle Paul are full of this mystery. Once the heart is stricken by the inconceivableness of the thought, into the consciousness of faith steps the *mysterium tremendum*.

The man courageous enough to safeguard the personality with which he was originally endowed cannot but will this mystery. Conflict arises only when man falls from his proper plane. Not the exalted thing, but the fallen is complicated. The Christian should be humble, yes, but never diffident.

X

DEATH

In the previous chapter we spoke of sin and forgiveness of sin. Now we must consider that dark thing which the New Testament seems to link so closely as to unite with it: death. What does death mean to Jesus?

One may look upon death, as did antiquity, as a shadowy, inexplicable fate hovering over existence and infusing it with melancholy. Or as science sees it: the simple fact of organic disintegration. Thus conceived, death belongs so intrinsically to life, that one might define life as the movement towards death. One may greet death ecstatically as the Great, the Unspeakable, the Dionysian Mystery in which life culminates; or one may relegate it to the farthest corner of the mind, crowding it to the very brink of the consciousness and behaving as though it were non-existent. Death may also be regarded as an ultimate way out of the labyrinth of existence, a leap to be taken calmly or in despair. But as soon as we compare any one of these conceptions with Jesus' words on the subject, it becomes obvious how differently he thinks.

He speaks of death seldom. This is the more surprising since death's defeat stands at the very center of the Christian consciousness. How impressively the saints, James and Paul, for example, speak of it. Yet Jesus mentions it rarely, and then with no particular stress, but simply stating a fact, as in the parable of the wealthy debaucher and the beggar Lazarus, who both die when the appointed time comes (Luke 16:22). Or the Lord speaks of death in connection with the Father's guidance of the world, as in the parable of the man who has brought in his harvest and rests, completely assured that now nothing can happen to him: "But God said to him, 'Thou fool, this night do they demand thy soul of thee; and the things that thou hast provided, whose will they be?' " (Luke 12:20). Another time Jesus tells the disciples that they are not to fear those who kill the body, but only him who after the earthly death can also destroy the soul (Matt. 10:28).

Finally we come to that strange passage in which a man comes to Jesus and expresses the wish to follow him, but asks leave first to go and bury his father (in the consciousness of the Old Testament, one of the most sacred duties). Jesus must have seen that behind the delay was something that could shackle the would-be disciple, and he gives the harsh, almost disdainful reply that simply shoves death aside: "Follow me, and leave the dead to bury their own dead" (Matt. 8:22).

But most surprising is the peculiar freedom we find in Jesus' attitude towards death. Not the freedom of the hero who considers death's victory the simple reversal of greatness; also not the freedom of the sage, who has perceived what is lost in death and what remains, and firmly stands his ground. Here is something else. Essentially Jesus knows himself independent of death because death has no claim on him. No part of him is "stung" by mortality; perfect fruit, he is sound to the core.

Because he is entirely alive Jesus dominates death. Death's superior, he voluntarily submits to it, he who has been sent into the world to change death's very essence in the eyes of God.

The freedom Jesus takes with death is most obvious in the raising of the three dead. We see it when he restores the son to the widow of Naim, effortlessly calling the youth back to life as he passes through the city gates (Luke 7:11–17). And when the Lord returns his little daughter to Jairus with such delicate, lovely ease—"the girl is asleep, not dead"—he seems to be playing with death. The terrible one obeys his almost bantering word, and withdraws as lightly as slumber from a child's lids at the waking hand of a mother. Finally,

the tremendous event that John describes in his eleventh chapter:
the resurrection of Lazarus.

He was Jesus' friend, brother of the sisters Mary and Martha. One
day a message comes from them: "Lord, behold, he whom thou
lovest is sick." But Jesus only remarks: "This sickness is not unto
death, but for the glory of God . . ." and he remains where he is another two days, allowing Lazarus to die. Then he proceeds on his
way with the words: "Lazarus, our friend, sleeps. But I go that I may
wake him from sleep." (Again death and sleep paired in one breath,
and certainly not poetically. Jesus' words are not those of a poet but
of a commander.) The disciples misunderstand. "Lord, if he sleeps,
he will be safe." Then Jesus says plainly: "Lazarus is dead; and I rejoice on your account that I was not there, that you may believe. But
let us go to him."

What must there have been in his look that made Thomas say im-
pulsively to the others: "Let us also go, that we may die with him."
They arrive at Bethany, to find Lazarus already in the tomb. In Jesus
we sense a constantly rising excitement. Martha hears of his arrival
and greets him with the mild reproach:

"Lord, if thou hadst been here my brother would not have died."

"Thy brother shall rise."

"I know that he will rise at the resurrection, on the last day."

"I am the resurrection and the life; he who believes in me, even if
he die, shall live; and whoever lives and believes in me, shall never
die." The words span heaven and earth: "I am the resurrection and
the life," I and no other. Everything depends on our accomplishing
within ourselves this "I am." If only Jesus' vitality were in us, we
should not know death. But that vital quality which in Jesus is not
only indestructible, but intrinsic and creative, has been destroyed in
us. Hence we die. Our death is not 'tacked on' to life, it is the direct
outcome of the kind of life we live. In our dying a condition already
present in our living asserts itself: a condition—as we see by contrast
with Jesus, the full measure of man—which should not exist. Mortality has no foothold in Jesus. For this reason, although he offered

himself up in the Eucharist and died the death on the cross, he exists only as "life": (for us, who are mortal, as "the Resurrection"). Thus the human being linked in faith to Christ possesses a life that will outlive death and that already here on earth reaches into eternity. It is as Christ himself once expressed it: "Amen, amen, I say to you, he who hears my word, and believes him who sent me, has life everlasting, and does not come to judgment, but has passed from death to life" (John 5:24).

But to return to Bethany: "Dost thou believe this?" Christ asks Martha. Martha does not understand (how could she before the descent of the Holy Spirit?) but she trusts him: "Yes, Lord, I believe that thou art the Christ, the Son of God, who hast come into the world." Then she calls her sister. Mary comes, apparently on her way to the tomb. Seeing Jesus, she falls at his feet; greets him with Martha's identical words. But when Jesus hears her speak them and the lamentation of the mourners accompanying her, he shudders. Death's challenge seems to thicken about him: the dying of his friend, the pain of those close to him, his own approaching end. The Lord accepts the challenge.

"Where have you laid him?" They lead him to the place. At sight of the tomb, again "groaning in himself" Jesus weeps. No impotent distress this, or mere venting of sorrow, but monstrous experience. The fate of the world is at stake as death and the Lord stand face to face. Jesus commands that the stone be rolled away. Martha reminds him of the four days that have passed since burial. "Have I not told thee that if thou believe thou shalt behold the glory of God?" She believes but does not comprehend. Jesus stands alone with all that he is, the only one intrinsically alive among so many mortals, hence also the only one who really knows what death means. He must break this dark power; but no one helps him, not even by understanding.

Turning to his Father, he praises him for the unheard-of power about to manifest itself; then he cries with a loud voice: "Lazarus, come forth!" ". . . With a loud voice"—why? In Naim it had been so easy, and at the bedside of the little girl a quiet word had sufficed. Why then the cry and the huge gesture? We recall the same mighty cry from the cross between the last word and death (Luke 23:46). Both issued from the same heart, the same calling, and are one and the same act. Here though is not only the miracle of resuscitation from death; behind the visible event, deep in the last recesses of the spirit, rages a battle, the contest we spoke of in the chapter on the enemy. It is against the enemy of salvation that Jesus warns. Christ conquers death by conquering him who reigns in death: Satan.

And he does not vanquish by magic, nor by superior spiritual force, but simply by being what he is: invulnerable to the root and vital through and through. He is life itself, that life which is grounded in perfect love to the Father. This is Jesus' strength. The cry was a surge of that vitality in an all-overpowering thrust of love.

And Jesus' own death? In the beginning he does not mention death. Had the people been open, the predictions of the prophets would have fulfilled themselves, and salvation would have been brought about bloodlessly, through gospel and faith. The face of history would have been completely different. As long as this possibility existed, Jesus seems not to have spoken of his own dying, or at least only in uncertain and tentative terms. But when the leaders hardened their hearts, and the masses failed him, Jesus turned—we do not know in which darkest hour—down the other road to world salvation: the road to Golgotha.

Now in the hour of Caesarea Philippi he speaks openly of dying, "But who do you say that I am?" After Peter has replied and the Lord has praised him come the words: "From that time Jesus began to show his disciples that he must go to Jerusalem and suffer many things from the elders and Scribes and chief priests, and be put to death, and on the third day rise again" (Matt. 16:21; 17; 20). How terrible this decision was, how much, in spite of the power of his will, his whole being revolted from death's strangeness and horror, is revealed by what follows the announcement, when Peter takes him aside and remonstrates with him: "Far be it from thee, O Lord; this will never happen to thee."

Jesus turns on him: "Get behind me, satan, thou are a scandal to me; for thou dost not mind the things of God, but those of men" (Matt. 16:22–23). Also at this time fall the heavy words about the grain of wheat that must sink into the ground and die, if it is not to remain barren (John 12:24) and the call of readiness for death: "But I have a baptism to be baptized with; and how distressed I am until it is accomplished!" (Luke 12:50). Lazarus' resurrection is also of this period. But always, reference to Jesus' own death is linked with resurrection, Good Friday with Easter Sunday.

From this alone it is clear that the death which Jesus dies is not, like ours, the destructive death of sin, but a death which he who is Lord of death voluntarily accepts from the hand of his Father: "For this reason the Father loves me, because I lay down my life that I may take it up again. No one takes it from me, but I lay it down of myself. I have the power to lay it down, and I have the power to take it up again" (John 10:17–18).

It is on the road to Jerusalem too that the mysterious interlude of the Transfiguration takes place: premonition of that which is to fulfill itself at Easter projected into the living moment. The dying of the Lord is always linked with the Transfiguration, for he dies in the abundance of life, not in weakness or decline.

This is also apparent the last night in the Garden of Olives, where the full horror of his end breaks over him. Fearful unto death, he nevertheless surrenders his will to the Father's. Christ the uncontaminated receives death only from the will of the Father, accepted in perfect freedom. For this reason he "drank of death" more deeply than we ever could. We submit to death by force: he *willed* it in the ultimate intimacy of love. That is why his dying was so difficult. It has been claimed that others have died worse deaths than Jesus Christ. This is not true. The purer, stronger the life that death overcomes, the more terrible the dying. Our life is always so corrupted by death, that we have no idea what real, whole life is. Jesus was so entirely vital that he could say: I *am* life; thus he alone could drain death to the dregs and still prevail against it.

After Golgotha, death was never the same. To believe in Jesus Christ means to share in his deathlessness, as he himself said we should: He who believes shall have life everlasting, even in death. The believer participates in true, in eternal life.

Full consciousness of what takes place, comprehension of death and of man's share in that which Christ has brought about may be found in St. Paul. In the fifth chapter of the Epistle to the Romans he says clearly: Through a man, Adam, sin came into the world; through sin, death. Death does not belong to the essence of human nature; it is pagan to claim that it does. Sin brings death because it tears people from God. Man's real life is in the sharing of "the divine nature" (II Peter 1:4) that sin destroyed, thus causing the first death. Since then we all die. Christ though exists not only in communion with divine nature, but in union with her. He himself is the life that overcomes sin and death.

XI

ETERNAL CONSCIOUSNESS

At the beginning of these meditations we stated that a history of Jesus, in the sense that one speaks of a history of St. Francis, is impossible. The very form of our knowledge of him (not chronologically noted recordings, but living proclamation) precludes such record.

How often Jesus visited the capital we do not know. Very likely, he was there often, but for the presentation of his tidings and their acceptance three visits are of principal importance. The first, probably immediately after his baptism and temptation, is reported by John in chapter two. With a few of his disciples, Jesus arrives at Jerusalem; incident of the cleansing of the temple, the leaders of the people cool but watchful. Then comes a second visit to Jerusalem, in the autumn apparently, for it is the time of the Feast of the Tabernacles. The events described by John in the seventh to tenth chapters are grouped about this visit, possibly also the healing at the pool of Bethsaida in chapter five. During this sojourn, the smouldering conflict breaks into the open. The Pharisees try to put Jesus out of the way, and he accuses them of denying God. Then he continues, partly through the pagan territory of Tyre and Sidon, back to Galilee. There too the storm is gathering. Possibly the proclamation of the Holy Eucharist was decisive; at any rate, the decision falls— against Jesus and his message. Henceforth, much of the public is hostile; even many of Jesus' disciples no longer follow him. Now Jesus keeps in the background, his teachings circling mainly about the hidden kernel of Christian existence. From this point on it is clear that he is being sent to his death. Once again he journeys to Jerusalem, this time for the Easter festival at which all things are to be consummated.

It is the decision in Jerusalem at the Feast of the Tabernacles, the decision known as the Judaic crisis, that we shall now discuss.

Jesus has performed one of his miracles, his "works" as he calls them. He has cured someone, perhaps the cripple at the pool of Bethsaida. The healing has taken place on a Sabbath, to the great excitement of the zealots, who accuse him of breaking the law. Jesus responds as he has on similar occasions, by showing them the ridiculousness of their arraignment: when a child is born so that the eighth day after its birth falls on a Sabbath, it is nevertheless circumcised on the eighth day; why therefore should one not also be healed on a Sabbath? They should interpret the law with common sense and try to judge with justice (John 7:22–24). Actually, it is not a question of the law that causes the trouble, but Jesus' claims regarding his mission. When he teaches in the temple all are astounded by his knowledge; they ask whence he has it, and who he is. But he produces no earthly authorization; he simply refers to his being sent by God: "My teaching is not my own, but his who sent me" (7:16). Such learning can be shared by anyone who enters into Jesus' relationship to him from whom it proceeds, surrendering his will to the Father, as Jesus himself has done.

"They therefore said to him, 'Where is thy father?' Jesus answered, 'You know neither me nor my Father. If you knew me, you would then know my father also' " (John 8:19–20). The Father is hidden in unapproachable light and reveals himself only through his Son. There is no other immediate approach to him. Thus no one who is a stranger to Christ can claim that he knows the Father, just as no one can know Christ, whose heart is not ready for obedience to the Father, and by such readiness "called." This he states clearly. Jesus knows himself one with the Father; sent by the Father, and teaching through the Father. His opponents demand proof, but he only replies: What you ask cannot be answered by external proofs.

You must enter into the interior oneness between my Father and me; your wills must be ready to accept the manner in which the Father lives and reveals himself in me. Otherwise, this mystery will be sealed to you, and you yourselves will remain locked in error and evil.

How terrible is the Pharisees' darkness is best shown by the wild passage in John seven: " 'Why do you seek to put me to death?' the crowd answered and said, 'Thou hast a devil. Who seeks to put thee to death?' " But Jesus knows what he is saying. Such obdurate disobedience to God cannot remain neutral; it turns to hate and the desire for blood. Actually, they do give orders to seize him, but his hour has not come (that hour ordained by the Father in which he is to surrender himself to the sinners voluntarily) and not one of the officers dares to lay hands on him (7:30).

On the last day of the festival (at the solemn rite in memory of Moses' bestowal of water in the desert) Jesus stands in the temple, and filled with the unspeakable abundance of the divine power surging through him, power enough to embrace and transform the whole world, calls in a loud voice: "If anyone thirst, let him come to me and drink. He who believes in me, as the Scripture says, 'From within him there shall flow rivers of living water' " (John 7:37–38). Summons straight from the kingdom of God longing to break into reality, it is directed at God's people and their leaders. Nor was its urgency unfelt: "Some therefore of the people of Jerusalem were saying, 'Is not this the man they seek to kill? And behold, he speaks openly and they say nothing to him. Can it be that the rulers have really come to know that this is the Christ? Yet we know where this man is from; but when the Christ comes, no one will know where he is from' " (John 7:25–27).

To this, Jesus: Yes, my earthly origin you know, but my essential, heavenly origin you do not know. Even as an earthly teacher, I do not come with my own message, for I am the Envoy of him who is eternally true. You recognize neither my mainspring nor my teaching, because you do not know him who sent me. But I know him, because I come from him, I root in him, I work through him. It is of him that I speak. (See 7:28–29.)

Again Jesus appeals to them, calling himself the light of the world. The Pharisees: But you remain alone with your claims—no one testifies for you! Jesus defends his title nevertheless: he who stands at the beginning of all things is necessarily his own witness. No one can bear witness to him, because everything that exists independently of him is outside reality. Thus he plants himself in his own claims, trusting himself not to "the wisdom of men" but to "the power of God" (I Cor. 2:4). Divine power is no blind force, but truth recognizable by anyone who steps into the world of living truth which Jesus, who *is* way, truth and life, has constructed (John 14:6). Not weighing of evidence is demanded here, but obedience to the self-revealing God. Then and then only, in faith, will it be evident that Jesus has after all one "witness" at his side: ". . . he who sent me testifies for me too, the Father" (John 8:18). God's testimony must have been tremendously effective, for on the strength of his words alone, "many believed in him" (John 8:30; Luke 4:32), though several hastened to reassert themselves.

Jesus promises: If you would be truly my disciples, keep my word, live in my word; then you will know the truth. The new existence will embrace you, and you will understand the self-revelation of the Father in his Son, and this truth will make you free (John 8:31–48).

Immediately contradiction flares: Make us free? We are sons of Abraham and have never been slaves!

Jesus: Everyone who sins is the servant of sin. Not until he who is above all servitude, the kingly Son of the Lord of earth, frees you, will you be really free. You are Abraham's sons—true enough, but only by his blood, not his spirit. Therefore you do not understand me; therefore your reserve turns to hatred and you desire my life. And again: I speak of things I have seen in my Father's house, but you do what your father has taught you.

They sense the awfulness of the charge and fall back upon Abraham: He is our father!

Jesus: If you were true sons of Abraham you would do as he did: believe. Instead, your disbelief turns to thirst for the blood of him who tells you the truth. You do the works of your real father.

They: Our flesh is not bastard flesh, and our spirit has but one Father: God!

Jesus: If God were your Father, you would love me and understand my words, for he it was who sent me. Why won't you understand? Because you have given your hearts to the other one, who is now your father: Satan. He was a murderer from the beginning and hater of truth—hence the hatred you bear me. Terrible this scene.

Jesus begins again: "Amen, amen, I say to you, if anyone keep my word, he will never see death."

The Jews: "Now we know that thou hast a devil. Abraham is dead, and the prophets, and thou sayest, 'If anyone keep my word he will never taste death.' Art thou greater than our father Abraham, who is dead? and the prophets who are dead? Whom dost thou make thyself?"

Against the ill will all around him Jesus can do nothing but reaffirm his position in that will which supports him: "If I glorify myself, my glory is nothing. It is my Father who glorifies me, . . . And if I say that I do not know him, I shall be like you, a liar."

In this hour of satanic hate, Jesus stands squarely in his Father's will, budging not by a hair's breadth. On the contrary, he drives truth to those ultimate consequences which to the enemy must seem blasphemous: " 'Abraham your father rejoiced that he was to see my day. He saw it and was glad.' The Jews therefore said to him, 'Thou art not yet fifty years old, and hast thou seen Abraham?' Jesus said to them, 'Amen, amen, I say to you, before Abraham came to be, I am.' They therefore took up stones to cast at him; but Jesus hid himself, and went out from the temple" (John 8:51–59). It is the inmost depths of Jesus' self-knowledge breaking through in speech, eternal consciousness of divine Sonship.

He who reads the Gospels with an open heart must feel the profound difference between the three first and that of John. This difference may trouble him. He will ask himself whether the Jesus of the Evangelists, Matthew, Mark and Luke, is the same as the Jesus of John. Aren't the two portraits contradictory, hence one right and the other wrong? How could they ever be an entity? For centuries historians have labored over the answer; we cannot go into the results of their research here, so we must formulate the question differently. If Jesus really was both true man and true Son of God, who can see him rightly? Only faith, belief, given by the same Father who spoke the Word of flesh that was to be believed. Now faith has always understood that the Jesus of the four Gospels was one and the same. It really should be self-evident that an existence of such unthinkable depths and immeasurable proportions could never be completely portrayed by any one artist, not even by the greatest genius. It must take shape gradually. Little by little the eye penetrates the darkness of the mystery, uncovering increasingly richer treasure. The longer Christian experience lasts, the more complete Christ's image will become. The more practiced the mind and the better trained by attacks of the enemy, the broader, bolder, clearer its recognition will be.

All the texts of the New Testament speak in the Holy Spirit; that is the decisive point. Where such foundations exist, all shades of meaning possible to human insight and expression are effective. Thus the Synoptics record immediate historical experience, which views Jesus as he might have been seen by any believer. To be sure, even here fall such far-reaching words as: "All things have been delivered to me by my Father; and no one knows the Son except the Father; nor does anyone know the Father except the Son, and him to whom the Son chooses to reveal him" (Matt. 11:27–29). St. Paul probably never saw the Lord face to face; he draws Christ's spiritual features as he has been taught by personal revelation—the Christ who thrones "at the right hand of God" and simultaneously lives and works in us: "And all things he made subject under his feet, and him he gave as head over all the Church, which indeed is his body, the completion of him who fills all with all" (Col. 3:1; Eph. 1:20–23).

Last of all writes St. John, now an old man. Once with his own eyes he had seen "the Word" who is life; had touched him with his hands, as he tells us so vividly in his opening epistle.

His Christ is painted from life—from the historical life in which he, John, personally participated. Since then, it has been constantly enriched by long years of Christian experience, of prayer, proclamation and struggle. Layer after layer of sacred reality has come to light. During the conflict with the first Gnostics who crop up about John, comes the hour to stress those features of the Lord only hinted at in the earlier Gospels; to develop thoughts in Christ's teaching that in the preceding records lie dormant as seeds. Thus in the earth of long apostolic, prophetic, and apocalyptical experience, they unfold to the total reality of Christ in all its "breadth and length and height and depth" (Eph. 3:18).

The Christ of the Synoptics and the Christ of St. John are one. The more deeply we penetrate into divine truth, the more clearly we see that John speaks the ultimate word indeed; word, however, which the others have prepared.

XII

REBIRTH IN WATER AND IN THE HOLY SPIRIT

It is St. John who describes the clandestine visit paid Jesus by Nicodemus, one of the rulers of the Jews, and who records the remarkable conversation that took place between them.

"Now there was a certain man among the Pharisees, Nicodemus by name, a ruler of the Jews. This man came to Jesus at night, and said to him, 'Rabbi, we know that thou hast come a teacher from God, for no one can work these signs that thou workest unless God be with him' " (John 3:1–2).

Since earliest Christianity, opinion has varied as to when, precisely, this meeting took place. Let us suppose the time to be that of the Feast of the Tabernacles. Jesus has just cured the man, crippled for thirty-eight years, at the pool of Bethsaida, and now, challenged by the priests and Pharisees, he has so openly revealed his divinity and taken his stand next the Father, that those who do not believe must consider his claims blasphemous.

Among the many opponents there are also individual Jews who accept Christ's word, or who—perhaps in spite of themselves—are attracted to him; Nicodemus is one of these. He longs to speak with the Master. How strong the feeling already prevalent against Jesus, is evident from the fact that the man does not dare to come by day.

Nicodemus has been shaken by Jesus' mysterious power; his wonderful teaching has struck home. He has sensed the miracles to be what in truth they are: a breaking through of power from above, visible signs of a new divine reality. Now he too wishes to be where this Stranger is, to share in his vision of the kingdom. That is prob-

ably what he means by his question: How may one become worthy
to behold the kingdom of God. Thereupon Jesus: " 'Amen, amen, I
say to thee, unless a man be born again, he cannot see the Kingdom
of God.' Nicodemus said to him, 'How can a man be born when he
is old? Can he enter a second time into his mother's womb and be
born again?'

"Jesus answered, 'Amen, amen, I say to thee, unless a man be
born again of water and the Spirit, he cannot enter into the Kingdom of God' " (John 3:3–5). In other words: What you desire is humanly impossible. To behold the kingdom of heaven, to reach the
point where the Envoy of that kingdom stands, is something that
man, unaided, can never do. Man is "world." As long as he thinks
by his own means, no matter how clearly, how exaltedly, he remains
world. He may struggle with all the moral strength at his disposal, he
will never surpass the summits of *earthly* good. No matter what values of nobility, traditional refinement and high culture he may lean
upon, he will always remain earth's prisoner. Something else must
take place: a new existence must be established—from above—
whence both the kingdom and its Envoy come. We can see only
that for which we have an eye; can grasp only that which is somehow related to us. Therefore, he who would behold the kingdom
must be reborn into a new existence.

Nicodemus does not understand. He takes Christ's words literally, physically: shall the adult revert to infancy, return to his
mother's womb? The answer seems obvious; all the more interesting
Jesus' reply. He does not say: Be sensible! Try to understand this
symbolically: an entirely new point of view must be gained, a fresh
start. No, precisely the provocative words are repeated. Christ insists: a new creation, a second *birth* must take place (naturally, in the
spirit). However, "spirit" here does not mean the opposite of body.
Nor is it recognition and wisdom, nor yet what later philosophy was
to call objective spirit: culture in all shades of the word's meaning.
In the language of Holy Scripture, man and everything concerned

with him is "flesh"—'from below.' The Spirit Jesus refers to comes 'from above,' it is sent by the Father: *Pneuma,* Holy Spirit. He is the third "countenance" of God. Through his power, the Word became flesh, that same power which flowed down upon Jesus at his baptism and upheld the Godman to the end. It is through him that our new birth is to take place.

What does the Spirit accomplish? It is not easy to say. One must delve into the lives of the prophets; for example, into a joyful passage like that in the first Book of Kings where the prophet Samuel says to young Saul: ". . . thou shalt meet a company of prophets coming down from the high place, with a psaltery and a timbrel, and a pipe, and a harp before them; and they shall be prophesying" (I Kings 10:5). Or into the account of Pentecost and its effects as presented in the Acts (2:1–21 and further). Or we should read what St. Paul has to say of the gifts of grace (14:12–14). These and other passages would give us an inkling of that mysterious and powerful Something that is meant here.

It is through the Spirit that the eternal Word creates and sustains the world; it is also through the Spirit that salutary love recreates what already exists, but 'crippled' in the state of sin. In the course of a lifetime, ever new strata of being are uncovered, down to the ultimate depth fixed at birth. There is no passing beyond this level. The older a man is, the more clearly he recognizes his natural limitations, the more he becomes rooted, even petrified within them. But the constantly creative Holy Spirit can stir the most static being to life and motion. He frees it from the prison of its first birth, kneading it to material for a new creation. As the liturgy of Pentecost prays, the boundaries of self-existence vanish in the new existence: "Send forth thy Spirit, and they shall be created, and thou shalt renew the face of the earth."

But the mystery plunges deeper. Between God and man stands the barrier of sin. God the Holy One, angered by Man's sinfulness, rejects him. The Holy Spirit lowers that barrier. 'Emerging' from

God's heart (actually he *is* God's heart), he carries holy life to man, lifting him back to the pristine purity of beginning. What results is no mixture of humanity with divinity, but new being: unthinkable, inexpressible, incredible—were it not for God's own word that this is so. Through the strength of this Spirit of Love, the creature enjoys community of life and of heart with his Creator.

This may at first sound like pious fancy. But in human existence there is an allegory for it: love. Take for example a man of a specific nature, occupation, environment, who has reached maturity within a specific set of conditions. For him all these things belong together, forming a unit, himself; all other people are another unit, 'the others,' who live 'over there.' Our man may be considerate, friendly, neighborly, but unconsciously he will always draw a line between himself and them: I, mine—as distinct from you, yours; them, theirs. But when he falls in love something astonishing occurs. The I-not-you, mine-not-thine barrier begins to dissolve. Now no particular virtue or effort is necessary to join the beloved; he is already 'there.' What is his suddenly belongs to the other, and what affects the other suddenly touches him, for a new unit has been created. It has not been superficially tied, nor has it come into being by a mixing or blending of the two; it was *born,* and its name is love. Something similar, however divinely different, happens between man and God, though here it is the love of God himself which is active, the Holy Spirit. He creates the new existence in which man lives in God, and God receives man into his own. Foundation of such love is Jesus Christ, the Son of God become man. Through faith and participation in the act of salvation any Christian may share in divine love: that is the new birth and the new life which springs from it.

Jesus says that the new birth will take place in water and in the Holy Spirit. John came and baptized with water, knowing that this was only preparatory: "I have baptized you with water, but he will baptize you with the Holy Spirit" (Mark 1:8). Since the memory of man water has been the dual symbol of life and death, womb and grave. Christ preserved the symbol, Christianizing it with the mystery of the Holy Spirit. Thus baptism came into the world. From it the new man steps—into the new beginning in faith and in grace. In the ceremony of baptism we are spiritually buried with Christ, that we may rise with him and receive our share in his life. Through it the new center of divine vitality to which St. Paul refers is established within us. That is the new birth which no possible considerations of why or wherefore, possible or impossible, right or wrong can turn back—any more than they can turn back an earthly birth.

"That which is born of the flesh is flesh; and that which is born of the Spirit is spirit. Do not wonder that I said to thee, 'You must be born again.' The wind blows where it will, and thou hearest its sound but dost not know where it comes from or where it goes. So is everyone who is born of the Spirit" (John 3:6–8). Here is mystery that cannot be penetrated from without. He who coldly watches the conduct of lovers, who notes how they think, react, who observes what delights or discourages them, but has no share in that renascence which has just unfolded to them, finds them not only incomprehensible, but downright foolish. He sees only their visible acts, detached from their source, impulse and direction. He who lives only in himself, in "the world," who has never ventured the step into the new existence, can see, hear, note the acts of one living in faith; but he will never understand their origin or purpose.

How is such a thing possible? asks Nicodemus, and isn't his question our own—all the helplessness of it, the longing, the discouragement? There on the one hand stands Christ with his chosen ones, radiating the beauty and plenitude of God; and here am I, entangled in myself, heavily forged to my own dark paltriness; how can I ever cross over to him? How, ever, escape from myself to share in all that is he? Jesus replies: You never will—alone. Do not hope to be able, however slowly, to comprehend. Do not reason thus: What he says is true, I must hasten to join him. This would be measuring Christ by your own standards, and it would not be he you encountered 'over there,' but yourself—you would have walked in a circle. No, you must let go; renounce all hope of self-illumination, fling the measuring-rod of reason and experience to the winds and venture the call: Lord, come—send me your Spirit that I may be recreated! Give me the new mind that I may grasp your spirit, the new heart, that I may grasp your love!

How do I know that this is possible? Because he who has "seen," who "has come down from heaven" warrants for it. You must take him at his word. But what if I am not that far, if I haven't yet such trust? Then you must wait and pray, if only to say: Lord, if you are he whom Scripture names, let me know you! Christ is our guarantor. Our part is simply to let go. Confidence in our own understanding, purity of attitude, excellence of personal effort, faithfulness to character, the sterling quality of the historical or cultural elements of the past—all this has been preparatory and important. But now the moment has come to put it aside. To become a Christian means to go to Christ *on the strength of his word alone;* to trust solely in his testimony. Blind acceptance of what remains unclear, unreasonable is part of this step and belongs essentially to the "foolishness" of the crossing over (I Cor. 1:23).

But what if I have already been baptized? If the second birth has taken place and I still stand before Christ instead of in him? Still hear and do not understand, still walk deep in earth and not "in heaven" (Phil. 3:20)? What then? Then a word from John's prologue to his Gospel might help: "But to as many as received him he gave the power of becoming sons of God; to those who believe in his name: Who were born not of blood, nor of the will of flesh, nor of the will of man, but of God" (1:12). It is good that this word exists, otherwise we should lose heart. It says: to be born again and to be a child of God in the full sense of the word is not yet one and the same thing, not any more than to have left the womb is to have attained the fullness of the human state. To be borne again in God is also only a beginning, an infancy. We are children of God when we are "born of water and the Holy Spirit," but we have yet to become the sons and daughters of God that we have been empowered to become. What can we do to further our spiritual maturity? A great deal: think, reflect, struggle for knowledge, clarity and virtue, fight our weaknesses, help our neighbors, perform our given tasks loyally, and much more. Yet even all this, alone, is not enough; the growth of divine life in us too must come from the source of our second birth: from the Holy Spirit, who must permeate our thoughts and struggles and deeds, and thus renew them. Again and again, therefore, we must supplicate: Eternal Beginning, Creative Spirit, recreate me! You who have begun me, complete me!

One thing about Nicodemus moves us strangely: that nothing more is said of him. He remains silent, but what he heard must have gone deep.

Jesus' words grow increasingly grave, but they are not accepted. It is clear that the responsible groups not only reject them, but also desire to destroy Jesus. This, humanity's crime (the second fall halfway through history, as the first was the prelude to history) Christ's love was to transform to the perfect sacrifice that insured salvation.

"And as Moses lifted up the serpent in the desert, even so must the Son of Man be lifted up, that those who believe in him may not perish, but may have life everlasting.

"For God so loved the world that he gave his only-begotten Son, that those who believe in him may not perish, but may have life everlasting. For God did not send his Son into the world in order to judge the world, but that the world might be saved through him. He who believes in him is not judged; but he who does not believe is already judged, because he does not believe in the name of the only-begotten Son of God. Now this is judgment: The light has come into the world, yet men have loved the darkness rather than the light, for their works were evil" (John 3:14–19).

Nicodemus was there when it took place. In the nineteenth chapter of the same Gospel we read: "Now after these things Joseph of Arimathea, because he was a disciple of Jesus (although for fear of the Jews a secret one), besought Pilate that he might take away the body of Jesus. And Pilate gave permission. He came, therefore, and took away the body of Jesus. And there also came Nicodemus (who at first had come to Jesus by night), bringing a mixture of myrrh and aloes, in weight about a hundred pounds" (John 19:38–39).

PART THREE

The Decision

I

THE BLIND
AND THE SEEING

We have already spoken of the clash between Jesus and the Pharisees in Jerusalem. It is probably to this that John refers as early as the fifth and sixth chapters, certainly in the detailed seventh to tenth. The conflict is so grave that henchmen are sent to arrest Jesus, but they return without having executed the order. The Pharisees: " 'Why have you not brought him?' The attendants answered, 'Never has man spoken as this man.' " Strange reply for constables! The divine authority of him whom they are supposed to seize, the power of his personality and words is so great that they dare not lay hands on him. Thereupon the Pharisees' significant: "Have you also been led astray? Has any one of the rulers believed in him, or any of the Pharisees? But this crowd, which does not know the Law, is accursed" (John 7:45–49).

The Hebrew race was divided into a caste-system descending steplike from the families of the high priests to the lowest 'half-breed' offspring of a Hebrew father and an alien mother. Another sharp fissure ran horizontally, cleaving the entire nation into two categories: those who knew the science of the law, the tenets of right and wrong, permissible and forbidden (in other words those acquainted with the law, symbolism, mysticism of the temple) and those who did not, the uninitiated and ignorant. The first group consisted of the intellectuals—the Scribes and Pharisees; the second of "the crowd." This intellectual dividing line cut so deeply that a man from the lowest level of society who knew the law stood higher than the ignorant son of a high priest. And now the most revered among the initiated say: None of us will have anything to do with the folly and blasphemy of this man. Only the masses, who are ignorant of the law, can find any good in him—curses on them! This gives us a clue to the revolutionary, the truly divine blessedness which Jesus pronounces over "the poor in spirit" (Matt. 5:3). "The crowd," despised and cursed by the erudite, were open to Jesus and his message. If only they had remained loyal, how unspeakably blessed they would have been—blessed with all the beatific joy of the Isaian prophecies!

Shortly after this incident, the Lord meets a blind man in the street and feels himself called upon by this brother living in darkness to perform works of light in the service "of him who sent me. . . . As long as I am in the world, I am the light of the world." Jesus spits on the ground (a practice common to ancient therapeutics, which attributed healing powers to spittle) kneads it with dust, spreads the resultant paste over the blind eyes, and commands the invalid to go and wash in the waters of Siloe. The blind man obeys and returns seeing.

There is a tremendous uproar. The man is brought before the Pharisees. They question him, and he replies: "The man who is called Jesus made clay and anointed my eyes, and said to me, 'Go to the pool of Siloe and wash.' And I went and washed, and I see." The miracle makes a profound impression. Some of the Pharisees side with the man capable of such wonders; the others however declare: "This man is not from God, for he does not keep the Sabbath." They ask the former blind man his opinion, and he gives the only answer he can after such an experience: "He is a prophet."

The matter is then referred to the high council. They refuse to believe that the man had been really blind, and they summon his parents, who testify that he is their son and had been blind from birth. But knowing that the council bans anyone who recognizes Jesus as the Messiah, they dodge the questions asked concerning the manner of the healing. Actually, the decision has already fallen, irrevocably; still the hearing continues.

"What did he do to thee? How did he open thy eyes?" The man grows impatient; he has already told them often enough. The facts are perfectly clear, but the interrogators have little interest in facts. They hope that by withholding official recognition of the healing and by heaping Jesus with calumny they can cover up the miracle. It blazes brightly before their eyes, but they do not see it, because they do not wish to see it, and they wrap it in a cloud of darkness so that no one else can. As for the embarrassing witness, they hope to intimidate him so that he will hold his tongue. But the man stands his ground. So they place him under ban: he is thrust out of the community, and his property is confiscated. When Jesus hears what has happened he goes to him:

"Dost thou believe in the Son of God?"

"Who is he, Lord, that I may believe in him?"

"Thou hast both seen him, and he it is who speaks with thee."

And the man who was born blind falls on his knees and worships. Jesus, however, turns to the bystanders: "For judgment have I come into this world, that they who do not see may see, and they who see may become blind" (John 9:1–39).

Extraordinarily impressive event! Here outer developments and inner sense, the immediate incident and its bearing upon the whole of Christ's works, are powerfully united. The key to this union lies in the words: "for judgment." They are reminiscent of similar ironic passages: "I have come to call sinners, not the just" (Mark 2:17); or of Jesus' jubilant: "I praise thee, Father, Lord of heaven and earth, that thou didst hide these things from the wise and prudent, and didst reveal them to little ones" (Matt. 11:25). The "little ones," minors in the eyes of the world, are to become knowing, just, great and free. Those, however, who consider themselves already great, who are loathe to relinquish their earthly knowledge, are adolescent fools and will remain so. Here behind the miraculous healing of the man born blind lies the same thought, only more powerfully, sharply focused. Jesus knows that he has come that "they who do not see may see, and they who see may become blind."

"Blind" are those who realize that with all their earthly insight and knowledge they stand in the dark before the divine, utterly incapable of comprehending the Essential. He who admits this truth to himself and to his God, encounters "the light of the world," who unfolds in him powers of heavenly vision. In its clarity he recognizes God's messenger, the new order, the budding new creation. And the more he sees, the more 'seeing' he grows, comprehending the things of God's kingdom more and more deeply and fully. Thus the inner eye feeds on what it sees, and the greater its strength, the greater the abundance that is revealed to it.

The 'seeing,' on the other hand, are those who in God's presence still cling to their earthly point of view, their earthly knowledge, earthly conception of justice, naively attempting to measure even the divine by their own standards. When the Son of God himself stands before them, they see only a rebel and proceed against all who believe in him with the heavy indignation of the righteous. And when the long awaited Christ performs his miracles before their eyes, they either refuse to see them or brand them works of Satan! Because they do not wish to see, demonstrations of God's power and love only seem to make them incapable of seeing. They become increasingly short-sighted and ultimately blind.

Seeing is more than indifferently reflecting (as a mirror reflects all that passes within range). It is a vital process that directly affects our lives. To see, *perceive,* means to receive into oneself, to submit to the influence of things, to place oneself within their grasp. Necessarily, the will mounts guard over the vision. One protection against precarious things is to look at them sharply, so as to discover their weaknesses; another is to look away, so as to remain unaffected by them. On the whole, we see what we choose to see; the selectiveness of the individual eye is a protective measure of life itself. This being true already on the natural plane, how much truer it is on the spiritual, with its cognizance of others, of the positions we take to the truths and demands thrust upon us. To see another human being as he really is means to lay ourselves open to his influence. Thus when fear or dislike moves us to avoid him, this reaction is already evident in our gaze; the eye caricaturizes him, stifling the good, heightening the bad. We discern his intentions, make swift comparisons, and leap to conclusions. All this proceeds involuntarily, if not unconsciously (in which case our powers of distortion, uncurbed by reason, do their worst). Seeing is a protective service to the will to live. The deeper our fear or distaste of a person, the more tightly we close our eyes to him, until finally we are incapable of perception or the profound German word for it, *Wahrnehmen:* reception-of-truth. Then we have become blind to that particular person. This mysterious process lies behind every enmity. Discussion, preaching, explanations are utterly useless. The eye simply ceases to register what is plain to be seen. Before there can be any change, a fundamental shift must take place in the general attitude. The mind must turn to justice, the heart expand; then only can the eye really begin to discern. Little by little the sheen of the object on which it rests strengthens its visual power, and slowly it recovers the health of truth.

Jesus Christ is the incarnate Son of God, flesh and blood Revelation in whom the hidden God is made apparent: ". . . no one knows the Son except the Father, and no one knows the Father except the Son, and him to whom the Son chooses to reveal him" (Matt. 11:27); "And he who sees me, sees him who sent me." He was "the true light" who enlightens "every man who comes into the world" he has made, and filled with purpose, and flooded with spiritual sun (John 12:45; 1:9–10). Thus he stands, showering radiance upon everyone who nears him. If that person is 'seeing' in the worldly sense, something in him is willed to seek the world and himself rather than the Messiah. His eye is fixed on world and self and remains so. Everything else that crosses into his vision is thrown out of focus, and if it registers at all, only as something suspicious, ugly, dangerous. Thus it can happen that a man opposes Jesus with all the passion of outraged reason, order and justice because the Jesus he sees before him really seems an abomination. His own eyes have so distorted the Light of the world, that he must reject him. That man is one of the unblessed who is "scandalized in me."

But is such blindness in the face of divine light possible? If it were a question of the acceptance or rejection of human brilliance, it would be understandable, but darkness before the clarity of God? There more than anywhere else! Since seeing is a vital act, since the will to existence stands close behind the eye, and every glance harbors a preconceived decision, the more it is a question of eternal destiny, the more dominant, decisive that will becomes. When Christ appears, everything is at stake. That is what he means by his: "For judgment have I come into this world. . . ."

When the Messenger of Revelation appears before mankind, he forces it to a decision—one that simultaneously affects himself (Creator placing his fate in the hands of his creatures!). Revelation presents no mere facts to be acknowledged, but truth, that once seen obliges. And it demands that this truth be accepted, that man surrender himself to it and enter into that which comes from God. He who really sees already approaches obedience. Thus the spreading of the gospel of truth necessarily separates people into two camps: the willing and the unwilling; those who wish to see and those who do not (hence, those who will see, and those who will lose their sight). It is to these spiritually blind that the words following the parable of the sower are addressed:

"Hearing you will hear, but not understand; and seeing you will see, but not perceive. For the heart of this people has been hardened, and with their ears they have been hard of hearing, and their eyes they have closed; lest at any time they see with their eyes, and hear with their ears, and understand with their mind, and be converted, and I heal them" (Matt. 13:14–15). This separating of the seeing from the unseeing may occur in various ways: the decision may come lightning-like at the first encounter, or gradually in a slow process of ripening. It may be made overtly or covertly, screened by careful feint, or veiled in sentiment and passion. But one way or another it must be made.

In the eighth chapter, Mark describes Jesus' healing of another blind man. The Lord lays his hands on the blind eyes: What do you see?

Men large as trees, but walking!

The sight-nerves have been greatly stimulated; the man is beginning to see, but objects are still blurred and disproportionate. Again Jesus lays his hands on the afflicted eyes, and now they see clearly and are healed. The incident is both reality and parable, or rather reality that stretches from the physical into the spiritual.

He who had lived in darkness was suddenly flooded with light that, pouring in through his eyes, dazzlingly illuminated everything within him. Then Jesus taught him to adjust himself to the new brightness both within and without: to perceive in the natural light also that other, holy light which contact with the light of the world had kindled. Jesus inflamed the man to a single blaze of light; first his eyes caught it, then his heart and blood, and finally that which the Lord calls "the soul": that state of readiness for God and his fire. "If thy eye be sound, thy whole body will be full of light." Practically in the same breath, comes the warning: "Therefore if the light that is in thee is darkness, how great is the darkness itself!" (Matt. 6:23).

The healing of the blind man gives us a key to the mystery of Jesus' rejection in Jerusalem, and we ourselves are advised to be "in fear and trembling" lest the light in us go out. We too stand 'in court'; for us too the decision must be made as to whether we belong to the 'seeing' whose inner eye is afflicted, or to the 'blind' whose 'eyes' have been opened. And our sentence falls over and over again—each time we hear a word of the Lord or encounter his truth, or feel called upon by his demands, for God weaves a ray of light, which effects either our vision or our blindness, into his every disposition of our lives. Woe to us if we are content with our intrinsic blindness!

Thus the decision in Jerusalem fell, and Jesus returned to Galilee. Those responsible, the priests and scribes, denied him, declaring that only the ignorant masses could possibly be expected to believe. Now the second decision nears: will the masses themselves accept him? When the rulers primarily responsible as representatives of the Covenant fail, only the masses can still save the day. Will they step forward and seize the initiative of faith?

II

THE SON OF MAN

At this time the Lord clearly expresses his salutary mission to mankind in the parable of the shepherd: "Amen, amen, I say to you, he who enters not by the door into the sheepfold, but climbs up another way, is a thief and a robber. But he who enters by the door is shepherd of the sheep. To this man the gatekeeper opens, and the sheep hear his voice, and he calls his own sheep by name and leads them forth. And when he has let out his own sheep, he goes before them; and the sheep follow him because they know his voice" (John 10:1–5).

The passage is a familiar one, though not a favorite. Let us be frank; the comparison of the faithful to a herd of sheep is embarrassing. Most of us are city-dwellers and unfamiliar with rural life, and even those who live in the country today have little idea of the importance of the herd in the consciousness of a pastoral people. Jesus' listeners, however, were men and women who still vividly recalled the founding fathers of their nation. Abraham, whom God had summoned to the new land, was a shepherd and lived with his sheep—a princely shepherd, whose herds were so vast that one land was too small to sustain them with those of his nephew Lot, and the one had to take the country to the right, the other that to the left (Gen. 13:6). Isaac was a shepherd, and Jacob, who served twice seven years for Rachel before he returned home with his blessed herds, wrestling with God on the way (Gen. 29; 32). When the years of famine came, and Jacob's sons removed to Egypt, Joseph, the youngest, presented his brothers to Pharaoh as shepherds, and the pasture-land of Gessen was alloted them (Gen. 47:3). It was as a no-madic, pastoral folk that Jacob's descendants wandered back through the desert, and even after they had become sedentary, the shepherd living among his flocks remained for them the prototype of human leaders. It is from this background that we must approach the para-ble of the man who shares the life of his animals. He knows how it is with them; notes every characteristic, every weakness. And they consider him their protector and guide, almost a member of the herd; they respond to his voice and follow his movements.

The Pharisees fail to understand the point of the parable, so Jesus enlarges upon it, underlining the specific features: "I am the good shepherd. The good shepherd lays down his life for his sheep. But the hireling, who is not a shepherd, whose own the sheep are not, sees the wolf coming and leaves the sheep and flees. . . . I am the good shepherd, and I know mine and mine know me, even as the Father knows me and I know the Father; and I lay down my life for my sheep" (John 10:7–15).

I know my sheep (the isolation of each individual) and my sheep know me; upon whom their very life depends. But the deepest words are those that follow: ". . . even as the Father knows me and I know the Father." At first we accept them in the sense usually sug-gested by St. John, but suddenly we pull up. A tremendous thought breaks in on us: Jesus is saying that the bond between himself and us is the same bond which binds him to the Father, in that perfect in-timacy and understanding of life shared in its entirety side by side. John speaks of this union in his opening words: ". . . and the Word was with God."

Father and Son—between them the inexpressible: duality with-out division. They gaze into each other's countenance, sharing the bliss of mutual love with none of the impotency of separation. Su-perfluous here the earthly makeshift of 'crossing over'; theirs is the autonomy of identical life. And now Jesus says that he knows us as he knows the Father! We begin to surmise what salvation must mean. It is the Lord of salvation speaking from the depths of his consciousness of mission. Sharply, impatiently, he sets himself apart from the others—from all others who have found their way in before him. None of them knows men as he knows them, "nor does anyone know the Father except the Son, . . ." (Matt. 11:27).

Now we understand better that humble and yet so exalted name that the Messiah goes by: Son of Man. No one is so warmly, so intimately, so excellently human as he. That is why he knows us, why his words strike the intrinsic in us. That is why man is more profoundly understood by Christ than he ever could understand himself. No wonder he can call his sheep by name! But then what about those others who also wish to help mankind—to teach wisdom, lead the way, fight for the truth behind our existence? Jesus says: I am the door to the sheepfold—door and shepherd. The shepherd comes in through the door. All others are thieves who sneak in to steal and kill and destroy. "I came that they may have life, and have it more abundantly" (John 10:7–10). He alone is the gateway to the essence of human existence. Anyone who would reach that essence must come through him. This is not meant figuratively but literally. The intrinsic form of all Christian being is Jesus himself. He who would penetrate to man's heart, to the core where all true decisions form, must pass through Christ. The thoughts of any other must be purged to blend with Christ's thoughts, his words with Christ's words. Then that other will think and speak truly, and his teaching will strike home. His intentions must be carried out as Christ would have wished them; his will must be fused with Christ's love. It must be Jesus Christ who speaks, not he; Jesus Christ who is presented, and no other. Then the depths of the soul, which "know" the Lord and obey his voice, will respond. That the metaphor of the door might swing its full weight, Jesus declares categorically: All others are "thieves and robbers." Terrible sentence! Nothing else is acknowledged, neither wisdom nor goodness, nor cleverness, nor pedagogy, nor pity.

Everything outside Christ is swept aside. Obviously, ultimate reality is at stake, and no confusion with human attributes—even the noblest—may be countenanced. Compared with the coming of the Messiah, the advent of any mere human is theft, robbery, violence and murder. What an unmasking of human nature! We do well to waste no time wondering whether also Abraham is meant, Moses and the prophets—"all" others; the words are there in black and white. But never mind the others, see to yourself. God has declared what you are when you go to others with your worldly wisdom; take his word for it!

But what if I have genuine knowledge and truth to share? The Lord replies: What you really want is not to share truth but to exercise power!

But if I wish to better others?

You don't; what you desire is to confirm yourself!

But I love my neighbor and want to do good to him!

You want self-satisfaction more! . . . Are we offended by the words "thief," "robber"? Let us be honest, how deeply must we penetrate human nature before we strike greed and violence? Christ says: Greed and violence are also to be found in the wiseman who teaches wisdom, in the preacher who preaches piety, in the teacher who educates, in the superior who commands, in the lawgiver who creates justice, in the judge who metes it out—in all of us! Only One is entirely free from them. One only speaks pure truth in genuine love and sincere devotion: Jesus Christ. He is the door to mankind and he alone!

The depth of the Lord's earnestness is indicated by the sentence: "I lay down my life for my sheep." Only he has access to man's deepest reality, because only he is prepared for perfect sacrifice. He is ready to die for his own. This is perhaps the first time that Christ mentions his death—not only the hatred and bloodthirstiness of his enemies, but that dying which was to insure salvation. Savior is he who comes to men both from God and from the roots of human existence; who willingly submits, if need be, to Golgotha. Jesus does not yet say that he is going to die; the decision in its entirety has not yet fallen. Only on his final journey to Jerusalem does he speak that openly. Here he refers generally to the ultimate sacrifice and to his readiness for it; not in a wave of enthusiasm or exaltation, not in a mood of fatalistic acceptance, but in perfect freedom: ". . . I lay down my life that I may take it up again. No one takes it from me, . . ." (John 10:17–18).

There is a profundity to these words which human understanding cannot plumb; still it is good to feel their existence, to sense something of the dynamism streaming from them. "Savior" "Godman" are lightly said; we do well to try to envisage the depths from which they spring; to know Christ as the One, everyone else merely 'the others'; to feel his roots plunging deep into humanity and deeper still into the timeless beginnings of God!

It is also said that the sheep heed the Shepherd, because they know his voice. Is it true that men recognize Christ's call and respond to it? In one sense it must be, for he has said so; yet much in me qualifies the statement. Actually I respond much more readily to the call of 'the others'; I neither really understand Christ's summons nor follow it. Therefore, in order that I may hear, he must not only speak, but also open my ears to his voice. Part of me, the profoundest part, listens to it, but superficial, loud contradiction often overpowers it. The opponents with whom God must struggle in order to win us are not primarily 'the others,' but ourselves; we bar his way. The wolf who puts the hireling to flight is not only outside; he is also within. We are the arch-enemy of our own salvation, and the Shepherd must fight first of all with us—for us.

Somewhere in Mark we find this sentence: "And when he landed, Jesus saw a large crowd, and had compassion on them, because they were like sheep without a shepherd." How well we understand these words: whenever we meet a crowd we are reminded of sheep without a shepherd. Man is a lost and erring creature who has forsaken the very fundaments of his being. Not because there are too few efficient or conscientious people who bother about the others—more would only mitigate the loneliness and isolation within existence. What is meant here is a sense of forsakenness that goes back much further. Existence itself is forsaken because it is as it is: estranged from God and sinking into nothingness. No human can rescue here, only Christ, the Godman, who has overcome the void.

III

THE LAW

After the events discussed in the preceding chapter, Jesus returns to Galilee. But there too the situation has changed. He no longer finds the joyful acceptance of earlier days, that open, fallow ground into which he could scatter the precious seed of his word and on which his miracles could flourish so naturally. Now there too suspicion hangs like drought over the land. Luke reports:

"And it came to pass, when he entered the house of one of the rulers of the Pharisees on the Sabbath to take food, that they watched him. And behold, there was a certain man before him who had the dropsy. And Jesus asked the lawyers and Pharisees, saying, 'Is it lawful to cure on the Sabbath?'

"But they remained silent. And he took and healed him and let him go. Then addressing them, he said, 'Which of you shall have an ass or an ox fall into a pit, and will not immediately draw him up on the Sabbath?' And they could give him no answer to these things" (Luke 14:1–6).

And again: ". . . when they saw that some of his disciples were eating bread with defiled (that is, unwashed) hands, they found fault. For the Pharisees and all the Jews do not eat without frequent washing of hands, holding the tradition of the ancients. . . .

"And he said to them, 'Well do you nullify the commandment of God, that you may keep your own tradition! For Moses said, "Honor thy father and thy mother," and, "Let him who curses father or mother be put to death." But you say, "Let a man say to his father or his mother, 'Any support thou mightest have had from me is Corban' " (that is, given to God). And you do not allow him to do anything further for his father or mother. . . .'

"Then he called the crowd to him again, and said to them, 'Hear me, all of you, and understand. There is nothing outside a man that, entering into him, can defile him; but the things that come out of a man, these are what defile a man. . . .'

" 'For from within, out of the heart of men, come evil thoughts, adulteries, immorality, murders, thefts, covetousness, wickedness, deceit, shamelessness, jealousy, blasphemy, pride, foolishness. . . .' " (Mark 7:1–23).

Luke continues:

"But the Lord said to him, 'Now you Pharisees clean the outside of the cup and the dish, but within you are full of robbery and wickedness. Foolish ones! did not he who made the outside make the inside too? Nevertheless, give that which remains as alms; and behold, all things are clean to you.

" 'But woe to you Pharisees! because you pay tithes on mint and rue and every herb, and disregard justice and the love of God . . . you are like hidden tombs, over which men walk unaware.'

" 'Woe to you lawyers! because you have taken away the key of knowledge; you have not entered yourselves and those who were entering you have hindered.'

"After he had said these things to them, the Pharisees and the lawyers began to press him hard and to provoke him to speak on many things, setting traps for him and plotting to seize upon something out of his mouth, that they might accuse him" (Luke 11:38–54).

Very likely these events are only a few among many similar ones. Very likely Jesus was asked more than once to help some sufferer on a Sabbath, and he was not one to refuse. Doubtless, his disciples were guilty of other breaches in the complicated observances of the day besides those recorded: forgetting to wash their hands before eating, or chewing ears of grain as they walked through the fields because they were hungry. They had weightier things on their minds than the protective fences of orthodox rules and regulations, and it is understandable that their ardor was not lavished on the intricate niceties of the law. At the least infringement, its protectors, the Pharisees, were immediately on the spot, eager to make the most of every irregularity. Realizing that Jesus did not share their attitude of reverence for legal formality, they spied upon him, minutely recording the slightest offense as evidence against him. And when the sentence finally fell it read: rioter and rebel, overthrower of the law. What was the law, precisely? We will never understand the destiny of the Lord before we have clarified the Biblical meaning of this word.

Millenia have passed since the event of the first sin. Scripture mentions a few names during this long period, rare individuals who remained true to God and who bore his name through the darkness. Then one is called, Abram; he is to leave his country and his people and establish a new beginning. Such dignity does the Creator attribute to man, his creature, that he enters into a covenant with him: he pledges him his word and promises loyalty for loyalty. Abraham, as God now names him, 'the ancient one,' is to become a great nation if he will only remain faithful to the word of God. God's blessing is to rest upon that nation. The greatness of Abraham is the greatness of his faith. He follows God into the dark, the inexplicable, holding fast to that faith through trial and uncertainty. He believes, and his trust is his justification.

Abraham's descendants, the nation which sprang from his loins, were also meant to live in such faith. God was to have been their supreme authority; he himself was to rule them; they had only to trust him and obey. This does not mean that life was to become idyllic—the trials of the patriarch's son, grandson and great-grandson speak clearly enough. Their faith would have been constantly proved, but it would have grown in the proving and ripened to maturity. With God as its sovereign, this people was to have led a holy life in his service.

The history of the first generations indicates the road it was to have taken. Then came Egypt, and Abraham's descendants found themselves in one of the great empires of the age, where they "sat over the fleshpots, and ate bread to the full" (Ex. 16:3). Their number increased rapidly and soon distrust and fear consolidated against them. They are considered a national danger, placed under exceptional law, and forced to heavy bonded labor. A great change also seems to have taken place within them: they have hardened their hearts against God; have lost their old eagerness to hear and obey his voice. They have become insubordinate and refractory, a "stiff-necked" race (Ex. 32:9). We have only to see how they treated the man sent by God, Moses. Thus begins a new chapter in sacred history. The possibility of serving God in free faith is gradually lost. God's determination to lead them to salvation remains unchanged, but his manner of doing so is completely revised: he gives them his law (Ex. 20). Once again, through Moses this time, he makes a covenant with them. Again he promises them an indestructible history, grace and salvation—no longer in the freedom of faith, but under the law.

The foundations of the law were laid on Sinai, but in the course of time, according to the historical and social needs of each century, the law developed until it had grown to such proportions that it filled every branch of life, indeed *became* the life of the nation. It regulated the contacts between man and man: between rulers and people, group and group, individual and family, tribe and tribe, Jew and Gentile. It disposed of the different branches of civil life: division of property, administration of justice and so on. It supervised the relations between man and God: the service of the temple, feast- and fast-days, and the sacred seasons. Of the many duties thus imposed upon the race, the most far-reaching and strictly observed were the ritualistic washings. They are difficult to describe, concerned as they were not with essentially ethical cleanliness, but with a religious cult. Whoever carefully observed the symbolic ritual (which before all else closely linked physical life to altar, sacrifice and cult) was "clean." Temple observances set a man apart for God. The process was formally prescribed, regulated down to the most minute detail. The result was a welter of rules and rites expressive of deep wisdom and insight into human nature, that of the individual as well as of the family and the nation. However, when we realize that not only the general welfare, but also eternal salvation depended upon strict observance, that failure to fulfill the Law meant banishment from the community and the wrath of God, it makes one's blood run cold to read the interminable list of commandments. And though these were already so numerous that they were difficult to keep, they were constantly elaborated and supplemented. A special caste, that of the scribes, the protectors of the Law, grew up around it. They probed its meaning, interpreted and applied it. They surrounded every paragraph with explanations and observations, which in turn gradually assumed the character of new laws, so that in the course of time a fine strong net held the whole of life in its meshes.

What was the meaning behind it all? Seen from the social, ethical, or (as this sometimes, strangely enough, occurs) from the hygienic point of view, the whole complex is incomprehensible. Its true sense is immediately religious. St. Paul, who himself had been a Scribe, and who had desperately experienced the rigors of the law on his own person, interprets it in his letters to the Romans and the Galatians, as well as in the Acts.

The people of Israel had been promised that the Messiah would be born of their stock. The Lord God had "pitched his tent" among them, and they were to bear him through history. Israel was a small race surrounded by the ancient, widely spread cultures of Egypt, Assyria, Babylon, Persia, Greece and Rome, all of them political and intellectual empires rooted simultaneously in age-old wisdom and beguiling sensuousness, and enhanced by the manifold beauties of art. Their tap-root, however, the content and justification of their existence, was their belief in gods: beings aglow with all the powers of earth, and blood and spirit. Today it is almost impossible to imagine the seduction which must have emanated from those old civilizations.

In their midst, completely alone, stood the Jewish people, who were expected to preserve their unique faith in the one, invisible God: faith which, if properly lived, must lead to gradual emancipation from the immediate world. This was the idea of their Law. Every moment of its existence, this people was to encounter the demands of its God. Everywhere stood his Law with its Thou shalt, thou shalt not! Everywhere the easy, natural thing to do was forbidden as "unclean"; and at every step one was reminded of the mysteries and sacrifices of the altar and of the promise of salvation, and constantly warned against failing to maintain them. Wherever it turned, this people was to feel the yoke of God's law; through personal effort and renunciation it was to grow ever more deeply into his service. God's imprint was to be stamped upon every phase of life; his hand was to shape its smallest part. Thus—not through any mere ethical consideration or education—the conscience was to be increasingly refined. In the midst of boundless worldliness one nation was to be able to distinguish between right and wrong as God saw them; was to stand ready to receive the word of those powers which voice the spiritual, the holy; was to incorporate values, practices of non-earthly origin into daily life. And one other thing; St. Paul himself gives us this disquieting interpretation: this people is to experience what sin is! (See the Epistle to the Romans, especially the fifth to seventh chapters.) Where there is no law, says the Saint, sin sleeps, the wickedness dormant in the recesses of our being passes unnoticed. Salvation presupposes longing for salvation, and longing for salvation recognition of that from which we are to be saved. The old Law could not be fulfilled, says St. Paul, because it was too severe; still it came from God, hence the feeling that fulfillment was necessary. The result was breach upon breach, and an entire race's painful realization of what it means to fail in the sight of God. From this knowledge that man cannot justify himself and therefore was lost was to come the conclusion that no one, unaided, can ever fulfill God's demands, and that consequently all are lost. The next step was the profound and still more general realization

that failure of the Law was only a part of human failure in its entirety. Thus slowly, the Messianic people was to be stripped of its illusions and prepared for the fullness of time and the advent of the
Messiah.

The Law itself, however, had undergone a strange history. After
Solomon it had fallen into oblivion. It was not until as late as the
seventh century that its text was rediscovered, and under King Josias
newly proclaimed (II Kings 22:10). From that time on it had a permanent place in the consciousness of the race: it was studied, interpreted, defended, and an ethos of loyalty-to-the-law was developed.
Now it really began to shape a people. Conscience grew profounder. Israel's triumphant bearing of the faith in the one God
through a pagan world was a miracle, and it was the Law that made
it possible. The quiet, candid, clean-hearted figures we meet in the
New Testament have all gone through its school.

Nevertheless, a strange perversion had also set in. The Law was
meant to take possession of the people for God; its every clause was
to lay his hand upon them. In reality, the people took possession of
the Law, making it a frame for their worldly existence. It was used as
a claim to greatness and authority in the world—God and his
promise were simply incorporated into the claim. Over and over
again the legalistic will of the priests and Scribes opposed the freedom of God. We see this freedom at work in the prophets, shaping
history as it saw fit. The representatives of the Law, however, oppose
divine will, try to force it to obey their own, until at last both kingdoms crumble, the people are carried off into exile, and after a brief
renascence under the Machabees, their political power ceases to
exist. With its passing, the voices of the prophets are silenced. From
the worldly viewpoint, the representatives of the Law have won.
They have succeeded in reducing God and his will to a guarantor of
the glory of human law. The lower the nation's outer power sank,
the prouder, more fanatical grew the hopes of the law-makers. With
them they faced Roman power, Greek culture, Asiatic seduction—
but also Christ. Thus the covenant founded on faith and grace, that

wonderful exchange of loyalty for loyalty, of trust for divine aid, became a documented charter of rights and demands.

To this was added that which Jesus mentions with such heaviness
of heart: hypocrisy and cant. On the outside, greatest delicacy of
conscience; on the inside, hardness of heart. Outer loyalty to the
Law; inner sin—and sin without admission of sin, with neither contrition nor the desire for salvation (Matt. 15:7; 22:19; 23:13–35).
Such then the attitude with which Jesus was confronted. Again and
again accusations are flung at him: he, the free and sovereign Son of
God has sinned against the Law; he has broken the commandments,
trampled upon tradition, transgressed against the laws of the temple,
betrayed the people and frustrated God's promise to Abraham's descendants. Everywhere his word, big with divine freedom, falls
upon hardened concepts. Everywhere the power of his love rico-
chets against an impenetrable armor. He who spoke from the fullness of a heart in which all the power and depth of God's creative
love are contained, was thronged by legal experts, watchmen and
spies whose sharpness of intellect and strength of will only seconded
their insidious cunning.

What terrible perversion of the divine has taken place—how terrible, is perhaps most apparent in the Pharisees' reply to the supreme
authority of Roman law when he instinctively observes that he finds
no fault in the accused: "We have a Law, and according to that Law he
must die, because he has made himself Son of God" (John 19:6–7).
So infernally perverted has the law of God become, that his own Son
must die by it!

Such was the Law, that flint from which the tremendous experience of a St. Paul could blaze. He had loved it with heart and soul,
served it with zeal. We first encounter him at the stoning of
Stephen, for which he has assumed full responsibility. Moreover, he
has acquired permission to exterminate the enemies of the Law in
Damascus (Acts 22:3–5; 7:58; 9:1–9). He has also taken himself to
task for the Law, sternly disciplining his body in the hope of fulfilling the sacred codex and thus finding salvation. When experience

proves this impossible, he becomes increasingly violent, until just before the gates of Damascus Christ breaks into his life, a lightning-stroke that hurls him to his knees—and freedom. In that moment he realizes the monstrous perversity of the Pharisees' attitude, and that all effort and will subjected to it can only lead to destruction and undoing. Comprehending at last the impossibility of self-salvation, he relinquishes all hope of it, and immediately the insupportable burden falls from his shoulders. Now he understands that salvation is a grace to be accepted in gratitude and faith; that only he who has thus received it awakens to his true self. And Paul has become a fiery defender of Christian freedom against oppression in the name of "the Law."

Has then the Law vanished? The old Law certainly. With Christ's coming its whole sense was lost, and St. Paul saw to it that it was eradicated from the Christian conscience. Nevertheless, as possibilities both the Law and its protectors, the Pharisees, remain.

As soon as a religious consciousness that preaches 'pure doctrine' comes into being, and with it an authority ready to spring to its defense, the danger of orthodoxy becomes acute. For what is orthodoxy but that attitude which considers obedience to the Law already salvation, and which would preserve the purity of the Law at all costs—even at the price of violence to the conscience? The moment rules of salvation, cult and communal pattern are fixed, one is tempted to believe that their strict observance is already holiness in the sight of God. The moment there is a hierarchy of offices, and powers, of tradition and law, there is also the danger of confusing authority and obedience with the kingdom of God. The moment human norms are applied to holiness, inflexible barriers drawn between right and wrong, the danger of laying hand on divine freedom, of entangling in rules and regulations that which falls from God's grace alone becomes considerable. No matter how noble a thought may be, once it enters the human heart it stimulates contradiction, untruth and evil. The same fate awaits that which comes from God. Order in faith and prayer, in office and discipline, tradition and practice is of genuine value; but it opens up negative possibilities. Wherever a decisive either-or is demanded in the realm of sacred truth; where the objective forms of cult, order and authority are all that count, there you may be sure, is also danger of "the Pharisee" and his "Law." Danger of accepting outer values for intrinsic; danger of contradicting attitude and word; danger of judging God's freedom by legal standards—in short, danger of all the sins of which Christ accuses the Pharisees.

The history of the Mosaic Law is a terrible warning. What had come, a holy thing, from God, was turned into an instrument of disaster. The moment definite revelation, the positive ordering of existence by God is believed, this possibility presents itself. It is good for the believer to know this, that, as a member of the second covenant, he may be spared the fate of the first.

IV

JESUS AND THE PAGANS

We know Jesus as the Savior and Lord. For us he is, at least traditionally, the norm of our spiritual life. Consequently we accept everything that happened to him as inevitable. True, the mysterious necessity mentioned by Luke "*Ought* not Christ to have suffered these things . . . ." (24:26) is part of his destiny, still it should have been otherwise, and it is incomprehensible that things went the way they did.

How was it, for example, with Buddha? He cleared his own way to the light, was recognized and accepted as a great master, and died surrounded by reverent friends and disciples, many of them men of the highest human and religious qualities. He himself considered death the fulfillment of his earthly mission. Or Socrates: his was the death of a true philosopher. Fundamentally he died not because his enemies so ordered it (it would not have cost him a single concession to go free) but because he desired to end a long philosophical life philosophically. Enthusiastically devoted pupils, Plato among them, carried on his spirit. How different it was with Jesus! How strange his life appears when measured by human standards. Nothing in it for such pat phrases as: he fought his way through to success; he blazed the way for his message and his mission; he ripened to maturity and fulfillment. Nothing of the superiority of a "great" life. Jesus has surrendered himself utterly, but even the self-sacrifice of the Holiest is hindered by incomprehensible narrowness and dark. No logical consequences here of a person being who he is. In Jesus we have the double mystery of an unspeakably exalted origin and a precipitation into the inexplicable tragedy of the all too human. And we begin to sense something of what takes place when God becomes not a classical hero, or overwhelming personality, or subduer of continents, but simply "man." Once the consequences of the Incarnation have been drawn from the divine standpoint, they assume an entirely different aspect—so different from the usual standards of greatness, that by comparison the figure of a Buddha or a Socrates seems almost artificial.

Wouldn't the divine greatness in Christ have been able to express itself quite differently if he had left the narrow confines of the country and history of Israel? Had he traversed the wide realm of the Roman Empire, or entered into the intellectual superabundance of Hellenic civilization, he would have been deeply understood by free and open minds and thirsting souls. What power his message and miracles would have had there! But such reasoning is human reasoning. Christ knew that he had been sent "to the lost sheep" of Israel. He was to bring the Gospel to the people of the covenant, and so doing meet his destiny.

This was no intrinsic necessity, but the will of the Father. Jesus' whole life was determined not by circumstance or by the structure of his personality, but by the will of God: mission in the most literal sense of the word. Accordingly he confined himself to the little nation of Israel and its history; delivering his message there and accepting its answer as his fate. Nevertheless, he was fully conscious of the world without, and its longing.

Apparently Jesus was strongly attracted to the pagans. This is clear from many passages, for instance from that on the Phoenician woman who came to him for help on his wanderings through Tyre and Sidon: "Now the woman was a Gentile, a Syrophoenician by birth. And she besought him to cast the devil out of her daughter. But he said to her, 'Let the children first have their fill, for it is not fair to take the children's bread and to cast it to the dogs.' But she answered and said to him, 'Yes, Lord; for even the dogs under the table eat of the children's crumbs.' And he said to her, 'Because of this answer, go thy way; the devil has gone out of thy daughter.' And when she went to her house, she found the girl lying upon the bed, and the devil gone" (Mark 7:26–30).

The words are harsh; shockingly so. But isn't this the harshness that binds the will to a different duty? Difficult because the heart threatens to strike? The woman seems to sense this and her own heart is wide enough to understand, her faith deep enough not to be put off. That is the beauty of the incident. Quietly she accepts and uses the humiliating metaphor; the Lord feels himself understood and loves her for it: "Because of this answer. . . ." She was a pagan. Similar encounters must have occurred often—whence otherwise the bitter complaint: "Woe to thee, Corozain! woe to thee, Bethsaida! For if in Tyre and Sidon had been worked the miracles that have been worked in you, they would have repented long ago in sackcloth and ashes . . . And thou, Capharnaum, shalt thou be exalted to heaven? Thou shalt be thrust down to hell! For if the miracles had been worked in Sodom that have been worked in thee, it would have remained to this day. But I tell you, it will be more tolerable for the land of Sodom on the day of judgment than for thee" (Matt. 11:21–24).

Jesus loved the pagans. Humanly speaking one might even say that he longed for them; obedience alone held him within the close boundaries of his mission.

Then we have the much quoted centurian (Matt. 8:5–13). He is a Roman, at any rate a pagan, though possibly a proselyte like Cornelius, that other captain referred to in the Acts. He seeks relief for his orderly; this fact alone makes a favorable impression: here is an officer who looks after his men. When Jesus offers to go with him, he declines: that would not be right, how could he receive such a guest? Besides, it is unnecessary. I am only an officer, but when I give a command it is carried out. You are—we can almost hear him say—the commanding general; order the sickness to leave, and it will obey! We feel Jesus' heart warm at these words. The sense of narrowness leaves him; suddenly he finds himself in the spaciousness of an upright nature and a faith that little dreams how beautiful it is. The pain of a Savior whom few have understood, of a heavenly Messenger slowly stifling in the restrictions he meets everywhere on earth, breaks out in the words: Believe me, nowhere in Israel have I found faith like this!

And we begin to realize how Jesus should have been received: with all the *élan* of a great and joyful readiness. How different the world would be today! Instead, it was as if everywhere he went barriers were laid across his path, snares and man-traps lay in waiting for him. Here a tradition, there a prohibition, yonder pedantic hair-splitting—narrowness, pettiness, misunderstanding all along the line, and suspicion and envy. His tidings are answered by doubt and protest; his miracles denied, suspected, and labeled either breaches of the law or works of the devil. They try to trap him, to maneuver him into opposition to the Law by misleading questions (Matt. 16:1; 19:3). The loneliness and isolation of this Son of God in chains is terrible to see.

What comes from God does not discriminate, qualify or limit, it overflows freely from his bounty. Here is no philosophical system, no complicated ascetic doctrine, but the fullness of God's love, that divine audacity with which the Creator gives himself to his creatures, demanding their hearts in return. Everything for everything; we cannot but admit the truth of this—and in so doing pronounce our own judgment. For are we any better than those others? Is our cowardice any less narrowing, our indolence any less oppressive; are our constant reservations and subtleties any less restricting? God give us his light and his candidness of heart!

Soon afterwards, in the parable of the sower, Christ indicates the fate of his message: seed that falls upon good earth, or upon shallow, or upon stony ground where nothing can grow. Obviously he means the varying degrees of the heart's readiness—or its lack. And still we do not grasp the full implication: the unspeakable tragedy of almighty truth and creative love doomed, for the most part, to sterility. "He who has ears to hear, let him hear!" The ominous cry also comes here, along with similar warnings. It is the moment of decision; we feel the steadily growing tension.

God's word cannot be shelved to wait until we have leisure for it. It is a living, challenging call, worker of destinies, and makes its own time. Where it strikes deaf ears it simply departs. At the end of the chapter on the centurion we read: "And I tell you that many will come from the east and from the west, and will feast with Abraham and Isaac and Jacob in the kingdom of heaven, but the children of the kingdom will be put forth into the darkness outside; there will be the weeping, and the gnashing of teeth" (Matt. 8:11–12). The hour in which the word is offered to the people of the covenant draws to a close; soon it will pass on to the others. The result is not only that those who have refused to hear no longer have the opportunity of doing so, but that they no longer *can* hear; they have closed their hearts, and the prophecy of Isaias is fulfilled: "because seeing they do not see, and hearing they do not hear, neither do they understand" (Matt. 13:13).

God's word is a command that brings with it the possibility of obeying. It creates its own "acceptable time." The hour rejected not only vanishes, but trails a wake of disaster. The point is a delicate one and we make it reluctantly, but the text must be interpreted. What have we ourselves done with the all-decisive opportunity? Painfully aware that the words are there for us too, we can only place ourselves under judgment, begging God to be patient. For the heart from which the rejected word turns, remains not only empty, but also hardened. Its owner settles down for good in the world; he may be efficient, clever, noble, almost anything, but he is closed to Christ's tidings. "For what does it profit a man, if he gain the whole world, but suffer the loss of his own soul?" (Matt. 16:26).

One of the great mysteries of God is his patience. He is the Lord; he does not act according to any law of justice applicable to all, himself included, he *is* justice. His will not only wills what is right, but what is right is his will—therein its supreme justice. When he commands and man disobeys, man pronounces his own judgment. And yet, God has also revealed that such judgment is but a part of his will in its entirety. Throughout the history of salvation, from Paradise to the present, runs the fearful message of God's judgment, but also the wonderful message of his patience. We dare not mitigate the decisiveness of the summons to faith, but if it stood alone, we should despair. However, the revelation of God's forbearance accompanies it. And it is really revelationary and ground for hope, for by it we know that God can prolong the crucial moment; indeed that he can send a new one, and with it another chance.

V

ATTACHMENT
AND DETACHMENT

After Jesus' return to Galilee from Jerusalem, a profound change in his manner of speaking and in the spiritual direction of his instructions to the disciples becomes apparent. Before, in the beginning of his public life, he strewed words, deeds and miracles lavishly into the joyful readiness of the throngs about him. Now everything is directed inward. His listeners are taught to recognize and grasp the intrinsic kernel of his gospel; he questions them on it, preparing them for the test that is to come. Many of the texts in Matthew fifteen and Luke twelve and sixteen illustrate this clearly.

Jesus has called the Pharisees hypocrites and left them. His disciples though have remained behind; they have mingled with the crowds and heard the reaction. Now they are frankly worried. " 'Dost thou know that the Pharisees have taken offense at hearing this saying?' But he answered and said, 'Every plant that my heavenly Father has not planted will be rooted up. Let them alone; they are blind guides of blind men. But if a blind man guide a blind man, both fall into a pit' " (Matt. 15:12–14).

Primarily, the disciples are afraid, for the Pharisees are powerful; but behind this simple fear lies something deeper. Scribe and Pharisee, priest and high council are the visible embodiment of traditional law. Their stand against Jesus brings his followers into a difficult conflict. The disciples are devoted to their Master, yet they cannot but revere the leaders and teachers of their people. That they are uneasy and ask themselves whether Jesus' claims are valid is only understandable. He himself answers: there is no authority but that which comes from God, and he has placed his mission in the hands of his Son. Jesus not only has authority, but *is* authority. Those in power, who failed to recognize him and lead the people to him are weeds "that my heavenly Father has not planted," blind men's blind guides. With these words Jesus clears the field for battle; the former authorities are simply swept aside. They still have outer power, but their spiritual leadership is no longer valid.

"But I say to you, my friends: Do not be afraid of those who kill the body, and after that have nothing more that they can do. But I will show you whom you shall be afraid of; be afraid of him who, after he has killed, has power to cast into hell.

"Yes, I say to you, be afraid of him. Are not five sparrows sold for two farthings? And yet not one of them is forgotten before God. Yes, the very hairs of your head are all numbered. Therefore do not be afraid, you are of more value than many sparrows.

"And I say to you, everyone who acknowledges me before men, him will the Son of Man also acknowledge before the angels of God" (Luke 12:4–8).

Here again Jesus draws his own closer. He makes them realize what the conflict is really about: him, the God-sent one, the sword of dissension; the Messiah, his message and his will, that in reality are the message, will of the Father. Acknowledge me! In the final analysis everything opposed to me and my Father is of no consequence! (It is, of course, important for immediate existence, for those who side with Christ will be ostracized from the community; their bread, possibly even their lives will be taken from them.) Yet the more deeply they realize that Christ is the essential, the less concerned they will be about everything else. Thus they are armed for the struggle to come, are given a foundation of eternal indestructibility. "Do not be afraid." Scribe and Pharisee, judge and potentate will be your enemies. You will think yourselves forsaken, but you will be safe and sound. Where? In the hands of divine Providence. We have already seen what that means: not the order of nature, which exists in itself, but that order which exists between God and those who give themselves to him in true faith. To the extent that a man recognizes God as his Father, that he places his trust in him and makes his kingdom the primary concern of his heart, to precisely that extent a new order of being unfolds about him, one in which "For those who love God all things work together unto good" (Rom. 8:28). And those who love God are those who hold fast to his Son. Tremendous word: condition for the realization of providential order is Christ himself! Those who acknowledge him need never fear; the very hairs of their heads are numbered. Therefore the disciples are not to fear persecution or death, for God is their personal protector. Their essence is invulnerable; though the body may be slain, the soul is preserved by its faith in Jesus Christ.

The soul too is faced with a decision: is it to be granted eternal life or sentenced to eternal death? For God can cast it into everlasting death; this alone men should fear. Those, however, who have acknowledged Christ will be counted among the living by his Father and will participate in eternal life. More, the decision—eternal life or death—lies in the hands of the same Jesus who is addressing them, Jesus of Nazareth who stands before them in mortal danger. The choice for or against him made in the paltriness of an earthly moment will decide their eternal destiny. What self-assurance pulsates here! Assurance of a victim whose fate is already sealed, yet who alone gives the world its intrinsic weight and meaning. Assurance of one rejected by worldly 'authority,' who knows himself the incarnate Word of the Father. Assurance of the Son of Man who is Son of God!

Scarcely has he finished speaking when someone asks: " 'Master, tell my brother to divide the inheritance with me.' But he said to him, 'Man, who has appointed me a judge or arbitrator over you?' And he said to them, 'Take heed and guard yourselves from all covetousness, for a man's life does not consist in the abundance of his possessions' " (Luke 12:14–15). And he tells them the parable about the man who fills his barns with a rich harvest and prepares to eat, drink and be merry in the assurance that nothing can happen to him, whereas in reality that very night his soul will be demanded of him.

"Thou fool, . . . and the things that thou hast provided, whose will they be?" Why does Jesus refuse to help this man, who has probably been unjustly treated by a violent brother? We can easily guess. He has been speaking of the all-essential, of what one must hold fast and what one must let go. The man had stood there listening, but thinking only of the house and land that are being withheld and how Jesus might help him to procure them. But Jesus turns on him: Who has made me your attorney? Don't you see how enmeshed you are in things of earth that have no permanence? And he tells the story of the wealthy land-owner so wise in worldly wisdom yet a fool in the eyes of God. Here again the sharp division between the essential and the non-essential. Bread or life—which is more important? Life, for when I am dead I no longer eat. Eternal possessions or temporal possessions—which are essential? Naturally the eternal ones, for the others will fade away. What, therefore, should a man do? He should concentrate on the things of heaven, letting those of earth take their own course. His holdings should be in eternity, not in time. This is possible only through faith in Christ, which lifts the soul into life without end. Faith enables man to carry earthly existence over into immortality.

Another time Jesus tells them the strange parable of the dishonest steward: "There was a certain rich man who had a steward, who was reported to him as squandering his possessions. And he called him and said to him, 'What is this that I hear of thee? Make an accounting of thy stewardship, for thou canst be steward no longer.'

"And the steward said within himself, 'What shall I do, seeing that my master is taking away the stewardship from me? To dig I am not able; to beg I am ashamed. I know what I shall do, that when I am removed from my stewardship they may receive me into their houses.' And he summoned each of his master's debtors and said to the first, 'How much dost thou owe my master?' And he said, 'A hundred jars of oil.' He said to him, 'Take thy bond and sit down at once and write fifty.' Then he said to another, 'How much dost thou owe?' He said, 'A hundred kors of wheat.' He said to him, 'Take thy bond and write eighty.'

"And the master commended the unjust steward, in that he had acted prudently; for the children of this world, in relation to their own generation, are more prudent than the children of the light. And I say to you, make friends for yourselves with the mammon of wickedness, so that when you fail they may receive you into the everlasting dwellings" (Luke 16:1–9).

The parable is really curious. A steward has been wasteful. His master demands that he show his accounts, and gives him notice. What is the man to do? No one will ever engage him as a steward again; he is not strong enough to be a farmhand and not humble enough to beg. So he calls his master's debtors together and reduces the sums they owe in the hope of winning their gratitude. He is just able to do this before his time is up. When his master hears of it, he is so impressed by the man's cunning, that he cannot but "commend" him. And now the astonishing moral of the piece: You should do likewise!

What, am I a wasteful steward?

Precisely, the Lord would reply.

Have I things which do not belong to me?

Yes!

Am I in a similar situation with no way out but to secure my future as the steward did?

Just as he did! . . . What does this mean?

The parable is not obvious. The clue to its meaning lies in the words "mammon of wickedness." Mammon is the Phoenician god of wealth; his name also means property. But why "of wickedness"? All wealth is wicked, "base wealth." All degrees of prosperity, which we regard so highly, are included in the sweeping judgment. Nor is Jesus differentiating between the honest fruit of hard labor and wealth accumulated effortlessly. He is not encouraging proficiency and integrity; is not suggesting a more just distribution of material goods. He is saying: No one really owns anything. Neither one dollar nor a million, neither one acre nor a hundred. Jesus' words have nothing to do with the ethics of work or the economic order of things. Rather they suggest other remarks of his: for example from the parable of the importunate friend. "Therefore, if you, evil as you are, know how to give good gifts to your children, how much more will your heavenly Father give the Good Spirit to those who ask him!" (Luke 11:13). Here again the Lord does not distinguish between good people and bad—all are bad; all, without exception, fall under the universal judgment. In the same sense we are all "base" owners. The baseness lies in the root of property itself. Sin has destroyed the possibility of natural ownership without fetters upon the owner or injustice to others. In the sight of God even the most innocent ownership is unjust. What Jesus is driving at is neither sociological nor economic. His words have nothing to do with secular morality; they simply state what sin has done: destroyed paradise. In paradise property of the one would not have been to the exclusion of others. Just how this could have been is beyond human understanding. We can only surmise it when we meet someone who in the love of Christ has really become selfless. In him the kingdom of God actually begins to take form, and paradise is not only regained, but regranted on a higher level.

Jesus then, is referring to things of faith, pointing to an existence in grace and the Holy Spirit long since lost through sin. Ever since, all human doing and owning is in itself 'unjust,' a state which cannot be essentially changed by economic or social reforms. It can only be raised in its entirety to the plane of faith, there to undergo conversion and salvation.

Now we begin to understand what Jesus means. The disciples are troubled about their property, and Jesus uses the occasion to bring home to them the true value of all earthly goods. They must learn to reach behind the individual need to the general, fallen state of humanity. They must understand that the only way to get at the problem is through Jesus Christ: once emancipated by him, to relinquish the whole idea of the *rights* of property, tending that which they happen to have in *caritate Christi*. When a man who has lived thus comes to his judgment, to that hour of complete self-recognition before God when excuse and argument stick in the throat, then the intrinsically fallen and "base" property he has used with love will come forward and testify for him. Those who have received help from him will say: He was merciful to us; Lord, be merciful with him!

In other words, here again Jesus is attempting to anchor the minds and hearts of his disciples in reality. He wants them to sense what counts in God's eyes and what does not; what he considers acceptable and what fallen. They are to complete the revaluation of existence that Jesus has begun. If they do this, they will be prepared for anything. If property they know to be "base wealth" (whatever its justification or cultural value) is taken from them for their love of Christ, there is no loss. Needless to say, this is spoken to believers, and is effective only to the degree that their belief is alive.

Thus Jesus roots his followers in the indestructible. Gently he immunizes them to all unreality: to the seeming authorities of the day, to the world's wise and powerful and traditionally revered, to the prevailing social and economic order, to the dangers that threaten property, limb and life. He is stripping them for the coming struggle: concentrating their forces, teaching them how to become invulnerable.

VI

NOT PEACE
BUT THE SWORD

We have just seen how, as the hour of decision approaches, Jesus fortifies his disciples, preparing them to remain steadfast and insisting on their being able to distinguish between the essential and the non-essential. Further words of his serve as practical illustrations: "And it came to pass as they went on their journey, that a man said to him, 'I will follow thee wherever thou goest.' And Jesus said to him, 'The foxes have dens, and the birds of the air have nests, but the Son of Man has nowhere to lay his head' " (Luke 9:57–58). Here is a believer who wishes to join Jesus. But he only warns him: Be sure you know what you are doing! He whom you want to follow has no home. The security others find under their own roof among their own people and possessions is not his. He must constantly be on the road; and not as other travellers, who leave home only to return to it shortly, he lives in homelessness. Can you do that: make your only habitation the will of God, your only security work for his kingdom?

And there was another who said, " 'I will follow thee, Lord; but let me first bid farewell to those at home.' Jesus said to him, 'No one, having put his hand to the plow and looking back, is fit for the kingdom of God' " (Luke 9:61–2).

Jesus seems to see that the man is sincere but weak. Actually, the wish to arrange his affairs at home is more than justified; but perhaps Jesus sees in it a threat to the decision just made; once back in his accustomed environment, this man may be unable to keep his resolution. So the Master faces him with his now-or-never. He who hesitates even for a moment to answer God's call is lost.

"And he said to another, 'Follow me.' But he said, 'Lord, let me first go and bury my father.' But Jesus said to him, 'Leave the dead to bury their own dead, but do thou go and proclaim the kingdom of God' " (Luke 9:59–60). Here Christ himself has summoned the man who asks only permission to perform a filial duty. But Jesus knows it is a case of everything or nothing and refuses. Let the past bury the past; you who've been called to the future owe the past nothing—not even the gesture of burial. These are harsh demands, yet they are not the expression of a fleeting situation, they are reiterated and intensified again and again: "If anyone comes to me and does not hate his father and mother, and wife and children, and brothers and sisters, yes, and even his own life, he cannot be my disciple. And he who does not carry his cross and follow me, cannot be my disciple" (Luke 14:26).

The will to follow the Lord is opposed here by the strongest ties that man knows: those of a father, mother, wife, children, brothers and sisters, of life itself. Jesus is not saying: If you wish to follow me you must renounce sin; he does not demand that one give up the ignoble pursuits of life to devote oneself to the noble; that one avoid wicked company and seek good; that affection be directed toward one's wife and family, and not away from them—this is precisely what he is *not* saying. Calmly, Jesus urges us to leave the closest, most vital and precious realities that exist for his sake! And as though this were not enough, he adds: He who does not *hate* these things—yes, himself and his own life included—is not worthy of me! What does this all mean?

What do we hate? That which is contrary to our will to life, the enemy. And now Jesus says: everywhere, in everything that touches you, cowers the enemy; not only in forbidden, base, or evil things, but also in the good, the great, and the beautiful. Only that which the Lord brings is excepted, and it does not come from earth. The differences between things are great, but they are all "of the world," and one point they all have in common: their alliance against Christ; holiness must be kept at a safe distance! The moment a man prepares to follow Christ, he becomes aware of the enemy in everything around him. Not only in the evil and the inferior, but also in the good and the great; not only outside, but inside, in himself first of all, because his whole attitude towards himself is prompted by sin. As long as he remains 'immune' to the kingdom of God, the contradiction is not evident. Man's relations to God are naively simple; he is sensible only of those differences which exist within the world: between great and small, exalted and base, precious and useless, creative and destructive. But when the other world begins to stir in him, he becomes suddenly aware of the fundamental difference that severs all earthly things, himself included from those which Christ proclaims. Therefore, the Lord warns all who would follow him to be certain that they understand clearly what they are about. As the parables remind us, the man who wishes to build a tower should reckon the cost in advance; the king who would go to war does well to count his soldiers first.

Here one might ask, But, Lord, you said you had come to bring peace! When you sent your disciples into the world you taught them to say: "Peace to this house!" How can you bring man into such conflict with himself and his whole existence? Christ anticipated the question: "Do you think that I came to give peace upon the earth? No, I tell you, but division. For henceforth in one house five will be divided, three against two, and two against three. They will be divided, father against son and son against his father; mother against daughter and daughter against the mother; mother-in-law against her daughter-in-law and daughter-in-law against her mother-in-law" (Luke 12:51–53).

The peace of Christ comes after the struggle. First the conflict. Even as we consider this, we feel the conflict he has brought into our own lives; we fight it off, though we know that it comes for our good. It is false peace, the self-satisfaction of the world that Jesus would destroy. Not that this world, torn as it is, is any too harmonious, far from it. But on one point all its conflicting members agree: that it is sufficient unto itself and determined to protect its worldliness.

Into this complacency Jesus flings his sword, severing the very ties that seem to hold life together. He questions everything that humanly speaking is self-understood, even the closest ties of flesh and blood. Once the unrest of Christ has been let into a man's heart, he becomes incomprehensible and a cause of scandal.

But, what actually flings the gauntlet and opens the battle? "The kingdom of heaven is like a treasure hidden in a field; he who finds it hides it, and in his joy goes and sells all that he has and buys that field.

"Again, the kingdom of heaven is like a merchant in search of fine pearls. When he finds a single pearl of great price, he goes and sells all that he has and buys it" (Matt. 13:44–46).

The man in the field lives in his own little world: his land, his plough and his harvest, his cottage and the life it shelters. His existence runs its own course, complete in itself and at peace. Suddenly his plough strikes against the pot of gold, and the world he has known is shattered. The treasure devaluates everything that had been naturally dear to him before, and he cannot wait to give up all he owns to possess it. The merchant has his business: buying and selling regulated by profit and integrity, by the wish to expand and the desire for security. Then he sees the pearl, recognizes its extraordinary costliness and flings caution to the wind. The pearls he owns seem small and mean by contrast, and he sells all he has to be able to buy the one.

In other words, what unleashes the struggle is no mere promise or command, but a tangible reality greater than any worldly reality and more precious, that suddenly blazes across the path. And this 'greater' 'more precious' are not simply higher rungs on a ladder of already existing values, they are incomparably higher than everything else, yet simultaneously at cross-purposes with the worldly values above which they tower—hence, the conflict. It strikes at cot and palace, at the fleeting human relationship and the great love, at indigent labor and the lasting creation. It is the sudden appreciation of that other costliness, acceptance of the summons to God's kingdom with all its splendors that sets off the struggle.

In Jesus' day, when that kingdom was still within reach, the words "followers of Christ" had a special significance: they meant those who literally followed him into the new creation. The follower had only to make himself free for the abundance at hand. Today the original interpretation of Christ's summons is inadequate, for in that sense the kingdom did not arrive. The fullness of time was not allowed to crystallize into the unending moment; it still hovers in a state of becoming, now not only over Israel, but over the entire world. To each of us comes the unrest of Christ, waiting to be let in, that the kingdom may follow after.

What this means to the individual cannot be stated generally. He who is called to renounce wife and children, in other words, to forego marriage, answers his summons one way; he whose vocation is marriage, another, and the disciples were rightly startled by the thought of a marriage-union dissoluble only by death (Matt. 19:10). Christian marriage is something quite different from the natural community of the sexes, and is no less based on sacrifice than is Christian virginity. Thus here too God's kingdom is possible only when each partner of the marriage-bond "hates" as fallen both himself and the other in the sense of the New Testament. For one called to poverty, "following" consists of renouncing property; for another, the correct use of property (and to be a Christian owner is anything but easy). St. Paul's possessing "as though not possessing" (I Cor. 7:29–31) when really applied and not used as a pious embellishment to a life of comfort, is possible only through the same knowledge of the enemy present in all property and the same powers of overcoming him that are necessary for renunciation. It is impossible to consider God as a Christian should with heart and head full of earthly business, society, worries or pleasures. At first it is a question of choice between good thinking and evil, right doing and wrong; soon, however, we realize that this is not enough; that we must also limit the good and beautiful things to make room for God. We cannot practice love in Christ's sense and at the same time accept the natural standards of honor and dishonor, self-respect and bourgeois estimation. On the contrary, we must realize how ego-centric, fallen and profoundly untrue those standards are.

What makes all this so difficult? Attachment to people and things and self, certainly. But not only this. What is much worse is that we do not really know why we should make the sacrifices demanded. The brain 'knows' perhaps—it has heard or read the reasons some-where—but the heart does not know. Intrinsically we do not un-derstand; the whole idea is foreign to the most fundamental part of us. Giving is not so difficult once I know what for. I can abandon a genuine value for the sake of a higher one, but that higher one I must feel, if it exists simply in the magnanimity of renunciation, I must *feel* that renunciation is wonderful. This is why we have the parables of the pearl and the treasure! As soon as the gold lies before me, it is not difficult to trade in house and belongings for it; but I must see it. Once the pearl is held out to me, I can sell everything to possess it; but it must really shimmer before my eyes. I am sup-posed to sacrifice life's realities for other realities, yet things and people touch me, overpower me, whereas the other realities seem unreal. How can I barter this firm bright world for a shadow? I am told that God's kingdom is precious beyond price, but I do not feel this. What good does it do a trader to be told that somewhere a fab-ulous pearl exists, and that he should sell all he has to acquire it? He must see it. The trouble is that we do not experience the costliness of what Christ brings! How are we to do battle for heaven when on the one side stand "the kingdoms of the world and the glory of them," on the other only a pale uncertainty?

But what can we do about it? First of all pray: "Lord, I do believe, help my unbelief!" (Mark 9:24). After all, we do sense something of the pearl and the treasure, let us then turn to the Lord of the divine treasury and ask him to show it to us. He can. He can so stir our hearts with the illimitable wealth of God, that they burn with desire, and we see clearly where the true values lie, choose easily between them and the things of earth. We should pray constantly, piercing the dark with prayer so that light can stream through. No matter what we do, some part of us must constantly remain on the *qui vive* for a sign from the other side. That is the "praying without ceasing" that is always heard.

But even that is not enough. God's word is not something that must be understood, completely, then acted upon; understanding and action go hand in hand. At first we understand very little. But if we put that little into practice, our comprehension grows, and from our increased comprehension springs ever greater and more perfect action. In this blessed circle, or rather spiral, a glimpse of the pearl will soon be ours, and we will begin to realize that the conduct which Christ calls "love" is more precious by far than that inspired by worldly virtue around us or by personal inclination. Then why not put into serious practice the little we do understand? For example, respond to injury not with only too natural anger, or with society's appraisement of "honor," but with the love of Christ; stake everything on love, which is sovereign and has its own laws, gives of its own wealth; forgive with forgiveness as pure and Christlike as possible. Then we will really understand much better what it is all about—for the first time, because essential values become clear only through practice. Now the pearl will shimmer before us, and the next time we shall be capable of more: of letting go more easily, of "selling" more magnanimously, of "hating" more honestly: what? Our instinct, our sensuality, our natural reactions, our self righteousness and all the apparently invulnerable standards of justice and honor. The more deeply we penetrate into the new order of being, the more we comprehend, and the more we comprehend, the more Christlike action will result. Already we know that to work for God is quite a different thing than to work merely for earthly ends: for survival, or from creative necessity, or the desire to serve an institution or an epoch. Work dedicated to God is governed by the will to place all one's acts entirely at his disposal, in order that he may use them to help realize the new creation.

Much depends on our seeing the actual applicability of Christ's demands. Perhaps the following expresses the essence of his message most aptly: "For he who would save his life will lose it; but he who loses his life for my sake will find it" (Matt. 16:25). We shouldn't immediately seize upon the extreme interpretation of the statement to excuse ourselves the more easily as not concerned. We are all concerned. The losing of "life" already begins in the little things of everyday existence; the so-called dying may be our victory in the coming hour over some passion.

He who performs my will, says the Lord, will understand my will. We have only to begin here and now, to experience personally the blissful spiral of doing, knowing, high-doing.

VII

THOSE WHOM HE LOVED

We have already spoken of the great loneliness in which Christ lived, its pain reflected in such speeches as: "The foxes have dens . . . and the birds of the air have nests, but the Son of Man has nowhere to lay his head" (Luke 9:58). The greatest of all graces is to love the Lord with a heart fully conscious of what it is about; to love not only "our dear Savior" in the impersonal sense which the phrase so often has, but Christ himself, corporeally and spiritually, as one loves an irreplaceable person to whom one is bound through thick and thin. The conviction that this person is simultaneously the eternal Logos, Son of the living God and Savior of mankind is grace unspeakable.

If we peruse the accounts of the Evangelists for a word of someone who loved him, not only as a drowning man loves his rescuer, or a disciple his master, but who loved the *person* Jesus of Nazareth, we do find something. Not that Christ ever had a genuine friend. How would that equality which is the basis of true friendship have been possible where the One is Envoy of the hidden God, himself the meaning of the world and Bearer of its salvation? Even if he did say to his disciples on parting: "No longer do I call you servants, because the servant does not know what his master does. But I have called you friends . . ." (John 15:15), this is pure gift, not the expression of a mutual relationship.

Still, there was one disciple among the Twelve who was particularly close to Jesus: John. As an old man looking back over the years, he refers to himself as "one of his disciples, he whom Jesus loved"

(John 13:23). A mystery of intimacy lies between them. We feel it in the profundity of his Gospel, which is poured from the heights of love's knowledge; above all, in the world-wide and yet intimate richness of his first Epistle.

There was also a woman: she whom the power of Jesus' personality and word had rescued from a life of dishonor. Luke tells her story in the seventh chapter. She is the "sinner" who wept at Christ's feet in the house of Simon the Pharisee, anointing them in a gesture of humility and love. This is probably the same Mary of Magdala John reported under the cross, who coming to the tomb early on Easter morning to honor the body of the Lord, is also the first to see and hear the Resurrected One (19:25; 20:11–18). This courageous, great, and ardent soul loved the Lord deeply, and she was also dear to him. We hear this in her desperate words to the "gardener," and in Jesus' reply: "Mary."

"Rabboni" (Master!)

Finally, there are three other people who in a simple, intimate way, are closely befriended with Jesus: the sisters and brother, Lazarus, Martha and Mary of Bethany. The Gospels mention them often, and when we read the passages word for word, attentive also to what is not said, we get a very clear picture of them.

Luke mentions them first: "Now it came to pass as they were on their journey, that he entered a certain village; and a woman named Martha welcomed him to her house. And she had a sister called Mary, who also seated herself at the Lord's feet, and listened to his word. But Martha was busy about much serving. And she came up and said, 'Lord, is it no concern of thine that my sister has left me to serve alone? Tell her therefore to help me.'

"But the Lord answered and said to her, 'Martha, Martha, thou art anxious and troubled about many things; and yet only one thing is needful. Mary has chosen the best part, and it will not be taken away from her" (Luke 10:38–42).

Something we note with surprise is that there is, after all, a man in the house, Lazarus. According to ancient custom, he was the head of the family and lord of the estate, yet we read "a woman named Martha welcomed him to her house." The one who ruled under that roof, apparently, was she, stout-hearted and friendly by nature, but domineering. Lazarus, on the other hand, must have been a thoughtful, serious person more intent upon the inner life than the outer; and one characteristic seems to stamp his whole life: his silence. We do not have a single word of his. In the presence of his energetic sister of the firm hand and brisk tongue, we feel doubly the unusual depth of this silence. There is one other in the New Testament who never speaks, whose presence is nevertheless particularly strong: Joseph, Mary's husband, and guardian of the divine Child. He does not speak; he reflects, listens and obeys. There is something powerful in him—a touch of that all-directing, quiet watchfulness of the Father in heaven. Lazarus too is silent, and we soon learn what kind of silence this is.

Then comes Mary. She has also willingly placed the reins of the household in her sister's hands. Probably she is younger; obviously of a quiet, introspective nature. When the Lord enters the house, and the duties of hospitality demand that everything possible be done for his comfort, she curls up at his feet and listens to him. Martha's complaint is not without grounds.

We see from the incident that Jesus is at home here. He is not treated with the mixture of shyness and reverence accorded elsewhere to the illustrious Master. If he were, Martha would hardly have dared to complain so openly. She addresses him as an old friend, and it is in the same spirit that he replies—though not quite as she expected! All the more joyfully must his words have rung through the heart of her sister.

In the chapter on death we examined the passage from St. John's eleventh chapter about the resurrection of Lazarus. Jesus' friend is critically ill; otherwise his sisters would not have sent for the Master. But Jesus does something that seems monstrous: he simply lets Lazarus die. We should stop and consider what this means! What must the Lord think of this silent man, that he requires him to suffer death, to appear before God's countenance, and at his summons, return to life! We begin to sense what lies behind the man's silence.

Then Jesus sets out for Jerusalem. Conscious in the spirit of all that is happening, he says to his disciples: Our friend Lazarus is asleep. But I am going there to waken him. The next words are strange. The disciples know exactly what "sleep" Jesus means—one does not go from Jericho to Bethany, which is near Jerusalem, to disturb the slumbers of an invalid! But they are afraid, for Jerusalem bristles with Jesus' enemies. So they pretend to take Jesus literally: Lord, if he is asleep, he will soon recover!

Jesus grows precise: Lazarus has died, and I am glad for your sakes that I was not there, that now your faith may be strengthened. Come, let us go to him!

In Bethany, Martha greets Jesus with the words: Lord, had you been here, my brother would not have died. Jesus promises resurrection; now for him to whom he is granting it, once, for all in the state of grace. Martha remarks somewhat too glibly that she knows her brother will be resurrected—on Judgment Day. Martha always has an answer. But she is a warm-hearted, impulsive creature, and sensing that Jesus wishes to see her sister, she summons her gently: The Master is here, and wishes to see you! Martha is not jealous.

Then Mary comes and weeps at his feet. Jesus says nothing, but a shudder passes through him. Then he asks: Where have you laid him? Arrived at the tomb, he commands that the boulder be rolled away. Martha, realistic as ever, is horrified and tries to intercede: But, Lord, the air must be foul by now, he has been dead four days! Jesus must reassure her: Did I not tell you that if you believe you will see God glorified?

And the unheard of happens: summoned by the omnipotent Word, Lazarus steps back into life. They free him from the bandages of death, and he returns with his sisters to his quiet house. Now his silence grows deeper than ever. And we read on, stunned by the blind brutality of the human spirit in revolt against God: "But the chief priests planned to put Lazarus to death also. For on his account many of the Jews began to leave them and to believe in Jesus" (John 12:11).

John mentions this decision in the course of his description of the banquet that Simon the leper gave for Jesus in Bethany, to which Lazarus and his sisters are invited: "Jesus therefore, six days before the Passover, came to Bethany where Lazarus, whom Jesus had raised to life, had died. And they made him a supper there; and Martha served, while Lazarus was one of those reclining at table with him.

"Mary therefore took a pound of ointment, genuine nard of great value, and anointed the feet of Jesus, and with her hair wiped his feet dry. And the house was filled with the odor of the ointment. Then one of his disciples, Judas Iscariot, he who was about to betray him, said, 'Why was this ointment not sold for three hundred denarii, and given to the poor?' Now he said this, not that he cared for the poor, but because he was a thief, and holding the purse, used to take what was put in it. Jesus therefore said, 'Let her be—that she may keep it for the day of my burial. For the poor you have always with you, but you do not always have me' " (John 12:1–8).

Here they are again, Jesus' three loyal friends: Lazarus, sitting silently among the guests, his very presence apparently a great attraction: "Now the great crowd of the Jews learned that he was there; and they came, not only because of Jesus, but that they might see Lazarus, whom he had raised from the dead" (John 12:9). Martha is as busy as ever, helping to serve the guests. But Mary brings a jar of costly salve, and performs a service of love whose beauty blesses all who learn of it. Matthew says she anoints the Lord's head with it; John, his feet. It matters little—the tenderness of the act fills the whole house with its fragrance. And though the disciples, who are "small folk," are shocked by the extravagance and the traitor sermonizes, Christ rewards the instinctive clairvoyance of this quiet, ardent soul with a unique monument: "Amen I say to you, wherever in the whole world this gospel is preached, this also that she has done shall be told in memory of her" (Matt. 26:13).

Only a few strokes of the pen, but we feel the warm power of Mary's heart. We have no difficulty accepting Jesus' word for it: She has chosen the better portion! Mary has grown very dear to the Christian consciousness. Her spirit, her way of life (confirmed by Jesus himself), have become the ideal of Christian contemplation. Human existence runs on two levels: exterior and interior. On the one, words are spoken and deeds performed; on the other, thoughts are thought, convictions formed, decisions made. The two belong together, fusing to make the one whole world of being. Both are important, but the inner level is the more important of the two, because all that is enacted on the outer has its roots within. Cause and effect lie outside; decisions come from the heart. Even in ordinary life the intrinsic enjoys precedence over the extrinsic. Already here it is the "one thing that is necessary," which before all else must be clear and ordered. When the roots are sick, a tree may continue to green for a certain time, but finally it dies. This is true of all life, but particularly of the life of faith. There too we have outer activity: speaking and hearing, work and struggle, creating and organizing, but the ultimate sense of them all lies within. Martha's work is balanced by Mary's reverence. Christianity has always placed the life struggling for inner truth and ultimate love above that intent on exterior action, even the most courageous and excellent. It has always valued silence more highly than words, purity of intent more than success, the magnanimity of love more than the effect of labor. Naturally, both must exist; where there is but one, the tension between inner and outer existence is destroyed, and life must deteriorate. If the leaves are taken from a tree, its roots do not save it from suffocation. Both are part of life, but the inner part is the decisive one. This is not always self-understood. Again and again the man of action feels Martha's complaint on his lips: Isn't the inner life really pious indolence, religious luxury? Doesn't need press in on us from all sides? Mustn't the battle be continued until it is won? Doesn't God's kingdom need above all selfless labor? Certainly, and the contemplative life itself does not always preclude the question. Often enough the danger Martha senses has become reality. Much pride, laziness, self-indulgence have masqueraded as 'Marianic'; much un-naturalness thus attempted to justify itself. And still Jesus' word about the better portion holds.

His own life is the perfect illustration. His public activity lasted three years, according to some, not quite two. During this time he fought for God's kingdom with word and visible sign. Before that, thirty whole years long, he kept silence. And even in the brief span of activity, a good portion of his time was spent in prayer and med-itation. We have only to read the Gospels, which are fragmentary enough, to see how often, particularly before great events, he with-draws to the mountains, desert, or "a quiet place" to pray. The choice of the apostles, the hour of Gethsemane are but a few exam-ples. All Jesus' acts are deeply embedded in silent contemplation. And the more violent our struggles, the louder the spoken word, the more conscientiously we work and organize, the more impor-tant it is to remind ourselves of this.

One day all the loud things will be still. Everything visible, tangi-ble, audible will come to judgment, and the great inversion will take place. The external world is inclined to consider itself the real world; it accepts the inner realm as a remote, somewhat degenerate addition in which the weakling takes refuge when he can go no fur-ther. One day the correction will be made. What is now silent will be clearly evident as the stronger thing; what is now hidden as the decisive. The heart will prove itself mightier than the hand, a man's essence weightier than his works. But things will not be entirely right until both worlds meet and blend. Then as much of the ex-trinsic will remain as is justified by the intrinsic; the rest will fall away. Only that will be received into the new creation which the spirit upholds as true.

VIII

SIGNS

We have seen how after the events in Jerusalem Jesus tries to ground the lives of his disciples in the indestructible so as to prepare them for the coming struggle. The Lord's own powers are mightily concentrated, and from his consciousness of the pending, ultimate decision, break overwhelming proofs of his omnipotence. There must have been moments when his presence was a terrifying thing. It is from this period that St. Matthew reports:

"When Jesus heard this, he withdrew by boat to a desert place apart; but the crowds heard of it and followed him on foot from the towns. And when he landed, he saw a large crowd, and out of compassion for them he cured their sick. Now when it was evening, his disciples came to him, saying, 'This is a desert place and the hour is already late; send the crowds away, so that they may go into the villages and buy themselves food.'

"But Jesus said to them, 'They do not need to go away; you your-selves give them some food.' They answered him, 'We have here only five loaves and two fishes.' He said to them, 'Bring them here to me.'

"And when he had ordered the crowd to recline on the grass, he took the five loaves and the two fishes, and looking up to heaven, blessed and broke the loaves, and gave them to his disciples, and the disciples gave them to the crowds. And all ate and were satisfied; and they gathered up what was left over, twelve baskets full of fragments. Now the number of those who had eaten was five thousand men, without counting women and children" (Matt. 14:13–21).

From all sides people have streamed to the man whose name is on every tongue. Their physical hunger is expressive of their spiritual. Jesus sees both, and performs the symbolic act of blessing bread and fish and distributing them. Thousands eat their fill, and quantities of food are left over. The meaning of the miracle is clear. It does not consist of the feeding of the crowd. From the practical standpoint, the disciples are quite right to suggest that the people go into the surrounding villages and buy food. No, the feeding of the thousands is a revelation of divine abundance. This is the gesture of the active, giving source of divine love; the nourishing of the bodies is but the prefiguration of the sacred nourishment soon to be proclaimed from Capharnaum.

Then Jesus withdraws. The populace is excited. It has interpreted the sign as Messianic and insists on making him king. But Jesus will have nothing to do with such kingship or kingdoms. Sending the disciples across the lake, he retires.

"And when he had dismissed the crowd, he went up the mountain by himself to pray. And when it was late, he was there alone, but the boat was in the midst of the sea, buffeted by the waves, for the wind was against them. But the fourth watch of the night he came to them, walking upon the sea. And they, seeing him walking upon the sea, were greatly alarmed, and exclaimed, 'It is a ghost!' And they cried out for fear. Then Jesus immediately spoke to them, saying, 'Take courage; it is I, do not be afraid.'

"But Peter answered him and said, 'Lord, if it is thou, bid me come to thee over the water.' And he said, 'Come.' Then Peter got out of the boat and walked on the water to come to Jesus. But seeing the wind was strong, he was afraid; and as he began to sink he cried out, saying 'Lord, save me!' And Jesus at once stretched forth his hand and took hold of him, saying to him, 'O thou of little faith, why didst thou doubt?' " (Mark 14:23–31).

The disciples have been caught in a sudden squall, and Jesus goes to them, walking over the water. He has been praying. (We can imagine what tremendous consciousness of power and oneness with

God must have surged within him after the demonstration of the feeding of the thousands.) As he prayed he saw "in the spirit" the danger his disciples were in. Thus, when the time had come to save them, the "fullness of time" as God sends it, and 'time' for the men in their extremity, he rose and went to them. Perhaps he did not even notice that at a certain point the coast ended and the water began. For the power spanned within him it was all one. The Book of Kings tells how Elias, probably mightiest of the prophets, after the year-long agony of punitive drought, the mighty proving of the altars, and his terrible sentence upon the priests of Baal, flays heaven for water. Long before the least cloud appears he says to Achab, the godless king: "Go up, eat and drink; for there is a sound of abundance of rain." And he bade his servant announce to Achab: "Prepare thy chariot and go down, lest the rain prevent thee." The king's chariot races homeward. In the endless downpour, amidst the crashing of thunder and the lightning's flares, stands Elias, fixed by the Spirit. Then girding himself, he runs before the royal chariot the long way back to Jesrahel. A man in the grip of the Spirit obeys other laws, must be measured by other than ordinary standards. Jesus is not only visited by the Spirit, he *is* the Spirit. What for mortals, even for those far advanced in faith, must remain an unspeakable miracle, is for him but natural expression of his intrinsic being.

When Jesus reassures the frightened disciples that it is indeed he and no ghost, Peter says: "Lord, if it is thou, bid me come to thee over the water." What do the words reveal? The desire for proof, and we admire the boldness of that desire, for if it is a ghost that stands there, the proving will be fatal; it is also evidence of faith, for Peter does believe. And finally, it is an example of that great, undaunted will to union with Christ which is the apostle's profoundest trait. So Jesus calls: Come! Peter, his eyes deep in the eyes of the Lord, steps overboard and sets his foot upon a wave. The water bears his weight. He believes, and his faith lifts him to the circuit of that power which flows from Christ. Christ himself does not "believe," he simply *is* who he is, God's Son. To believe means to share not what Christ believes, but what he is. Thus Peter participates in this power, is part of Jesus' act. But all divine action is living action, that rises and falls. As long as Peter's gaze holds that of the Master and his faith remains one with the divine will, the water carries him. Then the tension of his trust slackens; consciousness of his human limitations surges in on him, and he recalls the power of the elements. He hears the roar of the wind and feels the waves rock beneath his feet. It is the crisis. Instead of leaning the more heavily on the support from Jesus' gaze, Peter drops his eyes. Contact with the divine strength is severed, and he starts to sink. All that remains of the fleeting, world-conquering faith is the helpless cry: Lord save me!

Jesus: Faint-hearted one, why did you let doubt come near you?

The passage contains one of the most important revelations of the nature of faith. Attempts have been made to couple the advance of the fervent soul with that made by the intellect. For example: At some specific point in the journey of faith, the intellect bogs down. Realizing its position, it decides that it would be wisest to let Revelation pull it out of its quandary. Others have tried to explain faith by the will: The will in search of truth and worth arrives at the end of earthly values. Concluding that where these leave off, eternal values must begin, it accepts the tidings of them from the word of God. There is much truth in this, but the central truth lies elsewhere, for what the believing soul experiences is not a 'truth' or a 'value,' but a reality—*the* reality. Which? The reality of God in the living Christ. Only now, in the midst of everything that man may think or experience; in the midst of all that is known as "world," rises a point that does not belong to the world; a place into which one may step; a room one may enter; a power on which one may lean; a love to which one may give oneself. This is reality, different from the reality of the world, more real than the world. Faith is the act of seizing this reality, of building one's life on it, of becoming part of it.

The life of faith demands a revolution in our sense of reality. In our consciousness, which is not only entangled, but completely befuddled by the world, the body is more 'real' than the soul; electricity more real than thought; power more real than love; utility more real than truth. Together they form "the world"—incomparably more real than God. How difficult it is even in prayer to sense the reality of God! How difficult, and how seldom given us, the grace of contemplation in which Christ is more tangibly, powerfully present than the things of existence! And then to rise, to mix with people, perform the duties of the day, feel the tug of environment and public life and still to say, God is more real than all this, Christ more powerful, to say this spontaneously, absolutely convinced that it is so, how many can do this?

Living in faith, working in faith, practicing faith—that is what counts. Daily, earnest exercise of faith is what alters our sense of reality. *Experience* of genuine reality must be our aim. But that is auto-suggestion, someone objects. To this there is not much that can be said, little more than: You say that because you stand outside the experience. It is true that in the reforming of the consciousness all means of self-renewal are effective; nevertheless, it is not so much the technique that counts, as the actual result of that renewal. Enter into faith, and you will see clearly what it is we are striving for. And you will no longer talk of auto-suggestion, but of the service of faith and its bitterly needed daily exercise.

Such exercises are not easy. Those are rare hours in which eye is lost in eye, and the circuit of power looping between God and man is complete. Usually our unrest is stronger than Christ's paling features. Usually the water does not seem to bear our weight, and Christ's word that it does, sounds like pious symbolism. What happened to Peter in that hour happens daily in every Christian life. For to count for nothing the things the world holds dear, and for all-important what the world counts for nothing—simply on the word of Christ; to be contradicted again and again by those around us and by our own hearts within us, yet to stand fast, that is no easier than Peter's walking on the waves.

IX

BREAD OF LIFE

The sign of the feeding of the thousands shatters the narrowness that has been closing in on Jesus. The masses are beside themselves; here at last is the Messiah, and they press Jesus to become their king and to establish the promised kingdom. But Jesus knows only too well the kind of kingdom they mean and that it is not for him. So he sends his disciples back to Capharnaum by ship and slips away from the crowds to a hill above the sea to pray. We do not know what that prayer was; perhaps it was not unlike his prayer on Mount Olivet. A tremendous decision is nearing, and Jesus probably placed it at God's feet, uniting his will with that of the Father. Then, still inwardly exalted, he strides down to the coast and out upon the water. After the incident with Peter, he and the disciples land. The crowds have watched the disciples embark, and know that Jesus was not with them; also that no other boat had lain at anchor which could possibly have brought him across the sea. When they themselves arrive by ship or on foot and find him there they ask: "Rabbi, when didst thou come here?" (John 6:25).

The question expresses more than mere astonishment; there is an undertone of disappointment and indignation: We hailed you as the Messiah and wanted to make you king—why did you go away? Thus begins that strange event reported by John in chapter six. (We should read the whole chapter in order to feel the direct impact of Jesus' message and the indescribable isolation in which he lives.)

"Rabbi, when didst thou come here?"

Jesus hears at once what is behind their question. They do not seek him because of the sign he has worked, not because they have heard God speak through his lips or have perceived a flash from his coming kingdom, but because their earthly hunger has been stilled. They wish to secure the multiplier of loaves for their earthly kingdom, and to this end they claim him as their Messiah. Above all, this kingdom was to be one of material abundance: the grain was to grow so high that a man on horseback could not see over it; the grapes so huge that when pressed on the vine, rivulets of juice would stream from them. The multiplying of the loaves is taken as a guarantee of that Lubberland type of plenty to which the masses aspire; that is why they come. And it is precisely this material interpretation that Jesus wishes to avoid. He wants them to seek spiritual food, nourishment that will give them eternal strength and light, not momentary; he himself, the Son of Man, is there to mete it out to them.

"What are we to do in order that we may perform the works of God?" they ask. It is the classic question of the Old Testament: What must I do for God in order that God, in turn, will send his Messianic kingdom?

Jesus replies: "This is the work of God, that you believe in him whom he has sent." "The work of God" then, is faith in his Envoy. The Jews are not expected to perform this or that feat, to obey this or that law, but to throw themselves whole-heartedly into the great venture of the new relationship to God known as belief.

Sensing that something extraordinary is desired of them, they first demand to see Jesus' 'credentials': "They said therefore to him, 'What sign, then, dost thou, that we may see and believe thee? What work dost thou perform? Our fathers ate the manna in the desert, even as it is written, "Bread from heaven he gave them to eat." ' " Hasn't Jesus already performed miracles enough? Still the crowd insist upon the great Messianic sign: some act bearing the unmistakable stamp of heaven visibly descending from heaven. After all, the bread with which Jesus has just fed them is earthly bread. They want to see something entirely unrelated to earth, as spectacularly celestial as that bread which fell from heaven. At this point, Jesus' teaching takes a new bound forward.

"Amen, amen, I say to you, Moses did not give you the bread from heaven, but my Father gives you the true bread from heaven. For the bread of God is that which comes down from heaven and gives life to the world."

Moses' bread was no true celestial food, sustainer of divine life, and symbol of the new creation. This had been reserved for the gift of the new covenant. Paternal gift straight from heaven, this "Bread"—form, nourisher and preserver of eternal life in one—is none other than Jesus Christ himself. He has come from God to bring life to the world. The listeners apparently do not understand, but they mean well and stick to the point: "Lord, give us always this bread."

They are trying to understand, so Jesus tells them point blank: It is I who am the bread of life; he who comes to me will never be hungry, he who has faith in me will never thirst. He himself, the living being with all its readiness, his heart and soul and their immeasurable love, these are the life-giving nourishment. And men are to partake of them, to "eat" and "drink" through faith. Looking into their hearts Jesus adds: "But there are some among you who do not believe." They refuse to relinquish their standpoint; try to force his words into their preconceived mold, and when this fails, they are at a loss. They are unable to follow Jesus. So the Lord reveals the hidden meaning behind his words: "For I have come down from heaven, not to do my own will, but the will of him who sent me. Now this is the will of him who sent me, the Father, that I should lose nothing of what he has given me, but that I should raise it up on the last day. For . . . whoever beholds the Son, and believes in him, shall have everlasting life, . . ." Here we learn of God, the Unique in whom, however, there is sacred community of being. We are told of a Father and a Son and of a conversation in eternity of which we are the subject. The Father has sent his Son into the world to awaken eternal life in the chosen whom he is entrusting to him. Jesus is to preserve them, and one day, at the hour of Judgment, to resurrect them to the fullness of everlasting life.

This conversation is our eternal refuge, simultaneously root and sheltering branch of our temporary existence. It is the origin of our eternal destiny. With "fear and trembling" we read of those whom "the Father gives to me" of the terrible differences of predestination sprung from the impenetrable mystery of God's sovereign freedom. But believing, "hoping against hope," we trust our way into his love and fasten ourselves there firmly.

But the Jews "murmured about him because he had said, 'I am the bread that has come down from heaven.' And they kept saying, 'Is this not Jesus the son of Joseph, whose father and mother we know? How, then, does he say, "I have come down from heaven." '" Were Christ not who he is, they would be justly aroused, for what he is saying is unheard of. With the sensitiveness of those raised in the jealous belief in the one God, they notice immediately that a 'monstrous' claim is being made, and they attempt to ward it off with sharp realism. Jesus sees them huddling together suspicious and hostile, and he faces the attack: "Do not murmur among yourselves. No one can come to me unless the Father who sent me draw him, and I will raise him up on the last day. It is written in the Prophets, *And they all shall be taught of God.* Everyone who has listened to the Father, and has learned, comes to me; . . ."

In other words: You stand apart, watching from a distance, hence what I say sounds blasphemous, must sound blasphemous to you. You can understand only by coming over to me, but this only he can do who is enabled to by the Father who sent me. To be sent and to be called to him who is sent belong to one and the same work of redemption. The prophets have said the Lord will teach all. Now the moment has come; God will indeed instruct all who are ready to learn, and all who are willing to understand will understand and come to me, for they cannot approach the Instructor directly. No one can approach God. That is why an Envoy, "the Word," is necessary; he and he alone has direct contact with God for "the Word was with God" (John 1:1). He whose heart is open hears the Father in the Son, sees the Father in Jesus, and if he believes, is given eternal life.

And again the symbol of the bread: "I am the bread of life. Your fathers ate the manna in the desert, and have died. This is the bread that comes down from heaven, so that if anyone eat of it he will not die." And then comes a new leap forward in the thought—an unheard of leap: ". . . and the bread that I will give is my flesh for the life of the world." We understand only too well the resultant: "The Jews on that account argued with one another, saying, 'How can this man give us his flesh to eat?' "

Jesus has already proclaimed that he is the bread of life; that the 'eating' of the bread was faith; now he intensifies sharply the challenging literalness of the symbol. Instead of, "I am the living bread" he says, "and the bread that I will give is my flesh for the life of the world." He is speaking to Jews, people for whom sacrifice and the sacrificial feast is a daily event. They cannot help but be reminded of it, and their repugnance is understandable. Yet Jesus does nothing to soften the metaphor; he does not extenuate it by working it into a parable. On the contrary, he strengthens it: "Amen, amen, I say to you, unless you eat the flesh of the Son of Man, and drink his blood, you shall not have life in you. He who eats my flesh and drinks my blood has life everlasting and I will raise him up on the last day."

The thought is underlined again and again: "For my flesh is food indeed, and my blood is drink indeed. He who eats my flesh, and drinks my blood, abides in me and I in him." He who accepts them wins eternal life: intrinsic, invulnerable life already now in time; resurrection to blissful immortality later. But he who rejects this nourishment will have no life in him.

Consummation of Jesus' flesh and blood is closely bound to his own relationship to his Father: "As the living Father has sent me, and as I live because of the Father, so he who eats me, he also shall live because of me." The Holy Eucharist is the final link in the sacred chain of life-giving nourishment reaching from the remoteness of God into the here and now of human existence.

What is our own reaction to these words? If someone were to rise and address them to us, we should be horrified. Even if we had been prepared for them by teaching and miracle, we too should hardly know what to think. The Pharisees must have been thunderstruck. They could not believe their ears, were shocked, indignant, but also delighted to hear such 'monstrosities' from their hated enemy. It would be easy game to finish off one who spoke thus!

The many who first questioned Jesus have departed. The Pharisees are by this time doubtless convinced that they are dealing with one "possessed." Even "Many of his disciples therefore, when they heard this, said, 'This is a hard saying. Who can listen to it?' " Perhaps for some time they have not known what to make of Jesus' preaching; now at last they have decided: it is impossible to listen any longer to such blasphemy! "But Jesus, knowing in himself that his disciples were murmuring at this, said to them, 'Does this scandalize you?' " Are you disciples or not; are you willing to learn, or do you insist on judging right from the start, although it is only through blind acceptance of this beginning that all further comprehension of what is possible and what is not must spring? As for your precious understanding, what would it say "if you should see the Son of Man ascending where he was before?" If the unutterable mystery that shatters all earthliness were to reveal itself? . . . Those who are shocked have taken his words in the flesh rather than in the spirit. Promptly reminded of their animal sacrifices, they have made no attempt to reach the plane from which understanding would be possible. You are doing the same thing: judging without being in the position to judge. "It is the spirit that gives life; the flesh profits nothing. The words that I have spoken to you are spirit and life."

The sentence by no means weakens what has gone before. The fact that his words are spirit and life does not mean that they are to be taken as a parable. They are to be taken literally, concretely, but in the spirit; they must be lifted from the coarseness of daily physical life into the realm of sacred mystery, from immediate reality into the sacramental. Understood in the first sense, they must repulse; in the second, they are the holy truth of God, which, accepted in love, brings endless fulfillment.

Again the mind seeks the divine behind the event: "But there are some among you who do not believe." Jesus knew from the start which were those who did not believe, and which of them was to betray him. "This is why I have said to you, 'No one can come to me unless he is enabled to do so by my Father.' " And again there is a division: "From this time many of his disciples turned back and no longer went about with him."

Should they have understood? Hardly. It is inconceivable that at that time anyone could have grasped intellectually the meaning of these words. But they should have believed. They should have clung to Christ blindly, wherever he led them. They should have sensed the divine depth behind his words, known that they were being directed toward something unspeakably huge, and simply said: We do not understand; show us what you mean! Instead they judge, and everything closes to them. Jesus upholds his strand to the end. The time for the showdown has come and it must be carried to the ultimate consequences. The Lord demands a clearcut decision also from those closest to him. He is ready to dismiss his last followers if they fail: "Jesus therefore said to the Twelve, 'Do you also wish to go away?' " It is Peter who answers: "Lord, to whom shall we go? Thou hast words of everlasting life, and we have come to believe and to know that thou art the Christ, the Son of God." It is beautiful to see how Peter replies. He does not say: We understand what you mean, but: We hold fast to your hand. Your words are words of life, whether we understand them or not. At that moment, it was the only answer possible.

And still the sifting continues: "Jesus answered them, 'Have I not chosen you, the Twelve? Yet one of you is a devil.' Now he was speaking of Judas Iscariot, the son of Simon; for he it was, though one of the Twelve, who would betray him." Here we see that Judas has already inwardly rejected Jesus. His heart is already closed. To remain with the Lord in spite of this is the beginning of his betrayal. And it is already in acceptance of his coming fate that Jesus permits him to remain. It is terrible to watch the decision ripen with "the hour." One disciple after the other falls away, and the Master is left in growing isolation. But he does not swerve by a single word from what he has come to say. His message remains the same to the last, when "It is consummated!" (John 19:30).*

---

* To the unpracticed reader of St. John I should like to point out that his Gospel is arranged with minimum regard to logical sequence. More than a chain of cause and effect, his thought resembles ripples all departing from one point in eternity. They do not really follow one another, but lie concentrically one within the other and often overlap. R. G.

X

DESTINY AND DECISION

We have already inquired several times into Jesus' mission because it is the key to the understanding of his bearing and his fate. Let us put the question once more: to whom is his proclamation addressed? To whom does he pass on what the Father has placed in his hands? The only possible answer is: to everyone—to humanity as a whole and to every individual in it. His final instructions before ascending into heaven are: "All power in heaven and on earth has been given to me. Go, therefore, and make disciples of all nations, baptizing them in the name of the Father, and of the Son, and of the Holy Spirit, teaching them to observe all the commandments which I have given you" (Matt. 28:19–20). Still, this does not mean, as the modern might be inclined to suppose, that Christ was speaking directly to all humanity and to every receptive individual. Jesus' attitude is strictly historical; he is part of that great continuity which begins with Abraham, whose sense—stated for the first time in the opening verses of Genesis twelve and clearly repeated again and again—is directed to all mankind, but through the mediation of one particular designated race. Therefore, those primarily summoned are the descendants of Abraham under their official representatives: the people of God's covenant. It is to them that he who is the fulfillment of all God's promises addresses himself. If they accept him and his tidings, if they take the road he indicates to them, the promise made to Abraham and prophesied by the prophets will become reality. God's kingdom will be there in unreserved superabundance. Human existence will enter into a new phase: the entire world will be inflamed by the fires kindled here at the starting point. On the other hand, if they reject him, their decision will be valid not only for themselves, but for all mankind.

This thought makes no claim to infallibility; it is only an attempt to help us understand the sacred coherence of the whole. In any event, the idea is not easily accepted. *Can* humanity's fate be made to depend on a single nation, particularly when we consider the paltriness, the innumerable contingencies that are an inevitable part of our nature? Yet such an objection would not be only modern, but the logic of sin. Sacred history was constituted as a whole. Man's first decision was made by Adam. Here too we could ask:

What is Adam to me? The answer would be: Everything! All humanity was contained in the first man, was there from the beginning. Everyone participated in his decision, also you. And were our feelings to rebel, should we attempt to deny any such responsibility or to jeer skeptically at the idea as 'fantastic,' Revelation would probably reply: There you have it—the sin in you! If you lived in the truth, you would know that the claim to individual autonomy of being is in itself sacrilege. The individual exists only in close relation to the whole of mankind. Already in secular history we see again and again how one person sets or changes the direction of the lives of all. What he does, somehow the others do with him, through him. How much truer then must this be of the ancestor and head of the human race! If Adam had not failed, the foundation of all human existence would be other that it is. Certainly, each of us would be individually tried and proved, but under quite different circumstances.

If Abraham had failed, the promises attached to his faith would have been made void, and all mankind would have had to bear the consequences. This does not mean that salvation would have been lost, but the process of salvation would have been fundamentally different. Salvation does not take place on the natural level; or on the idealistic level, or on that of some exalted individual, but on the level of history and historical development. And what is history but decisions of the hour made by individuals and valid for all men for all time?

Similarly, the answer to the Messiah's call lay in the hands of certain individuals: the officials and those in power during the three years of Jesus' public life, as well as all those of that generation capable of individual decisions. This does not mean that certain people are better than others, or more pious, or more important to God; just as little as it means that salvation depended entirely on them. It does mean that the realization of universal salvation desired by God is brought about by the workings of the few upon history. This is the teaching of Revelation, and where we cannot understand we must feel the truth behind it.

Jesus himself submitted to this historical necessity. We have already mentioned how strongly he felt the pull of the world outside Palestine and the receptive hearts he knew to be there. But he also knew that the decision had to fall where he stood, in this nation hardened by need within, pressure without, and by long long waiting; among these people simultaneously perverted by realism and fantasticalness. He accepted the confines of their geographical borders in obedience, the monumental obedience of one fully aware that he was the Son of Man, Son of God, and *Logos* of the world!

We have seen how the decision first falls in Jerusalem: the hierarchy of the Scribes and defenders of tradition reject Jesus, branding him deluder and blasphemer. So he returns to Galilee. But there too the situation is changing. Expectation of the Messiah is at a high pitch and demands that Jesus satisfy it. Instead, the Lord faces the people with the truth, but they do not comprehend. The rulers should have, and when they failed to do so, the people ought to have shoved them aside and taken matters into their own hands. That was really the hour for a people's tribunal, for a divine revolution! But the masses also fail; disappointed, they allow themselves to be misled, and their enthusiasm collapses. The defection reaches deep into the ranks of Jesus' intimates. Even one of the Twelve turns traitor. But Jesus does not give up, he fights to the end. Even in Jerusalem during the last days, the battle continues. The essential decision though, has already fallen. Salvation must now be realized differently: no longer through the meeting of gospel with faith, of illimitable divine generosity with pure human acceptance; no longer through the evident arrival of the kingdom and the renewal of history; now the Father's will demands the ultimate sacrifice of his Son. The gospel of the Holy Eucharist already foreshadows this. The words about the eating of flesh and drinking of blood are suggestive of the sacrificial feast, and the form which the sacrament of union with Christ takes at the Last Supper rests entirely upon the sacrificial death of the Lord. The question whether the Eucharist would have been possible also if Christ had been accepted, now presents itself. Who knows? What form would it have taken? Who can say? All we really know is how it did come into being, as the feast of the new covenant in the body and blood of Christ.

It is difficult to speak of a possibility that did not materialize—the more difficult when already in the prophecies that non-materialization is envisioned. For Isaias speaks not only of the Messianic state of endless world fulfillment, but also of the slave of God, of his disgrace and propitiatory destruction, just as the prophetic preliminary form of the Eucharist, the Pasch, is also a feast of sacrifice. Thus the whole web of happenings, of those events that materialized and those that did not, those that should not have and did, is woven into the mystery of divine foreknowledge-and-volition. Our suppositions are only attempts from the periphery to penetrate more deeply into the darkest of all incomprehensibilities: the fact that our salvation is grounded in actual history.

The first unlimited possibility has been lost. Salvation now becomes identified with sacrifice. Thus God's kingdom does not come as it was meant to, in open history-revolutionizing fulfillment; it is to remain to the end of time suspended in the process of coming—its acceptance or rejection, progress or retrogression depending on the response of the individual or group in every period of world-history.

Is one really to suppose that God could not have changed the course of events? Was he really incapable of moving the hearts of this caste of priests, theologians and politicians so that they might understand what it was all about? Couldn't he have seized the masses, filled them with love of his Envoy, and established their wavering wills in genuine loyalty? After all, he is Truth, and Light, and the Spirit! The Holy Ghost came after Jesus' death—couldn't he have come a year earlier?

The questions are obviously foolish. Of course God could have done these things, but he did not choose to. A passage in the letter to the Philippians suggests why: ". . . who though he was by nature God, did not consider being equal to God a thing to be clung to, but emptied himself, taking the nature of a slave and being made like unto men. And appearing in the form of man, he humbled himself, becoming obedient to death, even to death on a cross" (2:6–8). God is Lord of the world and men, but his manner of entering the world and approaching men is not that of a Lord. The moment he descends to earth he becomes mysteriously weak. It is as though he has left his omnipotence outside the gates of his human existence. Once in the world, its forces seem stronger than he, seem to justify themselves against him.

In our own lives it is much the same. How is it that God permeates the universe, that everything that is comes from his hand, that every thought and emotion we have has significance only in him, yet we are neither shaken nor inflamed by the reality of his presence, but able to live as though he did not exist? How is this truly satanic deceit possible? Here in this mystery of the 'impotence' of God lies that special element we have already mentioned. It is this ultimate, terrible concentration of God's insistence on human freedom, however tragic its effects, with which St. John opens his Gospel: "In him was life, and the life was the light of men. And the light shines in the darkness; and the darkness grasped it not."

But why such insistence? Because human existence was designed to rest not only on divine creation and bountiful all-inclusive activity, but also upon human decision—precisely *because* God's omnipotence is crowned in the freedom of the individual to accept or reject him.

There are two kinds of freedom: a first and a second. The second consists of being free to act in truth and goodness: I recognize so clearly, so overwhelmingly who God is, that I have no choice but to accept him. This is the true freedom, but it presupposes the other, the primary freedom, which consists of my ability to accept God or to reject him. Fearful possibility, yet the gravity and dignity of human existence depends on it. God could not spare us the burden of this freedom. In order that it might exist, his own power had to be curtailed, for had he come to earth as the Omnipotent One, it would have been impossible to reject him (Cor. 8:9; Phil. 2:7). The first freedom is unnatural unless it is used as a springboard to the second. It is a crown which, laid at the feet of the only true king, is returned transfigured. How unnatural it is alone we see from the price God paid for it; nevertheless, it is essential.

From it comes the decision against Jesus: the second fall. A Yes! to God would have cancelled Adam's sin; the No! sealed it afresh. What this decision meant to Jesus is inconceivable. There is a passage in the Gospels that is an outpouring of his infinite hurt and anger: "Then he began to reproach the towns in which most of his miracles were worked, because they had not repented. 'Woe to thee, Corozain! woe to thee, Bethsaida! For if in Tyre and Sidon had been worked the miracles that have been worked in you, they would have repented long ago in sackcloth and ashes. But I tell you, it will be more tolerable for Tyre and Sidon on the day of judgment than for you. And thou, Capharnaum, shalt thou be exalted to heaven? Thou shalt be thrust down to hell! For if the miracles had been worked in Sodom that have been worked in thee, it would have remained to this day. But I tell you, it will be more tolerable for the land of Sodom on the day of judgment than for thee' " (Matt. 11:20–24).

How consciousness of all that might have been breaks out in these words, awareness of the unutterable bliss now lost! Possibly parables like the following also belong in this context.

"A certain man gave a great supper, and he invited many. And he sent his servant at supper time to tell those invited to come, for everything is now ready. And they all with one accord began to excuse themselves. The first said to him, 'I have bought a farm, and I must go out and see it; I pray thee hold me excused.' And another said, 'I have bought five yoke of oxen, and I am on my way to try them; I pray thee hold me excused.' And another said, 'I have married a wife, and therefore I cannot come.'

"And the servant returned, and reported these things to his master. Then the master of the house was angry and said to his servant, 'Go out quickly into the streets and lanes of the city, and bring in here the poor, and the crippled, and the blind, and the lame.' And the servant said, 'Sir, thy order has been carried out, and still there is room.' Then the master said to the servant, 'Go out into the highways and hedges, and make them come in, so that my house may be filled. For I tell you that none of those who were invited shall taste of my supper' " (Luke 14:16–24).

The supper is symbolical of God's magnanimity, of the all-inclusive community of grace. Which supper is meant here? That to which Moses delivered the initial invitation, which the people accepted in their acceptance of the covenant. Now comes the actual day of the feast, and the Messenger is sent out with the second invitation: to come at once, for the banquet is ready! But the Messenger is ignored; everything, apparently, is more important than the divine feast: land, cattle, women, property, power, pleasure. At this the anger of the host flares; he gathers together for his feast those despised by the guests for whom it was originally meant: the poor from the alleys of the city, the tramps from the hedges and fences, the publicans and sinners, the pagans and aliens.

How could two thousand years of divine schooling produce such paltry results? The mind staggers but finds no answer. St. Paul wrestled with this mystery with every fiber of his being. St. John flung himself so violently to Jesus' side, that the question was real to him only from God's point of view; he did not seem to experience it from that of man or of the Jewish race, as Paul did—to his unspeakable pain. It is not by chance that Paul discusses it in the letter addressed to the Christian community at the hub of a pagan world, the Epistle to the Romans. After he has written of grace, of selection and rejection, and the meaning of the Law, he speaks of the promise made to Abraham and the defection from the Messiah. Then comes the strange eleventh chapter:

"Has God cast off his people? By no means! For I also am an Israelite of the posterity of Abraham, of the tribe of Benjamin. God has not cast off his people whom he foreknew. Or do you not know what the Scripture says in the account of Elias, how he lodges complaint with God against Israel? *Lord, they have slain thy prophets, they have razed thy altars; and I only am left, and they are seeking my life.* But what does the divine answer say to him? *I have left for myself seven thousand men, who have not bowed their knees to Baal.* Even so, then, at the present time there is a remnant left, selected out of grace. . . . I say then: have they so stumbled as to fall? By no means! But by their offense salvation has come to the Gentiles, that they may be jealous of them. Now if their offense is the riches of the world, and their decline the riches of the Gentiles, how much more their full number! . . . partial blindness only has befallen Israel, until the full number of the Gentiles should enter, and thus all Israel should be saved, as it is written, *There will come out of Sion the deliverer and he will turn away impiety from Jacob; and this is my covenant with them, when I shall take away their sins.* In view of the gospel, they are enemies for your sake; but in view of the divine choice, they are most dear for the sake of the fathers. For the gifts and the call of God are without repentance" (Rom. 11:1–5; 11–12; 25–29).

The words are deep and heavy. They seem to say: the people of Moses have fallen away. Only a few have recognized the Messiah. The rest have denied him. What has happened to this people—has it simply been discarded? No, for election by God cannot thus be lost. Then what does it mean? St. Paul seems to think that something of that special glory which was to have come over Israel through its acceptance of the Messiah had now been transferred to others. He seems to continue the sense of the parables we have just quoted: since those first invited did not come, others sit in their place. Therefore the others should know that in a way, they have been saved through the calamity of those initially intended for salvation. Yet Israel lives on, still the bearer of the promise, only now it is conditional: this people will be given one last chance to accept the Messiah—then (let us stick to the metaphor) when the others have eaten their fill. When the predetermined number of pagans to be saved is complete, the question will again be put to the irrevocably chosen people. Then it will speak its Yes! Therefore, Paul admonishes the Gentile Christians, beware that you do not have too good a conceit of yourselves! In one sense you are living on the sin you condemn in others. Above all, you should be moved to profoundest gratitude; you should help prepare the ground for the coming renewal of the divine question to Israel. Every real Christian smooths the way which the chosen people will one day take to the foreground. Reading this part of the Roman Epistle, one begins to sense the meaning of destiny. The apostle's testimony throws mysterious light on the destiny of Jesus and of his race and of us all.

The Savior came because of Adam's sin. Because Adam sinned, God's love reached out in its most divine gesture of revelation: the offer of the covenant of faith with his people. When they deserted that faith, the covenant became a covenant of the Law. This was supposed to prepare them for the coming of the Messiah. It was through the Law that Israel established for herself a unique place in history; but it was also the Law which so hardened her, that when at last he whom she had been taught to expect arrived, she denied him.

Jesus ushered in the kingdom. It would have come into full bloom had the people accepted it. But the people failed and lost the kingdom which in the new order of things should have been theirs. Now others take their place, blessed by their fall. The Christians from the pagan world have been "grafted in" the sacred olive tree (Rom. 11:17). Now they are the chosen ones; nevertheless, the old pact remains. In the measure that the new Christians understand the way to salvation, that their love grows and is fruitful, the people who rejected Christ will approach conditions favorable for the repetition of Jesus' question. If, instead of an attitude of gratefulness and love, the grafted branch should consider itself blessed by *right,* then it too will become hard and its Christianity brittle.

We should remember this: God's kingdom is on its way. It is not tied to a certain historical hour; any hour may be its hour; anyone may usher it in. It presses for entrance on the heart of each individual; knocks at the door of every community and every enterprise. How ponderously destiny leans on the human race, fate woven of heaven and earth, of freedom and necessity, will and grace—no, entirely of grace! The heavy dregs of ignorance and sin that hold us down dissolve in the prayer of adoration at the end of Romans eleven:

"Oh, the depth of the riches of the wisdom and of the knowledge of God! How incomprehensible are his judgments and how unsearchable his ways! For *Who has known the mind of the Lord, or who has been his counsellor? Or who has first given to him, that recompense should be made him?* For from him and through him and unto him are all things. To him be the glory forever, amen."

PART FOUR

On the Road
to Jerusalem

I

THE MESSIAH

Part I of these meditations was concerned with the mystery of the beginning; Part II sketched the Lord at the commencement of his public ministry; Part III described the crystallization of the great decision. We tried to experience for ourselves something of the tragedy of rejection first by the authorities, then by the people. From that point on, Christ "steadfastly set his face to go to Jerusalem," where at journey's end, humanly speaking, must lie catastrophe.

Jesus had come to save his people, and through them, all peoples of earth. This salutary act should have been realized through faith and love, but they failed. The Father's mission remained unchanged, but the means of its accomplishment were changed profoundly. The bitter fate of death now became the new form of salvation—that which for us today is salvation *per se*. After Jesus' appointment of Peter as head of his Church, Matthew reports: "Then he strictly charged his disciples to tell no one that he was Jesus the Christ." (See Matt. 16:13–20.) Let us take one strand of the whole text, Jesus' question and the disciples' answer: Who do men say the Son of Man is? The disciples repeat the various opinions in circulation, linked, most of them, with the Apocalyptic thought of late Jewish history.

But who do you say I am?

And Peter's: You are the Christ, . . . Son of the living God. With prophetic solemnity Jesus confirms the reply. "*Maschiach*" Peter had said, in the Greek, "Christos," which is the equivalent of our "Messiah," "the Anointed One."

The first anointed one we meet in the Old Testament is Aaron, brother of Moses (Ex. 28:41). God commands that he be consecrated with holy oil and thus set apart as a high priest. When next we read of an anointing it is in connection with the refusal of the Jewish people to obey the voice of God through the direct medium of his prophet; they demand a king, and through Samuel, the last judge, God gives them one: King Saul, whom Samuel anoints (I Sam. 10:1). He is "the Lord's anointed," and after him David and Solomon and all the kings, and the succession of high priests after Aaron. Anointment is the laying on of hands in the name of God. The individual thus set apart remains what he is, with all his human weaknesses, yet he is somehow lifted above the level of everyday existence. Henceforth, he is the expression of God's majesty among men, who in turn are represented by the anointed one before the throne of heaven.

Above all, it is this role of go-between that the priest should suggest—not by his individual bearing; at least not primarily. The holiness meant here is no personal holiness, it is the reflected sanctity of office, and entirely independent of the representative's own worthiness. (Woe to him, naturally, if he does not try to become also personally worthy of the honor he bears, for then it will become his fate.) God is present in his anointed ones. The first book of Samuel tells how David, fleeing before Saul, unexpectedly finds his enemy at his mercy. David's friends urge him to make an end of the king, but shuddering at the thought, he refuses: ". . . that I may do no such thing to my master the Lord's anointed, as to lay my hand upon him, because he is the Lord's anointed" (I Kings 24:7).

Thus the double succession of the anointed continues: succession of the high priests throughout the entire history of the Jewish race; succession of the kings, until their line is extinguished in the Babylonian captivity. At the same time, the figure of another anointed one forms in the vision of the prophets, those men sent to declare God's will to priest and king, to warn them, defy them, and to foretell the judgment of heaven upon them. In the face of the actual corrupt king, they appeal to a future, mysteriously flawless being who will be the acme of royal perfection. More: he will be *the* Anointed One, simultaneously king and priest, God's Envoy, Executer of his saving and judging will, Bringer of the Kingdom, Teacher of Truth, Bestower of Holy Life, overflowing Vessel of the Spirit—the Messiah.

Jesus knows himself to be the Messiah, the Anointed One par excellence. He is *the* King. His realm consists of those human hearts that are devoted to God, of the world that such hearts have transformed. He is *the* Priest; he lifts to the Father hearts made malleable by love and purged by contrition and fills them with God's grace, that their whole existence may be one great mystery of union. And he does not act by force, but by the prophetic power and truth that is spirit and life (see John 4:24). The figure of the Messiah is immeasurably important. Not the word that he speaks, not the work that he performs, not the instructions that he gives are decisive, but what he himself *is*. Through him, the living one, heaven addresses earth, and man's will is directed to heaven. In him worlds meet and fuse. There is no immediate relationship based on forgiveness and homecoming between man and the God of Revelation; only via the Intermediary runs the road from man to God and from Holiness to us, and he is entirely selfless, living not for himself, but for the honor of his Father and the salvation of his brothers. "*Ich diene*" is the formula of his existence. His very essence is one of sacrifice; how that sacrifice is to be carried out depends on the course of history, which in turn is determined by the inseparably interwoven wills of God and man. The sacrificial act can be realized through simple love—if men will believe; it must be realized through destruction if they do not.

Anointment is the mysterious divine act by which the individual is lifted out of daily life and placed at the cross-roads between heaven and earth. This role is so perfectly fulfilled in Christ that all other anointing is only a foreshadowing of his. His anointment, prophesied in "the fullness of the oil," is the *Pneuma,* the Holy Ghost himself. Through him the Virgin conceived God's Son. In him the Messiah lives and works and speaks.

Thus it is only through the Holy Spirit that he can be recognized. When Peter answers Jesus' question with: You are the Christ, Son of the living God, Jesus responds with solemn triumph: Blessed are you, Simon son of Jona; it is not flesh and blood, but my Father in heaven who has revealed this to you. Enlightenment does not come from man's mind, but from the mind of God. For one superb moment Peter, knowing, stands where Christ stands, being. But for a moment only (we see how difficult it is to maintain such altitudes) until Jesus mentions the coming agony. Then Peter grabs his arm: "Far be it from thee, O Lord; this will never happen to thee." Angrily Jesus shakes him off and turns away: "Get behind me, satan, thou art a scandal to me; for thou dost not mind the things of God, but those of men" (Matt. 16:22–23). And Peter is back in his own territory, no longer capable of recognizing the divine. How moving it is that only now that he has resolutely turned his face toward Jerusalem, does Jesus speak openly of his intrinsic nature, closing his words with the stern command to tell no one that he is the Messiah. This is his essential message to the world, yet for a long time he does not mention it. The first to recognize him are the demons. These unfortunates, in whom an evil, non-earthly power is at work, immediately sense the Stranger who is not of this world, and his coming kingdom of salvation. Jesus threatens them, laying a strict charge on them not to make him known. Next it is the simple folk who acknowledge him. Their wisdom springs from a deeper source than that of the educated; they feel who he is. But he does not take them into his confidence. Why not? Why doesn't he tell them openly that he is God's Son? Why does he remain silent when they question him? Because he knows that they have no place for him. True, they expect the Messiah, but the Messiah of an earthly kingdom. A religious kingdom, a theocracy, yes, but they want merely the prolonging of the old covenant, not the dawning of the new, heavenly. Jesus knows that the moment he says "Messiah" he will be drawn into a network of illusions, so he remains silent and tries first to convert their hearts.

He does not succeed, so the message remains unspoken. Like a sealed missive, it is brought to the dungeon of John the Baptist, who has sent two of his disciples to Jesus for confirmation: " 'Art thou he who is to come, or shall we look for another?' And Jesus answering said to them, 'Go and report to John what you have heard and seen; the blind see, the lame walk, the lepers are cleansed, the deaf hear, the dead rise, the poor have the gospel preached to them' " (Matt. 11:3–6). John, who lives in the spirit of the prophets, understands. Likewise 'sealed' under command of secrecy, the revelation is made to Jesus' own disciples.

The Messiah is there, but the form his mission will be allowed to take depends on the readiness of the people. The coldness and reserve with which he is received do not permit him to become the Prince of Peace he should have been in the immeasurable abundance of the prophecies, and the total devotion of his soul, which was to have become apparent in illimitable, all-transforming love, is forced to remain in the power of the enemy. Thus "the Anointed One" becomes "the One who Perishes." His intrinsic sacrifice is turned outward, and the solemn revelation of his identity is linked with the dark annunciation of the coming agony, death and resurrection (Matt. 16:21).

Thus the Messianic High Priest is not allowed to lead all creation to God through the mystery of holy transfiguration, though many lines in the farewell speeches and in the first Epistle of John hint at what might have been. The mystery of divine abundance must be exchanged for the mystery of divine mortality. During the Last Supper Jesus gave himself to his disciples, body and blood, a sacrifice "poured out." Henceforth, the Eucharist remains: "For as often as you shall eat this bread and drink the cup, you proclaim the death of the Lord, until he comes" (I Cor. 11:26). The Messianic king's crown has become a crown of thorns.

And still, the divine decision remains unchanged. Indeed, we ask ourselves in all the earnestness of contrition whether it was not precisely by this *via mala,* which never should have been necessary, that the ultimate revelation of God's love and superabundance broke into holiest reality. Doesn't he himself suggest this in the words spoken after the Resurrection: "Did not the Christ have to suffer these things before entering into his glory?" (Luke 24:26). Yet who dares to say that he comprehends the divine freedom of this "have to"?

II

THE ROAD TO JERUSALEM

If one were to ask of the New Testament: What is Man? it would reply with the words of the apostle John: That creature whom God "so loved . . . that he gave his only-begotten Son . . ." (3:16). The answer immediately evokes a second: Man is that creature who dared to slaughter the Son God sent him. He who retorts: What have I to do with Annas and Caiphas? is still ignorant of the collective guilt that binds all men. Already on the historical plane one stands for all, and all have to bear the consequences of the deeds of the one; how much more so here where it is question of the great collectivity of deicide and redemption. Then Scripture gives still a third answer to the question: Man is that creature who now lives upon the destiny of Christ; him on whom God's love still rests, but also the responsibility for driving that love to death.

After Matthew has reported the evil clash between Christ and the Pharisees in which Christ accuses them of blasphemy against the Holy Spirit, he goes on to say that several Jews come to Christ and ask for a sign—not just any demonstration of supernatural power, but the great, specifically Messianic sign expected by the chosen people as the fulfillment of the promised kingdom.

"But he answered and said to them, 'An evil and adulterous generation demands a sign, and no sign shall be given it but the sign of Jonas the prophet. For even as Jonas was in the belly of the fish three days and three nights, so will the Son of Man be three days and three nights in the heart of the earth. The men of Nineveh will rise up in the judgment with this generation and will condemn it; for they repented at the preaching of Jonas, and behold, a greater than Jonas is here' " (Matt. 12:39–41). Already the shadow of possible rejection and death; the identical demand and answer appear in chapter sixteen. Again Christ's enemies have demanded a sign, but he only replies: " 'When it is evening you say, "The weather will be fair, for the sky is red." And in the morning you say, "It will be stormy today, for the sky is red and lowering." You know then how to read the face of the sky, but cannot read the signs of the times! An evil and adulterous generation demands a sign, and no sign shall be given it but the sign of Jonas.' And he left them and went away" (Matt. 16:2–4).

Jesus' position in the world being what it is, and his relations to people developing as they do, the possibility of his destruction gradually swells to what is practically a necessity. It is that 'must' which he himself often implies, for example in speaking of the baptism with which he is to be baptized "and how distressed I am until it is accomplished!" (Luke 12:50). What does it mean? One might suppose it to be that type of necessity which arises when the consequences of word and deed become so manifold that everything is crowded into one set direction. In this way catastrophe can become inevitable. However, Christ does not behave like a person about whose head storm-clouds are gathering. Such a person would change his course, or flee, or with a desperate act of the will prepare to go down with all flags flying. Nothing of the kind in Jesus' conduct. He could flee easily, but does not dream of doing so. There is not a word that suggests a change in tactics in order to win over the populace; also not a trace of desperation. Imperturbably he proceeds along the road he has taken. He sees his mission through to the end without a single diminution, consenting to his doom and thus transmitting to it the immeasurable, God-willed purpose of his coming: fulfillment of the act of salvation.

In Matthew sixteen we read that Jesus began to prepare his disciples for the end in Jerusalem, for his death and Resurrection; again in chapter seventeen: " 'The Son of Man is to be betrayed into the hands of men, and they will kill him; and on the third day he will rise again.' And they were exceedingly sorry" (17:21–22). And finally: "And as Jesus was going up to Jerusalem, he took the twelve disciples aside by themselves, and said to them, 'Behold, we are going up to Jerusalem, and the Son of Man will be betrayed to the chief priests and the Scribes; and they will condemn him to death, and will deliver him to the Gentiles to be mocked and scourged and crucified; and on the third day he will rise again' " (20:17–19).

Jesus' attitude to what is to come is without the slightest trace of self-surrender or desperation or enthusiasm or Bacchic longing for personal cessation of being. It is the very core of his will that speaks unshakable, terrible. Jesus was no cold Superman—he was more human than any of us. Entirely pure, unweakened by evil, he was loving and open to the core. His ardor, truth, sensitivity, power, capacity for joy and pain were unlimited, and everything that happened to him happened in the immeasurableness of his divinity. What then must have been Jesus' suffering! God of himself cannot suffer, yet he did suffer: in Jesus Christ it was God who suffered. Jesus' will to the passion is not to be broken, but at thought of it, his whole frame shudders in the grip of unspeakable pain. We feel it in his furious reply to Peter, when the disciple, well-meaning but puny of heart, tries to dissuade him from going to his death in Jerusalem: "Get behind me, satan, thou art a scandal to me; for thou dost not mind the things of God, but those of men." The will to sacrifice stands fast, but it has been torn from Jesus' human nature and is still throbbingly sensitive; he can bear no tampering with it. Doesn't Luke's account of the temptation in the desert close with the words, the tempter "departed from him for a while." Now he is back, speaking through the mouth of the disciple.

Why does Jesus mention what is to come, in order to turn the course of events? To find help or at least alleviation of the load on his heart? The Gospels show again and again how he tries to make his disciples understand; how after both rulers and people have rejected him, he desires that at least his own be with him. We hear how in Gethsemane he commands the little band to wait, taking only the three with him who are supposed to share his vigil: "Then he came to the disciples and found them sleeping. And he said to Peter, 'Could you not, then, watch one hour with me?' " (Matt. 26:40). And in Luke: "But while all marvelled at all the things that he was doing, he said to his disciples, 'Store up these words in your minds: the Son of Man is to be betrayed into the hands of men.' But they did not understand this saying, and it was hidden from them, that they might not perceive it; and they were afraid to ask him about this saying" (Luke 9:44–45). Three times we are told that they did not understand, and the fourth that they did not even have the courage to ask. What forsakenness!

Among Jesus' complaints against the Pharisees we find the parable of the rich man who planted a vineyard. He has let it out to vine-dressers, who later refuse to pay the promised revenue and mishandle the messengers sent to collect it. Accordingly he sends his own son, convinced that they will respect him. " 'But the vine-dressers, on seeing the son, said among themselves, "This is the heir; come, let us kill him, and we shall have his inheritance." So they seized him, cast him out of the vineyard, and killed him. When, therefore, the owner of the vineyard comes, what will he do to those vine-dressers?' They said to him, 'He will utterly destroy those evil men, and will let out the vineyard to other vine-dressers, who will render to him the fruits in their seasons.'

"Jesus said to them, 'Did you never read in the Scriptures, *The stone which the builders rejected, has become the corner stone; . . .' "* (Matt. 21:38–43). The meaning is clear enough. Christ is both Son and Corner-stone. The temple in all its mysterious freedom is not built, but the corner-stone is there of which Paul writes: "For other foundation no one can lay, but that which has been laid, which is Christ Jesus" (I Cor. 3:11). The building has begun; from the groundwork it grows slowly upward to the crowning cupola of the coming kingdom. How deeply Christ feels about the darkness ahead is evident in his words to the mother of the Zebedees, who comes to beg the Lord to give her sons places of honor in heaven: "You do not know what you are asking for. Can you drink of the cup of which I am about to drink?" (Matt. 20:21–23). Christ's "cup" is his fate, proffered him by his Father. In the last night the word appears again: "Father, if it is possible, let this cup pass away from me; yet not as I will, but as thou willst" (Matt. 26:39–40).

How strangely God's holy will and the unholy will of the world are intermingled! In another passage we see how good and evil both finally submit to divine command: "On that same day certain Pharisees came up, saying to him, 'Depart and be on thy way, for Herod wants to kill thee.' And he said to them, 'Go and say to that fox, "Behold, I cast out devils and perform cures today and tomorrow, and the third day I am to end my course. Nevertheless, I must go my way today and tomorrow and the next day, for it cannot be that a prophet perish outside Jerusalem" ' " (Luke 13:31–33).

First the curious words about Herod; they have a knowing, contemptuous ring; then the veiled "today and tomorrow, and the third day," not meant literally, but as periods of time in general human life and activity. Immediately they are repeated: "I must go my way today and tomorrow and the next day" up the road of destiny. And finally, the ghastly mystery of the law of necessity: ". . . it cannot be that a prophet perish, outside Jerusalem." All messengers from God have been murdered there; Jesus has mentioned this before: it was suggested in the words about the scandal of Nazareth, and stated plainly in the passage about the blood of the prophets (see Luke 4; Matt. 23:34–36). Afterwards, the city decorated their graves and claimed the honor of sheltering their tombs! Now this terrible necessity is about to be repeated. Jesus' message of love is unable to break it. Only by his act of offering up himself can he destroy its power. But, oh, the disappointment and pain of it!

"Jerusalem, Jerusalem, thou who killest the prophets, and stonest those who are sent to thee! how often would I have gathered thy children together, as a hen gathers her young under her wings, but thou wouldst not!" (Luke 13:34–35). To the end of human history (the end of sin) the impenetrable mystery of God's voluntary weakness will be walled in with darkness.

Mary's anointing of Christ's head with the precious spikenard is the perfect symbol of his readiness for sacrifice. The gesture is one of holy beauty, and he thanks her for it accordingly: "Amen, I say to you, wherever in the whole world this gospel is preached, this also that she has done shall be told in memory of her" (Matt. 26:10–13).

The words suggest melancholy, but in Jesus there is no such thing; only a plumbless sense of destiny, unspeakable pain that it should come as it did, and with the pain, a love that is neither tired nor embittered, but remains purest devotion to the end. Perfect knowledge and perfect love in one, and a freedom of heart quick to sense the fleeting delicacy of the woman's act, and to transform it into a lasting symbol. As Jesus and his apostles seat themselves at the final pasch, this readiness for sacrifice assumes holy proportions: "And when the hour had come, he reclined at table, and the twelve apostles with him. And he said to them, 'I have greatly desired to eat this passover with you before I suffer; . . .' " (Luke 22:14–15). It shouldn't be necessary to point out that there is not a trace of Dionysian urge to self-obliteration in Christ, but unfortunately for us heirs of modernity who live among sullied words and blurred thoughts, it is imperative that we clarify our thinking and speaking again and again. The desire of which Jesus speaks is part of the same determination to obey the paternal will that runs through his entire life: love that is truth, knowledge and obedient devotion (that state of heart which finds its purest expression in the prayer of Gethsemane).

After St. John describes Lazarus' resurrection he mentions an incident that belongs here: "The chief priests and the Pharisees therefore gathered together a council, and said, 'What are we doing? for this man is working many signs. If we let him alone as he is, all will believe in him, and the Romans will come and take away both our place and our nation.'

"But one of them, Caiphas, being high priest that year, said to them, 'You know nothing at all; nor do you reflect that it is expedient for us that one man die for the people, instead of the whole nation perishing.' "

Slowly the meaning of the passage emerges. The high council (those responsible for the decisions of the people) has assembled. Jesus has presented overpowering proof of his identity, but they see in it only danger to their position. Not one heart yields to the power demonstrated or to the warning voiced; their only concern is how to render that strange power innocuous. Finally the high priest rises and says: Don't you see that it is better for one man to die than for the whole nation to perish? John explains: "This, however, he said not of himself; but being high priest that year, he prophesied that Jesus was to die for the nation; and not only for the nation, but that he might gather into one the children of God who were scattered abroad. So from that day forth their plan was to put him to death" (John 11:47–43).

Supreme horror. The head of the nation reproves the responsible elite for not recognizing at once their obvious duty: to annihilate him whom it is 'right' to destroy, the Son of God! He must die that peace be reestablished and the people's fate sealed once and for all. Strangely enough, what Caiphas demands is precisely that which has now become the will of the Father, and consequently (in the purity of obedience) of the Son. The man's words have a double sense of which he is entirely unconscious; he is speaking prophetically. In the long chain of prophecies the enemy of God is given the last word: ". . . it is expedient for us that one man die for the people instead of the whole nation perishing." On our knees we agree: It is better, by the love of God it is better that this man die, than that we all be lost. And blessed be the eternal mercy that allows us to speak thus!

But what does it all mean? What are we humans? What is history? What is God? The last prophet stands there and speaks blindly—inspired by his sacred office—against his own lost heart!

Let us glance back over the prophecies. From them emerges a double figure of the Messiah. He is the King on the throne of David; the Prince of Peace, the powerful, glorious One whose kingdom knows no end (Is. 9:5–6); at the same time he is the slave of God, one who for our sins is despised, abused, and finally destroyed, whose suffering purchases our salvation (Is. 53:4–5). Both images are there, the two sides of the prophecy. Neither may be effaced, but can both be correct? It would be missing the sense of the whole mystery to say that Prince of Peace is meant only 'intrinsically'—as Prince of those hearts which have accepted the cross in unshaken belief; or that it means the transfigured one, who will be revealed once the slave has suffered his passion through to the end. Such interpretations do little justice to prophetic vision, which in reality holds both possibilities in suspension: that the people say Yes! but also No! That the Savior, who has placed his love at the mercy of human freedom, stride into opened hearts or to his death.

Does God know that it will end with the death of the Messiah? Certainly, from all eternity. And still it should not happen. Does he desire Jesus' death? Certainly, from all eternity. If the people close their hearts his love must take this road. Still, they should not close their hearts. It is obvious that with our human intelligence we shall never comprehend. God's eternal omniscience and our freedom of choice; that which should not be, but is; form which the act of salvation is supposed to take, and that which it actually does;—all this remains for us a hopelessly entangled mystery. What happens is simultaneously freedom and necessity: God's gift laid in human hands. To ponder these things makes sense only when we are able without disregarding truth to lift them to the plane of adoration. To be a Christian means to stand on that level. Indeed, one is Christian in the degree that one is open to these mysteries, that one accepts them in faith through the word of God, thus 'understanding,' willing, living them.

We have often spoken of the 'must' which led the Lord to his death; however, something is still lacking. When Jesus says: ". . . and the Son of Man will be betrayed to the chief priests and the Scribes; and they will condemn him to death" he does not look as he speaks at mankind in general, but at me. Everyone who hears Jesus speak of the 'necessity' of the road to Jerusalem, should substitute himself for the Scribes and Pharisees. That necessity is woven of the eternal Father, of Jesus and his mission, and of me—all that I am and do; not a distant nation a long, long, time ago. It is I, with all my indifference, refusals and failings, who strap the cross of Calvary to Christ's shoulders.

III

THE TRANSFIGURATION

The words with which Jesus informs his disciples more and more pressingly that he will have to suffer and die have something special about them. This is evident already earlier, when his enemies demand the great Messianic sign as proof of his identity. He retorts that he will give this unbelieving generation no sign other than that of the prophet Jonas. And there follows the mysterious hint: "For even as Jonas was in the belly of the fish three days and three nights, so will the Son of Man be three days and three nights in the heart of the earth" (Matt. 12:40). And in all three of the formal proclamations of his passion made on the final journey to Jerusalem he says that he will suffer and die and rise again.

When Luke says that the apostles did not understand, that his meaning was hidden from them, he means that for them the idea of a dying Messiah was simply inconceivable; yet even less conceivable must have been the idea of his Resurrection. Clarity came only with Easter: "And it came to pass, while they were wondering what to make of this, that, behold, two men stood by them in dazzling raiment. And when the women were struck with fear and bowed their faces to the ground, they said to them, 'Why do you seek the living one among the dead? He is not here, but has risen. Remember how he spoke to you while he was yet in Galilee, saying that the Son of Man must be betrayed into the hands of sinful men, and be crucified, and on the third day rise'" (Luke 24:5-8). From these words, as from the whole life of our Lord, one thing is evident: for Jesus there was no such thing as death alone. He accepted his death, spoke of it with increasing incisiveness, but always inseparably bound to resurrection.

Did Jesus live our human existence? Certainly. Did he die our death? Most assuredly; our very salvation depends upon his being like us in all things, sin excepted (Hebrews 4:15). Yet there is something behind his living and dying that is more than life and death in the nearest meaning of the words. Something for which we really should have another name, unless we limit the word "life" to the special sense it has in John, inventing a new word, a pale reflection of this, for all other purposes. An illimitable abundance and holy invulnerability in Jesus' person made it possible for him to be entirely one of us yet different from us all; not only to live our existence, but to transmute it, plucking the "sting" from both life and death (I Cor. 15:56).

What a strange phenomenon this thing called life! It is the *a priori* of everything, foundation of existence which, when threatened, responds with that unqualified reaction known as self-defense, which has its own laws. It is a miracle so precious that at times the sheer bliss of it is overwhelming. Life enjoys, abstains from, suffers, struggles, creates. It enfolds and permeates things, joins with other life, resulting not in a mere sum, but in new and manifold vitality. Foremost and fundamental, it is and remains an inexplicable enigma. For is it not strange that in order to possess one thing we must relinquish another? That in order to do anything of genuine value we must focus our attention on it and away from all else? That when we wish to do justice to one person we do injustice to all others, if only by not likewise accepting them into our range of heart, simply because there is not room enough for everyone? That when we experience any powerful sensation, then only in ignorance of what it is, the instant we try to understand it, the current is cut. Wakefulness is wonderful but tiring, and we long to lose ourselves in sleep. Sleep is pleasant, but how terrible to sleep away half our lives! Life is unity. It demands containment of things; demands that we preserve our entity in the superabundance around us, and yet that we throw the fullness of that entity into our slightest act. In all directions run the cracks. Everywhere we look we are faced with an either-or, this-or-that. And woe to us if we do not choose, for from the cleancut choice of the one or the other, depends the decency of existence. The moment we attempt to grab everything, we have nothing properly. If we try to do justice to everyone, we are just to no one, only contemptible. As soon as we reach out to embrace the whole, our individuality dissolves into nothing. Thus we are forced to make clear decisions, and by so doing—woe again!—to cut into our existence. Really, life has something impossible about it! It is forced to desire what it can never have. It is as though from the very start some fundamental mistake had been made, as evinced by everything we do. And then the dreadful transitoriness of it all. Is it possible that things exist only through self-destruction? Doesn't to live mean to pass over? The more intensively we live, the swifter the passing? Doesn't death begin already in life? With desperate truth a modern biologist has defined life as the movement towards death. Yet what a monstrosity to define life only as part of death! Is death then better ordered? Must we surrender our deepest instinct to Biology? Research has pointed out that early man experienced death quite differently from us. He by no means considered it something self-understood, as the necessary antipode of life. Instinctively he felt that death was not only unnecessary, but wrong. Where it occurred it came as the result of a particular cause, of a spiritual power of evil—even in cases of accident, old age, or death in battle. Let us wait a moment with our smile and with an open mind try to accept the possibility of the primitive's being closer to the truth than the professor.

Is death self-understood? If it were, we should accept it with a sense, however heavy, of fulfillment. Where is there such a death? True, here or there we find someone who sacrifices his life for some great cause; or another who has grown weary of the burden of life and accepts death with a sense of relief. But does the man exist who from the very essence of his vitality, consents to death? I have never met him, and what I have heard of him was poppycock. Man's natural stand to death is one of defense and protest, both rooted deep in the core of his being. Death is not self-understood, and every attempt to make it so ends in immeasurable melancholy.

Nevertheless, this life and death of ours belong together. When the romanticists attempted to make them the opposite poles of existence, comparing them with light and dark, height and depth, ascent and decline, this was aesthetic thoughtlessness under which lay a demonic illusion. But on one point they were right: our present forms of living and dying do belong together. They are two sides of the same fact—a fact which did not exist in Jesus.

In him there was something that towered above our little life and death. He lived more deeply and purely than it is ever possible for us to live. It has been pointed out that Jesus' life was poor and uneventful in comparison with that of Buddha through which streamed all the good things of earth, both material and spiritual: power, art, wisdom, family life, solitude, wealth and its renunciation, and above all, length of days, which enabled him to experience existence in all its breadth and depth. Strangely brief, almost fragmentary by contrast, Jesus' life and work. Yet how could it have been otherwise in a life whose essence was not richness, but sacrifice? Nevertheless, what Jesus did experience, every gesture, every act, every encounter, he experienced with an intensity that outweighted mere number and multifariousness. There was more to his meeting a fisherman, a beggar, a captain than in Buddha's acquaintance with all the strata of human existence.

Jesus really lived our life and died our death, real death (its terrors were only the more terrible for the divine strength and sensitivity of his life) yet everything was different both in his living and in his dying.

What decides the essence of a human life? In St. Augustine we find a thought which at first strikes us as strange, but which, carefully weighed, leads deep into existence. Asked whether the souls of men and the spiritual beings of angels are immortal, he answers: No.

Naturally, man's soul, being spirit, and hence indestructible, cannot die as his body dies; it cannot disintegrate. Still this is not yet immortality as the Gospels know it, immortality that comes not from the soul, but directly from God. (Unlike that of ox or ass, man's body receives its life from the soul; his essential vitality is carried over from his soul in an arc of flame.) The life of those souls who appear in Revelation, however, comes directly from God in the arc of flame known as grace. In that life, not only the soul, but also the body participates in grace, and the whole fervent being, body and soul, draws its life from God. That final stage then is true, sacred immortality.

God has shaped human life mysteriously indeed. Man's essence is meant to leap up to its God and return with the life it has taken from him. Man should live in a downward-sweeping movement that begins in heaven, not from earth upward, as animals do. His body should draw its sustenance from his spirit, his spirit from God; thus man's whole being would be infused with ever-circulating vitality. But sin has broken this entity; sin that was the will to autonomous existence, that desired "to be as Gods" (Gen. 3:5). And the arc of fire burned out; the ardent circle collapsed. True, man's rational soul, being indestructible, remains, but its indestructibility has become a shadowy *Ersatz*. The body also remains, since it is the soul's necessary covering, but it now covers a 'dead' soul, one no longer capable of transmitting to the body that life which God intended it to have. Thus life has become simultaneously real and unreal, ordered and chaotic, permanent and fleeting.

It is this that was different in Jesus. In him the flaming arc still burned divinely pure and strong, and not only as grace, but as Holy Spirit. His humanity lived from God in the fullness of the Holy Ghost, through whom he was made man, and in whom he lived to the end—and not only as a God-loving man lives, but as God and man. There is still more to this: only he can possess humanity like Christ's who not only clings to God, but who "is" God. Such humanity is alive in quite a different way from ours. The curve of fire 'between' the inseparable Son of God and Son of Man is that mystery behind Jesus' life and death that enabled him to live our human life and die our human death more profoundly than we ourselves. With him life and death assume new dimensions.

Matthew reports on the wonderful incident which took place on the last trip to Jerusalem.

"Now after six days Jesus took Peter, James and his brother John, and led them up a high mountain by themselves, and was transfigured before them. And his face shone as the sun, and his garments became white as snow. And behold, there appeared to them Moses and Elias talking together with him. Then Peter addressed Jesus, saying, 'Lord, it is good for us to be here. If thou wilt, let us set up three tents here, one for thee, one for Moses, and one for Elias.' As he was still speaking, behold, a bright cloud overshadowed them, and behold, a voice out of the cloud said, 'This is my beloved Son, in whom I am well pleased; hear him.' And on hearing it the disciples fell on their faces and were exceedingly afraid. And Jesus came near and touched them, and said to them, 'Arise, and do not be afraid.' But lifting up their eyes, they saw no one but Jesus only.

"And as they were coming down from the mountain, Jesus cautioned them, saying, 'Tell the vision to no one, till the Son of Man has risen from the dead' " (Matt. 17:1–9).

By "vision" here is meant the particular kind of vision outside the realm of hitherto known experience, with all the mysterious and disquieting traits of an act of heaven: light which comes from no natural source but belongs to the spheres of inner reality; likewise the "cloud," which has nothing to do with the meteorologic forms we know, but is something for which there is no satisfactory word—brightness that conceals rather than reveals, heavenliness unveiled yet unapproachable. Further visionary characteristic is the suddenness with which the figures appear and disappear, leaving behind them the emptiness of an earth abandoned by heaven. This vision then is nothing subjective, no suddenly projected inner picture, but response to a spiritual reality, as the senses daily respond to physical realities. The event does not merely descend upon Jesus, or take place within him; it also breaks from him, revelation of inmost being, arc of the live flame within him become apparent.

In the gloom of fallen creation the *Logos* blazes celestial light. But the dark asserts itself; ". . . grasped it not . . ." as John says in the opening of his Gospel. Thus Christ's truth and love, which long for nothing but the freedom to spend themselves, are forced back into his heart—sorrow God alone can measure and comprehend. Here on the mountain though, for one moment, they break through in all their radiant clarity. This was the Light which had come into the world and was powerful enough to illuminate it completely. On the way to death the glory of what may be revealed only after death breaks out like a jet of flame, burning illustration of Christ's own words on death and resurrection.

What is revealed here is not only the glory of pure, angelic spirit, but of the spirit *through the body,* glory of the spiritualized body of man. Not the glory of God alone, not a piece of disclosed heaven, not only the sheen of the Lord as it hovered over the ark of the covenant, but the glory of the God-Logos in the Son of Man. Life above life and death; life of the body, but issue of the spirit; life of the spirit, but issue of the *Logos;* life of the man Jesus, but issue of the Son of God.

The Transfiguration is the summer lightning of the coming Resurrection. Also of our own resurrection, for we too are to partake of that transfigured life. To be saved means to share in the life of Christ. We too shall rise again, and our bodies will be transformed by the spirit, which itself is transformed by God. In us mortals blissful immortality will once awaken; read the magnificent fifteenth chapter of the first Epistle to the Corinthians.

Such is the eternal life in which we believe. "Eternal" does not mean merely endless; we are that as spiritual creatures of God anyway, "by nature." But the general indestructibility of the soul is not yet the blissful, eternal life that Revelation describes. That comes to us from God. Actually, "eternal" life has nothing to do with the length of that life; it is not the opposite of transitory life. Perhaps we come closest to the truth when we define it as life which participates in the life of God.

Such life has received from him its conclusiveness, its all-inclusiveness, its unity in diversity, its infiniteness and immanent oneness (things that our present life lacks, protest as we may and must for the sake of that dignity with which God himself endowed us). In the new life such eternity exists for all, whether one is a great saint or the least "in the kingdom of heaven." The differences exist within eternity itself, where, admittedly, they are as great as the differences in love. This eternal life does not wait till after death to begin. It already exists. The essence of Christian consciousness is founded on its presence—through faith. The degrees of that consciousness are limitless and dependent on many factors: its clarity, strength, and "tangibility" (the depth to which it is actually experienced and lived). Whatever our measure, something of it is always behind our living and our dying, whether given by grace or seized by faith: something of that flaming arc which broke through for the first time on Tabor, to reveal itself victoriously in the Resurrection.

IV

THE CHURCH

Now Jesus, having come into the district of Caesarea Philippi, began to ask his disciples, saying, 'Who do men say the Son of Man is?' " He is told the various opinions in circulation, then asks who the disciples think he is, and Peter gives his historic answer, "Thou are the Christ, the Son of the living God." Jesus calls him blessed and entrusts to him the keys of the kingdom, names him the rock of his Church, against which "the gates of hell" shall not prevail. We know the passage almost by heart, still there remains one point that we should try to see more clearly.

Here for the first time Jesus declares himself openly and unmistakably the Messiah, and simultaneously he speaks with equal definiteness of his coming death. This hour is also the decisive hour of the Church. From now on three facts belong together: Jesus the Messiah, his death and his Church. Before that hour the Church did not exist, nor did she spring into being later as the result of historical development. Jesus himself founded her in the superabundance of his Messianic power.

The decision regarding the acceptance or rejection of his message has fallen; the Lord is on his way to death. The powers of evil have the upper hand, and the Church will be attacked by them; nevertheless, she will stand, rocklike. The two thoughts belong together, never to be separated.

To the reality of the Church belong other passages which it might be well to mention here, among them Jesus' words about his disciples' mission: "He who hears you, hears me; and he who rejects you, rejects me. . . ." (Luke 10:16). Something more than inspired men capable of inflaming hearts are being sent into the world; they are delegates equipped with full powers, for they bear their high office with them. They are already "Church."

Another time Jesus speaks of man's duty toward an erring brother. First one should tactfully speak to him alone. If he refuses to listen, one should approach him with one or two others, that the necessary warning gain weight. If he still remains refractory "appeal to the Church" (*Ecclesia*—the word is still something halfway between church and congregation) and means at least a body with authority. Then Christ continues, "but if he refuse to hear even the Church, let him be to thee as the heathen and the publican" (Matt. 18:15–17).

At the Last Supper Jesus instigates the holy mystery of the Eucharist already promised in Capharnaum (John 6). It is sacrifice and sacrament in one, mystery of the new community, heart of the new Church's new covenant. Its consummation is her vital heart-beat. (See Matt. 26: Acts 2:46.)

After the Resurrection, the Lord's memorable questioning of Peter on the shore; three times he asks him: Simon, son of John, lovest thou me? And three times, shamefully recalling his treachery, Peter replies: "Yes, Lord, thou knowest that I love thee." And each time he is commanded: "Feed my lambs," "Feed my lambs," "Feed my sheep" (John 21:15–16). That too is Church. Once Jesus had said to Peter: You are the rock; then: I have prayed for you, that your faith remain firm; when it is established, confirm your brothers (Luke 22:32). Now he says: Be the shepherd of lambs and sheep, of the whole world, which embraces both the weak and the strong. Church again, founded on the unity of its fundament; constituted with one head and one leader. 'Conceived' by the words spoken at Caesarea Philippi, the Church was not born until Pentecost, when the Holy Spirit fused the individual believers in Christ to a single, determined body with a consciousness of its own, fully aware that it lived in Christ and Christ in it: the Corpus Christi. And immediately he whom the Lord has appointed its rock and its shepherd rises

and speaks. His words are the first of the new-born Church (I Cor.;
Acts 2:14).

What does Church in Jesus' sense mean? The question is not easily answered, but that should not prevent us from trying; we must
constantly attempt to free ourselves from that false simplicity which
is nothing but a mirage-like 'comprehension' of conceptions that
have become habitual. We want to experience that renewal of faith
which comes when eyes are suddenly opened to the eternally new,
the eternally fresh that is in Christ, and again we return to the
thought that has appeared so often in our meditations: to the rejection of his message and the fundamental change in the course of his
life that resulted. From that point on, God's continued will to salvation is forced up Golgotha. But what if the people had accepted the
Lord? Would there have been a Church then?

Our religious individualism is tempted to say No! The individual
would then have turned to Jesus, would have been linked through
him directly with the Father. Nothing would have stood between
the soul and God as he is revealed in Christ. But this is not true. Let
us recall the "greatest and the first commandment," which demands
that the Christian love God with all his strength and his neighbor as
himself. Actually, the two commands are one; it is impossible to love
God without loving your neighbor. Love is a stream that flows from
God to me, from me to my neighbor (and not to one only, but to
all), from my neighbor back to God. This is no longer individualism, but vital communalism. Jesus once warned against domination
in any form: "But do not you be called 'Rabbi'; for one is your Master [Christ], and all you are brothers" (Matt. 23:8–12). This is the
beginning of the Christian "we." The faithful are to be bound to
each other in mutual fraternity. They are the family of God, in
which all are brothers and sisters and one the Father. St. Paul completes the thought with great depth and beauty when he calls Christ
"the firstborn among many brethren" (Rom. 8:29). The communal
spirit finds expression in the *ethos* of the Sermon on the Mount; in
the Our Father it crystallizes into prayer.

Is it enough that everywhere the individual is bound through Christ to God and to his fellows in sacred 'relationship'? Is the family of God the ultimate goal? We have already pointed out several times that Jesus addressed himself neither to the individual nor to humanity in general, but to a historical reality: the chosen people with all that belonged to the term: vocation, guidance, loyalty and apostasy. This the people which was to speak its Yes, whose decision was to enter into the new existence of grace. What then would have stood, firmly implanted in faith, would again have been that specific people. Unlike the old, natural covenant, the new would have been a covenant of the spirit—in history, hence with a nation, the spiritual nation of the New Israel, "a chosen race, a royal priesthood, a holy nation."

"Church" again, historical reality and all that is bound to it in the way of destiny and responsibility. Hence the earnestness of the decision to be made by God's 'family'; its new weight and dignity. This then the Church that was to stand at the heart of history, radiating, attracting, transfiguring. From every country, one after the other, a genuine community of blood was to rise, forming the one new spiritual nation. *Nation,* people—not group of individuals or heterogenous mass, but folk, product of a long history, vocation, guidance and destiny, and in its turn bearer of history, the history of God in the world. Ultimately, the number of mankind and of the new people of God was to be identical, for just as each racial and historical group was to be filled one by one with the spirit of the New Israel, so also unredeemed mankind was to be replaced by an all-inclusive family of the saved. But the arms of the Church were to stretch still further: the established beginning made here was to permeate and transfigure the universe. Paul's Epistles to the Romans, Ephesians, Colossians speak of this mystery. "Church" then, was to be converted mankind in a transfigured world: the new creation born of the Holy Spirit.

Yet this would not have taken place in a burst of formless enthusiasm. Throughout the process, apostolic office and mission, power and obedience, differentiation between authorities, mystery and the sharing of mystery are not to be thought away: ordered whole, and in that order and completeness, true Church. This is already made clear in the sending forth of the apostles before the decision has fallen. St. Paul compares the Church to a body with many parts; he speaks of the many graces or "varieties of gifts" in the one Spirit; of the manifold expressions coming from the one organic unity (see I Cor.). It is the same thought that Jesus expresses in the parable of the one vine and the many branches in John fifteen.

And there is still another image, this time from the prophecies, that of the Messianic Kingdom of New Jerusalem (Is. 65:17). Initially the actual city of Jerusalem is meant, which is then transfigured to the holy City of the Messiah. St. Paul also speaks of her, of "that Jerusalem which is above," the city freed by grace and faith, mother whose children are born into freedom, not into the slavery of the flesh as were the former children (Gal. 4:21–26). And finally in the Apocalypse the radiant Jerusalem, heavenly city, unit of sacred mankind (21:9–27). Here it is again, Church, the great congregation, spiritually ordered communal life as a powerful historical reality. In the words of the Apocalypse the metaphor of the city receives its ultimate impressiveness.

Is the Church we know today the same she would have been in the accepted kingdom of God? Church was to exist; Jesus wanted no individualistic piety. He wanted the *Ecclesia* based on confidence, freedom and love. This does not mean a bodiless 'spiritual church,' nor does it mean a purely pneumatological church incapable of taking its place in history. Always there would have been organization and order, differences of office and authority, leaders and led, ecclesiastic and layman, authoritative teaching and obedient acceptance—but in freedom, love and trust. Unfortunately, the second Fall occurred, rejection of God's Son, and ever since, the Church too has borne the marks: danger of mistaking sacred order for "law," danger of abusing it.

What then is the present Church? The fullness of grace functioning in history. Mystery of that union into which God, through Christ, draws all creation. Family of the children of God assembled about Christ, the Firstborn. Beginning of the new, holy people. Foundation of the Holy City once to be revealed. And simultaneous with all her graces, her dangers: danger of dominating, danger of "the law." When we speak of the Church we cannot ignore the fact of Christ's rejection, which never should have been. We cannot ignore the terrible means by which we came to salvation; the consequences have penetrated deep into existence. Accordingly, we have neither the Church we might have had, nor the Church we one day will have. We have the Church scarred by that most tragic of all decisions.

Nevertheless, she is and remains the mystery of the new creation, Mother constantly bearing and rebearing heavenly life. Between Christ and herself flows the mystery of love. She is his Bride. When St. Paul in his letter to the Ephesians speaks of the mystery of Christian marriage, he grounds it in the greater nuptial mystery of Christ and his Church. (The image should not be used lightly, for it is indeed a "high mystery" and renders the sacrament of human marriage only the more impenetrable.) The Church is the Holy City of the Apocalypse, blazing in an unutterable mystery of beauty and love, when suddenly transformed into a shimmering Bride, she steps down to receive the Bridegroom.

All this exists, and with them the flaws, the abuses, the rigors. We have no choice but to accept the whole, as it is. The Church is a mystery of faith and can be experienced only in love.

V

Moses and Elias

When we read the Synoptic accounts of the Transfiguration, we usually concentrate our attention on what happens to the Lord and on its relation to the Resurrection.
All too easily we overlook the appearance of the two men who are
seen conversing with him. What are they doing here, Moses and
Elias? One the lawgiver of the old covenant, the other the prophet
who, according to the first Book of Kings, did not die, but was spirited away into heaven. (For this reason late Jewish apocalyptical
writers concluded that he would return to earth before the appearance of the expected Messiah.) Still, there seems to be a special reason why precisely these two figures of Old Testament history are
selected. Why Moses and not Abraham? Why Elias and not Isaias or
one of the other prophets?

Yes, why not Abraham, that dynamic figure with whom faith
among men began in earnest? Abraham was a wealthy, childless man
who enjoyed high esteem in his own country. Then God summoned
him away. In his old age he was to become the father of a nation, the
beginning of a tremendous history. To this end he must leave everything and follow God. The command is no light one. It is not so
much the going away that is difficult; wanderlust was in the blood of
those people at the time; but the going in obedience to a promise utterly contrary to the laws of nature. This was Abraham's greatness,
his faith and his persistence in that faith even after a quarter of a century had rolled by and he had passed the hundred-year mark. Still
Abraham hoped. Unspeakably great then the fulfillment of the

promise when at last his son was born. Several years later the centenarian is again summoned by God to leave his home—this time to proceed to Mount Moria with the boy whom he is to sacrifice there without losing his faith in the promise that from his loins was to spring a great nation (Gen. 22). Thus Abraham becomes the "father of all . . . who believe" (Rom. 4:11). About him glows illimitable hope; before him inconceivable promise. God had told him those many years ago that he should look out into the Mesopotamian night at the stars; great as their superabundance would be the richness of the fulfillment with which the future was pregnant (Gen. 15:5). This then the quality of the hope and blessing in which the man had lived, yet it is not he who comes to speak to Jesus when the nation he has fathered fails. Had the Transfiguration taken place at the time of the Sermon on the Mount, when the tremendous possibilities of the promise were still alive, Abraham might have come. But not now. Now it was Moses who came. Why?

Court favorite until he had to flee the results of his death-blow to the Egyptian, Moses too was commanded by God to perform a specific mission: on Mount Horeb he was told to lead his people out of Egyptian captivity (Ex. 3). Moses demurred—probably because he realized what he would be in for. About the figure of Abraham is an air of divine largesse, spaciousness, illimitable possibility; on Moses presses the weight of a terrible yoke. His heavy tongue is only one expression of it.

The nation of Abraham is now reality; a large nation and a strong one, but enslaved, and Moses' task it is to guide it back to freedom. This meant not only liberation from Egyptian domination (God was with the Jews, and had they earnestly desired freedom, who would have been able to prevent them?). The trouble was that fundamentally they were not too discontented with their lot. Certainly, they had cried to God imploring his aid, but they would have considered an alleviation of their forced labor and improved living conditions a satisfactory answer to their prayer. The real problem was to shake these masses out of the torpor of an existence in which the necessities of life were provided for. After centuries of bondage they were now suddenly ripped out of their security and sent into the desert, into an unknown existence that demanded both courage and initiative. To free them from their own shackles, from their refractoriness and stupor, this was Moses' thankless task.

It required endless effort. While Moses spent forty days on Sinai in intense prayer and fasting, even while he stood in the presence of God, receiving from him the tablets of the law, terrible things were happening in the Hebrew camp at the foot of the mountain. Aaron, the high priest, had collected the people's jewelry and poured a molten calf, and when Moses descended from the heights he found them in the midst of a riotous cult. Incensed, he sent the stone tablets crashing to the ground (Ex. 32:19). The gesture is symbolical. Moses has been commanded to enforce the will of God— against the obdurate will of this people; to free them from their own servile tendencies. He has well been called the most plagued of men. The story of the forty years' wandering through the desert is the story of a never-ending struggle, not only with the hardships of nature and the assaults of hostile tribes, but also with the apathy and stubbornness of those he was leading. At first the people are enthusiastic, but soon discouraged. They bind themselves with sacred vows, only to forget everything when it comes to the test. They start everything well, but see nothing through, and the moment they meet with difficulties, the experience of God's great and terrible signs is completely forgotten; they react like any mass of humans under pressure, yes, more paltrily than other peoples in an armed march would have permitted themselves to react. Then again they are senselessly bold and plunge without warning headlong into disaster. Often one has the impression that they feel nothing of the glory of their march, that they are insensible to the power of the advancing God who hovers protectingly over them; that they are completely blind to the greatness of their leader. They make constant demands, are "stiff-necked," torpid, malicious. The record of the march to the Promised Land is the story of the desperately heavy struggle of a powerful, God-fearing will with the crushing burden of humanity. Moses had to carry the entire nation on his shoulders. He was, necessarily, the most patient of men.

Sometimes it is as though he has to bear the additional weight of God's wrath; when, for example, the Almighty loses patience and says to Moses: Let me destroy them! But the leader of this blind, unmanageable people stands his ground, even when blows rain upon him from both sides. He remains true to his terrible charge of middleman. However, the test is such a sore one, that once his faith fails: at the moment when he is required to call forth water from the rock and in his own eyes he appears ridiculous. As punishment, God assures him that he will lead his people to the border of the Promised Land, but that he himself will not cross over (Num. 20:12).

How obdurate this people was, is best shown by God's own appraisal of them: not one of those who had left Egypt as an adult was deemed worthy to behold the Promised Land; not one of them was considered fit for pioneer life. Only those who had begun the wandering as children and those born on the way were accepted (Deut. 1:34, etc.). Even Moses had to share this fate. God takes back nothing once said. He continued to speak to Moses "face to face, as a man is wont to speak to his friend" (Ex. 33:11); he remained his friend, but Moses' life too ends upon the mountain-top from which God shows him the land of milk and honey that he may not enter (Deut. 32:48–52; 34:1–6).

This then the man who appeared to Christ, to him who was to carry the cross of his people to the bitter end; Moses too they had failed to follow, in the flesh, into the new land of free divine dominion. Yet another leader had to die 'on the mountaintop' (this one for our sins, not his own) before the promised Country could become reality.

And Elias? It is not too much to call him the mightiest of the prophets. Not as a speaker; there is no record of exalted or path-blazing words from his lips. He left no book; hardly a sentence that in itself is anything out of the ordinary. Nor did he have any remarkable visions or revelations. Yet no other prophet looms as huge against the bottomless depths of divine mystery as Elias; nowhere in the whole history of prophecy do we find an existence of such huge proportions. However, it is encysted in the immediacy of the moment, and that moment is terrible.

It is the reign of King Achab, a man who so hated God, that down the centuries it was said that because of him God's wrath still hung over the people of Israel. There he stands in the Books of Kings, the prototype of rebellion, with him his wife Jezabel, who was even more hardened in wickedness than he (I Kings 16). It was she who erected everywhere the altars of Baal and taught her people the worship of idols; she who annihilated the priests of the Lord. For years Elias had to hide from her wrath. During Achab's reign darkness covered the land, the darkness of hell. It was against this dark that Elias had to hide from her wrath. During Achab's reign darkness covered the land, the darkness of hell. It was against this dark that Elias had been sent. He never was able to proclaim the tidings of the coming kingdom; he had to fight to the end against a wall of blackness, hardened disbelief; against the violence, blasphemy and bloodthirstiness that stalked through the land, Elias' life is one titanic struggle against the powers of evil. The spirit of the Lord seethes in him, lifting him high above the human plane, spanning his strength far beyond the human breaking point. Once the tension relaxes, he sinks to the desert sand like a spent animal and begs for death. But again the angel touches him, and strengthened by divine refreshment, he wanders forty days to Horeb, the holy mountain (I Kings 19:4–9). Thus he fights the terrible fight to the finish, relentlessly breaking the power of the idols, until at the given hour, the fiery chariot swings low and bears him off into the unknown (II Kings 2:11).

"And behold, two men were talking with him. And these were Moses and Elias, who, appearing in glory, spoke of his death, which he was about to fulfill in Jerusalem" (Luke 9:30–31). Moses who had known the hopelessness of all efforts to rip his people out of the captivity of their own hearts; Elias, who with both sword and spirit had charged the satanic dark. It is as though the weight of one and a half millennia of sacred history had been bundled together and laid upon the shoulders of the Lord. All the enmity against God, heritage of a thousand years of intractability and blindness he must now bear to an end. No wonder we are shocked when Peter, seeing the radiance, says to Christ: "Master, it is good for us to be here. And let us set up three tents, one for thee, and one for Moses, and one for Elias, . . ." (Luke 9:33). The Evangelist does well to add, "not knowing what he said." It is the comprehension of a child, who, witnessing something terrible and ignorant of what it is, thinks it beautiful because it shines.

Then comes the cloud and God's voice, and the disciples fall on their faces. Words die. Next we read: "And after the voice had passed, Jesus was found alone." Heaven closes again. The earth grows dark. Jesus continues his way alone.

In spite of their strangeness, two passages from this period give us an inkling of Jesus' attitude at the time: "And when they had come to Capharnaum, those who were collecting the didrachma came to Peter, and said, 'Does your Master not pay the didrachma?' He said, 'Yes.' But when he had entered the house, Jesus spoke first, saying, 'What dost thou think, Simon? From whom do the kings of the earth receive tribute or customs; from their own sons, or from others?' And he said, 'From others.' Jesus said to him, 'The sons then are exempt. But that we may not give offense to them, go to the sea and cast a hook, and take the first fish that comes up. And opening its mouth thou wilt find a stater; take that and give it to them for me and for thee'" (Matt. 17:23–27). Jesus is the King's Son, by right exempt from all such burdens; by right, he and his followers should live as lords in his Father's land. Instead: Let us pay the temple money, that they have no grounds for complaint against us!

And again Jesus' reply to Herod in St. Luke (13:31–33). The words peal like an echo from long-sunken ages. They could have stood in Genesis, or in some saga of forgotten heroism: "Behold, I cast out devils and perform cures today and tomorrow, and the third day I am to end my course." The three days of our transitoriness, today, tomorrow and the third day! And then the terrible irony: "for it cannot be that a prophet perish outside Jerusalem."

Law from the abyss of the human heart: no one sent by God's love to his people shall die a natural death, and nowhere shall he die unnaturally but in the holy city, where the temple stands, the throne of the heavenly Monarch's glory! Do we begin to sense something of the dreadful mystery that overshadows the Lord? To be a prophet is to know the meaning behind all events, to interpret them from God's perspective. Jesus is the fulfillment of all prophetic being. He is the heir of human history, the all-knowing one, who bears everything that is in his heart, who receives it into his will and consummates it. It is his mission to bring human fate with its sin and need to completion; to explore the limitations resulting from the freedom given the little creature man and not trespassed upon by the omnipotent Creator because he desires that freedom. It is Jesus' task to recognize the wickedness and fearfulness that issue from such freedom, things that should not be, need not be, yet since they do exist, must be expiated.

Here in the ultimate, stands the pure supreme readiness of Jesus' love in that double sphere of possibility and necessity to which the ancients shudderingly referred as fate, and which we know to be the love of God. Knowing down to the very root, willing in all the clarity of his decision, the Lord's heart sets this inmost mystery in motion, launching what is known as redemption, the new beginning.

VI

MYSTERY
AND REVELATION

Between the second and third announcements of the coming passion stands the parable of the wealthy worldling:

"There was a certain rich man who used to clothe himself in purple and fine linen, and who feasted every day in splendid fashion. And there was a certain poor man, named Lazarus, who lay at his gate, covered with sores, and longing to be filled with the crumbs that fell from the rich man's table; even the dogs would come and lick his sores. And it came to pass that the poor man died and was borne away by the angels into Abraham's bosom; but the rich man also died and was buried in hell. And lifting up his eyes, being in torments, he saw Abraham afar off and Lazarus in his bosom. And he cried out and said, 'Father Abraham, have pity on me, and send Lazarus to dip the tip of his finger in water and cool my tongue, for I am tormented in this flame.'

"But Abraham said to him, 'Son, remember that thou in thy lifetime hast received good things, and Lazarus in like manner evil things; but now here he is comforted whereas thou art tormented. And besides all that, between us and you a great gulf is fixed, so that they who wish to pass over from this side to you cannot, and they cannot cross from your side to us'" (Luke 16:19–26).

The account is thought-provoking. Above all, we are struck by the warning that eternity is being prepared now, in time. In these fleeting days of our worldly existence we are deciding our eternal existence. "I must do the works of him who sent me while it is day; night is coming, when no one can work" (John 9:4). Both beggar and worldling live forever; not simply as a continuation of their former lives, but as those lives are evaluated by God, once and forever. Decisive here was that the one through a life of privation and misery still held fast to God, whereas the other enjoyed himself and forgot both God and mercy.

But there is more to it than this, as the final sentences reveal. The damned one begs Abraham to send Lazarus to his brothers to warn them to think of their own hereafter. Abraham replies: for this they have Moses and the prophets: in other words, revelation as it stands in Holy Scripture and is taught daily. That will not help, pleads the other; what is read from Scripture or preached in the temple no longer has the power to impress. But should eternity itself in the form of a dead man confront them, they would take heed. But Abraham only remarks: If they do not heed Scripture and the teachings of the faith, they would also be unimpressed should someone return from death to admonish them. And we are reminded of that other Lazarus who actually made the dreadful return and lived among just such demanders of flesh and blood proof. And the result? They assemble the high council, who declares the sign dangerous to the welfare of the people and debates how it would best put Lazarus out of the way! (John 12:10–11). This leads us to the question: How *can* the reality of God make itself known to men? Is it easier for some people to grasp revelation than for others?

Why doesn't God speak to us himself, since he upholds and transfuses all being? Why must we depend on printed and spoken matter, on teachers and preachers? Why doesn't he himself stir my conscience into knowing where I stand with him? Why doesn't he let me sample the costliness of his promise with my whole sensitive being, then the clarity which brings peace and is the goal of everything would be mine? It is difficult to say: ultimately the reply will be: Because it is not God's will. Still, we can guess a little.

Certainly, God speaks through everything and to everything, also to me. Everything that is reveals him; everything that happens is an effect of his guidance and somehow affects the conscience; he *is* palpable at the core of me. But all this remains vague. It is not enough to live by, not to live as I feel I must. It is ambiguous and needs the ultimate clarification that can come only through the word of God, and this he does not speak to everyone.

Specific revelation of reality and God's will comes to me only through people. Divine Providence selects an individual with whom he communicates directly. The chosen one pays dearly for the grace; we have only to think of what has been said of the lot of prophet and apostle. In him we see what it means to stand in immediate contact with the word of God: how uncompromisingly it isolates him from the rest of humanity, strips him of the ordinary joys of existence. The one who has received the call passes it on to the next. "Thus speaketh the Lord God!" This is the way God has chosen to convey his will to us, and he who wants to understand, will. More; he will soon realize that this method of divine communication is the only one suitable to human nature. The idea that everyone is strong enough to bear immediate contact with God is false, and conceivable only by an age that has forgotten what it means to stand in the direct ray of divine power, that substitutes sentimental religious 'experience' for the overwhelming reality of God's presence. To claim that everyone could and should be exposed to that reality is sacrilegious. God is holy and speaks specifically only through his messengers. He who refuses to accept him through his chosen speaker, who insists on hearing his voice directly, shows that he either does not know or will not admit who God is, and who he himself.

We can also put it this way: God has established both man's essence and his salvation on faith. Faith, however, seems to come into the full power of its intransigence and purity only when applied to one sent by God. He who insists on hearing God himself shows that what he really desires is not to believe, but to know; not to obey, but to react to his own experience. It is entirely fitting and proper that man hear his God through his fellow men, for all lives are inextricably interwoven into the one great community of human existence. No one life is self-sufficient. My existence draws on the core of my being but simultaneously on others in order to exist. Plant-like, we sprout from our own seed, but we grow by feeding upon other growth. In the same way we arrive at truth through personal recognition; the 'ingredients' which go into that recognition, how-ever, are brought us by others. Man is humanity's way to life—and of course, to death. Man is humanity's way to God, and it befits us that God's word personally penetrate each of our hearts, but that it be brought to us by others. God's word through the lips of man: that is the law of our religious life. It demands humility, obedience, docility. At the same time, it is reassuring, this sharing of experi-ence, for the prophet does not simply pronounce words; he voices something that has passed through his own life. He, the called one, stands behind his words; his conviction carries them; on his faith the faith of the others is kindled. This is not essential, for the divine word exists in its own God-given power, independent of the private faith or doubt of the speaker. Still the speaker's faith is a help for the hearer.

In Christ, the living God speaks from our midst. Not as science speaks or cold law. God's Son does not write his message on the walls of validity, demanding that we read and obey. His thought is formed in his human intellect, experienced in his own heart, and sustained by his love. He is consumed by "the zeal" for his Father's house and burns for love of the Father's will. He is the living Word, and from his holy life at once human and divine flies the spark that lights the flame of our own faith.

To this day Christian faith glows from the warmth, security and love of truth which burned in Jesus' soul. The vitality of the divine word in him is other than that which so stirred the prophets. The prophet cried: Thus speaks the Lord God! Jesus says: But *I* say unto you . . . His word does not serve, it *is;* creative, activating force. The ardor with which Jesus lives the word he speaks, gives it its vital fire. We believe in Christian teaching as it was brought to us, warm from the lips of the Lord. Were we to attempt to isolate his word from the living person behind it, taking it for itself, it would no longer be the word God meant. Were we to apply a single statement of his directly, from "God" to hearer, it would cease to be Christian. Christ is not only Messenger, but also Message, "the Word" that we believe. What he says is what it is only because he says it; the Speaker whose speech is an act of self-revelation.

Good. But then the question returns, more pressing than ever: Why aren't we permitted to warm ourselves in Christ's fire? Why mayn't we hear his message from him? Since he is the living truth of God, corporeal Epiphany of the hidden Creator, why aren't we permitted to see him for ourselves? Weren't the men and women of his day incomparably more privileged than we? What wouldn't we give to hear the accents of his voice, to see him cross a street? What immeasurable assurance it would be to catch his eye and feel his power surge through us, to know with every cell of our being who he is? Why isn't this granted us? We must know.

Did those who saw him really have an advantage over us? Was "hearing" then fundamentally different from what it is today? One thing makes us pause: if it was so advantageous to personal faith to see the Lord, why did those of his day fail to believe? For with the exception of a very small group (possibly no larger than that of his mother, the two Marys and John) they did fail! Apparently then, it is erroneous to think that Jesus' bodily presence necessarily overcame resistance to belief. It is equally erroneous to think that immediate enthusiasm can replace the real essentials of faith: obedience, effort, responsibility. What would God's visible light make easier, the decision? The quitting of self for the things of God? Obedience? Surrender of soul? He who wishes to facilitate such things risks underestimating the earnestness of faith; he is prone to seek refuge from obedience in sensational religious 'experience.' Probably he also has false conception of what divine light itself is, humanly enough imagining it as an overpowering sensation straight from the realm of the religious rather than from that of simple Christian faith. If we suppose that direct contact with Jesus would have automatically eliminated the intrinsic risk and struggle that are the elements of genuine faith, we are far from comprehending the Master of souls! Never would he have permitted this. The person swept to him on a wave of enthusiasm would have to stand his test later. The unavoidable hour would surely come in which he would be forced to a fresh decision—without benefit of transport, in which he too would have to take the step from the 'direct experience of Jesus' to faith in Jesus Christ, the incarnate Word and Messenger of God. Isn't this precisely what was demanded of the Apostles at the Lord's death, then at his Resurrection, and above all, at Pentecost?

What then *is* really the Incarnation? It is the fulfillment of revelation, in which the unknown God makes himself known, the remote God suddenly steps into human history. Incarnation is literally what the word says: the living, actual Word of God, the *Logos,* Son in whom all the mystery of the Father is gathered, becomes man through the Holy Ghost. Do we see the essential now? *Becomes man*—not "enters into" a man. The Heavenly One is translated to the earthly scene; the Remote One becomes temporal reality. "And he who sees me" need no longer guess; he "sees him who sent me" (John 12:45). The Hidden One steps out into the open in human form, identifying himself with the form, content and sensory realm of the Word made man. Here is no place for dialectics which see in Jesus a mere human suddenly, at a whim of God's, transformed into the living No and Nevertheless of the divine Word. Such 'logic' is only a clumsy attempt to veil a secret disbelief: Christ was not really God's word in history; he couldn't have been literally God incarnate! No. Truth needs no mental acrobatics. He who hears Jesus' word hears God. Understanding is another question; it is possible to "hear, but not understand" (Mark 4:12).

Incarnation: the *"deus absconditus,"* hidden God revealed in flesh and blood—strange how this very self-revelation hides him from us! How difficult it is to accept as God's living messenger, as the long-awaited Messiah, this Son of Man whom we see eating, drinking, walking the streets; who is threatened by countless enemies; who *suffers.* How am I to recognize in this transient, already doomed figure the ultimate measure of being for all ages?

God speaking human words from human lips, speaking from a human destiny, opens eternal doors to us. To enter them is what is known as faith; it is to know too, who God really is: not the "absolute" but—let us dare the word—the "human" God. Precisely here lies our chief difficulty, in his humanity. God cannot be so! we protest. His flesh and blood is simultaneously revelation and veil. The tangible erects walls; that which makes revelation what it is also shapes our "stumbling block."

We know only too well how difficult it is to hear Christ solely through his messengers. And not only through those first inspired ones who had been his witnesses and whose words bore the power of the Holy Spirit, but through messengers of messengers, thousandfold removed. Spokesmen, moreover, who are not always swept along by their own vital conviction, sometimes indeed little more than hired teachers. We know what an added difficulty it is that the sacred word has been worked over and over by the centuries, and not without endless controversy and hatred and resistance; that it has been dulled by usage, lamed by indifference, abused by greed and the thirst for power. On the other hand, it is a help to know that so many have given their minds and lives to it; that two thousand years of history have lived in it; that so much humanity vibrates in the divine tidings.

Doesn't Christian community mean helping one another to understand God's word? Haven't we all known some person who has made Christ's message clearer to us, has taught us to pattern our lives more truly after his? Who is not grateful to some personage of the past, whether a great mind or a great saint or anyone who has taken his faith seriously?

When we reflect a little we begin to wonder whether Christ's contemporaries really had such an advantage over us? Was faith easier when Jesus wandered through Galilee, or after Pentecost when St. Paul preached in the cities, or during the persecutions, when the endurance of the martyrs blazed triumphantly, or in the centuries of the great saints of the middle ages, or now? A hundred years or five hundred, how much do they affect the eternal truth of God? To believe means to grasp what is revealed by the spoken word, the historical figure—through the veil that covers them both. The initial revelation must have been wonderfully powerful; but often insurmountable too the question: who is that man? Then the first barrier fell, barrier of God as a contemporary. After that he could be seen and interpreted only in retrospect, through the glowing experience of apostles stirred by the power of the Spirit. But the more this indirect revelation spread, the thicker, simultaneously, grew its veil, woven of the human weaknesses of its messengers and the distortions and abuses of human history. The problem of the later-comers, that of excavating the living Son of God from sermon, book and example, from the sacred measures of divine worship, from work of art, pious practice, custom and symbol, is difficult, certainly, but probably not more difficult than that of recognizing him in the son of a carpenter.

And the conclusion? Aren't we almost forced to conclude that faith's situation remains essentially the same? Always both are present: what reveals and what veils. Always the demands remain the same: that our desire for salvation meet the desire for our salvation voiced in the sacred word. Naturally, in the course of time much changes; at one period a specific obligation is easier, at another more difficult; but the essential demand remains unchanged: the hearer must discard the familiar ground of human experience and take the plunge into the unknown. Always he must lose his life in order to find it (Matt. 10:39). How this happens in each individual instance it is impossible to say. Fundamentally there is but one essential requirement: readiness on the part of the hearer to receive revelation. Something in him must keep constant watch, listening, straining for the reply to his unceasing *qui vive?* No longer may he find full satisfaction in this world; he must constantly be on the look-out for signs of the other. Then when one day that other actually presents itself, he will recognize it. The form of one approaching through a fog is at first ambiguous. It can be almost anyone. Only two will know him: he who loves him and he who hates him. God preserve us from the sharpsightedness that comes from hell. Let us keep to the keen perception of love, even if it is only that of beginning love; keep our desire to love one day with heart and soul for the coming of God's Son into our lives. Then when he does come, we shall recognize him. There is no rule for the manner of his coming, nor for the hour. It may be that the profoundest presentation has nothing to say to us, whereas a simple admonition or the magnanimity of a human heart may bring light. It can come instantly, but it may take years of waiting and perseverance in obscurity. Only persevere in the truth! It is better to continue to bear uncertainty, than to talk oneself into a decision that has no permanence. Genuine readiness already contains the seed of faith; untruth, on the other hand, that self-deception that pretends to views it does not really hold, and the violence with which we force ourselves to a creed which does not root in the heart, already contain the seeds of destruction.

This does not mean that doubts are already the beginning of a fall from faith. Questions can always arise to trouble us, particularly as they are usually afflictions of the heart that have assumed intellectual form. As long as our faith has not yet passed over to the beatific vision it will be constantly challenged—particularly in the glare of this over-enlightened all-destructive age, bare of vision and unwarmed by the glow of experience, where it can survive only by the sheer force of fidelity. Moreover, there are profound questions that return after every supposed solution, mysteries whose intrinsic meanings, not solved but lived, increasingly clarify the faith of those who live them.

VII

JUSTICE AND THAT
WHICH SURPASSES IT

Following the custom of the Orient, Jesus often employed parables, that favorite form of speech among peoples who think figuratively. The parable stimulates the imagination, which in turn illumines the sense behind the suggested image. However, that sense is not necessarily univocal, as is the abstract teaching, but complexly interwoven into life and the situation of the moment. Vital truth speaks here in a homophony of many voices, theme and accompaniment. In this form it is flexible, now stressing one note, now another. Thus the parable is a fluctuating, mobile thing and difficult to pin down. In a barren hour it remains dumb; indeed, it may even be an obstacle to understanding, serving that dark mystery touched upon in Matthew thirteen: "Hearing you will hear, but not understand; and seeing you will see, but not perceive."

We have heard most of the parables of the New Testament many times, usually so enveloped in the Lord's authority that unconsciously we accept them without giving much thought to our personal reactions. This one manifestly contains a complicated, contrary meaning, that must work itself out 'dramatically' in word and reaction, sense and opposing sense. Only in the clash of thesis and antithesis, is its full clarity released. Two often heard but by no means simple parables are those of the owner of the vineyard and the prodigal son, the latter to be found in Luke fifteen. A man has two sons. One day the younger demands his heritage (possibly from the maternal side). He is of age, and the father is forced to comply. The young man goes abroad with the money and in a short time has squandered it entirely. Reduced to bitter poverty and unable to find better employment, he gratefully accepts the job of swineherd on the estate of a wealthy landowner. (We must not overlook the odium Hebrews attached to this service, considering the animals unclean also from a religious point of view.) His lot is such a poor one, that the young man often begrudges the animals their coarse fare, and gradually he realizes what folly it was to leave home, where even his father's hired men lived better than he, for apparently his father is a just man, and takes proper care of those who work for him. Homesick and conscious of having failed his father as well as himself, he decides to return home and ask to serve there as a field-hand, since he has forfeited his right to be treated as a son. But upon his return he is received in a manner contrary to all expectations. His father hurries to meet him, replying to his words of self-condemnation with signs of love, and showering him with the attentions he would lavish upon an honored guest. Soon the whole house rings with rejoicing. When the elder son returns from the field and demands the reason for the festivity, he is told, and accordingly, is filled with indignation. He points out to his father how loyally he has served him, how little appreciated he has been, and how the parental treatment of the wastrel cries to heaven for justice.

"But he said to him, 'Son, thou art always with me, and all that is mine is thine; but we were bound to make merry and rejoice, for this thy brother was dead, and has come to life; he was lost, and is found.' "

How does the incident affect us? If we are not influenced by the moral pointed out by sermon and instruction, unconsciously we agree with the elder brother. Possibly he is venting an old grievance. Perhaps the younger son was a talented, charming person who stole the favor of all he met. He was imaginative and high-spirited, quick to receive and quick to give. Bored by the tedious labor at home he had left it to seek adventure. Probably the older son was the exact opposite: serious and conscientious. Perhaps he was not able to express himself well, was awkward and abrupt in his manner, so that he was constantly put in the shade by his younger brother, who was everybody's favorite. Yet it was the elder son who had to bear the responsibility and the main burden of the estate. The father had probably never thought of pleasing this undemonstrative, sober off-spring who seemed so entirely absorbed by his work, and he never would have asked for favors, whereas the younger one took every-thing that came his way as light-heartedly as he scattered gifts. How otherwise are we to explain the bitterness of the complaint that not even the smallest animal was ever slaughtered for his pleasure and that of his friends? When his younger brother set out into the world with half of their heritage, he left behind him one heart filled with rancor and disdain. Now the spoiled profligate is back, penniless, only to be received like a prince! The father's reply to his eldest's objections fails to impress.

But what if the father had agreed with him? If he had said to the homecomer: Go your way! You've had what you wanted! Then jus-tice would have been restored. The older brother would have been satisfied. Or would he? Completely? If he was a good man, certainly not. The sight of his brother would have robbed his peace. Contrary to all feeling of "justice" a not to be stilled small voice would have insisted that somehow he had missed a sacred opportunity.

Justice is good. It is the foundation of existence. But there is something higher than justice, the bountiful widening of the heart to mercy. Justice is clear, but one step further and it becomes cold. Mercy is genuine, heartfelt; when backed by character, it warms and redeems. Justice regulates, orders existence; mercy creates. Justice satisfies the mind that all is as it should be, but from mercy leaps the joy of creative life. That is why it is written that heaven rejoices more over one sinner who does penance than over a hundred just who have no need of it. High above all the stupidity and evil of mankind arches the spacious dome of mercy. When justice enters here insisting on its narrow rights it becomes repugnant. We catch the undertone in the gently disdainful words about the ninety-nine "just"; that heap of righteousness so excellent and respectable, is incomparably less than one penitent over whom the angels can rejoice (Luke 15:7).

If we look closely we begin to wonder whether perhaps justice's protest isn't in reality directed against penance. Does the person stiff with justice really want the sinner converted? Doesn't he somehow feel that he is thus escaping his just deserts, endangering the existent order? Wouldn't he prefer to see him remain locked in sin and forced to bear the consequences? Perhaps he considers the return to grace a more or less underhanded trick played at the expense of justice. What would things come to if everyone like that scamp there, after wasting half a fortune, extricated himself from the affair by turning virtuous! And actually, the true conversion does break the bounds of mere justice. It is a creative new beginning—in God, as theology teaches us, since the sinner alone and unaided is incapable of true repentance. According to the logic of evil, sin produces blindness, which leads to fresh sin, which in turn leads to deeper blindness, ultimately ending in complete darkness and death. Conversion breaks this vicious circle of cause and effect, and is thus already grace. If there is seraphic joy in heaven over the conversion of a single sinner, it is because that conversion is a victory of grace. To the so-called pure sense of justice, conversion is a scandal. For justice runs the risk of not being able to see beyond its borders to the realm of love and creative liberty where the renascent forces of the human heart and divine grace are at home. Woe to him who insists on living in mere justice! Woe to the world in which justice alone reigned!

But the truth is even stranger than this. Justice itself would suffocate if left isolated. What does justice consist of? Obviously, of giving each his due. It is not universal equality, but a vital order, taking into consideration the diversity of people and things. But to know what a man really deserves, one would have to be able to see to the bottom of his soul. Not having this capacity, if I wish to avoid new injustice, I can only give him the benefit of the doubt and regard him with the eyes of love. Only in the light and freedom created by love can the one under examination unfold to his full stature. Justice is unable to fulfill itself through its own strength; it needs the conditions created by love to come into its own. *Summum jus, summa injuria* is the old maxim: Justice supreme may be supreme injustice.

Thus the return of the younger son introduces an hour of destiny for his older brother. The parable adds nothing to the description of the incident, but it is self-evident that he is faced with a fundamental decision: if he insists upon justice only, he will force himself into a position of narrowness that will curtail his own liberty of heart and spirit. On the other hand, if he accepts the truth in his father's words, he will understand the true nature of conversion and pardon, and enter into the kingdom of creative freedom that lies above justice.

This parable was probably inspired by an actual incident. Perhaps Jesus himself had been touched by the good intentions of a "sinner," and drawing him to him, had scandalized the just. It might have been Zacheus, who like all publicans, was considered an enemy of the people, and the parable Jesus' reply to the general indignation against him.

A similar incident must have suggested the parable of the landed proprietor and the day laborers (Matt. 20:1–15). Early in the morning the owner goes to the market-place where the unemployed gather, and hires several men to work in his vineyards for the agreed wage of a denarius a day. In the course of the day he revisits the spot several times, each time engaging additional laborers, whom he promises a suitable wage. In the evening he pays off his hirelings, giving each a denarius—also the late arrivals. Seeing this, those who had come earlier hope for advantageous treatment, and disappointed to receive the same wage as the others, protest. But the landowner only replies: Friend, I do you no wrong. Did we not agree on one silverpiece? Take what is yours and go! I shall pay this late-comer as I see fit: the same to you. "Have I not a right to do what I choose? Or art thou envious because I am generous?" (Matt. 20:13–15).

Again our first reaction is, they are right to protest! Perhaps not before the law, for they will certainly receive only what was promised them, but simply for the sake of justice. For if those who have worked but a few hours receive the same as those who have toiled all day, their wage is devalued. And the landowner's answer is anything but placating: Can't I do with my money as I please? No, you cannot! There is a law concerning your money and your power, the law of justice. You and your property are subject to this higher law, and we accuse you before it!

Nevertheless, the proprietor's unwelcome reply hits the nail on the head. We begin to understand when we realize that he represents God. The parable means simply this: He who distributes work and wage and the various destinies of men is the Lord of all existence, God. He is the Creator, the Omnipotent, the Primal One. Everything that is, is his. There is no law higher than he. His decision is always valid. Do we agree? Sincerely? No. Even from God we demand justice. We expect his omnipotence to be curbed by his justice. This expectation is not irreligious. There is a whole book in the Bible on the self-assertion of justice in the face of God: the Book of Job. Job knows he has not sinned, at least not so as to have deserved anything like the terrible afflictions that have been sent him. Therefore he sees himself a victim of injustice. Job's friends appoint themselves his judges and declare that he must have sinned, for such misfortune can only be punishment. However, the palaver comes to a sudden end; they are disdainfully silenced by God himself, who personally appears to Job, wrapped in the mantle of living mystery, whereupon all discussion ceases. What does this mean? That we attempt to call God to order in the name of justice only as long as we are intrinsically ignorant of who he is. As soon as the essence of his holy being even begins to dawn on us, our objections wither away. For everything comes from God, has its roots in God. Justice is not a law superior to everything, God included, God *is* justice. As soon as justice ceases to be considered a thing in itself, it becomes a 'crystallization' of the living, divine essence. Never can it be an isolated platform from which man can confront his God; he who stands on its stands 'within' God, and must learn from him who is more than justice what living justice means.

All this cannot be stated abstractly: that God not only can but may do as he likes with his 'money'; that what he does is without exception or reservation good and just, regardless of how human heart or human head may react. More: that justice itself begins to exist truly only when rooted in divine volition; that it is none other than the expression of God's sovereign will, and comprehensible only in the degree that the believer approaches the God of whom these things are true.

The parable culminates in the words: "Or art thou envious because I am generous?" Divine liberty surpassing all judgment, fact that there is no higher instance to invoke; the whole is the mystery of God's goodness, of his bounty and love. The New Testament has another word for it: grace. Man is warned against locking himself in justice rather than opening his heart to the goodness of divine reason and action; he is told to surrender to grace, which is higher than justice, if he would be free.

A curious thing happens to the spokesman of justice in this parable. He is accused of envy. What a reply to one convinced that he has suffered an injustice! Instead of hearing as he expected, that untamperable right will be restored, he must learn that his real motive for intervening was inferior! Yet if we accept Scripture as God's holy word, we learn a strange rule about human nature: that when it becomes necessary to invoke justice, that irreproachable value and crystalline motive, almost always something is rotten in Denmark. Too often 'justice' is used as a mask for quite different things.

Human justice is highly problematical. It is something man should strive for but not lean upon. Perhaps we come closest to the true sense of the New Testament if we say that genuine justice is not the beginning but the end, and that the other justice so pompously displayed as the fundament of morality is a dubious thing. True justice is the fruit of bounty, and practicable by man only after he has been initiated into the school of divine love where he has learned to see people as they really are, himself included. Before one can be just, one must learn to *love*.

VIII

Unless You Become
as Little Children

A
t that hour the disciples came to Jesus, saying, 'Who then is greatest in the kingdom of heaven?' And Jesus called a little child to him, set him in their midst, and said, 'Amen I say to you, unless you turn and become like little children, you will not enter into the kingdom of heaven. Whoever, therefore, humbles himself as this little child, he is the greatest in the kingdom of heaven.' "

Here we catch a glimpse of the daily life that was lived around Jesus, with its human and all too human frailties. We also see how spontaneously, on the spur of the moment as it were, those teachings sprang into being which were to become valid for all times. The disciples are jealous of each other, anxious to secure their positions in the coming kingdom, which for them, though divine, is still inconceivable without the trappings of human rank and glory. St. Mark brings this out even more sharply: "And they came to Capharnaum. When he was at home, he asked them, 'What were you arguing about on the way?' But they kept silence, for on the way they had discussed with one another which of them was the greatest. And sitting down, he called the Twelve and said to them, 'If any man wishes to be first, he shall be last of all, and servant of all' " (see Mark 9:33–37).

Then in the twentieth chapter of Matthew we read the incident of the mother of the Zebedee sons, who shamelessly tries to extract from Jesus the promise that in the new kingdom her boys will sit upon his left and right! The disciples are conscious of their personal worth, and wish to be assured that it will be properly recognized and rewarded. The one has come to Jesus sooner than the others; a second is especially industrious, while a third enjoys high esteem in his native village. All are indignant when relatives intervene and brazenly attempt to take Jesus by surprise. In the heated exchange of words that follows, one thought is uppermost: who will be greatest in the kingdom? However, behind this thoroughly terrestrial question lurks a deeper one: What *is* the measuring-rod of value in paradise?

Jesus replies with a demonstration that in Mark's text is rendered with great precision: the Lord fetches a child, leads it into their midst, and seating himself, puts his arm around it: Look, you wrangling, self-interested, grown-ups here is the opposite of the lot of you! This child can teach you how to evaluate and behave! God's kingdom is not like the world's, where some command and some obey, where there are quick ones and slow ones, astute and stupid, those who succeed and those who fail. There it is the contrary! Jesus' jubilant words upon his apostles' return from their wonderfully fruitful missions suggests this same idea of complete revaluation: "I praise thee, Father, Lord of heaven and earth, that thou didst hide these things from the wise and the prudent, and didst reveal them to little ones" (Matt. 11:25–26). St. Paul is later to reiterate the same idea in his first Corinthian epistle: "For consider your own call, brethren; that there were not many wise according to the flesh, not many mighty, not many noble. But the foolish things of the world has God chosen to put to shame the 'wise,' and the weak things of the world has God chosen to put to shame the strong" (1:27).

In the child, life begins again with all its primeval freshness, regardless of the adult already installed and his adaptive measures. Thus in spite of natural affection, there is often a trace of secret, unconscious resentment in the attitude of the grown-up towards the child. This is why the picture is such a powerful one: not only does it impress itself upon the eye, it touches a vital nerve deep in our consciousness.

Ever since, the word about the necessity of rebecoming a little child has played an important role; it has been set up as the standard of Christian being, and rightly so. We must admit, however, that from this same source something weak and adolescent has crept into the Christian attitude: a dependency that is offensive. What then does Jesus mean when he sets up the child as model? If we read the full texts carefully, we see in them three distinct ideas.

One of them is in the words: "And whoever receives one such little child for my sake, receives me." To receive means to accept, to make room for, to respect. Unconsciously we reserve such regard only for the person who is able to prove himself; who accomplishes something, is useful and important. The child can prove nothing. It is only a beginning, has not yet accomplished anything; it is still only a hope. The child cannot force the adult to take it seriously. Real people are the grown-ups; the child counts only as a fraction. This opinion is not to be found solely among stern realists and egotists, but also—indeed often to a greater extent—among affectionate, motherly or pedagogic types; the form it takes here is that of excessive protectiveness. The usual attitude of the adult toward the child is one of either friendly or unfriendly disregard all too evident in the forced, playful tone which he feels obliged to assume toward the young one. To this Jesus says: You do not receive the child because it cannot enforce respect. For you it is unimportant. But let me tell you, wherever there is something defenseless, there am I! A divine chivalry protects that which is unable to protect itself and declares: *I* stand behind it!

Now the child moves in a completely different light. It is freed from the pot-pourri of genealogical, economic influences; from the simultaneous pride and envy, desire for self-expression and instinctive affection known as 'love of child,' and given its own intrinsic dignity as a potential Christian. Christ has said: *I* take it seriously— seriously enough to give my life for it. What you do to a child, you do to me!

The second thought: "But whoever causes one of these little ones who believe in me to sin, it were better for him to have a great millstone hung around his neck, and to be drowned in the depths of the sea." And again: "See that you do not despise one of these little ones; for I tell you, their angels in heaven always behold the face of my Father."

The child cannot compete with the ableness, experience, greater knowledge of the adult, and is defenseless when a grown-up wickedly poisons its mind, confuses its conceptions of right and wrong, plays upon its helpless senses, and destroys its natural modesty or reverence. In other words, the child is utterly at the mercy of the unscrupulous adult, whom Jesus warns: Beware! Where you see only a weak creature is, in reality, a divine mystery as delicate as it is holy. He who lays impious hands upon it does something so terrible that it would be better for him to have been put out of the way before like a dangerous animal.

This is one of the few texts in the Bible in which the guardian angels are mentioned, those protectors God has given man to watch over that which is holy in him. In the course of time the picture of the guardian angel has also been spoiled, as has so much that is great and beautiful in revelation. Out of the angel has grown a kind of governess who keeps children from falling off bridges or being bitten by snakes. The powerful creature of the Scriptures has degenerated into a sentimental, if not ambiguous picture-postcard figure. In reality, the angel is God's earliest creature, one of such insupportable majesty and power that when he appears to men his first word is: "Do not be afraid!" He himself gives the power to bear his presence. Concern for the welfare of the soul in his charge is shared between him and God; he protects it through error, pain and death. And now Christ says: You who would deflower the natural holiness of a child, beware! Behind him stands his angel, and behind him, God! When you harm a child, you make yourself a fearful enemy. He will keep silence; you will notice nothing at the time; but one day you will realize the immortal dreadfulness of the hour in which he became your enemy. Here in Jesus' words shines the sacred dignity of vulnerability.

And then the third and final thought: "Amen I say to you, unless you turn and become like little children, you will not enter into the kingdom of heaven." This then the prerequisite of heaven: child-likeness.

Yet what terrible abuse the word has suffered! What sentimentality, silliness, oppressiveness, what human and religious mediocrity have fed upon it! What weakness and dependency have excused themselves as "childlike"! What inability to associate with independent and mature people has referred itself to this adjective! It is high time to look closer at this word of the Lord!

What is it that the child has which the adult, in Jesus' eyes, so sadly lacks? What norm is this by which one's very suitability for heaven is measured? Certainly not childish charm; that would be a lyricism, something Jesus had nothing to do with. Innocence perhaps? But the child is not innocent. The Bible is much too realistic to call a child innocent. It knows human nature, and that even the one-day-old infant is a carrier of evil. And the small child? Already it contains all the ingredients of wrong-doing—to be sure, mainly dormant, though often astonishingly awake and active. No serious pedagogue can claim that children are innocent. The "innocent child" is an invention of grown-ups eager to stake a sentimental claim to the vanished purity of their own childhood.

If neither its charm nor its purity, what is it then that Jesus praises in the child? Apparently the exact opposite of the chief (and negative) characteristic of maturity. The grown-up seeks security, and in the process, becomes sly and hard. He is afraid, and fear abases. The child, on the other hand, does not yet have the instinct of self-preservation—at least not nearly so strongly; he lives in a world of unruffled trust. This attitude is no credit to him, for it springs from ignorance rather than virtue; nevertheless, it is there, and engenders an unconscious courage toward existence.

The adult has aims toward which he selects and applies his talents. He sees everything with an eye to its usefulness, thereby rendering everything unfree. He has intentions, and nothing so hampers existence, altering it for the worse, as these, which trammel action and falsify vision. The child has no intentions. (This is, of course, exaggerated; of course it has intentions too, as well as fear and everything else that grown-ups have, for it begins to grow up with its first breath.) Strictly speaking, the child too desires this and that; but for Jesus' purpose here, which is to illustrate an idea rather than demonstrate psychology, it is correct to say: the child meets reality as it is, with simple acceptance. Therefore in his presence things can move freely; he permits them to be themselves.

In the adult there is much unnaturalness. He does not leave life alone, but constantly tries to improve it. The result is what is known as culture and has many precious values, but values bought with artificiality and distortion. Between man and man, heart and heart, person and thing, everywhere loom intermediates, shutting out reality. Everywhere considerations, precautions break life's spontaneous *élan*. This, that and the other natural reaction "is simply not done"; the phrase stands at every walk of life, an invulnerable policeman, guarding it from itself. The child is completely natural. It says what it thinks—often to the embarrassment of the adults—and shows what it feels; hence it is considered ill-mannered. Manners, for the most part, conceal feelings rather than cultivate selflessness, understanding and love. The good manners of adults are heavy with dishonesty and guilt. By contrast, the child is simple and candid. This is due to no virtue on its part, but to the fact that it does not yet feel the inhibitions that make it so difficult for the adult to be honest. The child's honesty is untried, but it is there, a living reprimand.

The adult is self-centered; he is constantly examining, testing, judging himself. Herein lies the earnestness of life, which consists of a feeling of responsibility, conscious living. The immediacy of things and people is broken in the grown-up world, for the adult is constantly projecting himself between them and him. The child does not reflect. His life moves outside himself. He is open to the world and everything in it. Unconsciously he stands straight and looks straight at things as they really are. Then comes the change; gradually his open doors close upon a room of reflection and self-assertion of which he is the center.

In the child's attitude toward life lies his humility: as Jesus says, he does not count himself for much. He does not drag his small ego into the foreground; his consciousness brims with objects, people, events—not himself. Thus his world is dominated by reality: that which is and really counts. The grown-ups' world is cluttered with unrealities: with formalities and illusions and substitutes, intermediaries and trivialities all taken with tremendous seriousness. The child, accustomed to dealing directly with things as they are, is surprised and confused by the hardness and narrowness he confronts in his elders.

Naturally, here too, we must guard against exaggeration. We must not substitute the romantic notion of childish innocence with a new romanticism. Nevertheless, roughly speaking, this is what Christ means by childlike; this is the attitude of heart whose lack he so deplores in adults.

Because the child is natural, open, without intentions or fear of failing to assert itself, it is receptive to the great, revolutionary ideas in Christ's teaching of the kingdom. The same teaching is met with reserve by the maturer listener. His cleverness condemns it as impossible; his caution warns him of the consequences; his self-esteem is soon up in arms; his hard grasp cannot let go. He has encysted himself in artificialities, and fearful for his brittle little world, he prefers not to understand. Fear has made his eyes blind, his ears deaf, his heart dull; as Jesus would say, he is over-mature.

The Jewish people, the Pharisees and Scribes and high priests, how 'grown-up' they are! The whole heritage of sin with its harshness and distortion looms at us. How old they are! Their memory reaches back more than one and a half millennia, back to Abraham—a historical consciousness not many nations can boast. Their wisdom is both divine gift and fruit of long human experience; knowledge, cleverness, correctness. They examine, weigh, differentiate, doubt; and when the Promised One comes and prophecy is fulfilled, their long history about to be crowned, they cling to the past with its human traditions, entrench themselves behind the Law and the temple, are sly, hard, blind—and their great hour passes them by. God's Messiah must perish at the hands of those who 'protect' his law. From his blood springs young Christianity, and Judaism remains prisoner of its hope in the coming of One who has already come!

The child is young. It has the simplicity of eye and heart which welcomes all that is new and great and salutary; it sees it for what it is, goes straight to it and enters in. This simplicity, *naturalis christianitas,* is the childlikeness to which the parable refers. Jesus means nothing sentimental or touching; neither sweet defenselessness nor gentle malleability. What he values is the child's clarity of vision; the ability to look up and out, to feel and accept reality without ulterior motives. Fundamentally, the attitude of the child is precisely the attitude suggested by the word "believer": the natural attitude of a faith which is open to all that comes from God and ready to accept the consequences. In other words, something great and holy, and clearly not to be had for the asking. Not for nothing does the text read: ". . . unless you turn and become as little children . . ." unless you outgrow maturity, turn back to the beginning and build from the ground up. . . . This is a long and difficult process.

The spiritual childhood Jesus means emanates from God's fatherhood. Everything comes to the child from its father and mother, is related somehow to them. They are everywhere, the origin, measure and order of all things. The adult soon distances himself from his parents; in their place stands the world, irreverent, disinterested or hostile. Once the parents have gone, everything becomes homeless. For the child of God a fatherly Someone is again omnipresent; to be sure, he must not be distorted to a super-projection of an earthly father, but must remain who he is, as he has revealed himself: God our Father and Lord Jesus Christ who helps us to accomplish his will.

The childlike mind is the one that sees the heavenly Father in everything that comes into his life. To do this requires a great effort: wisdom must be sucked from the naked continuation of cause and effect; love from the accidental. To do this sincerely is difficult. It is the "victory that overcomes the world" of which St. John speaks. To become a child in Christ's sense is to reach Christian maturity.

IX

CHRISTIAN MARRIAGE
AND VIRGINITY

A nd there came to him some Pharisees, testing him, and saying, 'Is it lawful for a man to put away his wife for any cause?' But he answered and said to them, 'Have you not read that the Creator, from the beginning, made them male and female, and said, *For this cause a man shall leave his father and mother, and cleave to his wife, and the two shall become one flesh?* Therefore now they are no longer two, but one flesh. What therefore God has joined together, let no man put asunder.' They said to him, 'Why then did Moses command to give a written notice of dismissal, and to put her away?' He said to them, 'Because Moses, by reason of the hardness of your heart, permitted you to put away your wives; but it was not so from the beginning. And I say to you, that whoever puts away his wife, except for immorality, and marries another, commits adultery; and he who marries a woman who has been put away commits adultery.'

"His disciples said to him, 'If the case of a man with his wife is so, it is not expedient to marry.' And he said, 'Not all can accept this teaching; but those to whom it has been given. For there are eunuchs who were born so from their mother's womb; and there are eunuchs who were made so by men; and there are eunuchs who have made themselves so for the sake of the kingdom of heaven. Let him accept it who can' " (Matt. 19:1–12).

These words of the Lord have regulated the most vital forces of human existence for almost two thousand years and they continue to do so. But before we go into them more closely, let us glance at the Speaker. In all reverence, let us ask what these life forces meant to him, Jesus, and what part women played in his own life. The question is important; not only for our understanding of Jesus' character, but also for that of his mission as the bringer of salvation.

The religious personalities we encounter in history differ widely from one another on this point. Some have held the interrelation of the sexes to be simply evil and have done all they could to suppress if not to eliminate it. Others have incorporated it into their religion, have even made it the peak of religious experience. For some the whole problem of sex does not seem to exist; it has been completely stifled or consumed. And again there are those who wage an unceasing war against it to the end of their lives. When we consider Jesus in the light of these possibilities, we see at once that none of them applies to him. His personal desires and behavior are untouched by any such relationship; an unheard of freedom pervades everything he is and does; freedom so complete that the question does not even arise save when for some particular reason it is artificially posed. In his attitude toward the sexes there is no trace of struggle: he neither fears sex, nor hates it, nor despises it, nor fights it. Nowhere do we find anything to suggest that it was necessary for him to overcome it. The question presents itself: was he perhaps insensitive to it—there are people who know neither struggle nor victory in this regard because they are by nature indifferent? Certainly not! Jesus' personality is aglow with a profound warmth and vitality. Everything about him is wonderfully alive and creative. With what deep interest and sympathy he approaches people! His love for them is not willed, or merely dutiful, it streams spontaneously. Love is the mainspring of his being. When he fetches the child to show his disciples which bearing of heart is most acceptable to heaven, he takes it in his arms. Though he is tired after a long day, he insists that the children be permitted to come to him for his blessing, and apparently they feel completely at home with him. His disciples were no mere porters of his ideas, but were personally dear to him: "But I have called you friends. . . ." The hours of farewell brim with love.

John occupies a particular place in the Master's heart: "Now one of his disciples, he whom Jesus loved, was reclining at Jesus' breast." It would hardly have been the first time. When the Lord announces that one of them will betray him, they are so stricken that they dare not ask directly who it will be, and Peter signals John to inquire for them: "He therefore, leaning back upon the bosom of Jesus, said to him, 'Lord, who is it?' " (John 15:15; 13:21–25).

In the eighth chapter of Luke we read of the loyal care of the women about him, whose motherliness he doubtless repays with gratitude and kindness. In John eleven we become acquainted with the sisters and brother in Bethany whom Jesus "loved": Martha and Mary and Lazarus. The description of the feast in the following chapter shows how much Mary, Lazarus' sister, means to him, whereas the mutual warmth of affection between him and Mary Magdalen is revealed in the divinely beautiful scene in the garden after the Resurrection:

Mary!

My Master!

Yet no one whose eyes and heart are in the right place could possibly discover in any of these expressions of human love a trace of secret relationship or of suppressed desire. They are the words and gestures of warm, clear freedom. When we reflect on the figure of Jesus, we realize that everything about him is richly alive, and that all his powers are centered in the heart. From here they stream Godward in an unbroken flow drawn back to earth by the constant thirst for the "meat" and "drink" from above which Jesus' inmost being requires. Thus the sacred demand and surrender of the Father's love circulates between heaven and earth, working through the Son in acts of love towards his fellow men. That such power is transmitted from God to Christ to man so utterly without violence, detour, or ruse, but simply and naturally; that everything between them is of diamond clarity—precisely this is the unique and unspeakable mystery of Jesus' person. He whose teaching hardly touches on the relationship of the sexes has had a calming, clarifying, mastering influence on the problem unequalled in human history. The physical life of Christians should not be regulated according to the lights of this or that Christian personality or pedagogue, however great or saintly, but as Jesus himself would have regulated it. We must confront all men, doctrines, epochs with Christ Himself, who in everything, the attitude towards sex included, is alone "the way, and the truth, and the life" (John 14:6; see also 4:32).

But let us return to our text. The situation here resembles others we have already examined. The Pharisees (theologians, lawyers, the most orthodox of the orthodox) ask: Is it lawful for a man to put away his wife for any reason? The question is as insincere as the one they ask concerning the "greatest commandment." They are not interested in learning from Jesus; they hope to trap him with a question. An extensive casuistry on the subject already existed: on the grounds considered acceptable; when they weighed more, when less; which exceptions were to be recognized and so on and so forth in an endless and intricate network of differentiation and differing. Jesus' enemies hope that he who lays too much stress on the things of Providence—on cleanness of heart and on love rather than the law—will trip in its meshes and fall, publicly. But with a single gesture the Lord brushes the whole web aside, simultaneously lifting the problem to an entirely different level. Why bicker about the circumstances suitable or unsuitable to the divorcing of a wife? A man should divorce his wife under no circumstances at all!

Marriage was founded by God. God created man and woman with an eye to their union. Proper marriage forms a unit which comes from God himself; its partners are so close, also spiritually, that they are "one flesh," and everything that affects the one affects the other. Man can separate only that which he has joined; what God has joined is beyond man's reach. Man is free to marry according to his own will; that much lies in his power. But once he enters the state of matrimony, he binds himself to God by a bond he no

longer controls. That is the divine character of marriage, which can
become a blissful, invulnerable mystery of strength and peace—also,
admittedly, a ponderous fate.

Indignant, Jesus' questioners reply: Then why Moses' divorce
law? Because of your hearts' hardness. Because you know neither
love nor the constancy of love. Because you are selfish and sensual,
and if Moses had not made concessions, you would have revolted
against God, who was too merciful to allow this.

We have already pointed out that Moses' Law was not an expression of original divine will (as this was revealed to Abraham, or in
Paradise); it is the expression of a new order of things given fallen
humanity by God after the original order of faith and freedom has
been made void.

The disciples are aghast. Perhaps they are reminded of Jesus'
words from the Sermon on the Mount: "You have heard that it was
said to the ancients, 'Thou shalt not commit adultery.' But I say to
you that anyone who even looks with lust at a woman has already
committed adultery with her in his heart" (Matt. 5:27). Then what
a terrible bond marriage is! To be tied to one woman without hope
of release, and the mere lustful glance at another already adultery! To
this Jesus replies as he so often has: Not everyone can grasp this, but
only he to whom understanding is given. It is another form of: "He
who has ears to hear, let him hear" (Matt. 11:15), and it means that
what he has just said cannot be taken purely intellectually, humanly,
juristically, but can be understood and obeyed only with the help of
faith and grace.

Then the thought continues: there is an order of things for those
to whom understanding is "given" that is even farther removed than
marriage from the usual conception of the relationship between
man and woman: renunciation of all sexual intercourse. And that
there be no misunderstanding, Jesus differentiates clearly between
the involuntary celibate whom either man or nature has rendered
physically unfit for marriage, and the voluntary celibate "for
heaven's sake." There exists an order and form of existence in which

a person directs the entire strength of his love to God and his kingdom, returning through these to his fellow men. (There is still less about such love in the law-books—mystery even greater than that of marriage; let him understand who can!)

Both orders stem from the same root. Both uphold a great mystery in the face of mere nature. Both are greater than what the average intellect can grasp. Neither can be simply traced back to the senses, or to the heart, or to the law of human society; both are truly recognizable only through revelation, acceptable only through faith, realizable only with the aid of grace.

It is said that Christian marriage is well suited to the nature of man. This can be correctly, but also incorrectly interpreted. It is appropriate to human nature, certainly, but to that nature as it was when it still bore the clear stamp of divine will, when it was directed Godwards and permeated with his grace. To men and women living in Paradise it would have been natural that marriage, which is contracted in the freedom and love of hearts obedient to God, must be unique and perpetual. But for fallen man? Is the life-long bond between two people today something we can accept as natural—not after long rationalizing, sober consideration of its ends and values, its physical and spiritual advantages, but spontaneously, in affirmation of our own experience?

Primarily, nature is drive: the ceaseless urge to preservation and multiplication of self. But man's fallen nature has become divided, insubordinate, discordant, dishonest with its conscience, blind, violent, inconstant and perishable, and consequently these characteristics color the relationship of any two people founded on it. The heart too is "natural," vouching only for what it knows: the evident, present moment—not for what lies buried deep in the subconscious or in the future. The great theme of world literature is that of the heart's fickleness.

Is it then natural for a person, and possible on the basis of his own strength, to remain bound life-long to another in the face of changing events and circumstances of his own development and that of his marriage partner? The bond made in unredeemed freedom is apt to be loosened by that same freedom.

And man's conscience? His judgment, power of decision, loyalty? Are they still honest and dependable? He who claims they are is shutting his eyes to the truth. And even if it were true that moral liberty is enough to guarantee a moral bond, marriage is so much more than this! Its sense lies over and above the flow of instinct, in the existence of something that comes from elsewhere: a unifying energy that is not only stable and "good," but also eternal and holy. That two human beings after the advent of sin into the world, variable as they are, confused, ready to revolt against the grace in their hearts, receive this sacred unity into their conscience and will; that this bond maintains and transfigures their community of life in spite of all its human shortcomings and tragedy—this is not "natural" but conceivable only to him who has faith.

Assuredly, indissoluble marriage conforms to the most profound sense of nature, and in the final analysis, even with all the destruction and suffering it sometimes entails, is the only practicable form of marriage. Even so, it is an over-simplification to call it "natural." We only risk distorting its sacred sense, and degrading it to an ethical or social institution. On the other hand, marriage comprehended in the light of faith and lived in grace *becomes* 'natural' in a much higher sense, as the fruit of grace, the harvest of faith. It is not beginning, but end of Christian effort, and must be formed by the same power as that behind virginity: renunciation made possible by faith. Christian marriage is constantly renewed by sacrifice. True, it fulfills and enriches the lives of both partners through fertility and a ripening of the personality beyond the limits possible for each individually; not only through the fullness and creativeness of the joint life, but also through the sacrifices necessary to weather the temptations of brute instinct, inconstancy, never-ending disappointments, moral crises, changes in fortune and the general demands of a common life.

Marriage is not only the fulfillment of the immediate love which brings a man and woman together, it is also the slow transfiguration of that love through the experiences of a common reality. Early love does not yet see this reality, for the pull of the heart and senses bewitches it. Only gradually does reality establish itself, when eyes have been opened to the shortcomings and failures revealed by everyday life. He who can accept the other then, as he really is, in spite of all disappointments, who can share the joys and plagues of daily life with him just as he has shared the great experience of early love, who can walk with him before God and with God's strength, will achieve second love, the real mystery of marriage. This is as far superior to first love as the mature person is to the child, as the self-conquering heart is to that which simply allows itself to be conquered. At the cost of much sacrifice and effort something great has come into being. Strength, profound loyalty, and a stout heart are necessary to avoid the illusions of passion, cowardice, selfishness and violence. But how many long-married couples succeed in breaking through to this really triumphant love? We well understand why Jesus' words about marriage pass on to the alternative: virginity. Here the quality of non-naturalness already present in marriage breaks out into the open.

Man is certainly not encouraged by nature to renounce his desire to love and be loved, to sacrifice his fecundity. Yet what Jesus means by virginity is not the mere uncomplaining acceptance of a physical handicap or the duress of harsh circumstance; that would be making a valiant but scant virtue of necessity. Jesus means the voluntary renunciation of marriage; not out of weakness, or indifference, or for any philosophy of life, but solely "for heaven's sake." Once more precisely: not because any 'religious duty' commands it, but because it is a unique opportunity of becoming the participant of an immeasurable love offered by God to anyone who desires to belong to him entirely. Today with psychology turning its beam upon the hidden root and background of all human behavior, it is necessary to mention something further.

One might object that Christian virginity was simply a transplanting of the object of affections; that often for very complex reasons a human being unable to attain his natural partner seeks him in the sphere of religion. In other words, that when he loves "God" or "heaven" he unconsciously means the person he has lost. Where this is true (not only in falsely experienced isolated instances, or as a light accompaniment to the genuine religious motivation, but as the actual core of a man or woman's virginity) that virginity is a terrible thing. Then the human is only being cheated of the most vital part of his existence, and is offering God a disposition that is dishonest and unclean. It is in this light that non-believers usually regard virginity; and there are certain aspects of Christian life which sometimes justify their attitude; however, the essence of genuine virginity is quite other.

What Christian virginity is cannot be deduced from our knowledge of man, but only from revelation. Christ says that it *is* possible for the human being to concentrate all his powers of love honestly, purely on God, for he is such that he can be loved with all the plenitude of life; that he can become everything, beginning and end, of man's existence. Not as an *Ersatz,* not as a cloak for something else, nor as the object of a deflected human affection, but for his own sake. God is the sovereign Lover, he who loves and can be loved absolutely—indeed, in the last analysis, the only one who can be loved without reserve. Doesn't the experience of every loving heart, even the richest and happiest, concede the impossibility of complete fulfillment? Is it perhaps so, after all, that love cannot harness its entire force for any human need because no human is big enough to receive it; that it is impossible to embrace an earthly lover with perfect intimacy, because essentially he is always distant? Perhaps precisely through the never completely satisfactory experience of human love, man begins to sense the presence of another love, unrealizable on a merely earthly plane, to whom we not only can but must surrender our most intimate being—the love revealed by revelation. Here lies the secret of virginity. Compared with its tremendous mystery, all objections of psychology and ethics dwindle to pathetic presumption. This certainly does not mean that every individual is capable of realizing such love, and there is no fixed rule as to how it may be realized. "Not all can accept this teaching; but those to whom it has been given." The passage is valid here in its strictest sense: Christian virginity is a special garden within the reservation of grace in nature as it exists in Christian marriage.

The power that has created both states of life is the power of Jesus Christ. Christian marriage, like Christian virginity, is not the product of sociological truth, however evident; nor of moral and personal strength, however valuable; nor of immediate, personal religiousness, however genuine. None of these even touches the essential. Both states are tenable only through the strength of Christ. Christian marriage is possible only when between the two "gathered together for my sake" is Christ "in the midst of them" (Matt. 18:18–20). He gives them the strength to bear and forbear, love, overcome, forgive "seventy times seven" (Matt. 18:22).

This same strength, and no abstract "heavenly kingdom," makes virginity possible. Not "God" generally, but Christ and all that radiates from his specific person: the ineffable fulfillment of all our aspirations. There is no collective word for such wealth, neither *ethos* nor any other. The only word large enough to contain him is that by which he is called: Jesus Christ, living Son of God and supremely beautiful offspring of men, personification of life and love. Both Christian marriage and Christian virginity become incomprehensible the moment the Nazarene ceases to be their essence, their norm and their reality.

X

POSSESSION
AND POVERTY IN CHRIST

A nd as he was going forth on his journey, a certain man running up fell upon his knees before him, and asked him,
'Good Master, what shall I do to gain eternal life?' But Jesus
said to him, 'Why dost thou call me good? No one is good but only
God. Thou knowest the commandments: *Thou shalt not kill. Thou
shalt not steal. Thou shalt not bear false witness. Thou shalt not defraud.
Honor thy father and mother.*' And he answered and said, 'Master, all
these I have kept ever since I was a child.' And Jesus, looking upon
him, loved him, and said to him, 'One thing is lacking to thee; go,
sell whatever thou hast, and give to the poor, and thou shalt have
treasure in heaven; and come, follow me.' But his face fell at the saying, and he went away sad, for he had great possessions.

"And Jesus looking round, said to his disciples, 'With what difficulty will they who have riches enter the kingdom of God!' But the
disciples were amazed at his word. But Jesus again addressed them,
saying, 'Children, with what difficulty will they who trust in riches
enter the kingdom of God! It is easier for a camel to pass through
the eye of a needle, than for a rich man to enter the kingdom of
God.' But they were astonished the more, saying among themselves,
'Who then can be saved?' And looking upon them, Jesus said, 'With
men it is impossible, but not with God; for all things are possible
with God' " (Mark 10:17–27).

Like so many others, these words of Jesus have had a profound
and ever deepening and widening influence on Christian history.
They are closely related to those we examined in the foregoing

chapter: there it was a question of the ordering of sexual life, here of property. Before we go into them further, let us consider how they apply to the Lord himself.

According to Scripture, Jesus came of poor parents. Read Luke two: the temple offering of Mary and Joseph after Jesus' birth was a poor man's offering: two pigeons; they could not afford a lamb. Later he himself warns a young man who would follow him: "The foxes have dens, and the birds of the air have nests; but the Son of Man has nowhere to lay his head" (Matt. 8:20). The one passage reveals the economic situation in which he grew up; the other his manner of life as an adult.

Still, we must not confuse absence of means with actual need. The Gospels report that Jesus was provided with all that was necessary for his maintenance. Wealthy women among his followers saw to that. It is also written that the little group had a common purse, kept by Judias Iscariot. There was enough, therefore, from which to buy food and other necessities, as well as to provide alms. Nowhere a word about self-imposed austerities, such as penance or the rigors of spiritual exercises. Jesus does fast after his baptism, but this is not asceticism in the usual sense; it is rather the desire for extreme isolation in which to be alone with God (Matt. 4:3). Otherwise the Lord eats what he is served, uses what he needs, and speaks little about such things. At the wedding feast of Cana he presents his hosts with an abundance of finest wine—hardly an ascetic miracle! He does not preach abstinence to the hungry multitude, but feeds them amply and sees to it that the left-overs are cared for. We even have one report that shows how deeply appreciative Christ was of Mary of Bethany's luxurious gesture: the breaking of the alabaster box of costly salve which filled the whole house with its perfume. The spirit of love expressed by the beautiful act delighted and moved him, and when objections were raised that the money would have been more appropriately spent on the poor, he defended it (John 12:1–8). The same attitude of largesse is evident in Jesus' receptiveness to nature. Only an eye appreciative of the richness and glory of

God as revealed in the animal and vegetable worlds makes possible their telling use in the parables. Had Jesus been insensible to the beauties of earth, Satan's spreading them out before him would have been no temptation. The Lord is no ascetic. When he chides the Jews for their repeated objection of God's messengers he says: "For John came neither eating nor drinking, and they say, 'He has a devil!' The Son of Man came eating and drinking, and they say, 'Behold a glutton and a wine-drinker, a friend of publicans and sinners!'" (Matt. 11:18–19). John fasts and does penance. Jesus honors these, but does not practice them himself. Unique in Christ is not his renunciation of earth's costliness or the taking upon himself of all sorts of privations, but that he is free as no one has ever been before or since. Christ's greatness lies in his perfect freedom, that is clear and sufficient unto itself. Wonderfully free as he is of all desire, of all worry about property or livelihood, he is equally untouched by all cramp of opposition to things, of renunciation, and above all, of even the most unconscious resentment towards things he himself does not enjoy. This freedom is so natural to him that it almost escapes the attention; only gradually do we learn to recognize and appreciate it. Jesus' eye rests calmly on all things; he does not ignore beauty, but frankly accepts it for what it is: beautiful; and the good things of life for what they are: good. But all his powers of appreciation and love are directed to God with a naturalness that is the pure fruit of his union with God (as is all Christian "naturalness": not the beginning of effort, but its fulfillment).

Hence Christ's great influence on those who are open to him, and his power to inspire people to regulate their own possessions. This is the theme of the passage we began with. Someone rushes up to him, perhaps rather breathlessly; a young man according to Matthew, a ruler according to Luke. "Good Master," he says, "what shall I do to gain eternal life?" He has probably just witnessed Jesus' kindness to the children, and touched, desires to share his purity and obvious 'proximity' to God. Jesus answers with a rebuff: Why dost thou call me good? He does not reject the adjective for humility's sake—Jesus' humility is of quite another dimension. Didn't he calmly defy his enemies to find a single sin on him? Here, however, his ear seems to have caught a false note, a trace of sentimentality or attachment to the things of this world, so he directs him upwards: only God is good, the invisible, holy God. Orient your thoughts there! Then he hastens to add: "Thou knowest the commandments," and he names several—not only from the Decalogue; by "commandments" Jesus apparently means all the divine instruction contained in the Old Testament. The youth replies: I have already done all that—and from earliest childhood! The answer is perhaps a bit hasty; he should have considered it more carefully. According to Matthew he supplements it with: What more can I do? He must be sincere, for the Lord looks at him with love and says: "One thing is lacking to thee." Jesus sees that he really has tried to keep the commandments, and that nostalgia for the realm beyond them, tugs at his soul. To this grace-given desire Jesus responds with a look of encouraging love and the new counsel: "Sell whatever thou hast, and give to the poor, and thou shalt have treasure in heaven; . . ." If it is so with you, give everything away and follow me! Not: Give everything to your heirs, but to the poor—give it away completely. Make yourself entirely free and come with me!

Here, one after the other, two legitimate Christian attitudes to property are revealed. First, that based on the commandments: to own property; to be grateful for it; to manage it well and achieve something with it; to avoid dishonesty and injustice; to be decent to others and help dispel need. This order of existence is acceptable to God and leads to eternal life. If the youth had said: Lord, I have tried to do these things but have not completely succeeded; I shall try to do better. If he had consecrated his life to an ever more perfect realization of the commandments and attempted to manage and use his property in the spirit of the new teachings, something great from the Christian viewpoint would have come of it. But he wanted to do more; keeping the commandments in faith and with growing perfec-

tion is the ordinary Christian way of life valid for all. Something in
the young man yearned to surpass the Law, to enter the free realm of
magnanimity, of spiritual creativeness and novelty. It was this that had
driven him to Christ. Hence the Lord's encouragement: if this is
really your desire, go ahead and follow through! Then a special order
of things is valid for you, that will help you to concentrate all the
power of your love on God, to serve him not only in justice, but in
the absolute freedom of the heart that has stripped itself of everthing
that is not he. Then away with things and follow me! To make this
easier, Jesus turns on him a look of all-empowering love, including
him in the intimacy of all who share already now in the union with
his Father. If he trusts himself to Jesus, he will mount the steps of divine counsel higher and higher in the exceptional Christian life. But
the price is too great; the youth cannot cut himself free. His possessions, spread richly before his inner eye, tie him fast, and sorrowful in
the knowledge of a divine possibility lost, he returns home.

Two modes of life are outlined here: one the rule that is valid,
obligatory for all, the other a counsel direct from divine freedom to
be voluntarily accepted or rejected by the individual heart. This is
no question of natural decision. May no one presume to take such a
step on his own. One must be called, personally, not jointly, and the
summons must be weighed freely. "If thou wilt be perfect . . ." actually, he too is bound, for if he fails, he fails not only his own potentialities, but he turns a deaf ear to God. Hence the young man's
sadness. From this blend of vocation and freedom, of obligation and
magnanimity springs the order of perfection, that state of more than
ordinary Christian freedom which is the privilege of certain chosen
individuals. It is fulfilled by readiness to obey not the law, but the
vocation, and this readiness and vocation together form the new individual order, which binds as tightly, if not more tightly than the
general.

What is the relation of these two orders of existence to each
other? First of all, let us make it perfectly clear that both are good.
And good in the eyes of God. Also the first order leads to eternal

life, union with God, and there is nothing higher. It is contrary to
the sense of Scripture to regard the order of property (or marriage)
as not quite Christian: as an inferior state allowed those incapable of
a higher state based on divine grace rather than on natural strength.
It is important to see this; the text speaks clearly. When the wealthy
youth has gone, Jesus looks gravely at his disciples and says: How difficult it is for those who trust in their riches to enter the kingdom
of heaven! "It is easier for a camel to pass through the eye of a needle, than for a rich man to enter the kingdom. . . ." Hearing this,
the disciples are thrown into great consternation and ask: "Who
then can be saved?" Jesus does not mitigate his statement to comfort
them; on the contrary. Looking at them compassionately he says:
"With men it is impossible, but not with God; for all things are possible with God."

Anyone who wants to, must see what is meant. But why are the
disciples so concerned—they are not rich! They might have sympa-
thized with the young man, or possibly—if they were that
worldly—might have taken an unconscious pleasure in his chagrin.
But why, instead, this deep "consternation"? Why their fearful:
Then who can be saved? Apparently they include themselves among
the "rich," and Jesus agrees with them. For he does not condemn
wealth quantitatively; he does not say that great wealth is necessarily
worse than little. It is ownership *per se* that is the root of evil, and the
disciples feel at once that from Christ's viewpoint even a poor cot or
fishing sloop is not innocuous, that his warning goes for them too.
And now the Master continues: Only with the strength of God's all-
emancipating magnanimity and love can we renounce everything,
voluntarily take poverty upon us. This is obvious enough, yet we
should not forget to add: to hold property as it should be held, in
justice and love *without* being "rich" in the Gospel's sense, is likewise possible only through the same divine strength required to give
everything away. Property compromises the heart whether it consists of one dollar or a million, a patch of ground or a large estate.
However, one of God's immeasurable graces is that which makes it

possible for people living in this world of things to possess them "justly," in Christ, without forfeiting God's kingdom. . . .

We saw how Christian marriage, that insoluble lifetime bond between two people, is feasible only with the same divine aid that enables an individual to hold himself free of all ties in order to concentrate all his love and energy upon God. It is the same thing here: with God's help, property that would otherwise bind, can be used for freedom. St. Paul's much quoted word is still valid. Men should possess "as though not possessing" (I Cor. 7:29–31). To do this honestly without self-deception, is a great and difficult accomplishment. To become genuinely independent of things, really free from attachment to pleasure, from desire, fear, envy, niggardliness; to hold what one has as a gift of God, using it according to his will, that is frankly impossible, just as impossible as it is to be voluntarily poor or "blessed" in suffering and sorrow, or any other beatitude without God's very appreciable aid. We should even invert the question: Is it only ownership that is dangerous to the Christian? Certainly not; need (and suffering and sorrow) are too. Poverty is never a virtue in itself, but only a possibility for virtue—when practiced voluntarily, in the freedom of the heart and for heaven's sake. Mere need, self-limitation in themselves can make for spiritual barrenness rather than fertility; can lead to a new, special pride, pharisaism much worse than the pride in honest labor and justly acquired success. (There are people who renounce marriage only to become spiritual deserts, hard and haughty, hypocritical and violent against themselves and others; true misanthropes, because they have only suppressed their desires, instead of lifting them to the freedom of virtual sacrifice.) For such as these it would doubtless have been better to marry than "to burn" (I Cor. 7:9).

But let us return to our question: which of the two orders is the higher? He who can view the problem entirely without prejudice, influenced neither by personal reaction, nor by the biased attitudes resulting from the Reformation and modern naturalism, knows the answer: the order of perfection is superior. Not because the other is wrong, but because even the unschooled mind realizes at once that the exceptional value is higher than the common value; that a life which sacrifices everything to the search for God is more pleasing to him than one that also pursues various other interests. It is essential to intellectual integrity to admit this, even though one does not feel personally called to such a life. It is better not to belong to a higher plane of spiritual existence than to pull it down to one's own level. Besides, it is by no means self-understood that a person in the order of perfection actually lives up to that state and is intrinsically closer to God than another. His true rank depends on the purity of his intentions and the power of his will. There have been priests, for example, that were narrow-minded, cold, proud and violent; business men broad of view, warm-hearted, humble, reverent and refined. What has been said of the two orders of Christian life is valid not for the attitude of every individual in the respective order, but for the position of that order in the hierarchy of spiritual life. For the individual there is no such thing as a valid "caste-system" of human worth. Both orders come from the same divine plan and are realized with the strength of the same grace. Are they alien to each other?

Let us try to answer the question with an example: St. Francis understood the sense of the order of perfection as hardly another, and may be regarded as its purest most daring and creative representative, one who climbed high into the realms of the supernatural. When the Poverello of Assisi entered the house of a man of means and conquered him for Christ, what happened? Perhaps the rich man, fired by Francis' own example, also sold all he had and followed him. More likely, he stayed where he was. One thing though is certain; as long as the figure of his guest, the breath of his personality, the sound of his voice remained with him, he rejected any not quite straight deal; he did not press his debtors, or fail to help the needy and distressed who came to his door. Already we have part of our answer: the realization of the order of perfection operates as a living example in human society. It proves the possibility of freedom from property, reminding those who possess it that there is freedom to be had also among possessions. He who has entirely freed himself from things helps him who retains his belongings to use them properly. On the other hand, would Francis have been able to "marry" Lady Poverty with so much radiant enthusiasm and graciousness if he had come from a very poor house? I doubt it. His sacrifice possessed such a high degree of emancipating power because he knew the value of the things he renounced. He knew how beautiful the world is, how delightful abundance, with all its possibilities of enjoyment and munificence. That is the other part of the answer: the exceptional order is renewed again and again by the freedom of the human heart and the grace of God. However, if this order is to be genuinely emancipatory, humanly pure, spiritually sound and creative, then in the general consciousness of the times the order of Christian property must remain. It is the fertile field from which, when it pleases God, the flower of renunciation climbs into bloom.

The two orders are mutually dependent on each other. Only when marriage and property are seen in their true light and allowed to unfold their values freely, can virginity and poverty attain their purest form. Only when virginity and poverty are a real force in the general consciousness, are marriage and property protected from sinking into wordliness.

XI

BLESSING

In Chapter Ten Mark describes how children are brought to Jesus for his blessing. The Lord is tired and in need of rest, so his disciples attempt to secure it for him, but he is indignant: "Let the little children come to me, and do not hinder them, for of such is the kingdom of God." The blessing of the children is a lovely incident, whether thought-provoking or not. But what about the word of the man who confronts Christ so resolutely: We wish to bless, not be blessed! What does it mean? To desire to bless rather than supplicate sounds like revolt. What does blessing mean? What other instances have we of Jesus blessing? On the last evening during the feast of the Pasch, he blesses the bread and the chalice with the words that institute the mystery of the Eucharist (Matt. 26:26), and again after the Resurrection, just before his return to the heavenly Father we read: "Now he led them out towards Bethany, and he lifted up his hands and blessed them. And it came to pass as he blessed them, that he parted from them and was carried up into heaven" (Luke 24:50–51). According to Matthew and Mark, with the blessing he gave command to spread his message throughout the world.

Gestures heavy with meaning, this blessing of the children, of the bread and wine, of the apostles in the final hour. If we glance from here back at the Old Testament, we see the connection: blessing at the beginning and end of sacred history. On the fifth day of creation God spoke his blessing over the living creatures in the waters: "And he blessed them, saying: Increase and multiply, and fill the waters of the sea; and let the birds be multiplied upon the earth." On the sixth day, after he has created man in his own image as man and wife he blesses them: "Increase and multiply, and fill the earth, and subdue it, and rule over the fishes of the sea, and the fowls of the air, and all living creatures that move upon the earth" (Gen. 1:22, 28). And after all things have been created and found "good" by his all-seeing eye of truth, God blessed the seventh day, on which earth was completed, day of his own repose (Gen. 2:3). Then, however, the blessing is destroyed. Man sins and God curses him, and with him the earth and its fruits, and all his labors, and his wife's womb (Gen. 3:16–19).

At the end of time blessing will return, eternal blessing; with it, however, eternal malediction. To those who have believed in the name of Christ and who have tried to practice his love, the Judge of the World will say: "Come blessed of my Father, take possession of the kingdom prepared for you from the foundation of the world; . . ." But to those who have closed themselves to this love: "Depart from me, accursed ones, into the everlasting fire which was prepared for the devil and his angels" (Matt. 25:34, 41).

Between beginning and end, in the long period of human history, the blessing appears anew. Not the original blessing—that has been destroyed—but another which is given Noah after the mysterious flood, when God makes a covenant with him, foreshadowing the covenant to come. (See Genesis nine.) Then the real covenant, with Abraham, is sealed, and with it blessing upon all who are called and obey the call: Abraham's descendants are to be the bearers of sacred history, and some day in the impenetrable future, one of them will give birth to the Messiah (Gen. 12). It is in him that the second blessing will grow ripe and full.

Blessing is directed to living things. Inanimate things have their fixed measure; they remain as they are. Animate things though, contain a secret source from which flows the mystery of beginning. They grow and multiply. It is to this mystery of increase that blessing is applied: increase in the vitality of body and spirit, as proved by their fruits. Blessing stirs inner depths, unsealing some hidden spring. It can be applied to everything that has immanent life. Malediction is barrenness. It chills and closes, renders life inanimate and sterile: the cursed womb does not bear; the cursed field runs to weed; the cursed singer finds no new song. The blessing that the dying Jacob speaks over his sons is full of such bounty (Gen. 49:1–27).

Then there is another kind of blessing: that which accompanies man's doings. It brings 'luck.' It makes the eye see clearly, directs the word to the proper ear, causes the work to succeed. The Old Testament often speaks of such blessing. It is upon the head of Jacob, whose every undertaking is successful, and of Joseph, in whose hands everything flourishes; it rests upon the victorious weapons of David. With Esau and Saul it is different: they are unblessed.

Once the womb has borne fruit, the seed has sprouted, the work is begun, it is time for the crowning blessing of fulfillment. Existence is hardly favorable to completion. The paths of earth's activating forces cut into each other. One might speak just as correctly of universal chaos as of order. Sometimes malevolent forces seem to hover over a task, carefully preventing its completion. There is no guarantee that what is well begun will be well ended. When it is, then as the result of a particular blessing, a rare and wonderful thing. It is much more usual that the enemy intervenes: the form is broken, the promise fades, the necessary energy peters out, the lightning-bolt falls. Blessing is the power that releases the fertility of living things and brings them to fulfillment. Only he is blessed who can also create. Hence the desire to bless rather than be blessed would depose God.

But with this we are still only on the periphery of the subject. Not until Christ's advent do we learn what blessing really means. All the blessing that exists is focused on him, the Blessed One, to whom all power is given "in heaven and on earth" (Matt. 28:18). He himself is the living power of salvation from whom blessing streams. Three times Christ blessed specifically; actually, his whole existence was a fountain of "living water." And not for nothing did old Christian poetry sing of him as "Christus Sol," the radiant, warming, life-sending one. The three blessings in the New Testament are but three rays from his sun.

When the children are brought to him, he embraces them, lays his hands on their heads, and blesses—probably their physical and emotional development, their earthly destinies together, for they are inseparable. But the blessing goes deeper than mere corporal well-being, warmth of heart, and earthly success, penetrating to the profundity of God in man which is the fountainhead of the individual divine life. The ultimate sense of Jesus' blessing is that the "children of earth" become children of God, sons and daughters of the heavenly Father; that next their physical and intellectual fecundity, their spiritual develop; that their earthly struggles and labors may harvest invulnerable sheaves for heavenly barns.

At the Last Supper Christ takes bread and blesses it. No question here of kindling the festivity of a group of guests, or of seeking truth in the sanctifying of bread and beaker, or as at Plato's immortal Symposium, of consecrating an hour of friendship in which spirits, ignited by the spark from a great soul, take off in joint flight for the realms of eternal beauty. The bread is blessed that it may become the body of Christ, who offered himself in expiation of our sins; and the wine in the chalice is blessed that it may become his blood, poured out for the sins of the world (Luke 22:20; Matt. 26:28). Blessing opens the recipient to a fertility not of this world, a superabundance that comes neither from the plenitude of the spirit, nor from contact with higher powers, but solely from the redemptory love of God's Son. From it falls food and drink for the newborn life, giving strength for the toil and trials and struggles of the Christian day.

Finally Jesus blesses his disciples, that they may go out into the world not to build empires or to make history, but to carry the sacred message of love to men (Luke 24:50). The battle against worldliness is to be fought on all fronts; the seed of the new creation sunk into history. What this final blessing means is not clear until Pentecost, when the Holy Spirit brings its realization.

Who is Christ, the Spender of Blessing? Not one in the row of great healers and saviors. No new conjuror of the mysteries of winter's curse and summer's blessing, of the cycle of death and fecundity. He is Son of the living God, habitant of that eternal inaccessibility beyond the reaches of world myth and mystery (I Tim. 6:16). He does not step into man's world from that of nature, issuing neither from her light nor from her dark mystery of fertility, nor self-revealed from the silent depths of chaos. He comes impelled only by the free, pure decision of divine love, which knows no other law than itself. His blessing comes of that omnipotence expressed in the words: "All power in heaven and on earth has been given to me" (Matt. 28:18): power of sowing holy life; power of fertility and growth; power of protection, guidance and completion; power of judgment. Jesus' blessing redeems us from the curse. Not as the sun frees from darkness or the golden hero of a saga frees from the claws of the dragon. The curse is the judgment of the Lord and Creator of the world upon his mutinous creatures. It is not an independent power in itself aimed at God, it is the punishment God himself has placed upon the heart that has turned against him, and it is from this that Christ frees us. Evil is null and void before God. It is able to exist at all only because the creature whom God created good has become wicked, entangled in error and hardened by revolt. Christ's holy strength overcomes it. The battle is a bitter one, not because evil is difficult for God to conquer, but because man's heart refuses to learn.

Thus it is the voice of a petrification almost absolute which declares: We would be spenders of blessing, not blessed! It means we creatures would be creators, gods! God and Christ and salvation are rejected. Where this will dominates and is realized, man closes himself against that abundance which comes from sacred blessing. Then, though prosperity may seem to bloom and ripen, in reality there is desert. Then the sun also rises; spring still comes; deeds are accomplished and children born, but everything is sealed in eternal sterility.

XII

BELIEF IN CHRIST,
IMITATION OF CHRIST

A mong the instructions that Jesus gives the Twelve before sending them out into the world are the following: "Do not think that I have come to send peace upon the earth; I have come to bring a sword, not peace. . . . He who loves father or mother more than me is not worthy of me; and he who loves son or daughter more than me is not worthy of me. And he who does not take up his cross and follow me, is not worthy of me. He who finds his life will lose it, and he who loses his life for my sake, will find it" (Matt. 10:34–39).

Jesus' message is one of good will. He proclaims the Father's love and the advent of his kingdom. He calls people to the peace and harmony of life lived in the divine will. Yet their first reaction is not union, but division. The more profoundly Christian a man becomes, the deeper the cleft between him and those who refuse to follow Christ—its exact measure proportionate to the depth of that refusal. The split runs right through the most intimate relationship, for genuine conversion is not a thing of natural disposition or historical development, but the most personal decision an individual can make. The one makes it, the other does not; hence the possibility of schism between father and son, friend and friend, one member of a household and another. When it comes to a choice between domestic peace and Jesus, one must value Jesus higher; even higher than the most dearly beloved: father and mother, son and daughter, friend or love. This means cutting into the very core of life, and temptation presses us to preserve human ties and abandon Christ.

But Jesus warns us: If you hold "life" fast, sacrificing me for it, you lose your own true life. If you let it go for my sake, you will find yourself in the heart of immeasurable reality.

Naturally this is difficult; it is the cross. And here we brush the heaviest mystery of Christianity, its inseparableness from Calvary. Ever since Christ walked the way of the cross, it stands firmly planted on every Christian's road, for every follower of Christ has his own personal cross. Nature revolts against it, wishing to 'preserve' herself. She tries to go around it, but Jesus has said unequivocally, and his words are fundamental to Christianity: He who hangs on, body and soul, to "life" will lose it; he who surrenders his will to his cross will find it—once and forever in the immortal self that shares in the life of Christ.

On the last journey to Jerusalem, shortly before the Transfiguration, Jesus' words about the cross are repeated. Then, sharply focused, the new thought: "For what does it profit a man, if he gain the whole world, but suffer the loss of his own soul? Or what will a man give in exchange for his soul?" (Matt. 16:26).

This time the point plunges deeper. The dividing line runs not between one person and another, but between the believer or one desirous of belief and everything else! Between me and the world. Between me and myself. The lesson of the cross is the great lesson of self-surrender and self-conquest. Our meditations are approaching the passion of the Lord, so it is time that we turn to Christianity's profoundest, but also most difficult mystery.

Why did Jesus come? To add a new, higher value to those already existent? To reveal a new truth over and above existing truth, or a nobler nobility, or a new and juster order of human society? No, he came to bring home the terrible fact that everything, great and small, noble and mean, the whole with all its parts—from the corporal to the spiritual, from the sexual to the highest creative urge of genius—is intrinsically corrupt. This does not deny the existence of individual worth. What is good remains good, and high aspirations will always remain high. Nevertheless, human existence *in toto* has fallen away from God. Christ did not come to renew this part or that, or to disclose greater human possibilities, but to open man's eyes to what the world and human life as an entity really is; to give him a point of departure from which he can begin all over with his scale of values and with himself. Jesus does not uncover hidden creative powers in man; he refers him to God, center and source of all power.

It is as though humanity were one of those enormous ocean liners that is a world in itself: apparatuses for the most varied purposes; collecting place for all kinds of passengers and crew with their responsibilities and accomplishments, passions, tensions, struggles. Suddenly someone appears on board and says: What each of you is doing is important, and you are right to try to perfect your efforts. I can help you, but not by changing this or that on your ship, it is your course that is wrong; you are steering straight for destruction. . . .

Christ does not step into the row of great philosophers with a better philosophy; or of the moralists with a purer morality; or of the religious geniuses to conduct man deeper into the mysteries of life; he came to tell us that our whole existence, with all its philosophy and ethics and religion, its economics, art, and nature, is leading us away from God and into the shoals. He wants to help us swing the rudder back into the divine direction, and to give us the necessary strength to hold that course. Any other appreciation of Christ is worthless. If this is not valid, then every man for himself; let him choose whatever guide seems trustworthy, and possibly Goethe or Plato or Buddha is a better leader than what remains of a Jesus Christ whose central purpose and significance have been plucked from him.

Jesus actually is the Rescue-pilot who puts us back on the right course. It is with this in mind that we must interpret the words about winning the world at the loss of the essential; about losing life, personality, soul, in order to possess them anew and truly. They refer to faith and the imitation of Christ.

Faith means to see and to risk accepting Christ not only as the greatest teacher of truth that ever lived, but as Truth itself (John

16:6). Sacred reality begins with Jesus of Nazareth. If it were possible to annihilate him, the truth he taught would not continue to exist in spite of the loss of its noblest apostle, but *itself would cease to exist.* For he is the *Logos,* the source of Living Truth. He demands not only that we consent intellectually to the correctness of his proclamation—that would be only a beginning—but that we feel with all our natural instinct for right and wrong, with heart and soul and every cell of our being, its claims upon *us.* We must not forget: the whole ship is headed for disaster. It does not help to change from one side of it to the other or to replace this or that instrument. It is the course that must be altered. We must learn to take completely new bearings. What does it mean, to be? Philosophy goes into the problem deeply, without changing being at all. Religion tells me that I have been created; that I am continuously receiving myself from divine hands, that I am free yet living from God's strength. Try to feel your way into this truth, and your whole attitude towards life will change. You will see yourself in an entirely new perspective. What once seemed self-understood becomes questionable. Where once you were indifferent, you become reverent; where self-confident, you learn to know "fear and trembling." But where formerly you felt abandoned, you will now feel secure, living as a child of the Creator-Father, and the knowledge that this is precisely what you are will alter the very taproot of your being. . . . What does it mean to die? Physiology says the blood vessels harden or the organs cease to function. Philosophy speaks of the pathos of finite life condemned to aspire vainly to infinity. Faith defines death as the fruit of sin, and man as *peccator* (Rom. 6:23). Death's arm is as long as sin's. One day for you too its consequences and those of death's disintegration will have to be drawn. It will become evident how peccant you are and consequently moribund. Then all the protective screens so elaborately arranged between you and this fact will fall, and you will have to stand and face your judgment. But faith also adds, God is love, even though he allows sin to fulfill itself in death, and your Judge is the same as your Savior. If you were to reflect on this, over and over again until its truth was deep in your blood, wouldn't it make a fundamental difference in your attitude towards life, giving you a confidence the world does not have to give? Wouldn't it add a new earnestness and meaning to everything you do?

What precisely is this chain of acts and events that runs from our first hour through our last? The one says natural necessity; the other historical consequence; a third, something else. Faith says: It is Providence. The God who made you, saved you, and will one day place you in his light, also directs your life. What happens between birth and death is message, challenge, test, succor—all from his hands. It is not meant to be learned theoretically, but personally experienced and assimilated. Where this is so, aren't all things necessarily transfigured? What is the resultant attitude but faith?

Religion then! But there are so many, one might object; Christ is just another religious founder.

No; all other religions come from earth. True, God is present in the earth he created, and it is always God whom the various religions honor, but not in the supremacy of his absolute freedom. Earthly religions revere God's activity, the reflections of his power (more or less fragmentary, distorted) as they encounter it in a world that has turned away from him. They are inspired by the breath of the divine, but they exist apart from him; they are saturated with worldly influences, are formed, interpreted, colored by the historical situation of the moment. Such a religion does not save. It is itself a piece of "world," and he who wins the world loses his soul. Christ brings no "religion," but the message of the living God, who stands in opposition and contradiction to all things, "world-religions" included. Faith understands this, for to believe does not mean to participate in one or the other religions, but: "Now this is everlasting life, that they may know thee, the only true God, and him whom thou hast sent, Jesus Christ" (John 17:3). Men are to accept Christ's tidings as the norm of their personal lives.

My attitudes towards things to be done may be various. One follows the principle of maximum profit with minimum effort. This is the clever or economical approach. I can also consider a specific task in the light of duty, the fulfillment of which places my life on a spiritual and moral level. Christ teaches neither greater cleverness nor a higher sense of duty; he says: Try to understand everything that comes into your life from the viewpoint of the Father's will. If I do, what happens? Then I continue to act in accordance with cleverness and utility, but under the eyes of God. I will also do things that seem foolish to the world, but are clever in eternity. I will continue to try to act ethically, to distinguish clearly between right and wrong and to live in increasing harmony with an increasingly dependable conscience. All this, however, in the living presence of Christ, which will teach me to see things I never would have noticed alone. It will change my concepts and trouble my conscience—but for its good, stripping it of levity's self-confidence, of moral pride, and of the intellectual stiffness that results from too much principle-riding. With increasing delicacy of conscience will come a new firmness of purpose and a new energy (simultaneously protective and creative) for the interests of good.

Similarly, my attitude to my neighbor may be ordered from various points of view: I can consider others competition, and attempt to protect my interests from them. I can respect the personality of each. I can see them as co-sharers of destiny, responsible with me for much that is to come, and so on and so forth. Each of these attitudes has its place, but everything is changed once I understand what Christ is saying: You and those near you—through me you have become brothers and sisters, offspring of the same Father. His kingdom is to be realized in your relationship to each other. We have already spoken of the transformation that takes place when fellow citizens become brothers in Christ; when from the "you and me" of the world springs the Christian "we." Much could be said of the Christian's attitude to destiny and all that it implies in the way of injustice, shock and tragedy: things with which no amount of worldly wisdom, fatalism or philosophy can cope—and preserve its integrity. This is possible only when some fixed point exists *outside* the world, and such a point cannot be created by man, but must be accepted from above (as we accept the tidings of divine Providence and his all-directing love). St. Paul words it in his epistle to the Romans (Chap. 8): "Now we know that for those who love God all things work together unto good. . . ." This means an ever more complete exchange of natural security, self-confidence, and self-righteousness, for confidence in God and his righteousness as it is voiced by Christ and the succession of his apostles.

Until a man makes this transposition he will have no peace. He will realize how the years of his life unroll, and ask himself vainly what remains. He will make moral efforts to improve, only to become either hopelessly perplexed or priggish. He will work, only to discover that nothing he can do stills his heart. He will study, only to progress little beyond vague probabilities—unless his intellectual watchfulness slackens, and he begins to accept possibility for truth or wishes for reality. He will fight, found, form this and that only to discover that millions have done the same before him and millions will continue to after he is gone, without shaping the constantly running sand for more than an instant. He will explore religion, only to founder in the questionableness of all he finds. The world is an entity. Everything in it conditions everything else. Everything is transitory. No single thing helps, because the world as a whole has fallen from grace. One quest alone has an absolute sense: that of the Archimedes-point and lever which can lift the world back to God, and these are what Christ came to give.

One more point is important: our Christianity itself must constantly grow. The great revolution of faith is not a lump of reality fallen ready-made from heaven into our laps. It is a constant act of my individual heart and strength. I stand with all I am at the center of my faith, which means that I bring to it also those strands of my being which instinctively pull away from God. It is not as though I, the believer, stood on one side, on the other the fallen world. Actually faith must be realized within the reality of my being, with its full share of worldliness.

Woe to me if I say: "I believe" and feel safe in that belief. For then I am already in danger of losing it (see Cor. 10:12). Woe to me if I say: "I am a Christian"—possibly with a side-glance at others who in my opinion are not, or at an age that is not, or at a cultural tendency flowing in the opposite direction. Then my so-called Christianity threatens to become nothing but a religious form of self-affirmation. I "am" not a Christian; I am on the way to becoming one—if God will give me the strength. Christianity is nothing one can "have"; nor is it a platform from which to judge others. It is movement. I can become a Christian only as long as I am conscious of the possibility of falling away. The gravest danger is not failure of the will to accomplish a certain thing; with God's help I can always pull myself together and begin again. The real danger is that of becoming within myself unchristian, and it is greatest when my will is most sure of itself. I have absolutely no guarantee that I shall be privileged to remain a follower of Christ save in the manner of beginning, of being *en route,* of becoming, trusting, hoping and praying.

XIII

FORGIVENESS

The next to the last request of the Pater Noster runs: "And forgive us our debts as we forgive our debtors." Mark elaborates on the thought: "And when you stand up to pray, forgive whatever you have against anyone, that your Father in heaven may also forgive you your offences" (11:25). And Matthew adds directly to the words of the prayer: "For if you forgive men their offences, your heavenly Father will also forgive you your offences. But if you do not forgive men, neither will your Father forgive you your offences" (Matt. 6:14–15). Thus God's forgiveness of our sins depends upon our forgiveness or refusal to forgive others for the injustices they have committed against us.

After Jesus has spoken of fraternal, mutual correction, the text continues: "Then Peter came up to him and said, 'Lord, how often shall my brother sin against me, and I forgive him? Up to seven times?' Jesus said to him, 'I do not say to thee seven times, but seventy times seven'" (Matt. 18:21–22). Forgiveness should be no occasion, but our habitual attitude towards others. To drive this fundamental point home, Jesus illustrates his teaching with the story of the king who audits his accounts. Finding an enormous deficit in the books of one of his administrators, he commands that his property, family and person be placed under custody until the debt is paid. The man begs for mercy, and his master, who is magnanimous, cancels the debt. But the administrator has hardly left the room when he encounters a colleague who owes him an incomparably smaller sum. He seizes him, and deaf to excuse or plea, drags him to the debtors' court—in those days notorious for its harshness. The king learns what has happened, and angered by the man's heartlessness submits him to the same fate he has inflicted upon his debtor. "So also my heavenly Father will do to you, if you do not each forgive your brothers from your hearts" (Matt. 18:35).

Earlier in the same chapter Christ discusses what is to be done with one who refuses to see or admit his wrongs. It is up to you to straighten him out. If it is you he has injured, you must not simply ignore him in a mood of irritated moral superiority, but must go to him and do everything possible to make him understand and willing to clear things up. This will not be easy. If you come to him condescendingly, or pedantically, or in the role of the ethically superior, he will only consider you presumptuous. His opposition to your claims will entrench itself against the real injustice of your Pharisaic attitude, and the end of it all will be worse than the beginning. Therefore, if you wish to obey Christ, you must first free yourself of all 'righteous' indignation. Only if you forgive entirely, can you contact the true self of the other, whom his own rebelliousness is holding back. If you can reach this better self, you have a good chance of being heard, and of winning your brother. This then the great doctrine of forgiveness on which Jesus insists as one of the fundamentals of his message. If we wish to get to its root, we must dig our way there question by question.

What must we overcome in ourselves to be capable of genuine forgiveness?

First of all, deep in the domain of the purely natural, the sentiment of having to do with an enemy. This sense of the hostile is something animals have, and it reaches as far as their vulnerability. Creatures are so ordered that the preservation of the one depends on the destruction of the other. This is also true of fallen man, deeply enmeshed in the struggle for existence. He who injures me or takes something valuable from me is my enemy, and all my reactions of distrust, fear, and repulsion rise up against him. I try to protect myself from him, and am able to do this best by constantly reminding myself of his dangerousness, instinctively mistrusting him, and being prepared at all times to strike back. . . . Here forgiveness would mean first that I relinquish the clear and apparently only sure defense of natural animosity; second, that I overcome fear and risk defenselessness, convinced that the enemy can do nothing against my intrinsic self. Naturally, this does not mean that I close my eyes to danger, and it is self-understood that I do everything in my power to protect myself: I must be watchful and resolute. But the crux of the matter is forgiveness, a profound and weighty thing. Its prerequisite is the courage that springs from a deep sense of intimate security, and which, as experience has proved, is usually justified, for the genuine pardoner actually is stronger than the fear-ridden hater.

The desire for revenge is slightly more 'human.' It is not a response to mortal danger, but to the danger of loss of power and honor. The fact that the other was able to damage me proves that he was stronger than I; had I been what I should be, he never would have dared to attempt it. The impulse to retaliate aims primarily at reestablishing my self-respect by humiliating my enemy. I would rise by the other's fall. . . . To forgive him would mean to renounce this satisfaction, and necessitates a self-respect independent of the behavior of others because it lives from an intrinsic honor that is invulnerable. Again experience has shown that such an attitude also better protects my reputation, for my freedom blunts the point of the insult, thus disarming the aggressor.

One step closer to spiritual value is the desire for justice: order not of things and forces, but of human relations. That the individual receive according to his deserts and remain with these in the proper relationship to others and their deserts; that is justice. When someone does me an injustice, he disturbs that order there where it most vitally affects me, in myself. This is what arouses me. In the elementary desire for justice there is much that is simply primitive fear, for the just order is primarily protective. Wounded pride and the desire to avenge it are different; they are satisfied when they can take justice into their own hands. Fundamentally, what they demand is treatment conforming to one's personal dignity, and its simplest expression is the ancient law, "eye for eye, tooth for tooth" (Ex. 21:24). What the other has done to me shall be done to him; thus the wrong will be atoned, and order reestablished.

Here forgiveness would mean renouncing the right to administer justice oneself. To leave it to the authorities, to the state, to destiny and ultimately to God is the beginning of self-purification. But pardon really worthy of the name is much more: it is relinquishment of the wish to see punishment meted out at all. Quitting the questionable territory of desired pain for pain, damage for damage, atonement for guilt, one enters the open country of freedom. There too order exists, but of a different kind. It is not the result of weights and measures, but of creative self-conquest. Magnanimity, man's premonition of that divine power known as grace, rises to the surface. Forgiveness reestablishes order by acquitting the offender and thereby placing him in a new and higher order of justice.

But why should we act thus? The question really deserves to be posed. Why forgive? Why not simply establish justice? Wouldn't it be better? One answer is: forgiveness is more human. He who insists on his rights places himself outside the community of men. He would be judge of men rather than one of them, sharer of the common fate. It is better to remain within the circle of humanity and broaden heart and mind. Prerequisite is an innate altruism, and if we know people who have it, we also know how often it is accompanied by negative characteristics, by weakness, lack of dignity, indiscriminate negligence, disregard for truth and justice, even sudden outbursts of cruelty and vengefulness. . . . It has been pointed out that in reality, insistence on justice is servitude. Only forgiveness frees us from the injustice of others. To understand this attitude too requires a certain characteristic impersonality towards oneself and others; again with its negative counterpart: the tendency to disregard the rights and dignity of the individual. Much more could be said about the nobility of forgiveness and its accompanying values: generosity and magnanimity, and so on. This would all be correct, but still far from the pith of the New Testament's teaching.

Christ's exhortations are founded neither on social nor ethical nor any other worldly motives. We are told, simply, to forgive men as our Father in heaven forgives us. He is the primary and real Pardoner, and man is his child. Our powers of forgiveness are derived from his.

We beg the Father to forgive us as we forgive those who have been unjust to us. When you begin to pray, says the Lord, and suddenly remember that you have a grudge against someone, forgive him first! If you do not, your unforgiveness will step between you and the Father and prevent your request from reaching him. This does not mean that God forgives us because kindness to our neighbors renders us 'worthy' of his generosity. His pardon is pure grace, which is not founded on our worthiness, but creates it. *A priori,* however, is the opening of the heart for divine magnanimity: our readiness to forgive "our debtors." If we close it instead, we shut God's forgiveness out.

Briefly, forgiveness is a part of something much greater than itself: love. We should forgive, because we should love. That is why forgiveness is so free; it springs from the joint accomplishment of human and divine pardon. Like him who loves his enemies, the pardoner resembles the Father "who makes his sun to rise on the good and the evil, and sends rain on the just and the unjust" (Matt. 5:45).

Pardon reestablishes Christian fraternity and the sacred unity of the I-you-he (God). He who reasons from this height considers his neighbor's welfare precious, and to know him in the wrong is painful, as it is painful to God to witness a man's fall from his divine love. And just as God longs to win the lost one back (possible only through his aid in the form of grace), the Christian longs to help his brother to return to the community of sacred life.

Christ is forgiveness incarnate. We search in vain for the slightest trace of any reaction of his incompatible with pardon. Nothing of fear in any form is in him. His soul knows itself invulnerable, and he walks straight into danger, confident "because the Father is with me" (John 16:32). Vengeance is farthest of all from his thoughts. He is forced to endure unimaginable injustices, not only against his human honor, but also blasphemously directed against the honor of his Father. His sacred mission is called a work of Satan! His anger does flare, but it is divine wrath that blazes at the sacrilege, not desire for revenge. His self-confidence is untouched by the behavior of others, for he is entirely free. As for the weighing and measuring of justice, Christ came precisely for this, but he elevated it to the unspeakably higher plane of grace beyond weight and measure, dissolving man's own injustice in the divine solvent of genuine pardon. His message could not have been more personally delivered. He not only taught divine forgiveness, but demonstrated it on himself. All man's sinfulness against God gathered and precipitated blood upon the head of the "sign that shall be contradicted" (Luke 2:34). And Christ neither attempted to withdraw from the terrible rain, nor did he take personal offense; he recognized the injustice for what it was: an offense against God. He sealed the divine forgiveness he had come to bring by his own act of pardoning, offering his Father as expiation for humanity's sin, his own acceptance of the injustice heaped upon him: "Father, forgive them, for they do not know what they are doing."

And now we touch bottom: God's forgiveness did not occur as a mere pardon, but came as the result of Christ's expiation. He did not cancel mankind's sin, but reestablished genuine justice. He did not simply tear up man's frightful debt, but repaid it—with his own sweat and blood and tears. That is what Christian salvation means, and it is no isolated incident deep in the past on which we are still capitalizing, but the foundation for our whole Christian existence. To this day we live from the saving act of Christ, but we cannot remain saved unless the spirit of salvation is actively realized in our own lives. We cannot enjoy the fruits of salvation without contributing to salvation through love of neighbor. And such love must become pardon when that neighbor trespasses against us, as we constantly trespass against God.

XIV

CHRIST THE BEGINNING

I have come to cast fire upon the earth, and what will I but that it be kindled? But I have a baptism to be baptized with; and how distressed I am until it is accomplished!" (Luke 12:49–50). The words were probably uttered before Jesus crossed the Jordan to go to Jerusalem.

St. Paul speaks of the saving knowledge of Jesus Christ, which excels all else (Phil. 3:8). By this he does not mean knowledge in the sense of information or psychological insight, but that wisdom which springs from faith and love, fruit of the intimate contact with the soul of Christ when man's own soul suddenly becomes aware of whom it is embracing. And since Christ is power, the individual who so contacts him is transformed by the flow of divine strength. . . . If we call this central part of Christ's being his disposition, how, actually, is he disposed?

How can a man be disposed towards his fellow men? To start with the worst, he can despise them, taught by pride or disappointment, or sheer emotional exhaustion. He can fear them, or use them or benefit them. He can also love his fellows, and by giving himself to them, ripen to fulfillment of his own intrinsic being. Perhaps even creative love will stir in him, and he will venture everything, body and soul, breaking revolutionary paths for others to follow. What does Christianity say to all this? The answer is not easy to accept; indeed, for one without faith it is unacceptable. It runs: All these attitudes are enmeshed in the world, in the powers of evil, in the straits of fear and natural instinct, in intellectual and spiritual pride, in that which we over hastily define as "good." They can be good, even noble; but they are bonds nevertheless. The little freedom they enjoy is always limited by the borders of a world which is itself in chains.

Not so Christ. The purity of his disposition is not the result of a struggle against evil and victory over fear, nor is it instinctive physical purity or inborn spiritual nobility. In him the disposition of the Son of God is alive; purity which enters the world from above and is its new, spotless beginning. It is God's love that was made man. Not any man, but Jesus Christ, the Galilean, offspring of a specific race and age, of its social, political and cultural aspects, but so disposed that in the man Jesus faith finds the pure expression of divine sonship.

There is only one whom we might be inclined to compare with Jesus: Buddha. This man is a great mystery. He lived in an awful, almost superhuman freedom, yet his kindness was powerful as a cosmic force. Perhaps Buddha will be the last religious genius to be explained by Christianity. As yet no one has really uncovered his Christian significance. Perhaps Christ had not only one precursor, John, last of the prophets, but three: John the Baptist for the Chosen People, Socrates from the heart of antiquity, and Buddha, who spoke the ultimate word in Eastern religious cognition. Buddha is free; but his freedom is not that of Christ. Possibly Buddha's freedom is only the ultimate and supremely liberating knowledge of the vanity of this fallen world.

Christ's freedom is based not on negative cognition, but on the love of God; his whole attitude is permeated with God's earnest will to heal the world.

Everything in life is uncertain. The moment we demand more than mere probabilities, we are forced to admit that everything is questionable: people, things, works, knowledge. If we ask: Does anything really possess an ultimate, divine guarantee? the reply is: Yes, one thing does possess, *is* that guarantee, the love of Jesus Christ. It alone breathes such eternal purity, that the slightest doubt is equivalent to attack. What are the effects of this divine disposition?

What effects does one man have on another? His wickedness may destroy, his fear poison, his lust overpower and enslave. Or he may liberate, help, animate, create a sense of community and good works. His best talents may bring into being things of permanent splendor. All these are realities, and it would be folly to underestimate a single one. Nevertheless, there is a limit to man's possibilities: he can effect only things within the world. He can develop given possibilities; change and shape given conditions; he cannot change the world as a whole, for he is part of it. . . . He has no influence over being as such or its characteristics. He can change all manner of things on the surface of earth; earth itself escapes his power. Only one person ever seriously attempted to go farther: to lay hands on being—Buddha. He desired more than mere moral progress or peace outside the world. He attempted the inconceivable: himself part of existence, he tried to lift all existence by its "bootstraps." So far no Christian has succeeded in comprehending and evaluating Buddha's conception of Nirvana, that ultimate awakening, cessation of illusion and being. To do this one must have become entirely free in the love of God's Son, yet remain linked by a profound reverence to the great and mysterious man who lived six centuries before the Lord. One thing is certain: Jesus' attitude toward the world is basically different from that of Buddha: Christ is the Establisher of absolute beginning.

Not only does Jesus bring new truth, new means of moral purification, a doctrine of more crystalline charity to be established among men; his entry into this old world of ours launches the new. And not merely in the intellectual sense through the recognition of hitherto unknown truths, or in the psychological sense of an all-renewing inner experience, but actually. "I came forth from the Father and have come into the world. Again I leave the world and go to the Father. . . . I have overcome the world" (John 16). This is not the tone of one who has morally or religiously worked his way through to another, higher plane of existence. Nothing in the Gospels suggests that Jesus had to struggle through worldly captivity or uncertainty to the complete freedom he enjoyed. This is what makes every attempt to 'psychoanalyze Jesus' as ridiculous as it is impossible; in him there is no such thing as 'development of personality.' His inner life is the fulfillment of a fact: that he is simultaneously Son of Man and God. The person of Jesus is unprecedented and therefore measurable by no already existing norm. Christian recognition consists of realizing that all things really began with Jesus Christ; that he is his own norm—and therefore ours—for he *is* Truth.

Christ's effect upon the world can be compared with nothing in its history save its own creation: "In the beginning God created heaven, and earth." What takes place in Christ is of the same order as the original act of creation, though on a still higher level. For the beginning of the new creation is as far superior to the old as the love revealed in the incarnation and the cross is to the love which created the stars, plants, animals and men. That is what the words mean: "I have come to cast fire upon the earth, and what will I but that it be kindled?" (Luke 12:49). It is the fire of new becoming; not only "truth" or "love," but the incandescence of new creation.

How earnest these words are is clear from those that follow: "But I have a baptism to be baptized with; and how distressed I am until it is accomplished!" "Baptism" is the mystery of creative depths: grave and womb in one. Christ must pass through them because human hardness of heart does not allow him to take the other road. Down, down through terrible destruction he descends, to the nadir of divine creation whence saved existence can climb back into being.

Now we understand what St. Paul meant with his "excelling knowledge of Jesus Christ": the realization that this is who Christ is, the Descender. To make this realization our own is the *alpha* and *omega* of our lives, for it is not enough to know Jesus only as the Savior. With this supreme knowledge serious religious life can begin, and we should strive for it with our whole strength and earnestness, as a man strives to reach his place in his profession; as a scientist wrestles with the answer to his problem; as one labors at his life work or for the hand of someone loved above all else.

Are these directives for saints? No, for Christians. For you. How long must I wait? God knows. He can give himself to you overnight, you can also wait twenty years, but what are they in view of his advent? One day he will come. Once in the stillness of profound composure you will know: that is Christ! Not from a book or the word of someone else, but through him. He who is creative love brings your intrinsic potentialities to life. Your ego at its profoundest is he.

This is the literally all-excelling knowledge to which St. Paul refers. It springs like a spark from that "fire" Christ came to bring, streams like a wave from the "baptism" through which he had to pass. To know Christ entails accepting his will as norm. We can participate in the beginning which is he only by becoming one with his will. When we feel this we draw back, startled, for it means the cross. Then it is better to say honestly: "I can't, yet," than to mouth pious phrases. Slow there, with the large words "self-surrender" and "sacrifice"! It is better to admit our weakness and ask him to teach us strength. One day we shall really be able to place ourselves fully at his disposal, and our wills will really be one with his. Then we shall stand at the threshold of the new beginning. What that will mean we do not know. Perhaps pain or a great task, or the yoke of everyday existence. It can also be its own pure end; it is for God to decide.

Very likely after such an hour everything will seem to return to 'normal' and we will appear strange in our own eyes or fear that we have fallen from his love. We must not be confused, but hold fast to that hour or moment and continue our way. It will return; and gradually such moments will fuse to a permanent attitude something like that revealed in the words of the apostle: "For I am sure that neither death, nor life, nor angels, nor principalities, nor things present, nor things to come, nor powers, nor height, nor depth, nor any other creature will be able to separate us from the love of God, which is in Christ Jesus our Lord" (Rom. 8:38–39).

PART FIVE

The Last Days

I

ENTRY INTO JERUSALEM

In Bethphage, a place on Mount Olivet which they pass on the way to Jerusalem, Jesus sends the disciples ahead with a curious order: they are to go to the market-place, unbind an ass and her colt which they will find there, and bring them to him. Everything is as Jesus describes it, and when the owners protest, the disciples reply as instructed: ". . . the Lord has need of them," and they comply.

"Now this was done that what was spoken through the prophet might be fulfilled, *Tell the daughter of Sion: Behold, thy king comes to thee, meek and seated upon an ass, and upon a colt, the foal of a beast of burden. . . .* And they brought the ass and the colt, laid their cloaks on them, and made him sit thereon. And most of the crowd spread their cloaks upon the road, while others were cutting branches from the trees, and strewing them on the road. And the crowds that went before him, and those that followed, kept crying out, saying, *Hosanna to the Son of David! Blessed is he who comes in the name of the Lord! Hosanna in the highest!* And when he entered Jerusalem, all the city was thrown into commotion, saying, 'Who is this?' But the crowds kept on saying, 'This is Jesus the prophet from Nazareth of Galilee' " (Matt. 21:4–11).

This event is the prelude to the last six days of the Lord's life on earth. To understand it we must turn to the scholars of Old Testament history, who explain that it was customary to accompany pilgrims, particularly those who brought the seasonal first-offerings to the temple, in joyful procession through the city. Moreover, the population had got wind of Jesus' last miracle, the resurrection of Lazarus, for as St. John tells us, many had made the trip to Bethany just to see the one called back from death.

A profound excitement grips the city; the multitude flows towards the temple, and pours into its sacred precincts. Here the Synoptics report the cleansing of the Temple which John describes as part of Jesus' first visit to Jerusalem (John 2:14). Perhaps it is a second cleansing, for since the abuses continued, any number of 'sweepings' are possible. Invalids gather and Jesus heals them. Disciples, people from the street, children run through the halls calling again and again: "Hosanna to the Son of David!" And when the officials accost Jesus and demand to know whether he hears and approves the blasphemous words, he asks if they have never read that truth will be revealed by "the mouths of infants and sucklings." Luke adds the words of the Pharisees telling him to forbid them, and Jesus' reply: "I tell you that if these keep silence, the stones will cry out" (19:40).

The hour overflows with supernatural power. In these last days it is as if Jesus were gathering strength on strength preparing for the ultimate. He has just summoned Lazarus from the dead. His power has accompanied the disciples into the world, so that at their word strangers entrust their flocks to them. Now triumphantly he enters Jerusalem, fulfilling to the letter the prophecy of the coming Messiah. Until then he has refused to be called the Messiah and crowned king; now he proclaims himself the long awaited one. It is clear enough for all who have eyes to see. There is tremendous excitement. A steadily swelling stream of people, loud with the voices of adults and the cries of children, flows endlessly in the direction of the temple; it can no longer be stopped. Buyers and sellers in the temple are sent flying; the sick are healed; the hostile, who ask with what right all this is done, are silenced by the impact of the answer.

It is a prophetic event. Prophecy ceased a long time ago. Centuries have passed since Malachi last spoke. After that the voice faded and remained mute until in John, "one crying in the desert," it awakens one last time (Matt. 3:3). Now he too is dead. But the ghost of prophecy rises once more and seizes the multitude, and "in the spirit" the multitude beholds and interprets and acts. The prophetic experience lifts the historical barriers that hem in ordinary lives. Living in history, we experience only the present, the immediate. This is as it should be; it simplifies decision and directs action (for in this world only ignorance gives us the freedom necessary to act). Moving in prophecy, the Holy Spirit dissolves all limitations and enables the prophet, from his new, unhindered vantage-point, to see simultaneously what was, what is, and what is to be. For the prophet time is telescoped. Standing in the living present, he sees both past and future, for he is already part of eternity. Living in history, our interior life is hidden from one another. It is impossible to see, understand, grasp the inner life of another, save when it is self-revealed. This is also well; it is the foundation of modesty and respect and enables us to act, to take chances, to participate in the shaping of our destinies. If the inner existence stood open to view, history would be impracticable, for it can play its role only among masked players. In eternity, where souls are transparent, history no longer exists. The prophet, however, already sees into others, or rather, the Spirit so places him that he sees things from within. We see only appearances; their meaning is hidden. Once in a while their sense blazes out on us, briefly, only to reenfold itself in darkness. Thus we live in mystery and hope. To the prophet the meaning of things is revealed; for him there is no borderline between mystery and revelation.

But here we must make a distinction. There are also purely natural gifts of a similar order. Much that is premature and confused and erroneous has been claimed of clairvoyance, but that it exists cannot seriously be denied. This does not mean, however, that it is prophecy. One does not become a prophet by talent, but by the Spirit of God summoning to a special service. The prophet is sustained by the salutary will of God, and collaborates with him on his works and on the history resulting from them. Knowledge of the future is not what makes the prophet, but his ability to interpret history according to the salutary, divine will behind it, proclaiming this will in advance to history in the making. Prophecy is divine revelation of the sense of history.

It is with such prophecy that we are dealing here. Jesus acts—and the same Spirit that inspires his action moves in those about him, revealing to them its meaning. Simultaneously, their eyes see the Lord as he rides through the street, and their spirit sees what is behind the event. The physical eye and the spiritual are one. And those who so truly 'saw' in that hour were not the particularly talented, neither geniuses nor in any way the elite or the mighty, but 'the common people,' those who happened to be in the streets at the time. For the power that opened their eyes and hearts was not human power, but the Spirit of God moving among men. Indeed, it is "the little ones," possessors of the kingdom of heaven, as Jesus calls them, who are particularly free and open to the workings of the Spirit, for in them it can operate untrammelled by the consciousness of their own human value. This then is God's hour; were the masses to reject it, the stones beneath their feet would proclaim the Messiah. It is the last, God-given chance. Will those seized by its power also find the strength to act according to the Spirit? Will they after all force the gate of the kingdom which had seemed so hopelessly barred? When we look closely at the figure the Lord cuts as he rides along, and at the people running at his side, when we imagine ourselves actual witnesses of the scene, how true the words of the apostle seem: ". . . to the Jews indeed a stumbling-block, and to the Gentiles foolishness . . ." (I Cor. 1:23).

Here it is again, the "stumbling-block," "scandal," that so often reigned instead of love. It had already broken out in Nazareth. No matter what Jesus said—though he uttered words of divine power and profundity—invariably they were answered with stubbornness, distrust, and hate. No matter what he did—heal, help, pardon, shower with gifts—his thanks were hardness of heart, calumny, misinterpretation of his motives, blasphemy against the Spirit. Now again scandal rears its head. A high tide of enthusiasm floods the temple, washing away indifference, pain, and human suffering. One would suppose that nobody could resist its salutary power, and that the great community of hearts prerequisite to the founding of God's kingdom on earth would at last become vital reality. Instead, the Pharisees step to the fore and demand Jesus' legitimation! Indignant, they ask if he does not hear the blasphemous things his disciples are proclaiming; why he does not stop the nonsensical shouts of the children. They are so incapable of feeling the divinity of the hour, that after his reply about the stones proclaiming him were the others to be silenced, Jesus turns on his heel and leaves them.

And the foolishness unto the Gentiles? One interpreter writes that it is tempting to compare Jesus' entry into Jerusalem with the triumphal marches glittering with pomp and ceremony as we know them from the pages of Roman history. Jesus too is a victorious sovereign. His power is apparent to all. Cheering crowds surge towards the Omnipotent One, and the breath of divinity is in the air. And yet—suppose a high-ranking Roman officer in shining armor had trotted by just then on his blooded mount, his orderly troop behind him, a fragment of that great army which bore the power of Rome across the world. What would he have thought had he seen the poorly dressed man on his donkey, a coat as a saddle, the heterogenous crowd about him? The thought hurts, but that is how it was.

This then is how it is when God descends to men! The apparent folly and danger of it are so great that the just and orthodox prepare for legal condemnation. The event is not even clothed in the dignity of genuine poverty. That would have also been impressive, for side by side with the power of greatness there exists the moving or august power of poverty, which stirs by its own mysterious power. But it is not genuine poverty that accompanies Jesus—neither among his disciples nor in the cheering masses. It is simply the average crowd as it is to be found everywhere in workshop, store and street. Crowd in which we all could find our place—human reality, mediocrity bare of the pathos both of splendor and of misery.

How difficult it is to recognize the self-revealing God! How difficult to steer clear of the scandal to the worldly sense of propriety and righteousness!

II

INDURATION

After Jesus' entry into Jerusalem and his self-revelation in word and deed as the Messiah, we expect the following days to be filled with violent struggle. However, when we read the reports we are surprised. It is difficult to describe the Lord's bearing during those last days. What does he do, actually? Does he fight? He certainly does not concede an inch. To the end he upholds his claims, keeps all doors open to the possibility of being heard. The kingdom can still come. The leaders of the people can still accept him, or the people themselves turn to him. But Jesus also sees that the decision has already fallen, and that his road leads to death. He does not fight to win over the people or their leaders, nor does he retire into mere readiness for his fate. What does he do?

There is no other way of putting it: he completes his mission. Again he says what he has come to say, stresses what must be remembered, drives home God's demands. He follows no set plan of action, but speaks extemporaneously. He neither retreats nor advances; neither renounces a point nor attempts to gain one. He perfects his task—with his last breath: "It is consummated" (John 19:30). Thus these final, supreme days are at once wonderfully powerful, rich, decisive and yet astonishingly calm. Something of ultimate, universal importance is brought to a head and clarified.

On the evening of Jesus' triumphal entry into Jerusalem he does not remain in the city, but returns to Bethany. The next morning he goes again to the temple: "And when he had come into the temple, the chief priests and elders of the people came to him as he was teaching, and said, 'By what authority dost thou do these things? And who gave thee this authority?' " (Matt. 21:23).

The question *per se* is legitimate. Those responsible for the people's welfare and for the revelation guarded by the temple have not only the right, but the duty to examine anyone who comes with such tremendous claims. The reply is obvious; Jesus could have answered as he has before, by referring to the prophecies: "You search the Scriptures, because in them you think that you have life everlasting. And it is they that bear witness to me . . ." (John 5:39). Had they then asked how he could prove that it was he whom Scripture meant, he could have pointed to the miracles. But the Pharisees had already denounced the miracles as sin because they had often taken place on the Sabbath. Worse, they had been performed in a questionable if not satanic manner, and hence were evidence against Jesus! (See John 9:16; Matt. 12:10, 24.) The question as posed is prejudiced from the start; its sole aim is to place the interrogated one in the wrong.

Jesus is aware of this, so he replies with a counter-question: Where did John's baptism come from—from heaven or from men? John the Baptist as the last prophet had borne witness to Jesus. The purity of his divine mission is unquestionable. His life, his teachings, his death are still fresh in everyone's memory. Jesus' question allows of only one reply. So the Pharisees remain silent; they turn over in their minds what it would be cleverest to say, and finally hedge. They avoid the ground on which Jesus stands, clinging to their own earthly and political wills, and refusing to recognize the value of John's mission and the common reality to which he and Jesus have devoted their lives. Even humanly speaking, this crossing of swords ends in defeat for the Pharisees. Now they concentrate their forces for the fresh assault, this time sending courtiers from Herod's palace to ensnare Jesus: "Then the Pharisees went and took counsel how they might trap him in his talk. And they sent to him their disciples with the Herodians, saying, 'Master, we know that thou art truthful, and that thou teachest the way of God in truth, and that thou carest naught for any man; for thou dost not regard the person of men. Tell us, therefore, what dost thou think: Is it lawful to give tribute to Caesar, or not?' But Jesus, knowing their wickedness, said, 'Why do you test me, you hypocrites? Show me the coin of the tribute.' So they offered him a denarius. Then Jesus said to them, 'Whose are this image and the inscription?' They said to him, 'Caesar's.' Then he said to them, 'Render, therefore, to Caesar the things that are Caesar's, and to God the things that are God's' " (Matt. 22:15–22).

The young royalists accompanied by disciples of the Pharisees begin their cross-questioning courteously enough—even with flattery. Then comes the shot from the ambush. It is meant to be fatal whichever way the Lord answers. If he says tribute should be paid, he is an accomplice of the national enemy, and will be held up to the people as a traitor. If he says tribute should not be paid, he will be denounced to the Roman procurator as a rebel. Only twenty years ago, when the country was first occupied by the Romans, a certain Judas of Galilee had declared that the conquerors should not be acknowledged, and tribute refused. The revolt thus incited was quenched in blood. The whole subject of tribute is still dangerous enough.

Jesus hears the question, but does not walk into the trap. He demands a tribute-coin, a silver *denarius*. The Israelites have minting rights only for copper, not for silver and gold, so it is a Roman coin. Then give to the Roman what is his.

Jesus says nothing about paying or not paying tribute; nothing of the rights or wrongs of foreign occupation or obedience to its laws. He says judge for yourselves and do what is right. Precisely the same attitude he took when the man with the inheritance-suit came to him for help: "Man, who has appointed me a judge or arbitrator over you?" (Luke 12:14). He refuses to profane his mission by discussing worldly problems, for which they have their own judgment. They should decide for themselves, carrying their decisions before their consciences and before those in power. Actually, what he is saying is: over and above Caesar, regardless of who he is or what is his, stands God. That is Jesus' real answer. The question as such is calmly shoved aside because as it was formulated, it was directed against revelation, and precisely that passage which Christ's enemies had hoped to block—to the free area of his tidings—is ripped open. Here it is again, God's reality unfettered by pharisaic thinking, challenge of the approaching kingdom.

Silenced, the Pharisees retire.

They are the Conservatists of the country, the Orthodox; stubborn defenders of sacred tradition and passionate nationalists. Opposed to them are the Sadducees, highly cultivated cosmopolitans, sceptics, epicures. Until now they have held themselves aloof from the affair of the new Rabbi. His religious penetration, the exigency of his prophetic power are distasteful to them. But gradually they begin to consider him dangerous. They fear he might prove politically embarrassing—or even worse—that he might establish a religious dictatorship. Therefore, with ironical, superior mien, they also take a hand in the matter: "On that same day some of the Sadducees, who say there is no resurrection, came to him, and questioned him, saying, 'Master, Moses said, "If a man die without having a son, his brother shall marry the widow and raise up issue to his brother." Now there were among us seven brothers. And the first, after having married a wife, died, and having no issue, left his wife to his brother. In like manner the second, and the third down to the seventh. And last of all the woman also died. At the resurrection, therefore, of which of the seven will she be the wife? for they all had her.' But Jesus answered and said to them, 'You err because you know neither the Scriptures nor the power of God. For at the resurrection they will neither marry nor be given in marriage, but will be as angels of God in heaven. But as to the resurrection of the dead, have you not read what was spoken to you by God, saying, "I am the God of Abraham, and the God of Isaac, and the God of Jacob"? He is not the God of the dead, but of the living' " (Matt. 22:23–33).

The Sadducees believe neither in resurrection nor in the life hereafter, but only in the tangible present. In short, they are sceptics. The very manner in which they word their question is ironical, contemptuous, perhaps even slightly off-color. What will Jesus reply to these men, who don't care a fig for the answer, but wish only to ward off reality? He does exactly as he did before—exposes them with all their so-called knowledge as ignorant and malevolent, and points out that an afterlife in which they and their kind would feel at home does not exist, for it would be a mere continuation of their present existence. Above this entirely earthly realm, he points out, arches another, the real world. From there, from revelation, and the power of God, who is God of life, the true resurrection will come as a breakthrough into that life in which his messengers and those who hear them already live.

And again Christ's assailants are silenced, but untouched by his words; they do not open their hearts to him. They remain exactly as they were. Worse, they are ashamed, irritated, and retire to wait for the next opportunity.

And the Pharisees? At first they are pleased by the defeat of their traditional foes. However, they soon realize that it is high time to take more dramatic measures against this man whom the people admire and who definitely threatens to remain master of the situation.

So they lay fresh traps for him: which is the greatest commandment? The process is always the same: Jesus stands there, the incarnation of messianic reality. His word is vibrant with the power of the Spirit. About him gleams the aura of his miracles. The hearers have only to unstop their ears, stretch out their hands to seize the truth. But this is precisely what they refuse to do. They close themselves up tightly. They do not give the Lord a chance to approach them in his true capacity, but try to enmesh him in the tangle of earthly tradition and politics. If they succeed he is lost. He replies by ripping open the reality above them, but the result is terrible. They are mastered, yes, but in the negative sense of the word. They do not admit the vanity of their probing, and follow him into the freedom of the spirit, but are tactically defeated. The result is only wounded pride, renewed hatred, and another ambush.

Could it have been otherwise? Isn't it heroic but senseless optimism on Jesus' part to keep the possibility of acceptance open to the last? No. St. Mark reports the question of the greatest commandment slightly differently. In reply to Jesus' answer one of the Scribes says to him: " 'Well answered, Master, thou hast said truly that he is one and that there is no other besides him; and that he should be loved with the whole heart, and with the whole understanding, and with the whole soul, and with one's whole strength; and that to love one's neighbor as oneself is a greater thing than all holocausts and sacrifices.' And Jesus, seeing that he had answered wisely, said to him, 'Thou art not far from the kingdom of God.' " (Mark 12:32–34).

This man asked rightly and therefore understood the reply. His question came from the genuine desire for revelation. Here we see how it might have been. Thus all should have asked—and heard, or at least enough to turn the tide of history. For there lay the terrible drama of the moment—that so much depended on the conversion of this man or that! (Then, it was not question of the acceptance or rejection of constantly reiterated tidings, but whether or not God's Messenger was to be permitted to live!)

That he was not; that of so many questioners and hearers hardly one really wholeheartedly accepted him; that instead, with all the powers of intellect, with the long religious training of the Old Covenant, they kept him at a distance and their hearts hermetically sealed—that is a phenomenon for which the word tragedy hardly suffices. . . . It has been asked whether there is such a thing as tragedy in Christianity. If there were, then certainly in the figure of Jesus Christ—but, is there? Or in the figures of his opponents and of the Jewish people—but are they tragic? No, the word does not fit.

To tragedy belongs a world that is not in the hands of the living God. Its sense is that in this world nobility perishes because it is related either to weakness or to pride, but that in the very process of its destruction, it is exalted to the spheres of the "ideal" or of the "spirit." The pith of tragedy—in spite of all its sense of freedom and exaltation—is hopelessness. Behind ancient tragedy stood at least the hope of Advent; behind modern tragedy there is nothing but a dream, for the modern world is complete in itself and self-isolated from its Creator and Sustainer. Over it hangs the shadow of an awful (though to a large extent only aesthetic) earnestness, and it is precisely in the exaltation of its so-called ideal and spiritual spheres, that this artistic element is most sharply evident. Last paling shimmer of a once known, genuine kingdom of freedom—that of God and his grace—it is only a remnant that makes no demands and consoles only as long as it is not examined too closely. In Christian faith there exists neither a world complete in itself nor the spheres of the super-spiritual or ideal. All that exists are people and things in the sight of God. God is their Lord, but also their Savior; their incorruptible judge, but also a forgiving Re-creator and Renewer far excelling human hope. Human destiny is "tragic" when it fails its high possibilities; but actually, in the final Christian analysis, even such "failure" is caught up into the love and understanding of an all-redeeming, all-powerful God, omnipotent even over blame and misspent opportunity. This same God, though, is inexorable, and his judgment unswayed by aestheticism or tragic transfiguration. The earnestness of tragedy pales before the earnestness of the divine.

The Messiah who accomplished the redemption of man by his death is no tragic hero. The people that failed to recognize its Savior, destroying him instead in their blindness and hardness, is not burdened with a tragic destiny. It is no more tragic than was the fall of the first man; as little a tragic catastrophe as will be the Last Judgment. Here everything is real: not "dramatic"; man is a reality, and sin, and the sorrow that comes of it, and the ultimate consequence of sin—revolt against the only One who can rescue. But redemption is also real, and real consequently, the new beginning and grace that are its fruits.

III

GOD'S HUMILITY

Sometime or other the disquieting thought occurs to anyone who seriously endeavors to know Jesus' life: Is such a thing possible? The question does not arise facilely. For almost two thousand years the image of the Lord has moved men's minds and sentiments; accepting Jesus' incredible existence as the well-known and self-understood canon of right living, they have forgotten wonder. However, once one begins to probe beneath the surface of that existence, the question is bound to tap on the pane of consciousness: what is the real nature of Jesus, and what that of human life as determined by him? A centuries-old struggle against the supremacy of Christ has so undermined his prestige in the eyes of many, that today the mere question is often tantamount to refusal. Millions reject the conception of man drawn by Christ. All the more clearly then, must the believer be capable of recognizing the essence of that Christianity against which opposition turns with deepening and ever increasing violence—and not only in the hearts and minds of "the others," but also in ourselves. Only when we accept Christ and his radically new conception of man not merely by an act of will or for reasons of blind loyalty, but by vital conviction, are we Christians.

To understand antiquity's idea of man, we must examine its gods and heroes, myths and legends. In these we find the classical prototype of genuine man. Assuredly, side by side with the proud and the noble, we find the most repulsive crime, downfall and annihilation; nevertheless, all characters and events have one trait in common: the will to greatness, wealth, power and fame. This is the measure applied to all things, even to sacrilege and death. Anything opposed to it falls short of the authentically human. It comes under the rubric Second Class Humanity—small fry burdened with the problems of ordinary life, slaves. These are necessarily there, but they have no share in genuine humanity.

What a world of difference between this conception and that to which Christ has led us! Here grandeur of existence, human splendor are no longer measuring-rod. Much in the life of Christ is totally outside the pale of accepted antique values. The race from which Jesus springs is one of vanished glory; but he does not dream of reviving it. With him it is no question of the will to power, or fame as a philosopher, or the poet's glory. Jesus is poor. Not as Socrates is poor, with a philosophical flavor to his poverty, but literally poor. Not poor as one who has been struck down by fate, or as a great ascetic, through whose poverty a painful or mysterious greatness blazes, but poor simply in the sense of absence of needs (which, incidentally, are provided for).

Jesus' friends are in no way remarkable for their talent or character. He who considers the apostles or disciples great from a human or religious point of view raises the suspicion that he is unacquainted with true greatness. Moreover, he is confusing standards, for the apostle and disciple have nothing to do with such greatness. Their uniqueness consists of their being sent, of their God-given role of pillars of the coming salvation.

As for Jesus' own destiny—how disturbingly terrible it is! He teaches, but his teachings take root nowhere, not even among his own followers, for they do not understand. He struggles, but it is no genuine struggle, for the opposing forces never really clash. All he does and all that is done to him bears the stamp of mysterious failure. He does not end in grandiose enterprise, but in court. His friends do nothing—the impression Peter's conduct in Gethsemane and in the courtyard of the high priest must make on any *homme d'honneur* is pitiful. From the natural standpoint, Jesus' passion and death are only torturous and unbearable. We understand and shud-

deringly sympathize with the death of a great philosopher who dies
for his ideas; or that of the hero who goes down in battle, or of Caesar, who in the very act of mounting to the epitome of power falls
under the daggers of the conspirators. But how can one see without
revolt the proclaimer of divine wisdom being spat upon, or watch
the soldiers play their gruesome pranks, or witness a death intended
to annihilate not only the body of the Lord, but also his honor and
the mission for which he came? But the "scandal" neither begins
nor ends there. Before this there had been the "blood of the new
covenant," that mystery which as Jesus prophesied in Capharnaum,
would be intolerable to those who heard it (Matt. 26:28), and afterwards, the tremendous event of the Resurrection, which modern
science dismisses as fantastic or pathological. Nevertheless, this Eucharist is the central mystery of Christian life; this death has become
the fountainhead of salutary existence; this Resurrection has been
the all-transforming power now for almost two millennia.

How strange it all is! If we ask antiquity: What is the true nature of
man and how may it be realized?—the answer is: By a life of
grandeur. And what does Christianity reply to the same question?
(There is of course no such thing as 'the' Christian answer.) Anything is possible. Nothing necessarily precludes—neither the most
exalted existence nor the most shameful. Everything is summoned—
the entire, plumbless, unpredictable scale of human possibilities.
Everything, the noblest and the basest, receives from Christ new significance, for in everything lies the seed of new beginning. How
great the transformation of our conception of man through Christianity, is something we are again beginning to appreciate, now that
its validity is no longer generally accepted. Perhaps the moment is
not distant in which the Christian ideal, like that of antiquity during
the Renaissance, will overwhelm the modern consciousness with its
unspeakable plenitude.

Not only our idea of man has been modified by Christ, also our
idea of God. Through Jesus' life and teachings, the believer per-

ceives who God is. To the question about the Father Christ answers: ". . . he who sees me sees also the Father" (John 14:9). St. Paul identifies him as "The God and Father of the Lord Jesus" (II Cor. 11:31). But what is he like, this God? How does he compare with the Supreme Being of the philosophers? With the universal life of Hinduism, with the wisdom of all happening described in Taoism? With the human-superhuman abundance of Greek gods and their intense vitality and Olympian superiority? Even the Christian's conception of God is anything but self-understood. Two thousand years of intellectual and spiritual development have familiarized us with the "God and Father of the Lord Jesus" as the image of divine being. For some time, however, western culture has begun to desert this conception of the Supreme Power, and it is now evident why it had to be historically revealed.

What is he like, the God of Jesus Christ? Since he revealed himself in the person and destiny of Jesus, he must be like Jesus. What divine reality then is ours through our knowledge of the New Testament? From Socrates' figure radiates the sublimity of philosophical summits; from the Greek Pantheon the divinity of luminous heights or terrestrial depths; from the ranks of Hindu divinities, the universal-One-and-All behind all things; what message is there for us in the life of Jesus? What kind of Father becomes apparent in this Son who is so lamentably 'unsuccessful'? Who finds no better companions than a group of fishermen? Who succumbs to a caste of politically ambitious theologians? Who is arrested and 'liquidated' as a dangerous enthusiast and upstart? We forget, in the Incarnation, God did not merely fill a human being with his light, or carry him away in a surge of divine enthusiasm, he himself "came"—*in person* (John 1:11). What Christ did, God did. What Christ suffered, God suffered. The Father rejected no part of the life of his Son. The "I" behind the teachings and experiences of Jesus' life stands for "God" and reveals him; hence its inestimable importance to us. Moreover, the brief life of God on earth is no episode ending with Jesus' death; the band that connects him with humanity continues through the Resurrection and Ascension into all time. Never again is God to brush off the handful of finite being that was Jesus of Nazareth. Henceforth and to all eternity God remains the God who became man. This alone is so unheard of that something within us very nearly revolts. How can such 'behavior' be reconciled with genuine godhead?

Your thinking is false, says Christianity. You expect your human conception of man to answer to your conception of divinity, which in turn you try to reconcile with the personality and fate of Jesus. Thus you make yourself judge of what is essentially a manner of existence and point of departure outside human experience. You must reverse your whole approach to God and ask: With Jesus as he is, and his life as it was, how must the God he revealed be the "God and Father" of Jesus Christ? And the question must be constantly renewed, that our faith and love remain intensely conscious of the God who has summoned us.

Its answer confronts us on every page of Holy Scripture: He must be one who loves. Love does such things; it passes up the standards of usage and so-called reason. It begins anew and creates. We learn further that God is more than "the loving" one, more than the perfect fulfillment of all existing love, he is *Love itself.* Turned about, the logical consequence of our thought now recognizes the truth that what we call "love" is only the reflection, often distorted, of an attitude, a power whose real name is God. . . . When such a God enters human history, must he not necessarily shatter all traditional forms of existence? Mustn't his presence in an alien world seem strangely disquieting? That presence which is pulled down to the nadir of paltriness, only to rise again sky-high in a superabundance of glory surpassing anything ever known? That is correct; but in order to grasp all that the word "love" means here, we must examine another facet of it that has as yet escaped our attention.

Since God is love, is there anything love cannot do? Why doesn't he simply pour his light into men's spirit? Why doesn't his truth break in on it, truth that is simultaneously glory and irresistible costliness, that consumes men with desire for him? That would also be love—why then an existence like that of Jesus?

We answer: because of sin. But can sin hinder the all-powerful will of love? Can't God fill men with such horror of sin that they fly to him in contrition and love? Who is to say what is possible and what not? No, there must be something else in God that the word love does not cover. It seems that we must say, God is humble.

But first let us clarify the word. We use it to describe someone who bows to the grandeur of another; or who esteems a talent that surpasses his own; or who appreciates without envy another's merit. That is not humility but honesty. Difficult as it may sometimes be, such an attitude is no more or less than simple intellectual integrity. Humility, however, does not move upwards, but downwards. It does not mean that the lesser one respectfully acknowledges the greater, but that the greater reverently bends to the lesser one. By this profound mystery we can measure how far removed the Christian attitude is from any natural earthiness. That the great one kindly descends to the little one, gently respecting his importance, that he is touched by weakness and makes himself its defender—this much we comprehend. But humility beings only where greatness *reverently* bows before one who is not great.

Doesn't the great one degrade himself by such stooping? This is precisely what he does not do. Walking in humility, he is mysteriously self-confident and knows that the more daringly he flings himself away, the more certainly he will find himself. . . . Will his gesture be rewarded? Definitely. In his humble encounter with the little man, he learns to appreciate his intrinsic value. Not that he to whom he descends "also has his worth," but that his very unimportance possesses a special costliness of its own. To the humble one this is a great revelation. When St. Francis knelt at the throne of the Pope it was not an act of humility (since he believed in the papal dignity) but only of verity; he was humble when he bowed to the poor. Not as one who condescends to help them, or whose humanitarian instinct sees in every beggar a remnant of human dignity, but as one whose heart has been instructed by God flings himself to the ground before the mystery of paltriness as before that of majesty. He who does not see this must find Francis of Assisi *exalté*. Actually, he was only reproducing in himself the secret of Jesus.

When the Lord praises God because "'thou didst hide these things from the wise and prudent" and "didst reveal them to little ones" (Luke 10:21), this does not only mean that he is condemning pride by praising its opposite, or that he is holding up to men the incredibleness of the new divinity by destroying the existent standards—but that human nonentity itself is filled with grandeur and is precious to him. This is the attitude God brought with him to earth: ". . . learn from me, for I am meek, and humble of heart" (Matt. 11:29). Before the Last Supper he knelt before his disciples and washed their feet; not to debase himself, but to reveal to them the divine mystery of humility (John 13:4).

There is no other possibility: God himself must be humble. In him, the eternal, omnipotent, all-glorious One, must lie a readiness to prostrate himself before the infinite scrap of existence that we are in his eyes. Something in him must make him willing to assume the existence of an unknown human being from the village of Nazareth.

Is such a thing possible? Desirable? Isn't it unseemly folly? God himself replies, no. Already in the Old Testament he has said: It is my delight to dwell among the children of men. In all reverence, it must be mysteriously blissful for him to refind himself in the flesh-and-blood heart of the Nazarene. Here is a bliss the sense of which outstrips all measure, this assuming the responsibility for, experiencing the fate of, such an abandoned and questioned human life.

St. Paul touches on the same mystery when he says of Jesus: ". . . who though he was by nature God, did not consider being equal to God a thing to be clung to, but emptied himself, taking the nature of a slave and being made like unto men. . . . Therefore God also has exalted him and has bestowed upon him the name that is above every name . . ." (Phil. 2:6–9).

This then the humility of God—a stooping towards that which in his eyes hardly exists—humility possible only because he is everything that exists. Herein lies his ultimate glory.

"Did not the Christ have to suffer these things before entering into his glory?" From here, plumbless humility, he draws the splendor of that new creation of which John and Paul speak so prophetically.

This is what had to exist in addition to love, that Christian love might be. The love that sustained Jesus' life and according to St. John is God himself, is founded on such humility.

God then is the humbly loving One. What a reversal of all existing values—also divine! In truth, this God destroys everything that man in the pride of his revolt constructs of his own inspiration. Here ultimate temptation lifts its head: the impulse to say: "I will not bend the knee to such a God! To an absolute Being, to an all-inclusive Glory, to a Supreme Idea, a sublime Olympian, yes. To a humble God—no!" Christian humility though mirrors God's humility. It means above all that man accept his role: not Creator, but creature—and of a humble God. Man is not a noble being, not a beautiful soul or exalted spirit, but sinner, *peccator*. And as if this were not enough, sinner in the eyes of a humble Judge! Here we have it, expression of profoundest revolt in the often heard words—God is not to my taste. Humility means the breaking of this satanic taste-reaction, and bowing deeply, not only before God's majesty, but even more deeply before his humility: obeisance of all that is deemed great in the world before him whom the world despised. It means that as a natural human being conscious of health, beauty, strength, talent, intelligence and culture, he submits to him who from these familiar standards seems so questionable: Christ under the cross. To him who says of himself: "But I am a worm and no man: the reproach of men and the outcast of the people" (Psalm 21:7). This is the foundation and point of departure of Christian humility, never to be confused with the weakness of self-surrender or with ruse that purposely makes itself less than it is; still less with an inferiority complex. Humility and love are not virtues of degeneracy. They spring from that creative gesture of God which ignores all that is purely natural and are directed towards the new world in the process of creation. Thus a man can practice humility only to the extent that he is conscious of the grandeur, both actual and latent, that God has planted in him.

IV

THE DESTRUCTION
OF JERUSALEM AND
THE END OF THE WORLD

From the last days of Jesus' life the Gospels report also the following incident: "And as he was going out of the temple, one of his disciples said to him, 'Master, look, what wonderful stones and buildings!' And Jesus answered and said to him, 'Dost thou see all these great buildings? There will not be left one stone upon another that will not be thrown down!' "

Further: "And when you see the abomination of desolation, standing where it ought not—let him who reads understand. . . ." (Mark 13:1–2, 14).

And again, this time from Luke: "And when you see Jerusalem being surrounded by an army, then know that her desolation is at hand. Then let those who are in Judea flee to the mountains; and let those who are in her midst go out, and let those who are in the country not enter her. For these are days of vengeance, that all things that are written may be fulfilled. But woe to those who are with child, or have infants at the breast in those days! For there will be great distress over the land, and wrath upon this people. And they will fall by the edge of the sword, and will be led away as captives to all the nations. And Jerusalem will be trodden down by the Gentiles, until the times of the nations be fulfilled" (Luke 21:20–24).

Forty years later, Jesus' prophecy of the destruction of the holy city becomes historical reality.

What is proclaimed here is no mere political catastrophe. Naturally, it is that too, and is represented as such by the writers of history; Jesus, however, speaks of the event as a punishment of the city that has rejected the Messiah. During his last journey to Jerusalem again the words: "And when he drew near and saw the city, he wept over it, saying, 'If thou hadst known, in this thy day, even thou, the things that are for they peace! But now they are hidden from thy eyes. For days will come upon thee when thy enemies will throw up a rampart about thee, and surround thee and shut thee in on every side, and will dash thee to the ground and thy children within thee, and will not leave in thee one stone upon another, because thou hast not known the time of thy visitation' " (Luke 19:41–44).

Judgment, punishment—what is meant? Isn't world history world judgment? Definitely.

Every event has its consequences. Every considerate, dignified and just act renders peoples and nations prosperous; every senseless, unjust, unrealistic act destroys them. No impetus remains inconsequential movement; everything begun continues to its intrinsic end. What has been is the result of what was and prepares that which is to come. Thus there is a kind of continual judgment, often however, impenetrable and difficult to comprehend, particularly because the consequences of an action seldom rebound upon the heads of those responsible, but usually upon later generations. Often the form in which this 'judgment' falls is itself fresh injustice, evincing to those who look closely how profoundly the whole order of our existence has been destroyed. Such so-called judgment, however, is quite different from that which Jesus means and cannot be considered divine punishment for a certain fault. Should we say, for example, that Waterloo was God's punishment for Napoleon's presumption? Then the years of his fame must have been 'reward'—for what? No, that is not how things go. History is a highly complicated, incommensurable, interweaving cause and effect that in turn becomes new cause. To attempt to interpret it as divine judgment is a task that lies beyond human comprehension. The prosperity and "glory" of an age may in reality be chastisement; calamity, on the other hand, a sign of divine confidence, just as in the individual life, illness is not necessarily punishment, nor prosperity reward. When history is to be interpreted from God's point of view, he inspires a prophet through whom he himself may speak. We who live in history know only— no, believe (and this often only with great effort) that everything that happens to us comes ultimately from God, also when it occurs through the injustice of another. This is all we do know.

In world history there is only one nation of which it is possible to speak in terms of divine punishment—the Hebrew; for it was the sole nation whose earthly history was to be the direct result of its belief—or disbelief.

Isn't this true of all peoples? Doesn't the religious life always determine their deepest historical existence and with it the decisions that shape their temporal destinies? To be sure, the historical development of a race, whether it be Hindu, Greek or Roman, is conditioned by its religious attitude. Like artistic talent or military genius, religious life is rooted in a natural gift that is cultivated or neglected like any other. With the Jewish people this is not so. The Hebrews possess no religious history in the sense of natural development of original characteristics. Their evolution is unlike that of any other race before Christ; here there can be no talk of unfolding inherited religious traits or of schooling itself on the figures and teachings that have emerged from its own history. A truly Jewish religion would have been quite different from that which has actually come into existence. This people would have had certain religious experiences befitting their characteristics and would have tried to formulate them. At the same time it would have been influenced by the aborigines of the country, the Canaanites, as well as by the enormous polytheistic empires that flourished about them: the Babylonian, Assyrian, Persian, Egyptian and Greek. Thus a Semitic religion would have evolved largely similar to the others but with a stamp of its own. It would have gone the way of all religions—would have developed, purified itself, perhaps even approached a kind of monotheism, and then declined. But this is precisely what did not happen! At its beginning we find no "historical seed," no impulse upward from the root shaping first the blade; instead, there in all the richness and radiance of full maturity stands the ripe ear—figures whose greatness and purity are never to be surpassed in later Old Testamental history: Abraham and Moses. What takes place in them is no 'religious experience' emerging from the concentrated spiritual characteristics of their race, but God's summons to the Jewish people, the hand of the Lord in history. A holy Covenant is founded, first upon promise and faith, then upon law and obedience. What follows is an endless tug-of-war between the religious characteristics of this people (or of those who have influenced it) on the one side, and God and his truth and his law and his guidance on the other. In the sense then that Greek or Chinese religion exists, Jewish religion does not exist at all. What does exist is that nation's belief or disbelief: the struggle between divine revelation and the religious will of a people that accepts or rejects it.

The exterior history of Israel is the outcome of this struggle. It is the history of a people's obedience or disobedience to God; of its acceptance or rejection of the directives of his missionaries, lawgivers, judges and prophets; of its submission to his will or stubborn insistence on its own. When the Messiah, towards whom its whole history has been directed, finally arrives, Israel fails to understand the hour of its ultimate visitation "because thou hast not known the time" of salvation or "the things that are for thy peace," and achieves instead the fullness of disobedience. Punishment for this is the downfall of the city.

What an hour! Jesus knows that he is the Messiah and Bringer of salvation. He knows that in him alone is the possibility of all fulfillment—not only religious, but also historical; that all the promises of the past may be realized in him, yet he must watch this people closing itself to him! He cannot, will not force them, for the decision to salvation must be made in freedom. Therefore he must die and their judgment must fall. At this point begins the second part of Israel's history: the dispersion, with all the misfortune it brings upon her and others.

Behind the downfall of the Holy City looms a catastrophe of quite different dimensions: the downfall of the world.

"For in those days will be tribulations, such as have not been from the beginning of the creation which God created until now, nor will be. And unless the Lord had shortened the days, no living creature would be saved. But for the sake of the elect whom he has chosen, he has shortened the days.

"And then, if anyone say to you, 'Behold, here is Christ; behold, there he is,' do not believe it. For false christs and false prophets will arise, and will show signs and wonders, so as to lead astray, if possible, even the elect. Be on your guard, therefore; behold, I have told you all things beforehand.

"But in those days, after that tribulation, the sun will be darkened, and the moon will not give her light, and the stars of heaven will be falling, and the powers that are in heaven will be shaken. And then they will see the Son of Man coming upon clouds with great power and majesty. And then he will send forth his angels, and will gather his elect from the four winds, from the uttermost parts of the earth to the uttermost parts of heaven. . . .

"But of that day or hour no one knows, neither the angels in heaven, nor the Son, but the Father only. Take heed, watch and pray, for you do not know when the time is: just as a man, when he leaves home to journey abroad, puts his servants in charge, to each his work, and gives orders to the porter to keep watch. Watch, therefore, for you do not know when the master of the house is coming, in the evening, or at midnight, or at cockcrow, or early in the morning; lest coming suddenly he find you sleeping. And what I say to you, I say to all, 'Watch.' "

Again we must make distinctions. Men have attempted to understand the end of the world scientifically. They have asserted that the temperature of the globe would sink so far that life would no longer be possible; or that cosmic energy would neutralize itself, and the world would therefore cease to exist. There have been other hypotheses, but Jesus is referring to none of them. The end he means is no more the result of natural causes than Jerusalem's end is the result of mere historical necessity. The end of the world—like that of the Holy City—is a judgment, and comes, not from any natural development, but from the sovereign will of God.

This judgment is God's final word to sin, for God is not merely sin's demasker, not merely the guardian of moral law, but its avenger. God hates sin. At sight of it something mounts in him whose terribleness Scripture calls "the wrath of God." This swells until his patience reaches the breaking-point. The contrition of the sinner can disperse it—witness the saving of Nineveh through Jonas' preaching (Jonas 3). However, one day the measure will be full. When nothing lives on earth to justify it in God's holy sight, judgment will fall. (We are reminded of the destruction of Sodom and Gomorrha.) When not even that minimum number of the just exists in the cities to save them they will be lost. And not because historically speaking they were incapable of continuing existence, but because the wrath of God could no longer be contained (see Gen. 19).

The end of the world will come from a quarter whence few things come to the world—from there where revelation comes, and the Son and the Holy Ghost. Therefore it is senseless to ask how it will occur; it is an event from 'beyond' and accordingly incomprehensible. What Scripture has to say about it is not meant as a scientific explanation; Revelation is simply a series of pictures that suggest the shock to all existing orders and powers.

Saints Paul and John tell us, however, that through this violence the world will be transformed and the new heaven and new earth will appear. But they too are a mystery whose splendor only Christian hope can envision (Rom. 8:17–18; Apoc. 21:1).

When the modern hears of such things, he smiles. At best he accepts them as a profound myth. In his consciousness, the world is a given quantity, condition on which everything rests, absolute content. How can it then cease to be? For him an end of the world would be utterly meaningless, both from its own point of view and from God's—if he happens to believe in God. Here we sense the unreality of our modern conception of God and world, and we begin to realize how little claim the 'belief' of this late era can make to its name. For such believers, God is the ultimate consecration of existence; he is the activating mystery behind all things, an exalted Something somewhere "up there," far too removed to ever tamper with the reality of the world. He is a sacred impotence that satisfies the nebulous desires of human sensibility, but nothing that could really threaten the world with catastrophe.

And yet this is the meaning of Revelation: that the world is neither a given quantity nor a unique reality, but a part of creation that exists because its Creator so wills—for as long as he wills. Even its beginning is due not to any natural phenomenon relating to an eternal material or protoenergy, but to a voluntary act of God. He, her Creator, is also her Lord. Within the world God permits natural and historical necessity to reign; the world as a whole, however, is an autonomous piece neither of nature nor of history; it is God's property, of which he can dispose as he pleases—even if, in the meantime, it has become "modern" and ceases to believe in him.

Terrible irony! The scientific skeptic, the man of practical success, the philosopher of self-exalted worldliness all chuckle over such "fairytales." As if *God* could make an end of the world! This was precisely the amusement of the powerful and sophisticated in the days of the prophets, through whose mouths God proclaimed disaster over city and nation. They too considered themselves enlightened realists; reasoned along lines of fact and necessity—and the catastrophe came. And not for any objective cause that they had failed to predetermine because their logic had been insufficiently precise, not because they had not acted circumspectly enough; it came, simply from the same source that had called the prophets to announce its coming. Because the intellectual elite saw city and people only politically, the prophets' warnings were for them annoying and dangerous nonsense. The Hebrew people had been called upon—simultaneously its yoke and its glory—to fulfill its history not according to natural cause and effect, but in accordance with its faith. Thus it was from the least expected quarter, from the apparently non-existent, that its fate fell. It is the same thing today. For those who take only the natural or historical order of things seriously, every word about the end of the world is utter nonsense. Nevertheless, it will come; and not of itself, but of God. To accept this and to live accordingly, that is faith.

And again, what a situation! There stands the poor Rabbi from Nazareth who in a few days will be arrested, and says: The city will be destroyed! The world will be destroyed! And both because you have failed to accept the Son of God! The world will come to an end when your resistance to him has passed its fixed limit, and the measure of divine wrath is full. Signal to the catastrophe will be the sign of the Son of Man, the proclamation of his advent. . . . Really, it takes great faith to assent to this! It has been suggested that when Jesus realized that he was getting nowhere with his message, he took refuge in the incomprehensible; that by hoping for power in some nebulous future, he bridged the actual impotence of the hour. . . . Much could be said to this view—primarily that for all its cleverness, it is highly superficial. But the observation would hardly be decisive; everything depends on the answer to the question: "But who do you say that I am?" (Matt. 16:15). If we consider Jesus only the greatest of all religious geniuses, a man, not also divine, then his words are helpless ravings, and the terms "faith of Christ" and the "faith" of those who believe in him are nothing but abuses of the word. If, however, we recognize him as the actual Son of God the Creator and Lord, we do not presume to judge his words, because there is no standard by which to do so—neither scientific, historical, nor religious. They are their own standard. He is the First and the Last, and what he says is revelation (Apos. 1:17). Here faith begins. This is our answer to the world. We must remember that in the final analysis, faith has no legitimation but itself. Perhaps the modern Christian's 'arena' is this constant challenge to his words and beliefs by an incredulous world. To every answer faith gives, the world knows a different one. The world's conception of existence seems to grow increasingly complete, whereas the reasoning of faith continues to be looked at askance and is accordingly isolated. Thus it becomes more and more clear that the believer can prove his standpoint to the world only after death. This is not easy, but must be accepted, along with the mockery over faith itself, which the world can explain only as the self-consolation of its losers.

This is the faith in which we must exercise ourselves, even as in the fear of God. The end of the world and Judgment are not to be regarded as myths of a distant future, but as possibilities of God's wrath that keep astride of our own lives. We do not inhabit a safe, biological, historical and spiritual unit that goes its invulnerable way under the canopy of a harmless religious mystery called God, but like Jerusalem, both we as individuals and the world as a whole live under the ever-present possibility of judgment. Only when the protection that direct reality seems to give my obtuse senses has been partly withdrawn and the threat of God has become a personal reality, am I a believer in the full Biblical meaning of the word.

Modern thought has pushed all this to the background. The modern approaches the whole subject of the fear of God morally or with a peculiar shyness, because he does not see it for what it is: the fruit of sacred, threatening wrath mightier than the city of Jerusalem and mightier than the world. Therefore the Christian today does well to "practice" this too, sharpening his consciousness of the situation as seen from the standpoint of faith.

V

JUDGMENT

As part of those pronouncements which Jesus made about the end of time and of man and the world, we have his words about judgment:

"But when the Son of Man shall come in his majesty, and all the angels with him, then he will sit on the throne of his glory; and before him will be gathered all the nations, and he will separate them one from another, as the shepherd separates the sheep from the goats; and he will set the sheep on his right hand, but the goats on the left.

"Then the king will say to those on his right hand, 'Come, blessed of my Father, take possession of the kingdom prepared for you from the foundation of the world; for I was hungry and you gave me to eat; I was thirsty and you gave me to drink; I was a stranger and you took me in; naked and you covered me; sick and you visited me; I was in prison and you came to me.' Then the just will answer him, saying, 'Lord, when did we see thee hungry, and feed thee; or thirsty, and give thee drink? And when did we see thee a stranger, and take thee in; or naked, and clothe thee? Or when did we see thee sick, or in prison, and come to thee?' And answering the king will say to them, 'Amen I say to you, as long as you did it for one of these, the least of my brethren, you did it for me.'

"Then he will say to those on his left hand, 'Depart from me, accursed ones, into the everlasting fire which was prepared for the devil and his angels. For I was hungry, and you did not give me to eat; I was thirsty and you gave me no drink; I was a stranger and you did not take me in; naked, and you did not clothe me; sick, and in prison, and you did not visit me.' Then they also will answer and say, 'Lord, when did we see thee hungry, or thirsty, or a stranger, or naked, or sick, or in prison, and did not minister to thee?' Then he will answer them, saying, 'Amen I say to you, as long as you did not do it for one of these least ones, you did not do it for me.' And these will go into everlasting punishment, but the just into everlasting life" (Matt. 25:31–46).

No one discussing Christian truth today can speak as Christians were privileged to speak in earlier ages—in simple self-understood trust. The words we use and the thoughts among which we must move have been changed and devaluated. That is why Christian speech today invariably presents the problem of Christian differentiation. No longer can we simply say: Jesus teaches . . . or: according to Christian doctrine man is. . . . We must always be conscious of what the man or woman we are addressing involuntarily thinks or feels when he hears Christ's words—and not only "others," but we ourselves. Thus in order to get to the essential, we must distinguish between what Christ means and the natural reaction produced by his words; also when we speak of the judgment Jesus proclaims to the world.

Men have always known that something was wrong with human existence; that everywhere stupidity, injustice, deception and violence were at work. Consequently there was always the feeling that someday things must be set right and fulfilled. Some expected this clarification to come from human history itself: humanity by its own powers would fight its way through to a kind of divine existence. Let us allow this hope to die a natural death; it is flagrantly contrary not only to Revelation and Christian thinking, but also to the conclusions that must be drawn from a single honest glance at reality. We maintain our conviction that clarity can come only from God, after earthly life is over. But how is such a judgment to be imagined?

One might say: Throughout existence we find vain appearances and downright deception. A man is seldom rated by his fellow-men for what he really is. Often people of great value are poor, the honorable are unknown, and the questionable or utterly useless are wealthy and esteemed. Seldom does a person's appearance reveal his true nature. Even towards oneself there is much deceit. The self-appraising eye looks away at sight of the truth; the will hides its true intentions from itself and pretends to much that is non-existent. Thus judgment might well consist of the falling of the masks; the transparent appearance of all things as they really are. . . . We might also say: The inner reality of an individual should harmonize with the outer. The man who is pure should also be healthy; the good beautiful, the magnanimous strong and powerful of frame. Actually, it is quite different. Such unity is so rare, that an encounter with it seems like a fairytale. And it will never be otherwise. Neither physical-education nor spiritual formation will be able to change this radically, for the root of the disturbance goes deeper than human will. The cracks that run through personality will always be there—the stronger the personality, the deeper the cracks. Judgment could mean that disposition and being become one, that every human becomes in reality what he is by intention.

Or this thought: How rarely are life's promises kept, tasks completed, do human relations bear their fruit, does potential greatness become actuality. Again and again things break off and remain fragmentary. Life seldom receives the full, intelligent and loving approbation it desires. Even love is insufficient and illusory. Hence judgment could mean fulfillment; that every being might say: Everything in me that could be, has been perfected, has received its "yes" and its "no."

These suggestions, like many others, have their grain of truth—also of Christian truth. Many passages in Scripture, particularly in the Old Testament, support them. Still, what Christ says is different. In order that "judgments" such as these take place, things have only to appear before God's clarity. But what Jesus was referring to in the last days of his earthly existence was something else.

The judgment he means will not come through the falling away of time's constraint and the placing of all things in God's clarifying light, but through God's *advent*. Judgment is not the eternal consequences of divine government, but God's specific historical act— the last. After it, we are told, comes eternity. There is no action in eternity, only purest being and eternal fulfillment. And the God who is to come thus is Jesus Christ, he who is addressing us.

What unheard of consciousness of mission! There stands a man whose teaching has been rejected. The mighty have determined to put him to death; the real rulers of the country ignore him, letting things take their course; the people, who at first flocked to him, are gradually falling away. His friends are impotent; his fate is crystallizing—catastrophe lies just around the corner—and this man says: One day I shall return from eternity. I shall look through to the most hidden corner of every soul, shall judge what each is worth in the sight of God, and send him to his eternal destiny!

And according to what standards will he weigh him? According to how each has done his duty in his state of life, or struggled and suffered, or promoted good on earth? This too; but what is meant here and that through which the Christian conception of judgment differs from all other ethical or mythological conceptions, is something else. (Or is it that a man is judged by the number of people he has clothed and fed and comforted? This certainly, but Christ's words, primarily, mean something different.) The Judge will not say: You are saved because you have practiced love, you damned because you have closed yourself to it, but: Come, blessed of my Father. . . . For I was hungry, and you gave me food. Depart from me, you cursed, into everlasting fire. For I was thirsty and you did not give me drink. Not love, then, is the measure, but *that love which is directed to Jesus Christ*. He is Measure and Measurer. The thought is reiterated in that other stupendous sentence: "I am the way, and the truth, and the life" (John 14:6), and here again he is saying: The Good— that is I!

Inconceivable consciousness of being! We have only two choices: to see in one who speaks thus either a poor lunatic, or the living God, whose words, confounding human thought, are revelation.

Simultaneously we glimpse something of the earnestness of salvation. In daily life we deal with people as they come to us. But behind each of them, says Jesus, stands God. What we do to that person, we do to him. Thus in a sense that outrides all human sense, God has become our Brother. Not only by taking upon himself our sin, but because he has made himself the advocate of each and every one of us, and regards our interests as his own.

Man, even the ablest, is somehow forlorn, for sin has thrown him into a kind of homelessness. Christ came to make each life his own, and now all that happens to that life runs through him, to him, and receives in him its ultimate evaluation. The good that is done to another is done to him, Jesus, and receives in him its eternal evaluation—"reward," as Scripture calls it, in the misunderstood and yet profound sense we discussed earlier. The evil done to a person is also done to him, and he, the Judge, will determine its eternal reparation through forgiveness or punishment, whichever is right in his holy truth. Here is no ambitious dreamer who has exalted himself to the point of declaring that he is God, only to end in impotence, but true man as he came from the hands of the Creator; and simultaneously true Son of God. The Son of Man identifies himself with his "brothers"; he shares man's honor, and guarantees his eternal destiny. "It is now no longer I that live," St. Paul expresses this profound mystery, "but Christ lives in me" (Gal. 2:20).

Here lies the essential point of Christian eschatology, but it does not cover everything. The Biblical passages about the end of the world are strewn with parables likewise concerned with these ultimate things: parable of the thief who comes in the night (Matt. 24:43–44); of the good and faithful servant—or his opposite (24:45–51); of the wise and foolish virgins (25:1–13); of the five talents and the servants to whom they were entrusted (25:14–30). Here the different aspects of life have their word: conscientiousness in the fulfillment of daily duties; watchfulness in responsibility; loyalty to trust; and so forth. Everything a man is and has, what he does with it, how he acquits himself of his everyday duties—all this will be presented at his judgment. He will be judged with justice and love; the real measure of that judgment, however, is his love of his fellow men, which is love of Christ. That is why St. Paul says: "For the whole Law is fulfilled in one word: Thou shalt love thy neighbor as thyself" (Gal. 5:14). And why John writes throughout his first letter: "love one another," for this is the law.

When will Judgment come? No one knows, says the Lord—not even the Son. This knowledge is reserved to the Father and his counsel. It is not necessary to pull this word to pieces. It is part of paternal sovereignty "to know the times or dates which the Father has fixed by his own authority" (Acts 1:7). Judgment comes from the freedom of the Father, the Inaccessible One.

One thing we are told: it will come suddenly. Like the thief in the night, the master from his journey, the bridegroom from the wedding. This "suddenly" is the same kind of adverb as the "soon" of the Apocalypse and Paul's letters. It does not mean a brief span of time rather than a long one—not ten years instead of a thousand. This is how it was interpreted in the beginning, so that people thought Christ's return would take place in the next few years. In reality, any time is "soon" because all time is short, i.e., transitory. A thousand years before God are as a day, and all time as nothing, for he is eternity, but time passes. Whenever the end comes, it will be "soon." And people will say: "Now? Why now? We have scarcely begun to live! We haven't done any of the things that must be done, if everything is not to be lost! We have neglected the essential." Always it will be: "We have neglected the essential!" This is how Christ's "suddenly" is meant. Not as an accident comes suddenly, or lightning strikes, not as compared with an illness that grows slowly worse—Judgment will come with essential suddenness, because it has no precursive sign in the world itself. It will not be predictable by certain changes in temperature, or by signs of superannuation in the construction of society, but it will come when Christ comes; and Christ comes when he chooses. His return is God's final act, and cancels everything purely human, purely terrestrial. God's gaze is constantly upon earth, and his coming is a constant threat. When it will be carried out he alone knows, for he alone knows when the measure of his patience is full.

VI

BEHOLD, I COME . . .
TO DO THY WILL, O GOD

What did Jesus find in the Holy City he entered with his supreme claim? What powers were at work? What was the attitude of the people towards him? What his position in a situation drawing to its close?

First of all, there are those who call themselves "the Pure"—the Pharisees. From the point of view of character as well as politically, this is the strongest and most determined group, the real bearers of historical consciousness among the Jewish people. Still under the influence of the warlike Maccabeans, and convinced that the kingdom of Israel will spread from Jerusalem over the entire world, they are ready to stake everything on the realization of their dream. When Jesus appears on the scene, they feel at once that the reality of salvation for which he stands directly contradicts their own. Consequently, they consider him an enemy who must be eliminated, and apply all possible means to this end. . . . Then there is the group of Sadducees, hated by the Pharisees, whom they in turn cordially despise. Cosmopolitans, they have severed all ties with their own history and adopted Hellenistic culture; they are intellectually alert, have many-sided interests, and enjoy life. Their politics are international and conciliatory. Spiritually they are rationalists and skeptics. They consider Jesus an enthusiast—one of the many of his day. For a long time they ignore him completely, and their first clash with him comes late (see Matt. 22:24). And the people? Instinctively they sense the Messiah in this wonderful man, and press him to act. He resists, knowing that their conception of God's kingdom is essentially that of the Pharisees. The masses bring Jesus their problems and their sick; they listen to his words spellbound and are deeply shaken by his demonstrations of power. However, they are unable to reach a clear decision concerning him, but veer first in one direction then in another, as the mood of the moment blows them. There is no one there to help them to take a decisive step, so they remain the tool of those who happen to have the word. Finally, there are the various rulers; they see no reason why they should be forced into any decision. Jesus' compatriot, Herod, is a pleasure-loving, impotent despot. True, as we see from his discussions with John the Baptist, he is not insensible to religious personality, though he does not allow this weakness to interfere with his doings. For a lightly given 'word of honor' he sacrifices the last of the prophets. He is also interested in the new Prophet, as he would be in any new sensation; a fool the man who ever counted on the "fox" (Luke 13:32). As for the real representative of power in Palestine, Caesar's procurator, he has never even seen Jesus. He knows that the times are thick with wandering preachers and miracle-workers, and if he ever heard of "the carpenter's son," he probably held him for one of these.

This then the little world into which Jesus walked, proclaiming his message, working the miracles suggested by the people's distress or the spiritual demands of the moment. He exhorted, summoned, aroused. Not only did he attempt to drive home a teaching, demonstrate a way of salvation, proclaim a new interpretation of the kingdom; he tried to make men conscious of the stupendous reality knocking at their doors. *Now is the hour!* God's kingdom is at the gates of history, ready to enter. God has risen to his feet. The moment for sacred fulfillment is ripe. Come!

Looking closer, however, we see more. Jesus is flinging all his strength into this hour, advancing with all the love of which he is capable. He does not think of himself. He knows neither pleasure nor comfort; neither fear nor false consideration. He is completely and entirely messenger, prophet and more than a prophet. And still we do not gain the impression of a man working towards a fixed goal. . . .

Perhaps the reply is: What is at stake is too huge to be "worked" for. Such things happen of themselves—he only proclaims them, clears the way for them as all prophets have done. But is there in Jesus the restless drive that constantly spurred an Elijah? Has the Hand laid itself on him as it did on Jeremiah, who, still proclaiming the word of God, broke under its weight? No. Jesus is the bringer of the tidings of all tidings, but they neither crush nor drive him; he and his message are one. True, he is anxious that everything "be accomplished" (Luke 12:50); but this is his own intrinsic desire for consummation, not pressure from above. . . . Or is Jesus a fighter? One is tempted to imagine him one of those great and noble figures. But does he really fight? I do not believe so. Certainly, he had adversaries, but he never really considered them such or treated them accordingly. His real enemy was the condition of the world—and Satan, who supports it against God. But even Satan is no adversary in the full sense of the word, for Jesus in no way recognizes him as an equal. In the final analysis he does not fight—for that he is too serene.

We penetrate deeper into the soul of the Lord only when we see his deeds and his conduct from a central point of view outside the world. The moment we try to fit him into any familiar human category, all genuine recognition is destroyed.

After an initial period of apostolic plenitude both in word and deed, we see the crisis gathering, and how first in Jerusalem, then in Galilee, the decision falls out against Jesus. Once it is definite, he goes, not because he is forced to, or in desperation, but calmly resolved, to Jerusalem, and to the death he knows awaits him there (Luke 9:51).

We have already seen what takes place: the revelationary character of Jesus' entry, the spirit of prophecy upon the "multitude" who now breathlessly await the expected signs of the Messiah and the establishment of the kingdom. From the viewpoint of truth, they are hopelessly entangled in earthly expectations, and as soon as they see that their Messiah is politically powerless, their dream collapses. The Pharisees, who are prepared to go to any lengths, wait for this moment. They still fear the people, who feel essentially as they do, but the people attempt to force Christ to fit their conception of the Messiah, whereas the Pharisees are out and out hostile. All that separates the masses from their leaders is a misconception, but as long as it exists, the Pharisees must be cautious. Now the Sadducees and Hellenists also become uneasy. They fear a political embroilment and begin to discuss among themselves how this dangerous fanatic might best be stamped out. . . . What does Jesus do?

A man convinced of his high mission and placed in a similar position would have done everything possible to drive home the truth. He would have spoken with the priests, the Scribes, with those who had influence among the people; he would have taken Scripture to hand and clarified his identity with the aid of the Messianic prophecies. He would have attempted to recapture the hearts of the crowd, to reveal to them the essence of his teaching, and to win them over to his side. Is this what happens? No! Jesus does proclaim the truth, and his words are powerful and penetrating; but he makes nothing like the effort we expect of him. And his manner is anything but winning; it has something uncompromising about it, harsh and challenging. One eager to do everything in his power to swing a crisis in his favor does not speak as Jesus speaks. . . . The man we mentioned might also have reasoned thus: The time for persuasion is past; now for action! The adversary impermeable to reason must be met on his own grounds—force with force. He would have attacked each group at its weakest point. He would have played the Sadducees against the Pharisees and vice versa. He would have appealed to the people, would have warned them, stirred them to action, would have denounced their leaders and won them over. Or he would have realized that the odds were against him and flee. Jesus could easily have done so. The Pharisees even expected him to: "You will seek me and will not find me; and where I am you cannot come" (John 7:34–35). The Jews therefore said among themselves, "Where is he going that we shall not find him? Will he go to those dispersed among the Gentiles, and teach the Gentiles?" Our man would probably have done so. He would have gone to Alexandria or to Rome, certain of finding open ears there and hopeful of returning later under more favorable conditions. But this idea is totally foreign to Jesus. There remains one more possibility: that our man admit himself defeated and, according to his nature, exhausted, despairingly, or proudly die. Perhaps he would even fling himself into death, as into the mysterious counterpole of success, reckoning on the logic of death and life, catastrophe and new beginning. Nothing of all this applies to Jesus, though attempts were made into the period in which "the eschatological" was in vogue, to prove that when all possibility of earthly success was clearly out of the question, Jesus played upon the "success of a failure," on the mysterious intervention of God, hoping that from his death would come the fulfillment of all things. Actually, there can be no talk of this. Jesus does not capitulate; never is there the slightest trace of "breakdown," and it is as false to speak only of catastrophe, as it is to take his earthly failure in a bound of mystic-enthusiasm that tries to make a creative downfall of his death. This is unrealistically exalted and, by comparison with the truth, thin psychology. Here is something quite different.

What? If we follow the Gospel-reports of Jesus' last days closely, we find nothing of extreme concentration on a single goal; nothing of relentless effort or struggle in the usual sense of the word. Jesus' attitude is entirely serene. He says what he has come to say—unmitigatingly, objectively; not with an eye to its acceptance, but as it must be said. He neither attacks nor retreats. He hopes for nothing as humans hope and fears nothing. When he goes to Bethania by night and stays with friends because of the opposition against him, this does not mean that he fears his enemies, but simply that the ultimate is postponed because its hour is not yet ripe. Jesus' soul knows no fear, not only because he is naturally courageous, but because the center of his being lies far beyond the reach of anything fearful.

Therefore, he cannot really be called audacious in the human sense. He is only completely free for what in every minute of his life must be done. And he does it with unutterable calm and sovereignty.

The more closely we distinguish between Jesus and any other man, the more clearly we see that what is happening here is not measurable by human standards. True, it is conceived by human spirit, willed by human will, experienced by the most ardent and sensitive of human hearts; but its origin and the power with which it is consummated give Jesus a greatness outside human comprehension.

So God's will is done, and Jesus wills this will. It is humanity's second great test and failure—brought about by a specific people at a specific time, but because of our solidarity with all human existence, also to our woe.

VII

JUDAS

". . . and they took counsel together how they might seize Jesus by stealth and put him to death.

"Then one of the Twelve, called Judas Iscariot, went to the chief priests, and said to them, 'What are you willing to give me for delivering him to you?' But they assigned him thirty pieces of silver. And from then on he sought out an opportunity to betray him" (Matt. 26:4–5, 14–16).

Mention has been made of Judas himself earlier. John writes of Mary's anointing Christ for his death with costly nard. "Then one of his disciples, Judas Iscariot, he who was about to betray him, said, 'Why was this ointment not sold for three hundred denarii, and given to the poor?' Now he said this, not that he cared for the poor, but because he was a thief, and holding the purse, used to take what was put in it" (John 12:1–6).

In the report of the Last Supper we read: "When Jesus had said these things he was troubled in spirit, and said solemnly, 'Amen, amen, I say to you, one of you will betray me.' The disciples therefore looked at one another, uncertain of whom he was speaking. . . . 'Lord who is it?' Jesus answered, 'It is he for whom I shall dip the bread, and give it to him.' And when he had dipped the bread, he gave it to Judas Iscariot, the son of Simon. And after the morsel, Satan entered into him. And Jesus said to him, 'What thou dost, do quickly.' But none of those at the table understood why he said this to him. For some thought that because Judas held the purse, Jesus had said to him, 'Buy the things we need for the feast'; or that he should give something to the poor. When, therefore, he had received the morsel, he went out quickly" (John 3:21–30).

After the supper Jesus and his disciples go to Gethsemane. "Judas, then, taking the cohort, and attendants from the chief priests and Pharisees, came there with lanterns, and torches, and weapons" (John 18:3).

In Matthew we have the additional commentary: "Now his betrayer had given them a sign, saying, 'Whomever I kiss, that is he; lay hold of him.' And he went straight up to Jesus and said, 'Hail, Rabbi!' and kissed him." And Luke adds: "But Jesus said to him, 'Judas, dost thou betray the Son of Man with a kiss?' " (22:48). And Jesus is taken prisoner.

Finally, the report of Judas' end: "Now when morning came all the chief priests and the elders of the people took counsel together against Jesus in order to put him to death. . . . Then Judas, who betrayed him, when he saw that he was condemned, repented and brought back the thirty pieces of silver to the chief priests and the elders, saying, 'I have sinned in betraying innocent blood.' But they said, 'What is that to us? See to it thyself.' And he flung the pieces of silver into the temple, and withdrew; and went away and hanged himself with a halter.

"And the chief priests took the pieces of silver, and said, 'It is not lawful to put them into the treasury, seeing that it is the price of blood.' And after they had consulted together, they bought with them the potter's field, as a burial place for strangers. For this reason that field has been called even to this day, Haceldama, that is, the Field of Blood" (Matt. 27:1–8).

Judas, inhabitant of Carioth, the man who in the Christian consciousness personifies the most odious of traitors and the blackest of treachery, is one of Jesus' most intimate companions. We have also accustomed ourselves to this juxtaposition—next to Jesus, his traitor. Perhaps we have even construed a theory of the necessity of shadow at the side of light, of evil at the heels of sanctity, or some such idea.

If so, we have thought foolishly, for it is by no means necessary that treachery raise its head next "the Holy One of God" (Luke 4:34). Never should the Lord have been sold by one he called his friend. How could anyone who had been accepted by Jesus think and act as Judas did? The question has been discussed for centuries, and two answers prevail. The one says: Judas had a vocation; he recognized the Messiah in Jesus, possibly even the Son of God, but he was unable to purge his heart of its natural evil; he remained avaricious and sold his Master for money. Thus in a few dark strokes, the outline of the traitor *par excellence,* mythical simplification of evil. Possibly man's desire for a scapegoat to relieve his own conscience of its share in the terrible burden of Jesus' fate lurks behind this interpretation. . . . Next to this all too simple answer, there exists a very complicated one, which explains that Judas was a great soul, intimately acquainted with the dark profundities of existence. He believed in the Messiah, who, he was convinced, could reestablish the kingdom of Israel. When Jesus seemed to hesitate, Judas decided to force his hand. Exposed to mortal danger, Jesus would have no choice but to use his supernatural power, and the longed-for splendor would be there. . . . Or, one step further into the deeps, Judas knew that salvation could come only with the death of the Most Holy. Therefore, in order to save his fellow men, he willingly played the indispensable traitor, accepting contempt and damnation for the sake of world salvation. These are laborious considerations and have nothing in common with Scripture. They are the product of a romantic philosophy of evil which is contrary to the whole spirit of revelation. But also the first answer, though apparently based on a remark of the apostle John, is incorrect. It is over-simplified. Life is not that simple. Let us follow the text carefully, without making any more additions than are absolutely essential to our understanding of it.

Judas must have come to Jesus with the genuine desire to believe and follow him, otherwise Jesus would not have accepted him. At least, we find nothing of distrust or resistance on the Lord's part—

and still less of any thought of the 'necessity' of receiving his traitor
along with his other intimates. Therefore we must suppose that
Judas really was well disposed.

Like every other apostle, he brought his weaknesses with him.
Peter also had his; he was impulsive; his heart and tongue were forever running away with him—to his great good as well as to his
great detriment. He was inconstant. It took a real miracle of divine
power to make of Peter "this rock" (Matt. 16:18). By nature he was
far from rocklike. . . . Also John had his failings. Art and legend have
misrepresented him. He was anything but the delicate, affectionate
disciple of love. His mind soared higher than those of the other
apostles, but he was a zealot too and capable of all kinds of impa-
tience and harshness. We feel this when he calls down the fate of
Sodom upon Samaria, and there are other passages in his writing
that are terribly hard. That he so often spoke of charity and understood it so deeply is possibly due to the fact that he did not possess
it—at least not the charity of kindness, though there are also other
varieties. . . . Also Thomas was not perfect. Jesus' word to him
about the blessedness of those who believe without seeing, suggests
that at times he must have been close to unblessedness. . . . In the
same way, Judas too had his weaknesses, and the Evangelist—John it
is—describes one of them, probably the most conspicuous, with
great sharpness: he loved money. Thus his faith had to struggle with
avarice, his readiness to reform with inner bonds. Cupidity does
have something degrading about it. A generous heart beat in Peter,
for all his thoughtless impulsiveness, and in John's fanaticism burned
the ardor of genuine surrender. Even skeptical Thomas was honest
enough to give truth its due, once it had been revealed. But in Judas
there must have been a streak of meanness. How, otherwise, could
John call him hypocrite and thief? And how could Judas have conceived of such baseness as to seal his treachery with the kiss of
peace? But the possibility of salvation was also in him; Judas had received the vocation of an apostle and could have been one. But his
readiness to reform went lame. When this happened we do not

know; perhaps in Capharnaum when Jesus proclaimed the Eucharist, and so many hearers, disciples among them, took offence and turned from him (John 6:60–66). Jesus' most intimate circle must also have been deeply shaken, or he would not have asked: "Do you also wish to go away?" Not one of them was capable of belief in the fullest sense of the word. Peter dared the utmost of what they were capable when he rescued himself by a leap into blind trust: "Lord, to whom shall we go? Thou hast words of everlasting life" (John 6:68–69). We do not understand, but we believe in you, and for your sake we accept your words. Possibly this was the moment in which Judas' faith went out. That he did not leave, but remained as one of the Twelve was the beginning of his treachery. Why he stayed, we do not know. Perhaps he still hoped to muddle through inwardly, or he wanted at least to see how things would develop—unless he already dreamed of profiting by the situation.

By so doing, Judas placed himself in terrible danger. Holy existence, which thinks, judges, acts in God is not easily supportable. It is foolish to think that it is necessarily pure bliss to live in the presence of sanctity, particularly in the sanctity of God's Son; that there one couldn't help becoming good. Precisely there one can become a devil! The Lord himself says: "Have I not chosen you, the Twelve? Yet one of you is a devil" (John 6:71). Judas was not a devil from the beginning, as some claim; he became one, there in the presence of the Savior. Yes, *from* that presence "destined for the fall and for the rise of many" (Luke 2:34). Particularly after Capharnaum the situation must have been unbearable for him—always to feel this superhuman purity; always, and this was the most difficult, to be conscious of this divine will to sacrifice! Insupportable for one who did not love Jesus. For those not great in their own right, it is already difficult enough to bear human greatness—one should almost say to pardon it. But when it is religious greatness? Divine sacrifice? Where there is no pure readiness of faith and love to accept this sacred force as beginning and end, the atmosphere must become poisonous. In such a person a satanic irritation swells like a malevolent

tumor. He revolts against the tremendous power of the pathos unfolding before him and becomes increasingly spiteful and critical of
word and deed, until the mere presence of the saint, every gesture,
every inflection of his voice, becomes intolerable. Then it happens:
Judas finds himself the natural ally of the enemy. All his Pharasaic instincts awaken, and suddenly he sees Jesus as Israel's greatest danger.
Simultaneously his baser inclinations are aroused—a direct reaction
against what is now Jesus' exasperating nobility. Money again becomes all-important, an overpowering temptation, and finally the
most trivial incident, perhaps only an encounter, is all that is needed
to bring the latent treason to a head.

What did Judas' treachery consist of? Those in power wished to
arrest Jesus as inconspicuously as possible, because they feared the
masses, who were still under the impact of his entry into Jerusalem,
and Judas, who knew the Lord's personal habits, could tell the authorities where he could be seized without knowledge of the populace. The report of the Last Supper gives us an idea of Judas'
attitude at the time—of his doggedness, the insolence with which
he asks who is to betray the Lord: "Is it I, Rabbi?" (Matt. 26:25). His
baseness now has the upper hand. And again it is John—humanly
speaking, he must have mortally loathed Judas—who writes the terrible sentence: And after Jesus handed him the morsel, "Satan entered into him." The morsel was not the Eucharist; Judas did not
participate in the mystery of faith. What he received was an attention customarily paid by the host during the Paschal meal: a bunch
of bitter herbs, dipped in a bowl of *charoseth,* was handed one of the
guests as a token of affection. This last delicate gesture, which sealed
the end of their relationship, seemed to turn everything to stone. At
that moment "Satan entered" Judas Iscariot. After the deed came
repentance—overwhelming recognition of all that was lost. But this
consciousness could no longer alter the *fait accompli* that stared back
at Judas from the cold faces of those he had served. Strangely heart-
rending gesture of helplessness, this flinging down the silver in the
temple sanctuary! . . . Then the suicide.

Discussing Judas, we do well not to limit our attention entirely to him. He completed the treachery, but was he the only one touched by it? What did Peter do, whom Jesus had taken with him to the mountain of the transfiguration and declared the Rock and Keeper of the Keys? When the danger became acute, accosting him in the miserable form of the wench who kept the gates, didn't he declare: "I do not know the man!" (Luke 22:56–57). And did he not insist, denying it "with an oath" once, twice, thrice (Matt. 26:72–74)? What is treachery if not this? That he does not go down to his doom in it, but is able to rise again through contrition and reform is due only to the grace of God. . . . And John? He also fled, and the flight of one who had leaned on Jesus' breast must have weighed particularly heavily. True, he returned and stood under the cross, but that he was able to do so was likewise a gift. . . . All the others fled, dispersed like "the sheep of the flock" when the shepherd is struck (Matt. 26:31). . . . And the masses whose sick he had healed, whose hungry he had fed, whose burdens he had lightened—those in whom the Spirit had moved so that they had recognized him as the Messiah and cheered him—when it came to the choice, they preferred a highway robber! . . . And Pilate? What moves us so strangely in his conversation with Christ is that for a moment the skeptical Roman seems to feel who Jesus is. We sense something of the wave of sympathy that passes between them. Then cold reason returns, and Pilate washes his hands (Matt. 27:24). No, what came to the surface in all its terrible nakedness in Judas, existed as a possibility all around Jesus. Fundamentally not one of his followers had much cause to look down on Judas.

Nor have we. Let us be perfectly clear about this. Betrayal of the divine touches us all. What can I betray? That which has entrusted itself to my loyalty. But God—entrusted to me? Precisely. God did not reveal himself merely by teaching a truth, giving us commands to which he attaches consequences, but by coming to us, personally. His truth is himself. And to him who hears, he gives his own strength, again himself. To hear God means to accept him. To believe means to accept him in truth and loyalty. The God we believe in is the God who "comes" into heart and spirit, surrendering himself to us. He counts on the loyalty of that heart, the chivalry of that spirit. Why? Because when God enters the world, he puts aside his omnipotence. His truth renounces force, as his will renounces that coercive power which would set the consequences immediately after every deed. God enters the world defenceless, a silent, patient God. He "emptied himself, taking the nature of a slave" (Phil. 2:7). All the more profound his summons to the believer: Recognize an unassuming God! Be loyal to defenceless majesty! . . . And yet, aren't there many days in our lives on which we sell him, against our best knowledge, against our most sacred feeling, in spite of duty and love, for some vanity, or sensuality, or profit, or security, or some private hatred or vengeance? Are these more than thirty pieces of silver? We have little cause to speak of "the traitor" with indignation or as someone far away and long ago. Judas himself unmasks us. We understand his Christian significance in the measure that we understand him from our own negative possibilities, and we should beg God not to let the treachery into which we constantly fall become fixed within us. The name Judas stands for established treason, betrayal that has sealed the heart, preventing it from finding the road back to genuine contrition.

VIII

The Final Reunion

No marked event takes place in the period between Christ's entry into Jerusalem and the end. These are days of feverish tension for Jesus' adversaries, who are determined to rid themselves of the whole affair whatever the price; days of profoundest readiness for the Lord, who awaits the hour his Father has fixed. On Saturday, the great Sabbath, begins the eight-day Easter festival, during which no one will dare to take action against Jesus, because at this solemn time absolute repose is law. Thus the decision is forced to a head, for the authorities fear that the masses might take things in hand and do not wish to risk waiting until after the Easter festival. Friday is the great preparatory Feast of the Passover, and Jesus, who knows that by then he will no longer be able to celebrate it, anticipates it by a day, for he who calls himself Lord of the Sabbath is also Lord of the Pasch (Matt. 12:8).

St. Luke reports: "Now the day of the Unleavened Bread came, on which the passover had to be sacrificed. And he sent Peter and John, saying, 'Go and prepare for us the passover that we may eat it.' But they said, 'Where dost thou want us to prepare it?' And he said to them, 'Behold, on your entering the city, there will meet you a man carrying a pitcher of water; follow him into the house into which he goes. And you shall say to the master of the house, "The Master says to thee, 'Where is the guest chamber, that I may eat the passover there with my disciples?' " And he will show you a large upper room furnished; there make ready.' And they went, and found just as he had told them; and they prepared the passover."

The words gleam with the same prophetic mood we find in the description of the entry into Jerusalem: messengers are sent ahead who have been told precisely what they will find, what they are to do and say and reply, and everything takes place accordingly. As to the house in question, it is supposed that it was owned by the later Evangelist Mark, and was the one in which the disciples gathered after the death of the Lord, and where also the first Pentecost took place.

Jesus arrives there in the evening with the Twelve. To understand the situation better, let us recall the close connection that existed in those days between a teacher and his students, a master and his disciples; whether the leader was a philosopher, a religious personality, or anyone who gathered hearers and imitators about him. The master lived entirely with his followers, often for years at a time. Their relationship was human, spiritual, personal and religious in one. Thus hardly conceivable the intimacy and plenitude of that all-decisive evening which Jesus chose to spend in the smallest circle of his disciples, sharing with them the sacred Supper of the Passover.

What is Jesus' position among these twelve men? Simply that of one who knows. The disciples make a strangely helpless, one is tempted to say, immature, impression. They by no means take their place at his side. There is not a word of genuine participation in his trials. They do not understand the Master's thoughts, or the trend things are taking—or for that matter, Christ himself. Hence they are utterly overwhelmed by all that follows.

Jesus alone *knows,* and his loneliness in this knowledge is complete. Not that he distanced himself from them, or kept his secret to himself. He longed to have them understand, if only a little; the words in Gethsemane are heavy with that longing: "Could you not, then, watch one hour with me?" (Matt. 26:40). They could not. On the other hand, we must not think the disciples indifferent or selfish. It was simply beyond their strength. They were not with him in the intimacy of understanding, but stood before him, helpless. Towards the end, Jesus' surroundings seem to fade away, and in the great conversation with God known as the sacerdotal prayer, the

Son speaks alone with the Father (John 17). Yet there is no cold superiority in Jesus' attitude. The hour overflows with love: Jesus, ". . . having loved his own who were in the world, loved them to the end," says John at the opening of chapter thirteen. Now what had been promised in Capharnaum becomes reality: the Lord gives them that mystery of surrendered love and union so huge that when he first spoke of it, no one was able to grasp it. It is his "covenant," and his covenant is also his command; command of love reiterated in this ultimate hour together.

"This cup is the new covenant in my blood, which shall be shed for you. . . . For I have given you an example, that as I have done to you, so you also should do" (John 13:15).

And we understand why "he was troubled in spirit," who was forced to add: "but that Scripture may be fulfilled, 'He who eats bread with me has lifted his heel against me.' . . . Amen, amen, I say to you, one of you will betray me" (John 13:18–21). In the awfulness of the moment the bond between Jesus and the other disciples is palpably strengthened: "Now one of his disciples, he whom Jesus loved, was reclining at Jesus' bosom. Simon Peter therefore beckoned to him, and said to him, 'Who is it of whom he speaks?' He therefore, leaning back upon the bosom of Jesus, said to him, 'Lord, who is it?' Jesus answered, 'It is he for whom I shall dip the bread, and give it to him.' And when he had dipped the bread, he gave it to Judas Iscariot, the son of Simon" (John 13:23–26). And Judas took it and "went out quickly." And it was night.

Now Jesus is alone with those who really are his. He says: "I have greatly desired to eat this passover with you before I suffer; for I say to you that I will eat of it no more, until it has been fulfilled in the kingdom of God" (Luke 22:15–16). All that is in him, all he desires is to be consummated in the Eucharist instituted immediately after these words as an eternal memorial of his death for mankind: "Greater love than this no one has, that one lay down his life for his friends. You are my friends if you do the things I command you. No longer do I call you servants, because the servant does not know what his master does. But I have called you friends, because all things that I have heard from my Father I have made known to you. You have not chosen me, but I have chosen you, and have appointed you that you should go and bear fruit, and that your fruit should remain; that whatever you ask the Father in my name he may give you. These things I command you, that you may love one another."

As yet this alliance of love is small and hidden. Only the few about Jesus are conscious of it (though they do not understand its essence) those who in the great but already distant sense of the Old Testament are no longer "servants of God," but his "friends"; who participate in the intimacy of the divine presence that Jesus has brought so close. For only he can be a friend of God who knows God, and this is possible only through Christ his Son.

Then, in the fourteenth and fifteenth chapters of St. John, come the sacred passages about love, reiterated and deepened again and again. The love in question is no philanthropy or general love of goodness and truth, but that love which is possible only through him, Jesus Christ; that is directed to the Father and returns from him to our fellow-men: "He who has my commandments and keeps them, he it is who loves me. But he who loves me will be loved by my Father, and I will love him and manifest myself to him" (John 14:21). And again: "He who does not love me does not keep my words. And the word that you have heard is not mine, but the Father's who sent me" (14:24).

And yet again: "In this is my Father glorified, that you may bear very much fruit, and become my disciples. As the Father has loved me, I also have loved you. Abide in my love. If you keep my commandments you will abide in my love, as I also have kept my Father's commandments, and abide in his love. These things I have spoken to you that my joy may be in you, and that your joy may be made full.

"This is my commandment, that you love one another as I have loved you" (John 15:8–12).

The disciples will hardly have understood these words—not for nothing does the Lord promise to send them the Holy Spirit to enlighten them: "But when the Advocate has come, whom I will send you from the Father, the Spirit of truth who proceeds from the Father, he will bear witness concerning me" (John 15:26). But already now the disciples feel the proximity and power of God in their Master.

Nevertheless, we must not allow this scene to mislead us into overhumanizing Jesus, regarding it only as the leave-taking of a departing master. Two similar events have graven their image deep in human memory; in each a great master bids goodbye to his disciples. One of them anticipates this hour by four hundred years: the death of Socrates, as described by his pupil Plato in the dialogue "Phaedo"; the other, another two centuries back: the death of Buddha, as recorded in the "Collection" of Buddhistic texts from southern India. At first glance these two farewells seem to have much in common with the one just discussed: in each a master confronts death with the fruit of his labors during life. He passes on the essence of that life to his followers and consecrates them for the continuation of the work he has begun. And yet, what a difference!

Socrates, the great questioner deep in the uncertainty of all human reason, sought that pure philosophical cognition which for him was the divine. Unceasingly he had struggled to harmonize his life with eternal truth, and he felt at home and secure in that perfect harmony which he was now about to enter forever. This is what he taught his pupils, the possibility of finding such harmony, and he demonstrated his teaching with his own exemplary death. But Socrates refuses to claim any authority. He himself has recognized none, and he has no desire that others accept his word as final. Every pupil should depend on his own intellectual powers. Each should do what he, Socrates, has done: ferret out the truth. Though his mind and personality loomed far above the others, essentially he was one of them; indeed one of his disciples, Plato, surpassed the master.

With Jesus it is entirely different. He never sought truth or worked his way through a sea of uncertainty. He never struggled to embody eternal truth. He never said to his disciples: What I have done you can do, prepare to do the same. He is by no means one of a group—"one of us" yes, in that holy sense implied by his name, "Son of Man," our Brother and Savior—but always as one whose roots lie elsewhere, and who especially in the love-saturated hour of his leave-taking, identifies himself with the Father in heaven and the Spirit he is to send.

And Buddha? Omitting here the question where he leads to God and where away from him, and considering him only in the form to which he himself laid claims, that of a master, we do well to summarize his essence with the name he applied to himself, "the Enlightened One." He is convinced that he has discovered the law of illusion that reigns everywhere, but which only the extremely rare individual is privileged to perceive. Now it is manifest to all—through his life's work, which he has carried out to the end, thus perfecting himself. About his deathbed stand his disciples, some of them already profoundly entrenched in his world of thought. One last time he summons his strength and mounts all the steps of meditation. Fully conscious of the control he exercises over existence, at the moment he recognizes as his, he "lets go" the last frail bond that links him to life: "Nothing more exists." The disciples know that they have witnessed the fulfillment of a tremendous mystery.

Jesus, who was Truth, never sought it. Nor was he a "Perfect One" in the sense of one perfected. Humanly speaking, his life was not perfected, but destroyed in the plumbless mystery of his sacrificial destiny. Also intrinsically or religiously speaking, the term and all that goes with it does not fit him. There is nothing in his life that suggests it, and his last word, "It is consummated" means not that his life is fulfilled, but the will of his Father (John 19:30).

It is important to see these differences clearly, if nothing of the essential and unique in Christ is to be blurred or lost. Comparison with Socrates only proves how little comparable the two lives are. All that is noblest in the Greek soul is focused in Socrates, but his great spirit is more than a mere collection of virtues. Rarest and most difficult of achievements, it pursued intrinsic nobility not only to its ultimate consequence, but beyond, letting men sense how in an unimaginable effort bordering on the superhuman, even absolute virtue may be overcome. Alcibiades, the pupil who himself walked in the superabundance of Greek youth and beauty, compares his master to one of those ugly sileni which the sculptors of the day loved to fashion as shrine for the golden statue of a god; his physical bizarreness only served to enhance the harmony and beauty it enclosed. Socrates, "seducer"-to-the-heights of Athens' noblest youth and that of her neighboring Greek states—what a contrast between his gifted followers and the little group of fishermen about Jesus! How little Christ's words bear of a great culture! Its absence is palpable—sometimes to the brink of temptation!

Even more difficult is comparison with Buddha, that inconceivably great spirit who possessed all that existed of terrestrial splendor and forsook it to realize a religious existence of even greater cosmic dimensions than the philosophical spheres of Socrates and Plato— here again, how different Jesus! Indeed, asking in all reverence and only to adore the better, is there in Jesus himself that which in Buddha we call "religious greatness"? Might one not conclude that from the point of view of the path he climbed, of the profundity of his cognition, of his creative religious wisdom and sovereignty of style Buddha was superior? This would not only be a great error and profound temptation, but infinite nonsense, for all these things have nothing to do with Jesus Christ. He is the Son of the living God, the incarnate *Logos*. Seen against this one tremendous fact, all else is purely incidental. That so much in Christ seems to fail to measure up to earthly standards of genius is due only to the sacred Kenosis, entry of the omnipotent Word into the voluntary impotence of a genuinely shared human existence (Phil. 2:17).

Now we understand Jesus' position as he sits at table with his disciples one last time: it is not only that of the all-knowing one among the unknowing; also not merely that of the loving one among his friends. It is the Son of God breaking bread with fallen man—with a few whom he has selected from many—not wise and great, but expressly "little" and "humble." To the end he is completely alone.

This is the unfathomable mystery of the Last Supper. Around Socrates as he lies ready and waiting for death spreads an atmosphere which his disciples can only describe as "wondrous"—mixture of pain and joy, of the sadness of farewell and the conviction that here something was breaking through into the eternal; double sense of loss and indestructible union. The hour is wondrous but not incomprehensible. . . . In Buddha's death we have the solemn consummation of his evolution towards perfection; it opens a door through which all others may pass—who have the courage to do so. . . . In Jesus there is something else: a will capable of bearing all that is to come through to the end; a heart that has embraced the illimitableness of human sin and human suffering, yes; but how are we to express this inexpressible serenity of the abyss, incandescent ardor, this absolute self-control and readiness to descend to the nadir of the grave and beyond to new life? This willingness to *be* the grave in which the old may die, that the new and holy may come to life? Here is the inconceivableness of God incarnate. There is no logical or psychological frame into which he fits. We only destroy the mystery and with it Christianity and our own salvation by attempting to see Jesus along the lines of a Buddha or Socrates or any other great man. The mystery of Holy Thursday is the intrinsically impenetrable reality of sanctity descended from God as divinely unique as it is vulnerable.

IX

THE FOOTWASHING

In the report on Jesus' last reunion with his disciples we find the description of a strange incident that has seldom failed to make a deep impression on the Christian consciousness: ". . . Jesus, knowing that the Father had given all things to his hands, and that he had come forth from God and was going to God, rose from the supper and laid aside his garments, and taking a towel girded himself. Then he poured water into the basin and began to wash the feet of the disciples, and to dry them with the towel with which he was girded.

"He came, then, to Simon Peter. And Peter said to him, 'Lord, dost thou wash my feet?' Jesus answered and said to him, 'What I do thou knowest not now; but thou shalt know hereafter.' Peter said to him, 'Thou shalt never wash my feet!' Jesus answered him, 'If I do not wash thee, thou shalt have no part with me.' Peter said to him, 'Lord, not my feet only, but also my hands and my head!' Jesus said to him, 'He who has bathed needs only to wash, and he is clean all over. And you are clean, but not all.' For he knew who it was that would betray him. This is why he said, 'You are not all clean.'

"Now after he had washed their feet and put on his garments, when he had reclined again, he said to them, 'Do you know what I have done to you? You call me Master and Lord, and you say well, for so I am. If, therefore, I the Lord and Master have washed your feet, you also ought to wash the feet of one another'" (John 13:3–14).

In the antique world, guests invited to dine bathed and attired themselves freshly for the occasion. However, since everyone wore sandals, dusty feet were unavoidable—at least for those not in a position to maintain a litter. Hence, upon arrival, the guest was received by a slave, who washed his feet. (In Luke seven, Jesus refers to the custom in his remark to Simon, "I came into thy house; thou gavest me no water for my feet.") Obviously, the service was menial enough; the slave who performed it considered hardly worthy of so much as a glance. . . . The participants in the little paschal ceremony in Mark's house had arrived that morning on foot from Bethania and spent the whole day in the streets of Jerusalem. Very likely, by evening they were a bit the worse for wear. Neither their means nor the spirit of their community permitted them to keep a slave, and possibly their appearance at table left much to be desired. This then the natural background of the incident described. Jesus rises, girds himself with a towel, pours water into a basin and goes from one to another, kneeling to perform the service of the slave at the door. Now we understand the atmosphere—it must have been loaded with mortal embarrassment. Only Peter, whose heart so often runs away with his tongue, finds words: "Thou shalt never wash my feet!"

What does the scene signify? Clearly something profound. What could move a person to perform such a service voluntarily?

Good-natured helpfulness perhaps, readiness to serve. Or one could be conscious of the omission and free enough to take things in hand. But the moment described here is far too huge for any such slight motive. Again, there are people who instinctively seek the lowest possible place. Inner uncertainty or a feeling of inferiority drives them to perform the most menial services in order to attain a certain inner truth. It is self-understood that Jesus' nature knows none of these. On the contrary, after he has finished the task he says:

"You call me Master and Lord, and you say well, for so I am." He has acted in the full, pure consciousness of his authority. Or was Jesus only demonstrating how to overcome squeamishness and pride? At least one of the disciples might have thought of performing the service for his brothers, but if he did, he probably dismissed the idea, as a man of simple origin would be likely to—fearful that it would be beneath his dignity. By performing himself this slave's task, the Master burns the lesson once and for all into their hearts. The thought is clear, and Jesus' own words support it: "If, therefore, I the Lord and Master . . . that as I have done to you, so you should do also." But the moral is too obvious to cover the whole import of the act, too pedagogic. Christ never acts "moralistically." The idea that Jesus was constantly setting an example has done much to spoil his sacred picture. Of course he was exemplary, *the* model simply; but the figure of the Lord loses all spontaneity when it is constantly portrayed in pedagogic pose. Through such an interpretation something construed and unnatural creeps into his bearing—something fundamentally at odds with his true self. No, Christ lived among his disciples spontaneously, doing from moment to moment what was "right" without thinking particularly of the example he was giving. Because he acted unconsciously, genuinely, from his essence outward, not the other way around, all he did was perfect. He is exemplary because in him Christian life begins. He is its foundation, demonstrates what it stands for, and supplies the necessary strength to participate in it. "Imitation of Christ" does not suggest that he be literally copied—what unnatural and pretentious situations would be the result!—but that the Christian live in Christ, and learn from his spirit to do hour by hour what is right.

In an earlier discussion of how God approaches us through Jesus we concluded that he comes through love. But a God who was only the endlessly Loving One would not have acted as he did; there must be more to it than love, and we discovered that this "more" was humility. Humility is no human quality. The attitude of the little man who bows to the greater is one not of humility but of truth; genuinely humble is the greater man who bows before the lesser because in his eyes the little man has a mysterious dignity. To recognize this dignity, to gather it up and bow before it—that is humility. Humility springs from the Creator and is directed towards the creature;

tremendous mystery! The Incarnation is the fundamental humility on which all human humility rests (Phil. 2:5–10). That is what we have here in the footwashing. But the act goes deeper still. One can perform a service in the current sense of the word: as a necessity. Then it is simultaneously impersonal and decent, objective. Everything can be done from this approach, without the slightest trace of subjectivity. There is also the will to service which springs from an inferiority-complex and finds its expression in self-abasement. Obviously Jesus neither responds to an objective necessity nor deliberately degrades himself. The will behind his act comes from elsewhere.

St. Paul speaks of that which in all eternity motivates the Incarnation. Of God's Son he says: ". . . who though he was by nature God, did not consider being equal to God" (which he was) "a thing to be clung to, but emptied himself, taking the nature of a slave and being made like unto men" (Phil. 2:6–7). In the eternal Son, who was God and his Father's equal and fully conscious of that equality, stirs a desire beyond all psychology or metaphysics to "empty" himself of his glory and omnipotent bounty in order to descend to us as one of us. Jesus "came down" not only to walk on earth, but to penetrate to depths we can never measure—to the abysmal vacuum we know only after we have been genuinely, personally shaken by the full consciousness of what sin is: destruction of the Victim who expiates, redeems, and renews.

When we speak of the price of redemption we usually think of Jesus the man; of his human heart and body and soul, and all that salvation cost them. If we consider God in relation to this act, then usually only to add that his immeasurable sublimity in the divine person of the Savior is what gives Jesus' human sacrifice its all-redeeming power. At the preposterous idea of God's suffering, man stops short. And he is right; how could God suffer? We must not humanize him. And yet, something is missing. The plumbless earnestness of salvation ceases to be a full reality when we imagine Christ on Calvary in untouched exaltation. What we are about to say is false; yet statements seem to exist that are untrue but indispensable. Our salvation was not something God could bring about with a detached and effortless gesture; he felt its full weight. St. Paul speaks of *kenosis,* God's 'emptying' himself (Phil. 2:7). For there not Jesus the man is meant, but the *Logos,* that mysterious decision of the Divine to cancel his own Being in order to assume "the nature of a slave."

There are many varieties of nothingness. First of all, the clear and simple void meant when we say: God created the world out of nothing. This means that God was all in all, and that there was nothing besides him, the simple non-existence of any thing. Then came man's test, and he failed and sinned. Sin is more than mere blameworthiness. Man does not live because he happens to exist, as does the animal or stone; he lives towards fulfillment of the good that is in him. Through voluntary obedience to God's will, he is meant to realize his full capacities. Once man sinned, he was not the same person he had been before, only guilty, but his whole existence, down to the roots of his being became questionable. Instead of living towards God, he fell from him. Now he exists only in his headlong plunge from divine plenitude to nothingness; and not to the pure, positive nothingness that anticipated creation, but to the vacuum that follows on the heels of sin's destruction. Such destruction is never complete, for man, who did not create himself, cannot completely destroy himself through sin; nevertheless, total destruction remains the goal towards which the curve of existence eternally plunges. It is this immeasurably terrible and distant "point" that divine redemption had to reach (naturally not by sinning personally, but by "emptying" himself). To abandon himself to the void, to destruction—not his essential annihilation, but the destruction meant in Matthew's: "He who finds his life will lose it, and he who loses his life for my sake will find it" (10:39)—this is Christ's sacrifice.

That *God* took this sacrifice made possible and necessary by sin upon himself, not only Jesus the man, but the incarnate Son of God, this is the truth that Jesus' act on Holy Thursday so poignantly reveals: he who knows himself Lord and Master assumes the duty of a slave. And we catch a glimpse of that potent nothingness which overtakes and stops the abysmal plunge away from God. It is the nothingness from which the second creation is born: creation of the new man, his face towards God, and once more participating, through grace, in sanctity and reality. Like humility, also Christian sacrifice begins not with men, but with God. Just as only the great and saintly can practice truest humility, only the wealthy and all-powerful can practice purest sacrifice. It is this "divine virtue" of sacrifice on which Christian sacrifice is patterned. No wonder the disciples are perplexed! Everything is really upside-down! By comparison, all human "revaluation of values" is child's-play. The earnestness of Jesus' act is perhaps best measured by his remark to Peter: "What I do thou knowest not now; but thou shalt know hereafter. . . . If I do not wash thee, thou shalt have no part with me." Peter must participate in the mystery of divine surrender if he is to share in the life of Christ, for it is the kernel of Christianity. That is why the Lord adds: ". . . that as I have done to you, so you also should do." The disciples are not only to learn humility and fraternal love, they must actually participate in the mystery.

Every Christian one day reaches the point where he too must be ready to accompany the Master into destruction and oblivion: into that which the world considers folly, that which for his own understanding is incomprehensible, for his own feeling intolerable. Whatever it is to be: suffering, dishonor, the loss of loved ones or the shattering of a lifetime *oeuvre,* this is the decisive test of his Christianity. Will he shrink back before the ultimate depths, or will he be able to go all the way and thus win his share of the life of Christ? What is it we fear in Christianity if not precisely this demand? That is why we try to water it down to a less disturbing system of "ethics" or "*Weltanschauung*" or what have you. But to be a Christian means to participate in the life of Christ—all of it; only the whole brings peace. The Lord once said: "Peace I leave with you, my peace I give to you; not as the world gives do I give to you. Do not let your heart be troubled, or be afraid" (John 14:27). Peace comes only from living this through to the end. One way or another we must brush the depths Christ divinely plummeted, taste the dregs he drained to the last drop: "It is consummated" (John 19:30). From this unreserved realization of the Father's will comes the illimitable peace of Christ, also for us.

X

"Mysterium Fidei"

Human events spring from various depths. Some of them, like a simple purchase, exhaust their possibilities in the process of taking place; in others an experience out of the past may be revived, or a long chain of events brought to an end, or an old tension eased or misunderstanding clarified. Thus the associations of a particular event can penetrate ever deeper, or reach back, or grope ahead. The event that took place on Holy Thursday rises from immeasurable depths.

Jesus is with his disciples for the last time. The hour is heavy with the premonition of parting and of all the pain and dark to come. The little group has not assembled by chance, but to celebrate the Pasch together, solemn reminder of the Chosen People's exit from Egypt, when God's final and most dreadful plague, the smiting of the first-born, forced Pharaoh to let the captives go. The Easter Supper was instituted to commemorate this "high deed" of God. Upon this memorial supper of the Old Covenant, Christ founds the mystery of the new: the "mysterium fidei." On the other hand, the hour also reaches far into the future, to that unknown day ". . . when I shall drink it new with you in the kingdom of my Father" (Matt. 26:29).

The Book of Exodus reports: "And the Lord said to Moses and Aaron in the land of Egypt: . . . Speak ye to the whole assembly of the children of Israel, and say to them: On the tenth day of this month let every man take a lamb by their families and houses. . . . And it shall be a lamb without blemish, a male, of one year: according to which rite also you shall take a kid . . . and the whole multitude of the children of Israel shall sacrifice it in the evening.

"And they shall take of the blood thereof, and put it upon both the side posts, and on the upper door posts of the houses, wherein they shall eat it.

"And they shall eat the flesh that night roasted at the fire: and unleavened bread with wild lettuce.

"You shall not eat thereof any thing raw, nor boiled in water, but only roasted at the fire. You shall eat the head with the feet and entrails thereof.

"Neither shall there remain any thing of it until morning. If there be any thing left, you shall burn it with fire.

"And thus you shall eat it: You shall gird your reins, and you shall have shoes on your feet, holding staves in your hands, and you shall eat in haste; for it is the Phase (that is the Passage) of the Lord.

"And I will pass through the land of Egypt that night, and will kill every firstborn in the land of Egypt both man and beast; and against all the gods of Egypt I will execute judgments. I *am* the Lord.

"And the blood shall be unto you for a sign in the houses where you shall be: and I shall see the blood, and shall pass over you. And the plague shall not be upon you to destroy you, when I shall strike the land of Egypt.

"And this day shall be for a memorial to you: and you shall keep it a feast to the Lord in your generations with an everlasting observance" (Ex. 12:1–14).

For centuries the descendants of Abraham have lived in Egypt. They have become a great people, originally highly esteemed by the Egyptians, then feared and hated. Now treated as bondsmen, they perform invaluable slave labor for Pharaoh, who in spite of Moses' command from God, refuses to let them go. Plague after plague descends upon the land, but Pharaoh stubbornly refuses to yield, till finally the Lord deals the terrible death-blow to all firstborn of man and beast, from the son of the ruler to that of the lowest slave-girl.

God's own people are protected by the blood of the lamb on their gateposts commanded by Moses. A tide of grief sweeps the country; Pharaoh's will is broken, and he lets the Hebrews go.

In memory of this liberation and wondrous passage through the desert, the Pasch was celebrated annually, under strictest observation of the prescribed ritual, on the Friday before the great Easter Sabbath. The lamb was slaughtered in the early afternoon, and the meal began as soon as the first stars appeared in the heavens. Originally it was eaten standing, in travelling-garb, as prescribed by Moses. Gradually the strict ceremony assumed the form of a prolonged and joyful feast, which the participants, as was customary upon such occasions, ate reclining. During the repast, the host blessed the wine-beaker and passed it around four times. After the first cup, a kind of *hors-d'oeuvre* was served; after the second, the host distributed unleavened bread and bitter herbs. The first part of the "Hallel," Song of Praise, was then recited, and the lamb consumed. After the meal the third and fourth beakers were mixed and blessed, and the second part of the Hallel ended the ceremony. Thus also Jesus celebrated the Passover with his disciples, who constituted the prescribed Pasch community.

The last time he did not strictly adhere to the ritual. The very day was changed from Friday to Thursday, for was not he who called himself Lord of the Sabbath also Lord of the Passover? During the meal there were other, incomparably weightier, innovations. Matthew and Luke report: "And he said to them, 'I have greatly desired to eat this passover with you before I suffer; for I say to you that I will eat of it no more, until it has been fulfilled in the kingdom of God.' And having taken a cup, he gave thanks and said, 'Take this and share it among you; for I say to you that I will not drink of the fruit of the vine, until the kingdom of God comes.'

"And having taken bread, he gave thanks and broke, and gave it to them, saying, '(Take and eat) This is my body, which is being given for you; do this in remembrance of me' " (Luke 22:15–20, parentheses from Matt. 26:26).

St. Paul adds: "For as often as you shall eat this bread and drink the cup, you proclaim the death of the Lord, until he comes" (I Cor. 11:26).

The chalice St. Luke mentions is the third beaker to make the rounds during the paschal rite. And according to one beautiful version, after the words "Drink ye all of this" the following were added "for the last time according to ancient custom." Then Christ takes the bread, blesses it, breaks it; and what he passes to them is no longer mere pieces of unleavened Easter bread. He takes the chalice, blesses it; and what he hands them is no longer only the sacred drink-offering of the Pasch, but the mystery of the New Covenant just established. And all that takes place is not only the celebration of one high, fleeting hour; it is a sacred rite institutional for all time and constantly to be renewed until God's kingdom comes, and the Lord himself celebrates it again with his own in the unveiled glory of the new creation.

What has happened? For almost two thousand years men have prayed and probed and fought over the meaning of these words. They have become the sign of a community that is holier, more intimate than any other, but also occasion for profoundest schism. Hence, when we ask what they mean, let us first be clear as to how they should be taken. There is only one answer: literally. The words mean precisely what they say. Any attempt to understand them 'spiritually' is disobedience and leads to disbelief. It is not our task to decide what they should mean in order to express 'pure Christianity,' but to accept them reverently as they stand, and to learn from them what Christian purity is. When Jesus spoke and acted as he did, he knew that all he said and did was of divine importance. He wished to be understood, and spoke accordingly. The disciples were no symbolists, neither were they nineteenth- or twentieth-century conceptualists, but simple fishermen much more inclined to take Jesus' words literally—if not with crude realism, as they had at Capharnaum—than spiritually. Even generally speaking, the man of antiquity was accustomed to perceiving and thinking through the evidence of his senses rather than abstractly. As to Christ's gestures, every detail of these men's daily lives was saturated with cult, and they were accustomed to reading truth from sign and symbol. Aware of all this, the Lord yet spoke and acted as he did.

Like the propitiatory sacrifices common in Egypt at the time of the original passover, the Pasch was a ritualistic ceremony for which a living creature was slaughtered, that its blood might be used to guard the people against destruction. So much then for the background of Jesus' act. He takes bread, gives thanks, praises God for the grace it contains, and blesses it, as shortly before he had blessed the meal. Then he breaks the bread and hands it to the disciples, as he had offered this or that partaker of the Pasch a tid-bit as token of friendship and community. "Take and eat; this is my body." Here on the same table the sacrificial lamb had lain, nourishment of the Old Testament. Those present cannot fail to understand Jesus' words in the same sense: ritualistically and mysteriously, but realistically nevertheless. Then, just as he had blessed and passed round the chalice of the Pasch, whose wine was reminiscent of the blood of sacrifice, he now says: "All of you drink of this; for this is my blood of the new covenant, which is being shed for many unto the forgiveness of sins." The old alliance had been in the blood of the paschal lamb and the blood of the sacrifice on Sinai; the new is in Christ's blood.

It is certain that the disciples did not grasp the full meaning of what their Lord had done. But it is equally certain that they did not interpret it merely as a symbol of community and surrender, or as an act of commemoration and spiritual intervention, but rather along the lines of the first passover in Egypt, of the paschal feast they had just completed, and of the sacrificial rite celebrated day after day in their temples.

What had happened? Theology is constantly wrestling with the answer, yet one cannot avoid the feeling that this part of her effort has remained singularly unsuccessful. Perhaps it is just as well. In the holiest part of the Mass, in the midst of the transubstantiation, the

Church herself rings out the words, *"mysterium fidei!"* Where is the impenetrability of divine mystery more apparent than here? Let us too respect it rather than attempt to explain. Leaving the 'how' in all the density of its mystery, let us inquire only into the 'what.'

When a human being does something, his deed takes its place in history. Granted, it also bears a sense that outlives time—that by which it will be judged and transported into eternity. In one way, therefore, all action is permanent, elevated by the similarity of the individual to his Maker, and by the end to which God has assigned it. Generally speaking, however, human action is a part of time, and when its hour has passed, the act is also a thing of the past. With Jesus it was different. He was man and God in one, and what he did was the result not only of his human and temporal decision, but also of his divine and eternal will. Thus his action was not merely a part of transitory time, but existed simultaneously in eternity.

The earthly life of the Lord was drawing to a close; the treason had already been perpetuated. The rest was fulfillment of sacred destiny. Jesus' passion—which actually had started with the crisis in Galilee and was both temporal history and divine eternity—he now moulded in liturgic rite. As he spoke over the bread and wine, he himself, the soon-to-be-slaughtered-one with his love and his fate *was* word and gesture. And not only once, in the house of Mark, but forever, for when the Lord and bearer of all power "in heaven and on earth" (Matt. 28:18) said "Do this for a commemoration of me," he was instituting something that was to remain to the end of time. Hence, as often as those authorized to do so say these words, make this gesture, the identical mystery takes place, and the passion, whose stand is in eternity, is caught and 'brought down' in liturgical rite. In all truth may be said: This is his body, and his blood—this *is* Jesus Christ in his propitiatory dying! The liturgy is a commemoration, yes, but divine commemoration, not human imitation and memorial, not pious evoking of the past by a faithful congregation, but divine *in memoriam,* and fecund as only one other revealed act of the all-creative Father, that mystery of the infinitely holy passage: "In the beginning was the Word," eternal fruit of which is the living Son (John 1:1–2).

What then is the Eucharist? Christ in his self-surrender, the eternal reality of the suffering and death of the Lord immortalized in a form that permits us to draw from it vitality for our spiritual life as concrete as the food and drink from which we draw our physical strength. Let this stand as it is. Any attempt to 'spiritualize' or 'purify' it must destroy it. It is presumption and incredulity to try to fix the limits of the possible. God says what he wills, and what he wills, is. He alone "to the end" sets the form and measure of his love (John 13:1).

The institution of the Eucharist is also revelation. It reveals the true relation of the believer to his God: not before him, but in him. Among the farewell words that follow the sacred act we find: "I am the true vine, and my Father is the vine-dresser. Every branch in me that bears no fruit he will take away; and every branch that bears fruit he will cleanse, that it may bear more fruit. . . . As the branch cannot bear fruit of itself unless it remain on the vine, so neither can you unless you abide in me. I am the vine, you are the branches. He who abides in me, and I in him, he bears much fruit; for without me you can do nothing. If anyone does not abide in me, he shall be cast outside as the branch and wither; and they shall gather them up and cast them into the fire, . . . In this is my Father glorified, that you may bear very much fruit, . . . As the Father has loved me, I also have loved you. . . . If you keep my commandments you will abide in my love, as I also have kept my Father's commandments, and abide in his love" (John 15:1–10).

Words that must scandalize and revolt those closed to faith, but that to others are "words of everlasting life" (John 6:68; Mark 9:24).

In Luke's text there is a passage we must reread: ". . . for I say to you that I will not drink of the fruit of the vine, until the kingdom of God comes" (22:18). We hear it echoed in the words of a man whose travelling companion and pupil Luke was, St. Paul: "For as often as you shall eat this bread and drink the cup, you proclaim the death of the Lord, until he comes" (I Cor. 11:26). Full of mystery, they too point to an hour that is to come. We cannot very well know what they mean, for they indicate the future. What a prophet says becomes clear only after it has been accomplished; until then it can only be reverently remembered and hopefully foreknown. These words too will be clear only when the Lord has come. They suggest the heavenly banquet he will hold with his own when the kingdom has been established. There he will drink "the fruit of the vine" with them. It is the same mystery John once mentions when Jesus says that to him who believes he will come with his Father and "make our abode with him" (14:23). We are also reminded of similar parables of endless fulfillment in the Book of Revelation that follows. But there is little more to say. The promise must stand as it is; the heart alone can sense its meaning and wait for its realization.

XI

THE SACERDOTAL PRAYER

Reading the account of the Last Supper, we are moved by the love with which Jesus enfolds those he counts his own—but also by his isolation in their midst. A few light touches are sufficient to bring this out sharply: " 'A new commandment I give you, that you love one another: that as I have loved you, you also love one another. By this will all men know that you are my disciples, if you have love for one another.'

"Simon Peter said to him, 'Lord, where art thou going?' Jesus answered, 'Where I am going thou canst not follow me now, but thou shalt follow later.' Peter said to him, 'Why can I not follow thee now? I will lay down my life for thee.' Jesus answered him, 'Wilt thou lay down thy life for me? Amen, amen, I say to thee, the cock will not crow before thou dost deny me thrice' " (John 13:34–38).

Peter means what he says. He loves his Master and is ready to die for him. But Jesus looks through this love and sees that it is nothing he can count on.

The disciples listen to the Master, understand some connection, grasp the meaning of this or that metaphor and call out eagerly: Now we understand! Now we believe! But Jesus sees how it is with their understanding and their faith: no real clarity; no genuine conviction that will weather the coming storm.

Then the thought-provoking: "But I speak the truth to you; it is expedient for you that I depart. For if I do not go, the Advocate will not come to you; but if I go, I will send him to you" (John 16:7). The Spirit kindles the truth of Christ in the hearts and souls of the faithful. He takes what is Christ's and will "declare" it to you (16:14). But why the words "if I do not go, the Advocate will not come to you"? "Go" means die—must then Christ die to be understood? And why? Why can't he be understood now? We remember that many a genius has had to die before he was understood, so that the veil of proximity, the petty trials of everyday life, the all too human foibles of an immediate presence, could fall. But Jesus means something entirely different. Why must the Son of God die before he is comprehended? Why can't his living presence be understood? No, the "must" and "can't" and his own "it is expedient for you" cannot be explained away by psychology, for they are part of that dark mystery mentioned in the first chapter of John's gospel. Jesus was not recognized because men had shut themselves up in darkness. And if we understand rightly, it is added that the darkness took possession also of hearts desirous of knowing him. Even the Apostles were so constituted that Christ's spirit could not come to them directly, but for some inexplicable reason, Christ first had to pass through death.

According to paschal rite, the supper opened with the recitation of the first half of the great Hallel (Psalms 113–118); it was supposed to close with the second half. Instead, Jesus, "raising his eyes to heaven," utters the words of the sacerdotal prayer recorded in John's seventeenth chapter.

It is one of the holiest passages of the New Testament, and should be read with the concentrated powers of heart and spirit. Here too there is no logical sequence of thought, no because and therefore, but a simpler—or more complicated—pattern. A thought emerges and sinks back into the depths. A second appears, disappears, and the first returns. The source from which they spring and the unity into which they merge do not lie on the surface, but deep down under. What is revealed is not any chain of thought, but a fundamental reality, a truth, a plenitude of heart that ebbs and flows like the tides of a deep sea. The point of departure-and-return is the union of Jesus' human heart and spirit with his living divinity. Jesus' words must be read and retained; the new sentences constantly fused with those before. One must grope behind every thought deep into the inexpressible from which it rises, noting how the ineffable breaks through again and again in ever different form. What follows is no explanation. More than almost any other part of Scripture, this prayer lies beyond the reach of intellectual dissection. God alone can unveil it for him who asks for understanding.

"These things Jesus spoke; and raising his eyes to heaven, he said, 'Father, the hour has come! Glorify thy Son, that thy Son may glorify thee, even as thou hast given him power over all flesh, in order that to all thou hast given him he may give everlasting life. Now this is everlasting life, that they may know thee, the only true God, and him whom thou has sent, Jesus Christ. I have glorified thee on earth; I have accomplished the work that thou hast given me to do. And now do thou, Father, glorify me with thyself, with the glory that I had with thee before the world existed.

" 'I have manifested thy name to the men whom thou hast given me out of the world. They were thine, and thou hast given them to me, and they have kept thy word. Now they have learnt that whatever thou hast given me is from thee; because the words that thou hast given me I have given to them. And they have received them, and have known of a truth that I came forth from thee, and they have believed that thou didst send me.

" 'I pray for them; not for the world do I pray, but for those whom thou hast given me, because they are thine; and all things that are mine are thine, and thine are mine; and I am glorified in them. And I am no longer in the world, but these are in the world, and I am coming to thee. Holy Father, keep in thy name those whom thou hast given me, that they may be one even as we are. While I was with them, I kept them in thy name. Those whom thou hast given me I guarded; and not one of them perished except the son of perdition, in order that the Scripture might be fulfilled. But now I am coming to thee; and these things I speak in the world, in order that they may have my joy made full in themselves. I have given them thy word; and the world has hated them, because they are not of the world, even as I am not of the world. I do not pray that thou take them out of the world, but that thou keep them from evil. They are not of the world, even as I am not of the world. Sanctify them in the truth. Thy word is truth. Even as thou hast sent me into the world, so I also have sent them into the world. And for them I sanctify myself, that they also may be sanctified in truth.

" 'Yet not for these only do I pray, but for those also who through their word are to believe in me, that all may be one, even as thou, Father, in me and I in thee; that they also may be one in us, that the world may believe that thou hast sent me. And the glory that thou hast given me, I have given to them, that they may be one, even as we are one: I in them and thou in me; that they may be perfected in unity, and that the world may know that thou hast sent me, and that thou hast loved them even as thou hast loved me.

" 'Father, I will that where I am, they also whom thou hast given me may be with me; in order that they may behold my glory, which thou hast given me, because thou hast loved me before the creation of the world. Just Father, the world has not known thee, but I have known thee, and these have known that thou hast sent me. And I have made known to them thy name, and will make it known, in order that the love with which thou hast loved me may be in them, and I in them' " (John 17:1–26).

The prayer opens with an expression of Jesus' knowledge that "the hour has come" and the wish that he be glorified with the glory that was his before the world was born. Yet it is the hour of Jesus' death; then his glory must lie in his dying. The glory of God transcends form and measure. It is not only joyful, but terrible as well. That Jesus goes to his death in the purity of his oneness with the Father's will—that is glory. That afterwards, he rises again from death in the radiance of resurrection—that is the same glory, and identical with the glory that preceded creation and that will succeed it, for eternity remains the same, before or after.

Obedient to the paternal will, the Son "came unto his own" but they refused to accept him (John 1:10–11).

He spoke The Word through sermon and deed, but his message found deaf ears and had to remain in the air. He summoned mankind to share in divine life, in that unspeakable "we" of his sacerdotal prayer, but mankind declined, and the Messenger of love was left standing in immeasurable isolation. Now in this hour he is void and dumb with loneliness. Even the few he calls his own desert him; others cooperate in a satanic reversal of love's unity to destroy him: the union of scandal in which Pilate and Herod, Pharisee and Sadducee, ruler and people, the just and the criminal, Jew and Roman, disciple Judas (and how nearly the other disciples!) drop their quarrels to ally themselves against him. What would have happened if Jesus had not prayed that Peter's "faith may not fail," and that once converted, he would strengthen the others (Luke 22:31–32)? In this desolation Jesus turns to the one place where unity is mightier than division and security than doubt: there where the Father commands and the Son obeys; where the Son gives of himself, and the Spirit carries it into human hearts; there where the divine "we" of Father and Son through the Holy Ghost controls all things. Here are Jesus' roots; here is his peace, source of his invulnerable strength and union. From here, the beginning, Jesus departed into the world at his Father's command. Now, in the final hour, the Son tells his Father that he has accomplished the paternal will and glorified him on earth by his obedience.

That Jesus' task "is consummated" must be true, because he says so (John 19:30). Yet what a spectacle of failure! His word rejected, his message misunderstood, his commands ignored. None the less, the appointed task is accomplished, through obedience to the death— that obedience whose purity counterbalances the sins of a world. That Jesus delivered his message is what counts—not the world's reaction; and once proclaimed, that message can never be silenced, but will knock on men's hearts to the last day. Once introduced, the eternal kingdom, too, remains forever "at hand," ready to enter into time wherever faith opens a door, for Christ is "the way, and the truth, and the life" (Matt. 3:2; John 14:6). Jesus' coming changed the world. From now on it is and will remain the world in which Christ stands. Through this accomplishment the Father has been glorified.

A hand reaches out from divine unity into the fallen world. Possibly no other passage in Holy Scripture is so heavy with the sense of our plunge from grace as this. Not even St. Paul brings a word as hard as this word of Jesus: ". . . not for the world do I pray, but for those whom thou hast given me. . . ." Into this forlornness reaches the Father's hand, picks out those he will, and gives them to the Son. They are his. Jesus has taught them his message and the name of his Father. He has lost none of them but the son of perdition. Not even the implacable passages of the Epistle to the Romans speak with such harshness of the law of grace and the inviolate sovereignty of that divine will which chooses as it pleases, giving those it has selected to the Son—leaving the others so far behind that the Son does not even pray for them. We should hear these words often, and God grant us the fear without which we shall never enjoy salvation! The more deeply we understand them, the more unconditionally we should fling ourselves on God's mercy. Autonomous, he can choose whom he will; there is no such thing as a 'right' to be chosen, but nothing on earth should hinder me from pleading: Lord, let me be among your chosen, and my loved ones, and all mankind! Do not add: for I have done no real wrong. If you are tempted to, fear for your chances. Before this tremendous mystery it matters little whether or not you have done your duty, whether you are noble or base, possess this or that intrinsically important quality. Everyone should do what he can; every value retains its value; but in the face of this overwhelming mystery, such things are no longer decisive. You must know only this, but as profoundly as possible: that you are a sinner and lost. In this knowledge fling yourself on God's heart and say: Lord, will that I be chosen; that I am among those given to your Son never to be lost—my loved ones and I and all mankind!

Folly, isn't it? How could philosophy exist if everyone thought along such lines? If justice and order among men were so fashioned, they would not survive long. But that is precisely it: these thoughts are not of this world, and their 'folly' is due to the ineffable mystery of God's grace, which cannot be anthropomorphized without distortion.

In Jesus' eyes the Father has been glorified ostensibly by something meriting particular mention in this hour of closing accounts: by the fact that he has lost none of those entrusted to him. Everything was against their remaining faithful. Isn't it here, the terrible word: "Those whom thou hast given me I guarded; and not one of them perished except the son of perdition, in order that the Scripture might be fulfilled." Wasn't Judas also a chosen one? And nevertheless lost? What does this mean? Here thought stands still. There is only one point which we should try to see: that this is a warning, indication of the great danger of scandal and revolt facing the disciples. This very night, before the cock has crowed twice Peter will disavow his master—three times and under oath! This night they all will scatter and flee, so that none will be there to stand under the cross save John and a few women. . . . That they do not permanently abandon the Lord—that is the miracle of grace that glorifies God.

Jesus revealed to those who were given him the name of his Father. He told them, and they believed him, that Christ had been sent by that Father. He passed on to them his word, which is living truth. He communicated to them the glory God had confided to him. He gave them his love. All this is true—and still they remained as they were. Then what he gave his disciples must lie within them as seed lies in earth unconscious of its presence. In spite of their incomprehension, in spite of their cowardice, they contain divine truth! What proof of God's omnipotent grace! Later, after the Lord's death, the Spirit will descend, and his ardor will warm the seed, which will swell and green. Then their human will and understanding will grow together with the divine that the Lord has planted in them. It had been there all along, but intrinsically *they* were not really present. Once though, it will be in them, and they in it, and they will believe and bear witness—not knowing how the grace that had borne them through the abysmal dark could possibly be theirs.

This will be the beginning of the "we," that unspeakable mystery of union with which the sacerdotal prayer pulses: Father and Son united in the love of the Spirit. One life, one truth, one love, and yet three living and revealing loving Ones. Into this triple love-center those will be drawn who were carried by Christ's strength across the dark. Estrangement with the world, more, the world's hostility against all that is alien to her, will rest upon them (John 15:19). That is why Christ's enemies will kill him, because he is different from them. They will turn against those united to him with the same hatred, and will manage, one way or another, to do to them what they did to him. The disciples though must know themselves protected by the same unity in which Christ knows himself sustained and safe; now in this hour in which he is to give himself up to the world's hate.

Indescribable, the perspectives that Jesus' words open: "And the glory that thou hast given me, I have given to them, that they may be one, even as we are one: I in them and thou in me; . . . that the world may know . . . that thou hast loved them even as thou hast loved me" (John 12:22–23).

The plenitude of the new creation is hinted here, all that the letter to the Romans will later say about the one-time glory of the children of God (8:17–21); that the Epistles to the Colossians and the Ephesians will say about the coming re-creation; that the mysterious visions of the Apocalypse will proclaim of the new heaven and the new earth.

What lies between the hour in which the Lord reveals these things and the hour in which the Holy Spirit descends and the fulfillment of the promise begins must never be forgotten. Never should the Christian calmly accept Christ's death as "necessary" to salvation. If he does, a rigidity and inhumanity will creep into his faith that will destroy everything. For then the life of the Lord ceases to be genuinely lived, genuine coming and going and acting and willing and suffering fate!

XII

GETHSEMANE

Afeter saying these things, Jesus went forth with his disciples beyond the torrent of Cedron, where there was a garden . . ." (John 18:1) "according to his custom" adds Luke.

"And they came to a country place called Gethsemane, and he said to his disciples, 'Sit down here, while I pray.' And he took with him Peter and James and John, and he began to feel dread and to be exceedingly troubled. And he said to them, 'My soul is sad, even unto death. Wait here and watch.' And going forward a little, he fell on the ground, and began to pray that, if it were possible, the hour might pass from him; and he said, 'Abba, Father, all things are possible to thee. Remove this cup from me; yet not what I will, but what thou willest.'

"Then he came and found them sleeping. And he said to Peter, 'Simon, dost thou sleep? Couldst thou not watch one hour? Watch and pray, that you may not enter into temptation. The spirit indeed is willing, but the flesh is weak.' And again he went away and prayed, saying the same words over. And he came again and found them sleeping, for their eyes were heavy. And they did not know what answer to make to him" (Mark 14:32–40).

Then he went back again "And there appeared to him an angel from heaven to strengthen him. . . . And his sweat became as drops of blood running down upon the ground" (Luke 22:43–44). And he rose and returned a third time to the disciples and said to them: "Sleep on now, and take your rest! It is enough; the hour has come. Behold, the Son of Man is betrayed into the hands of sinners. Rise, let us go. Behold, he who will betray me is at hand" (Mark 14:41–42).

After Jesus had ended the sacerdotal prayer he and the little group walked down the hill and out of the city. According to tradition, the house in which the Last Supper had been held belonged to the family of the John who later was called Mark, Peter's assistant missionary and author of the Gospel that bears his name. He is believed to be the John who, "having a linen cloth wrapped about his naked body" was also there that last night (until he too was put to dramatic flight—Mark 14:51–52). Jesus, then, descended to the brook Cedron and crossed it—possibly at the same spot where nine hundred years earlier his ancestor, the ancient King David, had fled before his son Absalom. Then they walked up the valley until they came to a farm called Gethsemane. Jesus has often sat there with his disciples, teaching (18:2). Now they feel that things are drawing to a close, and are not surprised when he tells them to wait while he prays. They are quite accustomed to his leaving them in order to speak alone and undisturbed with God. Only the three who had recently been with him on the mountain of the Transfiguration, Peter, James and John, accompany him.

A terrible sadness overcomes the Lord—sadness "unto death" says Holy Scripture. Then Jesus tells also the three to wait—perhaps they are surprised to hear him say they should watch with him; it is probably the first time he has ever asked them to. Alone, he advances a few paces, falls on his face and prays.

This is no place for psychology. When guided by reverence and warmed by generosity, psychology is an excellent thing, doing much to help one human understand another. Here though it must fail, for it could only say that this was another instance of natural reaction: after the tension of tremendous religious concentration and the climb to dizzying spiritual heights of surrender, love and revelation— the collapse, depression. We have only to recall the life of the prophets to see what is meant. Psychology would explain Gethsemane similarly: the rejection by both the ruling class and the masses, the pilgrimage to Jerusalem with its tremendous experiences, the entry into the city, the terrible waiting of the preceding days, the treachery and the Last Supper—as a result of the prolonged strain now the breakdown. In the case of any human, fighting under duress for a noble cause, the analysis very likely would be correct, also (at least partly) for a prophet. But with Jesus any such explanation is bound to founder. If it is insisted upon, Holy Thursday is robbed of that weight and salutary power which can be sensed only in contrition and adoration. Here we can proceed solely through faith guided by revelation.

And it must be living faith—no mere passive acceptance of facts. We participate in this mystery only when we realize and admit that its content is our sin. Mankind's sin constantly being relived in our own deeds and omissions today and yesterday and always; in all our daily rebellion and lassitude, interestedness and sharpness; in the indescribable evil deep at the root of our whole attitude towards existence. We understand here as much as we understand that in the agony of Gethsemane the ultimate consequences of our sin had their hour. Not before we have surrendered ourselves to the dreadfulness of that hour will we understand, really, what sin is. In the measure that we comprehend sin, we comprehend Christ; and we comprehend our own sin only in the measure that we experience what he experienced when he sweated blood in the night.

What does faith tell us? Before all else who this man is there on his knees—the Son of God in the simplest sense of the word. For that reason he sees existence in its ultimate reality.

Wherever we encounter Jesus, it is as the Knowing One, as he who knows about man and world. All others are blind; only his eyes are all-seeing, and they see through to the very ground of human depravity. The forlornness Jesus beholds there embraces the whole of human existence. And he does not see it as one who has broken through to spiritual health and clarity with the help of grace. Jesus' knowledge of sin is not like that of fallen mankind; he knows about it as God knows—hence the awful transparency of that knowledge.

Hence his immeasurable loneliness. He is really the Seer among the blind, sole sensitive one among beings who have lost their touch, the only free and self-possessed one in the midst of general confusion.

Jesus' consciousness of the world's corruption is not grounded in the world and therefore prisoner of existence. It springs from above, from God, and enfolds the whole globe, seeing as God sees: around existence, through existence, outwards from existence. Moreover, Jesus' divine consciousness, before which everything is stripped and lucid, is not extrinsic, but intrinsic, realized in his living self. He knows with his human intellect, feels the world's forlornness with his human heart. And the sorrow of it, incapable of ripping the eternal God from his bliss, becomes in Christ's human soul unutterable agony. From this knowledge comes a terrible and unrelenting earnestness, knowledge that underlies every word he speaks and everything he does. It pulses through his whole being and proclaims itself in the least detail of his fate. Here lies the root of Christ's inapproachable loneliness. What human understanding and sympathy could possibly reach into this realm in which the Savior shoulders alone the yoke of the world? From this point of view Jesus was always a sufferer, and would have been one even if men had accepted his message in faith and love; even if salvation had been accomplished and the kingdom established alone by proclamation and acceptance, sparing him the bitter way of the cross. Even then, his whole life would have been inconceivably painful, for he would have been constantly aware of the world sin in the sight of a God he knew to be all holy and all love; and he would have borne this terrible and inaccessible knowledge alone. In the hour of Gethsemane its ever-present pain swells to a paroxysm.

The life of God is timeless and changeless; it is fixed in a present that is simple and illimitable. The life of men rises and falls like the tides. In the Lord there was both: eternal present and temporal fluctuation; thus also that inner pain will have had its ebb and flow, its variations in volume, pressure, and acuity. Now was the hour in which everything was to be "consummated."

Who knows how God the Father faced his Son in that hour? He never ceased to be his Father; the band of endless love between them which is the Spirit never broke; and yet—"My God, my God, why hast thou forsaken me?" (Matt. 27:46). If we do not prefer to pass over this in reverent silence, we must say that God permitted his Son to taste the human agony of rejection and plunge towards the abyss. Christ's terrible cry from the cross came from the bitter dregs of the consequence of his union with us. But the chalice was given him to taste already in Gethsemane, when, his consciousness of the abysmal forlornness of the world heightened by God's proximity, his Father began to 'withdraw' from him. It was then that Jesus' knowledge and suffering reached the frightful intensity evinced by his terror, agonized praying, and sweat of blood that streamed to the ground. In much the same way, a whirlpool on the surface of an ocean may be the visible sign of a catastrophe at its depths surpassing imagination.

Gethsemane was the hour in which Jesus' human heart and mind experienced the ultimate odium of the sin he was to bear as his own before the judging and avenging countenance of God; hour in which he felt the fury of the Father against sin *per se* as directed against himself, its porter, and therefore suffered the unspeakable agony of "abandonment" by holy God. We are humanizing again. Perhaps it would be better to be silent. But with God's help, possibly that hour in the garden will not be quite lost on us. There Jesus accepted the Father's will and surrendered his own. "His" will was not revolt against God, that would have been sin; it was simply the repulsion of a supremely pure and vital being against the role of scapegoat for the evil of a whole world; revolt against being the one, through no fault of his own but as the price of self-sacrificing love, on whom all God's anger must fall. To accept this was the meaning of his words, ". . . yet not what I will, but what thou willst."

There the real struggle took place. All that came afterwards was the realization of that hour, the actual execution of what had already been excruciatingly anticipated by heart and spirit. And in what solitude! So tremendous that we sense the fundamental guiltlessness of the disciples. In the face of such infinite suffering, their little capacity for compassion must have rebounded like the heart of a small child when the grown-ups are engulfed in some shattering experience: it turns aside, begins to play, or simply falls asleep. The fact that there is no alternative shows how hopeless Christ's isolation is.

No one has ever seen existence as Jesus saw it; neither before nor after. In that hour when his human heart lifted the world from its vapors of deception, he beheld it as otherwise only God beholds it—in all its hideous nakedness. What happened was truth realized in charity. And we are given the standpoint from which we too can see through and reject deception. For that is the meaning of salvation: seeing the world as Christ saw it and experiencing his repulsion of sin.

XIII

THE TRIAL

atthew's account of Jesus' capture and trial is given in chapter twenty-six; Luke's in twenty-two; Mark's in fourteen, and John's in eighteen. The records are simple and entirely convincing. Not a word of any occult power as counterbalance to the dreadfulness of the hour. Nothing exaggerated or glorified. It is not difficult to imagine how these reports would have read had the apostles chosen to dramatize them. Let us take them as they stand, line by line, careful to let nothing speak but the sacred record.

Jesus is still speaking to his disciples—the words about the "hour" that is now come—when Judas appears, accompanied by a large crowd sent by the high council. Some carry staves (probably they are members of the Sanhedrin troops, who are forbidden to bear arms) others, with swords, doubtless belong to the temple guard and have been commanded to maintain order.

Judas has arranged a signal with them—we cannot read the passage without being shaken by the plumbless baseness of that sign: "Whomever I kiss, that is he; lay hold of him." So he strides up to Jesus, greets him with a Peace-to-thee, Master—and kisses him. Jesus replies, "Friend, for what purpose hast thou come?" (Matt. 26:48–50). And according to Luke he adds, "Judas, dost thou betray the Son of Man with a kiss?" (22:48). And turning to the crowd he asks: "Whom do you seek?" And they reply: "Jesus of Nazareth." Jesus: "I am he." It is John who writes this, and also how, overcome by the unearthly majesty to the Lord, and profoundly shaken, they recoil and fall to the ground. Jesus repeats his question, and they answer as before. Then, simultaneously giving them free hand and protecting his followers, Jesus says: "I have told you that I am he. If, therefore, you seek me, let these go their way." Very likely it is to this imperious request that the disciples owe their lives (John 18:5–8).

Now the cohort closes in on Jesus. Peter, unable to bear the sight of the men's hands on the Lord, draws his sword and slashes right and left. But Jesus, like a grown-up calling a child to order, tells him to put up his blade. No earthly sword can possibly cope with the gravity of the situation. If he wished protection, other powers, infinitely triumphant, would come at his bidding, but "How then are the Scriptures to be fulfilled, that thus it must take place?" And he touches the ear of the wounded servant, and it is healed. Then the soldiers bind Jesus and lead him away (Matt. 26:51–54; Luke 22:51).

Terrified, the disciples flee—and not only for fear that they too might be sized; they are utterly dismayed and consternated. In spite of everything, up to this moment they have expected their Master to crush all opposition by some mighty sign of mission. When instead he is taken prisoner, they cannot help but conclude that he is not the victorious bearer of all power in heaven and earth that in their opinion the Messiah must be.

Jesus is led first to Annas, father-in-law of Caiphas, the ruling high-priest. He is apparently a man of such influence that the important case is at once referred to him. But without asking a single question, or taking any measure whatsoever, Annas sends the prisoner, still tied, to Caiphas, in whose home the first hearing is held.

Peter and John have followed at a distance. John is well known in the house of the high-priest and is able to accompany Jesus into the courtyard. Peter remains outside the door, waiting to see what will happen.

What goes on inside the courtyard is not yet the real trial, which according to Jewish law, can take place only in the daytime. It is a kind of preliminary hearing, and above all an opportunity for those in power to enjoy their victory. Thus the high-priest questions the prisoner as to his teaching and followers—we can well imagine his expression and the tone of his voice! Jesus realizes that he is not the least interested in truth, that the sentence has long since been determined, and that the hearing is only a lie and a mockery. So he refused to answer: "I have spoken openly to the world; I have always taught in the synagogues and in the temple, where all the Jews gather, and in secret I have said nothing. Why dost thou question me? Question those who have heard what I spoke to them; behold, these know what I have said" (John 18:20–21).

One of the servants, seeing an opportunity of distinguishing himself, slaps Jesus' face: "Is that the way thou dost answer the high priest?" But Jesus, with a calm weightier than any action, replies: "If I have spoken ill, bear witness to the evil; but if well, why dost thou strike me?" (John 18:22–23).

In the meantime, John has spoken to the wench who keeps the gates, and she has let Peter in. It is a cold night. Someone has kindled a fire in the inner court, and they all gather around it warming themselves, also Peter. The slave girl who has let him in sees him there and accuses him of being a friend of Jesus, and there follows the terrible scene of Peter's triple denial: "But he began to curse and to swear: I do not know this man you are talking about." And the cock crows the second time. Jesus, who is just being led out of the house to prison, "turned and looked upon Peter." And the disciple remembers his words: Before the cock crows twice, thou shalt deny me thrice! "And Peter went out and wept bitterly" (Mark 14:66–72; Luke 22:61).

The Lord is in prison, guarded by servants of the tribunal. Everyone knows who the captive is; the question whether or not he is the Messiah has stirred all Jerusalem. How baseness rears its head when sacred greatness, whose power it previously has been forced to concede, becomes impotent! From what evil depths must it spring, this hunger for revenge against holiness! . . . The guards bind the defenceless prisoner's eyes, strike him and mock: "Prophesy, who is it that struck thee?" It is in truth the "hour, and the power of darkness" (Luke 22:53), and one seems to sense an invisible, non-human force behind those who blaspheme and mock at the Son of God.

Early the next morning the high council is summoned—elders, Scribes and priests, all of them triumphant enemies at the high tide of their power. They have decided that Jesus shall be accused of blasphemy, since it is punishable by death. However, the Law precisely defines the crime: Blasphemy is the mention of God's name in slanderous speech, and as yet no evidence has been produced of the prisoner's guilt. Moreover, the charges brought against him are confused and contradictory. The figure and works of the Lord are so pure, that not even total unscrupulousness is able to wring a "crime" from it. Jesus does not answer a single charge and remains silent even when the high priest orders him to speak. The whole trial is a lie, just as earlier the questions with which the Scribes and Pharisees had attempted to trap him were lies. It would have been child's play to point out the contradictoriness of the accusals; to strengthen the impression of candidness which he could not fail to make on all who saw him; to seize the offensive against his accusers. It is painful to watch Jesus do absolutely nothing to retard his obvious fate—until we remember that he does not wish to retard it. In the night of Gethsemane he had accepted it, and what now happens, all that the harsh, hypocritical, cowardly, confused agents of Satan undertake against him, is only the form in which his Father's will finds expression. We will never understand what is happening until we experience the deep, resolute calm that is in Jesus. There is nothing oppressive about it. Nothing desperate or resigned. Nothing insolent. Here is only perfect calm, knowing, watchful, readiness for the ultimate.

When the high priest sees that they are getting nowhere he changes his tactics and suddenly flings the official formula at the accused: "I adjure thee by the living God that thou tell us whether thou art the Christ, the Son of God." Now Jesus answers. This is no trap, but an expression of the supreme authority of his people, and though hardened against God, this people comes from God and has a right to demand information on Jesus' origin and mission. It is the question that is to set his salutary destiny in motion, so he replies: "Thou hast said it. Nevertheless, I say to you, hereafter you shall see the Son of Man sitting at the right hand of the Power and coming upon the clouds of heaven." The high priest responds with the pathetic gesture that commonly established guilt: he rends his garments.

"He has blasphemed; what further need have we of witnesses? Behold, now you have heard the blasphemy. What do you think?" And they all cry: "He is liable to death" (Matt. 26:63–66).

Law and order have vanished. Violence and treachery remain. The claim to be the Messiah is simply accepted as proven blasphemy. No attempt is made to test the possible truth of the claim— neither legally, with questions as to how Jesus substantiates his statement, nor religiously, through examination by the wisest and most pious priests. The mere fact that the name of God appears in his answer is sufficient. An "offence" at last! Immediately it is registered and sentence pronounced. But there is one hitch: the Jewish nation has lost its judiciary sovereignty, and no longer has the right to pass sentence of death. Where this is necessary, the representative of the Roman state, the procurator, must both confirm the verdict of the Great Sanhedrin and execute sentence. So they bind Jesus again and lead him to the *Praetorium,* where Pontius Pilate holds his court of justice.

The accusers, anxious for their paschal purity, proceed as far as the courtyard, but not into the building proper, lest they become "unclean." . . . Hadn't Jesus mourned just this kind of formalism? "Woe to you, Scribes and Pharisees, hypocrites! because you clean the outside of the cup and the dish, but within they are full of robbery and uncleanliness" (Matt. 23:25).

The procurator familiar with the Jewish custom, descends to the courtyard. From the very first questions and answers we sense the mutual irritation and contempt. The Roman: Have you charges against this man?

The Jews: If we had none we would not have brought him to you.

Pilate: Then take him and judge him according to your own Law.

The Jews: We have no right to sentence to death (John 18:29–31). And they begin their accusals. These have changed on the way. Blasphemy is no longer mentioned; they fear the Roman would say it was not his affair. Instead, they charge Jesus with the offence which must appear gravest in the eyes of the occupation: sedition.

The Jews: We have found that he incites the people to revolt, encourages them to withhold the tax-money from Caesar, and calls himself king and Messiah! (They themselves would be only too glad to participate in a successful revolt against the foreign domination; but he who has preached: Give unto Caesar that which is Caesar's, is now accused of rebellion—precisely the word recommending obedience to Caesar is turned around for use against the accused!)

Jesus is silent. Also to the procurator's question as to what he has to say to the charges, and Pilate "wondered exceedingly" (Matt. 27:14). This is certainly anything but the usual behavior of defendants, excited, verbose, pathetic, insistent—who try anything and everything to save their lives. This man is silent. So Pilate takes him inside, where he can question him privately: "Art thou the king of the Jews?" Jesus replies with a strange counter-question: "Dost thou say this of thyself, or have others told thee of me?" (The accusers, in other words, who charge me with revolt against Caesar.) If you are only questioning me formally, as part of the trial, I have nothing to say. But perhaps you are asking because something in you desires to know. That something I will answer. But Pilate only replies haughtily: "Am I a Jew?" What is your Messiah to me? "Thy own people and the chief priests have delivered thee to me. What hast thou done?"

Nevertheless, Jesus sees that there are depths to this Roman, and he proclaims himself: He is King, yes, but his kingdom is "not of this world." If it were, "my followers would have fought that I might not be delivered to the Jews. But, as it is, my kingdom is not here."

"Art thou then a king?"

"Thou sayest it; I am a king. This is why I was born, and why I have come into the world, to bear witness to the truth." Now Pilate thinks he knows where he is: the man is obviously one of those wandering philosophers who deny the earthly realm in an attempt to establish an ideal realm of truth—a harmless utopian, to put it in modern speech. For the idea that what the stranger says might be actually true, in the trusting and passionate sense of the word, he has only the skeptical shrug of the cultivated of his day: "What is truth?"

Yet his judiciary eye sees clearly, so he goes outside and announces to the Jews: "I find no guilt in him" (John 18:33–38).

But the accusals grow only louder: "He is stirring up the people, teaching throughout all Judea, and beginning from Galilee even to this place" (Luke 23:5). At the word Galilee, Pilate sees a way out. As a Galilean, the accused is under the jurisdiction of Herod, who at the moment happens to be in Jerusalem. By sending the defendant to Herod for judgment, he would simultaneously flatter the nominal sovereign and rid himself of the unpleasant affair. And this Pilate does, but the accusers go along with Jesus.

Herod is delighted. He has heard much about Jesus and is eager to meet him. The tetrarch is interested in the religious and marvelous (as evinced by his strange friendship with John the Baptist—interest, however, which did not prevent him from beheading the last of the prophets when manoeuvred into an embarrassing predicament). Now he hopes to experience something extraordinary—possibly even a miracle! So he plies question on question, while the representatives of the supreme council stand by violently accusing. But Jesus never says a word. All of them, Sanhedrin, Rome's Procurator, Herod "the Fox" and the rest, can terrorize and murder as they will. They are only slaves (their violence proof enough) at best fallen slaves of God. After Herod has questioned a while in vain, his interest turns to mockery. He and his whole court make sport of this Messiah so obviously impotent, and garbing him in a jester's royal cloak, they send him, a living caricature of his claims, back to Pilate.

"And Herod and Pilate became friends that very day; whereas previously they had been at enmity with each other." The Evangelist states the fact calmly, stripping the human heart bare (Luke 23:7–12).

Now Pilate summons the populace and entire Sanhedrin and declares formally that the charges are groundless. Not only administrator of justice, but also a sound politician, he hopes to play out one power against the other: the masses against their rulers. According to an age-old custom, the governor annually pardoned one prisoner in honor of the Pasch; didn't they wish this harmless "king of the Jews" set free? Pilate knows why he asks as he does. The rulers are anxious to rid themselves of a rival, but it is to be expected that the masses love this man in simple garb with the calm, fearless face, and count him as one of their own. . . . Moreover, we read in Matthew the strange aside: "Now, as he was sitting on the judgment-seat, his wife sent to him, saying, 'Have nothing to do with that just man, for I have suffered many things in a dream today because of him' " (26:19). Pilate is skeptical but sensitive—possibly also superstitious. He feels the mystery, fears supernatural power, and would like to free the accused. He counts upon the masses to demand Jesus' release. There is a man in prison who has been really seditious—and in addition committed murder. His name is also Jesus, Jesus Bar-abbas.

Pilate: Whom shall I give free, Jesus the Bar-abbas, or the Jesus called Messiah? But the Procurator has reckoned falsely. The crowd collected outside is no real cross-section of the masses composed in the main of serious, hard-working, long-suffering, honest men and women, but mob, *plebs*. The High Council has seen to that, and its agitators are busily and successfully spreading 'public opinion' among them. So they yell: Bar-abbas!

Pilate tries to placate them: "What then am I to do with Jesus who is called Christ?"

All: "Let him be crucified!"

Pilate: "Why, what evil has he done?" Luke adds: "I find no crime deserving of death in him. I will therefore chastize him and release him." But they only bawl the louder: "Let him be crucified!" (Matt. 27:17–23). Pilate has Jesus flogged. Terrible contradiction of intent: those sentenced to crucifixion were first flogged to intensify the punishment! Actually, Pilate means well—if the word can be uttered at all in such connection. (For had his will been really earnest, he could have proven it by a just sentence.) The Roman knows mob psychology and thinks he can handle the situation; they must see blood flow; must have the satisfaction of inflicting pain, then they will be satisfied. So he has Jesus flogged; it is enough to remember that men often died at the flogging-post.

At sight of the horribly striped one, the soldiers, knowing that he has been accused of attempting to usurp royal dignity, suddenly recall an ancient comedy still well known in certain sectors of the Roman army—the Comedy of the Shadow-King. The figure was a remnant of a nebulously distant past. We have authentic record of a widespread primeval custom which demanded that a king (who was considered the savior of his kingdom and the living embodiment of Nature's mysterious powers of birth and death) was sacrificed before he could grow old that his blood might serve the regeneration and new fertility of his kingdom. Later the royal life was substituted by that of a prisoner, who for one day reigned as shadow king and was then offered up in his stead. Probably the soldiers dimly remembered the terrible and grotesque comic figure patterned after the one-time pagan redeemer from degeneration and death, and had him in mind when they played their cruel game with him who had come to save them all from the slavery of fallen nature with her categories of gods and goddesses.

"Then the soldiers of the procurator took Jesus into the praetorium, and gathered together about him the whole cohort. And they stripped him and put on him a scarlet cloak; and plaiting a crown of thorns, they put it upon his head, and a reed into his right hand; and bending the knee before him they mocked him, saying, 'Hail, King of the Jews!' And they spat on him, and took the reed and kept striking him on the head" (Matt. 27:27–30).

After they have had their will, Pilate comes out and speaks to the crowd and the Sanhedrin: "Behold, I bring him out to you, that you may know that I find no guilt in him." Jesus appears wearing the cloak and the crown of thorns, and Pilate says: "Behold, the man!" But the only answer he receives is: "Crucify him! Crucify him!" (John 19:4–5).

Pilate replies, there is no Roman law according to which this man could be condemned to death. If such a Jewish law exists, they should apply it. At this, they drop the charges brought to impress the Roman and fall back upon their own trial: "We have a Law, and according to that Law he must die, because he has made himself Son of God." The governor is startled. The time is one of religious upheavals; everywhere mysterious undercurrents flow. There is much talk of gods who come down to earth and walk unrecognized among men. The skeptic is suddenly shaken—perhaps the stranger there is such a one?

Again he takes him inside and questions him: "Where art thou from?" No answer. Pilate again: "Dost thou not speak to me? Dost thou not know that I have power to release thee?"

Jesus: "Thou wouldst have no power at all over me were it not given thee from above."

Pilate has no wish to become involved with the supreme powers. He desires to save the mysterious one and says so to the Sanhedrin. At this the accusers attack him where he is most vulnerable: If you free him, you are no friend of Caesar. For he would be king; he revolts against Caesar! Now their victory is assured. Religion is all very interesting; however, interest flags when the earnestness of daily living, when one's career, is threatened; when visions of messengers to Caesar's court at Rome with reports of dubious loyalty begin to form.

Pilate leads the accused outside and seats himself in the judge's seat. One last time, with an uncertainty that is impotent against the fanatical will of the accusers, he tries to save Jesus: "Behold your king."

But they sense their victory and only clamor: "Away with him! Away with him! Crucify him!"

Pilate: (we cannot help sympathizing with this weak man, bullied, against his better judgment, to injustice) "Shall I crucify your king?"

"We have no king but Caesar" (John 19:4–15).

Pilate gives up. After the symbolical, oh so paltry gesture of the hand-washing, he makes the ridiculous announcement: "I am innocent of the blood of this just man; see to it yourselves."

To this, the gruesome answer of the mob: "His blood be on us and on our children."

Pilate releases Bar-abbas and surrenders Jesus to their will.

The account rings with sacred truth. Never rhetorical, it is rendered simply and objectively. Not a word about Jesus' possible emotions; no hint of the author's reaction. We have only to imagine what a modern reporter would have made of the 'story' to feel the straightforwardness with which this event, upon which the eternal salvation of the world depended, is recorded. That is why it is so convincing, but also why it appears almost insignificant. Every sentence is packed with immeasurable content; but only so much is revealed as the individual reader's love and earnestness is capable of bringing to light. No wonder the pious masses have composed as accompanying commentary to these few terse pages, the prayerful, meditative, symbolic exercise of the Way of the Cross.

How strangely disturbing Jesus' conduct! We must shake off a two-thousand-year-old simplification of Christ as "our dear Savior," prototype of patience and love, long enough to realize how incomplete this representation, how little known he really is. What has happened? No mighty struggle has taken place; no particularly dramatic words have fallen; no mysterious greatness strong enough to influence the enemy has broken through—not even a negative power, sweeping aside all pretence and bodily flinging Jesus' haters upon him, to put an end to him then and there. No. Step by step the trial plods to its intended conclusion. And Jesus?

Apart from the cold calculation with which men responded to the holiest Being that ever walked on earth what is most disquieting about the whole account of the end is the sudden unanimousness of

Jesus' enemies, diabolical antithesis of the peace and harmony of God's kingdom. Pharisee and Sadducee are inherent foes, who spontaneously oppose each other on every issue. Yet on this they join hands. Tomorrow, when Jesus is in the tomb, they will resume yesterday's quarrel. . . . The masses know perfectly well that those in power despise them. More than once they have been on the verge of rebelling against their rulers and proclaiming Jesus king and Messiah. Yet now all consciousness of the Pharisees' contempt, all gratitude to Jesus, all enthusiasm have vanished; herdlike they follow the leaders. . . . Pharisees and Romans are cleft by an implacable hatred. For the defenders of heaven's sacred cause, the conquerors are the enemies of God and his Chosen People: idolators, blasphemers, untouchables. In their eyes the emperor, who claims divine dignity, is the embodiment of all abomination and sacrilege; yet during the trial they do not hesitate to remind Pilate of his duties to Caesar, and to use the Roman law for their own ends. To this hour, Pilate and Herod have been enemies: Pilate is hated as the representative of the power that has crushed Herod's sovereignty; Herod is for Pilate just another little oriental despot-troublemaker. Yet the Procurator eagerly seizes the opportunity to make a polite gesture. The intention is recognized and appreciated, and in the diplomatic exchange that takes place over the blood of Christ, the two become friends.

It is frightening to witness this hate-torn world suddenly united for one brief hour, against Jesus. And what does he do? Every trial is in reality a struggle—but not this one. Jesus refuses to fight. He proves nothing. He denies nothing. He attacks nothing. Instead, he stands by and lets events run their course—more, at the proper moment he says precisely what is necessary for his conviction. His words and attitude have nothing to do with the logic or demands of a defence. Their source lies elsewhere. The accused makes no attempt to hinder whatever is to come; but his silence is neither that of weakness nor of desperation. It is divine reality; full, holy consciousness of the approaching "hour"; perfect readiness. His silence brings into being what is to be.

None the less, in the dark a struggle is raging. The struggle against truth so self-evident, that the whole trial seems to have but one aim: to obscure truth long enough for the desired sentence to be pronounced without an outburst of truthful enthusiasm for Jesus or of truthful terror that would send men flying from the scene. There is no defence whatsoever, and the defendant declines to defend himself. In this turbulent hour only truth *per se* takes the stand, and therefore must be trampled beyond recognition before the sentence can fall. This is most evident in Pilate. It is not easy to do him justice. After all, he was the supreme judiciary authority in the country, and whatever Rome's callousness with regard to certain aspects of imperial domination, the law was always endowed with a majesty whose appearance at least every judge was obliged to protect. One might suppose that Pilate was simply without conscience. But this would not explain his behavior during Jesus' trial. Had he really lacked integrity, he could have directed the trial or have let it direct itself so that the sentence against Jesus would have been inflicted as against a dangerous agitator. Actually he does nothing of the sort. He insists upon the defendant's innocence—repeatedly, to the end—and then, fully conscious of the illegality of the decision, pronounces the sentence of death, and what a death! We are likely to overlook the contradiction, or to explain it away with Pilate's 'weakness.' This is insufficient. The procurator is sucked into the depths of "the powers of darkness," into a confusion so dark and deep that he is no longer sensible of the gruesome and ignominious folly he is committing.

XIV

Jesus' Death

O nce the sentence has fallen, everything goes its merciless way. The reader should take the Gospels and read for himself now, before we continue, the four reports. They are to be found in Matthew twenty-seven, Mark fifteen, Luke twenty-three, and John nineteen. He should not retreat before the horrors recounted here, but should read them through, will all the concentration of his heart, remembering that they were suffered for him.

Why did Jesus die? When a man dies in battle for his country, even (to the extent that the general mysteriousness of life allows) when he succumbs to a stroke of fate, the answer to the 'why' is more or less clear. Up to this point we understand. But with Jesus everything is different. He does not fall in battle. His strength does not collapse before superior, hostile forces. He is not the victim of malevolent misfortune. True, all these things participate in his end, but they are not its real inescapable cause, for which we must dig deeper. It is contained in the words: "This is my body, which is being given for you. . . ." and over the chalice: "This cup is the new covenant in my blood, which shall be shed for you . . ." (Luke 22:19–20). Here we have it—the *leit motiv* of the Pauline Epistles and content of Revelation: Jesus Christ has redeemed us through his death.

But what does it mean, 'redeemed'?

Holy Scripture opens with the words, "In the beginning God created heaven, and earth." And the catechism adds: Out of nothing he created them. This means that 'before' (one of those false words necessary for human logic, but of course not to be taken literally) God conceived and willed creation, nothing existed—neither matter nor energy nor images nor motives; not even the mysterious yearning for existence, but actually nothing!

God existed, and that was enough. "Beside" God nothing was, *is* necessary, for he is the "One and All." Even all that is 'in addition' to God comes from him: matter, energy, form, purpose, order, things, events, plants, animals, humans, angels—everything that is. Man can work with the stuff of reality or even recombine images in the unreal realms of fantasy. But he can never create from nothing, can add no single new thing (real or imagined) to those God has fashioned. For man nothingness is a blank wall. Only God, who can create from it, making things and placing them in reality, has genuine contact with it. For man nothingness is only the severance from things.

Thus God created man, who had no coherence, no life save in his Creator. Then man sinned; he attempted to free himself from this fundamental truth of his existence; attempted to be sufficient unto himself. And he fell away from God—in the terrible, literal sense of the word. He fell from genuine being towards nothingness—and not back to the positive, creative pure nothingness from which God had lifted him, but towards the negative nothingness of sin, destruction, death, senselessness and the abyss. Admittedly, he never quite touches bottom, for then he would cease to exist, and he who has not created himself is incapable of cancelling his existence.

God's mysterious grace could not leave man in such forlornness; it desired to help him home. It is not for us to discuss how he might have accomplished this. Our task is to hold to the text that accounts how it actually was done: in a manner of such sacred magnanimity and power, that once revealed to us, it is impossible to conceive of any other: in the manner of love.

God followed man (see the parables of the lost sheep and the missing groat in Luke 15) into the no man's land which sin had ripped open. God not only glanced down at him and summoned him lovingly to return, he personally entered into that vacuous dark to fetch him, as St. John so powerfully expresses it in his opening Gospel. Thus in the midst of human history stood one who was both human and God. Pure as God; but bowed with responsibility as man. He drank the dregs of that responsibility—down to the bottom of the chalice. Mere man cannot do this. He is so much smaller than his sin against God, that he can neither contain it nor cope with it. He can commit it, but he is incapable of fully realizing what he has done. He cannot measure his act; cannot receive it into his life and suffer it through to the end. Though he has committed it, he is incapable of expiating it. It confuses him, troubles him, leaves him desperate but helpless. God alone can 'handle' sin. Only he sees through it, weighs it, judges it with a judgment that condemns the sin but loves the sinner. A man attempting the same would break. This then the love, reestablisher of justice and willer of man's rescue known as "grace." Through the Incarnation a being came into existence who though human in form, realized God's own attitude toward sin. In the heart and spirit and body of a man, God straightened his accounts with sin. That process was contained in the life and death of Jesus Christ.

The plunge from God towards the void which man in his revolt had begun (chute in which the creature can only despair or break) Christ undertook in love. Knowingly, voluntarily, he experienced it with all the sensitiveness of his divinely human heart. The greater the victim, the more terrible the blow that fells him. No one ever died as Jesus died, who was life itself. No one was ever punished for sin as he was, the Sinless One. No one ever experienced the plunge down the vacuum of evil as did God's Son—even to the excruciating agony behind the words: "My God, my God, why hast thou forsaken me?" (Matt. 27:46). Jesus was really destroyed. Cut off in the flower of his age; his work stifled just when it should have taken root; his friends scattered, his honor broken. He no longer had anything, was anything: "a worm and not a man." In inconceivable pain "he descended into hell," realm in which evil reigns, and not only as the victorious breaker of its chains. This came later; first he had to touch the nadir of a personally experienced agony such as no man has ever dreamed. There the endlessly Beloved One of the eternal Father brushed the bottom of the pit. He penetrated to the absolute nothingness from which the "*re-creation*" of those already created (but falling from the source of true life toward that nothingness) was to emerge: the new heaven and new earth.

Christ on the cross! Inconceivable what he went through as he hung there. In the degree that we are Christian and have learned to love the Lord, we begin to sense something of that mystery of utter helplessness, hopelessness. This then the end of all effort and struggle! Everything, without reserve—body, heart and spirit given over to the illimitable flame of omnipresent agony, to the terrible judgment of assumed world-sin that none can alleviate and whose horror only death can end. Such the depths from which omnipotent love calls new creation into being.

Taking man and his world together, what impenetrable deception, what labyrinthian confusion, all-permeating estrangement from God, granitic hardness of heart! This is the terrible load Christ on the cross was to dissolve in God, and divinely assimilate into his own thought, heart, life and agony. Ardent with suffering, he was to plunge to that ultimate depth, distance, center where the sacred power which formed the world from nothing could break into new creation.

Since the Lord's death, this has become reality, in which all things have changed. It is from here that we live—as far as we are really alive in the sight of God.

If anyone should ask: What is certain in life and death—so certain that everything else may be anchored in it? The answer is: The love of Christ. Life teaches us that this is the only true reply. Not people—not even the best and dearest; not science, or philosophy, or art or any other product of human genius. Also not nature, which is so full of profound deception; neither time nor fate. . . . Not even simply "God"; for his wrath has been roused by sin, and how without

Christ would we know what to expect from him? Only Christ's love is certain. We cannot even say God's love; for that God loves us we also know, ultimately, only through Christ. And even if we did know without Christ that God loved us—love can also be inexorable, and the more noble it is, the more demanding. Only through Christ do we know that God's love is forgiving. Certain is only that which manifested itself on the cross. What has been said so often and so inadequately is true: The heart of Jesus Christ is the beginning and end of all things.

PART SIX

*Resurrection
and Transfiguration*

I

THE RESURRECTION

All the Gospels report a mysterious event which took place on the third day after Jesus' death. The character of the accounts is peculiar: they break off suddenly, cross-cut each other, contain contrasts and contradictions that are not easily clarified. Something extraordinary seems to be seeking expression— something that explodes all hitherto known forms of human experience. If we arrange the different texts in the probable order of events, the result is more or less as follows:

"Now late in the night of the Sabbath, as the first day of the week began to dawn, Mary Magdalene and the other Mary came to see the sepulchre. And behold, there was a great earthquake; for an angel of the Lord came down from heaven, and drawing near rolled back the stone, and sat upon it. His countenance was like lightning, and his raiment like snow. And for fear of him the guards were terrified, and became like dead men" (Matt. 28:1–4).

"And when the Sabbath was past, Mary Magdalene, Mary the mother of James, and Salome, bought spices, that they might go and anoint him. And very early on the first day of the week, they came to the tomb, when the sun had just risen. And they were saying to one another, 'Who will roll the stone back from the entrance of the tomb for us?' And looking up they saw that the stone had been rolled back, for it was very large" (Mark 16:1–4).

"But on entering, they did not find the body of the Lord Jesus" (Luke 24:3).

"She [Mary Magdalene] ran therefore and came to Simon Peter, and to the other disciple whom Jesus loved, and said to them, 'They have taken the Lord from the tomb, and we do not know where they have laid him.'

"Peter therefore went out, and the other disciple, and they went to the tomb" (John 20:2–3).

"And it came to pass, while they were wondering what to make of this, that, behold, two men stood by them in dazzling raiment. And when the women were struck with fear and bowed their faces to the ground, they said to them, 'Why do you seek the living one among the dead? He is not here, but has risen. Remember how he spoke to you while he was yet in Galilee, saying that the Son of Man must be betrayed into the hands of sinful men, and be crucified, and on the third day rise' " (Luke 24:4–7).

"But go, tell his disciples and Peter that he goes before you into Galilee; there you shall see him, as he told you" (Mark 16:7).

"And they remembered his words. And having returned from the tomb, they reported all these things to the Eleven, and to all the rest" (Luke 24:8–9).

"The two were running together, and the other disciple ran on before, faster than Peter, and came first to the tomb. And stooping down he saw the linen cloths lying there, yet he did not enter. Simon Peter therefore came following him, and he went into the tomb, and saw the linen cloths lying there, and the handkerchief which had been about his head, not lying with the linen cloths, but folded in a place by itself. Then the other disciple also went in, who had come first to the tomb. And he saw and believed; for as yet they did not understand the Scripture, that he must rise from the dead. The disciples therefore went away again to their home.

"But Mary was standing outside weeping at the tomb. So, as she wept, she stooped down and looked into the tomb, and saw two angels in white sitting, one at the head and one at the feet, where the body of Jesus had been laid. They said to her, 'Woman, why are thou weeping?' She said to them, 'Because they have taken away my Lord, and I do not know where they have laid him.'

"When she had said this she turned round and beheld Jesus standing there, and she did not know that it was Jesus. Jesus said to her, 'Woman, why art thou weeping? Whom dost thou seek?' She, thinking that he was the gardener, said to him, 'Sir, if thou hast removed him, tell me where thou hast laid him and I will take him away.' Jesus said to her, 'Mary!' Turning, she said to him, 'Rabboni!' (that is to say, Master). Jesus said to her, 'Do not touch me, for I have not yet ascended to my Father, but go to my brethren and say to them, "I ascend to my Father and your Father, to my God and your God" ' " (John 20:4–17).

The claim is stupendous: Jesus of Nazareth, Master of "the little group," he who was held by many to be the Messiah and had been put to death by his enemies, has returned to life. And not only to the existence Socrates described before his death when he told his followers that his soul would live on in a better and larger life; not only as the memory and example of a great man lives on in history, but in flesh and blood—reawakened to that same life (naturally in a new form) which death has destroyed.

Our feelings protest against this exigency of faith. If they do not, we have grounds to suspect ourselves of having accepted the account merely as a beautiful legend. For what is stated here is unheard of, and our immediate reaction has always been one of natural protest. No wonder the official report to the effect that while the guards slept, disciples had stolen the body, was believed by many! (Matt. 28:11–15).

In fact, attempts have been made over and over again to eliminate the Resurrection from the true accounts of Jesus' life, where it allegedly has no place. The methods employed are various. One of the earliest and most frequently used was the 'explanation' of deception: the followers of the Lord had resorted to a more or less pious trick; one had only to read the official proclamation for ample

proof. More serious are two modern theories. According to the
first, Jesus' disciples had believed in his Messianic mission with all
their souls. The more precarious the outer, historical situation grew,
the more tensely they upheld this belief. To the last Christ's followers desperately awaited the great victory over the enemy. When the
catastrophe came, everything was shattered. In the plumbless discouragement that seized them, one of those mysterious psychological defence-processes came to the rescue; from the subconscious
rose the triumphant certainty: the Lord lives! This conviction (a natural means of overcoming despair) produced visions of the object of
their desire—or more exactly—such visions, called into being by
the subconscious, were the foundation of the disciples' certitude.
Created by those most intimately involved, the Resurrection was
accepted by other believers, and so made its way into history.

The second explanation takes as its point of departure the Christian community. This little group, surrounded by strangers and enemies, felt the need of possessing a reality capable of consolidating it
from within and defending it against inroads from without; it
needed a central, divine figure and a redemptory event. And just as
other religious communities had their cults, in which some mythological fate was reenacted and assimilated in liturgic ceremony, so
also the early Christians created the supernatural figure whose sacred fate was to become the content of their cult and the measure
of their own existence: Christ the Lord. . . . From such religio-
psychological experience then, was he formed, this risen Christ so
different from the simple Jesus of Nazareth. Jesus had been a man, a
creative religious genius who had lived and died like other men, save
that his death had produced incomparably greater repercussions. It
was only the Easter experience that made him the "*Kyrios Christos,*"
the Lord Christ living in the souls of his followers, the spiritually
powerful, transfigured Lord of faith and coming Judge of the world.
There is no possible reconciliation between these two, Jesus and
Christ, though of course one may veil the clear facts by insisting that
faith alone is able to bring about such reconciliation—which is as

much as admitting that it exists only in the personal experience of the individual.

Much may be said against this argument. Not a word in Scripture suggests that the apostles ever expected a resurrection in any form; on the contrary, they rejected the thought, and were overwhelmed by the actual fact (which might also be explained away 'psychologically,' though it is not very probable that an idea so foreign to Jewish religious thought as an incarnate god who retained his corporality in the heavenly state would be Galilean fishermen's subconscious reaction to depression!). And finally, it should be pointed out that a mere religious experience might be sustained briefly over a period of spiritual torpor, or even for a few dramatic years, but that it never could become the world factor which Christianity today is—factor indissolubly bound to the Resurrection of Christ.

St. Paul—who did not go through the others' crisis—words it: "For if the dead do not rise, neither has Christ risen; and if Christ has not risen, vain is your faith, for you are still in your sins. Hence they also who have fallen asleep in Christ, have perished. If with this life only in view we have had hope in Christ, we are of all men the most to be pitied" (I. Cor. 15:17–19). In other words, with Jesus' Resurrection stands or falls Christian faith. It is no supplement to that faith, also no mythological development, briefly acquired for historical purposes, to be dropped without danger. It is the center of our religion.

The apostle's consciousness of this fact leads us back to Jesus himself: What did he have to say about it? Jesus often spoke of his death, particularly on the three special occasions during his last trip to Jerusalem; each time, however, he added that he would rise again. In these declarations the attitude towards death peculiar to Jesus is crystallized. The death that is valid for us is unknown to him. He knows only death followed by Resurrection: immediate, historical Resurrection.

With this we arrive at the supreme but also most difficult task of Christian thought: that of understanding the Lord's existence. The simplest Christian is given such understanding through participation in the community of grace, through faith and imitation. But what we are aiming at here is conscious, intellectual comprehension, for the mind is also summoned to service for Christ. (*A priori* is its willingness to submit to Christian 'baptism.') The problem of understanding the living Jesus Christ and interpreting his consciousness of self is extremely difficult. Two dangers face it: that of falling into purely human psychology, which simply discards all that lies outside its limitations, and that of dogmatizing: of claiming the supernatural without being able to make it apparent. Only he is really successful who on the one hand never loses touch with the living figure of the Lord, appreciating his humanity at every step; yet on the other, is constantly aware of the fact that this appreciation is at all times subject to explosion by something that is not only the greatness of genius or the dynamism of religious experience, but holy God himself.

The stand Jesus takes to the world is different from ours. His attitude to people is different from that of one person to another. His relation to God is not that of a believer. His consciousness of his own existence, of his living and dying is utterly different from ours, already conditioned by the coming Resurrection.

We are faced with an either-or that reaches to the bottom of existence. If we take ourselves as measuring-rod, our human lives, the world as it appears to us, our thoughts and reactions and attempt to judge Christ by them, can only conclude that the Resurrection was either the psychological result of a religious shock, or the product of a primitive community's desire for a cult. In other words, individual or mass self-deception. Then logic demands that this whole chapter of Jesus' life, with all its conditions and conclusions, be eliminated as swiftly as possible and a 'pure' Christianity formulated. Admittedly, what remains will be little more than very thin ethics and piety. This is one possibility. The alternative is to realize in our own lives what Christ's whole existence demands: faith. Then we understand that he did not come to bring us new but world-born truths and experiences, but to free us from the spell which the world has cast over us. This means that we hear and accept his demands; that we measure him by the standards he himself has taught us; that we *know,* once and forever, that he was not born to further this existence, but that a new existence was born in him. Thus we accomplish the complete reversal of faith, which no longer judges Christ with worldly eyes, but sees the world and everything in and around it with his eyes. Then we do not say: There is no such thing as the return to life of one who has died; therefore the Resurrection is a myth, but: Christ rose again; therefore resurrection is possible, and his Resurrection is the foundation of the true world.

In the Resurrection, that which had lain dormant from the beginning in the vital existence of the Son of Man and God becomes apparent. When we look back on our own existence, it seems like a movement begun in the darkness of childhood—as far back as memory reaches—which mounts gradually to the summit, only, more or less fulfilled or broken off, to descend. The curve of my existence begins with birth and ends with death. Before it lies darkness so complete that it seems incredible that I ever could have begun to exist at all. After it again dark, out of which gropes a vague sensation of hope. In Jesus this is not so. The arch of his existence does not begin with his birth, but reaches far behind it into eternity: ". . . before Abraham came to be, I am" (John 8:58). These are not the words of a Christian mystic of the second century, as has been claimed, but the direct expression of what was alive in Christ. And the arch does not break off in death, but continues, bearing his earthly existence with it, into eternity: ". . . and they will kill him; and on the third day he will rise again" (Matt. 17:22). For Christ, death—however burdened and agonizing and essential—is only a passageway to fulfillment. "Did not the Christ have to suffer these things before entering into his glory?" he asks the disciples on the way to Emmaus (Luke 24:26). The Resurrection is the blossoming of the seed he has always borne within him. He who rejects it, rejects everything in Jesus' life and consciousness that is linked with it. What then remains, is not worth faith.

But the Gospels clearly indicate visionary experiences! The disciples did have visions! True, only we must restore the full meaning to the word. What the reader of today involuntarily thinks when he sees the words "it was a vision" is not the same as what ancient readers thought. Yet the words have an ancient, not a modern, meaning. The valid sense, also for us, is that found already in the Old Testament. "Vision" means image, contemplation. And not merely as a private experience in the intimate life of the beholder, but as the entry of a higher reality into that experience. The disciples at the tomb, on the road to Emmaus, in the room in Mark's house, on the lake had visions, yes; but that means they beheld the living Lord. Beheld him as a reality in the world, though no longer of it, respecting the order of the world, but Lord of its laws. To behold such reality was different and more than to see a tree or watch a man step through a doorway. To behold the risen Christ was an experience that burst the bounds of the ordinary. This explains the extraordinary wording of the texts: the strangeness of Christ's "appearing," "vanishing," suddenly standing in the middle of a room or at someone's side (Mark 16, 9, 14; Luke 24, 31, 36). Hence the abruptness, fragmentariness, oscillation, contradictoriness of the writing—the only true form for content so dynamic that no existing form can contain it.

II

THE TRANSFIGURED BODY

When we read the Gospels' accounts of Easter and the weeks immediately following it attentively, we notice the dual character of the Christ portrayed. The difference between the risen Christ and Jesus before his death—indeed, between the risen Christ and all men—is carefully stressed. His presence is strange; his coming shocks, terrifies. Actually he no longer comes and goes, but "appears" and "vanishes" with disturbing suddenness. Corporal limitations no longer hamper him; the barriers of time and space have ceased to exist. He moves with a freedom impossible on earth. Yet the Evangelists stress equally the fact that this is the same Jesus of Nazareth. No mere spirit, but the corporal Lord who had lived among them. (The very first words about the Resurrection, the stone rolled away from the entrance of the sepulchre and the carefully folded burial clothes suggest substance.) Then we read how the disciples see him, feel his proximity, hear him, experience his body's compactness, touching the wounds from the nails and placing their hands in the gash in his side. The whole incident of St. Thomas, who at first does not believe, only then, overwhelmed, to fling himself at the feet of the Lord, lets us share in the tremendous mystery of Christ's corporality (John 20:24–29). The same intention leads to the description of his startling appearance in the room where his disciples are dining. They stare at him as at a ghost, until he quiets them by asking for something to eat and consumes it before their eyes (Luke 24:42). Again out on the lake, John sees a form on the beach: "It is the Lord." And Peter leaps overboard and swims to him, while the others follow in the boat. Nearing the shore they see a fire burning and a fish on the coals, and Christ divides the fish and partakes of it with them (John 21:1–14). Such things and more are reported of Christ's corporal reality, among them the memorable opening of St. John's first Epistle: "I write of what was from the beginning, what we have heard, what we have seen with our eyes, what we have looked upon and our hands have handled: of the Word of Life. And the Life was made known and we have seen, and now testify and announce to you, the Life Eternal which was with the Father, and has appeared to us. What we have seen and have heard we announce to you, in order that you also may have fellowship with us" (I John 1–3).

Again and again it is stressed: Here is something far out of the ordinary. The Lord is transformed. His life is different from what it was, his existence incomprehensible. It has a new power that comes straight from the divine, to which it constantly returns for replenishment. Yet it is corporal; the whole Jesus is contained in it, his essence and his character. More: his earthly life, passion and death are incorporated into it, as the wounds show. Nothing is sloughed off; nothing left behind as unessential. Everything is tangible, though transformed, reality; that reality of which we were given a premonition on the last journey to Jerusalem—the mysterious lightning-like flash of the Transfiguration. This was no mere subjective experience of the disciples, but an independent reality; no 'pure' spirituality, but the saturation, transformation by the Holy Spirit of Christ's whole life, body included. Indeed, only in the transformed existence, does the body fully come into its own. For the human body is different from the animal's and is only then fulfilled when it no longer can be confused with the animal body. The Resurrection and Transfiguration are necessary to the full understanding of what the human body really is.

If we continue to read—thoughtfully and reverently—we notice something else. Of all the apostles, who stresses most the corporal reality of the Resurrected Christ? He who most stressed the divinity of Jesus, John. He who proclaimed Christ as the *Logos,* the eternal Son, also traced the living features of his resurrected body. There were reasons for this. By the time John's Gospel was written, Christianity's message had spread so far that the moment had come for a clarification of the Christian essence. In addition, John had certain polemic reasons for his clear-cut statement: his writings had to face a powerful enemy: the pagan and half-Christian spiritualism of the Gnostics, who were convinced that God was spirit. However their conviction was so narrow and distorted, that they concluded that he was therefore anti-corporal, and that in his eyes all matter was impure. Consequently, they could not accept the Incarnation; insisting instead that a divine being, the eternal *Logos,* had descended from heaven and made his dwelling in the man Jesus. Through his mouth we were taught the truth and shown the way from the fleshly to the spiritual. When the man Jesus died, the *Logos* left him and returned to heaven. To this St. John says: God became man and remains man in all eternity.

To the question: What have we to do with the spiritualism of Gnostics?—the answer is: A great deal! Modernity is often completely confused by 'spiritualism.' In the preceding chapter we saw how it is constantly trying to explain away the Resurrection as deception; Jesus' divinity as mere religious experience; the figure of the resurrected Christ as the product of communal piety, in order to separate "the real" Jesus from the Christ of faith. Whether expressed historically or psychologically, as it is today, or mythologically, as it was at the time of the Gnostics, the argument remains the same. In reply, John erected two monumental landmarks. The first in the sentence: "And the Word was made flesh. . . ." (John 1:14). Not "entered into" a human being, but became that being, so that he was simultaneously human and divine; his deed God's deed; his fate God's fate, resulting in an indivisible unity of existence, responsibility and dignity. Not merely "And the Word was made man"—but, that there be no possible mistake, ". . . was made flesh"—the clarity is almost unbearable.

The second landmark is in John's proclamation: "This is now the third time that Jesus appeared to the disciples, after he had risen from the dead" (21:14). Not merely in the memory of his followers; not merely made manifest through the power of his teaching and his works, but in divine and human, spiritual and corporal reality— transformed, transfigured. God's Son did not discard his humanity, but took it with him into the eternal glory revealed in the Apocalypse and in the dying Stephen's vision, and referred to by St. Paul when he speaks of the risen Christ sitting on the right hand of God (Eph. 1:20; Rom. 8:34).

We do well to pause and consider what is being claimed, for it is truly unheard of; and if something in us is estranged or revolts, it should speak up, for it has the right to do so.

Who is God? The supreme Spirit, and so pure, that the angels by contrast are "flesh"! He is the Endless, Omnipotent, Eternal, All-inclusive One in the simplicity of his pure reality. The Unchanging One, living in himself, sufficient unto himself. What possible use could he have for a human body in heaven? The Incarnation is already incomprehensible enough; if we accept it as an act of unfathomable love, this life and death, isn't that sufficient? Why must we also believe that this piece of creation is assimilated into the eternity of God's existence? What for? A bit of earthliness lost and caught up into the tremendousness of eternity? Why doesn't the *Logos* shake the dust from him and return to the pure clarity of his free divinity? . . . Revelation defines such ideas as philosophy or worldly religion, to which Christian thought is by nature and definition diametrically opposed. But then what manner of God is this, with whom Resurrection, Ascension and throning on his right hand are possible? Precisely the kind of God who makes such things possible! He is the God of the Resurrection, and we must learn that it is not the Resurrection that is irreconcilable to him, but part of our thinking that is irreconcilable to the Resurrection, for it is false.

If we take Christ's figure as our point of departure, trying to understand from there, we find ourselves faced with the choice between a completely new conception of God and our relation to him, and utter rejection of everything that surpasses the limitations of a 'great man.' . . . We must also completely reform our idea of humanity, if it is to fit the mould Christ has indicated. We can no longer say: man is as the world supposes him to be; therefore it is impossible that he throne at God's right, but: since Revelation has revealed that the Son of Man does throne at God's right, man must be other than the world supposes him. We must learn that God is not only "supreme Being," but supremely divine *and* human Being; we must realize that man is not only human, but that the tip of his essence reaches into the unknown, and receives its fulfillment in his Resurrection.

It is the Resurrection that brings ultimate clarity to that which is known as salvation. Not only does it reveal who God is, who we are, what sin really means; not only does it indicate the way to new accomplishment for the children of God; we cannot even say that it 'only' propitiates sin, anchoring the superabundance of divine pardon in justice and love—but something greater, more vital, in the concrete sense of the word: resurrection consists of the transformation of the totality of our being, spirit and flesh, by the recreative power of God's love. Living reality, not only idea, attitude or orientation. It is the second divine Beginning—comparable only to the first, the tremendous act of creation. To the question: What is salvation; what does it mean to save, to have saved, to be saved—no full answer can be given without the words "the resurrected Christ." In his corporal reality, in his transfigured humanity he is the world redeemed. That is why he is called "the firstborn" of all creatures, "the beginning," "the firstborn from the dead" (Col. 1:15, 18). Through him transitory creation is lifted into the eternal existence of God, and God, now invulnerable, stands in the world, an eternally fresh start. He is a vital road that invites all to follow, for all creation is called to share in his Transfiguration—that is the essential message of St. Paul and St. John (see Ephesians, Colossians, and Luke 12). Early modernism manufactured a dogma to the effect that

Christianity was anti-corporal, that the body was the enemy of the spirit. This is true only in the limited sense of pagan antiquity, or of the Renaissance, or of our own epoch, where the body is detached from God. Actually, Christianity alone dared to draw the body into the inmost sphere of divine proximity. One of the most powerful and decisive passages of the New Testament states it clearly: ". . . because creation itself also will be delivered from its slavery to corruption into the freedom of the glory of the sons of God. For we know that all creation groans and travails in pain until now.

"And not only it, but we ourselves also who have the first-fruits of the Spirit—we ourselves groan within ourselves, waiting for the adoption as son, the redemption of our body" (Rom. 8:21–23).

Let us be sure we understand: the ". . . glory of the sons of God" is the work of Jesus Christ: the body's redemption.

We must revise our whole conception of what redemption is. Rationalism is still deeply rooted in us, with its insistence on the spiritual alone in after-life. But redemption is more than an intellectual process, an interior disposition or emotion; we must learn all over again to grasp its divine concrete reality. Redemption is an integral and vital part of man's existence; so much so that St. Paul (whom certainly no one can accuse of being a worshipper of the body) actually defines it as a process that begins with bodily renewal. This then the gloriously illustrated promise of the Resurrection! Hence Paul's ". . . and if Christ has not risen, vain then our preaching, vain too is your faith" (I Cor. 15:14).

Now we begin to understand what sacrament means. Were we not also among those in Capharnaum who protested: "How can this man give us his flesh to eat?" (John 6:53)? Why these strange words about the flesh and blood of Christ—why not "the truth" and "the love" of Jesus? Why not leave it at the first half of the promise in John six; are the tangible, if not material details, the eating of flesh and drinking of blood really necessary? Wouldn't remembrance of the Lord in all the purity and dignity of the spirit suffice? Why not? Because not only the spirit of Christ, but his resurrected flesh and blood, his whole, transfigured humanity *is* redemption! Because through the Holy Eucharist we participate again and again in this transfigured reality at once human and divine. Because communion in his flesh and blood is the remedy of immortality, the "*pharmacon athanasias*" as the Greek Fathers called it, of an immortality not only spiritual, but also corporal; of man caught up into the abundance of pure corporal *and* pure spiritual life in God.

III

BETWEEN TIME
AND ETERNITY

T he days between Christ's Resurrection and his return to the
Father are full of mystery. If we accept them as we should,
not as a legend, but as a vital part of our faith, then we must
ask what they mean in the life of the Lord, and what their significance in our own Christian existence.

These are the days between time and eternity. The Lord is still on
earth, but his feet are already detached, prepared to depart. Before
him unfold the reaches of everlasting light, but he still pauses here
in transitoriness. In the New Testament there are two figures of
Jesus; one "the carpenter's son" (Matt. 13:55). It is he who stands in
the midst of earthly events, who toils, struggles, submits to his destiny. He has his own personal characteristics—mysterious and inexplicable, certainly—and yet so unmistakably his that we almost
hear the tone of his voice, see the accompanying gesture. In the
main, it is the Gospels that portray this Son of Man. (See the Epistles and Revelation.)

The other 'nature' of Jesus is centered in eternity. Here all earthly
limitations have fallen away. He is free, divinely free, Lord and
Ruler. Nothing transitory, nothing accidental remains; everything is
essence. "Jesus of Nazareth" has become "Christ our Lord," the
eternal one whose figure St. John describes as it was revealed to him
on the Island of Patmos: "One like to a son of man, clothed with a
garment reaching to the ankles, and girt about the breasts with a
golden girdle. But his head and his hair were white as white wool,

and as snow, and his eyes were as a flame of fire; his feet were like fine brass, as in a glowing furnace, and his voice like the voice of many waters. And he had in his right hand seven stars. And out of his mouth came forth a sharp two-edged sword; and his countenance was like the sun shining in its power.

"And when I saw him, I fell at his feet as one dead. And he laid his right hand upon me, saying, 'Do not be afraid; I am the First and the Last, and he who lives; I was dead, and behold, I am living forevermore; and I have the keys of death and of hell.' "

St. Paul also describes him in the Epistle to the Colossians when he speaks of him: "He is the image of the invisible God, the first-born of every creature. For in him were created all things in the heavens and on the earth, things visible and things invisible, whether Thrones, or Dominations, or Principalities, or Powers. . . . For it has pleased God the Father that in him all his fullness should dwell, and that through him he should reconcile to himself all things, whether on the earth or in the heavens, making peace through the blood of his cross" (I Col. 1:15–20).

Here all concrete detail falls away. Not one familiar trait remains; hardly a human feature. Everything is strange and disproportionate. Is it the same Jesus who walked on earth? The days we are speaking of reply. Those few days of transition from time to eternity prove that he is one and the same here as well as there; that when Jesus of Nazareth entered "into his glory," he took with him his whole earthly existence, which continues to live in "Alpha and the Omega, the beginning and the end . . . who is and who was and who is coming, the Almighty" (Luke 24:26; Apoc. 1:8).

We recall Mary Magdalen at the tomb. She has gone there at dawn with the other women to anoint the body. Finding it open, and the grave empty, she runs to tell the disciples. Returned to the sepulchre, she searches for the body in great distress. Suddenly she sees the Lord, and taking him for the gardener says: "Sir, if thou hast removed him, tell me where thou hast laid him and I will take him away." At his voice, she recognizes him, falls to her knees and is about to embrace his feet when he says: "Do not touch me: for I have not yet ascended to my Father, . . ."

This is the Mary who with Christ's mother and the other Mary, mother of the later Evangelist Mark, and John (when all the others had flown, and the masses, crazed by the darkness of the hour, had likewise turned against Jesus) faced the storm of rage about her and the horrible agony of her own heart, standing fast under the cross until the end (John 19:25). Now this great soul, for whom nothing exists but her love, again stands before her Master. He calls her by name and she answers, their words vibrant with the tremendousness of all that has occurred since Golgotha. Everything is confirmed, transfigured.

"Do not touch me: for I have not yet ascended to my Father." But soon he will ascend and take his place at God's almighty right, to which he will bear all things that they may be fulfilled, also this love (John 20:15–17). Doesn't the meaning of this period of transition begin to clear?

None of the Apostles is so sharply characterized in the Gospels as Peter. He was better than 'great'—we have already discussed this—his was a deep and warm humanity. His heart was ardent, honest and generous, if also rash, and his talkativeness was constantly getting him into trouble. The Lord often had to take the wind out of Peter's sails, but the good-natured fisherman was never offended; he emerged from each humiliation as eager and affectionate as ever. On the last trip to Jerusalem it is he who answers Jesus' question as to who he is: "Thou art the Christ, the Son of the Living God," and the Lord gives him the keys of the kingdom, pronouncing him guardian of his Church. A moment later, however, as Jesus foretells his passion and death, Peter, all too human again, misses the point and violently protests, and must hear himself vehemently rebuked: "Get behind me, satan, thou art a scandal to me; for thou dost not mind the things of God, but those of men"

(Matt. 16:13–23). All Peter is in this incident. On the mountain of the Transfiguration, when the glory of the Lord, Moses and Elias at his right and left, breaks in on the disciples, Peter babbles of building three huts, one for Jesus, one for Moses and one for Elias. Three huts for these three? Jesus ignores the nonsense. . . . And finally, the terrible last night Jesus prophesies that before dawn the impetuous one who so boldly declares: "Lord, with thee I am ready to go both to prison and to death" will betray him thrice. Peter does not believe him, but it happens: a slave-girl gatekeeper scares him into it, and the Rock, seeing Jesus led past him on the way to prison, remembering, weeps bitterly.

But then there is a change of tone. Simon Peter and several other disciples go fishing on the Lake of Galilee. All night long they toil without catching a thing. In the gray of dawn they see someone standing on the coast who calls to them: "Cast the net to the right of the boat and you will find them," a multitude of fish—which they do. The disciple whom Jesus loved, John, says to Peter, "It is the Lord." And Simon Peter, pulls on his shirt, girds himself and jumps overboard to swim to land. The others follow in the boat, and they all breakfast together. After the meal Jesus says to Peter: "Simon, son of John, dost thou love me more than these do?" And Peter replies: "Yes, Lord, thou knowest that I love thee." Jesus: "Feed my lambs." Again: "Simon, son of John, dost thou love me?" "Yes, Lord, thou knowest that I love thee." "Feed my lambs." And a third time: "Simon, son of John, dost thou love me?" And Peter murmurs sadly: "Lord, thou knowest all things, thou knowest [also] that I love thee." " 'Feed my sheep. Amen, amen, I say to thee, when thou wast young thou didst gird thyself and walk where thou wouldst. But when thou art old thou wilt stretch forth thy hands, and another will gird thee, and lead thee where thou wouldst not.' Now this he said to signify by what manner of death he should glorify God. And having spoken thus, he said to him, 'Follow me' " (John 21:15–19). Here too an event from the past is recalled, trans-

figured, and continued. Peter too has changed. He no longer answers Christ with his old confidence. Humbler, shamefacedly when
Jesus repeats his question a second and a third time and he realizes
that he is being punished for his triple treason, he replies cautiously:
You know that I love you! . . . Jesus' promise at Caesarea Philippi is
confirmed: Peter is to remain the Rock and Keeper of the heavenly
Keys; he is to be shepherd of the entire flock of his Lord. All that has
been remains: Jesus remains, and Peter remains; but everything is
transfigured, and the passion through which Peter one day must pass
is indicated in the last words heavy with shades of Golgotha. The
Evangelist writing, John, is now almost a hundred years old; thirty
years have passed since Christ's prophecy was fulfilled, and Peter in
Rome followed his Master to the cross.

Then comes a brief passage so full of mystery and memories that
one easily loses the thread. John, the centenarian, recalls a detail of
that hour so many years ago. Peter, happy again now that he has
been pardoned, resumes something of his old garrulousness. After
hearing his own future prophesied, he points to John: "Lord, and
what of this man?" In the swift question we catch an undercurrent
of jealousy, in spite of the stout band of friendship between the two.
The old man, speaking of himself in the sentences that follow,
touches on the secret of his life, his special place in Jesus' love.

The Lord replies: "If I wish him to remain until I come, what is
it to thee? Do thou follow me" (John 21:21–23).

Why do these words go so deep? John is the exception. Between him and Jesus lies a profound mystery of love. He does not
say what the Lord's words mean, he only repeats them. They have
often been misinterpreted to indicate that John, like Elias, was not
to die, but to be spirited away into heaven. No, John himself insists, that is not what Christ said; he said only: "If I wish him to remain until I come, what is it to thee?" The passage is already heavy
with eternity as the aged Evangelist writes it one last time, without comment, putting it down carefully, word for word. . . . It is
the same John who writes of the Lord both as he walked on earth

and as he blazes from the unspeakable figures of eternity he has envisioned: the Rider of the white horse; the Lamb who breaks the seals of the Book.

There are other passages that also indicate the simultaneous preservation and transfiguration of all that has been. For example, Jesus' meeting with the disciples on the way to Emmaus, when they press the "stranger" to dine with them. He takes the bread, breaks it; they recognize him, and he vanishes. What do they recognize him by? Not by the mere act of bread-breaking (the customary right of host and honored guest) but by his particular manner of doing so: the gesture, glance and palpable kindness so unmistakably his have remained after death; Christ has taken them with him into the unknown (Luke 24:29–31).

The hour of the Ascension draws close; the disciples ask: "Lord, wilt thou at this time restore the kingdom to Israel?"

Jesus: "It is not for you to know the times or dates which the Father has fixed by his own authority" (Acts 1:6–7). Still the same, uncomprehending disciples. While Jesus walked on earth they did not understand him, and even now, to the last, they fail to comprehend. Once this blindness had been Jesus' sorest trial; we have only to recall his outburst on the lake when, lost in thought over the stubborn darkness and hatred of the enemy, he says suddenly: "Take heed; beware of the leaven of the Pharisees, and of the leaven of Herod" and the disciples (returning from the miracle of the loaves and fishes!) "began to argue among themselves, saying, 'We have no bread.' " Jesus: "Do you not yet perceive, nor understand? Is your heart still blinded? Though you have eyes do you not see, and though you have ears do you not hear? And do you not remember?" (Mark 8:15–18).

It is here again, the same old incomprehension. But the Lord no longer scolds, he only calms them. The situation is identical, but it is no longer pressed into the torturous experience of Jesus' struggle and suffering; it is released and carried over into the spacious serenity of eternal life. Misunderstanding then as now; rebuff then as now, yet what a difference!

It might be asked: Why this mysterious lingering on earth after the Resurrection? Why didn't the Lord return home directly? What was happening during those forty days?

Let us for a moment suppose that the Resurrection and the period afterwards had been only offshoots of morbid religious experience, legend or myth—what would those days have looked like? Doubtless, they would have been filled with demonstrations of the liberated one's power; the hunted one, now omnipotent, would have shattered his enemies; he would have blazed from temple altars, would have covered his followers with honors, and in these and other ways, have fulfilled the longings of the oppressed. He would also have initiated the disciples into the wonderful mysteries of heaven, would have revealed the future, the beginning and end of all things. But nothing of all this occurs. No mysteries are revealed; no one is initiated into the secrets of the unknown. Not one miracle, save that of Christ's own transfigured existence and the wonderful fish-catch, which is only a repetition of an earlier event. What does happen? Something completely unspectacular, exquisitely still: the past is confirmed. The reality of the life that has been crosses over into eternity. These days are the period of that transition.

And we need them for our faith; particularly when we evoke the great images of the eternal Christ throning at his Father's right, coming upon the clouds to judge the living and the dead, ruling the Church and the souls of the faithful growing from the depths of God-summoned humanity ". . . to the mature measure of the fullness of Christ" (Eph. 4:13). Such images place us in danger of losing the earthly figure of the Lord. This must not happen. Everything depends on the eternal Christ's remaining also Jesus of Nazareth, who walks among us until the day when all things will be enfolded in eternity; on the blending of borderless spirit with the here and thus and then of the process of salvation. In the Christ of the Apocalypse one vision holds this fast: the Lamb standing "as if slain" but alive (Apoc. 5:6; 1:18). Earthly destiny entered into eternity. Once and forever, death has become lasting life. But there is a danger that this truth dangle in space, enigmatic as a rune on an ancient stone. This period of transition deciphers the rune, gives us the key to the parable: All that has been remains in eternal form. Every word Jesus ever spoke, every event during his lifetime is fixed in unchanging reality, then and now and forever. He who is seated on the throne contains the past transfigured to eternal present.

IV

GOD'S COMING
AND GOING

The thirteenth to seventeenth chapters of St. John's Gospel cover Jesus' last conversations and speeches, loaded with deep meaning. For example: "You have heard me say to you, 'I go away, and I am coming to you.' If you loved me, you would indeed rejoice that I am going to the Father, for the Father is greater than I" (John 14:28). ". . . The Spirit of truth who proceeds from the Father, he will bear witness concerning me. And you also bear witness, because from the beginning you are with me" (John 15:26–27). . . . "I came forth from the Father and have come into the world. Again I leave the world and go to the Father" (John 16:5–8; 28). . . . "Now they have learnt that whatever thou hast given me is from thee; because the words that thou hast given me I have given them. And they have received them, and have known of a truth that I came forth from thee, . . ." (John 17:7–9). "And I am no longer in the world, but these are in the world, and I am coming to thee. Holy Father, keep in thy name those whom thou hast given me, that they may be one even as we are. . . . that they may have my joy made full in themselves" (John 17:11–13).

Amazing words and confusing. Aren't they saying that God's Son—who *is* God!—comes and goes? That the Holy Spirit—who again is God—will be sent, will come, and remain, the remaining stressed because he could also depart? And this coming and going is concerned not only with Jesus' humanity, but speaks also of him who is eternally with the Father; of him whom St. John meant when he said that the *Logos* was "with God"; that he was "the true light" come into the world but rejected by it. (See John 1:1; 9:11.) What does this mean? Can God 'come' and 'go'?

Perhaps the words are meant only figuratively, for popular or childish comprehension? Certainly not! This is no parable, like that of the Good Shepherd who has no peace until his lost sheep is safely back in the fold; these words were written by John, who was neither childlike nor popular. The masses hardly understood his eager, ardent, hard and exalted spirit. Had anyone ever suggested to him that his words were parables, he would certainly have replied: What I wrote I mean. The words stand for precisely what they say!

But perhaps it is not God himself who comes and goes, but only the effects of his grace? That, for example, a man 'distances himself' from God when he is impious, or torpid, or stubborn; then one day his heart softens; suddenly God seems to be 'near,' and joyfully the man says God has "come" to him? Nothing of the sort! Scripture has little use for such psychological 'explanations.' When the Bible means that God's help comes, it says so; here though it is God himself who comes.

Or are we dealing with a particularly difficult or exceptional part of Holy Scripture? If we check, we find that the whole Bible—from the first page to the last, from the oldest books to the most recent, from the narrative, descriptive to the contemplative, 'intellectual'— speaks thus. St. John, however, whom we are quoting, is precisely he who writes with the greatest penetration into the mystery of the eternal, unapproachable, all-inclusive God. Over and over again the Bible refers to God as one who sees and hears and takes into account; as someone far removed who comes to us; who comes and is with us, speaks and acts. If all this is a false form of expression, we had better leave the whole book and turn to the philosophers. But Scripture means what it says! And it describes God as it means to describe him!

How would we picture God if we were to conceive of him by ourselves—our best selves, naturally: in the purest reverence of the heart, the clearest power of our intellect; if we tried to express only the supremely exalted, perfect and holy? What would such a God be like?

He would be omnipresent. He would have nothing whatsoever to do with space and its limitations, for he would fill all dimensions. He would simply be; thus all places, realms would exist only in him or before him, or in his power. There would be no talk of 'coming' and 'going.' Whence could he who is everywhere come? Where should he go, whose existence is beyond all movement? This God of ours would bear everything in his power, and everything that is would carry his stamp, varied according to species and nature. All things would report him: stone and mountain, sea and firmament, tree and animal, child and adult, rich and poor, insignificant hireling and creative genius. And all events would bear him out, each in its own way. God's "word" in the Biblical sense would be superfluous—everything would be word, and it would be impossible to say this or that spoken or written phrase is his in a special sense. For him with ears to hear, all things would preach the glad tidings. Such a God would be of course Creator, and all that was created would also exist through him. What is, would be constantly affected by his omnipotent power; what happens, would happen through him—so entirely, that the mere existence of evil action would be an impenetrable mystery. There would be no place for a particular act of God; all acts would be his. There would be no special divine operation distinguishable from the general chain of events unwinding in his all-activating will.

The God so conceived would be pure, sublime, worthy of adoration; but it would destroy the reality given us by Christ's personal revelation. His Father is precisely that God who "comes" and "goes," "speaks" and "acts." The whole purpose of Jesus' life is to replace our human conceptions of God; not only the primitive, grotesque, but also the highest, purest and most refined. These above all. Certainly, God is omnipresent, exalted over time and space; yet he also can come when it pleases him; can live among us, and when the hour has struck, can depart and return—with a new countenance. . . . Certainly God bears all things, speaks through all things; yet at a certain period in history he also proclaimed an explicit message which demands differentiation and decision, and which separates mankind into the obedient and disobedient, believing and unbelieving. . . . Certainly, everything that occurs is activated by his eternal power beyond the reaches of time; yet there are specific acts of God in time; the acts founded in sacred history, which every human is invited to enter, but which he is also free to reject.

Revelation is the revealing of just such a God, who surpasses human thought. We can somehow manage to conceive of "absolute Being" alone. Also of gods, and the one God—powerful spirits that do this or that, are thus or so. But no one ever conceived the God of Scriptures as revealed in Jesus Christ: "the living God." He is a mystery, penetrable only through the mind of Christ. For that exists: understanding of something strange and foreign to us through a person. Love breaks open the seal on his heart and spirit. In communion with Christ's heart, our own is suddenly able to experience that of which it is incapable alone. Our spirit stretches to measure up to Christ's, and thereby grasps much that it never could have grasped by itself. He who believes in Christ thinks through him, feels the mysterious God who reveals himself in Revelation, the God of mystery and yet so familiar, so divinely superior both to "the gods" and the "Supreme Being" of human conception. Thought fails; only the word remains: "Philip, he who sees me sees also the Father" (John 14:9). The moment we think about Christ, independently, the sacred glory of God which reveals itself only through him, falls away and we think again humanly: of "the Absolute," "the World Principle," "Universal Order"—or, according to our temperament and the historical trend, "the God," in other words, God of gods, even though he is supposed to be unique.

We are commanded above all to love God. Can one love an Absolute Spirit? One who is only all-knowing, all-being, all-powerful? Certainly, as the Platonists loved supreme good; or as Eros longed for eternal value. But this is not the love of the New Testament, which is so different that it is difficult to express. The Gospels speak of the love of an affectionate child for its father, love of a son or daughter, in short, of a "human" love. They speak of a divine Brother, to whom one is bound by the clear love of a sister. They speak of the mystery of divine marriage. And we hear of the Consoler and Friend who is "with us" in the profound sense that Christ meant when he spoke of the Holy Ghost. Is such love possible to an Absolute Spirit? To be so loved, must not God "come" to meet me, become my destiny?

Can one pray to mere Absolute Spirit asking it for specific things, not only revering it, or resigning oneself to its will, but saying: Give me that? Does this not require the presence of a divine but kindred heart, a 'stooping' to hear and grant my prayer?

Is the Absolute Being really Providence? Not only in the sense that his omniscient power penetrates all things, but also in the sense of the New Testament, which reveals that in all that occurs a loving God is continually intervening, taking us by the hand, guiding us, and turning the world towards him who seeks before all else "the kingdom of God and his justice" (Matt. 6:33).

Now the words at the opening of this chapter begin to clear. We see that they are not parables, but realities—admittedly, realities beyond our full comprehension.

We have already probed the meaning of those strange days between Resurrection and Ascension during which the Lord lingered on earth. Now we see a further reason for them: that we might feel this pausing and passing over. That we might know that Christian existence is neither a cosmic process nor a historical necessity, but the free act of God. His acts are unhindered by natural law or the wheels of historical necessity. He acts, and it is all-important to hold fast to the supreme liberty of his action; it is better to seem to humanize God than to pull him down into universal determinism. In these passages on the sacred forty days, we experience something of the Son's descent from the Father and return to the Father; of his promise to send the Paraclete at a certain time, Pentecost, in a certain hour, the third, that he may remain with us until all time is fulfilled. We are meant to feel for ourselves something of this coming and going in the freedom of the sublime.

John also contains statements like the following: "But I speak the truth to you; it is expedient for you that I depart. For if I do not go, the Advocate will not come to you; but if I go, I will send him to you" (16:7). A necessity after all? If God the Son does not leave, God the Spirit cannot come. The words stand there in black and white, so they must be true; nevertheless, we will be careful not to 'understand' this necessity in any physical or intellectual sense, for it rises from the profoundest depths of God. The words themselves seem to stream to us from an immeasurable distance, extreme tip of a contact with the great mystery; outermost ripple of something that stirs within the Unapproachable. They are a call to adoration, promise of the mystery of divine life into which we shall once be drawn.

"Yet not for these only do I pray, but for those also who through their word are to believe in me, that all may be one, even as thou, Father, in me and I in thee; that they also may be one in us. . . . And the glory that thou hast given me, I have given to them, . . . that they may be perfected in unity, and that the world may know that thou hast sent me, and that thou hast loved them even as thou hast loved me.

"Father, I will that where I am, they also whom thou hast given me may be with me; in order that they may behold my glory, which thou hast given me, because thou hast loved me before the creation of the world" (John 17:20–24).

V

"I Go Away and I Am Coming to You"

The Lord's earthly mission and experience are not terminated by his death, but by the event recorded in the opening chapter of the Acts: "To them [the Apostles] also he showed himself alive after his passion by many proofs, during forty days appearing to them and speaking of the kingdom of God. And while eating with them, he charged them not to depart from Jerusalem, but to wait for the promise of the Father, 'of which you have heard,' said he, 'by my mouth; for John indeed baptized with water, but you shall be baptized with the Holy Spirit not many days hence . . . and you shall be witnesses for me in Jerusalem and in all Judea and Samaria and even to the very ends of the earth.'

"And when he had said this, he was lifted up before their eyes, and a cloud took him out of their sight. And while they were gazing up to heaven as he went, behold, two men stood by them in white garments, and said to them, 'Men of Galilee, why do you stand looking up to heaven? This Jesus who has been taken up from you into heaven, shall come in the same way as you have seen him going up to heaven' " (Acts 1:1–11).

With this, Jesus' temporal life comes to an end, but not his life itself. The Gospels show him incorporated into terrestrial existence, submitting to its conditions, bound by its limitations. When he is in one place, he is not simultaneously elsewhere; what he does at one moment is not done also at another. Event follows event—at least as far as the proclamation of Christ's tidings are concerned. Then comes the Easter experience. He who was dead rises to new life, and not only in the indestructibility of his essence, but in all his concrete humanity. He, Jesus Christ, the incarnate Son of God, returns, transfigured to be "with" his followers, though no longer so inseparable, for forty mysterious days. Now the Evangelists' manner of writing changes. Events oscillate back and forth, occurring here and suddenly there. The Lord appears and disappears, is unrecognizable and yet recognized by as earthly a gesture as his manner of breaking bread. We feel in the lines how he pauses on the sill between time and eternity. . . . Then another tremendous mystery equally difficult for human nature to grasp, the promised Ascension: "I came forth from the Father and have come into the world. Again I leave the world and go to the Father" (John 16:28). Jesus of Nazareth steps out of history into the realm of fulfillment where deed and destiny no longer exist, only eternally vital being. He departs—and returns in a new form, as he himself has prophesied: "I go away and I am coming to you" (John 14:28).

It is chiefly St. Paul who writes of this Christ returned: He sits in heaven at his Father's right, yet is also in us and we in him. He is in eternity yet in time, though differently from before, in the intimacy of becoming. And at the extreme edge of Christian history stands that ultimate event in which all that has been will be finished and fulfilled: Christ's return for Judgment. Then he will come in yet another form, in that of eternity. It is described in the Book of Revelation, but already hinted in St. Paul. Henceforth heaven will be everything.

What is the heaven into which Jesus was accepted on that first Ascension Day? The heaven that will once be all? In the Biblical account an upward movement is unmistakable; according to the Gospels, Christ seems to mount upwards from the earth. Is then heaven the summit of space? Certainly not. The spatial 'up' is only a figurative expression for something spiritual. In the sense of the New Testament, though we were to fly to Sirius, we should be no closer to heaven than we are on earth. Heaven is no more in the infinity of the cosmos than it is within earthly limits. "Heaven" is also not what is meant by celestial beauty or peace, though the word does suggest delicate spiritual emotions and things strange and rare in ordinary existence. But the Bible's heaven is something else.

To understand it, let us skip all approximations and go straight to the point: Heaven is the intimate reserve of holy God, that which St. Paul calls the "light inaccessible" which he inhabits, unapproachable for any creature (I Tim. 6:16). When we meet a person in the street or in a room, he stands there openly before us. We can look at him, photograph him, describe him, and can often guess a good deal of what is going on inside him. Withal, he is more or less 'public.' On one point, however, he remains impenetrable: his attitude towards himself, his manner of answering for himself and his acts. For the most part, man is absorbed by corporal, psychological, sociological realities; in other words, by public things. But there are certain moments when he retires into a corner of his being that is closed to others—into his most personal self. No one can violate that privacy; if it is to be opened, then only by opening itself. This is what happens in love, when a person not only permits himself to be observed, not only speaks about himself, but gives himself in vital exchange. If the other accepts him, likewise opening the way to his most intimate self, desiring the other more than himself, entering into pure contemplation and exchange, then the two intimacies unite in a single community open to both participants, but closed to everyone else. The greater and deeper the person and his experience, the less accessible this inmost realm will be. But what if it is not question of a person, but of God? God, the incommensurable, infinite, simple; essence of truth and holiness? His reserve is absolute. Nothing can even approach it. God is all light because he is Truth itself; all clarity, because nothing can overshadow him; he is the Lord, free and genuine Being to whom all that is belongs—yet inaccessible in his light, mysterious in his truth, invulnerable in his kingdom (I Tim. 6:16).

This intimate reserve of God is heaven, 'destination' of the risen Lord—and not only of his spirit, but of the whole resurrected Lord

in all his living reality. But how is this possible? God is acknowl-
edgedly pure Spirit (John 4:24). How can he assimilate anything
corporal?

God is Spirit, certainly. It stands written in the fourth chapter of
John, verse twenty-four. But let us not oversimplify! If God is spirit,
then my soul must be something else; or if my soul is spirit, I must
find another name for God. St. John means the same thing, for
when he says "spirit," like St. Paul, he has the Holy Spirit in mind.
In other words, by comparison with the Holy Spirit, body and soul,
matter and spirit, person and thing are all "carnal." Between all
these and the Living God lies not only the distance between Creator
and creature; not only the distance which divides life in grace from
life in nature; but also the infinite gulf between saint and sinner
which only God's love can bridge. Before this bottomless ravine, the
difference between earthly body and soul shrinks to insignificance.
That God pardons the sinner and accepts the creature into his holy
presence—that is the new and overwhelming message of Christ.
Once we have assimilated this truth, the additional incomprehensibility of God's accepting not only created spirit, but also created
flesh, no longer seems great. His salutary love is directed not exclusively towards the "soul," but towards man in his entirety. The new,
saved man is founded on the divine humanity of Jesus, and this humanity, begun in the Annunciation, was fulfilled in the Ascension.
Not until Jesus Christ has entered into the intimacy of the Father, is
he the perfect God-man.

So Jesus left—only in the same instant to return in new form. He
entered eternity, into the pure here and now of unshadowed reality,
into an existence that is entirely love, for "God is love" (I John
4:16). Ever since, Christ's manner of being has been that of love.
Hence, because he loves us—and that he does is the essence of his
sacred message—his going away into the fulfillment of love really
means that he is "with us" more fully than ever before.

Ascension Day will be succeeded by Pentecost, and in the Holy
Spirit the Apostles will speak of "Christ in us." The Lord thrones at

the right of the Father, far beyond the transitoriness of history, in calm, triumphant anticipation of the overwhelming victory of Judgment once to be apparent to all. At the same time, he is continually with us—behind every event, in the heart of every believer, in the core of collective faith, his Church. He is everywhere as power, guidance, union. When he left the historical realm of visible existence, a new Christian realm took form in the Holy Ghost: the intimate reserve of the faithful individual and the Church, give-and-take of their unity of love. Here in this inner life, Christ "is with us even unto the consummation of the world" (Matt. 28:20).

VI

IN THE HOLY SPIRIT AND
FAITH AND THE PARACLETE

We have just seen how the person Jesus Christ varied in his relations to man. At first, he is part of history, one of us. Then he dies, and the miracle takes place that overthrows all existent conceptions of the possible, yet is and remains the foundation of the Christian idea of man and his divine possibilities: the Lord rises from the dead to a new, transfigured existence. In the period of the forty days that follow it is as if he hesitated, still on earth, but ready to depart at any moment. Finally, he does leave, but with the promise: "I go away, and I am coming to you." And he goes and returns in a new form, more active and powerful than ever. The realm of the Christian soul unfolds—in the individual and in the Church. There Christ resides, living and ruling. From there he founds the new existence of the believer; from there he penetrates, saturates, renews him; directing his deeds and his destiny.

Christ in man draws man into himself. In the Holy Spirit, man shares in Christ's existence, which is the life of his life. The vital exchange between God and man established on that first Pentecost continues throughout time. This does not mean that man merely thinks of Christ or lovingly cherishes his image; what exists in him is the living reality of Jesus.

Man's desire to share in the life and destiny of another certainly exists, but even the profoundest union stops short at one barrier: the fact that I am I and he is he. Love knows that complete union, complete exchange is impossible—cannot even be seriously hoped for. The human 'we' capable of breaking the bonds of the ego simply does not exist. For the dignity and glory of man is precisely this: that with certain reservations he can say, "I am I and no other." My every act begins in me, who am alone responsible for it. True, this fact also limits: I must always be myself; must always put up with me. This necessity of being myself is what insulates me mercilessly from others. What is I, is not you; what mine, not yours. The very fact that each of us is a specific being, with its own center, own fate, differentiates and separates it from every other. In the love of Christ it is different.

The consciousness of Christ, and thus that of the whole New Testament, is founded on the reality of the one, loving God; but at the same time on the knowledge that this uniqueness exists in a form that outstrips our understanding. It is as though divine oneness had several faces.

On the one hand, God is called the "Father." Not only because he loves us, his creatures, paternally (love which would not necessarily penetrate to the innermost depths of his being), but because he fathered a Son equal to himself. Not only creative, but self-creative, he pours out his essence in a Second Person Intimate: Thou; thus forming the illimitable plenitude of his Being into a substantial Word who goes forth from him and returns to him.

Then again God is called "Son." Not because he made himself the Child of Man, taking form from man's life and heart (this would not necessarily penetrate to the core of divine Being), but Son because he is the living image of his Sire, "begotten, not made." In the Son, the mystery of the divine Father is made manifest: Face that confronts God's own as in a mirror. He is the Spoken Word of an omnipotent Speaker, Word that returns to the creative Mouth in the bliss of infinite fulfillment. Two countenances then in one God. Two Persons, distinct in all reality and truth, separated by their sacred, inexorable dignity, yet one God.

Between them exists something unknown to man that makes possible their existence as two separate Beings yet with one life, one essence unhampered by the limitations of self which protect and isolate all other life. Between Creator and Creator everything is open; the closed doors of individuality are non-existent. The given condition, likewise unknown to man, that makes this possible is of course perfection of person. Nothing created is completely self-possessed, and this lack is evinced by the creature's incapacity for perfect union with another creature, which only complete self-surrender could bring about. With God it is different. The sacred Two-in-God of whom we are speaking are entirely open to each other—so much so that they share a single life. The one lives so completely in the other, that there is not a pulsebeat, not a breath, not a spark that is not mutual. This must be the reason why each is so perfectly self-contained.

All this means that God is "Spirit"—not Understanding, Logic, Will, but Holy Spirit, *Pneuma*. It is in him, the Third Person of the Trinity, that Father and Son are powerfully individual, yet one. In the Spirit the Father engenders the clear image of himself in which he is "well pleased." In the Spirit, Jesus receives divine truth and reflects it back to the Father. In the Spirit, the Father pours out his essence, the Word, confident that in Jesus it will be invulnerable. In the Spirit, the Son receives the essence of his being from the Father, in his Word and yet Lord of himself.

This mutual exchange and autonomy in the Spirit is itself a Countenance. The Third Person who makes it possible for the One to find and possess himself completely in the Other is the Holy Spirit, who flashes through Scripture in the strange symbols of the descending Dove, Wind that blows where it will, mighty Tempest from the skies, and Tongues of flame (John 1:32; 3:8; Acts 2:2–3).

But all is a great mystery, and the symbols only make us feel it the more. It cannot be 'explained.' All we can do is to grope, reverently, in the darkness of Christ's words and existence.

Because God is so, and man was created in his image, man too longs to burst the bonds of his individuality without losing himself in another or in vague generalities; longs for something he can never attain alone: personal existence in community. In the paradisiac state of grace he possessed this quality, both in regard to God and to his fellows individually and collectively. That is why the triumph of the first man over sin would have benefitted all the generations that followed with conditions of grace; why the sin of the first man had to be the sin of all. With that sin, grace with its fruits was lost. Now man's longing cannot be fulfilled. Always the one must live at the cost of the other; deep-rootedness in self is paid with loss of community, and self-surrender with loss of freedom. Only in the Holy Spirit can this longing be stilled.

It is he who gave the Word human flesh. Through him Mary conceived God's Son. In the Spirit, an untrammelled oneness existed between God and the incarnate Jesus—intimacy no mortal can conceive. Jesus lived, taught, healed, suffered and died in the Spirit—and rose again, transfigured, as the Lord. Once the intimacy between the Son of God and the earthly Jesus was interrupted by the open revelation of their union: in the Transfiguration. The risen Lord is Jesus of Nazareth, in whom the Son of God is corporally revealed; in him the Word of the Father has become complete expression. After Jesus' return to the Father, the Holy Spirit made room in men's hearts for the transfigured Lord. Now he is in us and we in him—again in the Holy Spirit. Through grace we participate in Christ's loving relationship with the Father. Through Christ we know the Father and are known by him; we are containers and reflectors of his light and truth.

Only thus are we able to understand the relationship to one another that Christ demands of the saved. Also in mankind as a whole, as St. Paul says, this intimacy has been established—in the Church. She is the "body"; the individual members her limbs. Thus each is a member of the other, each the other's strength and aid (Rom. 12; I Cor. 12; Col. 4). What harms the one, harms all; what helps the one, furthers all, and each has a share in the other. All this is of course still veiled. Invisible, it must be believed. It is also not yet fulfilled, only begun. That is why so much remains difficult and contradictory. Everywhere we feel the closed doors to sacred revelation pushing outward from within. Everywhere the coldness and weight of self stifle the warmth of self-surrendering intimacy. To be a "neighbor" in the Christian sense means to suspend the I-not-you, mine-not-thine without the evil consequences of blurred or lost individuality and dignity. Genuine love of neighbor is impossible through human strength alone; it necessitates something new which comes from God and which surpasses the logic of mere human differentiation or unification: the love of the Holy Spirit among men. Christian love does not attempt to fuse the I and the you, or to impose upon them an attitude of selfessness that would annihilate the individual. It is the disposition of reciprocal openness and autonomy together, that simultaneous intimacy and dignity which comes from the Holy Ghost.

These thoughts all refer ultimately to the new creation—new man, new heaven, new earth—the resurrected universe. Everything will be open; infinitely open, and thus kept pure and venerable. Everything will belong to everyone, but purely, in freedom and reverence. All things will be one. We have Jesus' own word for it: All things shall be one, as the Father in the Son and the Son in the Father; as they are one in the Spirit, so shall men be one with each other in Jesus Christ (John 17:22–23).

Then the mystery of the sacred trinitarian life will saturate existence and will be all to all things. Creation will be absorbed into its Creator, and for the first time come into its own. This will be the work of the Holy Spirit, who will make everything that is his "bride."

"Many things yet have I to say to you, but you cannot bear them now. But when he, the Spirit of truth, has come, he will teach you all the truth. For he will not speak on his own authority, but whatever he will hear he will speak, and the things that are to come he will declare to you" (John 16:5–14).

One special function of the Holy Spirit is yet to be mentioned: he is to instruct the disciples in the entire truth of Christ.

Throughout the period of Jesus' public life his disciples have been with him. In antiquity the bonds between a philosopher or teacher and his followers were much closer than the family ties they supplanted; so it was with Jesus and his disciples. They were really "his own" and lived with him in close community. We never meet the Lord without his disciples, save when he withdraws into solitude to pray. They listen to his teaching, question him, observe his conduct towards rich and poor, sick and well, sorrowful and seeking. They wander from city to city, village to village with him, share his meals and accompany him when he is invited. They watch his face, feel the beauty of his gestures, vibrate with the intensity that flows from him, participate in his whole destiny. And we conclude that they must have profoundly understood him—perhaps not everything, but at least the vital kernel of his thought; that they knew who he was and what he wanted, and identified themselves with their Master and his desires. Yet time and again we are amazed to read how far from understanding him they actually were.

Of course one could say that the figure of the Lord and his message were too tremendous to be grasped in so short a time; that the disciples at least gradually advanced in understanding, pondering his teaching, discussing it among themselves, and slowly readjusting their lives to his message. But even that is untrue. The disciples' lack of comprehension is not due to the difficulties of the Lord's teaching, but to the faultiness of their relationship to him: they do not really *believe*. This is no reflection on their warmth and generosity. After all, they literally "left all and followed"—the Lord himself confirms this (Matt. 19:27–29). Still the essential is missing: they do not recognize him as God's Son. We must guard against blurring the words we use to define the all-decisive. "Faith" in the sense of the New Testament means not only religious trust, reverence, self-surrender, but something specific: man's relationship to Christ and to the God who speaks through him which Christ demanded. It does not mean the general respect one harbors towards a great religious leader, be he Buddha, Zarathustra, Moses or the Nazarene.

The word "*Fides*" is inseparable from "Jesus," the incarnate Son of God. With this begins the complete revolution of the heart, revaluation of values, reconstruction of the entire intellectual process that St. Paul so often preaches. And it is this that Jesus' disciples lacked so long. The ultimate requirement of faith was not there; hence the vastness of their incomprehension.

But after the tremendous experience in the upper room? There stands Peter before the excited crowd that has gathered around Mark's house to learn what has happened on this first Pentecost (Acts 2:14). To hear him speak one would think it was an entirely different person. Not only has he become enlightened, courageous, but his attitude towards Jesus is now that of one bearing witness to ultimate truth personally experienced and proclaimed with authority. Peter does not speak about Jesus, but *from* him. Because his relationship to the Lord is different from what it was, he himself is different. The questioning, self-surrendering seeker has become the proclaiming believer. How? Not by reflection, or private experience; not because after days of confusion and terror he has himself again under control, but because the Holy Spirit prophesied by Christ has literally received "of what is mine" and declared it "to you" (John 16:15).

How does recognition generally come? Who understands, for example, the mystery at once so vital and so moribund, so powerful and so questionable known as nature? Only he who lives in nature. He who has no immediate contact with her will never grasp her meaning. He may be a master in the natural sciences, of nature herself he will know nothing. Who understands music? He who has music in him. It is the same, only more so, with Christ. Only he can understand Christ who lives in that which comes from Christ.

Where does Christ come from? What does he live from? From what power does he draw his strength? From the Holy Spirit, by whom he was conceived in a Virgin's womb, and whose plenitude was poured over him at the baptism in the Jordan (Matt. 3:16–17). Time and again the mysterious power of the Spirit of God streamed overwhelmingly from Jesus' words and acts. The same power must also exist in a person, closely linking him to Christ, before he can believe. The Holy Spirit is he who makes faith possible.

The *a priori* to faith is inner renewal; indeed, faith consists of this act of renewal in Christ. Jesus announces specifically that only he can love and understand him who is reborn of God: "If I speak the truth, why do you not believe me? He who is of God hears the words of God. The reason why you do not hear is that you are not of God" (John 8:45–47).

In his natural state man is incapable of belief, which is an act of the new man, ". . . unless a man be born again of water and the Spirit, he cannot enter into the kingdom of God" (John 3:5).

The real proclaimer of Christian existence is St. Paul. His Epistles vibrate with the impact of his Christian experience. Notable is his differentiation between "the sensual man" and "the spiritual man" (I Cor. 2). By spiritual he does not mean the opposite of sensual: soul rather than body, but the new man redeemed by the Holy Spirit as opposed to the old, unredeemed. And he means the whole man, body and soul, inner and outer being; he means eating and drinking as well as science and music and all the other blossoms of culture, but also conscience and ethics and charity—all this is "sensual." And all of it must become "spiritual" in the Pauline sense: man's understanding, heart and will; his acts, his work, his feeling, and the life of his body. And now the saint adds: The spiritual man is a mystery. He can judge the sensual man, but cannot be judged by him. The living, believing Christian born of the Holy Spirit can understand the world, but the world will never understand him. This does not mean that he is more talented than others, wiser, stronger, of more independent character; nor does it mean that others cannot understand him because he does mysterious things or has strange and occult motives. No, the spiritual man is capable of understanding the world because he lives 'above' the world—thanks to the redemption of Christ and the roots that he has in Christ's freedom. Thus he gains a distance from the things of the world that no one rooted in it can gain—not even the most gifted. He inhabits a sphere detached, that of salvation established by the birth and death of Christ. Through grace the Christian is permitted to share in Christ's superior life, and through grace he is enabled (in the degree that he is truly Christian) to judge the world, no matter how simple, poor, or uneducated he happens to be. Through this same grace he is also 'removed' from the world, which simply ignores him. For the world sees only the man in him—possibly also something strange, disturbing, undefinably irritating. What that something is it cannot say without itself being converted, and then it would cease to be world in this sense. The Christian reproduces the existence of Christ in the form of grace-given participation in his life. . . . What has been said of the relationship of Jesus' contemporaries to Jesus is also valid for the relationship between believer and unbeliever today. Also to comprehend the Christian, one must be enlightened by the Holy Spirit, for the Christian existence is intelligible only through faith.

Is this presumption? Pretention? Certainly not! Who dares to presume that he is a Christian? We only hope that we are, well knowing that, save "with fear and trembling" (Phil. 2:12) it is impossible. Moreover, it is not a question of personal qualities, not of intelligence, or industriousness, or talent, or nobility or anything of the kind. The Christian can be outdone by the non-Christian on every score. He can "glory" in nothing but in Jesus Christ and his own desire for renascence (II Cor. 11:18). This is nothing magical; no initiation into dark mysteries; no penetration into higher forms of consciousness, but something very sober: conversion. If baptism means that the divine beginning is made in us, to become Christian means that we fulfill the promise of that beginning: that we reconsider all things in Christ; that we penetrate more and more deeply into his point of view; that our life is remodelled after his. Who dares to boast that this is so? One does not 'believe' from a distance. One cannot consider Christ and his teachings and decide to join forces with him, cross over to him. He must come and fetch us. We must ask him to send his Spirit that we may come to him. We must 'let go,' confident that he will catch us up into his love and draw us to him. If we honestly think and hope thus, we already have the beginning for which we hoped, for even the hope that he will help us to believe is possible only when he has somehow already granted it.

VII

Lord of History

One book of the New Testament recounts the earliest beginnings of Christianity: St. Luke's Acts of the Apostles. They report how Christ, who during his lifetime found no entry into human existence, was triumphantly borne into it by the Holy Spirit (for faith alone opens the door to God). In words that try to express something of the inexpressible, they describe the overwhelming Pentecostal event that burst the bounds of all ordinary experience.

"And when the days of Pentecost were drawing to a close, they were all together in one place. And suddenly there came a sound from heaven, as of a violent wind blowing, and it filled the whole house where they were sitting. And there appeared to them parted tongues as of fire, which settled upon each of them. And they were all filled with the Holy Spirit and began to speak in foreign tongues, even as the Holy Spirit prompted them to speak.

"Now there were staying at Jerusalem devout Jews from every nation under heaven. And when this sound was heard, the multitude gathered and were bewildered in mind, because each heard them speaking in his own language. But they were all amazed and marvelled, saying 'Behold, are not all these that are speaking Galileans? And how have we heard each his own language in which he was born? Parthians and Medes and Elamites, and inhabitants of Mesopotamia, Judea, and Cappadocia, Pontus and Asia, Phrygia and Pamphylia, Egypt and the parts of Libya about Cyrene, and visitors from Rome, Jews also and proselytes, Cretans and Arabians, we have heard them speaking in our own languages of the wonderful works of God.'

"And all were amazed and perplexed, saying to one another, 'What does this mean?' But others said in mockery, 'They are full of new wine' " (Acts 2:1–13).

The roaring from heaven was not noise in the earthly meaning of the word, any more than the "cloud" in the account of the Ascension was a meteorological formation. It was simultaneously heavenly light and impenetrable, heavenly darkness. Likewise the "sound" was that of celestial fomentation, downpouring superabundance. "Parted tongues as of fire"—stammering again, that tries to impart something of the mysterious power and light of that ardent angelic eloquence which settled upon everyone in the room. The disciples are converted, and their timorousness vanishes. Completely transformed, they become enlightened, resolute, and ready to preach, bear witness, and fight for the truth. The divine tempest sweeps also through others. Before the house a crowd of chance pilgrims from many lands has gathered, eager to learn what is happening. Peter steps to the door and declares: What you are witnessing is the fulfillment of the promise of Joel according to which the spirit of prophecy and of strength was to be outpoured upon all the faithful (Joel 3). Then he retraces the prophecies and shows how they have been realized through him whom the people, in the evil clutch of the powers of darkness, have betrayed unto death. The hearers are profoundly shaken. They accept the tidings, believe, receive baptism, and the young congregation, first-fruit of the Church is there (Acts 2:1–40).

At first, this congregation leads a quiet existence, outwardly still embedded in the traditional customs and ceremonies of the temple; actually it is far freer than it knows and already prepared to go its own way in the near future. The masses feel a sacred timidity towards these believers so evidently in the grip of the Spirit but they love them. Jesus' old enemies are unchanged, but they fear the people. Thus we read of two attacks against the Apostles, both of them unsuccessful (Acts 4:2; 5:17).

Nevertheless, a crisis is in the making. Originally the Apostles were in charge of everything, also the care of the poor, of widows and orphans. Soon, however, their duties swell to such proportions that the day comes when they are no longer able to cope with them. The service of the "tables" must not interfere with their essential task: proclamation, so they appoint assistants, men filled with the Holy Spirit to perform the services of practical charity. There are seven such men, one for each section of the city, and they are called deacons. One of them is Stephen. He must have been a wonderful man. There is something powerful, radiant about him. He too has been disfigured by tradition, which has tried to make of him, as of John, a sentimental enthusiastic youth. Actually he was a spiritual giant who challenged the enemy and left them helpless under the impact of his supernatural strength. Thus about him, the prodigy of the Holy Spirit, the old "scandal" gathers; it is as if the controversy in Nazareth at the beginning of Jesus' public teaching were being fought all over again (Acts 6:8–15; Luke 4:16–30).

Stephen is cited to court, where he makes the speech recorded in the seventh chapter of the Acts. Outwardly his words are strangely touching. They have something helpless about them, gauche and unpolished. He speaks as a simple man would, starting at the beginning of the beginning and losing himself in a mesh of details that allows no hope of ever reaching the end. At a certain point he notices this himself, and from there on rushes through to the conclusion. And still the effect is tremendous. It is not so much the words themselves (anything but extraordinary) but the roar and gleam of Pentecostal fire, which seems to ignite them. Stephen starts with the origin of sacred history, shows its homogeneous structure, reviews the prophecies and promises that to the present day hover over it, and closes: He whom Scripture has foretold times without number is the one you have murdered, Jesus of Nazareth. . . . At this all the repressed hatred of the enemy bursts into flame, and shaken with fury they gnash their teeth at him. "But he, being full of the Holy Spirit, looked up to heaven and saw the glory of God, and Jesus standing at the right hand of God; and he said, 'Behold, I see the heavens opened, and the Son of Man standing at the right hand of God.' But they cried out with a loud voice and stopped their ears and rushed upon him all together. And they cast him out of the city and stoned him. And the witnesses laid down their garments at the feet of a young man named Saul. And while they were stoning Stephen he prayed and said, 'Lord Jesus, receive my spirit.' And falling on his knees, he cried out with a loud voice, saying 'Lord, do not lay this sin against them.' And with these words he fell asleep. And Saul approved of his death" (Acts 7:54–60).

Something infinitely significant has happened. On Pentecost faith was born, and with it Christian existence. Consciousness of a life grounded in Christ, its beginning and end, opened people's eyes. The Christians looked about them, reviewing the past, not only that of individuals but in the collective form of human history; they recognized themselves as part of that history and claimed it for their own.

The history of the Old Testament is double. The one thread recounts how in the first half of the second millenium a little tribe wandered from Palestine into Egypt. There it remained, at first welcomed, then feared and oppressed, until finally, greatly increased and stoutly nationalistic, it returned to Palestine. The country of its origin had first to be reconquered; then after a period of confusion and violence, a royal house was established. A few centuries of tumult and injustice follow, and both parts of the realm succumb to the onslaught of their powerful eastern neighbors, the Babylonians and Assyrians. The Hebrews are deported, to return only after years of slavery, their strength broken. Brief revival in the struggles with the Syrians, then the Jews are conquered by the Romans and incorporated into their Empire.

That is history, but not yet the history of the Old Testament, which above all is the history of God on earth: of the covenant he sealed first with Abraham then with Moses. Through that covenant the Hebrew people became the chosen people of God, and hence-

forth its history is the record of their keeping or breaking their contract with him, not of their political, cultural, or even religious
powers. Naturally, the forces within them that seek self-expression
in autonomous, earthly history will reject the covenant and its demands. This is the reason for the strange double quality of Jewish
history with its two currents: the upper, essential stream that must be
lived in faith in divine revelation, and the undertow of the natural,
accidental course of events that constantly disturbs it. It is a difficult
existence and possible only with the grace that flows from there
where the covenant was authorized.

Prophet after prophet is sent by God to help his people understand
his sacred history; to take the plunge into faith and life in accordance
with the divine contract, in order that for the faith thus dared they
may be blessed with a national fulfillment far beyond their natural capacities as a tiny people surrounded by powerful empires. It was the
prophets who shaped the Old Testament's consciousness of history.
Through their words shimmered a distant figure: the Messiah; and an
equally distant future state: the Messianic kingdom. This was the radiant goal the prophets saw at the end of their dark passage; it was
their perennial hope. But their faith was not strong enough to sweep
the people with them against the tide of nature and the all-powerful
present. They were rejected, persecuted, killed; then, too late, their
writings collected and revered as sacred. We have heard the bitter
echo of their fate in the words of him whom they foretold (Matt.
23:29–35). The outcome of it all is dark and tangled: neither a great
natural historical development, nor genuine action in faith. Brief periods of prosperity and greening culture hint at what might have
been: the reign of David, the first years of Solomon, the eras of
Hosea and the first Machabees. But after each ascent, new decline.
And finally, when the one towards whom the whole sense of the
covenant was directed actually arrives, the nation and its leaders are
so involved and confused that they fail to recognize him.

Now, after such a past, young Christianity says: All that belongs to
us! Jesus, so briefly dead, has fulfilled the old history and begun the

new. He stands in the middle. All that has been was preparation for him, all that is to come works through him. Saints Paul and John go still further. They proclaim the return of this same Christ at the end of time to judge the world and give all history its ultimate sense, and they reveal him at the beginning of all eventfulness; before the beginning of time: John as the *Logos,* universal Creator; Paul as him in whom all things were founded.

And the covenant? The old has been accomplished. God kept his promise, in spite of all man's faithlessness. In Christ it is finally fulfilled and the new covenant is established between the Father in heaven and all who believe in him through Jesus Christ, covenant of faith standing fast in a world that holds it for scandal or folly. Now the promise is that of the coming kingdom; the new creation. There too a people; no natural race, but people in the Holy Spirit, as proclaimed in Peter's first Epistle: "You, however, are a chosen race, a royal priesthood, a holy nation, a purchased people; that you may proclaim the perfections of him who has called you out of darkness into his marvellous light" (2:9–10). Nation of all who believe in the Lord.

At Pentecost, consciousness of Christian history (arching back to the beginning of time and forward to the end of time) dawns. Since then for the most part it has gradually been lost. Much of Christian existence has been broken up into individual believers under some roof-organization. We all have reason to pray the Holy Spirit to send us new consciousness of our universal history, of our place in God's plan, organically rooted in the past and branching, flowering into the future.

VIII

RENEWAL

Among the Church's prayers to the Holy Spirit we find the promise of the psalmist: "Thou shalt send forth thy spirit, and they shall be created: and thou shalt renew the face of the earth" (Ps. 103:30). Something buried deep within us stirs at the words, for we are dissatisfied with our existence, eager to become new beings in whom we would at last find ourselves. We know perfectly well: not until we succeed in completely freeing ourselves from ourselves will we ever arrive at our true natures. Aren't fairy-tales man's attempts to escape to a different world? Isn't all fantasy and fable born of the desire to be someone else, if only in the imagination? Admittedly, it does not help much—not any more than theater-playing helps, or masquerading, or any other attempt to steal into a role not our own. The methods employed are various: for the one, constant change—whether of house, doctor, dress or occupation; for another, constant pleasure; a third attempts to lose himself in nature; a fourth in the excitement of adventure or war; a fifth seeks escape by recasting himself in the mould of a 'personality'; a sixth hopes to leave his old self behind through constant self-improvement, and so on. Always the same desire to emigrate from what one is to that which one is not; any change must be an improvement! And yet always the same disappointment. After the initial enthusiasm has worn off, the bonds of the old self press harder than ever. Everywhere, in pedagogic reform movements, in science's search for the fountain of youth, we find the same admission: one can develop intrinsic talents, but can *change* nothing.

There are experiences in which unknown possibilities seem suddenly to unfold; creative forces of which we were totally unaware. At times this urge seems to take hold of a whole culture. Our own epoch is full of this sense of innovation. Everywhere we meet the word 'new,' as though it stood for magic. And in reality? Is there anything really new under the sun? Furnishings, situations, points of view, certainly; but the foundation on which they rest? "As you began, so will you end," answers Hölderlin. Alone, one can never hope to escape from the narrowness of self into the breadth and newness of a higher existence in which that self finds its fulfillment and can say: At last I am the person I always suspected I could become! The world can give no such emancipation. The world is a circle complete in itself as a snake with its tail in its jaws; a never-ending, invulnerable round. Only from within and without simultaneously can the ring possibly be broken, hence only by Jesus Christ. In him God became man veritably, with all the consequences. He lived as we do, subject to all the necessities of nature, and to the human, national, historical, and cultural conditions of his time and place, precisely as we are. Every minute of his life he stood in complete obedience to the demands of the Incarnation. We are startled when we notice suddenly that even when tempted ("Command that these stones become loaves of bread") he never performed a miracle to lift the constraints of his accepted humanity; never eased his own poor or difficult situation, never overpowered his enemies, or forcibly broke their hardness of heart. Don't we wait vainly for something of the kind to happen—if only the enlightenment of his own disciples? Jesus lives his 'chains' through to the terrible end. His divinity relieved the world of none of its harshness, for his full experience of that harshness was the Father's will. But through his daily submission to the duress of existence, Jesus' humanity soars into the freedom of his divinity. One might almost say that his Ascension, the mounting of his sacred humanity into the spaciousness and liberty of God, took place not only actually, at the end of his life, but again and again spiritually during his earthly sojourn, when he crossed back and forth between heaven and earth in the *Sursum corda!* of prayer.

That is the one gateway out of the world. Everything else belongs to the illusion with which the world practices self-deception, arguing that because it is possible to burst earthly bonds momentarily with the weapons of fancy and imagination, the freedom thus gained is genuine! Illusion of dream and desire; illusion of the sentiment of infinity, of intrinsic revolution and renewal—in reality this is nothing but life's fine art of consoling us for the finality of our inborn limitations.

To believe means to be so rooted in Christ that he becomes the foundation of one's own existence, the beginning and end of the movement known as life, its measure, and source of strength. The extent to which we succeed depends on our loyalty and our power of sacrifice. Hence the believer does well to say, not that he is a Christian, but that he is trying to become one. The better he succeeds, the wider the doors of existence will open for him. He will be caught up into that 'crossing over' continually effected in Christ. The Lord once said: "I am the way, and the truth, and the life" (John 14:6). He who lives and moves in Christ takes the only road there is out of the labyrinthian tangle of the world into the freedom and new creation in God.

By this nothing magical is meant; no loosening of reality or escape from its limitations; neither mysterious inner experiences, nor extraordinary heavenly eruptions, but something entirely realistic and candid. No fact is changed in the life concerned; talents, health, family, social position, property and occupation remain what they were. The daily routine, people and circumstances, continue to make the same demands. Reality remains reality—yet everything is different because the door has opened and the crossing over to Christ is made possible.

How can this best be illustrated? When a person continues to live with others, simultaneously though also with Christ, his relations to the others will change, if only in that he becomes increasingly patient, more understanding, kinder, but also more alert, less gullible, and better able to judge character and worth, whatever his natural limitations happen to be. All this is true, but still not the essential difference. The person himself is changed by his daily contact with Christ, becoming more and more similar to his model. The believer remains in his profession; he remains the same trader, postman, doctor that he was, with the same duties. The machine does not function better in his hand than in that of another; the diagnosis is not easier than it was, yet work performed in Christ is somehow different. No longer over-estimated, but properly evaluated, it assumes a new dignity and earnestness; is performed with a new conscientiousness. The same holds true for worries and pain and all other human need. The difference is indefinable, visible only in the result: here an illness or loss borne with quiet heroism, there an old enmity healed. In Christ all things are changed.

The change is most clearly evident in those who undergo it with heroic thoroughness, the saints. Usually, however, first in retrospect, for those who worked and fought with them in life seldom dreamed the depth of the force from which they lived; many a saint has been unmanageable and difficult. Only after he has 'gone through,' does it become almost tangibly clear what has been going on: the process of his gradual surmounting of self and the limitations of his origin. Not that he created completely new conditions, or assumed a new personality. The reality and integrity of existence remained, even intensified, for no one takes reality as seriously as the saint, whose dangerous path allows of no fantastic experimentation. Any attempt to compromise with fancy would avenge itself mercilessly. Sanctity means genuine man's genuine liberation from self into the spaciousness of genuine divinity. *Genuine* liberation—this does not allow that from which he freed himself in the beginning to reappear, disguised, at the goal. And liberation into genuine divinity, God, does not take place through ecstasy or any religious *tour de force,* but through Jesus Christ. The saints are those who penetrate into the existence of Christ; who lift themselves, not by their 'bootstraps,' but by Christ's humanity to Christ's divinity.

These revelationary figures show us in clearer form what is taking place also in us—in a manner that is veiled and confused. Though our progress is constantly being interrupted and set back, it is real nevertheless. For it is Christ who makes the Christian possible; through him, who is both one with God and the way to God, the child of God is helped by grace to cross over into salvation. Assuredly, this must be believed—often against the constant evidence of our own insufficiency, always against the disbelief of the world. The world must disbelieve; how can it tolerate the existence of a Christian when it cannot tolerate Christ? Yet the Christian possibility must be believed in, in spite of the world. The extent to which our faith is and remains realized is the extent to which we "conquer" the world.

IX

THE NEW MAN

Before Pentecost the disciples had lived 'in the sight' of Christ; now they lived in him; before they had spoken about him; now they spoke through him. In letter after letter St. Paul illustrates the reality of this phenomenon: Christ's living and speaking in him, Paul, is not his special privilege, but the very essence of all apostledom, and—function and mission aside—of Christian existence in general. Paul is the privileged messenger of this doctrine. No one is more profoundly conscious of the essence of Christianity—of its grandeur and its obscurity—and his constant reply to all why's and wherefore's is: Because Christ lives in the Christian.

But let us examine more closely this curious thing called existence. The word means more than mere being; it means that I am myself and no other; I alone inhabit me, and no one can enter my habitation unless I open to him. In hours of spiritual plenitude and vitality I feel that I have myself well in hand, that I am master of myself. Herein lies my freedom and dignity, but also the ponderousness and solitude of my existence. We are speaking of purely human existence. To this Paul says: Christian existence is all this and more. Something has changed. Christian personality is not only the natural personality of an individual, but in addition to the solitude and freedom, the dignity and responsibility of the person, there is something else, someone else, Christ.

When you took baptism's plunge into faith, says the Saint, something fundamental happened: "Do you not know that all we who have been baptized into Christ Jesus have been baptized into his death? For we were buried with him by means of Baptism into death, in order that, just as Christ has arisen from the dead through the glory of the Father, so we also may walk in newness of life. For if we have been united with him in the likeness of his death, we shall be so in the likeness of his resurrection also" (Rom. 6:3–5).

And again: "Thus do you consider yourselves also as dead to sin, but alive to God in Christ Jesus" (Rom. 6:11).

And finally: "For you were buried together with him in Baptism, and in him also rose again through faith in the working of God who raised him from the dead" (Col. 2:12).

At birth you received your natural life from that of your mother. You were liberated from her womb into your own independent existence. This is a great mystery, at once intimate and harsh. But here another mystery is meant: the miracle of grace. You who were already born and lived, were drawn into the unutterable depths of another womb that is at once beginning and end. In the process, something belonging to you was lost: the false self-sufficiency of fallen man, and the isolation of him who has fallen away from God. You left the baptismal fount as a new person: a Christian, reborn into the new life of the children of God. In this existence you are yourself, but *in Christ*. He lives in you, and this is the guarantee of your most individual personality. With masterly simplicity and power the Epistle to the Galatians declares: "It is no longer I that live, but Christ lives in me" (2:20).

An astonishing statement. Is such a thing possible? Desirable? Christ is not only God's Son, but also man's; possessor of an individual soul and body—how can he then exist in me? St. Paul explains: When the Lord died and rose again, he remained who he was: Jesus Christ. However, his entire being assumed a new form: that of the Transfiguration. He became the spiritualized Christ, the mystical Christ—which does not mean that he was now spirit as opposed to body (mere essence, idea, impulse, power), but that his whole being, body and soul, was transfigured, released by the Holy Spirit from the prison of earthly corporality into the freedom of pure activity: "All flesh is not the same flesh, but there is one flesh of men, another of beasts, another of birds, another of fishes. There are also heavenly bodies and earthly bodies, but of one kind is the glory of the heavenly, of another kind the glory of the earthly. There is one glory of the sun, and another glory of the moon, and another of the stars; for star differs from star in glory. So also with the resurrection of the dead. What is sown in corruption rises in incorruption; what is sown in dishonor rises in glory; what is sown in weakness rises in power; what is sown a natural body rises a spiritual body.

"If there is a natural body, there is also a spiritual body. So also it is written, 'The first man, Adam, became a living soul'; the last Adam became a life-giving spirit. But it is not the spiritual that comes first, but the physical, and then the spiritual. The first man was of the earth, earthly; the second man is from heaven, heavenly. . . . Therefore, even as we have borne the likeness of the earthly, let us bear also the likeness of the heavenly" (I Cor. 15:39–49).

For this Christ no limitations exist—also none of person. He can inhabit the believer, not only so that he constantly thinks of Christ or loves him, but actually, as the human soul inhabits a body. Body and soul, Christ can inhabit the believer, for God's Son is not only Soul, Spirit, but holy glorious Reality, mystical *Corpus*. As such he is the renewer of life.

Because the Lord "is the Spirit" (II Cor. 3:17), he is also Love. The Spirit of God opens all things, permitting being to flow into being, life into life, me into you without violence or loss of individuality, freedom or dignity. The Spirit creates love, community of all that is good. He, Love, takes that which is Christ's and gives it to us for our own (John 16:15). He incorporates Christ himself into our lives: "For me to live *is* Christ and to die is gain" (Phil. 1:21).

Of the depths of this love: "Who shall separate us from the love of Christ? Shall tribulation, or distress, or persecution, or hunger, or nakedness, or danger, or the sword? Even as it is written, 'For they sake we are put to death all the day long. We are regarded as sheep for the slaughter.' But in all these things we overcome because of him who has loved us. For I am sure that neither death, nor life, nor angels, nor principalities, nor things present, nor things to come, nor powers, nor height, nor depth, nor any other creature will be able to separate us from the love of God, which is in Christ Jesus our Lord" (Rom. 8:35–39).

But doesn't such community dissolve all individuality, the loss of isolation cost us loss of self? One can determine the essence of God variously: he is the Founder of all intelligence and Creator of all being; Lord and Director of all events; the Omniscient, the All-just; the Holy One, the great Lover. . . . But other possible characterizations straight from the life of faith are also singularly fitting: God is the One of whom it can be said, that the more powerfully he activates an individual, and the more completely he penetrates his being, the more clearly that individual attains his own inherent personality. Seemingly a contradiction, actually this is the ultimate expression of the divine essence. For God is by no means "Another." It is not at all as if he stood opposite, and I had to choose between him or me. On the contrary, all that I am, I am through him. The more intensively he directs his creative powers upon me, the more real I become. The more he gives me of his love, the fuller my self-realization in that love. Christ is God in the pure, full sense of the word; the *Logos* through whom all things were created, myself included. Not until he inhabits me, do I become the being God meant me to be. For the creature, self-realization does not mean that it exists in itself, autonomously; the very desire to do so would border on revolt (that terrible and in heavenly eyes also ridiculous attempt to imitate God's sovereign independence). In reality, man's true ego is continuously fed by the creativity of God; man is most entirely himself in God, the *Logos,* Christ.

St. Paul says still more: Christ is the living form of Christian existence. Every human being bears a form within himself: that which binds his different characteristics, powers, activities to the unity that is he. Through it I, who at this moment am working, am the same who a few minutes ago was resting, and who, later, will go out with a friend. In change I recognize myself as the same; there is a fundamental form in me that finds expression in the diversity of my attitudes, a diversity so great that it often seems impossible to bring my manifold interests together under one skin. In what does the boy resemble the grown man? Yet they are one and the same because throughout a lifetime the same underlying form revealed itself as constant, though forever new. Now St. Paul adds: When you become a Christian you received a new figure into your being. (Being comprehends all that you are by nature: your body and your soul, all your acts and characteristics, your natural form included, in which your true and ultimate form will once express itself.) This figure is the mystical Christ as he lives and would reveal himself in your particular being, life, circumstances, work. Just as your soul is the shaper of your body, he is the shaper of your soul and body, the entity, you. In the Epistles to the Romans we read: "You, however, are not carnal but spiritual, if indeed the Spirit of God dwells in you" (Rom. 8:29). And similarly in the second Corinthian letter: "But we all, with faces unveiled, reflecting as in a mirror the glory of the Lord, are being transformed into his very image from glory to glory, as through the Spirit of the Lord" (3:18). The Epistle to the Ephesians (4:11–13) says of the shepherds and teachers of the Church: What makes a Christian Christian in everything he says and does is the living Christ in him; different in every individual and in every phase of that individual's life. Different in joy and pain, in work and social intercourse, nonetheless, it is always Christ. In every Christian, Christ relives his own life anew: first as a child, then as a mature and responsible adult. He lives and grows in each of us, that our faith may increase, our love may be strengthened, our Christianity constantly deepened.

Unheard of idea! It is; and supportable only in faith and the love that is one with him whom it recognizes as the Principle of all things, and essence of one's truest self, of that 'I' which is the child of God, and the 'Thou' which is its Father. That is why Scripture says: "No one comes to the Father but through me" (John 14:6).

Is this really true, considering that man is as he is? Has he changed by becoming Christianized? Has the Saint forgotten all the meanness and wickedness and paltriness that persist in man? There is an Epistle that speaks of unredeemed man, but also of the writer's bitter experience of that in Christians, himself included, which opposes redemption: "For I do not the good that I wish, but the evil that I do not wish, that I perform. . . . For I am delighted with the law of God according to the inner man, but I see another law in my members, warring against the law of my mind and making me prisoner to the law of sin that is in my members.

"Unhappy man that I am! Who will deliver me from the body of this death? The grace of God through Jesus Christ our Lord. Therefore I myself with my mind serve the law of God, but with my flesh the law of sin" (Rom. 7:18–25; compare I Cor. 3:3).

Can we still insist that all that has been said is true? By the resurrected Christ! For redemption and rebirth do not mean that an individual, as if by a stroke of magic, is renewed overnight, but that the beginning of his renewal is established. The wickedness is still there, but the new beginning as well. The Christian is a battlefield on which the struggle constantly rages between the "old man," rooted in his rebellious self, and "the new man," born of Christ. We must believe in spite of ourselves that we are reborn and bear Christ within us, and with him potential glory.

When we pass from the Gospels to the Epistles, we notice that the whole word so often used in the Gospels to express the whole of Christian existence, "imitation of Christ," seems to have vanished. What has become of it? It has been integrated into the passage just discussed. To be a follower of Christ does not mean to imitate him, literally, but to express him through the medium of one's own life. A Christian is no unnatural reproduction of Christ. (It is given to very few—as it was to St. Francis of Assisi—to bear the simultaneous yoke and glory of an almost identical route.) The task of the Christian consists of transposing Christ into the stuff of his own daily existence.

How differently profound Christian life from the life that is merely human! They are poles apart. One of the world's most fearful manoeuvres against the Christian is to rob him of his consciousness of this difference. It suggests that its attitude towards life is the only valid one, and that the Christian point of view is but one variety of it. It removes the two poles of Christian existence: the one planted in divine sanctity, the other in the wilderness of sin. The Christian who surrenders these two points (the height and depth of his faith), from which the vital tension of his Christianity depends, becomes more deplorable than the outright worldling. Here lies the fundamental task of spiritual education; one in which both the man of the intellect and the man of action must share: the reinstatement of the polarity of genuine Christianity in the consciousness, sensibility, and will of the believer.

X

ECCLESIA AND THE FIRSTBORN OF ALL CREATURES

". . . The mystery which has been hidden for ages and generations, but now is clearly shown to his saints. To them God willed to make known how rich in glory is this mystery among the Gentiles—Christ in you, your hope of glory!" (Col. 1:26–27).

In everyone is the same spirit of Christ, though differently expressed, so that each time it is the essential individual who thus develops his own nature. The Christian's individuality is not stifled by the presence of Christ within him, but on the contrary, spurred to genuine maturity. "Hidden with Christ in God," his essence is rendered invulnerable and inimitable even to the extent so intimately expressed in Revelation: "To him who overcomes, I will give the hidden manna, and I will give him a white pebble, and upon the pebble a new name written, which no one knows except him who receives it" (2:17).

This then Christian spirituality. It does not mean that a person turns inward, or strives to reach essential (psychological or spiritual) depths, but that Christ enters into his being, bringing his spirit with him, to remain as long as he remains, to depart when he departs. The same Christ who lives, I hope, in me, also lives in this and that and every believer. Hence the common, living genealogy in God through which we are related. We form the family of the children of God, among which stands Christ as the "firstborn" of many brothers (Rom. 8:29). Purest expression of this community is the

"Our Father" with its Christian "we." God's progeny, led by his eldest son, speak here to their common Father.

On the last day the Judge of all flesh will sentence every one of us to his right hand or his left, to blessing or to damnation, according to whether we have accepted or rejected him. When we ask what we have done to deserve this judgment, Christ will reply: "Amen I say to you, as long as you did it for one of these, the least of my brethren, you did it for me" (Matt. 25:40). In every believer we confront the Christ he bears within him, as St. Paul never tires of reminding us: "Wherefore, put away lying and speak truth each one with his neighbor, because we are members of one another . . . do not let the sun go down upon your anger: do not give place to the devil. He who was wont to steal, let him steal no longer, but rather let him labor, working with his hands at what is good, that he may have something to share with him who suffers need. Let no ill speech proceed from your mouth, . . . do not grieve the Holy Spirit of God, in whom you were sealed for the day of redemption. Let all bitterness, and wrath, and indignation, and clamor, and reviling, be removed from you, along with all malice . . . be kind to one another, and merciful, generously forgiving one another, as also God in Christ has generously forgiven you . . . walk in love, as Christ also loved us and delivered himself up for us an offering and a sacrifice to God to ascend in fragrant odor" (Eph. 4:25–5:2).

And still the essence of Christian oneness has not been completely stated. Among the Pauline Epistles, those addressed to the Ephesians and Colossians are particularly important and form the link between St. Paul and St. John.

"See to it that no one deceives you by philosophy and vain deceit, according to human traditions, according to the elements of the world and not according to Christ. For in him dwells all the fullness of the Godhead bodily, and in him who is the head of every Principality and Power you have received of that fullness" (Col. 1:18–20).

"Again, he is the head of his body, the Church; he, who is the beginning, the firstborn from the dead, that in all things he may have the first place . . . that through him he should reconcile to himself all things, whether on the earth or in the heavens, making peace through the blood of his cross" (Col. 2:8–10).

Here is the mystic Christ in yet another dimension. He not only inhabits the individual Christian personality, but omnipotent Creator of the world, rises to embrace all being. Not only the one or the other, but all mankind in its totality. This is eloquently proved in the experience of Pentecost. In that hour Christ permeated the whole of human existence, becoming its most vital and potent factor. The Church is not composed of this, that and the other believer; she was not born of the encounter of individuals of similar faith; she is not only a community of the faithful, but the visible expression of Christ's presence at the root of all human existence. The believer is an active organ in this totality, which is, however, entirely independent of him.

St. Paul has two images for this profound mystery of universal union. The one is the living body with its many members, an organic whole, controlled by the head, Christ. This head—here the Saint borrows his metaphor from ancient Greek medicine—is the activating principle of the whole. The forces at work in the various parts of the body all spring from the head, their common source and directive.

The other image is that of the temple. Each stone is a unit; all units together form the one great construction, so unified and fused by the genius of the architect, that each stone becomes an elemental part of the whole. Here again, the unifying power is Christ: living beauty and wisdom, force and idea; or (placed in a similar relationship to that of head to body) keystone, cornerstone that binds all others, foundation that supports them.

And the name of this whole is Church. The mystic Christ pulses through her. He is the Model after whom she was shaped; the plan after which she was constructed. And the power that sustains her is the Holy Spirit, as Paul declares in his first Corinthian Epistle: "But all these things are the work of one and the same Spirit, who allots to everyone according as he will" (I Cor. 12:12–13).

The Church is constructed differently from the individual. Her center is located elsewhere; the expression of her vitality is not the same; the rhythm of her slow development necessarily not our own; her struggles and crises are other than ours. Nevertheless, the Christ who inhabits her is the same Christ who lives in the individual. The Church too has her essence—as powerful as it is plumblessly profound: "Now, to him who is able to accomplish all things in a measure far beyond what we ask or conceive, in keeping with the power that is at work in us—to him be glory in the Church and in Christ Jesus down through all the ages of time without end. Amen" (Eph. 3:20–21). It is as if the intrinsic essence of the individual and that of the Church mutually perfected one another: the reserved depths of the isolated personality, and the great, all-inclusive profundity of the *Ecclesia*. Hers the divine science of truth, and the maternal womb into which the individual is drawn to be reborn as a child of God.

It is from Christ's presence in the soul and in the Church that St. Paul draws his conception of love. It has two aspects: first the love of one individual for another, flowing from the heart of a child of God to his brother or sister in Christ, and nourished by the manifold encounters of Christian existence. The Saint's correspondence with his favorite congregation in Philippi speaks beautifully of this aspect of love. Then there is the second kind of love: that which issues from the unity of life that permeates all members of Christ's Church. Paul refers to this love in his opening letter to the congregation in Corinth. There the different members have fallen into dispute—the result of spiritual jealousy. The waves that followed the descent of the Spirit at Pentecost have washed up special grace upon grace among the believers. To the one it was given to prophesy strange things in the mystic inspiration of the hour. To another to interpret the symbols of such prophecy, unintelligible to the uninitiated. A third was empowered to preach with singular forcefulness; a fourth to help and console, and so on. And now the bearers of these gifts—amazing confusion!—must have argued among themselves as to which was the most distinguished. St. Paul explains, thus smoothing the troubled waters: "Now there are varieties of gifts, but the same Spirit; and there are varieties of ministries, but the same Lord; and there are varieties of workings, but the same God, who works all things in all. . . . But all these things are the work of one and the same Spirit, who allots to everyone according as he will" (I Cor. 12:4–6, 11). In other words, it is one and the same power which produces all: the Holy Ghost; one and the same figure is revealed in all: Christ; one unit is the fruit of them all: the Church. And now St. Paul fills in the picture by showing how the different members of the body are interdependent. Neither foot nor hand is of the least value alone. Only as ordered parts of the whole can they live and serve one another. If any gift is supreme, then that of love; but love is no special, isolated function apart from the others. It is readiness to participate in the divinely activated whole, to serve all others. This is the theme of the famous thirteenth chapter, the canticle of love.

Viewed from here, love is the expression of the Church's unity. It is not the sentiment that binds one individual to another, but the unifying power of immense, all-permeating vitality. In this sense, to love means to be Church; to permit the life-stream of the *Ecclesia* to flow through oneself to others: "Put on therefore, as God's chosen ones, holy and beloved, a heart of mercy, kindness, humility, meekness, patience. Bear with one another and forgive one another, . . . But above all these things have charity, which is the bond of perfection. And may the peace of Christ reign in your hearts; unto that peace, indeed, you were called in one body. Show yourselves thankful. Let the word of Christ dwell in you abundantly. . . . Whatever you do in word or in work, do all in the name of the Lord Jesus, giving thanks to God the Father through him" (Col. 3:12–17).

The figure of Christ indicated in the Epistles to the Ephesians and Colossians has burst all bounds. He has grown wider than the world, and an all-permeating power streams from him. The meaning of all things is contained in him who stands before the beginning of time, before all beginning.

These texts suggest the opening chapter of St. John: "In the beginning was the Word, and the Word was with God: and the Word was God. He was in the beginning with God. All things were made through him, and without him was made nothing that has been made. In him was life, and the life was the light of men. . . . And the Word was made flesh, and dwelt among us. And we saw his glory—glory as of the only-begotten of the Father—full of grace and of truth" (John 1:1–4, 14).

Here too we confront the pre-temporal, the sense behind all things, the all-embracing; but that which renders Paul's Epistles so mysterious is missing. St. John is writing of the *Logos,* the Word of the speaking God—for God is not mute. We know by experience the power of speech, through which a sentiment within us takes form and becomes comprehensible to us. John teaches that it is much the same with God. He does not dumbly contain the plenitude of his Being, of his intelligence, vitality, bounty and bliss, but gives them expression in the Word, which is not addressed to another, but to himself. It remains within him, in the profoundest depths of his essence, yet is absolute reality. Human word is weak. Its strength lies only in its meaning, not its being, which is but a breath and swift to vanish, an image that takes form in speaker and hearer, then dissolves. The Word that God speaks lives and acts, is itself Someone. When God speaks to himself he is simultaneously Speaker and That Which is Spoken: Father and Son. This divine Word, uttered from all eternity (and as St. John says, eternally directed back to God, its Utterer) includes everything that is: the infinite Creator and all creation. More: all potential creation, for in it gleam the moulds of all possible forms. He who comprehends this Word, comprehends all. In order that this conception of the *Logos,* idea and source of all ideas, stand ready to serve sacred Christology, Greek thought labored for six centuries. Led by John, Christian thought, determined to reach clarity at any price, wrung order from chaos, conceiving primitive reality in eternal images. The thought is bold enough—but Paul's is bolder still. For John speaks of the eternal Son of God, of the *Logos per se;* Paul of that *Logos* become flesh and blood. It is he, the God incarnate that Paul places behind the beginning of all things. He, the God-man, is the Embracer of all that ever was or is or will be!

The mystery is particularly impenetrable since the *Logos* became man so long after the establishment of history. Who can say all it means? Only this much is clear: in divine vision man and his humanity are other than we suppose.

Such then the Firstborn of all creation. In him may be found the prototypes of all forms, beings, values. As white light contains all colors, the Word virtually contains everything distributed over the breadth of the universe, the length of time, the depths of intelligence, the peaks of the ideal. Christ is the creative hand of the Father into which are graven the lines of the world's destinies from the beginning on. Each line or thread is separate, yet together they compose the universal tapestry whose forms go back to him, the Weaver. In his hand lie also the decisions of grace, the impenetrable warp and weft of sacred history with its revelations, its prophecies and warnings, the infinite fabric of that which is to cooperate for the good of those who love God. What a thought!

Bearing all this within him, that same Christ entered into history, loved and died in the narrow confines of a human life. We have already seen how the power of the eternal Christ shapes the consciousness of the temporal Jesus. This is most evident in his speeches in Jerusalem: "Amen, amen, I say to you, before Abraham came to be, I am" (John 8:58), or in the farewell words: "And now do thou, Father, glorify me with thyself, with the glory that I had with thee before the world existed" (John 17:5).

St. Paul's Christ has cosmic proportions. He is no longer only the Lord of truth, Guide and Proclaimer of a new order. Here for the first time we begin to sense the scope of such words as: "I am the way, and the truth, and the life" (John 14:6). He *is* the truth, *is* all things; not only intellectually, but in a universal surreality; not only as Conceiver of all things, but as the Being into which they are drawn. Seen from here the Eucharist too receives its ultimate significance. The words: "He who eats my flesh, and drinks my blood, abides in me and I in him" (John 6:56), mean not only spiritual contact, an intrinsic sense of love and protection, but cosmic relationship. Man, and with him the world, should be *in Christo* in the whole literal truth of the word, for he, the incarnate *Logos,* is all-inclusive.

The objection that this is intellectual juggling, metaphysics stemming from Plato and Plotinus does not ruffle us, for it was to this end that Plato lived and thought: that the Christian, when he came, might find at hand the concepts necessary to his understanding of the Lord, and through faith in him, himself. Only here far more is said than any Platonic philosopher ever dared to say. The Apostle to the Gentiles teaches that Christ is the actual space, order, form, power that absorbs and transforms the believer and all existence.

Unconverted man lives in the visible world judging all that is or may be by tradition's experience and by the rules of logic. But when he encounters Christ, he must either accept him and his revolutionary approach to truth or lose him. If he attempts to judge also the Lord by the standards of common experience, he will soon notice that he is dealing with something outside experience. He will have to discard the norms of the past, and take Christ as his new point of departure. When he no longer attempts to subject Christ to immediate reason and experience, he will recognize him as the supreme measure of all possible reality. The intellect jealous for its own sovereignty rejects such recognition, which would put an end to its world-anchored self-glorification, and surrender it into the hands of the God of Revelation. This is the 'risk' any would-be Christian must take. If he takes it, a profound revolution begins. It may take a disquieting, even frightening form; may demand passage through stifling darkness and perplexity. All that until now has seemed certain suddenly becomes questionable. The whole conception of reality, the whole idea of existence is turned upside-down. Only the haunting question persists: *Is* Christ really so great that he can be the norm of all that is? Does the world really lose itself in him, or is the whole idea only another (magnificent) example of the human tendency to make that which it reveres the measure of all things; another proof of the blindness inherent in all love? Yet the longer the intellect continues to grope, the clearer it becomes that the love of Christ is essentially different from every other love. And to the degree that the searching individual experiences such spiritual revolution, he gains an amplitude, a superiority, a synthesizing power of reason that no natural insight can match.

With this, Christ's figure transcends all measure, for there is no measure outside him. That is why he is Lord of all being, its Judge and the norm of its judgment. What a man does for or against Christ is what decides his sentence. This the point of view that contains all others, that of goodness and justice included. In the Epistle to the Romans Paul says: "For I reckon that the sufferings of the present time are not worthy to be compared with the glory to come that will be revealed in us. For the eager longing of creation awaits the revelation of the sons of God. . . . For in hope were we saved. But hope that is seen is not hope. For how can a man hope for what he sees? But if we hope for what we do not see, we wait for it with patience.

"But in like manner the Spirit also helps our weakness. For we do not know what we should pray for as we ought, but the Spirit himself pleads for us with unutterable groanings. And he who searches the hearts knows what the Spirit desires, that he pleads for the saints according to God.

"Now we know that for those who love God all things work together unto good, for those who, according to his purpose, are saints through his call. For those whom he has foreknown he has also predestined to become conformed to the image of his Son, that he should be the firstborn among many brethren. And those whom he has predestined, them he has also called; and those whom he has called, them he has also justified, and those whom he has justified, them he has also glorified.

"What then shall we say to these things? If God is for us, who is against us? He who has not spared even his own Son but has delivered him for us all, how can he fail to grant us also all things with him? Who shall make accusation against the elect of God? It is God who justifies! . . . Who shall separate us from the love of Christ? Shall tribulation, or distress, or persecution, or hunger, or nakedness, or danger, or the sword? Even as it is written, 'For thy sake we are put to death all the day long. We are regarded as sheep for the slaughter.' But in all these things we overcome because of him who has loved us" (Rom. 8:18–37).

Here is the mystery of predestination. It is one of love, not of dreadfulness, and the Apostle's commentary to it ends in a paeon of praise: "Oh, the depth of the riches of the wisdom and of the knowledge of God! How incomprehensible are his judgments and how unsearchable his ways! For 'Who has known the mind of the Lord, or who has been his counsellor? Or who has first given to him, that recompense should be made him?' For from him and through him and unto him are all things. To him be the glory forever, amen" (Rom. 11:33–36).

XI

THE ETERNAL
HIGH PRIEST

O ne of the Pauline letters, the fourteenth, occupies a special place in his correspondence: The Epistle to the Hebrews. According to tradition, it was written not by the Apostle himself, but by a friend and assistant well acquainted with the world of St. Paul's thought, for its approach, its choice of words is not that of the other Epistles. Be this as it may, the broad, metaphysical sweep of the Saint is unquestionably there. The greater part of the letter is concerned with the person of Christ; Christ seen in his particular role of high priest. As such, he offers the sacrifice of the new covenant, which expiates our sin and redeems the world. Pauline theology makes of Christ a powerful, mysterious, for us, almost foreign figure. His strangeness is mainly due to the fact that for moderns, the whole sense of sacrifice has become blurred and remote. Both religious-philosophical thought and our own personal feelings tend to regard it as something belonging to a primitive, still imperfect stage of religious development long since replaced by a purer attitude towards our Creator. We are inclined to consider sacrifice unspiritual, if not downright questionable. Therefore, before we begin our study of the Hebrew Epistle, we must overcome this sense of strangeness by asking ourselves what the pure idea behind ancient sacrifice was.

In the Old Testament we meet with it everywhere. It was the question of sacrifice that divided the two sons of the first man: the one obedient to God, the other disobedient. It was during the sacrifice after the flood that God proclaimed his covenant with all who would be faithful to him. A sacrifice sealed the covenant with Abraham; likewise its renewal through Moses, the prophet and lawgiver, at whose side stood Aaron, the high priest. The whole order of religious life was regulated by sacrifice. It ran like a crimson thread through Hebrew history, both in its national totality and in the history of the individual. What is sacrifice? It is man's offering of something which belongs to him, something precious and without flaw. This he gives away; gives to God, to keep. To express the completeness of God's ownership and the cancellation of man's, the gift is destroyed: the beverage which man himself could have drunk is poured on the ground; the first fruits of his harvest are burned; the animal is slain, consumed by fire and thus transported to its Creator. One might ask what in heaven's name God is supposed to do with such gifts. Everything that exists was created by him, belongs to him; moreover, what use could he, the Infinite One, have for finite things? This is true, and the prophets themselves stress the fact: In the eyes of God the gift in itself is nothing. But the intention behind it? This is inspired by a sentiment of adoration, of thanksgiving, supplication, contrition or praise. The act of sacrifice is a concrete expression of man's recognized insignificance and his will to renunciation before the all-creative, omnipotent God who is the beginning and end of all things. It is a statement of who God is. If the sacrifice is offered in this sense, must it not be pleasing to him? If the attitude that inspires it is: God alone is all that really is, all created things exist only through his grace? If it concludes: Therefore it is self-understood that he rule, that things should retire to make room for him, to clear the way for his glory? This is the sentiment behind the words of the Apocalypse: "To him who sits upon the throne, and to the Lamb, blessing and honor and glory and dominion, forever and ever" (Apoc. 5:13).

But behind the sacrifice is something else: man himself. His consciousness of belonging to God has found terrible historical expression in human sacrifice. Here an intrinsic truth has been hellishly distorted, but truth it remains. The sacrifice says for him who offers it: Not I, creature, but thou, Creator! Its immolation would make room for God.

And immolation it is, not mere destruction; herein lies the second significance of the sacrificial act. Sacrifice is a passing over to God. In its deepest sense, to sacrifice means to enter into the life of God by renouncing the life of the world. We have a hint of the same idea even in secular life. The man who sacrifices himself for an ideal, for his country, or for some loved one, desires first of all to serve the object of his devotion. But behind this desire lies another which he is perhaps loathe to admit for fear of being considered fantastic; nevertheless, he is convinced that in some mysterious way his sacrifice simultaneously exalts what he is thus honoring, and gives him a share in that which has been exalted. Not only spiritually, but actually. How? It is impossible to say without merging in religion, for every sacrifice made for another or for a good cause is oriented towards God. In it lies the intrinsic hope that he who offers the sacrifice and he or that for which it is offered will be reunited, more intimately than ever, in the divine.

And now the Epistle to the Hebrews says: The sacrifices of the Old Testament prepare for the one infinite sacrifice of ultimate validity for the whole world—that of the Savior. That Jesus is conscious of his role of victim is obvious in his words at the Last Supper: Signifying the bread he says: "This is my body, which is being given for you." And of the wine: "This cup is the new covenant in my blood, which shall be shed for you" (Luke 22:19–20). Bread to be offered up, wine to be poured out "for you"—sacrifice in its purest form. Fundamentally, the letter to the Hebrews is nothing but a commentary to this sacrifice of all sacrifices: "Wherefore it was right that he should in all things be made like unto his brethren, that he might become a merciful and faithful high priest before God to expiate the sins of the people. For in that he himself has suffered and has been tempted, he is able to help those who are tempted" (Heb. 2:17–18). The priest must be one of those he represents. He must share their fate. For this reason God's Son became man, like us in all things, that his sacrifice might go forth from our midst. And again, he had to be different from us: "For it was fitting that we should have such a high priest, holy, innocent, undefiled, set apart from sinners, and become higher than the heavens. He does not need to offer sacrifices daily (as the other priests did), first for his own sins, and then for the sins of the people; for this latter he did once for all in offering up himself" (Heb. 7:26–28).

That which both in John and the Synoptics is so clearly underlined: Jesus' unconditional surrender to the paternal will, his passion for the Father's honor and unreserved readiness to defend it to the death, is evident here in its reversed form: in his complete surrender of self for mankind.

For it is not things that he sacrifices, not animals, not food or drink, but his own flesh and blood. And actually, not merely 'spiritually' as modernity would so often have it, not merely in the totality of his service to men, but in the mystery of literal annihilation. This is expressed in the fate placed upon him by the sinfulness of the world. What took place on Golgotha, with its earthly appearance of senseless destruction was the form in which the sacrifice was offered: "But when Christ appeared as high priest of the good things to come, he entered once for all through the greater and more perfect tabernacle, not made by hands (that is, not of this creation), nor again by virtue of blood of goats and calves, but by virtue of his own blood, into the Holies, having obtained eternal redemption. For if the blood of goats and bulls and the sprinkled ashes of a heifer sanctify the unclean unto the cleansing of the flesh, how much more will the blood of Christ, who through the Holy Spirit offered himself unblemished unto God, cleanse your conscience from dead works to serve the living God?" (Heb. 9:11–14).

Christ offers up himself, that God may be all in all: Thy will, not mine! Thus the words of sin: My will, not God's! are expiated. With this act, Jesus' humanity passes over into eternity. What he sacrifices is returned to him glorified. The Lord's way to death is his way to glory, and he takes us with him. By giving his life, he finds it, as he himself tells us—and not only his own but also ours (Matt. 10). He is the last Adam, in whom all mankind has its life, as it did in the first. And just as mankind was dragged into destruction by Adam's sin, it is lifted into life by Jesus' virtue. Faith and Baptism stand for burial with Christ, and resurrection with him to new life.

And now the tremendous thought: "For Jesus has not entered into a Holies made by hands, a mere copy of the true, but into heaven itself, to appear now before the face of God on our behalf; nor yet has he entered to offer himself often, as the high priest enters into the Holies years after year with blood not his own; for in that case he must have suffered often since the beginning of the world. But as it is, once for all at the end of the ages, he has appeared for the destruction of sin by the sacrifice of himself " (Heb. 9:24–26).

Once a year, on the day of the great reconciliation, the high priest was called upon to offer a propitiary sacrifice for the entire nation. With the blood of the victim he stepped from the temple courtyard into the holy of holies, the most sacred room of the temple, closed all other days of the year, as the sanctuary of the ark of the covenant. There, before the ancient covenant between God and Moses, seat of the divine throne of glory, he sprinkled the blood. Christ is true high priest. On the day of the veritable reconciliation, that first Good Friday, he stepped from the courtyard of existence, life, through the doorway of death into the veritable holy of holies: the glory of God, into which no other has entry. There he stands before the throne, offering up the victim that fulfills all things.

Mysterious, terrible image! Drawn from a flash of revelation that penetrates the profoundest intimacy of Christ—there where he stands alone with himself and his Father. In the power of his purity of heart, his veracity of spirit and the infinite love of his act, he faces God as high priest of the world. And though his sacrifice was made in time, in the historical hour of his death, it is celebrated eternally, in the endless present. Ages pass, immeasurable for human conception, but Christ remains standing, holding his sacrifice before the divine Presence until the end of all time. In the eyes of God, the millennia pass away and vanish as a day, but the sacrifice of Golgotha remains.

No other sacrifice exists. The service of the old covenant is ended. There where the Christian tidings have not penetrated, the pagan cults remain foreshadowings of the essential Sacrifice to come; where the sacred evangel has been proclaimed, they are demonic. In all eternity there remains but one true sacrifice, forever current in the words: "... do this in remembrance of me" (Luke 22:19). In holy Mass this offering centered in eternity is constantly renewed, for it cannot be repeated.

XII

The Lord's Return

S t. Paul speaks of the mystical Christ, the resurrected, transformed and transfigured "Spirit" independent of all human limitations of time and space; of the Christ borne by the Holy Spirit and activating all Christian existence. The description of his reality circles for the most part about two poles. The one is planted in the unapproachableness of God. "Therefore, if you have risen with Christ, seek the things that are above, where Christ is seated at the right hand of God. Mind the things that are above, not the things that are on earth" (Col. 3:1–2). There, 'above' thrones the Lord, clothed in the glory that was his before the world began (John 17:5). The same Christ is also in men, reliving his own life through the individual, as well as through the new race of the children of God. And still the power of his reality is not exhausted. He is also the One-who-is-to-come, present not only in the glorious isolation of God before creation, and in temporal history, but also at the termination of all things. And not only as a spectator, but as one with power, who will come "soon" to put an end to time (Apoc. 22:20).

It is predominantly the two Epistles to the Thessalonians that proclaim the second coming of Christ. "For the Lord himself with cry of command, with voice of archangel, and with trumpet of God will descend from heaven; and the dead in Christ will rise up first. Then we who live, who survive, shall be caught up together with them in clouds to meet the Lord in the air, and so we shall ever be with the Lord" (I Thess. 4:16–17).

The first Corinthian Epistle sounds the same chord: "Now this I say, brethren, that flesh and blood can obtain no part in the kingdom of God, neither shall corruption have any part in incorruption. Behold, I tell you a mystery: we shall all indeed rise, but we shall not all be changed—in a moment, in the twinkling of an eye, at the last trumpet. For the trumpet shall sound, and the dead shall rise incorruptible and we shall be changed. For this corruptible body must put on incorruption, and this mortal body must put on immortality (I Cor. 15:50–53).

We feel the visionary quality of the words. Paul experienced the full power and inexpressibleness of the vision of the returning Lord. He will come suddenly, in the wink of an eye. The trumpet will blare, that apocalyptic instrument whose sound once shattered the silence of Sinai, forbidding the people to approach its trembling heights; trumpets so shook the walls of Jericho that they dissolved under the omnipotent hand of God; seven trumpets (Revelation again) that will be the fanfare for the seven supreme agonies to break in upon the world. The Lord will descend from heaven to summon the dead from the earth. Those alive at the time will be transfigured to that state in which the resurrected Christ appeared to men as a promise of things to come. And all who belong to Christ will be caught up into the impenetrable mystery of coming union and fulfillment. Then will come Judgment.

For Paul, Christ's return is not only at the remote end of time, but makes itself felt already now. Already now Christian existence is troubled by the foreshadowing of that stupendous event. This is evident in several passages. Speaking of the Eucharist, for example, he says: ". . . the Lord Jesus, on the night in which he was betrayed, took bread, and giving thanks broke, and said, 'This is my body which shall be given up for you; do this in remembrance of me. . . . This cup is the new covenant in my blood; do this as often as you drink it, in remembrance of me. For as often as you shall eat this bread and drink the cup, you proclaim the death of the Lord, until he comes' " (I Cor. 11:23–26).

Celebration of the Holy Eucharist seems to be incomplete in itself; it points up and beyond. It is not only sacrifice and sacrament, but prophecy as well, and what it foretells is what Christ himself promised at the Last Supper: "But I say to you, I will not drink henceforth of this fruit of the vine, until that day when I shall drink it new with you in the kingdom of my Father" (Matt. 26:29).

Mysterious words! Who can say what they mean? We only feel that they stand for the plenitude of endless fulfillment—much like those others: ". . . and my Father will love him, and we will come to him and make our abode with him" and "If any man listens to my voice and opens the door to me, I will come in to him and will sup with him, and he with me" (John 14:23; Apoc. 3:20).

Christ's return also makes itself felt in the Christian's attitude to the things of the world. In the opening Corinthian letter Paul speaks of earth's genuine values: of marriage, property, culture: "But this I say, brethren, the time is short; it remains that those who have wives be as if they had none; and those who weep, as though not weeping; and those who rejoice, as though not rejoicing; and those who buy, as though not possessing; and those who use this world, as though not using it, for this world as we see it is passing away. I would have you free from care. He who is unmarried is concerned about the things of the Lord, how he may please God" (I Cor. 7:29–32).

These are the much-quoted lines that are supposed to express the Apostle's contempt for the world and human values, especially for marriage. Actually, there can be no talk of any such thing, for the Saint is not speaking generally; his words are no expression of principle, but are inspired by the conviction that Christ's return is imminent. He is certain that he himself will live to see it. Hence, in view of the stupendous, world-transforming event already at the door, the things precious to the world as it stands today are unimportant. So he preaches: Do not bind yourselves. Be free for the great moment of the transformation! It is the same attitude we find in the Acts of the Apostles: many sell all they own and give the returns to the Apostles to distribute among the poor. With the Lord so near, what is the good of property? Just as little as this gesture implies communism (or any attitude at all towards possessions other than that of the futility of all possessions in view of the Lord's return) does it imply a fundamental devaluation of marriage. After all, it was Paul who grounded the institution of marriage in the divine by likening it to the sacred bond that exists between Christ and his Church (Eph. 5:20–28).

Throughout Paul's Epistles runs the sentiment: the Lord is coming soon, then everything will be different! This is what gives early Christianity its intensity. Then conversion meant participation in the Christian's readiness for something about to happen. All who refuse to be converted are as blind and thoughtless as those who lived before the flood. Only the Christian is aware of humanity's true situation; only he is ready. Hence the watchfulness, power and unreserved enthusiasm of those first Christian centuries; hence their sweeping devaluation of all that is transitory. This is perhaps the profoundest difference between the age of the New Testament and our own, and it leads us straight to the question: When will the Lord come?

As we have said, St. Paul thought soon, during his lifetime. In the other Corinthian passage just quoted he wrote in the first person plural: ". . . and the dead shall rise incorruptible and we shall be changed." Then, gradually, his conviction was transformed. Christ's delay and the calm of his own increasing years taught him to reckon with the possibility that he would no longer be alive for the great advent. And he writes to the Philippians: ". . . in accord with my eager longing and hope that in nothing I shall be put to shame, but that with complete assurance now as at all times Christ will be glorified in my body, whether through life or through death.

"For to me to live is Christ and to die is gain. But if to live in the flesh is my lot, this means for me fruitful labor, and I do not know which to choose. Indeed I am hard pressed from both sides—desiring to depart and to be with Christ, a lot by far the better; yet to stay on in the flesh is necessary for your sake" (Phil. 1:20–24).

What a difference in tone from that of the first Thessalonian Epistle that we examined! The urgency has subsided. Beneath Christianity's layer of heroic *charitas,* as the Saint conceived it, the sharp eye will discover the less dramatic demands of everyday Christian life and the writer's dawning understanding of its permanent place in history. Once the mind has plunged deeper into the sense of the Lord's admonition, it realizes that his "soon" cannot be measured in terms of time, since he himself had said that no one but the Father knew the day or hour (Matt. 24:36). Moreover, Paul enumerates certain specific events that must take place before the Lord comes: the predestined number of heathen must have entered into the fold, and the Hebrew nation must have been converted. When this will take place is an open question: "For I would not, brethren, have you ignorant of this mystery, lest you should be wise in your own conceits, that a partial blindness only has befallen Israel, until the full number of the Gentiles should enter, and thus all Israel should be saved, as it is written, 'There will come out of Sion the deliverer and he will turn away impiety from Jacob; and this is my covenant with them, when I shall take away their sins' " (Rom. 11:25–27).

The Antichrist too must have made his appearance: "Let no one deceive you in any way, for the day of the Lord will not come unless the apostasy comes first, and the man of sin is revealed, the son of perdition, who opposes and is exalted above all that is called God, or that is worshipped, so that he sits in the temple of God and gives himself out as if he were God. Do you not remember that when I was still with you, I used to tell you these things? And now you know what restrains him, that he may be revealed in his proper time. For the mystery of iniquity is already at work; provided only that he who is at present restraining it, does still restrain, until he is gotten out of the way" (II Thess. 2:3–7).

These things have not as yet occurred, and who can say when they will?

The early Christian congregations' conviction that Christ's return was imminent makes much that is different in their lives and attitude understandable. Little by little that conviction faded. The pressure under which they lived, their ardent longing to surrender themselves completely to the new existence about to be established, decreased. The contempt and persecution to which they had been subjected began to disappear, and gradually a Christian society and culture by nature dependent not on termination, but on permanency, took root. Then with modernity the traditional *Weltanschauung* was entirely revised. Under the banners of science, cosmic and historical existence assumed a new autonomy, and its intrinsic laws. Faith in Christ's coming to terminate the world was made to seem senseless.

It is hardly an exaggeration to say that also among Christians profound consciousness of the Lord's return has become a rarity. Between preoccupation with the last things and present reality stands the wall known as the scientific viewpoint. But doesn't this entail an essential loss to Christian faith? Christianity has long since taken its place as Christian culture in the world, where it has become an integral part of the whole, and where it is only too inclined to share the general conception of a world to be ended by natural phenomena. Thus Christianity today lacks the tension which lent its early centuries their clear-cut decisiveness, their ardor and *élan*. The fact that most of the early Christians were converted as adults also did much to increase the earnestness and enlightened clarity of their faith. Nevertheless, faith in Christ's coming is not dead, and all faith has a certain, seed-like dormancy. It can rest for centuries only suddenly to put forth root and leaf. Perhaps before this can happen, Christianity must lose some of its complacency. The term 'Christian culture' must be purged of all that is questionable in it. The gulf between Revelation and the world must reopen. Perhaps a new period of persecution and outlawry must come to shake Christians back to a living consciousness of the values for which they stand. Such a period might also enliven belief in Christ's coming. It is difficult to say. Different elements of Christian truth have different seasons. At times they are powerfully felt, at others they recede into the background, seem to lose their importance and lustre, only to reappear in response to some new vital need.

PART SEVEN

Time and Eternity

I

THE BOOK OF REVELATION

J esus' life began in eternity. After his death, as all four Evangelists report, he is reborn to a new life. During forty days he lingers on earth, then ascends into heaven, whence he descended in the Spirit to reign in the heart of the individual and in the Church. Once, however, he will come in still another form, openly, to judge the world and put an end to history. Then creation and history will be caught up into eternity, and Christ himself will be the eternal life of the saved and the light of redeemed creation. This is the outline of the life of "Jesus, the Christ." The Book of Revelation reveals the ultimate and eternal part of that life.

A certain amount of knowledge is essential to the understanding of this book. One must know something of the milieu in which it was written: both of late Judaism, with its sense of menace and expectation hovering over all things, and of the early Christian congregations' relations to the world in which they found themselves. Furthermore, the Apocalypse is rich in symbolism and artfully constructed according to a mystic and liturgical plan difficult to appreciate without specific knowledge. We cannot go into such questions here; the reader interested in them should consult books on exegesis. Our task is to point out two particular characteristics of the final book of Scripture which are of great importance to our study. First of all: the Book of Revelation is a book of consolation; not a theology of history or of the ultimate things, but the consolation that God, at the end of the apostolic era, desired to place in the hands of his Church. She was badly in need of it. The Roman state had declared Christianity its enemy. Hostilities had long since followed one another. The Acts of the Apostles recount one incident almost immediately after the first Pentecost, and the large-scale persecutions under Emperor Nero had already spilled much blood. But at that time, the particular essence of the faith had not yet been recognized. To the popular mind, Christianity appeared to be either one of the many new streams of religious thought, or simply another offshoot of Judaism. It is noteworthy that Nero's persecutions were directed originally against the Jews, and only later spread to the Christians (when the Roman state realized what a power Christianity itself was rapidly becoming and forced it to choose between paganism and extermination). Now began the real Christian persecutions, which lasted over two hundred years. We should note the date. The first century, under Domitian, is the one in which the Apocalypse was written. In the opening chapter, verse nine, we read: "I, John, your brother and partner in the tribulation and kingdom and patience that are in Jesus. . . ."

How does God console? Not by saying: Your trials are not really so terrible; they are terrible, and he sees them as terrible. Nor does God promise miraculous intervention. History has its time and its power, also history directed against God, and he does not cancel them. But over and above earthly reality, he gives us a glimpse of heavenly reality. Over and above the storm and press of historical power, appears the One against whom it is directed, the silent, waiting Christ. Eternity is his. He sees everything, weighs everything, from the first secret stirrings of the heart to the ultimate effects of the accomplished act, and writes it down in the "scroll" of his infallible knowledge. And once the hour that marks the end of time for all things will strike, and things will cease to be, but Christ will live on. All flesh will appear before him, and he will disclose every human act, evaluate every soul once and forever. That is God's consolation, the comfort of faith there for all hearers who have "overcome" in faith. It is not applicable to tomorrow, or next year, or to this life at all, but after death in eternity, and it helps precisely as much as he to whom it is given lives in the reality of God and Christ and eternity.

The consolation of the Apocalypse is rendered neither in theological argument, nor in summaries of future history, nor in practical councils or maxims, but in images and symbolic events which should be correctly understood. One can approach them intellectually, digging into the secrets of numerology: the significance of seven, twelve, four-and-twenty. One can study the symbolism of the gems: of jasper and beryl and sardonyx. One can meditate on the meaning behind the animal forms that appear: lamb and dragon. All this is to the good, but remains sterile as long as the author's own introduction has not been fully and earnestly assimilated: "I, John, your brother and partner in the tribulation and kingdom and patience that are in Jesus, was on the island which is called Patmos, because of the word of God and the testimony of Jesus. I was in the spirit on the Lord's day, and I heard behind me a great voice, as of a trumpet, saying, 'What thou seest write in a book, and send to the seven churches, to Ephesus, and to Smyrna, and to Pergamus, and to Thyatira, and to Sardis, and to Philadelphia, and to Laodicea.'

"And I turned to see the voice that was speaking to me. And having turned, I saw seven golden lamp-stands; and in the midst of the seven lamp-stands One like to a son of man, clothed with a garment reaching to the ankles, and girt about the breasts with a golden girdle" (Apoc. 1:9–13).

Here we are told that the writer of the Apocalypse has been in an ecstasy, transported "in the spirit," as the prophets had been when they received the visions recorded in their books—a subject we have already discussed. The images in the Book of Revelation, then, are visions. In chapter five for instance: "And I saw, and behold, in the midst of the throne and of the four living creatures, and in the midst of the elders, a Lamb standing, as if slain, having seven horns and seven eyes, which are the seven spirits of God sent forth into all the earth" (Apoc. 5:6).

How can a slaughtered lamb live? How can it have seven eyes and seven horns? We can help a little by saying that it is a symbol of Christ. He had died and was resurrected; was dead therefore, and yet alive. Obviously, eyes are organs of sight; he though, who sees all things, has seven eyes, because seven is the sacred number of entirety. He also enjoys omnipotence in heaven and on earth; hence the seven horns (in Biblical language the horn is synonymous with force). All this is correct, yet remains lifeless and non-essential. Nor do we get any further by attempting to recreate these images as they are described—with simple exactitude, as if they were natural objects. Artists have tried to picture Revelation in this fashion, but we have only to glance at Albrecht Dürer's Apocalypse to realize the futility of the method.

We must try some other way. If not in the natural world, where can such a thing as a mortally wounded animal that is dead and yet overwhelmingly alive exist? In the dream world. There it might stand, simultaneously living and dead, inexplicable yet intrinsically understood. There a creature might appear that (we feel it) sees with unheard of visual power; everything about it sees; it has eyes all over. And it is powerful with all its being. Everything about it is weapon and horn and blow. We could encounter such a being in dreams, and though the mind protested, a knowledge deep within us would be satisfied. Why is this so? Because in dreams the substance of things disappears. A profounder vitality emerges, seizes the forms of things, and transforms them—and not only as the artist's fantasy, always conditioned by ambient reality, transforms, but so that the very limits of the possible and impossible cease to exist. Critical reason is silenced; the ebb and flood of the inner life hold sway: the hidden will of the senses, the intrinsic meanings of existence ignored by the waking consciousness. All this labors with tangible forms; reveals itself in them half veiled yet shimmering through the veil. Somehow initiated, the 'inner man' of the sleeper feels the message of the image even when he is incapable of expressing it.

Something similar happens in the vision—similar with the essential difference that the state we are now describing is determined from 'above,' from God. it is not the product of sleep's relaxation, in which the mind and its criticism, the will and its control are suspended; here the spirit of God seizes a person, lifts him out of himself, and makes him the instrument of something beyond the reaches of human judgment and will. Everything, the raw material of general existence, the personal life of the prophet, things, events, images—all are utilized by the divine spirit as means of expression. In dream, man's imagination functions in the service of some obscure impulse. In the vision, the spirit of God transforms the shapes of earthly existence to express a divine idea. Such images stand in an atmosphere, are of a quality, move in a manner as different from those of human existence as the state of sleep is different from that of wakefulness. The images in a vision emerge from a stream of omnipotence; they fluctuate, merge, and sink back into the flow. What they reveal is the mystery of an unutterably holy life, of fulfillment beyond all measure, of an inexpressible coming, a transforming and perfecting through God: briefly, the completely "new."

In the same chapter we find the words: "And I saw upon the right hand of him who sits upon the throne a scroll written within and without, sealed with seven seals. And I saw a strong angel proclaiming with a loud voice, 'Who is worthy to open the scroll, and to break the seals thereof?' And no one in heaven, or on earth, or under the earth, was able to open the scroll or to look thereon. And I wept much, because no one was found worthy to open the scroll or to look thereon" (Apoc. 5:1–4).

Why does the man weep with his whole being? All of us, sometime or other, have experienced a powerful dream. There stood or lay something—perhaps a book or scroll—on a table. It is closed, and the dreamer, knowing with all his soul that everything depends on its being opened, tries to open it, but in spite of his most heartbreaking efforts, he does not succeed. He is beside himself. Were

someone to ask him why he weeps, he would point to the book:
The book—don't you see? *It can't be opened!*

In dreams the barrier between here and beyond, between self and
other falls. One vitalizing current streams through all things, and the
dreamer feels both intimately related to all he beholds, and a
stranger to it. In his dream he encounters, startled into recognition,
his profoundest, most intimate and unknown self. What he beholds
is a book, but also the whole meaning of his life and its integrity. Or
perhaps a lamp-stand, candlestick stands before him, and someone
says: That is the person you love. That is your happiness. If the candlestick were to fall, your joy would be shattered! He would not say:
The candle's flame is a symbol of your happiness, because happiness
is bright and warm and vulnerable as the flame that tips a tall candle,
but: The flame *is* your happiness! The dreamer hears the words,
wonders perhaps for a moment, and then understands: Naturally, it
must be so! And with all his being he trembles for the frail flame
flickering in the wind, for in the dream his very life flares simultaneously in him and there on the tip of the candle.

For the visionary it is much the same, save that he does not experience in dream, but "in the spirit." And what streams through him
and the images he beholds is not natural life with all its instincts,
hopes and terrors, but the new sacred life from God. This it is that
speaks from the images before him, and when the scroll cannot be
opened, agony cramps his soul. To understand the Apocalypse, one
must first of all free oneself from the conception of things' rigidity.
Gradually animated, they must mingle and flow, and the reader must
surrender himself to the movement. He must entrust the things of
daily life to its power, quietly following its course. He must learn to
listen, to be docile of spirit, accepting the images as they come,
opening his heart to their meaning, harmonizing all his being with
them. Then the degree of understanding willed by God will be his.
Once he has made this intrinsic approach to the Apocalypse, not before, careful study of its symbols, its construction, its historical background will be wonderfully profitable.

II

HE WHO REIGNS

The Book of Revelation opens with a great vision. St. John on Patmos beholds ". . . seven golden lamp-stands; and in the midst of the seven lamp-stands One like to a son of man, . . . But his head and his hair were white as white wool, and as snow, and his eyes were as a flame of fire; his feet were like fine brass, as in a glowing furnace, and his voice like the voice of many waters. And he had in his right hand seven stars. And out of his mouth came forth a sharp two-edged sword; and his countenance was like the sun shining in its power.

"And when I saw him, I fell at his feet as one dead. And he laid his right hand upon me, saying, 'Do not be afraid; I am the First and the Last, and he who lives; I was dead, and behold, I am living forevermore; and I have the keys of death and of hell. . . .' " (Apoc. 1:12–18.)

Powerful image! The seer, swept by a tide of persecutions to the desert island of Patmos, is seized one Sunday by the Spirit, and lifted into a state of visionary experience that comes directly from God. Then he hears a voice behind him. (We feel the suddenness, unexpectedness, ubiquitousness of the vision.) He turns around "to see the voice that was speaking to me," and his eye falls on the seven golden lamp-stands, in their midst "one like to a son of man." He is not the trumpet-like "voice" that first addressed the visionary; that was the voice of the vision itself, the signal to man. He who stands among the lamp-stands speaks differently. His voice is "like the voice of many waters"—not proclamatory like the trumpet, but overflowing with the fullness of earth. He is "like" a son of man, yet indescribable, his hair "as white wool, and as snow"—the similes mix to give an unearthly impression of brilliance and purity felt rather than seen. The feet of the sitting one are like fine brass "in a glowing furnace." We are reminded of the paintings of an artist who possessed as few others the gift of capturing the visionary with his brush: Matthias Grünewald. The Resurrected One on his Isenheim Altar has limbs that glow from within, and a face that is not lighted, but sends forth light.

Under the impact of the vision, the seer breaks down. The images have overwhelmed his natural life, shaking him limp with emotion and terror. But they also infuse the strength with which to bear them. The Son of Man leans over, places his right, the powerful, reigning hand, upon the unconscious beholder, and draws him to his feet. "Do not be afraid." In the same breath he reveals who he is, and that too is visionary, for the reality that comes from beyond can be comprehended only upon self-revelation. No road leads to it, only from it. No natural experience or earthly logic can explain it, it must speak for itself: I AM! Vision, image, light in which it appears, eye with which it is beheld, strength with which it is supported—all these are a single unity.

It is Christ who reveals himself as "the First and the Last," he who existed before all creation and who will continue to exist after it has passed away. . . . More: he is the activating Last, just as he is the activating First. Everything that was ever created has been created through him, and through him, likewise, all finite things will come to their end; not through themselves or any natural expiration, but ended by him who began them. He is also the Living One, who stands above life and death, which his reality has reformed—hence the keys to death and to hell that he holds. He is mightier than the untried powers of existence, for he has personally experienced what lies between birth and death, overcoming it because he is endless Life and Love.

Certain traits of the vision are presented with particular power: "And out of his mouth came forth a sharp two-edged sword." Impossible to picture this realistically. The sword is continuously flashing forth in an unbroken gesture of aggression and threat. And from his mouth! We have only to turn to Dürer's representation of the act to see that it cannot be literally imagined but only spiritually comprehended. "And he had in his right hand seven stars," the angels of the seven churches. What is meant by "angels" are the bishops, those sent to the seven congregations of the church to protect, guide and enlighten them. Not only do the stars represent the guiding stars of the Christian groups because the men who fill these positions must be visibly radiant with ardor and spiritual light that they may be a help to all; no, they "are" those "angels." The Bishop of Ephesus and the first star in the hand of the Son of Man are one and the same. . . . This is also true of the lamp-stands. These tall light-bearing pillars are the congregations, their life and luminous reality. Later the words: ". . . or else I will come to thee, and will move thy lamp-stand out of its place, unless thou repentest" prove the mysterious unity (2:5).

It is Christ revealing himself. The same Christ who lived on earth and died and rose again. Now he lives in eternity, and all that has ever been lives on in him. He wanders among the seven lamp-stands above all things, over and above the hue and cry of existence.

He who still lives in earthly tribulation asks with the Psalmist: "Arise, why sleepest thou, O Lord? Arise, and cast us not off to the end" (43:23). Human existence often seems deserted. God appears not to exist. Men are able to act against his will with impunity. They blaspheme, they say that God is dead, and no thunderbolt falls from heaven. Sometimes it seems as if really there were nothing outside this world; as if it were only the longing of the ambitious, the comfort of those who have come too short, the self-defence of the weaklings that invented God. The Book of Revelation shows him above things; not isolated in Olympian remoteness, where, blissful in himself, he strolls over the clouds, disdainful of the miserable swarms below, but walking among the light pillars of his congregations. Those who on earth were found foolish because they believed in him are placed after death in eternity, in the presence of God. Earthly powers may seem to be their own lords; history may appear as the workings of human will. In reality, it is Christ who is Lord of both. Apparently Christianity is delivered up to the pagans. In reality, God himself protects it. Though it appears the victim of chance, in everything that occurs—even its destruction—an eternal sense is being fulfilled, an invulnerable idea which only the disloyalty of Christians can touch. Nothing can harm the golden light-bearer: no enemy, no event, no accident. The Lord watches over it. No one can lessen its radiant significance; but should he whose existence is thus symbolized become unfaithful, the Lord "will move thy lamp-stand out of its place." Then the sovereign power of the Lord will be felt. The opening vision is followed by seven letters dictated by Christ to his visionary and addressed to the seven churches. They are meant first of all for the specific congregations of Ephesus, Smyrna, Pergamus, Thyatira, Sardis, Philadelphia and Laodicea; then for all congregations, all hearths of heavenly fire on earth, all cells of the mystical body, however numerous, for seven is the sacred number of entirety.

The letters are all patterned alike. First the name of the bishop addressed: "To the angel of the church at Ephesus write:" then comes the name of the speaker, and in the given form of self-identification the endless abundance of Christ's power is made manifest: "Thus says he who holds the seven stars in his right hand, who walks in the midst of the seven golden lamp-stands. . . ." "Thus says the First and the Last, who was dead and is alive. . . ." "Thus says he who has the sharp two-edged sword. . . ." "Thus says the Son of God, who has eyes like to a flame of fire, and whose feet are like fine brass. . . ." "Thus says he who has the seven spirits of God and the seven stars. . . ." "Thus says the Holy One, the true one, he who has the key of David, he who opens and no one shuts, and who shuts and no one opens. . . ." "Thus says the Amen, the faithful and true witness, who is the beginning of the creation of God. . . ."

The attributes of sovereignty are proclaimed with powerful uniformity, as the divine-human Master of the universe to whom "All power on heaven and on earth has been given . . ." reveals himself (Matt. 28:18).

Then: "I know thy works and thy labor and thy patience . . . [thou] hast endured for my name, and hast not grown weary." "I know thy tribulation and thy poverty, but thou art rich. . . ." "I know where thou dwellest, where the throne of Satan is; and thou holdest fast my name. . . ." "I know thy works; thou art neither cold nor hot. . . ." Here speaks the knowledge of him who sees all things, good and bad, appearance and essence. There where the golden lamp-stands are nothing is hidden.

And everything is judged: "But I have against thee, that thou hast left thy first love. . . ." "But I have a few things against thee, because thou hast there some who hold the teaching of Balaam. . . ." "But I have against thee that thou sufferest the woman Jezebel, who calls herself a prophetess, to teach, and to seduce my servants, to commit fornication, and to eat of things sacrificed to idols." "I know thy works; thou hast the name of being alive, and thou art dead." ". . . Because thou sayest, 'I am rich and have grown wealthy and have need of nothing' and dost not know that thou art the wretched and miserable and poor and blind and naked one."

The letters also contain both summons to reform and threat of punishment: "Remember therefore whence thou hast fallen, and repent and do the former works; or else I will come to thee, and will remove thy lamp-stand. . . ." "In like manner repent, or else I will come to thee quickly, and will fight against them with the sword of my mouth." "And I gave her time that she might repent, and she does not want to repent of her immorality. Behold, I will cast her upon a bed, and those who commit adultery with her into great tribulation, unless they repent of their deeds." "For I do not find thy works complete before my God. Remember therefore what thou hast received and heard, and observe it and repent." "I counsel thee to buy of me gold refined by fire, that thou mayest become rich, and mayest be clothed in white garments, and that the shame of thy nakedness may not appear, and to anoint thy eyes with eye salve that thou mayest see. As for me, those whom I love I rebuke and chastise."

All the letters exhort the bishops to persevere and overcome. We must be sure that we understand the word: to overcome the world's resistance to that which is from God. This resistance is so great that the believer is continually tempted to believe that his faith is alien to earth and senseless. Danger of scandal in other words, of the sense of folly and unnaturalness in the eyes of the world and our own eyes. To overcome is to persevere to the end in spite of everything, to carry faith through all 'impossibilities.' Thus God's message is infiltrated into the world, realized in the world, and the new creation is begun.

To extract wisdom from apparent folly; to believe in the new that is to come in spite of all evidence to the contrary—this is too much for man alone. He can perform this act of faith only through the spirit of God. Hence in all Epistles the sentence: "He who has an ear, let him hear what the Spirit says to the churches." He says that it is possible to overcome.

And he proclaims immeasurable fulfillment: "Him who overcomes I will permit to eat of the tree of life, which is in the paradise of my God." "To him who overcomes, I will give the hidden manna, and I will give him a white pebble, and upon the pebble a new name written, which no one knows except him who receives it." "And to him who overcomes, and who keeps my works unto the end, I will give authority over the nations. And he shall rule them with a rod of iron, . . . and I will give him the morning star." "He who overcomes shall be arrayed thus in white garments, and I will not blot his name out of the book of life, but I will confess his name before my Father, and before his angel." "He who overcomes, I will make him a pillar in the temple of my God, and never more shall he go outside. And I will write upon him the name of my God, and the name of the city of my God—the new Jerusalem, which comes down out of heaven from my God—and my new name." "He who overcomes, I will permit him to sit with me upon my throne; as I also have overcome and have sat with my Father on his throne."

We shall speak of the meaning of these promises in a later chapter.

III

THRONE
AND THRONING ONE

The first three chapters of Revelation form the introduction. They reveal Christ as the Lord of history, walking, all-seeing among the golden "lamp-stands" of his churches. With the fourth chapter begins the heart of the Apocalypse: the vision of the last things. I beg the reader to read verses one to eleven before we examine the sentences separately.

The seer says that he "looked." What he saw was nothing visible to the natural eyes of anyone living among natural objects, nor was it a formation of his fantasy. The vision takes place outside the visionary when he is seized by the spirit of God and rendered capable of a higher visual power. Then what he is meant to see unrolls before his eyes.

The seer is "in heaven." We have already considered what that is: neither the space between the stars, nor a particularly intrinsic state of soul, but the holy transcendency of God. Heaven is where God is alone with himself; it is the unapproachable light into which the visionary has been transported by his vision.

"In heaven . . . a door standing open." It is futile to reflect intellectually upon the meaning of this image. One must ask those who have experienced such things; they will affirm that they do exist— not only doors leading from one spiritual realm to another, but the walls that separate them. Some doors between the known and the unknown can be opened by the seer himself through purging, concentration, patience, effort. Others can be opened only from within. This door is opened for the seer, and the trumpet-like voice that had spoken so mightily at the beginning of the vision bids him enter. We are not told who it is that speaks; it is simply the "voice" summoning the spirit, like that which called John the Baptist in the desert. It commands: "Come up hither," for that also exists—'up' and 'down' and 'across' in the spirit: expressions of the height of the spirit, and the depth of its profundity, and the immeasurable breadth of its all-inclusiveness. The spirit is vital, holy, creative, renovating; in it exist a multitude of powers, events, differentiations—far more than in any earthly reality.

At the sound of the voice, immediately the seer was "in the spirit": lifted out of himself into a higher reality previously inaccessible. That is the coming "up hither" simultaneously commanded and made possible by the commander. In the unapproachable light of heaven stands a throne. He who sits on it is like a blazing jewel. No further details are given—neither as to form nor face; everything seems to be lost in the radiance. All that is said is that Someone thrones there in costly glory.

Around the throne runs a rainbow "like to an emerald." (Image flows into image, suggesting the inexpressible.) About the central throne stand twenty-four seats or lesser thrones on which twenty-four elders sit clad in white garments, gold crowns on their heads. He who thrones in their midst is God, the Creator and Father. The twenty-four are the personification of humanity before God. Elders, not youths. Youth does not comprehend the essence of humanity, whose ultimate crowning is old age: the fulfillment of all perseverance, season in which the heights and depths of human existence have been measured and all things brought to maturity.

From the throne issue "flashes of lightning, rumblings and peals of thunder"—symbolic of the destructive, commanding, all-shaking omnipotence of God. Seven lamps burn before the great throne. We have already encountered them. They are the seven spirits of God, the seven congregations: reality of his kingdom scattered over the world.

Before the throne "a sea of glass like to crystal": an infinity of radiance. At center before the throne stand the four mysterious creatures.

They resemble those in the Old Testament vision of the prophet Ezechiel (1:5). Heavenly creatures "full of eyes"; they are all gaze, sight, clarity and depth of comprehension. These are the Cherubim. Where has their strange terribleness vanished? What is left of them in the popular consciousness today in the form of "cherubs" is little more than a sentimentality. Animal figures. We have yet to reflect on the significance of the animal in the presence of the divine. The first is a lion, or rather "like a lion," for it cannot really be named. The second resembles a calf; the third has a human face; the fourth suggests a flying eagle. Each has six wings—tremendous soaring power; in other words, power to scale the heights of the spirit and to measure its breadth. The wings are strewn with eyes, and their every height-, every depth-, every breadth-overcoming vision is given voice in a mighty never-ending cry of amazement and adoration: "Holy, holy, holy, the Lord God almighty, who was, and who is, and who is coming." Cry of superhuman dimensions from superhuman creatures stunned by eternal reality. The All in All pierces the heart of their being, from which their essence streams in a thunderous, unbroken cry.

As often as the creatures cry out, the elders fall on their faces before him who is seated on the throne; casting the crowns of their dignity at his feet, they worship his eternal life. We are told that the creatures cease their cry neither by day nor by night, and each time it sounds, the ancients fall down and adore. Something infinite is groping for expression, act continuously renewed in the perfect simplicity and silence of eternity.

Among the wealth of details in this vision, one detail stays the attention: on the throne sits Someone. The modern no longer knows what a throne is, nor how one sits on a throne, how one *thrones.*

Looking back, we encounter the mighty throning depicted in Egyptian sculpture. What quiet power emanates from these statues of gods and rulers! We find it again in early Greek art, and (Christianized) in the mosaics of the first Christian centuries and in the stone figures of the opening middle ages. Then it vanishes. Personages no longer throne—they merely sit. And even the sitting be-comes more and more restless. The ancient throning was not stiff—its movement lay in the potential power of the figure, in its stillness, intensity. Now movement flings itself to the surface. Sitting has be-come careless, a flighty interim between coming and going. Some-thing at the very root of our lives has changed.

When we ask a man today what he considers life, the answer will always be more or less the same: Life is tension, flinging oneself to-wards a goal; it is creation and destruction and new creation. It is that which rushes and foments, streams and storms. Thus the modern finds it difficult to realize that also the omnipotent present is life; in-tensity of gathered forces; power that vibrates in stillness. For him life is linked to the flow of time. It is change, crossing over, the constantly new. Life resting in permanency and bordering on the eternal is be-yond his comprehension. When he considers God, he thinks of the restlessly creative one. Indeed, he is inclined to see the Maker himself in an unending process of becoming that arches from an infinitely dis-tant past into an infinitely distant future. The God of the pure present, immutable, realizing himself in the reality of his existence, does not appeal to him. And when he hears of an eternal life in which all meaning is to fulfill itself, he is likely to grow uncomfortable: what does one do with an existence in which 'nothing happens'? The throne stands for the majesty of the God of the immaculate present. It stands for him who lives in eternal stillness, who in the timeless sim-plicity of his will created, sustains, and reigns over all things. Before his countenance, earthly toil and struggle is but passageway, and their claim to be genuine life superlative nonsense.

This then the image of God that dominates Revelation. God does not speak; he silently contains the meaning of all things. God does not act, but all power to act comes from him. All things have been made by him; all events have been willed by him. Not even his face or form is visible, only a blaze of costliness that the eye is unable to penetrate; yet all form that is takes its shape and significance from him. He appears to be merely present; yet those who see truly, the four living creatures and the twenty-four elders, are shaken by the universality of his activating power. They render him the honor that is alone his due: adoration.

All that happens, happens in God's presence, but it is the Son who acts. We have already seen him "who walks in the midst of the seven golden lamp-stands" as the Ruler of history (Apoc. 2:1). Soon he will appear as the Lamb who has accomplished redemption and therefore possesses the meaning of existence; who by surrendering himself, has drawn all creation into the nuptials of eternal life. We shall also see the Rider of the white horse leading his throngs to victory; the Judge passing sentence on history from his high white throne; and finally, him to whom the Apostle at the end of the Apocalypse calls, "Come, Lord Jesus!"

He who thrones has sent forth this Son, who acts through him, performing his paternal will. To him Christ returns, placing all things back in his hands.

IV

Adoration

In a powerful image the twenty-four elders, representatives of all humanity before God, clothed in festive garments and crowned with gold, rise, prostrate themselves, and place their crowns at the feet of the throning One, crying: "Worthy art thou, O Lord our God, to receive glory and honor and power; for thou hast created all things, and because of thy will they existed, and were created" (Apoc. 4:9–11).

The act of standing is a timeless human gesture. It says: I am. Here I stand, strong and determined to defend my rights—if necessary, by force. He who adores, sacrifices this independent attitude. Originally, prostration was the vassal's expression of self-obliteration before the power of his lord. Here the same idea is transposed to the spiritual plane. The worshipper's whole person says: Thine the power, not mine! Rise and reign! There where the worshipper stands, in the sphere of his personality, God alone should rule, he who really *is*. The act of worship has plumbless depths. This clearing the way for God, this will to see in him all genuine being and power can become increasingly pure, complete, essential; the 'space' allowed him ever freer and more vast.

But this is only one side of adoration, and it has two. Physical power is unequivocal: the storm is stronger than I, so I must cede; sickness is stronger than I, so I succumb. The enemy is stronger than I, so I am conquered. This is so obvious, that if I have resisted honorably, my defeat is no disgrace. But when it is a question of the inner person and his dignity, it is another story. It is one thing to bow, outwardly, to superior force; quite another to do homage to it inwardly, to prostrate my intrinsic personality before it. This is permissible only when that power is answerable before truth, justice, and goodness. Let us for a moment make a ridiculous supposition: that God, the supreme power and immeasurable reality, were only brute force—nothing else. Then it would be wrong to abase myself before him. Though he were to destroy my life, my person would have to refuse him adoration. He who is adored must not only have power, but must also be worthy of that power. This is precisely what is expressed by the text: "Worthy are thou, O Lord our God, to receive glory and honor and power. . . ." (Apoc. 4:11).

Why is he worthy? Because he has "created all things" and therefore must be all good, all true and all holy. His holiness is what makes him worthy of his omnipotence. Now adoration makes sense: not only the body bows before God, but the soul. Not only domination of feeling, but act of the free individual. What he honors is not simply God's reality and illimitable power, but his sacred truth and goodness. Hence to prostrate oneself before him is more than inevitable; it is right. To worship God is good because it expresses a truth that is as eternally fresh as it is plumbless. That is why the dignity of person is not only preserved in the act, but grounded in it, for man's dignity is a product of truth, and when he bows before God he acts in truth and its freedom.

The act of adoration has something infinitely genuine, beneficent, constructive about it—something salutary. Many associations meet here. In the realm of the spirit there is fervor, depth, height, intimacy, creative energy. Everything that exists in the tangible world, exists, far more genuinely, in the spiritual. There too perfect purity exists. Spiritual purity is a very great thing. The body has its purity, the heart as well; likewise the soul has its purity, the source of its health.

The purity of the spirit is dependent upon truth. A spirit is pure when it makes clear-cut distinctions between great and little, good and bad; when it refuses to bend yes into no and no into yes, but keeps them undistorted by a straight either-or. This doesn't mean that with the resultant clarity the good is also already accomplished and the bad avoided; it means something much more elementary: that virtue is never called vice, and vice virtue. Purity of spirit lies at the beginning of things, there where the first stirrings set in, where conceptions of being and doing are formed. It is that initial authenticity in which the true meaning of words is grounded and their relation to each other is corrected, their edges are trimmed. Spirit becomes impure through essential dishonesty. When it attempts to call evil good, it becomes essentially corrupt. A lie is always evil, but worse than its conscious evil is loss of the fundamental sense of truth. The spirit that errs is not yet impure—for example when it judges facts falsely, uses words incorrectly, confuses images. It is impure when it is indifferent to truth; when it no longer desires to think cleanly or to measure by the standards of eternity; when it no longer knows that the dignity and honor of truth are its own dignity and honor; when it besmudges the sense of words—which is the sense of things and of existence itself—robbing them of their austerity and nobility.

From uncleanliness of spirit a man can sicken; a completely different kind of sickness from that of an accident or contagion, different from that which results from disorder of the functions or of the nerves. The one causes physical illness, the other 'psychic' in the careless use of the word. What is usually meant by the term is a sickness of the braincells or derangement of the instincts. *Can* the spirit itself sicken? It can—through its relation to truth. Not already by sinning against truth; but easily enough by deserting or cancelling truth, by subordinating it to 'necessity,' by screening it in a fog of ambiguousness. Then the spirit sickens. It would be difficult to say how many so-called psychic illnesses are not really the results of a genuine psychic disorder: of a rupture between the spirit and the truth from which it stems, for as the spirit lives from truth, the body and its sensibility live from the spirit.

Divine worship protects the purity of spirit. As long as a person bows his head before his Maker as before one "worthy" because he is holy and true, that person will be immune to intrinsic deception. Health and purity of spirit are man's greatest forces, but also, as human nature now is, his most vulnerable and seducible. They need protection. Some sure means of distinguishing between true and false, pure and impure must exist. That a person fails to do the right thing after he has recognized it is serious, and he will be called to judgment because of it. But incomparably worse is a breach with truth itself: intrinsic deception readable in the eyes because it has taken hold of the spirit. That is why something must exist in which the truth of the heart can constantly renew itself, in which the spirit can be cleansed, the eye cleared, the character strengthened. And there is: adoration. Nothing is more important for man than to incline his spirit before God, personally to experience the truth that is God—this is great and sacred and salutary for body and soul.

In these meditations we have not often spoken of practical things. Our attention was concentrated almost entirely on attempting to understand Christ. Here though we must touch on the practical, because it concerns the ultimate foundation of our whole existence. We should make a point of regularly practicing worship. There are two hours in the day that are particularly suitable: early morning and evening. Today we no longer feel their full significance, because the fall of darkness and the return of light have not the power over us that they had over people who lived more intimately with nature and the sun. Yet we are still instinctively conscious of evening as a foreshadowing of the end of our earthly existence, just as we associate a sense of new life with early morning. These are the hours that naturally invite worship, and we should use them, whether or not we happen to feel the urge. For prayer is not solely an expression of inner life, it is also an act of self-discipline. Adoration does not often come spontaneously; it must be learned, and to this end practiced. We should kneel, center all our thoughts on the fact that God is and reigns; that he is worthy of omnipotence, worthy to be God—perhaps then we too will discover great joy in this contemplation that has inflamed so many saints.

If we need words of adoration we should look for them in Holy Scripture, here in the Apocalypse, for example, in the psalms, and in the books of the Prophets. Perhaps we find words of our own, or incline our hearts mutely under the weight of the knowledge and reverence they contain. Even when we are tired, inert, definitely unmoved to worship, it is something to place ourselves in God's presence and to remain there for a while with a feeling of—to use the humblest word—respect. Such moments will work their way into our consciousness, bringing their truth with them; particularly if they are permitted to bear fruit in our daily lives, helping us to refrain from an untruth because God is Truth, or to act with justice towards another because God thrones in holiness.

V

THE LAMB

God dominates every move in the Apocalypse, but indirectly; he whom he sent forth, Christ, is the immediate impelling force. In the opening chapter of Revelation we encounter him under the golden lamp-stands. The fifth chapter reveals him in a second form, that of the Lamb.

"And I saw a strong angel proclaiming with a loud voice, 'Who is worthy to open the scroll, and to break the seals thereof?' And no one in heaven, or on earth, or under the earth, was able to open the scroll or to look thereon. And I wept much, because no one was found worthy to open the scroll or to look thereon.

"And one of the elders said to me, 'Do not weep; behold, the lion of the tribe of Juda, the root of David, has overcome to open the scroll and its seven seals.' And I saw, and behold, in the midst of the throne and of the four living creatures, and in the midst of the elders, a Lamb standing, as if slain, having seven horns and seven eyes, which are the seven spirits of God sent forth into all the earth. And he came and took the scroll out of the right hand of him who sat upon the throne. And when he had opened the scroll, the four living creatures and the twenty-four elders fell down before the Lamb, having each a harp and golden bowls full of incense, which are the prayers of the saints.

"And they sing a new canticle, saying, 'Worthy art thou to take the scroll and to open its seals; for thou wast slain, and hast redeemed us for God with thy blood, out of every tribe and tongue and people and nation, and hast made them for our God a kingdom and priests, and they shall reign over the earth.'

"And I beheld, and I heard a voice of many angels round about the throne, and the living creatures and the elders, and the number of them was thousands of thousands, saying with a loud voice, 'Worthy is the Lamb who was slain to receive power and divinity and wisdom and strength and honor and glory and blessing.' And every creature that is in heaven and on the earth and under the earth, and such as are on the sea, and all that are in them, I heard them all saying, 'To him who sits upon the throne, and to the Lamb, blessing and honor and glory and dominion, forever and ever' " (Apoc. 5:1–14).

The Lamb stands "in the midst" of the throne, the four creatures and the elders. In other words, he stands before him who sits on the throne, God. All things are created by God and placed before him; they are borne and supported by him, seen and judged. The Lamb also stands before him who thrones, for the Son of God has entered into creation. Christ lived "before God"; not only actually, as a man in time and space, but because he loved the Father and lived in obedience to him. At the same time he is himself God; hence the elders' adoration both of him upon the throne and of the Lamb before it.

We know the figure of the Lamb through the liturgy and Christian art and through Holy Scripture itself; not only in the Book of Revelation, but also in St. John's Gospel, the Savior is represented as the Lamb (1:29, 36). Still perhaps we question the symbol. God's Son represented by an animal? Then we remember that also the Holy Spirit was seen in the form of a dove. What does this mean?

In what form could God be appropriately represented? Our first reaction to the question replies: Not in any! He is "the Fashionless One," as the mystics called him: he who is, who acts, who fulfills and beatifies; whom no form can contain. One can say only what he is not: He is not heaven, not ocean, not tree, not a person, nor anything that can be named. He is he; his self-created Word and the heart's intimate yet strange experience of him are to be believed. Nevertheless, he must be expressed in some form. To see him only as the Fashionless One would be at first very pure; but it would lead to his gradual disappearance from our lives. We must name him; must indicate him through forms, and this is precisely what Scripture does.

In what form would God seemingly be least appropriately represented? Isn't the almost instinctive reply, "In the human?" Why? Because it is our own, the most familiar and the most profoundly tempting. Tempting because it would be so easy to say: God is a being similar to man; he is immeasurably huge and powerful, but a being much like we are—as the Greeks, and many other polytheistic peoples, imagined their gods. The reversed temptation is also there: to say, One who appears in the form of a human being cannot be God—as the rigid monotheism of the Jews, of Islam and rationalism insist. Christianity runs the danger of scandal by saying: God "was made flesh." Yet this is the Alpha and Omega of her message. Jesus' human form is the revelation of the living God. In the profoundest sense of the word, God is a 'human' God; though he never for an instant ceases to be he who cannot be confounded with men. This word about his humanity comes not from us, but from himself, by his own revelation.

But then what form would most appropriately express God? The answer is doubtless: That furthest removed from man—empty space, for example. (It is a powerful idea of Islam's this representing the presence of God in her mosques by a room stripped of image and implement.) Or perhaps the spaciousness of heaven. Or silence. Or a rocky slope, or the sun. The power of such mute things is great— so great that it can lead to magic. Between this inanimate realm and man stands the animal. It is familiar to us because it is alive, as we are, yet unknown. We know how animals behave, we dominate and exploit them. Yet they remain a mystery. Does an animal ever regard us as one man regards another? It is necessary to be regarded in order to be understood—and to understand. Understanding comes only with the interchange of the 'I' and 'you' through the regard. The animal knows no such interchange. It regards the human either as an advantage or as a danger. It may flee him or accept him; may draw him into its circle, possibly even grow to consider him part of its life; never does it look him deep in the eye, for this is reserved for human exchange. Yet for man the animal is somehow a revelation. Human traits, dispositions, instincts, psychological reactions are often astoundingly evident in certain animals. How often does it suddenly dawn on us—Why, he looks like a fox, horse, vulture! Or the other way around—in fox, horse, tiger this or that human quality seems to be startlingly at home! Isolated from moderating, pacifying, human influences, these qualities seem like elemental forces.

This is precisely the point we wanted, for something similar is valid also in connection with God. Because the animal is closer to nature and her forces, because it is not a person, but simply a living being, it can express divine traits in a manner that is superhuman. Thus Christ appears in the figure of the Lamb. The image was familiar to early Christian readers. In southern countries the Lamb is the animal most used for nourishment; it was also the usual sacrificial offering, particularly in the cult of the Old Testament. That is why its image is so suggestive of the Savior, as one who surrendered himself into the hands of the enemy, to be consumed upon the sacrificial altar. Let us recall what has already been said of the nature of the vision. It is thus that we must imagine the Lamb, feeling within us the white helplessness of the delicate, defenceless creature like one "slain." Death in its heart, yet filled with a power that reaches to the core of existence, it emerges, unknown, bizarre from the impenetrability of God, yet movingly familiar. One artist, Matthias Grünewald, has succeeded in suggesting this image. The Lamb under the cross in his great painting of the crucifixion is an apocalyptical creature.

The text also speaks of its power. The Lamb alone is capable of breaking the seals of the scroll. Human existence is full of questions. "What is that?" asks the child. The adult replies with some logical explanation that hardly tells the child what it wants to know, and if it seems satisfied with the answer, then only because its ear has caught something more than the syllables spoken. What the child is after is the essence of the object in question; this no one can give. Adam could and did when he named the animals, "for whatsoever Adam called any living creature the same is its name" (Gen. 2:19). Adam called it by its essence, which escapes us. Even more difficult is the question, "Why is that?" Why the dissatisfaction, suffering, destruction, guilt? Science has no answer; neither has philosophy, though the problematic is her special field. Or isn't it problematic that over and over again people enthusiastically celebrated on all sides gravely step to the fore with 'the answer,' yet throughout the centuries the problem remains unmitigated, unshaken? ". . . No one was found worthy to open the scroll or to look thereon." The world is so deeply sealed in the enigma, that its solution can come only from elsewhere. Not simply from God; to say so is unchristian; for fallen man "God" himself is questionable. Not from the Father, then; he who thrones behind the Cherubim does not speak directly. He does not open the scroll; it lies closed in his right hand. He gives it to him who is able to open it, Christ the Lamb. He has the power to open the scroll, because he has suffered the world and her questions through to the end without ever succumbing to her. He can answer. And not with this or that teaching, but with the light that falls from his person over all things. In the measure that the believer surrenders himself to Christ, the seals fall away, and he knows the sense of the answer, even if he is unable to express it.

It is said that the Lamb ransomed the world from its bonds: from the captivity of the senses, of pride, of the subtle seduction of action, of the power of death. For there is slavery in all these, bonds that weigh heaviest when man considers himself most free. The Lamb has delivered the world of them all, because he personally penetrated them to the root. We have already spoken of the dark void into which Christ worked his way, redeeming at every step, making kings and priests of his redeemed, crowning them with power and sanctity. And not only the one or the other, not only the talented, or those of the chosen race, but men, women and children of all tongues, lands and nations. From all walks and stages of human existence he has selected them, his enfranchised ones, to form his great new nation of the saved. Their number is legion.

In the seventh chapter we again meet the image of the Lamb and his redemptory power: "After this I saw a great multitude which no man could number, out of all nations and tribes and peoples and tongues, standing before the throne and before the Lamb, clothed in white robes, and with palms in their hands. . . . And one of the elders spoke and said to me, 'These who are clothed in white robes, who are they? and whence have they come?' And I said to him, 'My lord, thou knowest.' And he said to me, 'These are they who have come out of the great tribulation, and have washed their robes and made them white in the blood of the Lamb. Therefore they are before the throne of God, and serve him day and night in his temple, and he who sits upon the throne will dwell with them. They shall neither hunger nor thirst any more, neither shall the sun strike them nor any heat. For the Lamb who is in the midst of the throne will shepherd them, and will guide them to the fountains of the waters of life, and God will wipe away every tear from their eyes' " (Apoc. 7:9–17).

Here it is not from servitude, but from guilt that man is saved. They "have washed their robes and made them white in the blood of the Lamb" and are liberated from the tribulations of existence: from hunger and thirst, from the stress of the sun, and from all sorrow, for they are redeemed to the fullness of life.

And once again in the opening verses of chapter fourteen: "And I saw, and behold, the Lamb was standing upon Mount Sion, and with him a hundred and forty-four thousand having his name and the name of his Father written on their foreheads. And I heard a voice from heaven like a voice of many waters, and like a voice of loud thunder; and the voice that I heard was as of harpers playing on their harps. And they were singing as it were a new song before the throne, and before the four living creatures and the elders; and no one could learn the song except those hundred and forty-four thousand, who have been purchased from the earth. These are they who are not defiled with women; for they are virgins" (14:1–4).

Here surges the mighty retinue of those who belong to the Lamb in a special bond of love: who have foregone all other love for his. The content of their existence is expressed by two acts: these intimates of the Lamb follow him wherever he goes and sing a canticle only they can learn.

VI

The Seven Seals

In the right hand of the throning One lies a scroll with seven seals that no one can open. It contains the meaning of existence and of the future. Before the throne stands the Lamb, death impotent in it. It has overcome and redeemed; hence its power over the seals. It takes the scroll and opens. Now begins the first chain of events depicted in the Book of Revelation.

"And I saw that the Lamb had opened the first of the seven seals, and I heard one of the four living creatures saying, as with a voice of thunder, 'Come!' And I saw, and behold, a white horse, and he who was sitting on it had a bow, and there was given him a crown, and he went forth as a conqueror to conquer.

"And when he opened the second seal, I heard the second living creature saying, 'Come!' And there went forth another horse, a red one; and to him who was sitting on it, it was given to take peace from the earth, and that men should kill one another, and there was given him a great sword.

"And when he opened the third seal, I heard the third living creature saying, 'Come!' And I saw, and behold, a black horse, and he who was sitting on it had a balance in his hand. And I heard as it were a voice in the midst of the four living creatures, saying, 'A measure of wheat for a denarius, and three measures of barley for a denarius, and do not harm the wine and the oil.'

"And when he opened the fourth seal, I heard the voice of the fourth living creature saying, 'Come!' And I saw, and behold, a pale-green horse, and he who was sitting on it—his name is Death, and hell was following him. And there was given him power over the four parts of the earth, to kill with sword, with famine, and with death, and with the beasts of the earth.

"And when he opened the fifth seal, I saw under the altar the souls of those who had been slain for the word of God, and for the witness that they bore. And they cried with a loud voice, saying, 'How long, O Lord (holy and true), dost thou refrain from judging and from avenging our blood on those who dwell on the earth?' And there was given to each of them a white robe; and they were told to rest a little while longer, until the number of their fellow-servants and their brethren who are to be slain, even as they had been, should be complete" (Apoc. 6:1–11).

Four steeds: white, red, black and fallow, like their riders. The four mounted ones signify, or rather are, four powers: dangers, events to come.

When the fifth seal is opened an altar suddenly appears. It was not mentioned before. "Under" it are souls that cry out with loud voices. Let us recall the nature of the vision, that which could appear to us in dream: something looms high, altar-like; we are permitted to see under it a space crowded with living beings held captive. They press against one another, cry out for something. Each is given a "white robe," expression of a pure and festive existence, and told that an end has been set to his suffering, that he should be patient.

The breaking of the sixth seal reveals new images of horror, terrible processes about to rock the foundations of human existence, rendering all who are alive: rich and poor, powerful and impotent, master and hireling equal in their terror. And the words that Christ spoke in his sermon on judgment, prophecy of the coming catastrophe, ring out: "Then they will begin to say to the mountains, 'Fall on us,' and to the hills, 'Cover us!' " (Luke 23:30).

"After this I saw four angels standing at the four corners of the earth, holding fast the four winds of the earth, that no wind should blow over the earth, or over the sea, or upon any tree. And I saw another angel ascending from the rising of the sun, having the seal of the living God; and he cried with a loud voice to the four angels, who had it in their power to harm the earth and the sea, saying, 'Do not harm the earth or the sea or the trees, till we have sealed the servants of our God on their foreheads.' And I heard the number of those who were sealed, a hundred and forty-four thousand sealed, out of every tribe of the children of Israel; of the tribe of Juda, twelve thousand sealed; of the tribe of Ruben, twelve thousand; of the tribe of Gad, twelve thousand; of the tribe of Aser, twelve thousand; of the tribe of Nephthali, twelve thousand; of the tribe of Manasses, twelve thousand; of the tribe of Simeon, twelve thousand; of the tribe of Levi, twelve thousand; of the tribe of Issachar, twelve thousand; of the tribe of Zabulon, twelve thousand; of the tribe of Joseph, twelve thousand; of the tribe of Benjamin, twelve thousand sealed" (Apoc. 7:1–8).

The angels hold back the four winds (weather-forces of the four points of the compass) to prevent them from breaking loose; thus a protective area is formed. Into this descends an angel, carrying the "seal" of divine election. This is the sign of those who belong to God, who have been seized by God and bear his mark upon and within them. (Baptism and Confirmation are seals, preparatory for the ultimate seal to come!) Those signed with the seal are God's elect mentioned in Christ's judgment speech: even they would succumb to the agony of these last terrors, were not God's hand upon them. They have been chosen from the twelve tribes of "the children of Israel," in other words, from all humanity. From each tribe twelve thousand. Twelve is the number of universality. Twelve times twelve further magnifies the sum, and "thousand" multiplies it again past all count.

In the midst of catastrophe the dynamic multitudes of the saved. Souls without number have been called to the fullness of life. The content of their existence is God: he who sits upon the throne is with them; they serve him, led by the Lamb, who guides them to the waters of life, and we are reminded of the words about the One Shepherd and the one flock.

Then follows the loosening of the seventh seal: "And when he opened the seventh seal, there was silence in heaven, as it were for half an hour.

"And I saw the seven angels who stand before God, and there were given to them seven trumpets. And another angel came and stood before the altar, having a golden censer; and there was given to him much incense, that he might offer it with the prayers of all the saints upon the golden altar which is before the throne. And with the prayers of the saints there went up before God from the angel's hand the smoke of the incense" (Apoc. 8:1–4).

First, silence "as it were for half an hour"—half of a short lapse of time. Then seven angels stand before God's inmost presence. They are given seven trumpets. The trumpet is a mysterious instrument—symbol of the eruptive power of God. Remember the trumpets that blared from Sinai, that shattered the walls of Jericho? Their fanfare sounds in the Last Judgment.

The seven trumpets proclaim a new series of events, and we begin to recognize the general structure of the Book of Revelation: the introductory vision brings the vision of the scroll with the seven seals; the breaking of the seals is followed by the first seven events; from out the seventh event step seven angels with trumpets, who in turn proclaim seven new events. Thus one chain of images issues from the other.

What does it all mean? Not that these figures will once actually appear as described on earth. On the contrary, the apocalyptical riders symbolize recurrent aspects of earth's existence, characteristics of world-evolution with the incidents that mark it. They do not gallop that one ultimate hour through history, but again and again. Whenever certain events take place, it is they, the horsemen, who ride over the world.

Apocalyptical riders—what, exactly, does the adjective signify? Not merely something predicted, but something suggestive of the sense of our transitoriness in the face of eternity, of what becomes of temporal existence when eternity rises to replace it. From our own human outlook we are apt to feel that existence is complete in itself; that it is the primary, natural, self-understood reality which is the point of departure for all things. Behind it is nothing. Once the natural explanation for a thing has been given, it seems comprehensible and proper. The eternal, on the other hand, is apparently secondary, a mere backdrop that can be sensed, hoped or feared; never definitely known, for its existence is too uncertain. One may take it or leave it. It is possible to say—perhaps even with conviction—that it is non-existent, that the temporal is everything.

In the realm of the Apocalypse, the eternal stirs, swells to a tremendous power that pushes in our neat little doors. The temporal, which only a moment ago seemed so self-sufficient and safe, begins to totter. Its very 'naturalness' vanishes, and it reveals itself as it is: transitoriness in revolt, existing as though God were non-existent. Ripped from its self-complacency and suddenly strange and terrified, its profound questionableness becomes evident. The apocalyptical is that which reveals temporality's true face when it has been demasked by the eternal. It was given to St. John to behold this. No pleasurable favor, this gift of the visionary eye. He who has it can no longer look upon the things of existence without trembling at sight of 'the hair' by which they hang. He lives under the awful pressure of constant uncertainty. Nothing is safe. The borders between time and eternity melt away. From all sides eternity's overwhelming reality closes in upon him, mounting from the depths, plunging from the heights. For the visionary life ceases to be peaceful and simple. He is required to live under duress, that others may sense how things really stand with them; that they not only learn that this or that is to take place—still less the futile details of the time and circumstances—but that they may possess the essential knowledge of what all existence undergoes at the approach of the eternal. Only he reads the Apocalypse properly who leaves it with some sense of this.

It is impossible to define the apocalyptical riders separately, for their symbols overlap. It is said that the last is death, but the second and third also bring death in their train, and war is followed by famine. Let us simply call them figures of dread. But why apocalyptical? We might say, because they proclaim the final terrors, which the Lord indicated in his sermons on the Last Judgment. But Christian instinct has at all times recognized in the Four, riders who ride all years, at all hours, over the earth. Not only are they something to come, already now, they *are*.

Let us try to interpret them. The first rider is given the bow of victory, and he sets out to conquer. We might say: this is he who leads truth to victory, penetrating power that triumphs over illusion and assorts all things according to their true worth. How does he accomplish this? Perhaps, as has been suggested, through history: world history as world judgment? Perhaps in the course of history all things work themselves out into clarity, so that good and bad, true and false are discernible? How is it then that obscurity over precisely these points seems to be an integral part of history, and that clarity in one place is always paid with darkness in another? The distinction meant here is something else: clarification of values, justification of good, judgment pronounced upon human works—yes, but so that herein the ultimate light from God breaks through. The gleam of this prophetic light, precursor of the great ultimate enlightenment to come, this is the "apocalyptical" behind all catastrophe. Admittedly it is given only to few, to the visionary and to those rendered profoundly discerning by faith, to "read the signs of the times" (Matt. 16:3). The word of the visionary, however, does help the Christian with a sense for these things towards clarity.

The next rider, on the red horse, is War. This does not mean that war in itself is apocalyptical. It becomes so because from God's viewpoint, its killing and destroying are a horrible consequence of man's fall. It is the same with the third rider, who is perhaps Hunger, and with the fourth, who is supposed to be Death: death and decay and the agony of death's night. These are the scourges of humanity; they are not meant to be accepted as 'facts,' or as social evils that must be outlawed, or philosophically as elements of historical life, or ethically, as punishment for past sin—but simply as a revelation of the final horrors. They are the first ripples of the ultimate flood, announcements of the coming God-sent catastrophe in which everything sinful, false and degenerate in man will be laid bare.

Similar reflections are suggested by the event that follows the breaking of the next seal. That human beings must suffer for the truth and the name of God is something we naturally regard as terrible. But the fifth vision reveals still more. We hear the victims of violence cry to heaven for revenge, hear heaven reply: Be patient, even though nothing seems to happen! Do not be deceived by God's silence! God is silent, and men think their power assured. In reality its limits have long since been set. Injustice steadily increases; when in God's eyes the measure is full, vengeance will come. The menace of this supreme chastisement flashes 'apocalyptically' in every scene of general violence, regardless of place or hour.

The vision of the sixth seal, on the other hand, seems to apply directly to the ultimate convulsions of the world, for the world was not naturally created and is not naturally sustained, but was created and continues to exist by the free will of God. Hence it will not come to any 'natural' end, but to the end provided by God. And because sin has heaped up such a terrible balance, which it continues to pile higher and higher, that end will be necessarily dreadful: utter destruction and judgment. Yet he who opens the seals—we must not forget this—is the Lamb. The last things occur through him, in connection with him. It is he who gives all things their ultimate character, who judges and fulfills.

VII

THINGS

The reader of Revelation is bound to notice the quantity of objects scattered throughout the Book: in the first vision the seven golden lamp-stands and seven stars, the tree of life and the crown woven from its leaves, the white pebble with the name upon it, the pillars in the temple of God, the communal feast; in the second vision the throne, the twenty-four elders with crowns and white garments, harps and censers; the sealed scroll, the Lamb and the four creatures. Then come the four riders on their four mounts. Many forms of nature are revealed: heaven, earth, seas, winds, stars, sun and moon, tree and seed. Multitudes gather with palm-leaves in their hands. Seven trumpets are distributed, and the divine seal is affixed. The Enemies of God also appear in various forms, with them the instruments of judgment and vengeance, thunder and lightning. An angel hands the seer a scroll which he is told to devour; then a reed with which he is commanded to measure a temple. A woman blazes across the sky, and an eagle sweeps to her aid. A sickle harvests the ripe grain, and the vats receive their grape. Seven vials or bowls of divine wrath pour out horrible plagues. And at last, the heavenly city sparkles in gold and crystal, jasper, pearl, emerald, sapphire, and endless nameless brilliance and glory. What does it mean, this multiplicity of things in eternity? Revelation describes the dislodging and consuming of time by the eternal—why this mass of earthly objects?

The Everlasting, God and his kingdom, speak constantly to man; were it otherwise, life would be senseless. But how does the Divine express himself?

Doubtless, the 'purest' manner of communication would be the simple stirring of the inner man by God, without word or image. There are people who are intensely conscious of his presence in and about them, who know themselves in his protection, under his guidance—all without the least image or 'voice' and yet with perfect clarity. In others this consciousness is less clear; in many it is entirely lacking, though one might also suppose that God speaks to every human being, whether he listens or not. For somewhere in every individual is that which the spiritual masters called the ground of the soul, the spirit's edge, the inner spark. It is not difficult to imagine that the silent divine eloquence continues unbrokenly in all of us, unnarrowed by the limits of form or sound; that this isolated existence of ours in the midst of so much strangeness, this dangling in senseless chance is only bearable because constantly, whether we register them or not, secret tidings of reassurance trickle through to us. We have been taught that we owe our existence to the eternal word of the Father; thus we may well suppose that on the groundfloor of our being the quiet converse between ourselves and him continues, and that it is from here that we draw our certainty of life's sense. True, the paternal word is spoken into noise and confusion, for man is no pure reality capable of receiving divine truth without misunderstanding and distortion. Vanity, stupidity, imagination use the flow of divine meaning for their own purposes, and not only in worldly things, but also in religious. We have good cause to remind ourselves constantly that our piety too is badly in need of redemption. Everything evil in man functions also (there all the more powerfully) in his religion. Thus the hidden word within us remains dark and confused until the clear, luminous Word manifests itself to us and is accepted by us: Jesus Christ.

God can also address us in a manner diametrically opposed to that just described: through all that is and occurs. For all things continuously stream from him; his creativeness does not simply set them down and leave them to run themselves, it sustains them. St. John tells us that all things were created by God and received from his word their being, truth and value. Thus everything is a mouth-piece through which the eternal speaks: every tree and creature, the breadth of heaven and the sea, the implement before me and the food I eat. There are people to whom this thousand-tongued language speaks clearly. Some are aware of the tidings of things only during certain hours, moments of their lives; some perhaps never.

We must all at least sense them, for otherwise existence would be unbearable. What is it that brings us into contact with things, gives us understanding of them? Not their concepts, but an intimate relationship between us. Perhaps we understand things only because we hear in them the quiet stream of the hidden, eternal word. I really believe that this is so; otherwise, we should be unable to comprehend and to love; we should be excluded from the great unity. If this intrinsic reassurance of God were to be suddenly plucked from all things without destroying them, how terrifying all the incomprehensible, unlovable instruments of death and sorrow about us would be! But we must be careful not to pollute and darken the divine converse with our own impurity and darkness; not to confuse it in our confusion, distorting it to fit our pride and pleasure, dragging it down into our worldliness, instead of adjusting our lives to its truth! We seldom stop to realize that such treatment of divine reassurance is the worst kind of highway robbery. Here in the domain of things too, we are in desperate need of redemption. It is a great mistake to believe that man can find truth in himself or in the things around him easily. It is not uncommon for someone particularly honored for his profundity and natural piety to suddenly break out with statements about God and Christ that are so false, so incomprehensibly distorted, that one is stricken by the heaven-shocking questionableness and unredeemed preposterousness of his views. Above the thousand-voiced chorus of God's word, the unique word of Revelation must sing its clear, unmistakable solo. It must separate and clarify; must open the ear and teach the heart with obedience and love. Then, not before, can the inspired accompaniment of things and their message be understood.

There is a third manner in which God can converse with man. He who is not only the hidden God, the completely unimaginable One without form or image, but the sovereign Lord of all things, has also spoken in plain words to living, historic men, in such and such a manner, at such and such a time, through specific human intermediaries. Finally, the eternal Word himself entered the world, became man, and remains to this day in our midst, speaking through human lips.

That God desired to communicate himself to us not only intrinsically, formlessly, but through a specific person; that he speaks not only in the countless shapes of existence, but also in the seeming arbitrariness of a historical advent; now, not always; thus, not in all manners; unique Word, yet valid for all time—this is admittedly difficult for the human mind to grasp and still more difficult to concede. Here lies the danger of scandal. Christ said what he wanted to say. We cannot question it, demanding why this and not that? He worked the miracles that his creative freedom held for opportune, and no human judgment is competent to weigh them. He suffered the fate shaped by the unique conditions of the hour, one that could have been different had he and the Jews so desired. He selected certain Apostles; he might have chosen differently, or not at all. He founded the Church in her particular form. She could have been entirely different; could also have not been founded. She watches over and distributes seven specific sacraments—no others, and seven, not two or ten. So it stands, the explicit, historical, personal, incarnate Word of God in time, from which the other means of divine expression receive their direction and clarity.

Now we begin to see what the things in the Apocalypse mean. In the realm of the incarnate Word, in the clarity of redemption, the implicit word of the *deus absconditus,* the hidden God, awakens, as does the divine word concealed in created things. These become pure and free. The inner voice is protected; the outer remains uncontaminated. Thus all things become luminous, their message audible. Through things eternity rises and thrusts itself into time. New creation, founded in the act of universal salvation and furthered by faithful living, obtains fulfillment and reveals itself. That which is only sensed in the ordinary Christian existence—the oneness of the wordless, inner speech of God, his sign-language in all created things, and the Word, Christ, with his clear, spoken Message—here becomes blazingly evident.

In the new creation God's holy otherness will stand in itself, independent of all earthly imagery (though confirmed by the things that bear witness to his divine creativeness), and purified, sealed in the truth of the incarnate Word. "For in him were created all things in the heavens and on the earth, things visible and things invisible, whether Thrones, or Dominations, or Principalities, or Powers. All things have been created through and unto him, and he is before all creatures, and in him all things hold together. . . . For it has pleased God the Father that in him all his fullness should dwell, and that through him he should reconcile to himself all things, whether on the earth or in the heavens, making peace through the blood of his cross" (Col. 1:16, 17, 19–20).

VIII

THE CHRISTIAN SENSE
OF HISTORY

The breaking of the last seal is followed by a new chain of visions, that of the seven angels with trumpets (Apoc. 8). Whenever a horn is blown, a new chastisement falls upon man. At the first blare, hail, fire and blood rain upon earth, destroying part of all growing things. At the second, something like a flaming mountain is cast into the sea, staining it far and wide blood-red. When the third trumpet sounds, a burning star falls into the rivers, poisoning a portion of all the sweet water of earth. At the signal of the fourth, the constellations lose a part of their light. An eagle sweeps through heavenly space crying "Woe, Woe, Woe to the inhabitants of the earth!" because of the three trumpetings to come! (Apoc. 8:13). His cry is strangely appalling, for the plunging star, Satan, the fallen angel, has been given the key to the bottomless pit: the power of destruction against mankind. And immediately an army of infernal locusts pours over the world, causing men gruesome torture. When the sixth trumpet blares, legions of demonic beings are turned loose to torment humanity. At this point, interim-acts are introduced. An enormous angel composed of heavenly bodies descends to earth. His voice calls down the thunder and causes it to speak, though what it says dare not be recorded. The mighty angel prophesies further horrors. Then he hands a scroll to the seer and commands him to eat it. It will be at once sweet and bitter, for the things to come are simultaneously consoling and dreadful. After this the visionary is given a reed and told to measure the temple of God and his destinies: knowledge, in other words, of the future of the temple and of time. Two prophets, "witnesses," filled with the power of word and deed, appear. They are killed and lie for a long time unburied; then, to the terror of their enemies, they are resurrected. At the seventh trumpeting we read: "And the seventh angel sounded the trumpet; and there were loud voices in heaven saying, 'The kingdom of this world has become the kingdom of our Lord and of his Christ, and he shall reign forever and ever'" (Apoc. 11:15). This is the signal for the ultimate things, and for Christ to intervene.

What follows is introduced by a "sign": "And a great sign appeared in heaven: a woman clothed with the sun, and the moon was under her feet, and upon her head a crown of twelve stars. And being with child, she cried out in her travail and was in the anguish of delivery" (Apoc. 12:1–2). A dragon dreadful to behold likewise appears in the heavens. It waits to devour the child about to be born. But the threatened woman is removed to a desert, where she is protected and cared for. This is the vision of Christ's birth, the blazing sign of the nations. The dragon is clearly Satan. The vision may be variously interpreted: for example, as the evocation of the birth of the Lord, against which the Demon revolted. Another interpretation of the Church fathers is that God tested the angels after creating them by showing them the future incarnation of his Son. Lucifer rebelled because he felt it beneath his dignity to serve (his subordinate in rank) the Son of Man, and was accordingly expelled from heaven. Be this as it may, the vision of the Incarnation introduces the last things. They unfold beneath its symbol. First the battle of Michael and his angels against the dragon, whereby the dragon is vanquished and falls. From the deeps he calls up a terrible creature, the first apocalyptical beast. We have already spoken of the animal form expressive of human characteristics and sentiments as well as of a superhuman essence. Here is the antithesis: revelation of the Antichrist. He will be a man of stupendous talents and spiritual force, of great knowledge and might. He will also be filled with religious power. Indeed, he will even have a certain resemblance to Christ, for it will be said also of him that he is mortally wounded and yet alive, in other words, that he has sacrificed himself and vanquished, so that there will be something perversely redemptory about him that is directed against the living God and his Christ. The beast defies God, blaspheming against him and his name. All men save those registered in the book of the Lamb submit to its power. Then a second beast appears, rising out of the land. Outwardly it resembles a lamb, but it speaks like a dragon. It proclaims the Antichrist, erects his image, performs miracles, and persuades men to worship him. Perhaps we are meant to see in this animal the evil counterpart of him who proclaimed the Savior, the Precursor, John. From all sides, from all races and clans, the beast summons men, leading them to the Enemy of God.

Opposed to this vision of the Antichrist and his precursor is the image that follows: the Lamb erect upon Mount Sion. "And I saw, and behold, the Lamb was standing upon Mount Sion, and with him a hundred and forty-four thousand having his name and the name of his Father written on their foreheads" (Apoc. 14:1). Figure against figure, sovereign against sovereign. But let us recall a point already underlined: the images that loom here face to face are not of equal greatness; not for example, the blazing, virtuous Christ on the one hand and an equally timeless, darkly evil Antichrist on the other. The one is as little the other's 'equal' as Satan is God's. He who claims the contrary blasphemes—or is simply ignorant. There is no independent power against God; nothing in existence that could even come into question as his counterpart, or his Son's. Everything that is or ever was is God's creature. The creature though is free and can turn evil, and since God respects freedom, bad will has terrible power—as long as time endures.

Then three angels appear, flying across the cope of heaven and proclaiming the tidings of the one God and the hour of his judgment. On a white cloud a being "like to a son of man" rides into view. He wears a gold wreath and carries a sickle.

"And I saw, and behold, a white cloud, and upon the cloud one sitting like to a son of man, having upon his head a crown of gold and in his hand a sharp sickle. And another angel came forth out of the temple crying with a loud voice to him who sat upon the cloud, 'Put forth thy sickle and reap, for the hour to reap has come, because the harvest of the earth is ripe' " (Apoc. 14:14–15).

Now a new chain of events unwinds. Seven angels are given golden vessels filled with the wrath of God. They step out of the temple and pour, one after the other, the contents of their vessels over the earth, the sea, the rivers, the Euphrates River; over the sun, the throne of the beast, into the air. Each time dreadful, all-exterminating plagues ensue. Men die in agony, but the wicked remain unconverted.

From the mouths of the dragon and the beast and the false prophet (possibly these last two are meant as one) issue three demons. They collect the rulers of earth "for the battle on the great day of God Almighty" (Apoc. 16:14).

Then the seer is transported into the desert, where he beholds a voluptuous woman seated on a third beast as scarlet as her gown and "full of names of blasphemy." She is clothed in luxurious splendor and is called "Babylon the great, the mother of the harlotries and of the abominations of the earth. And I saw the woman drunk with the blood of the saints and with the blood of the martyrs of Jesus" (Apoc. 17:5–6). The figure doubtless stood for the city of Rome: incarnation of sensuousness, violence, pride, and imperial power, culture in revolt against God—but also for every earthly power that rebels against the divine.

What now comes is judgment over Babylon, which is destroyed. Also the dragon—Satan—is vanquished by an angel and cast into the void for a thousand years. Now begins the thousand-year kingdom of God on earth, millenium of peace in which God rules. Then, one last time, the dragon is released. The final struggle rages, ending with eternal victory over the enemies of God.

A great white throne rises into view, and before the face of him who sits upon it "earth and heaven fled away" and there was no place found for them (Apoc. 20:11). It is the Judge. He summons the dead to life and judgment, and time comes to an end. The old passes; eternity is open. The new heaven and the new earth shine forth, and all that is God's is united in the New Jerusalem.

Thus it unreels, the process of the last things long prepared, in images so tremendous that we can only hint their significance. What we are beholding is the Christian conception of history. What does it look like, history in Revelation?

Perhaps we should first ask: Can history's meaning be recognized at all? Some say it is its own meaning. History's curve is read variously. Many hold that its peak lies behind us in a distant golden age; that we are on the downward plunge to ultimate catastrophe. Others expect to find it in the future, apogee of a steadily mounting line of progress. Still others insist that history is void of meaning; that it is a chance labyrinth of tangled powers and processes. Man alone can give it meaning by ordering its chaos through his enlightenment, stamping it with his will. Under the hand of a powerful personality a historical sense flares up, only to flicker out once that hand is removed. Whichever opinion one might share, Revelation's conception of history is none of these. All three are theories that should be seriously considered, for all contain their truth and their error. For Revelation, however, history's sense lies in the fulfillment of salvation.

From God's point of view, salvation means that his will has fulfilled itself, and the predestined number of the elect is full; from man's viewpoint, that he has decided for or against Christ. This double process of God's 'bringing home' the elect, soul by soul, and of man's essential decision one way or the other, continues progressively to the predetermined limits of time. When the fullness of time has been attained, the end will come. From the Christian standpoint then, all historical events have but one purpose: to clearly illustrate this decisive aspect. They are but constantly new situations in which it may be realized. If anything further on the subject of history can be said, then certainly not that during its course mankind grows better or worse, but that the object of the decision forced upon it is revealed with increasing clarity; that the option it-self becomes increasingly inescapable, the forces flung into the bat-tle ever weightier, the Yes! or No! increasingly fundamental.

One day the Antichrist will come: a human being who introduces an order of things in which rebellion against God will attain its ul-timate power. He will be filled with enlightenment and strength. The ultimate aim of all aims will be to prove that existence without Christ is possible—no, that Christ is the enemy of existence, which can be fully realized only when all Christian values have been de-stroyed. His arguments will be so impressive, supported by means of such tremendous power—violent and diplomatic, material and in-tellectual—that to reject them will result in almost insurmountable scandal, and everyone whose eyes are not opened by grace will be lost. Then it will be clear what the Christian essence really is: that which stems not from the world, but from the heart of God; victory of grace over the world; redemption of the world, for her true essence is not to be found in herself, but in God, from whom she has received it. When God becomes all in all, the world will burst into flower.

IX

The Great Sign
in Heaven

"And a great sign appeared in heaven: a woman clothed with the sun, and the moon was under her feet, and upon her head a crown of twelve stars. And being with child, she cried out in her travail and was in the anguish of delivery. And another sign was seen in heaven, and behold, a great red dragon having seven heads and ten horns, and upon his heads seven diadems. And his tail was dragging along the third part of the stars of heaven, and it dashed them to the earth; and the dragon stood before the woman who was about to bring forth, that when she had brought forth he might devour her son. And she brought forth a male child, who is to rule all nations with a rod of iron; and her child was caught up to God and to his throne. And the woman fled into the wilderness, where she has a place prepared by God, that there they may nourish her a thousand two hundred and sixty days.

"And there was a battle in heaven; Michael and his angels battled with the dragon, and the dragon fought and his angels. And they did not prevail, neither was their place found any more in heaven. And that great dragon was cast down, the ancient serpent, he who is called the devil and Satan, who leads astray the whole world; and he was cast down to the earth and with him his angels were cast down.

"And I heard a loud voice in heaven saying, 'Now has come the salvation, and the power and the kingdom of our God, and the authority of his Christ; for the accuser of our brethren has been cast down, he who accused them before our God day and night. And they overcame him through the blood of the Lamb and through the

word of their witness, for they did not love their lives even in face
of death. Therefore rejoice, O heavens, and you who dwell therein.
Woe to the earth and to the sea, because the devil has gone down to
you in great wrath, knowing that he has but a short time.'

"And when the dragon saw that he was cast down to the earth,
he pursued the woman who had brought forth the male child. And
there were given to the woman the two wings of the great eagle,
that she might fly into the wilderness unto her place, where she is
nourished for a time and times and a half time, away from the serpent. And the serpent cast out of his mouth after the woman water
like a river, that he might cause her to be carried away by the river.
And the earth helped the woman, and the earth opened her mouth
and swallowed up the river that the dragon had cast out of his
mouth. And the dragon was angered at the woman, and went away
to wage war with the rest of her offspring, who keep the commandments of God, and hold fast the testimony of Jesus" (Apoc.
12:1–17).

Powerful image, this figure of the woman garbed in sun, crowned
with stars, the moon her footstool. New life big with the future is
about to be born. The dragon crouches, ready to devour it, but sacred powers guide and protect it. We guess the significance easily
enough: what is envisioned here is the birth of the Saving Infant for
whom all creation has been waiting. The enemy's one desire is to
destroy it, but the divine aegis is over it. Perhaps we are meant to be
reminded of Herod and the period of refuge in Egypt. Then the
meaning shifts, for the woman is not only the Mother of the Savior,
but great holy Mother Church; her children, whom the dragon pursues, are the faithful.

Up to this point the vision is understandable enough; understandable too that now, before the gigantic struggle of the last days
begins, the symbol of Christ's birth flames across the heavens. More
difficult to interpret is the manner of its appearance. Why is it written across the heavens? The robe of sun, crown of stars, the moon
underfoot? Heaven is the sphere of the intransitory, arched about

the transitoriness of earth. The sun is the orb of day, life, height, of luminous order and measure. The moon is the orb of night, regulator of the tides of the sea and the blood; mistress of the hidden life-forces deep in earth. According to ancient belief, the stars are the quiet blazing letters of destiny and power. What has the Incarnation to do with all of these?

Let us transport the vision to a clear alpine night in which the stars really appear like cosmic powers, worlds framed in space rolling their way along immutable paths. Then let us recall the myths of countless peoples in which heroes pleasing to the divinity were lifted, and taking their destiny with them, were fixed in some constellation. Thus man and his fate, that so vulnerable and yet so significant scrap of life and eventfulness, is exalted to an eternal image beyond the reach of all history, itself now an eternal shaper of history. That we dare not conceive of the birth of the Saving Child and its appearance in the Apocalypse as an astral myth need hardly be mentioned. We have only attempted to suggest the immeasurable canopy of space against which it appears, as well as the character and power with which it is imbued.

What does this signify? That Jesus Christ, who was born in Nazareth, lived in Palestine; who taught, suffered, died and rose again, blazes above the world an eternally valid 'constellation' that lights and directs all creation; that he is "sign," prototype, meaning, measure and order of all that is. The Redeemer's existence is not encysted in the psychological, moral, intrinsically religious; primarily it is related to Being. It is not limited by geographical or racial boundaries, but enfolds the universe. The Savior's being is ordered by the same power that created all things; his works are part of the same impulse that brought the world into existence. At the risk of scandalizing the exponents of "pure Christianity," let us venture the conclusion: Christ is a cosmic reality.

We have two witnesses on which to lean: Saints John and Paul—both of them sources of mortal embarrassment to the pure religionists. The first testimony is to be found at the opening of St. John's

Gospel; the second in St. Paul's Epistles to the Colossians and Ephesians. According to John, Christ is the *Logos.* All things plunge the
roots of their being into his essential being, drawing their true life
from him. He entered this world that he might be its light and sun.
Such thoughts are comprehensible only when spanned between the
inner, individual life and the cosmic; between personal depth and
world-embracing breadth; between subjective experience and objective being; between the intellect and reality. This is a fact, and it
is futile to distort it. Paul refers to the same thing when he speaks of
Christ as the "firstborn of every creature"; when he writes that all
created things have been created by him, exist in and through him;
that he comprehends all that is in heaven and on earth and under the
earth, gathering it to a mystic unity, his "body," the Church. Here
we have not only *Weltanschauung,* experience, enlightenment, ethos;
but being, reality, world, new creation. This it is that burns its great
sign across the heavens.

But aren't we distancing ourselves from the simple meaning of
the Gospels and from the pure reality of Jesus? Isn't this after all
more like mysticism and metaphysics? We must not be intimidated.
The simple meaning of the Gospels—what is it? The pure reality of
Jesus—which? The Gospels are anything but simple in the sense
meant in the objection. Jesus is not at all the pure figure which criticism suggests. Behind these tenets stands a dogma—a shadowy,
modern, man-made dogma—according to which Christian essence
means pious humanism. The Gospels, however, know nothing of
the sort, and before they can be made to read so, piece after piece
must be eliminated on the excuse that it had crept in under foreign
influence or was the product of collective elaboration. What then
would be the significance of Revelation, or of faith? Then we
human beings would be taking it upon ourselves to decide what is
or is not divine. Then redemption would lose its power, for this self-
doctored Christ would no longer redeem, but would only confirm
our will. No, only one attitude towards Revelation is valid: readiness
to hear and to learn. Who is Jesus Christ? He who steps forth from

Revelation. Where is Revelation? In Scripture, taken as a whole and in each separate part. And what is Scripture? What the Church gives us. We have no right to eliminate a single word; to do so would endanger the whole. The Bible's every affirmation, every trait it reveals of Christ's figure places on us the duty to broaden, deepen, if necessary completely transform our conception of him. If this conception should be shattered in the process, burst the bounds of our good measure, then the Lord has but proved himself Lord of our measure, greater than ourselves, and it is time to sink to our knees and adore.

But if he is really the all-powerful One standing at the beginning and end of time, in history and in eternity, in us and above us in heart and heaven, is it possible that he can be denied, blasphemed, even—incomprehensible mystery—overlooked and forgotten? It is possible—this and more. For it is also possible for God, the one Reality, to exist, and for man, his own creature to declare: God is dead! Man can behave as if God did not exist. He can act, judge, proceed as if nothing existed but himself, man, and the animal, and the tree and the earth. It is possible for man (who has a vital soul through which he exists as man, through which he is joyful or sorrowful) to insist that he is soulless. All this is possible because seeing and understanding, serious contemplation and acceptance of reality are vital processes, hence dependent on man's will and profoundest disposition. Thus also his capacity for negation is illimitable.

X

VICTOR, JUDGE, PERFECTER

The events of the Apocalypse are conditioned entirely by the figure of the Lord. The reader distracted by the wealth and variety of the images may fail to notice this. However, once he reflects on the exact plan of the whole, he will see that the person of Christ dominates everything—so much so that all the action in the Book of Revelation can be grouped about the different apparitions of the Lord. After the initial revelation of him who wanders among the golden lamp-stands dictating his epistles to the churches, the image of the Lamb moves to the fore, to remain there throughout the visions of the seven seals, possibly also throughout those of the seven trumpets. Then begins the chain of the last things, introduced by the great sign in the heavens, the Mother with the divine Child and her persecution by the dragon; ending with the triumphant figure of the Lamb on the summit of Mount Sion, surrounded by his elect. After this the plagues are poured from the seven bowls of wrath, and the vision is climaxed by the destruction of Babylon and the prophecy of the nuptials of the Lamb. Finally, the consummation and the last events, interspersed with five swift visions of Christ, which we shall now discuss.

"And I saw heaven standing open; and behold, a white horse, and he who sat upon it is called Faithful and True, and with justice he judges and wages war. And his eyes are as a flame of fire, and on his head are many diadems; he has a name written which no man knows except himself. And he is clothed in a garment sprinkled with blood, and his name is called The Word of God. And the armies of heaven, clothed in fine linen, white and pure, were following him on white horses.

"And from his mouth goes forth a sharp sword with which to smite the nations. And he will rule them with a rod of iron, and he treads the wine press of the fierce wrath of God almighty. And he has on his garment and on his thigh a name written, 'King of kings and Lord of lords' " (Apoc. 19:11–15).

The rider on the white horse wars and wins with the aid of the sword of his mouth, his word. He *is* the eternal Word of the Father. He 'speaks' implicitly in form and gesture, deed and fate, his very existence informing us who God is. He also speaks explicitly, by word of mouth, as when he proclaims the tidings, witnesses to God before his enemies, sends forth his emissaries, and commands the Church to speak out to the end of time. And what he says is truth; "the Faithful," the "True" are names of the Lord. How is it possible then that the divine Word is not believed?

Truth is the foundation of existence and the bread of the spirit, yet in the realm of human history it is separated from power. Truth counts, but power forces. What truth lacks—and the nobler it is the greater the lack—is immediate power. The lesser truths retain some measure of power because instinct and necessity confirm them; we have only to think of those ethical truths which apply to our own immediate needs to see this. The loftier the truth, the weaker its direct, activating force, the less need for the spirit to surrender itself to that force voluntarily, in freedom. The nobler the truth, the more easily it can be shoved aside or ridiculed; the more dependent it is upon spiritual chivalry.

This applies to all truth; particularly, however, to sacred truth, which stands in constant danger of "scandal." The moment it enters the world, it lays down its omnipotence, entering in the apparel of a helpless slave. Not only because sacred truth ranks highest in the scale of veracity (and is, therefore, according to the law just mentioned, lowest in power) but also because it comes from the grace of divine love, which calls sinful man to conversion, it irritates him to revolt. Only for this reason was the phenomenon described in St. John's Gospel possible: "In him was life, and the life was the light of men. And the light shines in the darkness; and the darkness grasped it not" (1:4–5). Once though, truth and power will be inseparable. Then truth will have as much power as it has validity and value, and the higher it stands, the greater will be its force. Stupendous event— fulfillment of all spiritual longing! The immeasurable truth of God: immeasurable power, the holy truth of God: holy, destructive, revolutionary, reconstructive power that will dominate all things!

How will this come about? Through the word of Christ. Through his word spoken in history's last hour and valid for all eternity: the law, space, light and air of ultimate existence. Truth's first word was weak—as weak and defenceless as Jesus himself, the self-appointed slave of mankind. Thus the powers of darkness could easily reject it. Truth's second word will be as forceful as its sense, which is omnipotent. Dreadful hour for its enemies! Everything in us that shrinks from the light will have to go, for there will be no more shade. Now untruth can exist because truth is feeble, just as sin can exist because God allows our free will room (incomprehensible 'space') in which it is able to decide against him. Now for "yet a little while"—as little as that indicated by the "soon" of the Second Coming—it is possible to err and to lie. However, once truth comes into power, untruth will no longer be able to exist, because all existence will brim with truth and light. Deception will be crowded out of the universe, subsisting only in one inexpressible form: damnation. For those who long for truth, for that in us which loves it, what a liberation! It will be an experience similar to that of a suffocating man suddenly lifted into pure, clean air. All existence will flower into freedom and beauty, for as St. Thomas Aquinas says, beauty is the splendor of truth become reality. Such realization is the victory for which Christ contends with the "two-edged sword" of his mouth.

"And I saw a great white throne and the one who sat upon it; from his face the earth and heaven fled away, and there was found no place for them. And I saw the dead, the great and the small, standing before the throne, and scrolls were opened. And another scroll was opened, which is the book of life; and the dead were judged out of those things that were written in the scrolls, according to their works. And the sea gave up the dead that were in it, and death and hell gave up the dead that were in them; and they were judged each one, according to their works.

"And hell and death were cast into the pool of fire. This is the second death, the pool of fire. And if anyone was not found written in the book of life, he was cast into the pool of fire" (Apoc. 20:11–15).

We should compare this vision with the eschatological figures described by the Lord in his great sermons on judgment (to be found in the early Gospels). They belong together, forming one apocalyptical high-point. The vision of St. John reveals several complementary images, among them the great white throne which looms bright and terrible into space; image of him who thrones upon it, unnamed but designated by the reverence he inspires; and finally, the powerful scene of universal resurrection: death and the sea and the profoundest depths of earth rendering their dead so that all may stand before the Seat of Judgment, to be judged by the entries under their names in the books of blame and of the life-giving mercy of God. Most shattering of all are the words about the holy Countenance before whom heaven and earth will have fled, "and there was no place for them." Such the majesty of him who has flung his power into his truth. This is judgment. It is the probing, testing point of the Judge's blade in all being. The apocalyptical offensive of the eternal, holy One, against transitory history, *coup* that convulses the world. It lifts her off the hinges of her security, out of the placidness of her existence so completely, that heaven and earth "flee"—flung out as nonexistent (and herein the true sense of good and evil becomes apparent) until creative grace catches them up and receives them in the form of the new heaven and the new earth, into itself.

One day we too shall be resurrected and placed before the awful white throne. Everything on which we formerly leaned, behind which we formerly hid will disappear. All camouflage, trenches, arms. All earthly guards and allies. All rights, honors, works, successes and anything else that has helped us to avoid the truth. All these will fall away, vanish under the penetrating ray of the Judge. We ourselves shall wonder whether we still really exist. No place will be found for our poor being. The same Power that created us will weigh us to see how much of us actually *is,* for genuine existence is possible only through truth and justice, faith and love; our existence, then, will be appallingly questionable. We shall feel ourselves being undermined by nothingness, sucked down towards the void. Only our naked conscience will stand before God's gaze. May his mercy sustain us in that hour!

Victor and Judge have appeared in all their splendor. They are succeeded by the Lamb; this time as the Bridegroom of the eternal City. Then come the words: "And he said to me, 'Do not seal up the words of the prophecy of this book; for the time is at hand. He who does wrong, let him do wrong still; and he who is filthy, let him be filthy still; and he who is just, let him be just still; and he who is holy, let him be hallowed still. Behold, I come quickly! And my reward is with me, to render to each one according to his works. I am the Alpha and the Omega, the first and the last, the beginning and the end!' " (Apoc. 22:10–13).

Beginning that was before all things; End that will succeed them; he through whom all things were created and perfected.

In the final act every sentiment, every thought, every action will be drenched in light. Above all, man's most secret intentions will be disclosed: his fundamental attitude towards Revelation and God's will. If, ultimately, he believed, was receptive, loved good, he will be reckoned to the "men of good will" (Luke 2:14), and Christ himself will cause the full, sweet being to ripen round this sound kernel. Nothing will be lost; everything fulfilled—from this central point. With that which constituted the decisive characteristics of his earthly self, he will be perfected and established in his eternal form to live forever in the sight of God. If, on the other hand, he closed himself fundamentally to God, refused faith, rejected obedience, then whatever he did and experienced will be determined from this core of rejection. In all eternity he will remain a part-reality, a spiritual fragment living the non-life of "second death."

Judgment, the fulfiller of existence, is infallible. Appearances are torn down. Imitation, irrevelance crumble away. Truth alone remains. Man becomes precisely that which eternal mercy and his own will have made him. The remotest, finest consequences are drawn. The individual becomes completely himself, fashioned entirely of his own deeds, his own attitude. The ultimate unifying of his being takes place—here, before the throne. In this unprotected encounter with God, man receives himself; completely, finally. While on earth, where he had only himself, he could deceive that self, fly from him. Here though he is himself undivided and unconcealed. He no longer yearns for his own truth, he no longer needs to collect or unravel the loose ends of his being. Through God he has become the exact product of his earthly existence, without a single shadow of obscurity. And so he remains throughout eternity, though it is false to use the word remains here, which would be speaking in time; so he simply *is.*

Then we read: "I, Jesus, have sent my angel to testify to you these things concerning the churches. I am the root and the offspring of David, the bright morning star. . . . Let him who hears say, 'Come!' And let him who thirsts come; and he who wishes, let him receive the water of life freely. I testify to everyone who hears the words of the prophecy of this book. If anyone shall add to them, God will add unto him the plagues that are written in this book. And if anyone shall take away from the words of the book of this prophecy, God will take away his portion from the tree of life, and from the holy city, and from the things that are written in this book" (Apoc. 22:16–21).

XI

PROMISE

The epistles directed by the One among the lamp-stands to the churches—first to the seven congregations of Asia Minor, then to the universal Church—contain knowledge, judgment, praise and threat. Then at the end of each letter, words of promise. In the letter to the bishop of Ephesus: "Him who overcomes I will permit to eat of the tree of life, which is in the paradise of my God" (Apoc. 2:7). In that to the bishop of Smyrna: "Be faithful unto death, and I will give thee the crown of life" (Apoc. 2:11). To the bishop of Thyatira: "And to him who overcomes . . . I will give authority over the nations. And he shall rule them with a rod of iron . . . and I will give him the morning star" (Apoc. 2:26–28). And to the bishop of Sardis: "He who overcomes shall be arrayed thus in white garments, and . . . I will confess his name before my Father, and before his angels" (Apoc. 3:5). And to the bishop of Philadelphia: "He who overcomes, I will make him a pillar in the temple of my God. . . . And I will write upon him the name of my God, and the name of the city of my God . . . and my new name" (Apoc. 3:12–13). To the bishop of Laodicea: "He who overcomes, I will permit him to sit with me upon my throne; as I also have overcome and have sat with my Father on his throne" (Apoc. 3:21).

The symbols speak for themselves, deeply stirring man's intrinsic longing for life, genuine value, happiness. Then, however, it becomes evident that they all refer to that future fulfillment which Jesus calls the treasure in heaven, the pearl of price: union with God.

The tree stands for that death-overcoming vitality promised to the first human beings on condition that they triumph over temptation. The wreath is a joyful emblem of victory through faith. The hidden manna is the bliss of God's self-revelation to man; the white pebble with the name, the individual's personal summons by God to receive his word of love. Power over the nations will be given those who remain true in spite of persecution for their fidelity to Christ. The morning star, sacred earliness, is the astral glory of man fulfilled. The white robe is festive attire. The names recorded in the book of life and read aloud by the Father and his angels are the names of the elect. He who is made pillar in the temple of God, the Christ, is one destined to participate in the eternal construction of divine love; he can never be broken out of his sacred place. The name of God engraved in the pillar is God himself; it is what gives the chosen one his true essence. The seat upon the throne is a share in Christ's Ascension, promise of eternal harmony with the divine. This vein of luminous promise runs throughout the Apocalypse. Again and again those struggling for their faith are encouraged: Hold fast to the end! Be loyal! Conquer, and fulfillment beyond measure will be yours!

Connected with this bright vein of promise and also running the full length of Revelation, is the gleam of preciousness that sparkles through the text.

At the very start we see the gold of the seven mighty lamp-stands, and of the girdle of the Son of Man, crowns, harps, censers of the same costly metal. The angels are handed gold trumpets and gold vials from which they pour out God's wrath upon the earth. The combination of white garments with gold jewelry produces an effect of particular sumptuousness and sanctity. We know from history that the ancients loved to fashion the statues of their gods from gold and ivory, thus lending them a special richness suggestive of heaven and holiness. They must have been superhumanly beautiful, these Zeus-figures! In the visions we have the same holy, festive colors— white robes with golden girdles, crowns and utensils. Against all this costliness rise images of overwhelming splendor: "And behold, there was a throne set in heaven, and upon the throne One was sitting. And he who sat was in appearance like to a jasperstone and a sardius, and there was a rainbow round about the throne, in appearance like to an emerald" (Apoc. 4:2–5). The whole scene blazes with precious jewels that blind our eyes to the countenance of the Throning One. Even the glory around his throne gropes for expression in a strange fusion of similia. Further inexpressible preciousness is experienced in the vision of the heavenly Jerusalem. She is built of gold transparent as pure glass. Her streets too are of crystalline gold, and each of the twelve gates is hewn from a single pearl. Her walls are constructed of twelve varieties of precious stone. Here is a superabundance no longer assimilable by the eye; it can only be sensed.

When we put down the Book of Revelation we are left with a shimmer behind the eyelids, the power of costliness vibrant in the heart. This is part of the promises just described; the brilliance constantly breaking through guarantees their one-time fulfillment.

One thing more should be mentioned here: the apocalyptical masses. The word does not mean accumulations of disordered individual beings—helplessness and chaos—but organic units. Perhaps we would do better to say armies, choruses, powerful vital ensembles that incorporate the individual existence.

Thus we hear of the Lamb, whose throne is thronged with choruses of angels: "thousands of thousands" of them. Innumerable thousands in other words, for these numbers are the highest with which ancient thought (more interested in significance than endless prolongation) chose to deal. To the angels are added "every creature" in heaven and earth and under the earth and in all the seas, and in everything that is in them (Apoc. 5:11, 13). An endless canticle of praise streams from their throats. In chapter seven we read of the "hundred and forty-four thousand" with the sign of the servants of God on their foreheads. They have been gathered from the twelve tribes of the sacred nation. Twelve is the all-inclusive number,

squared and multiplied here by thousands: for antique sentiment in-
numerable masses multiplied once again later in the vision by the
"great multitude which no man could number, out of all nations
and tribes and peoples and tongues, standing before the throne and
before the Lamb, clothed in white robes, and with palms in their
hands" (Apoc. 7:9). We should feel their presence—these armies
with their flowing white vestments and the never-ending ripple of
waving fronds. From their throats too surges praise. And again, the
Lamb standing on the summit of Sion, the "hundred and forty-four
thousand" around him. They follow him wherever he goes singing
a "new song" that pours from hearts overflowing with the newness
of life (Apoc. 14:3). Chapter nineteen speaks of the voice of "a great
crowd . . . as the voice of many waters" (Apoc. 19:1, 6). Then the
heavens open, the Rider of the white horse appears, behind him the
celestial legions likewise on white horses and gowned in white
robes.

So it goes throughout the Apocalypse: choruses, crowds, armies,
masses—a continuous roaring, storming, thundering. And yet, the
promises in the epistles are addressed to individuals. Each time they
are introduced with the words: "to him who overcomes . . ." a latent "thou." And "thy" name graven on the white pebble that God
gives you—not your Baptismal name, but divine expression of your
truest essence and known only to him and to you, this is apocalyptical intimacy. In the heavenly masses, each member remains an individual, each carries his white stone; yet he is also an organic part
of the whole, of one single tide-like movement, one voice of praise.
That is what is important here. It too is superabundance, and belongs with the rich promises of fulfillment and the fire of costliness.

The Apocalypse seethes with holy, infinite, eternal life. Again and
again in the epistles we read: "He who has an ear, let him hear what
the Spirit says to the churches." It is the life of the Spirit speaking—
not of the intellect—Holy Spirit, worker of resurrection and transfiguration. Everything has become visible reality, body, thing,
world.

And everything is oriented towards Christ. He dictates the epistles. He sends fulfillment. Near the end of the Book stand the words of the Spirit and the Bride: "It is true, I come quickly!" Request made by the Spirit "with unutterable groanings" (Apoc. 22:7; Rom. 8:26). The costliness presses Christwards. The holy city in all her glory presents herself to her Lord, a Bride decked out for her Bridegroom. Choruses gather about him. Legions follow at his heels.

XII

THE SPIRIT
AND THE BRIDE

The row of apocalyptical visions closes with the great, shimmering image of the heavenly Jerusalem.

" 'Come, I will show thee the bride, the spouse of the Lamb.' And he took me up in spirit to a mountain, great and high, and showed me the holy city Jerusalem, coming down out of heaven from God, having the glory of God. Its light was like to a precious stone, as it were a jasper-stone, clear as crystal. And it had a wall great and high with twelve gates, and at the gates twelve angels, and names written on them, which are the names of the twelve tribes of the children of Israel. On the east are three gates, and on the north three gates, and on the south three gates, and on the west three gates. And the walls of the city has twelve foundation stones, and on them twelve names of the twelve apostles of the Lamb.

"And he who spoke with me had a measure, a golden reed, to measure the city and the gates thereof and the wall. And the city stands four-square, and its length is as great as its breadth, and he measured the city with the reed, to twelve thousand stadia: the length and the breadth and the height of it are equal. And he measured its wall, of a hundred and forty-four cubits, man's measure, that is, angel's measure. And the material of its wall was jasper; but the city itself was pure gold, like pure glass. And the foundations of the wall of the city were adorned with every precious stone. The first foundation, jasper; the second, sapphire; the third, agate; the fourth, emerald; the fifth, sardonyx; the sixth, sardius; the seventh, chrysolite; the eighth, beryl; the ninth, topaz; the tenth, chrysoprase;

the eleventh, jacinth; the twelfth, amethyst. And the twelve gates were twelve pearls; that is, each gate was of a single pearl. And the street of the city was pure gold, as it were transparent glass.

"And I saw no temple therein. For the Lord God almighty and the Lamb are the temple thereof. And the city has no need of the sun or the moon to shine upon it. For the glory of God lights it up, and the Lamb is the lamp thereof. And the nations shall walk by the light thereof; and the kings of the earth shall bring their glory and honor into it. And its gates shall not be shut by day; for there shall be no night there. And they shall bring the glory and the honor of nations into it. And there shall not enter into it anything defiled, nor he who practices abomination and falsehood, but those only who are written in the book of life of the Lamb.

"And he showed me a river of the water of life, clear as crystal, coming forth from the throne of God and of the Lamb. In the midst of the city street, on both sides of the river, was the tree of life, bearing twelve fruits, yielding its fruit according to each month, and the leaves for the healing of the nations.

"And there shall be no more any accursed thing; but the throne of God and of the Lamb shall be in it, and his servants shall serve him. And they shall see his face and his name shall be on their foreheads. And night shall be no more, and they shall have no need of light of lamp, or light of sun, for the Lord God will shed light upon them; and they shall reign forever and ever" (Apoc. 21:10–22:5).

Again a symbol. For the man of antiquity, the image of the city expressed a supreme reality. Particularly for Greek thought, the clearly ordered, limited area was more highly appreciated than unpatterned limitlessness. It pictured even the totality of existence not as an endless All, but as cosmos, the beautifully shaped and controlled universe. For the Greek, then, the city was more than endless masses of land and people. The city with her environs, her various buildings grouped harmoniously within the clear-cut borders of her walls; busy, flourishing stronghold regulated by a wise and just government—this image symbolized the goal of all Christian striving: redeemed existence. The historical Jerusalem also plays a role here, metropolis of sacred history, place of the Temple and seat of God's glory, which prophecy tells us will exist forever; capital that had to fall because of her people's treachery, but is spiritually resurrected in the New Jerusalem of the Church. The image is exalted past expression by the superabundance of its costliness. Splendor on splendor fills its walls. Nothing is kept back; everything is open to the light. This city has no temple; everything is temple; the heart of God itself forms the holy of holies in which all things stand. It needs neither sun nor moon. The same brilliance which once indicated the divine Presence above the ark of the covenant blazes everywhere. All peoples stream to the city. The wealth of creation is brought to her, but nothing unjust finds its way to her gates. The river of the waters of life flows through her; the tree of life, that grew in paradise, stands thousandfold and all-productive on its shores. Here God's countenance is uncovered, and his eternal name, expression of his holy Being, is stamped like a seal upon the foreheads of the inhabitants.

The vision speaks of the ultimate content of existence and object of our hope: the new creation. This had its beginning in the incarnation of the living man, Jesus Christ. His beginning is made in everyone who believes in Christ. St. John writes: "Behold what manner of love the Father has bestowed upon us, that we should be called children of God; and such we are. This is why the world does not know us, because it did not know him. Beloved, now we are the children of God, and it has not yet appeared what we shall be. We know that, when he appears, we shall be like to him, for we shall see him just as he is" (I John 3:1–2).

In every believer flows the spring of the new glory. If we take this word seriously, faith is not easy. Everything in and around us contradicts it, often with arguments difficult to refute. It can be pointed out that the greatest power and weightiest deeds come from elsewhere. We might be asked the embarrassing question, "whether the redeemed shouldn't *look* more redeemed?" But after all, the stupendous claim is not of our making, nor proved by our existence; we have it from Revelation, from God's own words. The Christian himself must struggle to sustain the promise against his own not-too-convincing personal experience. This is what John means when he says that our true selves are yet hidden—not only to others, but to ourselves. Nevertheless, the intrinsic splendor is there and grows in spite of all weaknesses.

St. Paul says that this promise of coming glory is not exclusively man's, but includes all creation. In his Epistle to the Romans he writes: "For I reckon that the sufferings of the present time are not worthy to be compared with the glory to come that will be revealed in us. For the eager longing of creation awaits the revelation of the sons of God. For creation was made subject to vanity—not by its own will but by reason of him who made it subject—in hope, because creation itself will be delivered from its slavery to corruption into the freedom of the glory of the sons of God. For we know that all creation groans and travails in pain until now.

"And not only it, but we ourselves also who have the first-fruits of the Spirit—we ourselves groan within ourselves, waiting for the adoption as sons, the redemption of our body. For in hope were we saved" (Rom. 8:18–23).

Here again the intrinsic beginning, the potential glory of man. Into this potentiality dumb creation pushes its way that it too may have a share. Thus an intrinsic beginning is made also in the realm of things. Something invisible to the eye grows and ripens toward the day of Revelation.

All this is expressed in the vision of the heavenly city. It is the image of new creation, grown from the seed of the Beginning, which is Christ, through every human life, through the course of history, through all the processes of cosmic evolution, to ultimate maturity. The Apocalypse says: "And I saw a new heaven and a new earth. For the first heaven and the first earth passed away, and the sea is no more. And I saw the holy city, New Jerusalem, coming down out of heaven from God, made ready as a bride adorned for her husband. And I heard a loud voice from the throne saying, 'Behold the dwelling of God with men, and he will dwell with them. And they will be his people, and God himself will be with them as their God. And God will wipe away every tear from their eyes. And death shall be no more; neither shall there be mourning, nor crying, nor pain any more, for the former things have passed away.'

"And he who was sitting on the throne said, 'Behold, I make all things new!' And he said, 'Write, for these words are trustworthy and true' " (Apoc. 21:1–5).

There is wonderful movement in the vision: the city "coming down out of heaven from God." This is no descent from nobility to baseness, but the movement implied by such expressions as: "The monarch descended the steps of his throne." It is the "coming down" of majesty, graciousness; that flow of angelic light round the head of the seated Madonna which Matthias Grünewald caught in the oils of his Isenheim Altar—endlessly streaming abundance of blessing and beauty.

Then the scene changes again: "And I saw the holy city . . . made ready as a bride adorned for her husband" (Apoc. 21:2). Now the splendor becomes all love. The whole of creation, "the bride," runs to meet Christ in joyful anticipation. The New Testament seldom mentions these intimate things. In St. Paul we find a few allusions to them; also, if we look carefully, in St. John—that is all. The above passage broaches the subject most openly: the entirety of new creation will be in a state of love. In the final chapter of the Apocalypse stand the words: "And the Spirit and the bride say 'Come!' " Syllable of infinite longing uttered by both. Through the Spirit, from the fullness of his love, Christ, the Beginning of all life, shapes creation, his bride, to awake at the end of time to the full maturity of love. It is the Spirit too that teaches creation love; that brings about the transformation, the receptiveness, the union. Here on earth we speak of intrinsic things: soul, sensibility, heart; and extrinsic objects, events, world. In the new unity this difference vanishes. The body will no longer be only 'outside,' the soul 'inside,' but the transfigured body will also manifest itself in the soul, and the soul will find perfect self-expression in the body. Likewise things—trees, animals, oceans, stars, world—will no longer remain exterior objects, but will enter into the heart of God and a hitherto inconceivable unity with him in which neither Creator nor creature loses its essential being; yet no division will separate them. Once, with "the mind of Christ," which the Apostle promises we shall be given, we shall be able to comprehend this mystery. The huge heart of the God-man, which once lived in terrible solitude, 'abandoned' by all, even by the Father, will triumphantly enfold all things that will exist in it, manifesting its radiance everywhere. Everything will be transparent, luminous. Interior and exterior will be no more, only the presence of the reality that is love. Love is the permanent state of creation. Identity of interior and exterior: that is heaven.

And it is Christ who brings all this about. His supreme self-revelation in the Apocalypse is in the image of the Bridegroom, to whom all things are bride. Wonderful summary! His grace begins in each a new life, for the all-renewing Spirit is sent by him, through whom all things are transfigured. In a transport of bliss creation hastens to meet him, decked out like a bride for her husband.

Thus the chain of christological visions: vision of him who wanders among the lamp-stands, of him who thrones on the white throne, of the Lamb on the mountain-top surrounded by infinite legions, of the constellation in the skies and the Rider of the white horse—these mighty symbols culminate in the simple intimacy of the name once given God on earth: " 'I, Jesus, have sent my angel to testify to you these things concerning the churches. I am the root and the offspring of David, the bright morning star.' . . . He who testifies to these things says, 'It is true, I come quickly!' Amen! Come, Lord Jesus!"

CONCLUSION

In the course of these reflections we included many questions and objections, faced many uneasy reactions, conscious that none of them could be confronted by the intellect alone, for the essence of true understanding is not a fruit of argument, but of obedience and faith. We attempted to prove nothing, only to clear the way for Revelation. Here again in this last chapter a question, perhaps *the* question, takes form: Can such a being as the Jesus Christ sketched in these paged exist? The answer is contained in the question. It runs: In history only that is possible which is humanly possible. If we accept only the human in Jesus Christ, then naturally, the greater part of the New Testament becomes a mere web of speculations and pious legends woven about the figure of the historic Nazarene. It may have its sense in the religious needs of the individual, or even of a church or of an age; but it cannot be called truth. The truth of Christ reaches only as far as human possibility, and it is the task of science to discover where this lies.

This opinion has of course many variations, but one thing should be clear from the start: all of them destroy both the fundament and the essence of Christianity. Origin and content of the Christian consciousness spring from one source only: the self-revelation of the living God as he himself addresses us. The essential Word through whom he speaks, the ultimate reality through whom he reveals himself is Jesus Christ. If he is really the incarnate revelation of the omnipotent God, then no human criticism is valid. Then one cannot say: such and such are the limits of possibility; hence this or that in the traditional figure of Christ must be rejected. Then only one attitude towards him is justifiable: readiness to hear and to obey. Not because of any lack of independence or of perspicacity, but because criticism of Christ according to human standards is utterly senseless.

One might parry with the first claim in new form: what you have described is the Christ of faith. Naturally he is good and just and all the rest of it, but he has nothing to do with reality. He may have some place in the realms of religious consciousness, symbolism, cult, or subjective Bible interpretation, but the historical Jesus is something entirely different. Only science can engrave his true likeness. Christian faith must reject both the Jesus of historical research and the pseudo faith which such a Jesus would imply. There is only one true Jesus Christ: the God-man of full uncrippled Christian belief. And faith is as essential to our understanding of him as the eye is to color and the ear to sound. From the start Jesus demanded of all would-be followers a clear Yes! or No! to the demands of faith he made upon them—affirmation or rejection, not a little of each. This point is essential and needs no further illumination, though it is interesting to call attention to the complete nullity of the figure known as "the historical Jesus." When we measure it with the necessary objectiveness and by its own standards we can only be amazed that human intelligence can possibly contribute such a person with the effects that Jesus actually produced.

Christ came to redeem us. To do this he had to inform us who God is, and what man is in the sight of God; and this in such a way that the doors to our conversion are flung open, and we are given the strength to enter into the new. He who succeeds in this cannot be substantially judged by men. The moment man assumes the right to decide how his redeemer is or is not to be, that redeemer is reduced to human limitations, and the given conditions of human existence, as well as the whole sense of redemption, is lost. If redemption exists at all, it necessarily demands that the competence of human judgment halt before him who announces and accomplishes it. And not only relatively, with the 'special consideration' due to greatness or genius, but fundamentally, because he is the Redeemer. A 'savior' with human limitations is hardly worth believing in. Anyone with the least idea of what Christian life demands in the way of conversion and sacrifice knows this. If the genuine Jesus Christ were no more than the greatest of men, it would be better to hack our way alone through existence.

For Christ there is no norm; he himself is the Establisher of all norms. Once we meet him the only way he can be met, in faith; once we renounce all personal judgment, letting Scripture speak with the full weight of its authority, every line of the New Testament suddenly comes alive. The Son of God and man escapes all categories—also those of the genius or religious founder. He steps out of eternity, the unknown, an immeasurable Being revealed to us bit by bit through the word of his messengers or through some personal trait. He himself surpasses all description, though so many have attempted to tell us of him—the synoptics, Saints Paul and John and James and Jude—all speak stammeringly. And if the portrait they trace are not identical, then only because Jesus Christ can never be intellectually unified. Faith alone senses the incomprehensible oneness of his many-faceted reality with its beatific promise of eternity.

Understanding of Christ requires a complete conversion, not only of the will and the deed, but also of the mind. One must cease to judge the Lord from the worldly point of view and learn to accept his own measure of the genuine and the possible; to judge the world with his eyes. This revolution is difficult to accept and still more difficult to realize, and the more openly the world contradicts Christ's teaching, the more earnestly it defines those who accept it as fools, the more difficult that acceptance, realization. Nevertheless, to the degree that the intellect honestly attempts this right-about-face, the reality known as Jesus Christ will surrender itself. From this central reality, the doors of all other reality will swing open, and it will be lifted into the hope of the new creation.